Beiträge zum
ausländischen öffentlichen Recht und Völkerrecht

Herausgegeben von

der Max-Planck-Gesellschaft
zur Förderung der Wissenschaften e.V.,
vertreten durch Prof. Dr. Anne Peters
und Prof. Dr. Armin von Bogdandy

Band 303

Jens T. Theilen

European Consensus between Strategy and Principle

The Uses of Vertically Comparative Legal Reasoning in Regional Human Rights Adjudication

Nomos

The Deutsche Nationalbibliothek lists this publication in the Deutsche Nationalbibliografie; detailed bibliographic data are available on the Internet at http://dnb.d-nb.de

a.t.: Kiel, Univ., Diss., 2020

ISBN 978-3-8487-8091-4 (Print)
978-3-7489-2509-5 (ePDF)

British Library Cataloguing-in-Publication Data
A catalogue record for this book is available from the British Library.

ISBN 978-3-8487-8091-4 (Print)
978-3-7489-2509-5 (ePDF)

Library of Congress Cataloging-in-Publication Data
Theilen, Jens T.
European Consensus between Strategy and Principle
The Uses of Vertically Comparative Legal Reasoning
in Regional Human Rights Adjudication
Jens T. Theilen
497 pp.
Includes bibliographic references.

ISBN 978-3-8487-8091-4 (Print)
978-3-7489-2509-5 (ePDF)

1st Edition 2021

Published by
Nomos Verlagsgesellschaft mbH & Co. KG
Waldseestraße 3–5 | 76530 Baden-Baden
www.nomos.de

Production of the printed version:
Nomos Verlagsgesellschaft mbH & Co. KG
Waldseestraße 3–5 | 76530 Baden-Baden

ISBN 978-3-8487-8091-4 (Print)
ISBN 978-3-7489-2509-5 (ePDF)
DOI https://doi.org/10.5771/9783748925095

Onlineversion
Nomos eLibrary

For T.T. and I.T.

Acknowledgments

This study started life as a doctoral dissertation, submitted to the University of Kiel in September 2019, with the viva taking place in July 2020. Case-law and literature were updated for publication in January 2021. I would like to thank my supervisor, Prof. Dr. Andreas von Arnauld, not only for his feedback on my dissertation but also for his support in many ways throughout the years. Thanks are also due to Prof. Dr. Nele Matz-Lück for her comments as second examiner of the dissertation, and to Prof. Dr. Anne Peters and Prof. Dr. Armin von Bogdandy for accepting the final product to be published in the present series.

Throughout the process of writing my dissertation, I was lucky enough to have the support of many people both in Kiel and beyond. Heartfelt thanks go to my friends and colleagues at the Walther Schücking Institute for their company and feedback throughout the years, notably Dr. Stefan Martini, Sinthiou Buszewski, and Katharina Wommelsdorff. Particular thanks to Wiebke Staff and Isabelle Haßfurther for bringing some joyous utopianism to Kiel!

Thanks are also due to all those who offered feedback at the various conferences, workshops, and seminars at which I presented on the topic of European consensus. Dr. Vassilis Tzevelekos and Dr. Panos Kapotas in particular provided support and encouragement even at a very early stage.

In late 2017, I spent several months at Queen Mary, University of London, where Prof. Dr. Merris Amos and Dr. Paul Gragl were kind enough to read and comment on several draft chapters, and many others likewise offered helpful feedback. Dr. Isobel Roele's questions at the staff seminar were particularly helpful, as were the many avid discussions (years ago in Oxford and again in London!) with Dr. Violeta Moreno-Lax.

For reading draft chapters, summaries, or related papers and providing detailed feedback, I would also like to thank Prof. Dr. Shai Dothan, Prof. Dr. André Nollkaemper, and Prof. Dr. Ben Golder. A special thanks to Prof. Dr. Janneke Gerards for repeatedly taking the time to offer feedback and advice.

I have also profited greatly from inspiring conversations with friends and colleagues at many a conference and workshop, whether in the context of European consensus, human rights in general, or other topics altogether – and for that matter over dinner and via Skype or e-mail. I would like to thank, in particular, Prof. Dr. Eva Brems, Prof. Dr. Philip Allott, Dr. Kay Lalor, and Dr. Damian Gonzalez-Salzberg. Thanks also to Prof. Dr. Sigrid Boysen for her invaluable support during the final phases of the dissertation.

And of course, none of this would have been possible without those who provided the foundations for me to pursue a doctorate in the first place and who have continued to offer material and emotional support over the last few years, especially in times of exertion and grief. My greatest thanks to my friends and family for every small – or large! – loving gesture. Thank you to Babs and Ulli for the welcoming homeliness of a writing retreat in Kassel, to Erika for her unconditional love and support in so many ways, and to Felix, for everything.

Table of Contents

Chapter 1: Justifying Concrete Norms in Regional Human Rights Law: The Uses of European Consensus in the Court's Processes of Justification

I. *Human Rights Adjudication: High Stakes and Little Guidance*

The European Court of Human Rights (ECtHR) finds itself, it must be said, in a rather awkward position. It receives applications from any person claiming to be the victim of a human rights violation by one of the States parties.[1] Provided that the admissibility criteria for such applications are fulfilled, the Court is bound to provide an interpretation of the European Convention on Human Rights (ECHR) which resolves the matter, either confirming or denying a human rights violation. And the stakes are high: human rights are, after all, the "last utopia", commonly regarded as "the highest moral precepts and political ideals" and aiming to set "an agenda for improving the world, and bringing about a new one in which the dignity of each individual will enjoy secure international protection".[2] This kind of utopian mindset may sometimes fade into the background in the everyday bureaucracy of a notoriously overworked court, but it is never entirely absent. One court, comprised of forty-seven judges, is responsible for giving legally binding judgments on the particulars of the last utopia in the European context.

There is, then, an enormous responsibility resting on the shoulders of the ECtHR's judges. Legal interpretation, in the words of Robert Cover, "takes place in a field of pain and death".[3] The violent implications of law perhaps become particularly clear in the case of human rights – but their utopian connotations make them appear not only as a field of pain and death, but also as a field of hopes and dreams. The ECtHR must navigate its way through these fields by adjudicating on a breath-taking array of issues. Are civil servants entitled to form trade unions and to engage in col-

1 Article 34 of the Convention for the Protection of Human Rights and Fundamental Freedoms.

2 Samuel Moyn, *The Last Utopia. Human Rights in History* (Cambridge, Mass.: Belknap Press of Harvard University Press, 2012), at 1.

3 Robert M. Cover, "Violence and the Word," (1986) 95 *Yale Law Journal* 1601 at 1601.

lective bargaining?[4] Do various practices of mass surveillance conflict with the right to private life?[5] Are States obliged to provide for a way of obtaining gender confirmation surgery?[6] Is it permissible to hang up crucifixes in State-school classrooms,[7] or to prohibit the wearing of a headscarf in universities?[8]

In terms of formal legal sources, most commentators agree that there is little guidance provided to the ECtHR in adjudicating questions such as these. Like constitutional courts at the national level,[9] the ECtHR cannot refer to an intricate web of laws to apply; instead, its formal reference point is exclusively the ECHR. The human rights there enshrined, furthermore, are formulated as norms at a very high level of generality: accordingly, "the core activity of international human rights treaty application involves subsuming particulars under generals in the domain of the relationship between the State and the individual".[10] The ECHR itself may constitute an uncontroversial starting point, at least insofar as it is clearly the ECtHR's mission to interpret it,[11] but it is generally perceived as vague,[12]

---

4 ECtHR (GC), Appl. No. 34503/97 – *Demir and Baykara v. Turkey*, Judgment of 12 November 2008.

5 ECtHR, Appl. Nos. 58170/13, 62322/14 and 24960/15 – *Big Brother Watch and Others v. the United Kingdom*, Judgment of 13 September 2018.

6 ECtHR, Appl. No. 27527/03 – *L. v. Lithuania*, Judgment of 11 September 2007.

7 ECtHR (GC), Appl. No. 30814/06 – *Lautsi and Others v. Italy*, Judgment of 18 March 2011.

8 ECtHR (GC), Appl. No. 44774/98 – *Leyla Şahin v. Turkey*, Judgment of 10 November 2005.

9 See Robert Alexy, *Theorie der Grundrechte* (Frankfurt: Suhrkamp, 1994), at 501.

10 Başak Çalı, "Specialized Rules of Treaty Interpretation: Human Rights," in *The Oxford Guide to Treaties*, ed. Duncan B. Hollis (Oxford: Oxford University Press, 2012) at 531.

11 Articles 19 and 32 ECHR.

12 E.g. Janneke Gerards, "Judicial Deliberations in the European Court of Human Rights," in *The Legitimacy of Highest Courts' Rulings*, ed. Nick Huls, Maurice Adams, and Jacco Bomhoff (The Hague: T.M.C. Asser Press, 2009) at 416; Magdalena Forowicz, *The Reception of International Law in the European Court of Human Rights* (Oxford: Oxford University Press, 2010), at 361; Angelika Nußberger, "Hard Law or Soft Law - Does it Matter? Distinction Between Different Sources of International Law in the Jurisprudence of the ECtHR," in *The European Convention on Human Rights and General International Law*, ed. Anne van Aaken and Iulia Motoc (Oxford: Oxford University Press, 2018) at 50; Aileen McHarg, "Reconciling Human Rights and the Public Interest: Conceptual Problems and Doctrinal Uncertainty in the Jurisprudence of the European Court of Human Rights," (1999) 62 *Modern Law Review* 671 at 679; see also Sandra Fredman, "For-

and thus "the trouble starts" when specifying its contents at a more specific level.[13]

And yet, the ECtHR must, in every case before it, make this troublesome conversion from the general to the specific: for one thing, it must interpret the guarantees of the ECHR so as to decide whether they have been violated in specific cases or not and, for another, it must justify the result it reaches.[14] A great variety of considerations might play a role within these processes of interpretation and justification. To provide but a few examples: in some cases, the ECtHR's own case-law might point in a certain direction – but new issues might crop up, or older cases might be considered outdated or wrongly decided in the first place. The ECtHR's function as a court established to protect the human rights of individuals might prod it towards broad interpretations – but more human rights need not equal better human rights, and democratic processes within individual States might be thought of as the better way of deciding where to draw the boundary lines. States might signal, deliberately or not, that they will react badly to certain expansive rulings – but should this be a consideration to take into account, or would it not run counter to the ECtHR's role of protecting the individual from the State?

From what we can gleam from the justifications which the ECtHR offers for its judgments, a form of reasoning to which it attaches considerable importance relies on the positions taken collectively by the States parties to the ECHR. This way of reasoning has become known as "European consensus" (or simply "consensus"). As the Court itself put it in the landmark case of *Demir and Baykara v. Turkey*:

---

eign Fads or Fashions? The Role of Comparativism in Human Rights Law," (2015) 64 *International and Comparative Law Quarterly* 631 at 632-633; see further infra, IV.5.

13 Saladin Meckled-García, "Specifying Human Rights," in *Philosophical Foundations of Human Rights*, ed. Rowan Cruft, S. Matthew Liao, and Massimo Renzo (Oxford: Oxford University Press, 2015) at 300; see also, in the context of European consensus, Panos Kapotas and Vassilis Tzevelekos, "How (Difficult Is It) to Build Consensus on (European) Consensus?," in *Building Consensus on European Consensus. Judicial Interpretation of Human Rights in Europe and Beyond*, ed. Panos Kapotas and Vassilis Tzevelekos (Cambridge: Cambridge University Press, 2019) at 4.

14 Article 45 (1) ECHR; Rule 74 (1) lit. h Rules of the Court; see generally on the abstract and the concrete in the ECtHR's judgments Janneke Gerards, *General Principles of the European Convention on Human Rights* (Cambridge: Cambridge University Press, 2019), at 31 et seqq.

> The consensus emerging from specialised international instruments and from the practice of Contracting States may constitute a relevant consideration for the Court when it interprets the provisions of the Convention in specific cases.[15]

This formulation is particularly revealing since it very clearly identifies the main function of European consensus as a mechanism of mediating between the general norms contained in the ECHR ("the provisions of the Convention") and the individual judgments which the ECtHR must render ("specific cases"). The Court thus needs to move from a general norm to a concrete norm;[16] and it is in the process of that move that European consensus potentially becomes relevant ("may constitute a relevant consideration").[17]

The basis of my interest in European consensus lies in the fact that it seems to constitute a relevant consideration, indeed arguably *the* relevant consideration, in a number of high-profile cases – especially when compared to comparative reasoning by other courts, it seems to be invested with normative force in an unusually strong manner.[18] Quantitatively speaking, it may not be the kind of reasoning most frequently deployed by the ECtHR – indeed, according to Kanstantsin Dzehtsiarou over 95% of its judgments make no reference to it.[19] But those cases in which it *does* pop up are often Grand Chamber cases of considerable importance, or other judgments dealing with particularly controversial and potentially far-reaching issues – cases in which "the Court develops and clarifies the standards of human rights protection of Europe".[20] Moreover, despite an outpouring of academic criticism ever since the ECtHR first started making

---

15 ECtHR (GC), Appl. No. 34503/97 – *Demir and Baykara*, at para. 85.

16 In Kelsenian terminology: see e.g. Hans Kelsen, *Reine Rechtslehre*, 2nd ed. (Vienna: Deuticke, 1960), at 243-244.

17 See Esin Örücü, "Whither Comparativism in Human Rights Cases?," in *Judicial Comparativism in Human Rights Cases*, ed. Esin Örücü (London: UKNCCL, 2003) at 239.

18 Jens T. Theilen, "Levels of Generality in the Comparative Reasoning of the European Court of Human Rights and the European Court of Justice: Towards Judicial Reflective Equilibrium," in *Building Consensus on European Consensus: Judicial Interpretation of Human Rights in Europe and Beyond*, ed. Panos Kapotas and Vassilis Tzevelekos (Cambridge: Cambridge University Press, 2019) at 394.

19 Kanstantsin Dzehtsiarou, *European Consensus and the Legitimacy of the European Court of Human Rights* (Cambridge: Cambridge University Press, 2015), at 21.

20 Ibid., 23; Sionaidh Douglas-Scott, "Borges' *Pierre Menard, Author of the Quixote* and the Idea of a European Consensus," in *Building Consensus on European Consensus. Judicial Interpretation of Human Rights in Europe and Beyond*, ed. Panos

use of European consensus, many commentators have greeted it with "effusive enthusiasm".[21] Within the array of controversial and conflicting considerations for interpreting the ECHR set out above, European consensus is seen by many as a reasonable compromise and a promising solution – a form of guidance for the ECtHR which seems relatively clear-cut as well as both justifiable and acceptable.

In contrast to this, my intuition is that European consensus constitutes, one might say, *too much* of a compromise in at least two different senses, which I introduce below and then elaborate upon in much of what follows: first, that it mediates between different kinds of normativity and thereby makes the contradictions of legal argument disappear from view and, second, that it provides a way in which principled and strategic considerations can be brought together in a way which disguises the tensions between them. By providing this kind of compromise and distracting from the tensions inherent in the argumentative structures of regional human rights law, a strong focus on consensus orients the ECtHR away from potentially more transformative results and forms of reasoning. Before turning to these aspects, the present chapter serves first and foremost to lay the groundwork for what follows by providing more detail on the ECtHR's use of European consensus. I begin by discussing a few examples from the Court's case-law (II.) and elaborating on what I take to be the key characteristics of European consensus (III.). I will then introduce the theoretical framework which will guide the remainder of my inquiry, developing it in relation to critical international legal theory and different perspectives on human rights (IV.), and finally provide a brief outline of the chapters to come (V.).

II. Introducing European Consensus

I define European consensus as a form of comparative legal reasoning which refers vertically to the positions taken by the States parties to the ECHR, viewed through the prism of collectivity. Before elaborating on this definition, I would like to provide a few examples from the ECtHR's

---

Kapotas and Vassilis Tzevelekos (Cambridge: Cambridge University Press, 2019) at 176.

21 Paolo G. Carozza, "Uses and Misuses of Comparative Law in International Human Rights: Some Reflections on the Jurisprudence of the European Court of Human Rights," (1998) 73 *Notre Dame Law Review* 1217 at 1218.

case-law so as to give a feel for the way in which the Court makes use of consensus.

Early references to European consensus can be found even in cases now four decades old. Though less formalised and substantiated than current references would typically be, these cases already capture the spirit of European consensus. For example, in *Marckx v. Belgium*, the ECtHR considered the distinction between "legitimate" and "illegitimate" children. It noted that the ECHR "must be interpreted in the light of present-day conditions" and, with regard to the case at issue, that

> the domestic law of the great majority of the member States of the Council of Europe has evolved and is continuing to evolve, in company with the relevant international instruments, towards full juridical recognition of the maxim "mater semper certa est".[22]

The Court proceeded to hold that the distinction at issue lacked a reasonable justification, and found a violation of Article 14 in conjunction with Article 8 ECHR. In a similar vein, when ruling two years later on the criminalisation of consensual gay sex in Northern Ireland, it noted that it "cannot overlook the marked changes which have occurred in this regard in the domestic law of the member States".[23]

For a more recent case, consider the ECtHR's judgment in *Schalk and Kopf v. Austria*, which no longer concerned criminalisation, but rather partnership rights of same-gender couples. The increased professionalisation of the Court's comparative endeavours becomes quite clear here:[24] under the general heading of "The Facts", the judgment contains a section entitled "Comparative Law".[25] It refers, first, to the right to marriage found in Article 9 of the Charter of Fundamental Rights (CFR) of the European Union (EU) and to the Commentary on that article, as well as several EU directives. It then gives an overview of the "state of relevant legislation in Council of Europe member States". Although this section does not explic-

22 ECtHR (Plenary), Appl. No. 6833/74 – *Marckx v. Belgium*, Judgment of 13 June 1979, at para. 41.

23 ECtHR (Plenary), Appl. No. 7525/76 – *Dudgeon v. the United Kingdom*, Judgment of 22 October 1981, at para. 60.

24 Paul Mahoney and Rachael Kondak, "Common Ground. A Starting Point or Destination for Comparative-Law Analysis by the European Court of Human Rights?," in *Courts and Comparative Law*, ed. Mads Andenas and Duncan Fairgrieve (Oxford: Oxford University Press, 2015) at 119 and 126.

25 On consensus as factual, see Chapter 2, II.3.; and on its relation to comparative law, see infra, III.

itly cite specific laws or provisions of domestic law, it is nonetheless fairly detailed. For example, after enumerating those States that grant same-gender couples access to marriage and to other registered forms of partnership, it also mentions ongoing reforms, the rough temporal framework for past reforms, and the main legal consequences deriving from various forms of partnership. States are presented in groups depending on the common positions between them, in relation to the States parties to the ECHR as a whole: for example, the ECtHR mentions that "six out of forty-seven member States" grant same-gender couples equal access to marriage and that thirteen of them provide for other forms of registered partnership.[26]

In developing its argument for the conclusion which it reaches in the judgment (the section entitled "The Law"), the Court then repeatedly refers back to the comparative references in has thus introduced. The first prong of the case concerned Article 12 ECHR (the right to marry) – essentially determining whether that right can be claimed by same-gender couples. The ECtHR notes that the applicants' case rests not so much on a textual or historical interpretation of Article 12, but "on the Court's case-law according to which the Convention is a living instrument which is to be interpreted in the light of present-day conditions". As in *Marckx*, it then connects the living instrument doctrine to European consensus, arguing that despite "major social changes" in the way marriage is conceptualised, "there is no European consensus regarding same sex marriage" since "no more than six out of forty-seven Convention States" allow it. Article 9 CFR is also discussed in this context, with the ECtHR noting its deliberately broad wording (no reference to "men and women", as in Article 12 ECHR) but also the caveat that the right to marry is "guaranteed in accordance with the national laws" governing its exercise, and the agnostic position taken in the Commentary on the CFR with regard to same-gender marriage. The ECtHR concludes from this – "[c]onsequently" – that Article 12 ECHR is applicable to the applicants' complaint but that, "as matters stand, the question whether or not to allow same-sex marriage is left to regulation by the national law of the Contracting State" – and hence that there was no violation of Article 12.[27]

---

26 ECtHR, Appl. No. 30141/04 – *Schalk and Kopf v. Austria*, Judgment of 24 June 2010, at paras. 24-34.

27 Ibid., at paras. 57-64; this part of the ECtHR's reasoning in particular has, understandably, generated much confusion: see e.g. Loveday Hodson, "A Marriage by Any Other Name? Schalk and Kopf v Austria," (2011) 11 *Human Rights Law Review* 170; Sarah Lucy Cooper, "Marriage, Family, Discrimination & Contradic-

A similar dynamic emerges in the Court's discussion of the second prong of the case, which concerned a potential violation of Article 14 in conjunction with Article 8 ECHR. The ECtHR refers back to its comparative analysis at several points. First, it establishes the applicability of Article 14 by bringing same-gender relationships within the scope of Article 8 not only by reference to "private life" but also – in contrast to its previous case-law[28] – to "family life". Its argument is based on "a rapid evolution of social attitudes towards same-sex couples" as reflected in legal recognition afforded in "a considerable number of member States" as well as "a growing tendency to include same-sex couples in the notion of 'family'" in "[c]ertain provisions of European Union law".[29]

Having thus established the applicability of Article 14 in conjunction with Article 8 ECHR, the ECtHR moves on to discuss whether they were complied with. Lack of same-gender marriage was not considered a violation any more than it was under Article 12; the more controversial aspect of this prong of the case was whether Austria should have provided an alternative means of registered partnership earlier than it did.[30] In this respect, the judgment discusses at length the margin of appreciation to be accorded to Austria; its scope is established by reference to several factors, including "the existence or non-existence of common ground between the laws of the Contracting States".[31] The ECtHR notes "an emerging European consensus towards legal recognition of same-sex couples" which "developed rapidly over the past decade". However, it also holds that:

> Nevertheless, there is not yet a majority of States providing for legal recognition of same-sex couples. The area in question must therefore still be regarded as one of evolving rights with no established consensus, where States must also enjoy a margin of appreciation […].[32]

---

tion: An Evaluation of the Legacy and Future of the European Court of Human Rights' Jurisprudence on LGBT Rights," (2011) 12 *German Law Journal* 1746.

28 ECtHR, Appl. No. 56501/00 – *Mata Estevez v. Spain*, Decision of 10 May 2001.

29 ECtHR, Appl. No. 30141/04 – *Schalk and Kopf*, at paras. 92-95.

30 Austria's Registered Partnership Act came into force on 1 January 2010, i.e. before the ECtHR's judgment in June of that year; from that point onwards, this aspect of the case was a moot point; the ruling thus concerned the period before 1 January 2010.

31 ECtHR, Appl. No. 30141/04 – *Schalk and Kopf*, at para. 98.

32 Ibid., at para. 105.

The Court concluded that Austria did not have to introduce registered partnerships for same-gender couples any earlier than it did, and found no violation of the Convention.

If there is such a thing as a "typical" use of European consensus, then *Schalk and Kopf* can, in many ways, be considered to exemplify it. It contains a relatively detailed comparative overview of the domestic laws of the States parties to the ECHR as well as other legal commitments, in this case EU law. It integrates these into its reasoning at several points, both in determining the scope of the ECHR's provisions and when assessing compliance with them. It refers to both existence and "non-existence" of European consensus and draws differing conclusions. It connects consensus to other doctrines commonly used by the Court, particularly the margin of appreciation and the notion of the ECHR as a living instrument. And it becomes quite clear that consensus can constitute a highly relevant consideration within the ECtHR's reasoning.

Schalk and Kopf thus provides a feel for the way in which European consensus forms part of the ECtHR's reasoning. However, it must also be emphasised that the use of consensus remains, in many ways, difficult to pin down and there are thus limits to the way in can be grasped by describing any one case (or group of cases). Indeed, part of my argument in later chapters will be that the way in which consensus is operationalised depends on certain normative tensions and its use will therefore differ according to epistemological shifts and the kind of normativity foregrounded in any given judgment. Nonetheless, before adding such nuance I think it helpful to first provide a more detailed analysis of the kind of reasoning described by reference to "European consensus". The next section therefore builds on the examples just given to distil some key characteristics of consensus.

III. Key Characteristics of European Consensus

I would submit that, whatever the flexibility involved within the ECtHR's reasoning,[33] certain conditions must be fulfilled in order to speak meaningfully of "European consensus". They relate to the definition which I offered above: pro memoria, I understand consensus to mean a form of *comparative legal* reasoning which refers *vertically* to the positions taken by the

33 Rightly emphasised by Kapotas and Tzevelekos, "How (Difficult Is It) to Build Consensus on (European) Consensus?" at 3.

States parties to the ECHR, viewed through the prism of *collectivity*. I now propose to briefly discuss the three key characteristics of consensus which this implies.

First, European consensus makes use of *comparative legal* reasoning[34] – in fact, the ECtHR itself regularly introduces the materials used to establish consensus under the heading of "comparative law".[35] The implication is that consensus refers to "legal norms existing outside the Convention itself":[36] they do not directly form part of those legal norms which the ECtHR is tasked to interpret – i.e., the Convention – but they *are* considered legal or at least quasi-legal norms within other legal systems, whether domestic or international.

European consensus is sometimes understood in a broader sense, encompassing not only reference to legal norms but also other types of consensus. In that vein, Laurence Helfer influentially distinguished between "three distinct factors" used "as evidence of consensus" within the ECtHR's case-law: "legal consensus, as demonstrated by European domestic statutes, international treaties, and regional legislation; expert consensus; and European public consensus".[37] The first is the kind of consensus already discussed in the examples above. The second kind refers to the opinions of those deemed "experts" in any given area, for example to

34 An aspect which is reflected even in many article titles: see e.g. Mónika Ambrus, "Comparative Law Method in the Jurisprudence of the European Court of Human Rights in the Light of the Rule of Law," (2009) 2 *Erasmus Law Review* 353; Christos L. Rozakis, "The European Judge as Comparatist," (2005) 80 *Tulane Law Review* 257; Christopher McCrudden, "Using Comparative Reasoning in Human Rights Adjudication: The Court of Justice of the European Union and the European Court of Human Rights Compared," (2012-2013) 15 *Cambridge Yearbook of European Legal Studies* 383-415; Sabine Gless and Jeannine Martin, "The Comparative Method in European Courts: A Comparison Between the CJEU and ECtHR?," (2013) 1 *Bergen Journal of Criminal Law and Criminal Justice* 36.

35 Supra, text to note 25.

36 Ida Elisabeth Koch and Jens Vedsted-Hansen, "International Human Rights and National Legislatures - Conflict or Balance?," (2006) 75 *Nordic Journal of International Law* 3 at 12.

37 Laurence R. Helfer, "Consensus, Coherence and the European Convention on Human Rights," (1993) 26 *Cornell International Law Journal* 133 at 139 (footnotes omitted); see also Birgit Peters, "The Rule of Law Dimensions of Dialogues Between National Courts and Strasbourg," in *The Rule of Law at the National and International Levels. Contestations and Deference*, ed. Machiko Kanetake and André Nollkaemper (Oxford and Portland: Hart, 2016) at 221.

"[m]edical and scientific considerations".[38] The third kind of consensus refers to the bulk of public opinion across Europe, though rarely substantiated by empirical evidence such as polls. The ECtHR's reference to evolving "attitudes" in *Marckx*[39] is sometimes read as an example of this.[40]

The ECtHR's case-law also demonstrates the multitude of possible connections between these three approaches to consensus. Medical and scientific considerations, for example, can influence public opinion or themselves be influenced by prevailing social standards, and they can also be recorded in the context of international organisations such as the World Health Organization, thereby gaining "wide international recognition"[41] not only in terms of medical expertise, but also in legal or quasi-legal terms. Public opinion and legal consensus can influence one another[42] and are often cited side by side, as in the above example of *Schalk and Kopf* when the ECtHR posits "a rapid evolution of social attitudes towards same-sex couples" and relates it to their legal recognition.[43]

For all this, however, legal norms remain by far the most commonly cited factor to establish consensus within the ECtHR's case-law,[44] with the two other factors or other types of consensus only occasionally playing a significant role. It is this specifically legal form of consensus which many commentators – and increasingly, it seems, the ECtHR itself – rely on to interpret the ECHR and justify the ECtHR's decisions. It is consensus in the sense of comparative legal reasoning, too, which is commonly located "out there",[45] as a factor which might guide the ECtHR's judges rather than being constructed by them, and hence considered to hold such

38 ECtHR (GC), Appl. No. 28957/95 – *Christine Goodwin v. the United Kingdom*, Judgment of 11 July 2002, at para. 81.

39 ECtHR (Plenary), Appl. No. 6833/74 – *Marckx*, at para. 41.

40 George Letsas, *A Theory of Interpretation of the European Convention on Human Rights* (Oxford: Oxford University Press, 2007), at 77-78.

41 ECtHR (GC), Appl. No. 28957/95 – *Christine Goodwin*, at para. 81; see also ECtHR, Appl. Nos. 79885/12, 52471/13 and 52596/13 – *A.P., Garçon and Nicot v. France*, Judgment of 6 April 2017, at para. 139.

42 See generally Susan Marks, "International Judicial Activism and the Commodity-Form Theory of International Law," (2007) 18 *European Journal of International Law* 199 at 207.

43 Supra, note 29.

44 Shai Dothan, "Judicial Deference Allows European Consensus to Emerge," (2017) *Chicago Journal of International Law* 393 at 399.

45 The notion that law is "out there" in the sense of being independent of lawyers' use of it is a common target of criticism by critical legal scholars; in the present context, I borrow it, in particular, from Günter Frankenberg, "Critical Comparisons: Re-thinking Comparative Law," (1985) 26 *Harvard International Law Jour-*

promise as a relevant consideration in the interpretation of the ECHR. It is this type of consensus, accordingly, which will constitute my focus in what follows.[46]

The classification of consensus as a form of comparative legal reasoning is crucial, but also potentially misleading since it is somewhat idiosyncratic. One key point in that regard is the particular combination of the court making use of comparative reasoning and the comparative materials referred to: European consensus, as used by the ECtHR, relates specifically to the laws of the States parties to the ECHR. This is what I term its *verticality*,[47] for it means that the comparative materials used to establish European consensus originate in precisely those States which "fall within the jurisdiction of the court in question", in this case the ECtHR.[48] A similar form of verticality can be observed, for example, when the European Court of Justice (ECJ) refers to the constitutional traditions of the EU Member States to establish general principles of EU law.[49]

This verticality clearly distinguishes European consensus from the horizontal comparative references sometimes made between, for example, the constitutional courts of different States – these operate "among legal systems that belong to the same level".[50] If there is to be any parallel in the reasoning of national courts, it is that of federal courts that make compara-

nal 411 at 423, whose reflections on comparative law in general seem quite apt in the context of European consensus; the topos of consensus as "out there" will reemerge infra, IV.5.; see also, in the national context, John Hart Ely, *Democracy and Distrust. A Theory of Judicial Review* (Cambridge, Mass.: Harvard University Press, 1980), at 63.

46 For a brief discussion of its limits and relationship to expert consensus, see Chapter 6, particularly sections IV.5.-6.

47 On vertical comparative law in general, see e.g. Aleksandar Momirov and Andria Naudé Fourie, "Vertical Comparative Law Methods: Tools for Conceptualising the International Rule of Law," (2009) 2 *Erasmus Law Review* 291 at 295; in the context of European consensus, a more common distinction than that between vertical and horizontal references seems to be between "internal" and "external" comparative materials, which is related but not identical to my point here: see further Chapter 6, IV.4.

48 Hanneke Senden, *Interpretation of Fundamental Rights in a Multilevel Legal System* (Cambridge: Intersentia, 2011), at 115.

49 See generally Theilen, "Levels of Generality in the Comparative Reasoning of the European Court of Human Rights and the European Court of Justice: Towards Judicial Reflective Equilibrium" at 393-394.

50 Philipp Dann, Maxim Bönnemann, and Tanja Herklotz, "Of Apples and Mangoes. Comparing the European Union and India," (2016) *Indian Yearbook of Comparative Law* 3 at 6.

tive reference to a "national consensus" among various state laws;[51] tellingly, the ECtHR's use of consensus has often been compared to the US Supreme Court's search for a national consensus.[52] On the international plane, the verticality of consensus resonates with the recently re-burgeoning field of "comparative international law" which emphasises, inter alia, the direct relevance of the comparative method for the ascertainment and interpretation of international law.[53] European consensus may be considered a prime example of comparative international law in that sense.[54]

This is not to say that the ECtHR does not make use of comparative legal reasoning more generally – it certainly does,[55] although less frequently than it relies on European consensus. Sometimes it refers horizontally to other regional systems of human rights protection, for example to the American Convention or to the case-law of the Inter-American Court of

---

51 E.g. Supreme Court of the United States, *Roper v. Simmons*, 543 U.S. 551 (2005).

52 Mary Ann Glendon, *Rights Talk. The Impoverishment of Political Discourse* (New York: The Free Press, 1991), at 152-153; Jeffrey A. Brauch, "The Dangerous Search for an Elusive Consensus: What the Supreme Court Should Learn from the European Court of Human Rights," (2009) 52 *Howard Law Journal* 277; John L. Murray, "Consensus: Concordance, or Hegemony of the Majority?" (Dialogue between judges, European Court of Human Rights, 2008), at 28-34; Senden, *Interpretation of Fundamental Rights*, at 119-122; Dzehtsiarou, *European Consensus and the Legitimacy of the European Court of Human Rights*, at 172-175; Jaka Kukavica, "National Consensus and the Eigth Amendment: Is There Something to Be Learned from the United States Supreme Court?," in *Building Consensus on European Consensus. Judicial Interpretation of Human Rights in Europe and Beyond*, ed. Panos Kapotas and Vassilis Tzevelekos (Cambridge: Cambridge University Press, 2019).

53 Anthea Roberts et al., "Comparative International Law: Framing the Field," (2015) 109 *American Journal of International Law* 467 at 470; see also Momirov and Naudé Fourie, "Vertical Comparative Law Methods: Tools for Conceptualising the International Rule of Law" at 296; for an early example, see Michael Bothe, "Die Bedeutung der Rechtsvergleichung in der Praxis internationaler Gerichte," (1976) 36 *Zeitschrift für ausländisches öffentliches Recht und Völkerrecht* 280.

54 See Roberts et al., "Comparative International Law: Framing the Field" at 470; Samantha Besson, "Human Rights Adjudication as Transnational Adjudication: A Peripheral Case of Domestic Courts as International Law Adjudicators," in *International Law and... Select Proceedings of the European Society of International Law, Vol. 5*, ed. August Reinisch, Mary E. Footer, and Christina Binder (Oxford: Hart, 2016) at 62.

55 For a spotlight on this kind of reasoning, see Carla M. Zoethout, "The Dilemma of Constitutional Comparativism," (2011) 71 *Zeitschrift für ausländisches öffentliches Recht und Völkerrecht* 787.

Human Rights.[56] Sometimes it also refers – diagonally, as it were[57] – to the domestic laws of States not party to the ECHR.[58] I will bracket these kinds of comparative references in what follows, not because I take them to be any less important but because, as used by the ECtHR, they operate within a different logic than that applied to vertically comparative reasoning – the use of European consensus, in other words, involves different kinds of normative tensions and is supported or opposed for different reasons than other comparative references, in part due to its verticality.[59]

A further and related idiosyncratic feature of European consensus is that the vertically comparative materials on which it is based are assessed by the ECtHR *through the prism of collectivity*.[60] This is to say that the Court not only deals with similarities and differences among the laws of the States parties – this would be par for course in most if not all comparative endeavours[61] – but also *groups* the comparative materials accordingly and sets them in relation to one another according to the relative size of those groups. The very term "European consensus" implicitly reflects not only the aspect of verticality ("European") but also of commonality or collectivity ("consensus").[62] Similarly, both aspects shine through in the reference

56 E.g. ECtHR (GC), Appl. No. 69698/01 – *Stoll v. Switzerland*, Judgment of 10 December 2007, at para. 111.

57 Contrast Anne-Marie Slaughter, "A Typology of Transnational Communication," (1994) 29 *University of Richmond Law Review* 99 at 111, who formally includes States outside a transnational court's jurisdiction under the umbrella of "vertical communication" – but admits that such cases may in fact have more in common with horizontal communication (ibid.).

58 E.g. ECtHR (GC), Appl. No. 28957/95 – *Christine Goodwin*, at paras. 84-85; ECtHR, Appl. Nos. 18766/11 and 36030/11 – *Oliari and Others v. Italy*, Judgment of 21 July 2015, at paras. 65 and 178; ECtHR (GC), Appl. Nos. 60367/08 and 961/11 – *Khamtokhu and Aksenchik v. Russia*, Judgment of 24 January 2017, at para. 19 as well as the dissenting opinion of Judge Pinto de Albuquerque in that case, at para. 32.

59 See in particular Chapter 2, II.2. and Chapter 3, IV.1.-2.

60 Emphasised e.g. by Senden, *Interpretation of Fundamental Rights*, at 67 in fine; Kanstantsin Dzehtsiarou, "What Is Law for the European Court of Human Rights?," (2017) 49 *Georgetown Journal of International Law* 89 at 101.

61 See David Kennedy, "New Approaches to Comparative Law: Comparativism and International Governance," (1997) *Utah Law Review* 545 at 546; Carozza, "Uses and Misuses of Comparative Law" at 1233.

62 As many commentators have noted, the term "consensus" is otherwise understood to imply unanimity; in the context of European consensus, however, it usually refers only to State majorities: see Dzehtsiarou, *European Consensus and the Legitimacy of the European Court of Human Rights*, at 11-13; Luzius Wildhaber, Ar-

to "the existence or non-existence of *common ground* between the laws of the Contracting States" as it is found, inter alia, in *Schalk and Kopf*.[63]

Several points follow from this combination of verticality and collectivity. For one thing, there are clearly pragmatic limits to the level of detail at which the Court's comparative endeavours can be conducted.[64] These pragmatic constraints (e.g. time constraints and language barriers) are well-known from any kind of engagement with comparative law and often exacerbate a lack of proper contextualisation of "foreign" law, particularly in light of the preconceptions through which it is usually approached. The ECtHR finds itself in a relatively privileged position compared, for example, to national courts – like other transnational courts, it might be considered a "legal melting pot" or "laboratory" for comparative law[65] precisely because of its vertical placement "above" the States parties and hence its international composition. However, this cannot come even close to mitigating the pragmatic constraints of any comparative endeavour which aims to set the laws of not just two or three, but of *forty-seven* States (as well as any applicable norms of international law) in relation to one another across a broad range of subject-matters in various judgments.

European consensus differs from most attempts at comparative law in that, in a sense, it *embraces* this lack of contextualisation. One way of putting this succinctly (though it only captures part of the issue) is that the ECtHR is not usually concerned with the reasons for any given legal norm, but merely with the substantive position which it implies with regard to

---

naldur Hjartarson, and Stephen Donnelly, "No Consensus on Consensus? The Practice of the European Court of Human Rights," (2013) 33 *Human Rights Law Journal* 248 at 257; critically Murray, "Consensus: Concordance, or Hegemony of the Majority?" at 45; see further on the implications of this Chapter 3, IV.3.-4. and, on numerical issues involved in establishing consensus, see Chapter 5; see also Douglas-Scott, "Borges' *Pierre Menard, Author of the Quixote* and the Idea of a European Consensus" at 173, noting the "positive tenor" of the term "consensus" which (misleadingly!) suggests "a lack of dissent or disagreement, an absence of strife".

63 Supra, note 31 (emphasis added).

64 For an overview of some challenges, see Dzehtsiarou, *European Consensus and the Legitimacy of the European Court of Human Rights*, at 101-114.

65 Fernanda G. Nicola, "National Legal Traditions at Work in the Jurisprudence of the Court of Justice of the European Union," (2016) 64 *American Journal of Comparative Law* 865 at 868 (on the ECJ).

the matter at hand.[66] It is these substantive positions which are then added up, as it were, and to which the prism of collectivity is thus applied. While there are a few counter-examples and ample room for flexibility, in particular, with regard to level of generality at which the comparative analysis is conducted,[67] this kind of outcome-oriented approach to collectivity leads to the kind of "counting" which is commonly associated with European consensus:[68] States are grouped according to whether the position read into their legal system accords with the view of the applicant before the ECtHR – or not.

The implications of this grouping differ according to whether commonality is deemed to be present and, if so, depending on which position it favours. European consensus is a form of reasoning which is notoriously Janus-faced in the sense that it can be used to argue in two directions[69] – what has been called the "rein effect" and the "spur effect", respectively.[70] The prior refers to cases in which the ECtHR either identifies a majority position *against* the applicant or a lack of a clear majority one way or the other. In these cases, (lack of) consensus constitutes an argument against a violation of the Convention – it reins in the Court, as it were. Conversely, when the ECtHR identifies a clear majority in *favour* of the applicant, then it "spurs" the Court towards a more expansive approach, and consensus is used as an argument for a violation of the Convention. *Schalk and Kopf*

66 Dzehtsiarou, "What Is Law for the European Court of Human Rights?" at 121; see also Kanstantsin Dzehtsiarou and Vasily Lukashevich, "Informed Decision-Making: The Comparative Endeavours of the Strasbourg Court," (2012) 30 *Netherlands Quarterly of Human Rights* 272 at 290-291.

67 See further Chapter 7, II.

68 Dzehtsiarou, *European Consensus and the Legitimacy of the European Court of Human Rights*, at 175.

69 See e.g. Gerards, "Judicial Deliberations in the European Court of Human Rights" at 430; Yutaka Arai-Takahashi, "The Margin of Appreciation Doctrine: A Theoretical Analysis of Strasbourg's Variable Geometry," in *Constituting Europe. The European Court of Human Rights in a National, European and Global Context*, ed. Andreas Føllesdal, Birgit Peters, and Geir Ulfstein (Cambridge: Cambridge University Press, 2013) at 89; Paul Mahoney, "Marvellous Richness of Diversity or Invidious Cultural Relativism?," (1998) 19 *Human Rights Law Journal* 1 at 5; Eva Brems, *Human Rights: Universality and Diversity* (The Hague et al.: Martinus Nijhoff, 2001), at 412; Samantha Besson and Anne-Laurence Graf-Brugère, "Le droit de vote des expatriés, le consensus européen et la marge d'appréciation des États," (2014) 25 *Revue Trimestrielle des Droits de l'Homme* 937 at 942-943; in more detail Dzehtsiarou, *European Consensus and the Legitimacy of the European Court of Human Rights*, at 24-30.

70 Wildhaber, Hjartarson, and Donnelly, "No Consensus on Consensus?" at 251.

offers an example of the rein effect (although it also contains elements of the spur effect, e.g. in the use of consensus to establish a broad understanding of "family life"), while *Marckx* or *Demir and Baykara* can be seen as examples of the spur effect.

As a consequence of this bifurcation, it comes as no surprise that the use of consensus is criticised on different grounds in either case.[71] The more controversial scenario in practice seems to be the rein effect: many critics of European consensus are concerned about its use in relation to the specific subject-matter of human rights,[72] for they see a contradiction or at least a tension between vertically comparative legal reasoning and the idea of human rights. Since human rights are (seen as) conceptually focussed on the individual, it is those cases in which consensus is used to argue against the individual applicant – i.e., cases involving that rein effect – that take centre-stage when this line of criticism is followed. Conversely, the spur effect of European consensus relates to those cases in which consensus is used as an argument against the respondent State – here, the main line of criticism therefore relates to the fact the positions taken by a majority of States are transposed onto those States who find themselves in a minority.

European consensus finds itself caught between these diametrically opposed kinds of criticism; but precisely because of its Janus-faced nature, the applicability of either line of criticism in any given case will depend on whether the ECtHR identifies common ground among the States parties or not. As I will argue in what follows, this leads to the possibility of instrumental allegiances between consensus and other approaches to reasoning. But it also demonstrates that consensus is situated at the interstices of different approaches to interpretation, and thus caught up in persistent tensions owing to different kinds of criticism. The next section will introduce these tensions in more detail, situating them in relation to human rights theory and (critical) international legal theory more generally.

---

71 Carozza, "Uses and Misuses of Comparative Law" at 1228-1229; Vassilis Tzevelekos and Kanstantsin Dzehtsiarou, "International Custom Making and the ECtHR's European Consensus Method of Interpretation," (2016) *European Yearbook on Human Rights* 313 at 326; Kapotas and Tzevelekos, "How (Difficult Is It) to Build Consensus on (European) Consensus?" at 14.

72 E.g. Letsas, *A Theory of Interpretation of the European Convention on Human Rights*, at 9; Jan Kratochvíl, "The Inflation of the Margin of Appreciation by the European Court of Human Rights," (2011) 29 *Netherlands Quarterly of Human Rights* 324 at 354.

IV. European Consensus and Critical International Legal Theory

1. Different Perspectives on Consensus: Structuralist Methodology

One facet of the academic discourse surrounding European consensus which struck me when I first began research on this topic is the way in which the debate can be very clearly structured by ideal-type, diametrically opposed starting assumptions. This is particularly so in cases involving the rein effect: the standard criticism of consensus takes it to task for endorsing unjustifiable restrictions, particularly on minority rights; for paradoxically giving normative force to the very States parties whose laws the ECtHR is supposed to be supervising; and for replacing moral truth with mere factual consensus.[73] In defence of consensus, this approach is derided as claiming a ludicrous "status of philosopher kings with ultimate moral authority" for the ECtHR;[74] disagreement about moral matters such as human rights is emphasised; and hence the vertically comparative reference to democratically underlaid legal norms is regarded as essential rather than paradoxical: "There are democratic and epistemic benefits to enlisting domestic institutions in forming the content of Convention rights".[75] Distrust of States clashes with trust of States, and an epistemology predicated on substantive argument about moral truth clashes with an emphasis on disagreement and political solutions to moral problems.

With regard to the spur effect, the epistemological differences are slightly less marked, but a common perspective is no more forthcoming. One might regard consensus as a "hegemony of the majority" of States parties, and hence as contemptuous of the mores, heritage, culture and democratic processes within those States who find themselves in a minority.[76] One might, conversely, argue that giving too much weight to the decisions of individual States would negate the point of a regional system of human rights protection, hence shifting the focus back to a Europe-wide compari-

---

73 E.g. Letsas, *A Theory of Interpretation of the European Convention on Human Rights*, at 74.

74 Andrew Legg, *The Margin of Appreciation in International Human Rights Law: Deference and Proportionality* (Oxford: Oxford University Press, 2012), at 115.

75 Clare Ryan, "Europe's Moral Margin: Parental Aspirations and the European Court of Human Rights," (2018) 56 *Columbia Journal of Transnational Law* 467 at 480.

76 Murray, "Consensus: Concordance, or Hegemony of the Majority?" at 45-47.

son.[77] Nationalist and internationalist precommitments pull commentators towards either of these perspectives, which remain difficult to bring into conversation with one another.

Finally, many proponents of European consensus argue that the combination of the rein effect and the spur effect allows for the development of regional human rights standards while increasing the ECtHR's "legitimacy", in the sense of support for its judgments by the States parties and hence better chances at implementation.[78] This kind of argument operates on a different plane from the other controversies just mentioned, since it incorporates a strategic element into the ECtHR's reasoning which is geared at generating support for the Court in the long term. While this kind of argument has become extremely influential, some starkly oppose it, maintaining that it is "based on an overstated fear" that the ECtHR might lose its legitimacy, and that "[p]iecemeal evolution" of its case-law in accordance with European consensus cannot be reconciled with a principled account of human rights.[79] Again, there is a sense that the issue can be approached from diametrically opposed starting assumptions – either a matter of principle or strategy. A combination of the two is difficult to achieve without sweeping significant normative tensions under the rug.[80]

To put a spotlight on these differing perspectives and their various precommitments, epistemologies, idealisations, and implications I borrow from a structuralist methodology in the sense suggested by Martti Koskenniemi – a form of analysis which aims to bring to the surface the "deep structure" of "more familiar phenomena" of social life so as to understand them better.[81] Accordingly, the analysis which follows operates, for the most part at least, on the *meta-level* compared to the various perspectives just mentioned. My hope is that by making the theoretical implications of the various perspectives involved in debates on consensus more explicit, it

77 Gerald L. Neuman, "Import, Export, and Regional Consent in the Inter-American Court of Human Rights," (2008) 19 *European Journal of International Law* 101 at 115.

78 Dzehtsiarou, *European Consensus and the Legitimacy of the European Court of Human Rights*, chapter 6.

79 Letsas, *A Theory of Interpretation of the European Convention on Human Rights*, at 124.

80 Although many proponents of European consensus, to my mind, do just that; for a criticism of this tendency, see Chapter 10.

81 Martti Koskenniemi, "What is Critical Research in International Law? Celebrating Structuralism," (2016) 29 *Leiden Journal of International Law* 727 at 727-728; on structuralism and critique, see further Chapter 11, IV.1.

will become possible to get a better grasp of the role which European consensus plays within the ECtHR's case-law, and for that matter of the ECtHR's reasoning more generally. I thus build on the assumption explicated by Panos Kapotas and Vassilis Tzevelekos, according to which debates about European consensus are "closely linked to the wider discourse on the philosophical foundations of human rights and to the limits of judicial review", and ultimately to foundational questions underlying all "liberal democratic polities".[82]

Accordingly, much of what follows is "devoted to disentanglement"[83] – to disentangling different approaches to European consensus within the ECtHR's case-law from one another and setting them in relation to different approaches to human rights more generally by connecting doctrine and theory. The ECtHR itself famously "eschews abstract theorising"[84] and has offered only rare and partial indications of why it uses European consensus.[85] Partly due to this, I will draw to a significant extent on academic literature to establish the main tenets of different perspectives on European consensus, and only then turn back to the ECtHR's case-law to assess how they might be said to impact upon the use of consensus in more detail.[86]

It is worth noting, however, that my references to literature on human rights theory are not only faute de mieux, but also a deliberate move to underline its practical importance. Theoretical accounts may sometimes seem (overly) abstract, but they have the potential to influence how we think about and assign meaning to human rights, and hence to bring ideas into circulation which in turn influence how the ECtHR's judges conceive of their own role. In that sense, human rights theory is by no means discon-

---

82 Kapotas and Tzevelekos, "How (Difficult Is It) to Build Consensus on (European) Consensus?" at 14.

83 Martti Koskenniemi, *From Apology to Utopia: The Structure of International Legal Argument* (Cambridge: Cambridge University Press, 2005), at 4.

84 Alastair Mowbray, "The Creativity of the European Court of Human Rights," (2005) 5 *Human Rights Law Review* 57 at 61; see also Angelika Nussberger, *The European Court of Human Rights* (Oxford: Oxford University Press, 2020), at 73.

85 See Senden, *Interpretation of Fundamental Rights*, at 265-266; Kapotas and Tzevelekos, "How (Difficult Is It) to Build Consensus on (European) Consensus?" at 9; see more generally Fredman, "Foreign Fads or Fashions? The Role of Comparativism in Human Rights Law" at 633.

86 Chapters 2 to 4 build primarily on literature whereas chapters 5 to 8 focus on case-law. Chapters 9 and 10 return to academic commentary to discuss the issue of legitimacy.

nected from human rights practice: "analyses affect outcomes".[87] To render that connection more explicit is precisely what a structuralist analysis aims for by "bring[ing] to the surface that underlying world of beliefs that controls our institutional practices".[88] Human rights theory can be considered one of the manifold fora in which the "world of beliefs" underlying the ECtHR's practices is developed and through which it might be grasped.

2. Human Rights between Apology and Utopia

Before turning to theory dealing explicitly with human rights, however, I would like to briefly discuss Koskenniemi's own structuralist account of international legal argument in his path-breaking monograph, *From Apology to Utopia*, so as to then demonstrate its relevance in the area of human rights. While the bulk of the argument in the following chapters will be critically oriented only in a relatively weak sense,[89] it has been strongly influenced by critical international legal theory of the kind put forward by Koskenniemi, and accordingly I think it is a helpful place to begin so as to both explicate the intellectual debt and highlight areas of divergence.

Koskenniemi identifies two patterns of justifying positions taken within international legal argument. The first is "descending": it is based on the fact that, in order to uphold its normativity, international law must be capable of overriding individual State will. The latter is "ascending": it assumes that international law is based on States' will so as to ensure its concreteness, in contrast to some kind of natural morality.[90] Either kind of argument can be used to challenge the other – descending argument "cannot demonstrate the content of its aprioristic norms in a reliable manner" and hence seems (overly) utopian when challenged on the basis of State will,

87 Susan Marks, *The Riddle of All Constitutions. International Law, Democracy, and the Critique of Ideology* (Oxford: Oxford University Press, 2000), at 5.

88 Koskenniemi, "What is Critical Research in International Law? Celebrating Structuralism" at 733.

89 As is *From Apology to Utopia* itself, since it provides a structuralist critique of international law without a strong political (e.g. femininst, anti-capitalist, etc.) critique of the structural biases which go along with it; see Michele Tedeschini, "The Politics of International Lawyers: Whose Legacy Is at Stake? Reflections on Martti Koskenniemi's Series on 'The Politics of International Law'" (Critical Legal Thinking, 2019), available at <http://criticallegalthinking.com/2019/07/15/politics-of-international-lawyers-whose-legacy-is-at-stake-martti-koskenniemi/>. I will elaborate on this point in Chapter 11, II.

90 Koskenniemi, *From Apology to Utopia*, at 17 and 59.

whereas ascending argument privileges State will in a way which makes it open to doubt whether law is "effectively constraining", hence appearing (overly) apologetic.[91] As a result, international legal argument oscillates between these two patterns of justification in a way that renders it radically indeterminate, i.e. merely a formal structure for making arguments but "singularly useless" insofar as the choice between differing substantive outcomes is concerned.[92]

From Apology to Utopia deals with "the classical law of peace, concerned with the relations of sovereign States vis-à-vis each other" and thus largely brackets the field of international human rights law.[93] As Frédéric Mégret has shown at length, however, its claims are no less applicable to international human rights law than they are to international law at large.[94] Similar argumentative structures, although concerned more with capturing the notion of human rights in general than with specific legal interpretations, are also reflected in the popular juxtaposition of so-called "moral" and "political" theories of human rights and reactions to it. The prior kind of theory, represented in particular by James Griffin, takes up the popular idea of rights "that we have simply in virtue of being human" and hence make scant reference to State will.[95] The latter kind of theory, originating in the work of John Rawls and developed in particular by Charles Beitz, "takes the doctrine and practice of human rights as we find them in international political life as the source materials for constructing a conception of human rights".[96]

Each of these two accounts carries diametrically opposed weaknesses. The prior constitutes "top-down theorizing" which refers "to human rights

91 Ibid., 60.

92 Ibid., 67-69.

93 Ibid., 14.

94 Frédéric Mégret, "The Apology of Utopia: Some Thoughts on Koskenniemian Themes, with Particular Emphasis on Massively Institutionalized International Human Rights Law," (2013) 27 *Temple International and Comparative Law Journal* 455; from Koskenniemi's own writings on human rights, see in particular Martti Koskenniemi, "The Effect of Rights on Political Culture," in *The Politics of International Law* (Oxford: Hart, 2011) at 134.

95 James Griffin, *On Human Rights* (Oxford: Oxford University Press, 2008), at 2.

96 Charles R. Beitz, *The Idea of Human Rights* (Oxford: Oxford University Press, 2009), at 102, building on John Rawls, *The Law of Peoples* (Cambridge, Mass.: Harvard University Press, 1999).

practice at most as a test case [...] or as something to criticize"[97] and hence remains open to the charge of utopianism, for it lacks concreteness. The latter avoids this problem as it is clearly "practice-responsive",[98] but conversely has difficulties in establishing a sufficient degree of normativity and slides all too easily into apology.[99] It comes as no surprise that those who attempt to navigate a middle path between moral and political accounts focus on the legal dimension of human rights: the law "qua normative practice" evokes the familiar oscillation between ascending and descending argument.[100]

As I read it, Koskenniemi's dichotomy of ascending and descending argument is deliberately based, at least in the first instance, entirely on formal considerations, i.e. the reliance on or opposition to State will.[101] It is because of this formality, a kind of internal logic, that it becomes possible to claim that these two sets of argument "are both exhaustive and mutually exclusive".[102] This approach is entirely apt insofar as the general structure of international legal argument is concerned, since it relates directly to the twin demands of normativity and concreteness which aim to distinguish international law from its "neighbouring intellectual territories", particularly morality and politics.[103] The emergence of specifically legal accounts of human rights in explicit contrast to moral and political accounts only confirms this pattern.

For present purposes, however, I am interested not only in the dichotomy of ascending and descending argument, but also in *further differentia-*

97 Samantha Besson, "Human Rights: Ethical, Political... or Legal? First Steps in a Legal Theory of Human Rights," in *The Role of Ethics in International Law*, ed. Donald Earl Childress (Cambridge: Cambridge University Press, 2012) at 216.

98 Alain Zysset, *The ECHR and Human Rights Theory: Reconciling the Moral and Political Conceptions* (Abington: Routledge, 2017), at 7.

99 But see the discussion in Beitz, *The Idea of Human Rights*, at 104-106.

100 Besson, "Human Rights: Ethical, Political... or Legal? First Steps in a Legal Theory of Human Rights" at 217; see also Allen Buchanan, *The Heart of Human Rights* (Oxford: Oxford University Press, 2013), at 11.

101 Although the broader connections to liberal social theory are very much a part of his argument, as the brief overview of his structuralist approach above indicates. See also explicitly e.g. Koskenniemi, *From Apology to Utopia*, at 66 and 600; for emphasis of this point, see e.g. Outi Korhonen, "New International Law: Silence, Defence or Deliverance?," (1996) 7 *European Journal of International Law* 1 at 24; see also infra, note 187, and, on the connections which critical international legal theory typically draws between law and broader social phenomena, see further Chapter 11, IV.1.

102 Koskenniemi, *From Apology to Utopia*, at 59.

103 Ibid., 16.

tion between the rationales for supporting one or the other (or both),[104] so as to more specifically investigate (some of) the various *uses* of European consensus in that context.[105] My aim, in other words, is not to challenge the more general structure described by Koskenniemi but to elaborate on how it is used in the context of regional human rights law, particularly with regard to European consensus. I retain from his account the focus on *mutually exclusive* patterns of justification – I will sometimes express this by speaking of *different kinds of normativity*. This aspect explains the sense of diametrically opposed starting assumptions which I mentioned above. Because I investigate different rationales for supporting (or opposing) the use of European consensus, however, my framework will be less formal than Koskenniemi's, and hence I make no claim that the different perspectives I discuss are exhaustive. I will focus on two main sets of considerations, which I introduce in the following two subsections: principled and strategic considerations.

3. Morality-focussed and Ethos-focussed Perspectives

The different perspectives which I gather under the umbrella of "principled" considerations have been most extensively explored in constitutional law and political theory at the national level. The main dichotomy at issue

---

104 A variety of different rationales is discussed, for example, by Andreas Føllesdal, "A Better Signpost, Not a Better Walking Stick: How to Evaluate the European Consensus Doctrine," in *Building Consensus on European Consensus. Judicial Interpretation of Human Rights in Europe and Beyond*, ed. Panos Kapotas and Vassilis Tzevelekos (Cambridge: Cambridge University Press, 2019) at 200-208; on the "diverse roles" of consensus see also Kapotas and Tzevelekos, "How (Difficult Is It) to Build Consensus on (European) Consensus?" at 1.

105 My use of "use" is deliberate, and largely inspired by Sara Ahmed; as she notes, it "often points beyond something even when it's about something" (Sara Ahmed, "Uses of Use. Diversity, Utility and the University" (2018), available at <https://www.youtube.com/watch?v=avKJ2w1mhng>, at 0:09:20), thus allowing for easy differentiation between rationales underlying consensus. I also hope that the use of "use" will foreground the element of construction involved (again echoing Ahmed, we might say that it expresses not only a relation, but an activity): consensus *is used by legal actors in certain ways*, rather than constituting some pre-discursive essence. For a use of use similarly foregrounding this latter aspect (with regard to law more generally), see Martti Koskenniemi, "Epilogue. To Enable and Enchant - on the Power of Law," in *The Law of International Lawyers. Reading Martti Koskenniemi*, ed. Wouter Werner, Marieke de Hoon, and Alexis Galán (Cambridge: Cambridge University Press, 2017) at 410.

is sometimes presented, somewhat simplistically, as one of "democracy" versus "human rights".[106] I say "somewhat simplistically" because both concepts are, of course, subject to widely varying interpretations and each can be supercharged with the other. It is commonplace to note, for example, that democracy worthy of the name needs human rights of some sort – elections, by themselves, are "underdeterminative of democracy".[107] Conversely, human rights require democratic appropriation and specification if they are not to remain formal and paternalistic guarantees.[108] Any position taken within constitutional argument can thus claim to represent "true" democracy and human rights:[109] it is important to keep in mind that these notions are, in Edward Said's memorable phrase, "by no means simple and agreed-upon concepts that one either does or does not find, like Easter eggs in the living-room".[110]

I do think that democracy and human rights can and should work in tandem but, for present purposes, I am more interested in the tensions which can arise between them insofar as they are understood as "two logics which are incompatible in the last instance",[111] specifically as logics which entail not only differing understandings of substantive concepts such as

---

106 For example, John Rawls, *Political Liberalism: Expanded Edition* (New York: Columbia University Press, 2005), at 5 builds on Constant and juxtaposes the liberties of the ancients ("political liberties") with those of the moderns ("basic rights of the person"), though he acknowledges that this is a "stylized contrast".

107 Thomas Carothers, "Empirical Perspectives on the Emerging Norm of Democracy in International Law," (1992) *Proceedings of the American Society of International Law* 261 at 264.

108 A point made very emphatically by Ingeborg Maus, *Menschenrechte, Demokratie und Frieden. Perspektiven globaler Organisation* (Frankfurt a.M.: Suhrkamp, 2015).

109 Conor Gearty, "Building Consensus on European Consensus," in *Building Consensus on European Consensus. Judicial Interpretation of Human Rights in Europe and Beyond*, ed. Panos Kapotas and Vassilis Tzevelekos (Cambridge: Cambridge University Press, 2019) at 449; Martti Koskenniemi, "'Intolerant Democracies': A Reaction," (1996) 37 *Harvard International Law Journal* 231 at 231; for example, Ian Cram, "Protocol 15 and Articles 10 and 11 ECHR - The Partial Triumph of Political Incumbency Post-Brighton?," (2018) 67 *International and Comparative Law Quarterly* 477 at 479 claims that "strict supranational review of national decision-making" is "a *sine qua non* of democratic self-government" (emphasis in original).

110 Edward W. Said, *Orientalism* (London: Penguin Books, 2003), at xiv.

111 Chantal Mouffe, *The Democratic Paradox* (London and New York: Verso, 2005), at 5; see also Dimitrios Kagiaros, "When to Use European Consensus: Assessing the Differential Treatment of Minority Groups by the European Court of Human Rights," in *Building Consensus on European Consensus. Judicial Interpretation of Human Rights in Europe and Beyond*, ed. Panos Kapotas and Vassilis

equality but also radically different epistemologies. I draw inspiration, in particular, from the juxtaposition of different "traditions" or "grammars" in the writings of Jürgen Habermas and Chantal Mouffe. While these two writers draw very different conclusions from that juxtaposition,[112] both capture the same basic tension in a particularly evocative manner, and in such a way that connections can usefully be drawn to the debates surrounding European consensus. I will call the two different perspectives at issue the *morality-focussed perspective* and the *ethos-focussed perspective* respectively,[113] partly to underline the differing epistemologies and partly to avoid more loaded terms such as "liberalism" and "republicanism" which is Habermas's way of framing the issue.[114] (Insofar as I do occasionally talk of liberalism, it tends to refer to the "larger worldview"[115] which I take both the morality-focussed perspective and the ethos-focussed perspective, as well as most of the legal human rights project as a whole, to form part of.)

The morality-focussed perspective emphasises the importance of prepolitical rights to ensure moral self-determination. Because they are conceived of as prepolitical to avoid a "tyranny of the majority", the "moral-cognitive moment" is dominant in determining those rights;[116] for lack of reference to the will of any particular political community, they are

Tzevelekos (Cambridge: Cambridge University Press, 2019) at 287 who speaks of "[t]wo conflicting schools of thought".

112 Habermas aiming for reconciliation and Mouffe emphasising paradox; I will touch further upon this in a moment, and again in Chapter 7, IV. and Chapter 11.

113 I will sometimes use these terms in the singular form and sometimes in the plural, without assigning much weight to the distinction. The singular form captures the stylized form of each perspective, though without meaning to detract from different approaches within them which the plural renders more visible; see also infra, V.

114 See generally Jürgen Habermas, *Between Facts and Norms*, trans. William Rehg (Cambridge: Polity Press, 1996), at 99; Jürgen Habermas, "Versöhnung durch öffentlichen Vernunftgebrauch," in *Die Einbeziehung des Anderen. Studien zur politischen Theorie* (Frankfurt a.M.: Suhrkamp, 1999) at 89; see also Jürgen Habermas, "Volkssouveränität als Verfahren," in *Faktizität und Geltung. Beiträge zur Diskurstheorie des Rechts und des demokratischen Rechtsstaats* (Frankfurt a.M.: Suhrkamp, 2014) at 610; confusingly, Habermas uses the same distinction in a different (though arguably related) sense in Habermas, *Between Facts and Norms*, at 296 (see his footnote 10, at 549).

115 Duncan Kennedy, *A Critique of Adjudication (fin de siècle)* (Cambridge, Mass.: Harvard University Press, 1997), at 5.

116 Habermas, *Between Facts and Norms*, at 100.

"moral-universalistic".[117] The ethos-focussed perspective, by contrast, holds that "the ethical-political will of a self-actualizing collectivity is forbidden to recognize anything that does not correspond to its own authentic life project": thus the "ethical-volitional" moment predominates,[118] and rights are assumed to gain normativity in "ethical-particularistic" contexts.[119] In contrast to the universalising beam of the morality-focussed perspective, ethically oriented approaches thus rely on a form of normativity which is *relative* to certain groups.[120]

The transnational context of the ECtHR further complicates the picture. Whereas ethical normativity is most commonly derived from particularities, traditions or democratic procedures within individual States, the ECHR covers not one but forty-seven States. Ethical normativity can thus be grounded in different macrosubjects – either individual States or the *community of States parties as a whole*. I take this latter approach to be the essence of one line of argument commonly adduced to justify reference to European consensus: for lack of democratic procedures at the transnational level itself, vertically comparative references viewed through the prism of collectivity constitute the next-best stand-in for grounding ethical normativity.

In light of this, we can reformulate some of the controversies surrounding the rein effect and the spur effect of European consensus which I described above.[121] Criticism that the rein effect of consensus detracts from moral truth and the proper protection of minority rights is based on the morality-focussed perspective, the argument being that the ECHR should instead be read as prepolitical in the sense of being clearly removed from domestic politics and the laws which they give rise to.[122] The diametrically opposed defence of European consensus as carrying democratic and epistemic benefits and quite rightly relating the ECtHR's decisions to the laws of the States parties to the ECHR is based on the ethos-based perspective.

---

117 Mouffe, *The Democratic Paradox*, at 129.

118 Habermas, *Between Facts and Norms*, at 100.

119 Mouffe, *The Democratic Paradox*, at 129.

120 To avoid confusion, I should note that "moral" and "ethical" are sometimes used as synonyms; thus, Griffin's personhood account of human rights (supra, note 95) is sometimes called "ethical" rather than "moral" (in contrast to "political" accounts). My usage of the terms here is, by contrast, based on the contrast between (universalising, cognitive) moral and (relative, volitional) ethical normativity.

121 Supra, IV.1.

122 See Chapter 2.

Yet so is the criticism of the spur effect of consensus: here, the complaint is that consensus overrides the ethos of the respondent State. Proponents of European consensus argue based on a different kind of ethical normativity, grounded not within an individual State but derived from European consensus for all the States parties taken together: I call this a *pan-European ethos*.[123]

We can relate the distinctions made so far back to Koskenniemi's framework by noting that the opposition between the ethical-volitional and the moral-cognitive perspectives is mirrored in ascending and descending patterns of justification in that it reflects the fundamental distinction between the "categories of will and knowledge" as the basis for argument.[124] On the more substantively loaded accounts which form the basis of my enquiry, however, the morality-focussed and ethos-focussed perspectives not only represent different patterns of justification but also incorporate different, more substantively oriented rationales for arguing based on or in opposition to State will. The prior sets out to vindicate prepolitical human rights and moral self-determination, whereas the latter emphasises the importance of civic self-organisation and equal political participation.[125] Specifying these rationales creates space to distinguish (or "disentangle") them from alternative rationales for supporting (or opposing) the use of European consensus, such as those discussed in the following subsection.

A further difference in how I will frame the tensions surrounding European consensus compared to the Koskenniemian account pertains to the different kinds of ethical normativity just described. Within the dichotomy of apology and utopia, European consensus could be said to occupy a paradigmatically ambiguous role, for it contains elements of both ascending and descending argument.[126] The intuitive connection, at least to me, is to ascending argument – consensus is based, after all, on the positions taken by the States parties to the ECHR. The controversies surrounding the rein effect exemplify this role, for the use of consensus is opposed precisely because it seems overly apologetic.[127] However, in cases involving the spur effect, European consensus also serves to override the will of indi-

---

123 See Chapter 3.

124 Koskenniemi, *From Apology to Utopia*, at 422.

125 See also Gearty, "Building Consensus on European Consensus" at 467, whom I read as half-way in between the formal and the substantive by juxtaposing "normativity" and "democratic will".

126 Carozza, "Uses and Misuses of Comparative Law" at 1232.

127 This aspect was my primary focus in connecting the Koskenniemian structure to European consensus in Theilen, "Levels of Generality in the Comparative Rea-

vidual States, and it can thus serve as the "revenge of utopia against the unfortunate laggards" among the States parties.[128]

The distinction between State will in general and individual State will – or, differently put, the distinction between different macrosubjects within which ethical normativity is grounded – thus assumes a crucial place in evaluating the use of European consensus. To foreground this distinction, I will re-adjust the dichotomy of ascending and descending patterns of argument to a *triangular* model in which consensus as an expression of a pan-European ethos is not presented as middle-ground between two poles, but rather forms its own pole which stands in tension with both moral normativity as well as ethical normativity based on individual national ethe. Describing consensus as a form of ethical normativity showcases certain affinities and differences within (what is then conceptualized as) the triangular tensions at issue: while its Janus-faced nature opens up opportunities for different instrumental allegiances with other kinds of normativity depending on the case at hand,[129] consensus builds on an ethos-focussed rather than a morality-focussed epistemology.

A further reason to accentuate the notion of a pan-European ethos is that it foregrounds the specifically regional character of the ECHR, an aspect which has barely been touched upon in human rights theory.[130] The intuitive connection to the States parties drawn by vertically comparative legal reasoning prompts the idea that consensus might be a way of filling this lacuna by "articulating regionally specific conceptions of shared human rights concepts, or interpreting locally identified human rights norms".[131] There is a fuzzy feeling of a European identity, with the States parties as "members of [a] club"[132] and the ECtHR using consensus to identify "fundamental values that bind European Countries together and

---

soning of the European Court of Human Rights and the European Court of Justice: Towards Judicial Reflective Equilibrium" at 415-416.

128 Mégret, "The Apology of Utopia" at 488.

129 See further Chapter 4, III.3.

130 Critically Zysset, *The ECHR and Human Rights Theory: Reconciling the Moral and Political Conceptions*, at 19-22; for a rare account of European consensus which centres the issue of how it relates to "sense of regional identity" and the exclusionary effects of such a construction, see the brilliant article by Claerwen O'Hara, "Consensus, Difference and Sexuality: Que(e)rying the European Court of Human Rights' Concept of 'European Consensus'," (2020) *Law and Critique*.

131 Neuman, "Import, Export, and Regional Consent in the Inter-American Court of Human Rights" at 106 (on the Inter-American Court).

132 Dzehtsiarou, "What Is Law for the European Court of Human Rights?" at 124.

give concrete expression to what it is to be European".[133] As with any supposedly common identity, I would suggest that it is important to ask who constructs it and what its exclusionary effects are. What of those within the States parties whose positions are not reflected in the laws making up consensus? What of those whose democratically formed positions are not represented by those States forming an alleged consensus? What of those outside Europe who are impacted in various ways by the interpretations of the ECtHR but never considered as part of European consensus in the first place?[134] But however one answers these questions, the element of a common regional identity emerges within the ECtHR's reasoning, for better or worse, in part through the use of European consensus – and the notion of ethical normativity at the pan-European level aims to capture this.

The way in which consensus has developed as an expression of a pan-European ethos which mediates between apology and utopia as its own prong within triangular tensions is one of the senses in which European consensus can be deemed to constitute a compromise between different perspectives on the interpretation of the Convention. Such a compromise need not, in and of itself, be a problem, but it may carry certain downsides. With regard to the national level, Mouffe holds that the interaction between the morality-focussed and ethos-focussed perspectives "installs a very important dynamic" in which each constantly challenges and subverts the hegemonic idealisations of the other; she therefore deems their paradoxical articulation to have "very positive consequences".[135] If European consensus is given too much weight within the triangular tensions which occur at the transnational level, then this potential for mutual contestation is lost and the idealisations involved in the use of consensus cannot be sufficiently challenged. I will therefore argue that it is important, at a minimum, to counteract the "compromise" of European consensus with other forms of reasoning.

133 Michael O'Boyle, "The Future of the European Court of Human Rights," (2011) 12 *German Law Journal* 1862 at 1866.

134 See Eyal Benvenisti, "The Margin of Appreciation, Subsidiarity and Global Challenges to Democracy," (2018) 9 *Journal of International Dispute Settlement* 240 at 245-247.

135 Mouffe, *The Democratic Paradox*, at 44-45; see in more detail Chapter 11, IV.2.

4. Strategic Considerations and Consensus as Legitimacy-Enhancement

In theory, the suggestion that use of European consensus should be accompanied and indeed challenged by other kinds of reasoning is somewhat uncontroversial: academic commentary is replete with references to consensus as a *rebuttable* presumption,[136] or to doctrinal figures such as "core rights" which establish a kind of "consensus-free" zone.[137] The ECtHR's case-law similarly contains manifold indications that considerations other than European consensus play a role, for example by virtue of other factors influencing the width of the margin of appreciation which it accords to the respondent State.[138] Yet besides the notion of a pan-European ethos which may constitute one rationale for giving normative force to European consensus, there may be other reasons for doing so, and these reasons arguably have a tendency to smooth over potential counter-arguments to European consensus and therefore consolidate its position as a particularly strong argument.

Broadly speaking, one might say that the kind of rationales I have in mind belong to the realm of what, in Rawlsian terms, one might call *non-ideal theory*. As Rawls put it in *The Law of Peoples*, at issue here are "questions arising from the highly nonideal conditions of our world with its great injustices and widespread social evils".[139] With whatever principles of justice are deemed ideal in mind, non-ideal theory thus seeks to identify transitional "policies and courses of action that are morally permissible and politically possible as well as likely to be effective".[140] Simply put, it grapples with the non-ideal conditions which pertain in practice and tries to formulate pragmatic, but not incoherent responses to them.

Non-ideal considerations are not traditionally acknowledged by courts (though this is not to say that judges do not consider them in practice).[141] Insofar as they are explicated, they usually pertain to what in non-ideal theory would be called the danger of "rug-pulling", i.e. taking into consideration those "cases where people base life plans or important activities on the

---

136 Dzehtsiarou, *European Consensus and the Legitimacy of the European Court of Human Rights*, at 27 and 119.
137 See Chapter 4, III.2.
138 See Chapter 8, III.2.-3.
139 Rawls, *The Law of Peoples*, at 89.
140 Ibid.
141 On the distinction between processes of discovery and justification, see infra, IV.5.

reasonable expectation that the rules will remain unchanged".[142] Legal doctrine knows this issue through the doctrine of legitimate expectations, or through the related principle of legal certainty.[143] European consensus is sometimes used to argue against legitimate expectations of a finding of no violation despite precedent to that effect, as when the ECtHR held in *Bayatyan v. Armenia* that a "shift in the interpretation of Article 9" to encompass a right to conscientious objection was "foreseeable".[144] The key difference to the usual debates about both non-ideal theory and legitimate expectations is that we are not dealing, here, with individuals' "life plans" but rather with the foreseeability of a change in interpretation *for the States parties*.[145]

This does raise a number of interesting and little discussed questions on the role of precedent within the ECtHR's case-law, the extent to which changes must be "foreseeable" for the States parties in order to be justified, and the conservative implications of such an approach. I will mostly leave this branch of non-ideal theory aside, however, so as to focus primarily on a different kind of non-ideal consideration which seems to increasingly hold sway with regard to constitutional adjudication in general,[146] but also enjoys incredible popularity with regard to European consensus in particular. For this line of reasoning, the issue is not so much whether the result of any given decision is morally permissible (as in ideal theory, and also when legitimate expectations are at issue), but whether it is likely to be effective or whether it will, rather, face opposition which might detract both from its implementation and from support for the ECtHR in general.

---

142 A. John Simmons, "Ideal and Nonideal Theory," (2010) 38 *Philosophy & Public Affairs* 5 at 20.

143 See generally Andreas von Arnauld, *Rechtssicherheit: Perspektivische Annäherungen an eine "idée directrice" des Rechts* (Tübingen: Mohr Siebeck, 2006); in the context of the ECHR, see Patricia Popelier, "Legitimate Expectations and the Law Maker in the Case Law of the European Court of Human Rights," (2006) *European Human Rights Law Review* 10.

144 ECtHR (GC), Appl. No. 23459/03 – *Bayatyan v. Armenia*, Judgment of 7 July 2011, at para. 108; Kanstantsin Dzehtsiarou, "European Consensus and the Evolutive Interpretation of the European Convention on Human Rights," (2011) 12 *German Law Journal* 1730 at 1744 calls this a mitigation of the "surprise effect" of evolutive interpretation.

145 Contrast the case-law of the ECJ on legitimate expectations as summarised in Tim Maciejewski and Jens T. Theilen, "Temporal Aspects of the Interaction between National Law and European Union Law: Reintroducing the Protection of Legitimate Expectations," (2017) *European Law Review* 706 at 713-714.

146 See Roni Mann, "Non-ideal Theory of Constitutional Adjudication," (2018) 7 *Global Constitutionalism* 14.

The ECtHR, after all, is not detached from broader political structures and power constellations within Europe.[147] If this has ever been in doubt, it became amply clear over the course of the last few years, for example in the context of high-level conferences on reform of the ECtHR such as those in Brighton (2012) and Copenhagen (2018).[148] These conferences have led, in particular, to increasing emphasis on notions such as the margin of appreciation or subsidiarity.[149] On their own terms, these concepts could be read as part of the principled oscillations described above, e.g. as giving stronger weight to national ethe;[150] but the kind of political discourse surrounding the reform of the ECtHR suggests that they also constitute a way of exerting pressure on the Court to conform to the positions of some States parties for less-than-principled reasons.[151]

With this context in mind, it is often said that the use of European consensus will contribute to the ECtHR's "legitimacy" in the sense of gaining or retaining the support of the States parties:[152] besides its democratic credentials, a further rationale adduced in its support is therefore its (purported) *legitimacy-enhancement*. Ultimately, this approach to consensus sees it as a *strategic* move to deal with the non-ideal conditions and power constellations within which the ECtHR finds itself.[153]

Within the Koskenniemian framework discussed above, strategic elements are just as likely to motivate moves between descending and ascending patterns of justification as more principled considerations are; if anything, particularly for the kind of "pragmatic middle-ground" which European consensus exemplifies, "strategic action" is assumed to be the relevant

147 Mikael Rask Madsen, "Rebalancing European Human Rights: Has the Brighton Declaration Engendered a New Deal on Human Rights in Europe?," (2018) 9 *Journal of International Dispute Settlement* 199 at 221.

148 For a more long-term overview, see Ed Bates, "Activism and Self-Restraint: The Margin of Appreciation's Strasbourg Career… Its 'Coming of Age'?," (2016) 36 *Human Rights Law Journal* 261.

149 Most notably in terms of positive law, Protocol No. 15 to the ECHR will add a reference to the margin of appreciation to the ECHR's Preamble.

150 See, in the context of the reform process, Cram, "Protocol 15 and Articles 10 and 11 ECHR - The Partial Triumph of Political Incumbency Post-Brighton?" at 484; and, more generally, Chapter 8, IV.

151 Critically e.g. James A. Goldston and Shirley Pouget, "The Copenhagen Declaration: How Not to "Reform" the European Court of Human Rights," (2018) *European Human Rights Law Review* 208.

152 Dzehtsiarou, *European Consensus and the Legitimacy of the European Court of Human Rights*, at 143.

153 See Chapter 9, II.5.

(though often undisclosed) rationale.[154] Strategy is introduced, in accordance with the radical indeterminacy of law, as a point of contrast to the ostensible "constraining force of the decision process"[155] – to emphasise, in other words, that decisions are not "produced by law".[156] Indeed, once the indeterminacy of law is accepted as a starting point, positing any kind of "principled" counterpoint to strategy seems suspect since it cannot be legally justified without renewed oscillation between descending and ascending argument: "In the search for justifiability, again, every argument is vulnerable to the logic of apology and utopia".[157]

The reason I nonetheless introduce a clear analytical distinction between principled and strategic considerations is to gain a position from which it *becomes possible to also criticise strategic moves*. I do not understand principled considerations as fixed in the sense of being mandated by any kind of legal constraint; but the indeterminacy of formal legal argument does not imply the equal desirability of all substantive results proposed.[158] Accordingly, my point is merely that, *whatever* the decision as to the "best" judgment in substance is based on in ideal terms (e.g., morality-focussed or ethos-focussed considerations), this can and should be distinguished from strategic considerations which might prompt an institution such as a court to make strategic concessions.[159] Departing from principle for reasons of strategy may be a desirable course of action in some cases – but it need not be, and this is a question worth discussing, however difficult it may be.

I adopt this framework, in other words, not due to any belief that it is somehow ontologically grounded or an analytical necessity, but because of the effects I hope it will have with regard to the debates surrounding European consensus.[160] Succinctly put, I want to introduce a sense that the rationale for making use of consensus matters – it matters, for example,

---

154 Koskenniemi, *From Apology to Utopia*, at 598 (in footnote 98).

155 Ibid.

156 Ibid., 570; see also e.g. Kennedy, *A Critique of Adjudication (fin de siècle)*, at 2, where strategy is directly linked to ideological (i.e. non-"legal") considerations.

157 Koskenniemi, *From Apology to Utopia*, at 598.

158 Quite the opposite, in fact: to my mind, critical international legal theory, at least insofar as it is concerned with "legal" results at all, is geared at opening up possibilities so as to allow for "better" decisions in the sense that they do not inadvertently reproduce structural biases; see further Chapter 11, IV.1.

159 See Mann, "Non-ideal Theory of Constitutional Adjudication" at 40.

160 For the move from whether knowledge is true to what knowledge *does*, see Eve Kosofsky Sedgwick, "Paranoid Reading and Reparative Reading, or, You're So Paranoid, You Probably Think This Essay Is About You," in *Touching Feeling: Affect, Pedagogy, Performativity* (Durham: Duke University Press, 2002) at 124.

whether consensus is given normative force because it reflects the results of democratic procedures within the States parties, as discussed above, or because it is regarded as a strategy to influence the future behaviour of the States parties, attempting to retain their support and encourage implementation of the ECtHR's judgments. My sense is that academic commentary on European consensus is increasingly conflating the two – if not explicitly, then at least in the sense that the ECtHR's legitimacy is regarded as indispensable and the use of consensus is, in turn, considered a crucial way of retaining that legitimacy.[161] Because the ECtHR commonly refers to consensus without specifying its rationale for doing so, it furthers or at least does not counteract this tendency.

This is the second sense in which I worry that European consensus may constitute too much of a compromise – it is taken to embody non-ideal considerations, and strategic concessions in particular, in such a way that counterarguments to the idealisations of a pan-European ethos are derided as "los[ing] touch with reality".[162] Strategic concessions as such are not, I think, inherently problematic; but blurring the lines between ideal and non-ideal theory in such a way that they become well-nigh indistinguishable in the fulcrum of European consensus and leave little room for contestation may well be. The perspective of legitimacy provides only for a form of "pseudo-normativity".[163] To compromise by giving it too prominent a role in human rights adjudication runs the risk of effectively minimising the emancipatory potential of the ECHR and lending credence to critical assessments that "[g]overnments have taken power over the idea of 'human rights' without really surrendering to them".[164]

5. The Indeterminacy of Processes of Justification

To tie up this section, let me return once more to the definition of European consensus which I offered above: consensus as a form of comparative

---

161 See Chapter 10.

162 Dzehtsiarou, *European Consensus and the Legitimacy of the European Court of Human Rights*, at 117-118; for further examples in this vein, see Chapter 10, III.3.

163 Martti Koskenniemi, "Law, Teleology and International Relations: An Essay in Counterdisciplinarity," (2011) 26 *International Relations* 3 at 18; see also Martti Koskenniemi, "Legitimacy, Rights and Ideology: Notes Towards a Critique of the New Moral Internationalism," (2003) 7 *Associations* 349 at 372.

164 Philip Allott, *Eutopia. New Philosophy and New Law for a Troubled World* (Cheltenham: Edward Elgar, 2016), at 228.

legal reasoning which refers vertically to the positions taken by the States parties to the ECHR, viewed through the prism of collectivity. A crucial part of this definition which I have not so far commented on is the classification of consensus as a kind of "reasoning". I have also spoken of the "use" of consensus, of giving consensus "normative force", or, taking up the ECtHR's formulation in *Demir and Baykara*,[165] of consensus as a "relevant consideration". A common and similarly ambiguous starting assumption is that consensus constitutes a *method of interpretation*.[166] In this subsection, I would like to briefly reflect more explicitly on what these formulations refer to.

The traditional dichotomy in this regard is between processes of discovery and processes of justification.[167] The prior describes the deliberation among the ECtHR's judges leading up to the decision finally announced in the form of a judgment. With regard to European consensus, we know that, as a general matter, comparative studies which form the basis of consensus-type arguments are carried out upon request from the judge-rapporteur by the ECtHR's Research Division.[168] Accordingly, European consensus forms part of the ECtHR's reasoning in the sense that it is included in the judges' deliberations before a decision is reached. More specific information (especially with regard to individual decision-making processes) is

165 Supra, note 15.

166 This, too, is reflected in *Demir and Baykara*, see ibid.; see also e.g. Vassilis Tzevelekos and Panos Kapotas, "Book review of Dzehtsiarou, 'European Consensus'," (2016) 53 *Common Market Law Review* 1145 at 1145; Fiona de Londras and Kanstantsin Dzehtsiarou, "Managing Judicial Innovation in the European Court of Human Rights," (2015) 15 *Human Rights Law Review* 523 at 541; Rozakis, "The European Judge as Comparatist" at 270; Maija Dahlberg, "'The Lack of Such a Common Approach' - Comparative Argumentation by the European Court of Human Rights," (2012-2013) 23 *Finnish Yearbook of International Law* 73 at 79; contrast Zysset, *The ECHR and Human Rights Theory: Reconciling the Moral and Political Conceptions*, at 133, describing consensus as "a method of *justification* rather than a method of *interpretation*" (emphases in original).

167 Richard A. Wasserstrom, *The Judicial Decision. Toward a Theory of Legal Justification* (Stanford: Stanford University Press, 1961), at 27; for a similar distinction see Niklas Luhmann, *Recht und Automation in der öffentlichen Verwaltung. Eine verwaltungswissenschaftliche Untersuchung* (Berlin: Duncker & Humblot, 1966), at 51.

168 See in more detail Dzehtsiarou, *European Consensus and the Legitimacy of the European Court of Human Rights*, at 86-88; Dzehtsiarou also introduces consensus as "a tool of interpretation" which "the ECtHR uses *in its decision-making*" (ibid., at 1, emphasis added) and states that it "supports the Court in *finding* the meaning of the Convention rights" (at 153, emphasis added).

generally unavailable, however, due to the confidentiality of deliberation.[169]

The process of justification, by contrast, refers to the reasons put forward in the public sphere to support the ECtHR's decisions, specifically the reasoning it offers as part of its judgments. Particularly in response to legal realist critiques which stressed the influence of non-legal factors ("politics", "ideology", "career interests", etc.) within the process of discovery, the process of justification has often been presented as the more relevant aspect of adjudication. For one thing, given the confidentiality usually associated with the process of discovery, the public justification offered for judicial decisions is often all we have to go on, as it were.[170] More foundationally, and partly as a consequence of this, discovery and justification are considered functionally distinct: "A judicial opinion is not an institutional record documenting a mental process, but rather an elaborated ratiocination of a decision through reasons considered valid and appropriate", inter alia to expose it "to evaluation and contestation on its own terms".[171]

As categorical as these distinctions may appear in theory, it is worth noting that there are also multiple points of contact. For example, one might argue that there is, legal realist critiques notwithstanding, an expectation that the justification for a decision will, by and large, be a good faith depiction of the grounds which actually motivated it within the process of discovery. Conversely, concerns about its justifiability will reflect back on the kind of deliberations which lead to the decision in the first place.[172] Insofar as the use of European consensus is concerned, the ECtHR itself has occasionally drawn explicit connections – as when it noted, in the justification for its decision in *Kafkaris v. Cyprus*, that "*[i]n reaching its decision the Court has had regard* to the standards prevailing amongst the member States

---

169 Rule 22 (1) Rules of the Court.

170 MacCormick therefore speaks of "at least ostensibly justifying reasons": Neil MacCormick, *Legal Reasoning and Legal Theory* (Oxford: Clarendon Press, 1978), at 14-16.

171 Mann, "Non-ideal Theory of Constitutional Adjudication" at 25; see also Joxerramon Bengoetxea, Neil MacCormick, and Leonor Moral Soriano, "Integration and Integrity in the Legal Reasoning of the European Court of Justice," in *The European Court of Justice*, ed. Gráinne de Búrca and J.H.H. Weiler (Oxford: Oxford University Press, 2001) at 44.

172 See generally Andreas von Arnauld, "Zur Rhetorik der Verhältnismäßigkeit," in *Verhältnismäßigkeit*, ed. Matthias Jestaedt and Oliver Lepsius (Tübingen: Mohr Siebeck, 2015) at 282-283; Robert Alexy, *Theorie der juristischen Argumentation*, 7th ed. (Frankfurt a.M.: Suhrkamp, 2012), at 282.

of the Council of Europe":[173] in other words, it mentioned its process of discovery as part of its process of justification.

In the context of comparative reasoning more broadly, it is generally acknowledged that the comparative materials mentioned during the process of justification form only a small part of those considered during the process of discovery.[174] Legal realist critiques have therefore re-emerged under the heading of "cherry-picking" – roughly speaking, the charge that comparative references are broadly considered during the process of discovery but cited only opportunistically within the process of justification, i.e. insofar as they cohere with the result advocated for by the judges.[175] However, while the notion of "cherry-picking" is sometimes mentioned in discussions of European consensus,[176] the brunt of the debate has been elsewhere. After all, a further point which distinguishes consensus from comparative reasoning more generally is the *regularity* with which it is referred to within the ECtHR's judgements – to the point that high-profile judgments which deal with general issues but do not mention consensus stand out and are immediately seized upon for criticism.[177]

---

173 ECtHR (GC), Appl. No. 21906/04 – *Kafkaris v. Cyprus*, Judgment of 12 February 2008, at para. 101 (emphasis added).

174 Stefan Martini, *Vergleichende Verfassungsrechtsprechung. Praxis, Viabilität und Begründung rechtsvergleichender Argumentation durch Verfassungsgerichte* (Berlin: Duncker & Humblot, 2018), at 81.

175 Richard A. Posner, "The Supreme Court 2004 Term. Foreword: A Political Court," (2005) 119 *Harvard Law Review* 32 at 88; Antonin Scalia, "Keynote Address: Foreign Legal Authority in the Federal Courts," (2004) 98 *Proceedings of the American Society of International Law* 305 at 308.

176 Janneke Gerards, "The European Court of Human Rights and the National Courts: Giving Shape to the Notion of 'Shared Responsibility'," in *Implementation of the European Convention on Human Rights and of the Judgments of the ECtHR in National Case-Law. A Comparative Analysis*, ed. Janneke Gerards and Joseph Fleuren (Cambridge et al.: Intersentia, 2014) at 45; Senden, *Interpretation of Fundamental Rights*, at 127-128; Shai Dothan, "The Optimal Use of Comparative Law," (2014) 43 *Denver Journal of International Law and Policy* 21 at 39.

177 The chamber judgment in ECtHR (Second Section), Appl. No. 30814/06 – *Lautsi v. Italy*, Judgment of 3 November 2009 is exemplary of this: see e.g. the reaction by Zoé Luca, "Case of Lautsi v Italy. Religious Symbols in Public Schools and the (Lack of) Margin of Appreciation," (2010) 17 *Maastricht Journal of European and Comparative Law* 98; for criticism from within the ECtHR itself, see e.g. ECtHR (GC), Appl. No. 54012/10 – *Mihalache v. Romania*, Judgment of 8 July 2019, concurring opinion of Judge Pinto de Albuquerque, at para. 10; see generally on the kind of case in which consensus is used supra, I.

Therefore, while the "selective use" of consensus can occasionally be criticised,[178] it is not usually the main point of interest. The primary focus, instead, lies on *how* consensus is used. How is the prism of collectivity applied to vertically comparative law, i.e. when does lack of consensus turn into consensus?[179] Which comparative materials form the basis of this evaluation?[180] What are the criteria for comparison and which conclusions are drawn from this?[181] How is consensus set in relation to other forms of reasoning within the ECtHR's judgments?[182] All of these questions are discussed by reference to the ECtHR's judgments in which "reliance [on comparative materials] is made expressly",[183] i.e. in relation to the process of justification.[184] Even when different rationales for the use of European consensus are at issue, as in the oscillation between strategy and principle mentioned above, these rationales may not be explicit within the ECtHR's judgments but they constitute a meta-justification for the use of consensus, which *does* appear explicitly. Insofar as I do not specify otherwise, then, my primary focus in what follows will be on processes of justification rather than discovery.

This brings us back, finally, to the Koskenniemian framework, which likewise focusses on justification. Koskenniemi takes legal realist critiques and the resulting distinction between processes of discovery and processes of justification as his starting point and aims to demonstrate that *even* processes of justification provide *only* for a formal language or "grammar" but do not produce substantive outcomes.[185] Hence the claim that international law is radically indeterminate as a consequence of contradictory ascend-

178 See e.g. Paul Johnson, *Homosexuality and the European Court of Human Rights* (Abingdon: Routledge, 2013), at 82, citing ECtHR, Appl. No. 36515/97 – *Fretté v. France*, Judgment of 26 February 2002 (which makes use of consensus) and ECtHR (GC), Appl. No. 43546/02 – *E.B. v. France*, Judgment of 22 January 2008 (which "ignored" it).

179 See Chapter 5.

180 See Chapter 6.

181 See Chapter 7.

182 See Chapter 8.

183 Legg, *The Margin of Appreciation*, at 131.

184 See also R. St. J. Macdonald, "The Margin of Appreciation," in *The European System for the Protection of Human Rights*, ed. R. St. J. Macdonald, Franz Matscher, and Herbert Petzold (Dordrecht: Nijhoff, 1993) at 123.

185 Koskenniemi, *From Apology to Utopia*, at 25 and 570; see also Korhonen, "New International Law: Silence, Defence or Deliverance?" at 10; Thomas Skouteris, "Fin de NAIL: New Approaches to International Law and its Impact on Contemporary International Legal Scholarship," (1997) 10 *Leiden Journal of International Law* 415 at 418-419.

ing and descending patterns of justification, rather than in some meaningful sense "objective": "International legal discourse is incoherent as it incorporates contradictory assumptions about what it is to argue objectively about norms".[186]

It may seem rather trivial to transfer this framework to the ECHR, albeit with the modifications discussed above, and thus to insist on indeterminacy in the context of human rights – while the radical implications of the indeterminacy thesis for central tenets of liberalism, and by extension for the concept of human rights, certainly remain underappreciated,[187] human rights *are* at least commonly perceived as particularly "vague" or "abstract" and in that more limited sense indeterminate.[188] Yet not only is there a world of differences between these perspectives on indeterminacy; my sense is also that in any case, perhaps paradoxically, European consensus emerges as an *attempt to reinstate a kind of objectivity* within the ECtHR's processes of justification even if or rather precisely *because* they are otherwise acknowledged to be relatively indeterminate.[189] It is claimed, for example, that any "departure from the solutions supported by [consensus] is profoundly problematic":[190] here, consensus seems to be conceived of as a factor external to the ECtHR's judges,[191] binding upon them and somehow predetermining the substantive result of any given case, not merely a formal means of articulation within the grammar of regional human rights law.

---

186 Koskenniemi, *From Apology to Utopia*, at 63.

187 Ntina Tzouvala, "New Approaches to International Law: The History of a Project," (2016) 27 *European Journal of International Law* 215 at 229; see also Ntina Tzouvala, *Capitalism as Civilisation. A History of International Law* (Cambridge: Cambridge University Press, 2020), at 35.

188 See supra, I., particularly note 12; for the move from the "truism" of "linguistic openness" to a stronger sense of indeterminacy, see Koskenniemi, "The Effect of Rights on Political Culture" at 147; more generally on different approaches to indeterminacy Cameron A. Miles, "Indeterminacy," in *Concepts for International Law. Contributions to Disciplinary Thought*, ed. Jean d'Aspremont and Sahib Singh (Cheltenham: Edward Elgar, 2019); in the context of human rights, see also Frédéric Mégret, "Where Does the Critique of International Human Rights Stand? An Exploration in 18 Vignettes," in *New Approaches to International Law: The European and American Experiences*, ed. José María Beneyto and David Kennedy (The Hague: T.M.C. Asser Press, 2012), nothing that human rights as a body of law "does not even try to have the pseudo rigidity of rules".

189 On different senses of objectivity, see e.g. Chapter 3, II., Chapter 5, I. and V., and Chapter 10, III.2.

190 Dzehtsiarou, "What Is Law for the European Court of Human Rights?" at 130.

191 See also Chapter 5, V.

By disentangling various perspectives on European consensus as well as different rationales for using it, I hope to counteract this tendency. Echoing Koskenniemi, my aim is thus to free legal actors from the preconception that they are constrained by the law – or by (a certain understanding of) European consensus – which not only gives them "a mistaken picture of the epistemic standing of their beliefs but also of the possibilities for transformative action",[192] as well as downplaying their own responsibility for the decisions they reach. Differently put, in the specific context of this study: my purpose is to underline that neither consensus (all its tempting compromises notwithstanding) nor other traditional forms of legal reasoning should exhaust the imaginative space which human rights are capable of opening up.[193]

V. *Outline of the Following Chapters*

The remaining chapters will take up and elaborate on the argument roughly traced above. I begin on the level of principle, juxtaposing the morality-focussed perspective and the ethos-focussed perspective. Chapter 2 introduces the prior: its criticism of European consensus as an infringement on prepolitical human rights, but also its less starkly dismissive attitude in cases involving the spur effect. Chapter 3 contrasts this approach with that of the ethos-focussed perspective, particularly its insistence that a moral-cognitive epistemology falls prey to widespread disagreement about rights and that ethical-volitional approaches are therefore more appropriate. I trace the move from individual national ethe to a pan-European ethos as exemplified by European consensus, and connect it to the internationalist commitments implied by institutionalising a regional system of human rights protection. Grounding normativity in a pan-European ethos, however, also raises difficult questions as to how a common European identity can be identified without significant homogenisation.

Frédéric Mégret has noted how apology and utopia are not only "ideal conceptual parameters of international jurisprudence", but also often represent "embodied audiences", with e.g. governments tending towards apology while civil society organisations tend towards utopia.[194] Much the same is true of the morality-focussed and ethos-focussed perspectives with

192 Koskenniemi, *From Apology to Utopia*, at 538.
193 See Chapter 11.
194 Mégret, "The Apology of Utopia" at 483.

regard to different groupings within society at large, but also with regard to academic literature: some authors come down very strongly in favour of one or the other and thus, in a sense, embody a relatively "pure" form of that perspective. For all the dangers of "mutual caricature",[195] I think it is useful to begin by taking up these ideal-type accounts, particularly because they exemplify the different starting assumptions which I described above. Nonetheless, I would also emphasise at the outset that most accounts carry elements of different perspectives. By grouping various authors together as proponents of "the" morality-focussed or ethos-focussed perspectives, I do not mean to flatten out important differences between them; the grouping merely serves illustrative purposes.

Chapter 4 provides more nuance in that regard, for it explores the triangular tensions which result between European consensus (based on the notion of a pan-European ethos) and both moral normativity as well as ethical normativity based on individual national ethe. I argue, first, that these tensions cannot be dissolved by means of reconceptualization as it is offered, for example, by the so-called "epistemic" account of consensus. Rather, the differing epistemologies and idealisations involved lead to the kind of oscillation between different perspectives which is by now familiar from the Koskenniemian framework, and which I will demonstrate by reference to the example of core rights. I also discuss the consequences of conceptualising the tensions at issue as triangular, specifically the sense of compromise which arises from the possibility of instrumental allegiances between normativity grounded in a pan-European ethos and other forms of normativity, depending on whether the rein effect or the spur effect is operationalised.

The following chapters set out to assess how these triangular tensions play out within the case-law of the ECtHR. I should note immediately that such an assessment is likely to exhibit a selection bias at least in some form[196] – given the large number of cases decided by the ECtHR and the recurring reference to European consensus, it has become well-nigh impossible to provide a truly exhaustive analysis (to say nothing of a complementary analysis of cases *not* involving consensus). In any event, my interest is primarily in the tensions inherent in the ECtHR's reasoning, not in quan-

---

195 Cécile Laborde and John Maynor, "The Republican Contribution to Contemporary Political Theory," in *Republicanism and Political Theory*, ed. Cécile Laborde and John Maynor (Malden, Mass.: Blackwell, 2008) at 2.

196 See Tzevelekos and Kapotas, "Book review of Dzehtsiarou, 'European Consensus'" at 1148.

titative analysis. Still, the way in which consensus is used and hence its place within these tensions may shift within different lines of case-law or according to subject-matter. There is room for further, more specific studies on this point; for present purposes, I broadly take cases spanning a wide range of contexts and Convention provisions into account.[197] Given the controversies most often raised in the context of consensus, however, I will take a special interest in minority rights, and cases involving the right to private life under Article 8 ECHR, in particular, will occupy a prominent role.[198]

A preliminary difficulty in approaching the case-law with an aim to investigating tensions within the ECtHR's reasoning is that the Court only rarely presents European consensus in such a way that it conflicts with the substantive result of the case. I therefore begin by exploring the flexibility inherent in the construction of consensus itself and the way in which this relates to morality-focussed and ethos-focussed considerations. Chapter 5 considers numerical issues: how many States parties are necessary to identify (lack of) consensus, and accordingly to operationalise the rein effect or spur effect? I argue that the conventional account of consensus involves an asymmetry in favour of the rein effect which reflects the concerns of the ethos-focussed perspective, but that other cases, particularly those involving "trends", incorporate more morality-focussed elements into the establishment of European consensus. Chapter 6 further complicates the picture by showing how not only domestic law, but also international law may be considered part of European consensus, and how this may lead to a shift in emphasis within the triangular tensions at issue. Chapter 7 picks up the crucial but little discussed question of how to frame the issue to which consensus is applied, particularly the level of generality at which consensus is referred to and how this relates to (whatever is construed as) the issue before the ECtHR. I suggest that shifts in the level of generality at which consensus is used, too, can be connected to the triangular tensions involved in the ECtHR's reasoning or, as a more general framework within liberal theory, to the notion of a reflective equilibrium – which has the ad-

197 See the overview in Dzehtsiarou, *European Consensus and the Legitimacy of the European Court of Human Rights*, at 17-20.

198 The particular importance of consensus in the context of the limitation clauses of Articles 8-11 has often been noted: see e.g. Aaron A. Ostrovsky, "What's So Funny About Peace, Love, and Understanding? How the Margin of Appreciation Doctrine Preserves Core Human Rights within Cultural Diversity and Legitimises International Human Rights Tribunals," (2005) 1 *Hanse Law Review* 47 at 50; Brauch, "The Dangerous Search for an Elusive Consensus" at 279.

vantage of disavowing reliance only on one specific interpretation of consensus at a certain level of generality, but remains limited by its coherentist approach.

Chapter 8 broadens the scope of analysis and considers consensus in relation to other doctrines within the ECtHR's case-law, specifically the notion of autonomous concepts and the controversial margin of appreciation. The latter, in particular, showcases the potential for oscillation between a pan-European ethos and either the morality-focussed perspective or individual national ethe. While any perspective can thus be undermined by switching to the alternate epistemologies of another, the juxtaposition of autonomous concepts, on the one hand, and the margin of appreciation, on the other, also demonstrates that an uneasy stability may emerge in practice – not because it is in any sense legally necessary but because certain doctrines gain prominence within the ECtHR's case-law. A strong emphasis on consensus emerges as one of the current hallmarks of said case-law.

As mentioned above, however, my sense is that it is not primarily – or at least not solely – the principled considerations of the ethos-focussed perspective which lead to the naturalisation of European consensus as identifying a clear substantive outcome for the ECtHR to endorse. Rather, the popularity of this line of argument is due in large part to the notion of consensus as legitimacy-enhancement. I tackle this approach in Chapter 9, setting out its background assumptions and core tenets before pondering whether the goal of retaining the support of the States parties can truly be achieved by incremental development of the ECtHR's case-law based on European consensus. I argue that supporting consensus due to its ostensible legitimacy-enhancement constitutes a form of abstract strategizing since it is disconnected from strategic considerations that are specific to any given case.

This has certain advantages and disadvantages, but the primary point which I will focus on is how abstract strategizing relates to the relationship between principle and strategy in conceptualising European consensus. In Chapter 10, I argue that there are persistent tensions between taking a principled stand and allowing strategic concessions, and that the conflation of the two in discussions on European consensus contributes to a normalisation of strategic concessions which severely limits the emancipatory potential of human rights. Accordingly, I close with a plea to move away from the notion of consensus as legitimacy-enhancement – not so as to prevent strategic concessions entirely, but so as to become more aware of their costs and to acknowledge the responsibility of the ECtHR's judges, here as elsewhere, to *decide* where to take human rights rather than hiding behind certain understandings of what is deemed "realistic".

The red thread running through this study will be a focus on the contingent nature of European consensus – contrary to claims that it is an "objective" or "natural" method to use, "inherent" in regional human rights law, or "realistically" a necessary point of reference, my goal is to open up space for rethinking human rights in more transformative ways. This can be considered a rather standard approach to denaturalising current institutional practices, and part and parcel of many critically minded analyses in international law and elsewhere.[199] The question then follows, however, where a critique of European consensus should take us. There is a very real danger of co-optation here – that an argument against (the objectivity of) consensus might be taken to be an argument in favour of other forms of legal reasoning, and ultimately amount to little more than a plea for a slight shift within the ECtHR's processes of justification, otherwise content to leave things to business as usual.

To avoid this impression, I shift gears in the final chapter and move from an argument geared primarily at intervening in relatively specialised debates on European consensus to a broader consideration of the role of human rights courts such as the ECtHR within processes of social transformation. I provide a brief overview of the way in which the indeterminacy thesis outlined above can be connected to political critiques of human rights, of the consequences of such critiques for the way in which we approach legal and specifically judicial discourse, and specifically of possible uses of vertically comparative law beyond the narrow ambit of European consensus which distance themselves from the argumentative structures otherwise prevalent in regional human rights law. I suggest that vertically comparative law could be understood as what I call a "reflective disruption of equilibrium" – a way of foregrounding inconsistencies and paradoxes within European public culture so as to unsettle concepts otherwise left unquestioned. While by no means a panacea, my hope is that this mode of reasoning might create imaginative space for considering a more future-oriented and open jurisprudence of regional human rights.

---

199 See Susan Marks, "False Contingency," (2009) 62 *Current Legal Problems* 1, also noting its limits; for further reflections on the limits of denaturalization *as such*, see Jens T. Theilen, Isabelle Hassfurther, and Wiebke Staff, "Towards Utopia - Rethinking International Law," (2017) 60 *German Yearbook of International Law* 315 at 328.

Chapter 2: Morality-focussed Perspectives: European Consensus as an Infringement on Prepolitical Rights

I. Introduction

I begin with the criticism of European consensus. By setting out the perspective of those commentators who argue *against* its use, it will become possible from the very beginning to highlight areas of tension in which the use of consensus is particularly controversial, and to tease out the epistemological perspective to which consensus is arguably a deliberate counterpoint. I therefore focus, in this chapter, on what I will call the *morality-focussed perspective* on regional human rights adjudication, which underlies the most popular grounds for criticising European consensus: the worry that its use will undermine the substance of regional human rights protection, particularly insofar as minority rights are concerned.

Within the national context, Habermas introduces the morality-focussed perspective as follows. Its proponents "conceive human rights as the expression of moral self-determination" and "postulate the priority of human rights that guarantee the prepolitical liberties of the individual and set limits on the sovereign will of the political legislator".[200] This position has been highly influential in political morality and, above all, in theories of individual rights. It resonates with the idea, already mentioned in Chapter 1 in the context of moral theories of human rights, that individuals have rights merely by virtue of being human.[201] As Amartya Sen has put it, there is "something deeply attractive in the idea that every person any-

---

200 Habermas, *Between Facts and Norms*, at 99-100.

201 E.g. in different ways Griffin, *On Human Rights*, at 48; John Finnis, *Natural Law & Natural Rights*, 2nd ed. (Oxford: Oxford University Press, 2011), at 198; Michael Boylan, *Natural Human Rights. A Theory* (Cambridge: Cambridge University Press, 2014), at 13; Jack Donnelly, *Universal Human Rights*, 3rd ed. (Ithaca and London: Cornell University Press, 2013), at 7; in the context of European consensus: Brauch, "The Dangerous Search for an Elusive Consensus" at 288; see also the description of this position by Gearty, "Building Consensus on European Consensus" at 448-449.

where in the world, irrespective of [...] territorial legislation, has some basic rights".[202]

Of course, the rights contained in the ECHR are not, in a strict sense, prepolitical or (merely) moral: The Convention itself was, after all, created by the consent of the States parties.[203] It could thus be argued "that the ECHR itself is a form of consensus";[204] the ECtHR sometimes makes use of this perspective when emphasising the particular importance of some provisions, as when it argues that Article 2 ECHR (the right to life) "enshrines one of the basic values of the democratic societies making up the Council of Europe".[205] Proponents of the morality-focussed perspective acknowledge and indeed emphasise the consent of the States parties to be bound by the ECHR:[206] their point is not to reduce the legal qualities of the ECHR to a purely moral account. The point, rather, is that moral principles should guide the interpretation of the Convention and the justification of the ECtHR's decisions. Thus identified and justified, the concrete norms of regional human rights law set by the ECtHR would be prepolitical in the double sense of, first, restraining politics at the national level based on, second, moral considerations rather than European consensus.

In this chapter, I will follow this juxtaposition between the morality-focussed perspective and European consensus to give shape to the prior and, by virtue of contrast, the latter. I begin with the morality-focussed perspective's focus on the prepolitical rights of intra-State minorities – its concerns about prejudice, a "tyranny of the majority" and the conception of "minority" at play (II.1.). Because of the transnational vantage point of the ECtHR, these concerns must be broadened to encompass not only in-

---

202 Amartya Sen, "Elements of a Theory of Human Rights," (2004) 32 *Philosophy & Public Affairs* 315 at 315.

203 On the tension inherent in this, see further Chapter 6, III. in the context of human rights law more generally.

204 Christian Djeffal, "Consensus, Stasis, Evolution: Reconstructing Argumentative Patterns in Evolutive ECHR Jurisprudence," in *Building Consensus on European Consensus. Judicial Interpretation of Human Rights in Europe and Beyond*, ed. Panos Kapotas and Vassilis Tzevelekos (Cambridge: Cambridge University Press, 2019) at 77.

205 ECtHR (GC), Appl. No. 56080/13 – *Lopes de Sousa Fernandes v. Portugal*, Judgment of 19 December 2017, at para. 164.

206 See the commitment-based argument in George Letsas, "The ECHR as a Living Instrument: Its Meaning and Legitimacy," in *Constituting Europe. The European Court of Human Rights in a National, European and Global Context*, ed. Andreas Føllesdal, Birgit Peters, and Geir Ulfstein (Cambridge: Cambridge University Press, 2013) at 136.

tra-State majorities, but also other domestic processes and institutions such as courts. The rationale for opposing European consensus, however, remains similar to that for opposing majority decisions in matters affecting the relationship between majority and minority within any given State: The verticality of European consensus, on the basis of the morality-focussed perspective, appears paradoxical because the ECtHR refers back to the very States parties it is supposed to be supervising (II.2.). More generally, this implies a role for regional human rights law in which the ECtHR is conceived of as primarily critical and confrontational: any given State party's political decisions and legal system could be subject to review by the Court, and European consensus is conceptualised as merely the sum of these parts, and hence likewise subject to criticism rather than a justificatory element for the ECtHR. This, in turn, implies an epistemology which strongly emphasises the is-ought distinction and follows a strict form of normativity which leaves no room for elements which are conceived of as factual (II.3.).

In principle, these critical points apply to any use of European consensus; but because the primary concern of the morality-focussed perspective is to prevent the infringement of prepolitical minority rights, it takes issue, in particular, with the rein effect of consensus which prevents the vindication of such rights.[207] The morality-focussed perspective's take on the spur effect, which constitutes an argument *in favour* of finding a violation of the Convention, is more ambivalent: While European consensus is still not accorded independent force as a normative argument, it seems less suspect and is sometimes admitted as a secondary consideration so long as it corroborates independently established normative standards (III.). This raises the question of how to establish these standards in the first place, and who should be competent to do so: questions which will lead us towards the morality-focussed perspective's main rival, the ethos-focussed perspective (IV.).

II. Morality-focussed Criticism of European Consensus

1. Minority Rights and the Tyranny of the Majority

When Habermas introduces the morality-focussed perspective as based on "the priority of human rights that guarantee the prepolitical liberties of the

207 For the distinction between rein and spur effect, see Chapter 1, III.

individual and set limits on the sovereign will of the political legislator", he notes that its proponents "invoke the danger of a 'tyranny of the majority'" to justify such limits. Indeed, the dangers of majority rule for such pre-political rights have long been highlighted. Alexis de Tocqueville popularised the phrase "tyranny of the majority" which Habermas mentions.[208] It was taken up, for example, by John Stuart Mill who referred to it as "among the evils against which society requires to be on its guard": there is always the danger, he argues, that the ruling majority may oppress those in the minority within a certain society.[209] The majority, in brief, cannot be *trusted* to uphold minority rights.[210]

This morality-focussed preoccupation with the relationship between intra-State minorities and majorities has been the main ground for criticism of European consensus, particularly insofar as its rein effect is concerned – indeed, the "tyranny of the majority" has explicitly been cited as the underlying problem in that regard.[211] Concerns have been aired, in particular, by Eyal Benvenisti. He does not necessarily oppose the use of European consensus in general, but sees it as "inappropriate when conflicts between majorities and minorities are examined"[212] since consensus refers back to the approaches of the States parties but minority values are "hardly reflected in national policies".[213] In other words: national laws are made by intra-State majorities, so they should not be given normative force in the reason-

208 Alexis de Tocqueville, *Democracy in America: Historical-Critical Edition of De la démocratie en Amérique*, trans. James T. Schleifer (Indianapolis: Liberty Fund, 2010), vol. II, chapter 7.

209 John Stuart Mill, "On Liberty," in *On Liberty and Other Essays* (Oxford: Oxford University Press, 1991) at 8; but see also his cautioning note on the conservative misuse of the phrase "tyranny of the majority" in John Stuart Mill, "De Tocqueville on Democracy in America [II]," in *The Collected Works of John Stuart Mill, Volume XVIII - Essays on Politics and Society*, ed. John M. Robson (Toronto: University of Toronto Press, 1977) at 156.

210 See Ely, *Democracy and Distrust. A Theory of Judicial Review*, at 103; Ely's theory is hardly a paradigmatic example of the morality-focussed perspective (see infra, note 241), but in this regard, at any rate, there is a certain affinity.

211 Arai-Takahashi, "The Margin of Appreciation Doctrine: A Theoretical Analysis of Strasbourg's Variable Geometry" at 96; see also Kapotas and Tzevelekos, "How (Difficult Is It) to Build Consensus on (European) Consensus?" at 13 in footnote 51 on the "omnipresen[ce]" of the counter-majoritarian question in debates on consensus.

212 Eyal Benvenisti, "Margin of Appreciation, Consensus, and Universal Standards," (1999) 31 *New York University Journal of International Law and Politics* 843 at 847 (on the margin of appreciation).

213 Ibid., 851.

ing of the ECtHR which should rather aim to counterbalance national inequalities.[214] To do otherwise would be to further enhance "the inherent deficiencies" of democratic systems.[215]

It is seldom made clear how exactly an intra-State "minority" should be defined (and, of course, its use may vary from one author to the next). On a broad understanding, the protection of human rights by a court such as the ECtHR is conceptually and inescapably concerned with the protection of minorities since it contrasts with majority decisions previously made by individual States;[216] this would be a *functional* understanding of minorities as encompassing any stances that happen to not receive political support at a certain moment. But this is not usually what motivates the concern with minority rights that drives the morality-focussed position:[217] rather, its proponents make use of a more loaded understanding of minorities.

Benvenisti, for example, makes it clear that he does not necessarily oppose the use of European consensus when "certain matters that affect the general population in a given society" are at issue: he cites restrictions on hate speech and statutes of limitations for actions in tort as examples.[218] His understanding of "minorities" is thus more circumscribed than the functional view. He refers to minority *groups* that "tend to be *persistently* outvoted" because they belong to certain ethnic, national or religious communities, or to other "political outcasts" with distinct interests such as gay persons or persons with disabilities.[219] More recently, Benvenisti has also drawn attention to other "outsiders" such as refugees or asylum seekers.[220] Although there is no precise definition, then, the focus is laid on those minority groups that have been traditionally disenfranchised in some way.

---

214 Ivana Radačić, "The Margin of Appreciation, Consensus, Morality and the Rights of the Vulnerable Groups," (2010) 31 *Zb. Prav. fak. Rij.* 599 at 600; Joanna N. Erdman, "The Deficiency of Consensus in Human Rights Protection: A Case Study of Goodwin v. United Kingdom and I. v. United Kingdom," (2003) 2 *Journal of Law and Equality* 318 at 346.

215 Benvenisti, "Margin of Appreciation, Consensus, and Universal Standards" at 847.

216 See Robert Spano, "Universality or Diversity of Human Rights? Strasbourg in the Age of Subsidiarity," (2014) 14 *Human Rights Law Review* 487 at 488.

217 See Mark Tushnet, *Taking the Constitution Away from the Courts* (Princeton, N.J.: Princeton University Press, 1999), at 159.

218 Benvenisti, "Margin of Appreciation, Consensus, and Universal Standards" at 847.

219 Ibid., 848-849 (emphasis added).

220 Benvenisti, "The Margin of Appreciation, Subsidiarity and Global Challenges to Democracy" at 242; see also Buchanan, *The Heart of Human Rights*, at 119-120.

Similarly, Helen Fenwick has noted that giving normative force to European consensus can "lead to acceptance of detrimental treatment of groups traditionally vulnerable to discrimination, including women and sexual minorities".[221]

Both the focus on these traditionally disenfranchised minority groups and the morality-driven concern with ensuring their prepolitical rights also emerge clearly in the argument of George Letsas, specifically in the way he builds on the jurisprudence of Ronald Dworkin in criticising the use of European consensus. Since Dworkin's approach and the context in which it was developed remain pertinent in discussing the controversies surrounding European consensus, it may be helpful to recap them in some detail. Dworkin's theory of rights stands in the tradition of anti-majoritarianism mentioned above: he argues that rights must be prepolitical since they would be devoid of purpose if defeated by an appeal to the majority will. Therefore, on his view, a right "must be a right to do something even when the majority thinks it would be wrong to do it, and even when the majority would be worse off for having it done".[222] Rights are crucial because they represent "the majority's promise to the minorities that their dignity and equality will be respected".[223]

Dworkin developed this argument partly as a response to utilitarianism, a theory that is well-known for being hostile to individual rights given its emphasis on the aggregated good of society as a whole.[224] The argument goes roughly as follows. The appeal of utilitarian theories, according to Dworkin, lies in their ostensible egalitarian nature: everyone's preferences

---

221 Helen Fenwick, "Same-sex Unions at the Strasbourg Court in a Divided Europe: Driving Forward Reform or Protecting the Court's Authority via Consensus Analysis?," (2016) *European Human Rights Law Review* 248 at 249; see also Holning Lau, "Rewriting Schalk and Kopf: Shifting the Locus of Deference," in *Diversity and European Human Rights. Rewriting Judgments of the ECHR*, ed. Eva Brems (Cambridge: Cambridge University Press, 2012) at 248.

222 Ronald Dworkin, "Taking Rights Seriously," in *Taking Rights Seriously* (London: Bloomsbury, 2013) at 234; see also Ronald Dworkin, "Rights as Trumps," in *Theories of Rights*, ed. Jeremy Waldron (Oxford: Oxford University Press, 1984) at 166.

223 Dworkin, "Taking Rights Seriously" at 246.

224 See Bentham's infamous dictum that rights are "nonsense on stilts": Jeremy Bentham, "Nonsense upon Stilts, or Pandora's Box Opened," in *The Collected Works of Jeremy Bentham*, ed. Philip Schofield, Catherine Pease-Watkins, and Cyprian Blamires (Oxford: Oxford University Press, 2002) at 330; the classic rights-based response to utilitarianism is John Rawls, *A Theory of Justice: Revised Edition* (Cambridge, Mass.: Belknap Press of Harvard University Press, 1999) e.g. at 24.

are counted equally.[225] At first sight, it might seem that such a view concords with Dworkin's likewise egalitarian approach. However, Dworkin draws a distinction between personal and external preferences. The prior are directly connected to one's own situation, while the latter refer to one's own preferences regarding the situation and opportunities *of other people*.[226] Such external preferences, Dworkin argues, distort the allegedly egalitarianism of utilitarian reasoning: because they make one's opportunities depend on the preferences of other people, different ways of life are not seen as inherently equal but rather dependent on the approval of others.[227] The argument thus reconnects to the anti-majoritarian purpose of rights that Dworkin favoured from the very beginning: utilitarianism fails because it makes individual rights dependent on the external preferences of a society's majority.[228] This is also the gist of Dworkin's famous conceptualisation of rights as "trumps": it gives rights a reason-blocking function which excludes external preferences and hence (insofar as it involves those external preferences) utilitarian reasoning as a ground on which decisions may be based.[229]

Especially in his earlier works, Dworkin seems to deny normative force to any kind of external preferences. However, he also gives special attention to certain situations: in particular, he does not oppose, in theory, a utilitarian argument based solely on personal preferences – but he does claim that utilitarianism will usually fail because personal and external preferences cannot be untangled, which is "especially true when preferences are affected by prejudice".[230] Prejudices are understood as judgements which run counter to foundational moral ideas indicating the moral equality of all persons rather than their inferiority based on morally irrelevant characteristics.[231] H.L.A. Hart brought this aspect to the fore by insisting that only certain kinds of external preferences are normatively problematic in the first place – those influenced by the kind of prejudice which

225 Dworkin, "Rights as Trumps" at 154.

226 Dworkin, "Reverse Discrimination" at 281.

227 Ibid., 282.

228 On Dworkin's connection of utilitarianism and majoritarian democracy, see H.L.A. Hart, "Between Utility and Rights," (1979) 79 *Columbia Law Review* 828 at 837-838; see also, more generally, Jeremy Waldron, "Rights and Majorities: Rousseau Revisited," (1990) 32 *Nomos* 44 at 45-46 and 51.

229 Dworkin, "Reverse Discrimination" at 283; see also Dworkin, "Taking Rights Seriously" at 242; Dworkin, "Rights as Trumps" at 158.

230 Dworkin, "Reverse Discrimination" at 283.

231 Dworkin, "Liberty and Moralism" at 299.

(though Hart does not emphasise this aspect) Dworkin initially integrated into his theory only in a second step, as a device for connecting personal and external preferences. In Hart's own terms, their problem is not one "of the mere externality of the preferences that have tipped the balance but of their content: that is, the liberty-denying and respect-denying content".[232] Dworkin's response to this is not entirely clear: on the one hand, he does not concede Hart's point; but on the other, his response is noticeably devoid of reference to "external preferences". Instead, he retains his anti-majoritarian focus by denying normative force to what is now called "the majority's moralistic preferences about how the minority should live"[233] and again refers to the background assumption that people must be treated as equals.[234]

A further aspect of note in Dworkin's approach is that he refers, throughout, to discrimination as it exists in current societies. The examples he chooses reflect this point: he refers above all to racial minorities and homosexuality, i.e. to minority groups similar to those that Benvenisti is concerned with.[235] The element of disenfranchisement they face is reflected in the fact that prejudices against them are said to be "widespread and pervasive".[236] This is why, in his early writings, Dworkin could make the jump from opposing external preferences to opposing utilitarianism as a whole: he assumed that prejudice such as racism is so inextricably entwined with personal preferences and economic structures that it can never be shown that the utilitarian argument would succeed in the absence of prejudice.[237] In his later writings, too, he advocates rights as a prepolitical bar to legislation in those cases where "the ordinary political process is antecedently likely to reach decisions that [...] could not be justified, in political theory, except by assuming that some ways of living are inherently wrong or degrading".[238] This *likelihood* of prejudiced decisions – later explicitly based

232 Hart, "Between Utility and Rights" at 843; see similarly John Hart Ely, "Professor Dworkin's External/Personal Preference Distinction," (1983) *Duke Law Journal* 959 at 985.

233 Dworkin, "Rights as Trumps" at 161; he also speaks of "political preferences" (at 158); in Ronald Dworkin, *Law's Empire* (Oxford: Hart, 1986), at 384-386, the focus is directly on preferences arising from prejudices.

234 Dworkin, "Rights as Trumps" at 162.

235 On the significance of this point in understanding Dworkin's theory as a whole see Kennedy, *A Critique of Adjudication (fin de siècle)*, at 127-129.

236 Dworkin, "Reverse Discrimination" at 284.

237 Ibid., 285.

238 Dworkin, "Rights as Trumps" at 163

on an argument from history[239] – is an empirical assessment referring to the regular discrimination of certain minority groups.[240]

All this illustrates the difficulty in pinning down a precise understanding of those "minority" rights which the morality-focussed perspective takes as central when it invokes the "tyranny of the majority". Although the point of departure is the individual – *any* individual – and there are vestiges of the broad, functional understanding of a "minority", for example in Dworkin's early insistence that *any* external preferences should be trumped by rights, the focus ultimately shifts to a more restricted understanding. While not an exact definition, Dworkin's account helps to crystallise two characteristics of a minority in this more loaded sense: firstly, it is discriminated against in a way that suggests its alleged moral inferiority, in contrast to the fundamental idea of moral equality (a *normative element*);[241] and secondly, there is widespread prejudice against it embedded within society (an *empirical element*, often backed up by a historical retrospective). The exact formulations of both these elements may vary, but the reference to both of them is recurring, both in Dworkin's writing and in other references to minorities.[242]

As mentioned above, George Letsas has explicitly built on this Dworkinian framework in order to develop a criticism of European consensus.[243] He takes up the typically liberal anti-majoritarian framework for rights, arguing that "it makes no sense to allow the majority itself to decide

239 Dworkin, *Law's Empire*, at 384 and 396; see also the appeal to history by Arai-Takahashi, "The Margin of Appreciation Doctrine: A Theoretical Analysis of Strasbourg's Variable Geometry" at 96; Buchanan, *The Heart of Human Rights*, at 90.

240 See Hart's criticism that on Dworkin's view, rights will depend on what "prejudices are current and likely at any given time in any given society": Hart, "Between Utility and Rights" at 840; Dworkin would accept this as a positive aspect of his theory: Dworkin, *Law's Empire*, at 396.

241 Ely differs from fully-fledged proponents of the morality-focussed view by denying that the normative element is necessary: Ely, *Democracy and Distrust. A Theory of Judicial Review*, at 153-154; the appeal to normative self-evidence within the very same passage, however, makes this approach questionable; see also Paul Brest, "The Substance of Process," (1981) 42 *Ohio State Law Journal* 131.

242 See also Lourdes Peroni and Alexandra Timmer, "Vulnerable Groups: The Promise of an Emerging Concept in European Human Rights Convention Law," (2013) 11 *International Journal of Constitutional Law* 1056 at 1059 on descriptive and prescriptive aspects of "vulnerability".

243 Letsas, *A Theory of Interpretation of the European Convention on Human Rights*, at 5 and 110-119.

what rights individuals have in controversial legal cases".[244] On the basis of Dworkin's theory of rights, the morality-focussed objection to European consensus can be put as follows. Rights should be seen as trumps that prevent certain reasons – in particular, prejudiced external preferences – from unfolding normative force.[245] It follows that European consensus should not be used in interpreting the ECHR because "consensus in each Contracting State – and across Contracting States generally – is bound to contain hostile external preferences" vis-à-vis certain minorities such as gay people, trans persons, or those adhering to unpopular religions.[246] Because such minorities are commonly discriminated against and "cannot bring about a change in domestic law through legislative process" (the empirical element),[247] the national laws that make up European consensus are likely to reflect the intra-State majority's view that they "should not enjoy some liberty on the basis that their plan of life is inferior" (the normative element).[248] Simply put: the use of consensus "might well give effect to biased and prejudiced considerations"[249] – precisely those considerations that rights as trumps are supposed to prevent from gaining normative force.[250]

The criticisms by Benvenisti and Fenwick, discussed above, can also be viewed through this framework. Benvenisti refers to "traditional" minorities that are "persistently" outvoted and other "political outcasts": groups that are commonly disenfranchised, as I noted above, which constitutes the empirical element. The normative element is more implicit in his account, but it shines through, for example, when he describes gay people as "seek[ing] society's recognition and respect" – recognition and respect which, it remains unsaid, is currently being denied on the basis of the al-

244 Ibid., 119; see also Letsas, "The ECHR as a Living Instrument: Its Meaning and Legitimacy" at 123.

245 Letsas, *A Theory of Interpretation of the European Convention on Human Rights*, at 102.

246 Ibid., 121.

247 Letsas, "The ECHR as a Living Instrument: Its Meaning and Legitimacy" at 123.

248 Letsas, *A Theory of Interpretation of the European Convention on Human Rights*, at 121.

249 George Letsas, "No Human Right to Adopt?," (2008) 1 *UCL Human Rights Review* 135 at 149; see similarly (less focussed on minorities, but likewise questioning States' good intentions) Paul Martens, "Perplexity of the National Judge Faced with the Vagaries of European Consensus" (Dialogue between judges, European Court of Human Rights, 2008), at 58.

250 George Letsas, "Strasbourg's Interpretive Ethic: Lessons for the International Lawyer," (2010) 21 *European Journal of International Law* 509 at 540.

leged immorality of gay people.[251] Both the normative and the empirical element are likewise present in Fenwick's reference to "groups traditionally vulnerable to discrimination":[252] discrimination, in its loaded sense as different treatment that is *unjustified*,[253] carries the normative element within it, while the *traditional* vulnerability to discrimination encompasses the empirical element. Fenwick's account is also helpful in that it explicitly includes women as a group traditionally vulnerable to discrimination,[254] thus making plain that talk of "minorities" need not be understood in a numerical sense. Small numbers may be an indication of political disenfranchisement;[255] however, given how deep-rooted and pervasive the discrimination of women is, their numbers alone cannot be decisive.[256] Insofar as both the normative and the empirical element are considered to be present, proponents of the morality-focussed perspective are likely to invoke the danger of a hegemony of the majority regardless, in principle, of how many people are concerned.

Finally, it is worth noting that many of the examples discussed thus far pertain to minorities that can be subsumed under what is commonly called "identity politics", i.e. minorities with an allegedly coherent group identity. Certainly the "assess[ment of] group identity claims" is often made "according to the unfounded presumptions and stereotypes held by dominant cultural groups"[257] so that this is one important case of a minority in the more loaded sense discussed here; the examples commonly given by critics of European consensus (women's rights, gay rights, trans rights, rights of disabled persons, rights of ethnic or religious minorities) reflect

---

251 Benvenisti, "Margin of Appreciation, Consensus, and Universal Standards" at 848; see also his description of the majority as "questioning [the] different culture and tradition" of ethnic minorities.

252 Supra, note 221.

253 See ECtHR (Plenary), Appl. Nos. 1474/62 et al. – *Belgian Linguistics Case (Merits)*, Judgment of 23 July 1968, at para. 10.

254 Fenwick, "Same-sex Unions at the Strasbourg Court in a Divided Europe: Driving Forward Reform or Protecting the Court's Authority via Consensus Analysis?" at 249; see also, in the context of European consensus, Radačić, "Rights of the Vulnerable Groups" at 600; and, more generally, Dworkin, "Liberty and Moralism" at 299; Dworkin, *Law's Empire*, at 386.

255 Benvenisti, "Margin of Appreciation, Consensus, and Universal Standards" at 848; Letsas, "The ECHR as a Living Instrument: Its Meaning and Legitimacy" at 123.

256 Lau, "Rewriting Schalk and Kopf: Shifting the Locus of Deference" at 248.

257 Avigail Eisenberg, *Reasons of Identity. A Normative Guide to the Political & Legal Assessment of Identity Claims* (Oxford: Oxford University Press, 2009), at 2.

this. However, the examples given also demonstrate that a "minority" can be understood more broadly, so long as a case can be made out that both the normative and the empirical element discussed above are present with regard to a certain person, group, situation or practice.[258] Benvenisti mentions those who "seek better procedural guarantees of due process in criminal trials",[259] and Letsas points to the confiscation and seizure of obscene books or paintings as involving the moralistic preferences of the majority.[260] Ian Cram sees a counter-majoritarian role for the ECtHR in cases involving unpopular or dissenting opinions.[261] Ambiguities thus remain, depending on how broadly both the normative and the empirical element are interpreted.

We may summarise these arguments as follows. A hallmark of the morality-focussed perspective is its embrace of prepolitical rights that serve to protect individuals against their subjugation by majority rule. Critics of European consensus take up this perspective to ensure the protection of minority rights by the ECtHR. This may be understood to refer, in particular, to those groups or practices that have traditionally been subject to discrimination and prejudice which denies their moral equality – although

258 While this will not be a focus of mine in what follows, it is important to at least note in passing that ostensibly broad understandings nonetheless retain the typically liberal focus on civil and political rights at the expense of socio-economic rights; one can "watch most fundamental-rights theorists start edging toward the door when someone mentions jobs, food, or housing", as Ely memorably put it (Ely, *Democracy and Distrust. A Theory of Judicial Review*, at 59); an explicit example in the context of the ECHR is Letsas, *A Theory of Interpretation of the European Convention on Human Rights*, at 129-130; critically on the prioritisation of civil and political rights e.g. Benjamin Authers and Hilary Charlesworth, "The Crisis and the Quotidian in International Human Rights Law," (2013) 44 *Netherlands Yearbook of International Law* 19; Madeleine Rees and Christine Chinkin, "Exposing the Gendered Myth of Post Conflict Transition: The Transformative Power of Economic and Social Rights," (2016) 48 *New York University Journal of International Law and Politics* 1211; Marks, *The Riddle of All Constitutions*, chapter 3; the latter is particularly interesting in the present context, for Marks emphasises the exclusionary effects of socio-economic injustice within democratic processes, which casts a stark light on the absence of such rights in discussions of democratic "outcasts" by liberal proponents of the morality-focussed perspective.

259 Benvenisti, "Margin of Appreciation, Consensus, and Universal Standards" at 849.

260 Letsas, *A Theory of Interpretation of the European Convention on Human Rights*, at 121.

261 Cram, "Protocol 15 and Articles 10 and 11 ECHR - The Partial Triumph of Political Incumbency Post-Brighton?" at 497.

the exact meaning remains fuzzy, and the border between a functional and a more loaded understanding of "minorities" is thus not clearly delineated. Whatever the precise understanding of minorities at issue, the worry is that the States parties' legal systems will reflect discrimination against them – so the ECtHR should not refer back to those legal systems by incorporating European consensus in its reasoning. For the morality-focussed approach, the point of regional human rights is to prevent the discrimination of intra-State minorities – if necessary, against the prevailing majority opinion.

2. Regional Human Rights Law and Distrust of States

In light of the above, it is clear that the morality-focussed view sees it as one major purpose of human rights law to give legal voice to the concerns of minorities that would otherwise struggle to be heard. This is reflected in the criticism of consensus as giving too much normative force to intra-State majority views – a perspective that builds strongly on liberal positions developed in the national context. One can further develop that criticism by shifting one's perspective to the ECHR as a specifically regional instrument of human rights protection. Where Habermas described the morality-focussed view, in the national context, as setting limits on "the sovereign will of the political legislator",[262] the more transnational perspective would be that the ECHR sets limits on the sovereign will of States.

The additional transnational aspect can be exemplified by the transition from Dworkin's approach (initially developed for national law) to that of George Letsas (specifically developed for the ECHR). Dworkin argues that the purpose of (national) law and rights is "to guide and constrain the power of *government*".[263] Letsas takes up the gist of this approach, now formulated in transnational terms: "the purpose of human rights treaties is [...] to prescribe what a *state* may not do to its own people".[264] Note that I do not intend to set up these specific formulations in strict opposition to one another: in fact, Letsas himself has elsewhere combined them by refer-

262 Habermas, *Between Facts and Norms*, at 100.
263 Dworkin, *Law's Empire*, at 93 (emphasis added).
264 Letsas, *A Theory of Interpretation of the European Convention on Human Rights*, at 9 (emphasis added); see also ibid. at 72-73; on the importance of purposive interpretation, see Letsas, "Strasbourg's Interpretive Ethic: Lessons for the International Lawyer" at 533.

ring to the accountability of *States* for the violation of rights that individuals have against their *government*.[265] My point is, rather, that the transnationality of the ECHR adds another layer of complexity to the problem.[266]

The transnational aspect of the morality-focussed view takes up the verticality of European consensus that was mentioned in Chapter 1.[267] If human rights are, as Letsas supposes, about constraining States' choices, then why take a comparative survey of those very States to establish what those constraints should be? The verticality of consensus is central here, for it seems paradoxical, when evaluating State conduct, to accord any normative force to precisely that State conduct in the form of European consensus.[268] Carozza has summarised what many proponents of the morality-focussed perspective take to be the main problem: "To base the content of obligations on what the states are actually doing has the potential to amount to no more than a vulgar form of positivism, one that certainly contravenes the spirit of international human rights' normative aspirations and idealism."[269] Or, as Örücü succinctly put it: "Can the ECHR be led by

---

265 Letsas, "Strasbourg's Interpretive Ethic: Lessons for the International Lawyer" at 540.

266 The procedural side of this includes the requirement to exhaust domestic remedies, Article 35 (1) ECHR, which means (national) judges will typically have already been involved in the matter before the case reaches the ECtHR; on the inclusion of courts in the national ethos that the morality-focussed perspective is sceptical of, see more generally infra, text to notes 277-279.

267 Chapter 1, III.

268 On the paradoxical aspect, see Yutaka Arai-Takahashi, *The Margin of Appreciation Doctrine and the Principle of Proportionality in the Jurisprudence of the ECHR* (Antwerp et al.: Intersentia, 2002), at 196; Antje von Ungern-Sternberg, "Die Konsensmethode des EGMR. Eine kritische Bewertung mit Blick auf das völkerrechtliche Konsens- und das innerstaatliche Demokratieprinzip," (2013) 51 *Archiv des Völkerrechts* 312 at 329; and, at least "at first glance" (my translation), W.J. Ganshof Van der Meersch, "La référence au droit interne des Etats contractants dans la jurisprudence de la Cour européenne des droits de l'homme," (1980) 32 *Revue internationale de droit comparé* 317 at 319.

269 Carozza, "Uses and Misuses of Comparative Law" at 1228; see similarly Macdonald, "The Margin of Appreciation" at 124; Jeffrey A. Brauch, "The Margin of Appreciation and the Jurisprudence of the European Court of Human Rights: Threat to the Rule of Law," (2004-2005) 11 *Columbia Journal of European Law* 113 at 146; Arai-Takahashi, *The Margin of Appreciation Doctrine and the Principle of Proportionality in the Jurisprudence of the ECHR*, at 195; François Ost, "The Original Canons of Interpretation of the European Court of Human Rights," in *The European Convention for the Protection of Human Rights. International Protection versus National Restrictions*, ed. Mireille Delmas-Marty (Dordrecht et al.:

what it is to govern?"[270] Precisely because of this verticality, consensus is seen as "incompatible with the Convention's aim of providing protection of certain fundamental rights"[271] or as an "obstacle for the effective protection of Convention rights".[272]

What all these criticisms reveal is, at heart, a *distrust* of States – as Marko Milanovic has provocatively summarised Antonio Cassese's views, "States cannot be trusted [...]. It is perhaps only a slight exaggeration to say that states are the enemy, the problem that needs fixing".[273] The reasoning for that distrust runs in parallel, at a more general level, to that we have already encountered in the morality-focussed perspective on the tensions between intra-State minorities and majorities. Within that focus on individual States, one argument in favour of prepolitical rights was that majorities should not be the judge in their own cause.[274] In particular, on the Dworkinian approach sketched above, the problem is that majority decisions are likely to contain prejudice against certain minorities. Whether this is the case should not be judged by the majority itself, since "one is less likely to recognize these illegitimate grounds in [one]self than in others".[275] One possible way of institutionalising minority rights is therefore the creation of a relatively strong constitutional court, or other forms of judicial or for that matter non-judicial oversight vis-à-vis the majoritarian legislature.[276]

However, especially when prejudice against certain minorities is strong, constitutional and other forms of review may still fail to provide redress: judges, being recruited from much the same societal strata as legislators,

Kluwer, 1992) at 308; McHarg, "Reconciling Human Rights and the Public Interest: Conceptual Problems and Doctrinal Uncertainty in the Jurisprudence of the European Court of Human Rights" at 691; see also (as advocatus diaboli) Angelika Nußberger, "Auf der Suche nach einem europäischen Konsens – zur Rechtsprechung des Europäischen Gerichtshofs für Menschenrechte," (2012) 3 *Zeitschrift für rechtswissenschaftliche Forschung* 197 at 206.

270 Örücü, "Whither Comparativism in Human Rights Cases?" at 239.

271 Daniel Regan, "'European Consensus': A Worthy Endeavour for the European Court of Human Rights?," (2011) 14 *Trinity College Law Review* 51 at 52.

272 Radačić, "Rights of the Vulnerable Groups" at 600.

273 Marko Milanovic, "On Realistic Utopias and Other Oxymorons: An Essay on Antonio Cassese's Last Book," (2012) 23 *European Journal of International Law* 1033 at 1046.

274 Dworkin, "Constitutional Cases" at 175; Letsas, *A Theory of Interpretation of the European Convention on Human Rights*, at 119.

275 Dworkin, "Liberty and Moralism" at 303.

276 See Dzehtsiarou, *European Consensus and the Legitimacy of the European Court of Human Rights*, at 118-119.

may fall prey to the same prejudices.[277] Benvenisti has argued that in those cases where the national judicial process – "itself dominated by judges of the majority" – fails to protect such groups, "international judicial and monitoring organs are often their last resort and only reliable avenue of redress".[278] In this way, distrust is extended, from the transnational vantage point, to individual States as a whole. In avoiding the use of European consensus, the aim is to not only prevent intra-State political majorities (legislative majorities or the "government", in the phrasing by Dworkin and Letsas cited above), but also States as a whole from being judges in their own cause.[279]

It is true, of course, that the use of European consensus does not necessarily equal giving the States parties carte blanche to do as they please entirely. Proponents of consensus argue, in particular, that the danger of circumventing human rights standards is mitigated by the fact that consensus refers not to a single respondent State but rather to the community of States parties as a whole.[280] This has not convinced critics that minority rights will be any less endangered, but it has important conceptual implications. Dworkin's argument dealt with distrust of the government within an individual State, especially within the United States of America. Why should there be occasion for distrust? As we saw above, empirical support for Dworkin's assumptions was derived from his referral to forms of prejudice and discrimination actually found within society, particularly in light of historical retrospective: his focus was on groups that have been "historically the target of prejudice" in the United States.[281]

---

277 See Ely, *Democracy and Distrust. A Theory of Judicial Review*, at 168.

278 Benvenisti, "Margin of Appreciation, Consensus, and Universal Standards" at 848.

279 See (albeit in a different argumentative context) Buchanan, *The Heart of Human Rights*, at 113.

280 E.g. Neuman, "Import, Export, and Regional Consent in the Inter-American Court of Human Rights" at 115; see also the more critical stance taken by proponents of European consensus on what they call "internal consensus" within a single State: e.g. Kanstantsin Dzehtsiarou, "Does Consensus Matter? Legitimacy of European Consensus in the Case Law of the European Court of Human Rights," (2011) *Public Law* 534 at 552 (basing his argument on the tyranny of the majority); Fiona de Londras and Kanstantsin Dzehtsiarou, "Grand Chamber of the European Court of Human Rights: A, B & C v Ireland, Decision of 17 December 2010," (2013) 62 *International and Comparative Law Quarterly* 250; more on this move from national ethe to a pan-European ethos in Chapter 3, IV.3.

281 Dworkin, *Law's Empire*, at 396.

Similar arguments based on historical failures are made when criticising European consensus: for example, Carozza has stated that the "history of the human rights movement makes it lamentably obvious that even large groups of states might share similar internal norms that all violate some basic aspect of human dignity".[282] But, given the transnational context, the focus has shifted. If certain forms of discrimination were to be found only in individual States, then the consensus argument would, in fact, serve to protect the minority in question – it would unfold its "spur effect" rather than the "rein effect" we are considering here. As Carozza rightly emphasises, the empirical assumption underlying criticisms of European consensus is therefore that the majority of national laws will reflect prejudices vis-à-vis the *same* minorities. This is why Letsas claims not only that hostile external preferences will be found within the legal systems of individual States parties to the ECHR, but "across Contracting States generally".[283] The underlying empirical assumptions are given a broader reach.

In sum: the morality-focussed approach builds on a distrust of States due to which their actions must, on this view, be constrained. The presumed purpose of the ECHR reflects this: it is proposed that the human rights contained therein, prepolitical precisely in order to be removed from the political arenas tainted by distrust, serve to constrain the behaviour of States. The argument in favour of prepolitical minority rights discussed in the last section then emerges as a paradigmatic example of this more general approach – a case where distrust of the majority is seen as particularly appropriate. When transferred to the transnational level in criticising the use of European consensus, this involves the assumption that the States parties to the ECHR will fall prey to *similar* prejudices, tainting their national laws in such a way that they should not be given normative force even when viewed collectively.

3. The Is-Ought Distinction and Strict Normativity

Taking the morality-focussed view implies a certain epistemological approach – as Habermas put it, "the moral-cognitive moment predominates".[284] Such epistemological assumptions come through very clearly in

282 Carozza, "Uses and Misuses of Comparative Law" at 1228.

283 Letsas, *A Theory of Interpretation of the European Convention on Human Rights*, at 121.

284 Habermas, *Between Facts and Norms*, at 100

morality-focussed criticism of European consensus, and this subsection is dedicated to spelling them out. Not all those cited above as articulating morality-focussed reasoning will necessarily have in mind a particular, principled epistemological approach, of course; their concern may be more pragmatic, with epistemological elements following as an afterthought from the focus on minority rights. Therefore, it will once more prove helpful to put the spotlight on the argument of George Letsas, for its proximity to Ronald Dworkin's jurisprudence gives it a theoretical foundation that is particularly well-developed and thus lends itself to analysis.

Developing the framework that Dworkin had devised at the national level, Letsas argues that "the ECHR enshrines human rights that are both legal and liberal [...]. Legality and liberalism are objective values of political morality that should shape and guide the interpretation of the ECHR".[285] These objective values take pride of place, leading Letsas to conclude that "legal truth transcends communal understanding and acceptance".[286] He develops the slogan: "Truth Not [...] Consensus".[287] At a more general level, Dworkin later put the matter thus: "I believe that there are objective truths about value. I believe that some institutions really are unjust and some acts really are wrong no matter how many people believe that they are not."[288]

There are two aspects of particular note here. The first is the explicit reliance on "objective values of political morality" or moral truth. The belief that such a strong form of normativity should guide the ECtHR is commonplace among critics of European consensus, though often mentioned only in passing. Consider the following examples: "the Court should be guided by the values of autonomy, equality and human dignity, on which international human rights law is based, rather than on the question of consensus";[289] "it would be preferable for the Court to set out autonomous standards of Convention norms and abandon its search for consensus among the Contracting States";[290] "instead of using mathematical formula, the better approach to an autonomous interpretation of the convention is

285 Letsas, *A Theory of Interpretation of the European Convention on Human Rights*, at 5.
286 Ibid., 52.
287 Ibid., 74; see further infra, III.
288 Ronald Dworkin, *Justice for Hedgehogs* (Cambridge, Mass.: Belknap Press of Harvard University Press, 2011), at 7-8; on the "language of objectivity", see Dworkin, *Law's Empire*, at 81.
289 Radačić, "Rights of the Vulnerable Groups" at 600 (and see also at 611).
290 Regan, "A Worthy Endeavour?" at 52.

to look to its inherent values".[291] What all these quotations have in common is some approving reference to *normative* standards ("the values of autonomy, equality and human dignity", "autonomous standards", or "inherent values" of the Convention), which are then contrasted to the reliance on consensus.

This brings us to the second point: the way in which European consensus is *contrasted* to such normative standards. Arguing as a devil's advocate against consensus, Judge Angelika Nußberger has made this particularly clear by posing the question: is it permissible to derive normative conclusions (how *ought* the ECHR's provisions be interpreted) from the factual circumstances of what the law *is* in the States parties?[292] She is referring, of course, to the old distinction between the *ought* and the *is*. Generally seen as having been firmly established as an epistemological axiom by David Hume,[293] it has served as the baseline for legal theories as different as those of Dworkin[294] and Hans Kelsen.[295] It is no surprise, then, that it should also resurface in the argument advanced by Letsas. While interpretation is conceptualised as inherently normative, European consensus is there introduced as a factual element based on "empirical inquiries".[296]

Needless to say, Letsas recognises that the gap between norms and facts can be bridged: as he puts it, "facts are relevant if [...], in the chain of justification, there is ultimately a fact-independent normative reason making them relevant".[297] So the heart of his argument is found in the reasons *not* to make consensus relevant in the justification of the ECtHR's decisions – in particular, as discussed above, to avoid the reference to prejudiced exter-

291 Beate Rudolf, "European Court of Human Rights: Legal status of postoperative transsexuals," (2003) 1 *International Journal of Constitutional Law* 716 at 721.

292 Nußberger, "Auf der Suche nach einem europäischen Konsens – zur Rechtsprechung des Europäischen Gerichtshofs für Menschenrechte" at 206.

293 David Hume, "A Treatise of Human Nature," in *Hume. The Essential Philosophical Works* (Ware: Wordsworth, 2011) at 409; for historical contextualisation, see e.g. Finnis, *Natural Law & Natural Rights*, at 37.

294 E.g. Dworkin, *Justice for Hedgehogs*, at 17 and 44.

295 E.g. Hans Kelsen, *General Theory of Law and State*, trans. Anders Wedberg (Cambridge, Mass.: Harvard University Press, 1945), at 37.

296 Letsas, "Strasbourg's Interpretive Ethic: Lessons for the International Lawyer" at 540; see also Frances Hamilton, "Same-Sex Marriage, Consensus, Certainty and the European Court of Human Rights," (2018) *European Human Rights Law Review* 33 at 34-35 ("fact-dependent approach").

297 Letsas, "Strasbourg's Interpretive Ethic: Lessons for the International Lawyer" at 534; this can be assumed to be the case with regard to the empirical element of identifying relevant minorities, as discussed above.

nal preferences. The formal logic of the is-ought distinction is not itself central. It is nonetheless interesting that Letsas and other critics of consensus frame their arguments along these lines, for the *rhetoric* of the is-ought distinction coheres neatly with the overall approach of the morality-focussed perspective. While this kind of rhetoric is not out of the ordinary for any account which seeks to establish a form of normativity reaching beyond law as it currently stands, the way in which the is-ought distinction is brought to bear on European consensus is perhaps particularly revealing by virtue of how it positions consensus within the relations between the ECtHR and the States parties to the ECHR. To demonstrate, let me once more return to the context in which Dworkin developed the theory of rights on which Letsas builds.

One of the examples that Dworkin frequently recurred to was the vindication of gay rights, specifically the decriminalisation of homosexuality. When he first advocated his theory of rights as trumps, this was a controversial and much-discussed issue. The mainstream debate had been kick-started by the so-called Wolfenden Report, published in 1957, which among other things recommended the decriminalisation of "homosexual behaviour between consenting adults in private".[298] Lord Devlin disputed this conclusion in his Maccabaean Lecture, where he argued that any society is dependent on a "common morality" and may therefore properly legislate on how its members should live their lives.[299] This "common morality" is established from "the viewpoint of the man in the street": a "reasonable" or "right-minded" person.[300] Note that the requirement of reasonableness is *not* understood in the neo-Kantian sense (as *reason-able*) now so familiar to us from its central position in the theory of John Rawls.[301] Rather, Devlin is explicit that a society's "common morality" is established not by philosophical argument or reason but that it should be taken as it stands and "may be largely a matter of feeling".[302] In this way, he arrives at his infamous conclusion that if a society views homosexuality as "a vice so

298 Report of the Departmental Committee on Homosexual Offences and Prostitution (1957), at para. 62.

299 Patrick Devlin, "Morals and the Criminal Law," in *The Enforcement of Morals* (Indianapolis: Liberty Fund, 2009) at 10; for the overall structure of the argument see ibid. at 7-8.

300 Ibid., 15.

301 E.g. Rawls, *Political Liberalism*, at 48-50; see further Chapter 5, II.

302 Devlin, "Morals and the Criminal Law" at 15.

abominable that its mere presence is an offence", then it may criminalise (or, in his words, "eradicate") it.[303]

Devlin himself recognised that, in a sense, this approach makes morality and immorality a question of fact[304] – rather than arguing for a certain position on normative grounds, he would lead us to examine what a given society's current stance on the issue is. Much of the criticism levelled against Devlin focussed on this aspect. H.L.A. Hart, in particular, cited the distinction between "positive" and "critical" morality: the prior referring to the "historical fact"[305] of a morality "actually accepted and shared by a given social group", the latter used to criticise it.[306] Devlin's approach is seen as problematic in large part because it gives such strong force to positive morality and thereby "withdraws [it] from the scope of any moral criticism".[307] The essence of Dworkin's argument in response to Devlin is, in this respect, very similar to that of Hart. He, too, distinguishes positive from critical morality – in his terms, morality in the "anthropological sense" referring descriptively to the attitudes of a certain group, and "in a discriminatory sense" which contrasts with "prejudices, rationalizations, matters of personal aversion or taste, arbitrary stands, and the like" found in anthropological morality and is used normatively for "justification and criticism".[308] The connection to his broader theory of rights as trumps is immediately clear: on Dworkin's terms, Devlin's argument fails because it is dependent on the factually ascertained anthropological morality which is bound to contain the kind of prejudiced external preferences that should

303 Ibid., 17; for a thorough and recent criticism, see Martha C. Nussbaum, *From Disgust to Humanity. Sexual Orientation & Constitutional Law* (Oxford: Oxford University Press, 2010).

304 Devlin, "Morals and the Criminal Law" at 23; see also Devlin, "Democracy and Morality" at 91 and 100.

305 H.L.A. Hart, *Law, Liberty, and Morality* (Stanford: Stanford University Press, 1963), at 24.

306 Ibid., 20; see also Boylan, *Natural Human Rights. A Theory*, at 117 where he criticises accounts of rights in "*descriptive* terms" by noting that on those terms, "[n]o definitive *reason* can be given" (emphases in original); for an application of the notion of critical morality in the context of the ECtHR, see Christopher Nowlin, "The Protection of Morals Under the European Convention for the Protection of Human Rights and Fundamental Freedoms," (2002) 24 *Human Rights Quarterly* 264.

307 Hart, *Law, Liberty, and Morality*, at 73; H.L.A. Hart, "Immorality and Treason," in *Morality and the Law*, ed. Richard A. Wasserstrom (Belmont: Wadsworth Publishing, 1971) at 53-54.

308 Dworkin, "Liberty and Moralism" at 297.

be given no argumentative weight.[309] This is precisely the aspect that George Letsas has taken up at the transnational level.

What emerges from all this is the sense that by classifying something as a fact, the morality-focussed perspective sees it as something to be criticised. It has been said that the is-ought distinction itself is historically related to the increased freedom of the human mind which allowed it to gain a "critical edge".[310] Hart and Dworkin explicitly contrast the factually understood positive or anthropological morality with "critical" morality. On this account, anything that *is* remains under scrutiny whether it *ought* to be differently.

Now law is widely recognised as combining both factual and normative elements. Habermas famously indicated as much in the title of his monograph on the discourse theory of law, *Between Facts and Norms* (*Faktizität und Geltung*),[311] and Koskenniemi opens *From Apology to Utopia* by pointing to the relevance, for international law, of both "descriptive theories about the character of social life among States and normative views about the principles of justice which should govern international conduct"[312] – in brief, the tension between "facts and norms in international life".[313] Law can be understood as an institutionalised amalgam of facts and norms. When in action, however, it tends to define itself by its regulatory and hence normative force: it "perceives facts as what actually happens, and requires the separation of rules and facts in the sense that the former prescribe the regulation of the latter".[314]

Accordingly, when it is law itself that is being scrutinised by another (usually hierarchically superior) law, then the tendency will be to emphasise the normativity of the latter, but conversely, the factual element of the prior: Kelsen called this the *relativity* of the is-ought distinction.[315] A clear example may be found within human rights law itself, or even within in-

309 Ibid., 304.

310 Larry Siedentop, *Inventing the Individual. The Origins of Western Liberalism* (London: Penguin, 2015), at 218.

311 Habermas, *Between Facts and Norms*; orig. Jürgen Habermas, *Faktizität und Geltung. Beiträge zur Diskurstheorie des Rechts und des demokratischen Rechtsstaats*, 5th ed. (Frankfurt a.M.: Suhrkamp, 2014).

312 Koskenniemi, *From Apology to Utopia*, at 1.

313 Ibid., 4.

314 Alexander Orakhelashvili, *The Interpretation of Acts and Rules in Public International Law* (Oxford: Oxford University Press, 2008), at 111.

315 Hans Kelsen, "Natural Law Doctrine and Legal Positivism," in *General Theory of Law and State* (Cambridge, Mass.: Harvard University Press, 1945) at 393.

ternational law more generally: it is quite uncontroversial that the law of the respondent State in judicial proceedings before regional or international courts be treated as a matter of fact.[316] While nobody would deny that the very same national law is also imbued with normativity within its own legal system, its factual side is emphasised because, in the concrete situation before an international court, it is not itself setting standards but rather being measured against the standards of international law. It is not criticising but being criticised.

Consider now the extension of this approach to European consensus. Given how the ECtHR makes use of it within its reasoning, one might consider that "the real question here is the interpretation and application of the Convention" and hence emphasise the normative side of national laws.[317] One might also retain the focus on the factual element, but introduce it as part of a fact-dependent epistemology rather than the strictly binary is-ought distinction.[318] The morality-focussed approach instead sees European consensus as a factual element within that distinction, and thus distances itself from it even within its epistemological assumptions. By likening consensus to the way in which the law of the respondent State is treated before the ECtHR, the morality-focussed approach draws attention to the fact that it is made up of the national laws of other States parties, *each of which could likewise become a respondent before the ECtHR on the same issue*. The epistemological framework of the morality-focussed view thus rhetorically brings the "critical edge" of the is-ought distinction to bear on

316 Paul Gragl, *The Accession of the European Union to the European Convention on Human Rights* (Oxford: Hart, 2013), at 115; see also Orakhelashvili, *The Interpretation of Acts and Rules in Public International Law*, at 112.

317 Tobias Thienel, "The Burden and Standard of Proof in the European Court of Human Rights," (2007) 50 *German Yearbook of International Law* 543 at 558; contra: Alix Schlüter, "Beweisrechtliche Implikationen der margin of appreciation-Doktrin," (2016) 54 *Archiv des Völkerrechts* 41 at 61; this micro-debate concerns the issue of whether consensus should be established by reference to the law of (factual) evidence or to the principle of "iura novit curia" according to which (normative) legal conclusions are drawn by the Court itself; given its specific doctrinal context pertaining to the ECtHR's rules of procedure, it is only indirectly related to the epistemological issues considered here. For the same reason, the ECtHR's own introduction of the comparative materials that make up consensus under the heading "The Facts" (see e.g. Dean Spielmann, "The European Court of Human Rights: Master of the Law but not of the Facts?" (Speech to the British Institute of International and Comparative Law, 2014)) is not conclusive within a broader context.

318 Zysset, *The ECHR and Human Rights Theory: Reconciling the Moral and Political Conceptions*, at 137; see further Chapter 3, II.

European consensus and serves to illustrate the distrust of States that underlies its approach.

This way of framing the issue not only underlines once more the substantive criticism of consensus, it also ties in with what Habermas called the "moral-cognitive" approach.[319] Normativity is conceptualised as prepolitical and thus independent of volitional elements, the latter being relegated instead to the realm of facts (the "facticity of the existing context", as Habermas puts it[320]). The morality-focussed approach stands in the Kantian tradition according to which, as Seyla Benhabib has summarised it, rights claims are "not about what there *is*", but rather, emphatically, "about the kind of world we reasonably *ought* to want to live in".[321] What *ought* to be can only be known by virtue of normative argument; but such argument can be better or worse.[322] Whether it is adequate must in turn be established by further argument, and so forth. One must proceed in this purely normative and ultimately circular fashion for lack of other possibilities[323] – an aspect that will become particularly relevant in considering the ethos-focussed perspective's response to this epistemology. For now, we may conclude by recalling that the morality-focussed approach allows a categorical distinction to be made between permissible normative argument and factually conceptualised "positive morality": only on normative terms could the latter become relevant.[324] Since the national laws making up European consensus are regarded as tainted by prejudice and thus distrusted, no such bridge between norms and (what is taken to be) facts is built, and consensus is, as a result, considered to have no normative force whatsoever.

319 Supra, note 284.

320 Habermas, *Between Facts and Norms*, at 156.

321 Seyla Benhabib, "Another Universalism: On the Unity and Diversity of Human Rights," in *Dignity in Adversity: Human Rights in Troubled Times* (Cambridge: Polity Press, 2011) at 66 (emphases in original); Habermas names Kant as an example of a more morality-focussed view: Habermas, *Between Facts and Norms*, at 100-101.

322 See the comments on Kantian morality in Philip Allott and others, "Thinking Another World: 'This Cannot Be How the World Was Meant to Be'," (2005) 16 *European Journal of International Law* 255 at 273.

323 Dworkin, *Justice for Hedgehogs*, at 37-38.

324 Letsas, "Strasbourg's Interpretive Ethic: Lessons for the International Lawyer" at 534; see Hart, *Law, Liberty, and Morality*, at 17 and 82.

III. Ambivalent Morality-focussed Perspectives on the Spur Effect

As will have become clear at this point, the main concern of the morality-focussed perspective is the use of human rights law to protect intra-State minorities. Accordingly, critical engagement with European consensus by morality-focussed commentators has been overwhelmingly focussed on its rein effect. When (lack of) consensus "reins in" the ECtHR, it points towards a finding of no violation and may thus, on the morality-focussed view, prevent the acknowledgment of minority rights by giving argumentative weight to intra-State majorities. This has been the main focus of academic criticism of European consensus.

The opposite constellation, in which the spur effect of consensus is employed and it thus provides an argument in favour of finding a violation, has been less discussed by commentators adopting the morality-focussed perspective. Since the spur effect of consensus does not justify a restrictive understanding of the right at issue, it is simply perceived as less relevant – or, more dramatically, as less dangerous. Some critics of European consensus simply do not mention the spur effect at all, but rather focus exclusively on the rein effect and the wide margin of appreciation which it implies.[325] However, it seems clear that the broader theoretical implications of reasoning based on European consensus – for the justification of the ECtHR's judgments and the conceptualisation of regional human rights law as a whole – do not disappear simply because it is used to argue in favour of a violation of the Convention, rather than a finding of no violation. It is thus worth investigating the spur effect from the morality-focussed perspective in more detail.

Perhaps the most obvious approach is to simply replicate the position reached with regard to the rein effect of consensus, i.e. to argue against according it any normative force whatsoever. This would amount to a principled refusal of using European consensus in any context, insisting instead on purely normative argument relating to the right at issue in substance. Indeed, in many critical commentaries one finds such a rhetoric of rejecting consensus *per se*. For example, Jeffrey Brauch argues that use of consensus "endangers human rights" – the primary concern, as usual, is clearly with its rein effect – but continues without further distinction that rights should be protected "no matter what current opinion polls or national

325 E.g. Benvenisti, "Margin of Appreciation, Consensus, and Universal Standards".

laws reflect".[326] Similarly, the slogan of George Letsas – "Truth Not Current Consensus"[327] – makes no distinction between the rein effect and the spur effect in its rejection of consensus; indeed, the fact that it opposes the reference to *current consensus* (in favour of the applicant), and not merely a lack of consensus, underlines its principled opposition to according normative force to consensus in any context. Letsas's opposition to "rights inflation", i.e. the expansion of rights beyond those required by his liberal theory,[328] also implies that he does not approve of the spur effect of consensus, which might expand rights in precisely this way and only serves – on Letsas's account – to dilute the importance of human rights.

Others seem, at least at first glance, to take a different approach. Junko Nozawa has been the most explicit in this regard. Reviewing the ECtHR's case-law on gay rights, her main argument is typical of the morality-focussed perspective. Building on a prepolitical conception of human rights, she opposes the use of consensus in its rein effect due to its negative impact on intra-State minorities: "where there is no uniformity in the discriminatory practice of states on the basis of sexual orientation," as she puts it, the rein effect of consensus "has detrimental effects for the protection of fundamental human rights".[329] However, Nozawa does not oppose the spur effect of consensus: "a clear consensus [in favour of the applicant] remains an important marker for the Court in determining objective standards consistent with its evolutive interpretation".[330] She does not explain this approach in detail, but one important point would seem to be that there is less danger of perpetuating national prejudice when consensus is employed in favour of the individual applicant.[331] A similar motivation might be read into certain extra-judicial comments of Christos Rozakis:

326 Brauch, "The Dangerous Search for an Elusive Consensus" at 289; see also Brauch, "The Margin of Appreciation and the Jurisprudence of the European Court of Human Rights: Threat to the Rule of Law" at 146; Regan, "A Worthy Endeavour?" at 52.

327 Letsas, *A Theory of Interpretation of the European Convention on Human Rights*, at 74.

328 Ibid., 129; see critically infra, note 1640.

329 Junko Nozawa, "Drawing the Line: Same-sex adoption and the jurisprudence of the ECtHR on the application of the "European consensus" standard under Article 14," (2013) 29 *Merkourios* 66 at 67.

330 Ibid., 73; see also the overall gist of Helen Fenwick and Daniel Fenwick, "Finding 'East'/'West' Divisions in Council of Europe States on Treatment of Sexual Minorities: The Response of the Strasbourg Court and the Role of Consensus Analysis," (2019) *European Human Rights Law Review* 247.

331 See the juxtaposition at ibid., 74-75.

while not opposed to the use of European consensus in principle, he argues that "in situations where there is no consensus, the Court is free to [...] produce its own reasoning",[332] i.e. to use the kind of substantive argument that is dear to the morality-focussed perspective rather than giving normative force to European consensus in its rein effect. Its use with regard to the spur effect, in contrast, does not seem to trouble him.[333]

My impression is that these ostensibly differing approaches within the morality-focussed perspective – the principled rejection of consensus in any context on the one hand and its possible acceptance when used in favour of the applicant on the other – reflect a certain ambivalence and difference of emphasis rather than deep-rooted disagreement. To clarify, let me return once more to the approach of George Letsas, whose account of the spur effect of consensus is tied up with the analysis of certain key judgments by the ECtHR, but nonetheless shines light on the morality-focussed perspective's take on the spur effect more generally. For example, on his reading of *Marckx v. Belgium*, the ECtHR's mention of "common ground [...] amongst modern societies"[334] was "a mere addition to a chain of substantive reasoning"[335] – the substantive reasoning being, qua Letsas, the crucial aspect.

This becomes even more clear on his reading of the Court's judgment in *Dudgeon v. the United Kingdom*, which makes reference to "a better understanding, and in consequence an increased tolerance, of homosexual behaviour" as reflected in the decriminalisation of "homosexual practices" across Europe.[336] This amounts to a use of European consensus in its spur effect, since the consensus among the States parties was in favour of the applicant – but Letsas points out that the Court "takes contemporary understanding in Member States to be *better* and not merely different than the time when anti-homosexual legislation was enacted".[337] The description of

332 Christos L. Rozakis, "Through the Looking Glass: An "Insider"'s View of the Margin of Appreciation," in *La conscience des droits: Mélanges en l'honneur de Jean-Paul Costa* (Paris: Dalloz, 2011) at 536.

333 See his description of the spur effect at ibid., 535-536; Rozakis, "The European Judge as Comparatist" at 272; Rozakis's view is further discussed, in juxtaposition with the ECtHR's usual approach, in Chapter 5, III.2.

334 ECtHR (Plenary), Appl. No. 6833/74 – *Marckx*, at para. 41.

335 Letsas, *A Theory of Interpretation of the European Convention on Human Rights*, at 78.

336 ECtHR (Plenary), Appl. No. 7525/76 – *Dudgeon*, at para. 60.

337 Letsas, *A Theory of Interpretation of the European Convention on Human Rights*, at 79 (emphasis in original).

consensus as "better" implies its normative evaluation and thus points, once again, to the *primacy of substantive reasoning rather than reliance on consensus as such*.

Whatever one makes of this as an analytic account of the ECtHR's approach,[338] I think it accurately captures the morality-focussed perspective's own take on the spur effect of European consensus and, in fact, can be used to elucidate the ambivalence mentioned above. Because of the primacy of substantive argument, the spur effect of consensus is accepted (only) in so far as it reflects the result which said argument would, in any case, espouse:[339] the existence of European consensus in favour of the applicant can "only corroborate a pre-existing standard inherent in the convention".[340] For example, Ivana Radačić criticises the rein effect of European consensus for its detrimental effects on the rights of vulnerable groups and recommends that the ECtHR should "look instead at the international human rights instruments or progressive developments in comparative jurisprudence on the issue in question".[341] While less focussed on identifying a majority among the States parties than the ECtHR usually is, this nonetheless constitutes an endorsement of the use of "comparative and international law as an indication of a consensus".[342] The key qualifier, however, lies in the adjective "progressive".[343] Like the notion of "better" consensus on Letsas's reading of Dudgeon, it implies an independent normative standard (expressed, in this case, through the temporal lens of progres-

338 See further Chapter 5, IV.

339 See Letsas, "Strasbourg's Interpretive Ethic: Lessons for the International Lawyer" at 531.

340 Rudolf, "European Court of Human Rights: Legal status of postoperative transsexuals" at 721; see also (for "intangible rights") Martens, "Perplexity of the National Judge Faced with the Vagaries of European Consensus" at 65; and see (though empirically rather than normatively) Besson and Graf-Brugère, "Le droit de vote des expatriés, le consensus européen et la marge d'appréciation des États" at 949; Mahoney and Kondak, "Common Ground" at 121.

341 Radačić, "Rights of the Vulnerable Groups" at 612.

342 Ibid., 605, citing *Marckx* and *Goodwin* as examples over the following pages; see similarly Regan, "A Worthy Endeavour?" at 63; Letsas arguably takes a similar approach, though more focussed on international law (on which, see further Chapter 6): Letsas, "Strasbourg's Interpretive Ethic: Lessons for the International Lawyer" at 540-541; Letsas, "The ECHR as a Living Instrument: Its Meaning and Legitimacy" at 122.

343 For similar vocabulary in the Court's case-law, see e.g. ECtHR (GC), Appl. Nos. 60367/08 and 961/11 – *Khamtokhu and Aksenchik*, at para. 86 on "social progress", as well as the concurring opinion of Judge Turković in that case, at para. 11.

sion) against which the developments in question must be measured before being admitted into the Court's reasoning.[344]

In Dworkinian terms, one might thus conceptualise references to European consensus as a case of concurrent rather than conventional morality. Both involve an agreement on a normative rule, but while the actors involved in the prior "do not count the fact of that agreement as an essential part of their grounds for asserting that rule", those involved in the latter do.[345] By acknowledging references to European consensus only when the direction of the substantive argument is already clear, proponents of the morality-focussed perspective regard it as an aspect that is concurrent to their reasoning, but not essential to it. In a sense, this ties in neatly with the general epistemological assumptions of the morality-focussed perspective: as discussed above, it conceptualises consensus as an issue of fact which should have no place in normative reasoning, unless the gap between the is and the ought is bridged by "a fact-independent normative reason making [it] relevant".[346]

However, one might question the argumentative relevance of European consensus, even in its spur effect, for the morality-focussed views just described.[347] If the normative force of consensus is entirely dependent on its evaluation as a "good" or "progressive" consensus, then it does not have normative force in and of itself at all: rather, it would constitute what oth-

---

344 For a general discussion of normatively loaded qualifiers describing developments in international law as progress, see Tilmann Altwicker and Oliver Diggelmann, "How is Progress Constructed in International Legal Scholarship?," (2014) 25 *European Journal of International Law* 425 at 432-434; on narrativisation as a legitimising factor of ideology, see Marks, *The Riddle of All Constitutions*, at 19-20. I have previously critiqued a particularly strong instance of such temporal rhetoric in Jens T. Theilen, "Pre-existing Rights and Future Articulations: Temporal Rhetoric in the Struggle for Trans Rights," in *Cambridge Handbook of New Human Rights. Recognition, Novelty, Rhetoric*, ed. Andreas von Arnauld, Kerstin von der Decken, and Mart Susi (Cambridge: Cambridge University Press, 2020).

345 Dworkin, "The Model of Rules II" at 73; see also the discussion in Dworkin, "Rights as Trumps" at 162.

346 Supra, note 297.

347 See Gerards, "Giving Shape to the Notion of 'Shared Responsibility'" at 44 (in footnote 132): "doubtful [...] whether such an application can still be considered an example of purely consensus-based reasoning"; see also Dinah Shelton, "The Boundaries of Human Rights Jurisdiction in Europe," (2003) 13 *Duke Journal of Comparative and International Law* 95 at 134; Kapotas and Tzevelekos, "How (Difficult Is It) to Build Consensus on (European) Consensus?" at 12.

er commentators have deemed a merely "decorative"[348] use of consensus. My point here is not to raise charges of cherry-picking in the sense of discussing potential disparities between processes of discovery and processes of justification;[349] rather, I am interested in the ambivalence of the morality-focussed perspective with regard to the reference to European consensus within the ECtHR's judgments (i.e. its process of justification) in cases involving the spur effect.

Based on the above analysis, I would suggest that the conceptualisation of consensus as a form of concurrent morality is the main source of this ambivalence. On the one hand, the spur effect is perceived as less of a danger to the rights of intra-State minorities than the rein effect – or even, in cases like *Dudgeon*, to assist in justifying such rights. On the other hand, consensus is not given independent normative force as part of that justification, so its presence seems somewhat out of place: as Dworkin warned in a different context, it may "distort the claim" being made in cases of concurrent morality when societal consensus figures in the justification of the normative claim.[350] Or, differently put: decorative references to comparative law are seldom (if ever) *purely* decorative but rather take on an argumentative function by virtue of their very inclusion in a Court's process of justification.[351] This oscillation between normative relevance and irrelevance accounts for the morality-focussed perspective's ambivalence when faced with the spur effect of European consensus.

IV. Interim Reflections: Tackling Prejudice

To summarise: the morality-focussed perspective focusses on prepolitical rights of minorities in order to prevent their subjugation by intra-State majorities. In the context of European consensus, this distrust of intra-State majorities is extended to a distrust of States more generally; they are con-

---

348 Dahlberg, "'The Lack of Such a Common Approach' - Comparative Argumentation by the European Court of Human Rights" at 88.

349 See Chapter 1, IV.5.

350 Dworkin, "The Model of Rules II" at 73

351 See Ed Bates, "Consensus in the Legitimacy-Building Era of the European Court of Human Rights," in *Building Consensus on European Consensus. Judicial Interpretation of Human Rights in Europe and Beyond*, ed. Panos Kapotas and Vassilis Tzevelekos (Cambridge: Cambridge University Press, 2019) at 53; Dahlberg, "'The Lack of Such a Common Approach' - Comparative Argumentation by the European Court of Human Rights" at 94.

ceptualised as potential respondents whose laws as they stand should be scrutinised with a view to changing and improving them, rather than giving them normative force by way of European consensus. The ECtHR, on this view, should identify the values of political morality underlying the ECHR, and justify its decisions by reference to those values rather than the factually-oriented argument based on consensus. The case for this is particularly clear when the rein effect is at issue, since it may prevent the ECtHR from finding a violation where minority rights could otherwise have been protected. The morality-focussed perspective takes a more ambivalent position on the spur effect, which seems less likely to directly endanger minority rights in this way even though it still does not cohere with the morality-focussed perspective's underlying epistemology.

Rather tellingly, criticism of consensus along the lines just sketched is often voiced in comments dealing specifically with individual cases or lines of case-law[352] – academics dealing primarily with substantive rights, one might hypothesise, have had copious contact with the various forms of

---

352 Some examples on gay rights: Nozawa, "Drawing the Line: Same-sex adoption and the jurisprudence of the ECtHR on the application of the "European consensus" standard under Article 14" at 73-75; Fenwick, "Same-sex Unions at the Strasbourg Court in a Divided Europe: Driving Forward Reform or Protecting the Court's Authority via Consensus Analysis?" at 249 and 270; Hodson, "A Marriage by Any Other Name? Schalk and Kopf v Austria" at 173; Emmanuelle Bribosia, Isabelle Rorive, and Laura Van den Eynde, "Same-Sex Marriage: Building an Argument before the European Court of Human Rights in Light of the US Experience," (2014) 32 *Berkeley Journal of International Law* 1 at 18; on religious minorities: Tom Lewis, "What not to Wear: Religious Rights, the European Court, and the Margin of Appreciation," (2007) 56 *International and Comparative Law Quarterly* 395 at 405; Kristin Henrard, "How the European Court of Human Rights' Concern Regarding European Consensus Tempers the Effective Protection of Freedom of Religion," (2015) 4 *Oxford Journal of Law and Religion* 398 at 414; Antje von Ungern-Sternberg, "Anmerkung zu S.A.S. ./. Frankreich - Burkaverbot," (2015) *MenschenrechtsMagazin* 61 at 63; on criminalisation of incest: Shu-Perng Hwang, "Grundrechtsschutz unter der Voraussetzung des europäischen Grundkonsenses?," (2013) *Europarecht* 307 at 314; on trans rights: Rudolf, "European Court of Human Rights: Legal status of postoperative transsexuals" at 721; Erdman, "The Deficiency of Consensus in Human Rights Protection: A Case Study of Goodwin v. United Kingdom and I. v. United Kingdom" at 346; Jens T. Theilen, "Beyond the Gender Binary: Rethinking the Right to Legal Gender Recognition," (2018) *European Human Rights Law Review* 249 at 256-257; on data protection: Karen C. Burke, "Secret Surveillance and the European Convention on Human Rights," (1980-1981) 33 *Stanford Law Review* 1113 at 1133; on free speech: Cram, "Protocol 15 and Articles 10 and 11 ECHR - The Partial Triumph of Political Incumbency Post-Brighton?" at 493-494.

prejudice obstructing the development of such rights and therefore have less patience for the relatively formal argument from consensus,[353] instead placing their hopes on the ECtHR as an external institution which might instigate change. One might see this as an appeal to what Amartya Sen has called "open impartiality": the invocation of judg(e)ments from those "outside the focal group" in order "to avoid parochial bias".[354] In this case, the focal group would be the States parties to the ECHR, and the ECtHR would be conceptualised as external to them, and hence more impartial, by virtue of its status as a court that is both counter-majoritarian and transnational – "an international court distanced from local politics".[355]

The idea of open impartiality may indeed be one important reason for States to submit to scrutiny by a transnational court.[356] However, for the cases under consideration here, it is taken as a given that the ECtHR has jurisdiction; the question is, rather, whether it should refer to European consensus in exercising it. As argued above, the distrust of consensus implies that the majority of national laws will reflect prejudices vis-à-vis the *same* minorities; it also implies that not only intra-State majorities, but also national judges are likely to fall prey to prejudices. Against that backdrop, the ECtHR's impartiality-qua-remoteness seems less plausible: why should the ECtHR's judges, themselves elected by the States parties (Article 22 ECHR), be exempt from otherwise widespread prejudice?[357]

---

353 This need not, of course, imply a principled epistemological position against consensus in any context, but may instead be restricted to certain (minority) rights in certain scenarios: see supra, II.3., and further Chapter 4, III.2.

354 Amartya Sen, *The Idea of Justice* (London: Penguin Books, 2010), at 123.

355 Paulo Pinto de Albuquerque, "Plaidoyer for the European Court of Human Rights," (2018) *European Human Rights Law Review* 119 at 126; see also Egbert Myjer, "The Succes[s] Story of the European Court: The Times They Are A-Changin'?," (2012) 30 *Netherlands Quarterly of Human Rights* 264 at 270; Masuma Shahid, "The Right to Same-Sex Marriage: Assessing the European Court of Human Rights' Consensus-Based Analysis in Recent Judgments Concerning Equal Marriage Rights," (2017) *Erasmus Law Review* 184 at 193-194.

356 A point which is sometimes made even by critics of the morality-focussed perspective: see Richard Bellamy, "The Democratic Legitimacy of International Human Rights Conventions: Political Constitutionalism and the European Convention on Human Rights," (2014) 25 *European Journal of International Law* 1019 at 1039.

357 See in the national context Jeremy Waldron, *Law and Disagreement* (Oxford: Oxford University Press, 1999), at 299; Richard Bellamy, "Republicanism, Democracy, and Constitutionalism," in *Republicanism and Political Theory*, ed. Cécile Laborde and John Maynor (Malden, Mass.: Blackwell, 2008) at 183.

The ECtHR's track record on minority rights does not necessarily serve to allay such doubts. While it has undoubtedly contributed to their advancement is some cases, other judgments have been highly restrictive. In some of these latter cases, at least, it was the substantive reasoning of the Court itself that arguably perpetuated prejudice, while it either did not mention consensus at all – as when it infamously took up anti-Muslim stereotypes and opined that wearing a headscarf "is hard to square with the principle of gender equality"[358] – or it twisted consensus in such a way as to fit the general picture – as when it upheld a burqa ban in public spaces and claimed lack of consensus on the issue in blatant contradiction of the quasi-unanimity in favour of the applicant among States parties' legal systems.[359] Against the backdrop of these and similar judgments, charges of islamophobia have repeatedly been raised against the ECtHR.[360] In various dissenting opinions – typically more overt and expressive than the majority judgment[361] – individual judges have also made flagrantly homophobic remarks.[362] The list could be extended, but the general implication is clear: the ECtHR's transnational status does not shield it from the very prejudices it is supposed, on the morality-focussed view, to combat.

This insight need not undermine criticism of consensus based on the morality-focussed view: two wrongs hardly make a right, and one might well argue that giving normative force to consensus, at least insofar as its

358 ECtHR, Appl. No. 42393/98 – *Dahlab v. Switzerland*, Decision of 15 February 2001, at p. 463.

359 ECtHR (GC), Appl. No. 43835/11 – *S.A.S. v. France*, Judgment of 1 July 2014, at para. 156; more generally on cases of quasi-unanimity, see Chapter 5, III.1.

360 E.g. Alicia Cebada Romero, "The European Court of Human Rights and Religion: Between Christian Neutrality and the Fear of Islam," (2013) 11 *New Zealand Journal of Public and International Law* 75; see also Ratna Kapur, *Gender, Alterity and Human Rights* (Cheltenham: Edward Elgar, 2018), at 124; Jens T. Theilen, "Towards Acceptance of Religious Pluralism: The Federal Constitutional Court's Second Judgment on Muslim Teachers Wearing Headscarves," (2015) 58 *German Yearbook of International Law* 503 at 518.

361 Kenji Yoshino, "Of Stranger Spaces," in *Law and the Stranger*, ed. Austin Sarat, Lawrence Douglas, and Martha Merrill Umphrey (Palo Alto: Stanford University Press, 2010) at 220-221.

362 ECtHR, Appl. Nos. 48420/10, 36516/10, 51671/10 and 59842/10 – *Eweida and Others v. the United Kingdom*, Judgment of 15 January 2013, joint partly dissenting opinion of Judges Vučinić and de Gaetano, at para. 5 (contrasting "gay rights", in scare quotes, with fundamental human rights); ECtHR, Appl. Nos. 67667/09 et al. – *Bayev and Others v. Russia*, Judgment of 20 June 2017, dissenting opinion of Judge Dedov, e.g. at p. 40 (implying a connection between homosexuality and paedophilia).

rein effect is concerned, only exacerbates the problem. Simply put: the ECtHR's judges may or may not be prejudiced with regard to a certain minority group or practice, but the rein effect of European consensus would in either case constitute an obstacle to overcoming prejudice. With regard to the spur effect, things are, again, a tad more complicated. On the one hand, in its pure form, the morality-focussed perspective would continue to admit it, if at all, only as a form of concurrent rather than conventional morality. However, the problem of prejudice among the ECtHR's judges points towards a slightly different position, based on an observer's rather than a (hypothetical) judge's standpoint: perhaps the spur effect of European consensus could also prod the Court to find violations where individual judges' prejudices might otherwise give them pause?[363]

Posing this question refocuses our attention on the institution that makes the decisions at issue in practice. This line of thinking raises questions of who should be in a position to decide what constitutes prejudice and which prepolitical rights minorities have – in other words, who takes on the Herculean role of reaching a decision within the theoretically endless string of normative argument envisaged by the morality-focussed view? Asking what kind of reasons the ECtHR *should* use involves a tendency to conflate the observer's standpoint with that of a (hypothetical) judge: it is tempting to simply argue that the Court *should*, of course, neither make reference to national laws that discriminate against intra-State minorities, nor discriminate itself! But how to deal with disagreement between the observer and the judges as to, for example, what constitutes discrimination? Such questions lead us to the ethos-focussed perspective, which is the subject of the next chapter.

---

363 See Daniel Peat, *Comparative Reasoning in International Courts and Tribunals* (Cambridge: Cambridge University Press, 2019), at 161-162; however, the malleability of consensus casts some doubts on this line of argument; see e.g. Johnson, *Homosexuality and the European Court of Human Rights*, chapter 3; on various ways in which this malleability manifests, see Chapters 5 to 7.

Chapter 3: Ethos-focussed Perspectives: From National Ethe to a Pan-European Ethos

I. Introduction

European consensus, at this point, may seem like a rather disastrous undertaking: it endangers the prepolitical rights of intra-State minorities, paradoxically builds on the positions taken by the very States which the ECtHR is supposed to be supervising, and blunts the critical edge of the is-ought distinction. In the face of these charges, it is time to turn to the arguments adduced in defence of European consensus. I will argue in this chapter that, whereas European consensus is commonly criticised on the basis of the morality-focussed perspective discussed in the preceding chapter, its defence is typically proffered from what I termed the *ethos-focussed perspective*.[364]

At this point, I must provide a brief indication of what I mean when I speak of a subject's *ethos*. The meanings of the word in its original Greek are multiple and complex, so it carries a certain inherent ambiguity. Perhaps the most generalisable and accessible translation renders it to mean "character": for example, Aristotelian rhetoric understands ethos (as opposed to pathos and logos) to refer back to the speaker's character, i.e. their wisdom, virtue and good will.[365] But "character" can also be understood in a broader, less literal sense as relating to a subject's particularities in other contexts – most importantly, the distinctive values held dear by a certain person or society which shape their attitude towards moral questions. Ethical normativity eschews the universal aspirations of the morality-focussed perspective and focusses instead on norms valid only *in relation* to a certain person or group.

The focus is therefore, as Habermas has put it, on the "ethical-political will of a self-actualizing collectivity" which gives voice to "its own authentic life project".[366] The ECtHR might be said to have applied the idea of a

364 Or (and often in addition) on the basis of notions of legitimacy which I discuss in Chapters 9 and 10.

365 The distinction is introduced in Aristotle, *Rhetoric*, Book I Chapter 2, and the ethos is developed further in particular in Book II.

366 Habermas, *Between Facts and Norms*, at 100.

State's ethos when it referred, in the *Belgian Linguistics* case, to "those legal and factual features which characterise the life of the society in the State".[367] As discussed in Chapter 1, the juxtaposition of morality-focussed and ethos-focussed perspectives is based on Habermasian terminology; but even as both "morality" and "ethos" are sometimes used interchangeably, the distinction between universalising and relative normativity is usually quite clear. Thus, one standard formulation of the ECtHR refers to the competence of national judges to gauge "the 'exact content of the requirements of morals' in their country";[368] the Court has also spoken of "the moral ethos or moral standards of a society as a whole".[369] Given the reference to standards *of a certain society or country*, both these formulations establish normativity in relation (only) to a specific group or macrosubject, and hence form part of what I will call ethical normativity.

Throughout this chapter, I will trace the implications of such a relative form of normativity to the debates surrounding European consensus, particularly insofar as it could be said to respond to the critical points raised by the morality-focussed perspective. I begin by outlining the epistemological approach of the ethos-focussed perspective: it challenges the morality-focussed perspective's reliance on substantive moral reasoning by pointing to persistent disagreement about human rights (II.). Ethical normativity provides an alternative; the question then becomes how it should be identified. As the citations just mentioned indicate, this issue has received the most sustained attention with regard to ethical normativity developed *within individual States*; I therefore set out main lines of the debate in that context (III.). Briefly put, while some ethos-focussed accounts have focussed on pre-existing cultural commonalities and traditions, the overwhelming majority of modern accounts instead (purport to) locate a State's ethos in the values expressed by way of its political system and legislative acts. In that vein, Pheng Cheah has described ethical normativity as referring to "binding substantive forms of ethical self-understanding that are arrived through consensual procedures of law enactment and political decision making"; it is *by means of these procedures* that ethical norms "give objective embodiment to the concrete life of a political community".[370]

---

367 ECtHR (Plenary), Appl. Nos. 1474/62 et al. – *Belgian Linguistics Case (Merits)*, at para. I.B.10.

368 ECtHR (GC), Appl. No. 57813/00 – *S.H. and Others v. Austria*, Judgment of 3 November 2011, at para. 94; see further on this line of argument infra, note 492.

369 ECtHR (Plenary), Appl. No. 7525/76 – *Dudgeon*, at para. 47.

370 Pheng Cheah, *Inhuman Conditions. On Cosmopolitanism and Human Rights* (Cambridge, Mass.: Harvard University Press, 2006), at 150.

Having identified these general tenets of the ethos-focussed perspective, I turn to its application in the context of the ECHR, particularly with regard to the ECtHR's use of European consensus. One might imagine different ways of conceptualising ethical normativity at the transnational level – one option would be to refer to materials from regional organisations such as the Council of Europe (CoE), a possibility which I will return to in Chapter 6. For now, I retain the emphasis on democratic procedures at the national level as significantly more developed than any form of transnational democracy. In light of this point of emphasis, the ethos-focussed perspective takes a bottom-up approach to regional human rights law and conceptualises it as a form of cooperation between, rather than confrontation of, the States parties (IV.1.). European consensus then emerges as the continuation of this cooperation-based approach within the justification of concrete human rights norms: because it refers back to the legal systems of the States parties, it provides the ECtHR with a way of incorporating the results of democratic procedures at the national level into its reasoning; and the use of consensus could therefore be considered justified on democratic grounds (IV.2.).

Yet this involves a shift in perspective. Even as it builds on individual national ethe, European consensus also goes beyond them since it approaches the legal orders of the States parties through the lens of commonality. I will argue that this is the consequence of internationalist commitments, and that it implies a shift from national ethe to the notion of a *pan-European ethos* (IV.3.). The implication is that, particularly in cases involving the spur effect, European consensus becomes an instrument of harmonisation: it overrules the position of some States parties based on the combined democratic credentials of the position of *other* States parties (IV.4.).

It follows from all this that the use of European consensus could be considered justified as a form of ethical normativity based on a pan-European ethos building on democratic decisions made within the States parties, which in turn is due to the institutional context of the ECtHR as a regional human rights court without its own supporting democratic structures. It will also have become clear, however, that this is not an uncontroversial statement even on the ethos-focussed perspective's own terms, since it involves a shift away from the traditionally favoured macrosubject of the State in which democratic procedures are more pronounced; simultaneously, the morality-focussed perspective would continue to advocate for a different approach altogether. I conclude the chapter by reflecting on the dual difficulties facing the notion of a pan-European ethos, with particular reference to underlying assumptions of homogeneity at both the national and the transnational level (V.).

II. Against the Morality-focussed Perspective: Differing Epistemologies

Before returning to the notion of a pan-European ethos, I must establish some core elements of the ethos-focussed perspective more generally. An essential point which is common to any kind of ethical normativity is the distinct epistemological approach, which differs radically from that of the morality-focussed perspective and both explains and (on its own terms) justifies the differing focus. This section will therefore spell out that epistemology in more detail and, in particular, set it in contrast to the Dworkinian epistemology introduced in the last chapter – which, pro memoria, assumes that normative questions must be answered by further normative argument, itself contingent on yet further argument, and so forth. As Dworkin himself put it, this "may seem unhelpful, because it supplies no independent verification",[371] meaning that people will continue to disagree about which reasons are actually adequate. Dworkin noted that the question of whether a legal or moral question has an objectively true answer must be distinguished from the question of whether that truth can be demonstrated.[372] Although arguing in favour of the infamous "one right answer" thesis in response to the prior question, he always acknowledged the possibility and prevalence of disagreement in response to the second.[373]

Most proponents of European consensus do not take issue directly with the first prong of this epistemology – there is little indication that they take an entirely sceptical approach to morality.[374] Many have, however, been more preoccupied with the second prong of Dworkin's account: the lack of demonstrable proof in response to normative questions. This focus has an impressive pedigree: consider, for example, Jean-Jacques Rousseau,

371 Dworkin, *Justice for Hedgehogs*, at 37.

372 Dworkin, *Law's Empire*, at ix.

373 Dworkin, "Hard Cases" at 105; Dworkin, "Can Rights be Controversial?" at 336; for one contextualisation, see Kennedy, *A Critique of Adjudication (fin de siècle)*, at 35-36 and 123.

374 Explicitly Samantha Besson, "The Authority of International Law - Lifting the State Veil," (2009) 31 *Sydney Law Review* 343 at 375; see also Dzehtsiarou, "European Consensus and the Evolutive Interpretation of the European Convention on Human Rights" at 1743 (acknowledging the "moral value of human rights").

who provides a prototypical early account of the ethos-focussed perspective. "Doubtless", he says, "there is a universal justice emanating from reason alone", a justice which "comes from God"; however, "if we knew how to receive so high an inspiration, we should need neither government nor laws".[375] Rousseau therefore argues against a purely normative approach, since it leads only to circular argument "without arriving at an understanding".[376]

These considerations provide a different perspective, for example, on the debate on morality and law that followed the publication of the Wolfenden Report. In the last chapter, we considered Hart's and Dworkin's criticism of Lord Devlin, according to which his reliance on "positive morality" undermined critical engagement with the status quo. Devlin, however, approached the issue from an entirely different angle: while accepting "a man's own conscience" as "*for him* the final arbiter", he was concerned about the consequences of foregrounding that conscience, in the form of critical morality, for *society at large*.[377] With clear echoes of Rousseau, Devlin's argument for this conclusion was based on the prevalence of disagreement about moral issues: there could be no basis for privileging critical over positive morality when "men of undoubted reasoning power and honesty of purpose have shown themselves unable to agree on what the moral law should be".[378] (The positions of women or people of other genders, apparently, were not considered relevant in the first place.)

This approach is given its clearest modern presentation by Jeremy Waldron. He does not dispute the existence of objective moral truth in Dworkin's sense, but argues that, whether it exists or not, it is simply *irrelevant* since there is no way of uncontroversially accessing it.[379] His starting point is, instead, that "[t]here are many of us, and we disagree about jus-

375 Jean-Jacques Rousseau, *The Social Contract*, trans. G.D.H. Cole (Milton Keynes: Jiahu Books, 2013), at 49.

376 Ibid.

377 Devlin, "Democracy and Morality" at 92.

378 Ibid., 93.

379 Waldron, *Law and Disagreement*, at chapter 8; Waldron is here concerned primarily with moral realism, but see ibid. at 168-9 on Dworkin; see also Samantha Besson, *The Morality of Conflict. Reasonable Disagreement and the Law* (Oxford: Hart, 2005), at 45; Bellamy, "The Democratic Legitimacy of International Human Rights Conventions: Political Constitutionalism and the European Convention on Human Rights" at 1022 and 1024; Legg, *The Margin of Appreciation*, at 114; see also the commentary by Jürgen Habermas, "On Law and Disagreement. Some Comments on 'Interpretative Pluralism'," (2003) 16 *Ratio Juris* 187 at 189.

tice".[380] Waldron's account is particularly relevant in the present context because he explicitly extends its scope to cover human rights: from a wholly ethos-focussed perspective, there is no ground to make any kind of epistemological exception for rights. They are just as controversial as other issues – if not in their abstract formulation, then certainly in the concrete application which is of interest for the reasoning of the ECtHR.[381] In fact, Samantha Besson has argued that in the case of the ECtHR, adjudicating cases pertaining to 47 States parties, it is even more important to take disagreement about the issues before the Court into account.[382]

The upshot of all this is that while Dworkin's epistemological account is not necessarily rejected,[383] the ethos-focussed perspective approaches the issue from an entirely different direction.[384] If moral truth is regarded as irrelevant and disagreement foregrounded instead, then there is no ground on which to distinguish between the merits of the various views which constitute that disagreement. The spotlight is shifted, in other words, from the universal validity which the morality-focussed perspective claims under the auspices of (cognitive) reason to the *person* whose reasoned *but disputed* views are at issue. From that perspective, it becomes "something of an insult",[385] "unpleasantly condescending"[386] or "flagrantly elitist"[387] to put one's own opinion above that of anybody else when making decisions

---

380 Waldron, *Law and Disagreement*, at 1; in this respect, Ely is closer to the ethos-focussed perspective: see Ely, *Democracy and Distrust. A Theory of Judicial Review*, at 57-58.

381 Jeremy Waldron, "The Core of the Case Against Judicial Review," (2005-2006) 115 *Yale Law Journal* 1346 at 1366-1369; Waldron, "Rights and Majorities: Rousseau Revisited" at 53; Waldron, *Law and Disagreement*, at e.g. 198 and 245; see specifically on the ECHR ibid., 12.

382 Samantha Besson, "European Human Rights, Supranational Judicial Review and Democracy - Thinking Outside the Judicial Box," in *Human Rights Protection in the European Legal Orders: Interaction Between European Courts and National Courts*, ed. Patricia Popelier, Catherine Van de Heyning, and Piet Van Nuffel (Cambridge: Intersentia, 2011) at 136.

383 Of course, some philosophers also draw that stronger conclusion. This does not seem to be a common view among proponents of European consensus, however; and the practical consequences for that topic would in any case be similar.

384 See Waldron, *Law and Disagreement*, at 160-161.

385 Ibid., 15; see also Waldron, "Rights and Majorities: Rousseau Revisited" at 71.

386 Waldron, *Law and Disagreement*, at 303.

387 Ely, *Democracy and Distrust. A Theory of Judicial Review*, at 59.

which affect society (or, in the case of the ECtHR, even a large number of societies).[388]

As an example, consider the case of minority rights. There is disagreement over which minorities should be protected or empowered by law, and in which fashion. Dworkin would insist that there is a correct answer to an interpretive controversy about rights, particularly minority rights, and that it must prevail over other, prejudiced views.[389] Waldron holds precisely the opposite: "The most dangerous temptation is [...] to treat [an opposing view] as beneath notice in respectable deliberation by assuming that it is ignorant or prejudiced".[390] As argued in the preceding chapter, however, the claim of prejudice is central to the morality-focussed perspective's rationale for protecting minority rights. Furthermore, it implies a normative element: minorities are understood as subject to prejudice based on denial of equality, rather than a justified form of differential treatment. It is that normative element that the ethos-focussed perspective treats differently in light of its focus on disagreement: since the normative element is bound to be controversial, it may not be assumed; and any claim of prejudice is itself subject to disagreement.[391]

The epistemological shift in perspective may be best exemplified by the different understandings of *objectivity* used by the morality-focussed and

388 See Steven Wheatley, "On the Legitimate Authority of International Human Rights Bodies," in *The Legitimacy of International Human Rights Regimes. Legal, Political and Philosophical Perspectives*, ed. Andreas Føllesdal, Johan Karlsson Schaffer, and Geir Ulfstein (Cambridge: Cambridge University Press, 2013) at 102-103.

389 See Chapter 2, II.

390 Waldron, *Law and Disagreement*, at 111; see also Devlin, "Democracy and Morality" at 91 and 96, as well as Koskenniemi's critique of Philip Allott, arguing that a weakness of his writing lies in "a downplaying of the importance of actual disagreement, indeed the characterization of it in terms of the error or perhaps 'madness' of one (or both) of the parties": Martti Koskenniemi, "International Law as Therapy: Reading The Health of Nations," (2005) 16 *European Journal of International Law* 329 at 338-339.

391 See Waldron, "The Core of the Case Against Judicial Review" at 1398 and 1403-1404, where he acknowledges by reference to the *Carolene Products* footnote four that "prejudice against discrete and insular minorities" might lead to cases in which his argument fails since the preconditions which he posits (particularly what amounts to an assumption of good faith voting: see further infra, III., and Chapter 4, III.1.) do not hold, but also implies that this constellation should only be considered in rare and ultimately negligible ("non-core") cases, instead emphasising the importance of not all-too-hastily side-lining reasonable disagreement about rights.

ethos-focussed perspectives.[392] The prior is concerned with moral objectivity: not usually in the sense of moral realism (as giving moral claims "a bizarre metaphysical base"), but referring to moral claims as established through normative argument rather than "mere reports of taste".[393] The ethos-focussed perspective, as discussed over the course of the last paragraphs, bypasses the issue of moral objectivity since it considers it unverifiable. By focussing instead on agreement and disagreement, it takes (what it conceptualises as) *an issue of fact* as its starting point.[394] For all the practical and theoretical difficulties involved, facts are regarded as empirically verifiable and hence objective in a more relevant sense.[395]

The controversies surrounding European consensus exemplify the differences between the two approaches. While Letsas invokes the critical edge of the is-ought distinction to argue against consensus in favour of purely normative reasoning based on "objective" values of political morality,[396] proponents of consensus point to disagreement about the requirements of morality.[397] Proposals for the ECtHR to follow a morality-focussed approach have been criticised as assigning it the role of a Platonic philosopher-king,[398] and it is suggested that the ECtHR's reasoning "cannot rest solely on the moral superiority of human rights, because, as Waldron has rightly argued, people can disagree about rights".[399] Since there is no uncontroversial way to establish moral truth, the ECtHR is said to face "an

392 See critically Koskenniemi, *From Apology to Utopia*, at 16, 63, 513 and, for a connection to the epistemological issues under consideration here, 516; see generally on the Koskenniemian framework Chapter 1, IV.

393 Dworkin, *Law's Empire*, at 81; see also Ronald Dworkin, "Objectivity and Truth: You'd Better Believe It," (1996) 25 *Philosophy & Public Affairs* 87, esp. at 98.

394 Besson, *The Morality of Conflict. Reasonable Disagreement and the Law*, at 65.

395 See Waldron, *Law and Disagreement*, at 178.

396 Letsas, *A Theory of Interpretation of the European Convention on Human Rights*, at 5.

397 Besson, "European Human Rights, Supranational Judicial Review and Democracy - Thinking Outside the Judicial Box" at 136.

398 See Legg, *The Margin of Appreciation*, at 115, criticising the Letsas-Dworkinian epistemology; for Dworkin's own wry take on philosopher-kings, see Ronald Dworkin, "A New Philosophy for International Law," (2013) 41 *Philosophy & Public Affairs* 2 at 6.

399 Dzehtsiarou, *European Consensus and the Legitimacy of the European Court of Human Rights*, at 154; see also Dahlberg, "'The Lack of Such a Common Approach' - Comparative Argumentation by the European Court of Human Rights" at 77; Carmen Draghici, "The Strasbourg Court between European and Local Consensus: Anti-democratic or Guardian of Democratic Process?," (2017) *Public Law* 11 at 14; Kristin Henrard, "How the ECtHR's Use of European Consensus Consid-

epistemological quandary";[400] it must provide "some *more objective* and palpable grounds other than a moral reading".[401] European consensus provides those grounds because it refers to States parties' laws which are "on the books" and thus injects a verifiable, "objective element" into the Court's reasoning.[402] The meaning of objectivity has shifted from a normative to a factual understanding: unlike purely normative reasoning, consensus refers to "empirical evidence"[403] – to "external circumstances that can be verified".[404]

Given this affinity towards factual objectivity, it is hardly surprising that proponents of consensus are less concerned with the is-ought distinction. While they do not deny the fallacy of deriving an *ought* directly from an *is*, they emphasise that "there is no fallacy in informing the *ought* with the *is*"[405] and the "manifold connections" that exist between (factual) practice

---

erations Allows Legitimacy Concerns to Delimit Its Mandate," in *Building Consensus on European Consensus. Judicial Interpretation of Human Rights in Europe and Beyond*, ed. Panos Kapotas and Vassilis Tzevelekos (Cambridge: Cambridge University Press, 2019) at 160.

400 Legg, *The Margin of Appreciation*, at 115.

401 Dzehtsiarou, *European Consensus and the Legitimacy of the European Court of Human Rights*, at 154 (emphasis added); see also at 142.

402 Brems, *Human Rights: Universality and Diversity*, at 419; Mahoney and Kondak, "Common Ground" at 120 and 139; Draghici, "The Strasbourg Court between European and Local Consensus: Anti-democratic or Guardian of Democratic Process?" at 13; Nozawa, "Drawing the Line: Same-sex adoption and the jurisprudence of the ECtHR on the application of the "European consensus" standard under Article 14" at 73 in fine; ECtHR (GC), Appl. No. 57813/00 – *S.H. and Others*, joint dissenting opinion of Judges Tulkens, Hirvelä, Lazarova Trajkovska and Tsotsoria speaks of "objective indicia used to determine consensus", which is echoed e.g. by Kukavica, "National Consensus and the Eigth Amendment: Is There Something to Be Learned from the United States Supreme Court?" at 366; see also (though acknowledging the limits of the ostensible objectivity of consensus) Janneke Gerards, "Pluralism, Deference and the Margin of Appreciation Doctrine," (2011) 17 *European Law Journal* 80 at 109-110.

403 Örücü, "Whither Comparativism in Human Rights Cases?" at 239; Paul Mahoney, "Judicial Activism and Judicial Self-Restraint in the European Court of Human Rights: Two Sides of the Same Coin," (1990) 11 *Human Rights Law Journal* 57 at 74 (also "objective evidence").

404 Dzehtsiarou, "European Consensus and the Evolutive Interpretation of the European Convention on Human Rights" at 1734 (footnote 31); see also Peat, *Comparative Reasoning in International Courts and Tribunals*, at 177 ("comparative law provides an objectively verifiable benchmark").

405 Samantha Besson and Alain Zysset, "Human Rights Theory and Human Rights History: A Tale of Two Odd Bedfellows," (2012) *Ancilla Iuris* 204 at 216.

and normative decisions.[406] As Alix Schlüter has succinctly put it, "facts make law".[407] Just as Devlin was unapologetic about the facticity of positive morality and Habermas emphasised the facticity of the volitional moment on which the ethos-focussed perspective relies, so too the relevance of laws-read-as-facts is conceptualised by proponents of European consensus as a positive attribute, for it avoids the pitfalls of the morality-focussed perspective and its over-reliance on substantive reasoning.

III. National Ethe: From Traditions to Democratic Procedures

If there is no epistemology that allows for the mitigation of disagreement,[408] then the question becomes how to achieve concerted action in spite of it (the "circumstances of politics").[409] The argument traced so far merely counters the strictly normative approach of the morality-focussed perspective and suggests that an alternative approach would be preferable. I have mentioned that European consensus seems to avoid the pitfalls associated (from the perspective of proponents of consensus) with the morality-focussed perspective, but this only demonstrates that European consensus avoids some forms of criticism; it does not yet supply a positive argument *in favour* of using European consensus. To examine whether such an argument can be adduced, we must delve deeper into different ways of approaching the ethos-focussed perspective – for much depends on which ethos is regarded as relevant and how it is constructed.

To that end, consider once more the distinction between morality-focussed and ethos-focussed perspectives. Habermas describes the prior as assigning rational will-formation to the individual subject, which is why on that view "the individual's moral autonomy must reach through the political autonomy of the united will of all" in the form of prepolitical human rights.[410] By contrast, the ethos-focussed perspective is said to assume

406 Von Ungern-Sternberg, "Die Konsensmethode des EGMR. Eine kritische Bewertung mit Blick auf das völkerrechtliche Konsens- und das innerstaatliche Demokratieprinzip" at 326 (my translation).

407 Schlüter, "Beweisrechtliche Implikationen der margin of appreciation-Doktrin" at 55.

408 Waldron, *Law and Disagreement*, at 178.

409 Ibid., 102, developing the Rawlsian "circumstances of justice": see Rawls, *A Theory of Justice*, at 109-110; see also Bellamy, "Republicanism, Democracy, and Constitutionalism" at 167.

410 Habermas, *Between Facts and Norms*, at 103.

that "the rational will can take shape only in the macrosubject of a people or nation", so that priority must be given to "the self-conscious realization of the ethical substance of a concrete community".[411] As mentioned in the introduction of the chapter, ethical reasoning thus eschews the universalising claims of the morality-focussed perspective in favour of a form of normativity which is *relative* to a certain macrosubject. For example, Waldron conceptualises law as aspiring not to justice tout court, but to "justice *of a community*",[412] Besson argues that it modulates moral rights to adapt them to the "moral-political circumstances of life in a [specific] polity",[413] and Cheah describes the "ethical realm" as the "political morality of the state of its (national) public sphere".[414]

Several of these formulations identify a people, nation or State as the relevant macrosubject, which clearly chimes with the dominant tradition within Western political theory. Before considering whether the ethos-focussed approach can be broadened to accommodate different macrosubjects, particularly at the transnational level, I would like to examine in more detail how the "self-conscious realization of the ethical substance" is thought to take place within individual States, particularly insofar as the relationship between intra-State majorities and minorities is concerned.

Let us begin, once again, with Rousseau.[415] We saw above that, while he does not dispute the existence of moral principles of justice, they cannot be ascertained by humans in a way that would foster agreement. Justice, "to be admitted among us", must therefore be "mutual" – it must be introduced in the form of general laws, in the making of which "the whole people decrees for the whole people".[416] These laws give birth to what Rousseau calls, in another passage, "the morality of a nation".[417] Such an understanding need not be expressed unanimously, however[418] – once a society is constituted by the unanimous social contract itself, majority vote

411 Ibid.

412 Waldron, *Law and Disagreement*, at 6.

413 Besson, "Human Rights: Ethical, Political... or Legal? First Steps in a Legal Theory of Human Rights" at 240.

414 Cheah, *Inhuman Conditions. On Cosmopolitanism and Human Rights*, at 150.

415 For the centrality of Rousseau within the Habermasian framework, see Habermas, *Between Facts and Norms*, at 100; Habermas, "Über den internen Zusammenhang von Rechtsstaat und Demokratie" at 299; see also, with a different emphasis, Habermas, "Inklusion - Einbeziehen oder Einschließen? Zum Verhältnis von Nation, Rechtsstaat und Demokratie" at 164-166.

416 Rousseau, *The Social Contract*, at 49.

417 Ibid., 161.

418 Ibid., 35 (at footnote 6).

suffices to enact a law. The argument goes as follows: the citizens do not vote based on their individual interests, but rather state their opinion as to what the general will requires, i.e. they vote in the interest of the collective on which approach would best encapsulate the common good. Being outvoted, on those terms, means simply that one was mistaken as to what the general will requires.[419]

According to Rousseau (at least on some readings of him), this approach functions best when there is a certain level of homogeneity among the people united by a social contract: he argues that the "same laws cannot suit [...] many diverse provinces with different customs" and that small States with strong social ties will have a greater chance at succeeding in self-government.[420] The collectivity thus gains a particularly prominent place in his theory, individuals being "fuse[d] together", as Habermas puts it, in "the ethos of a small and perspicuous, more or less homogenous community integrated through shared cultural traditions".[421]

The ethos-focussed view, on this account, finds the self-understanding or ethos of a group in its pre-existent culture and tradition, though it may be further developed by way of the social contract.[422] Glimpses of such an approach can sometimes be found in the ECtHR's case-law, as when it held, in *M.C. v. Bulgaria*, that "perceptions of a cultural nature, local circumstances and traditional approaches" must be taken into account.[423] In the passage just cited, Habermas also draws a connection between this kind of "shared cultural traditions" and a *homogenous* community. The notion of homogeneity has since developed a long tradition of influence within political and legal theory, ranging from the uncompromising and exclusion-

---

419 Ibid., 135.

420 Ibid., 61; for an illuminating summary in this regard, see David Miller, "Republicanism, National Identity, and Europe," in *Republicanism and Political Theory*, ed. Cécile Laborde and John Maynor (Malden, Mass.: Blackwell, 2008) at 133-136 and 139.

421 Habermas, *Between Facts and Norms*, at 102; see also Habermas, "Volkssouveränität als Verfahren" at 611.

422 For a more positive elaboration of Rousseau in Habermasian terms, focussing on the latter aspect, see Habermas, "Inklusion - Einbeziehen oder Einschließen? Zum Verhältnis von Nation, Rechtsstaat und Demokratie" at 163-164 and 166; Annelien de Dijn, "Rousseau and Republicanism," (2015) *Political Theory* 1 at 15.

423 ECtHR, Appl. No. 39272/98 – *M.C. v. Bulgaria*, Judgment of 4 December 2003, at para. 154.

ary postulate of national homogeneity by Carl Schmitt[424] to various rather more subtle mentions of "relative homogeneity" e.g. by Ernst-Wolfgang Böckenförde,[425] Hans Kelsen,[426] and – controversially – the German Federal Constitutional Court.[427]

Given the vagueness of any notion of homogeneity in light of the countless (and often cross-cutting) human differences and similarities,[428] it is difficult to evaluate the merits of such more nuanced formulations of the concept; but in any case, its popularity has dwindled significantly in the face of the undeniable lack of homogeneity in modern societies[429] as well as the unpleasant aftertaste left by the Schmittian undertones of the concept.[430] Habermas, for example, has argued extensively against any role for homogeneity in theories of political will formation,[431] rightly emphasising that "behind such a façade [of alleged homogeneity] there lurks the hegemonic culture of the dominant part" of society.[432] Chantal Mouffe has

424 E.g. in Carl Schmitt, *Der Begriff des Politischen* (Berlin: Duncker & Humblot, 2009).

425 See Mirjam Künkler and Tine Stein, "State, Law, and Constitution. Ernst-Wolfgang Böckenförde's Political and Legal Thought in Context," in *Ernst-Wolfgang Böckenförde: Constitutional and Political Theory. Selected Writings*, ed. Mirjam Künkler and Tine Stein (Oxford: Oxford University Press, 2017) at 12-14, as well as the essays by Böckenförde collected and translated in that volume.

426 Hans Kelsen, *Allgemeine Staatslehre* (Berlin: Julius Springer, 1925), at 324.

427 German Federal Constitutional Court, Judgment of 12 October 1993, BVerfGE 89, 155, at 186.

428 See Gertrude Lübbe-Wolff, "Homogenes Volk - Über Homogenitätspostulate und Integration," (2007) 27 *Zeitschrift für Ausländerrecht und Ausländerpolitik* 121 at 127.

429 Ibid., 126; of course, this does not in and of itself resolve the issue: see e.g. Marks, *The Riddle of All Constitutions*, at 65 on how it can be ideologically shrouded, and Mouffe, *The Democratic Paradox*, at 18-19 on the necessity of a move from the "fact" of pluralism (Rawls) to fully acknowledging difference "as the condition of possibility of being".

430 See J.H.H. Weiler, "Does Europe Need a Constitution? Demos, Telos and the German Maastricht Decision," (1995) 1 *European Law Journal* 219 at 223, arguing that the German Constitutional Court's reference to Hermann Heller in the above-mentioned decision (note 427) served only to conceal a Schmittian framework.

431 Habermas, *Between Facts and Norms*, at 200; Habermas, "Inklusion - Einbeziehen oder Einschließen? Zum Verhältnis von Nation, Rechtsstaat und Demokratie" at 159.

432 Habermas, "Der europäische Nationalstaat - Zu Vergangenheit und Zukunft von Souveränität und Staatsbürgerschaft" at 142.

similarly held that homogeneity can always be "revealed as fictitious and based on acts of exclusion".[433]

In light of these insights, modern proponents of the ethos-focussed view typically disavow any reliance on (national) homogeneity;[434] instead, they explicitly take diversity and disagreement among individuals as their starting point and regard democratic processes based on alternating majorities as the most adequate way of overcoming the conceptual break between individual and collectivity.[435] In that vein, Jeremy Waldron has argued that jurisprudence should take up the challenges that law must face in a diverse society,[436] and that, to that end, it must "be careful to avoid building in any premise of ethnic and cultural homogeneity as a prerequisite in our models of politics and legislation".[437] Democratic self-governance combined with a political culture of human rights, albeit not prepolitical as on the morality-focussed view, are said to avoid the exclusionary effects of Schmittian theory and instead combine, in the best way possible, the diverse sub-groups and varying positions within a society.[438]

Against that background, the focus on a society's ethos is given a different twist: it switches from presuppositions of homogeneity to diversity and inclusion, from historically appropriated traditions to a communality continually constructed by way of majoritarian legislation.[439] Volitional self-realisation by way of democratic procedures thus emerges as the ethos-focussed counterpoint to the morality-focussed perspective's emphasis on cognitive reason: Rousseau emphasised the importance of general laws,[440] and Devlin appealed to "democracy and universal suffrage" to substantiate his reliance on positive morality, arguing that "in the end the will of the

433 Mouffe, *The Democratic Paradox*, at 19.

434 I will return to the notion of homogeneity in the transnational context infra, V.

435 Laborde and Maynor, "The Republican Contribution to Contemporary Political Theory" at 16; see also Besson, *The Morality of Conflict. Reasonable Disagreement and the Law*, at 1 and 155; Zysset, *The ECHR and Human Rights Theory: Reconciling the Moral and Political Conceptions*, at 222.

436 Waldron, *Law and Disagreement*, at 74; see also e.g. Lübbe-Wolff, "Homogenes Volk - Über Homogenitätspostulate und Integration" at 127; Habermas, "Inklusion - Einbeziehen oder Einschließen? Zum Verhältnis von Nation, Rechtsstaat und Demokratie" at 172.

437 Waldron, *Law and Disagreement*, at 75.

438 See Habermas, "Inklusion - Einbeziehen oder Einschließen? Zum Verhältnis von Nation, Rechtsstaat und Demokratie" at 166.

439 Ibid., 164 ("future-oriented popular sovereignty").

440 Supra, note 416.

people must prevail".[441] Arguments such as these turn on formally egalitarian considerations: every person's view is given equal respect by counting it equally as part of the decision-making process.[442]

The hallmark of this emphasis on democratic self-government within a community is that it assumes what Habermas, commenting on Rousseau, calls "political virtues"[443] – that citizens actually will vote with the common good in mind, rather than being led astray by self-interest or prejudice. This characteristic of the ethos-focussed view is carried over to its more modern formulations: for example, in Jeremy Waldron's account it is assumed that votes are conducted in good faith, reflecting "considered and impartial opinions",[444] even if that assumption has "an aspirational quality".[445] This approach ties in with the focus on disagreement and scepticism about moral-cognitive epistemology: where the morality-focussed perspective would distrust majority decisions since they are liable to contain prejudiced external preferences, the ethos-focussed perspective not only emphasises the lack of proof for any given moral position but also replaces the distrust of majorities with the assumption of their good faith[446] – indeed, in a sense it must do so because, on its own terms, there is simply no uncontroversial normative standard available for assessing whether a certain position lacks good faith. Accordingly, the ethos-focussed perspective considers it important to "respect and trust the ability of each of us collective-

---

441 Devlin, "Democracy and Morality" at 91-92; contra: Hart, *Law, Liberty, and Morality*, at 77-81; Dworkin, "Liberty and Moralism" at 304.

442 Waldron, *Law and Disagreement*, e.g. at 109 and 114; Zysset, *The ECHR and Human Rights Theory: Reconciling the Moral and Political Conceptions*, at 218; Besson, "The Authority of International Law - Lifting the State Veil" at 354.

443 Habermas, *Between Facts and Norms*, at 102; see also Samantha Besson and José Luis Martí, "Law and Republicanism: Mapping the Issues," in *Legal Republicanism: National and International Perspectives*, ed. Samantha Besson and José Luis Martí (Oxford: Oxford University Press, 2009) at 23 (acknowledging that the danger of a tyranny of the majority would otherwise loom large).

444 Waldron, *Law and Disagreement*, at 12-14; see also Besson, *The Morality of Conflict. Reasonable Disagreement and the Law*, at 252.

445 Waldron, *Law and Disagreement*, at 14; see also ibid., 305; Waldron, "The Core of the Case Against Judicial Review" at 1379; Jeremy Waldron, "Democratic Theory and the Public Interest: Condorcet and Rousseau Revisited," (1989) 83 *The American Political Science Review* 1322 at 1326-1327; see also Joshua Cohen, "An Epistemic Conception of Democracy," (1986) 97 *Ethics* 26 at 33; Bellamy, "Republicanism, Democracy, and Constitutionalism" at 159 and 162.

446 Waldron, *Law and Disagreement*, at 221-222; Waldron, "Rights and Majorities: Rousseau Revisited" at 64-65; Miller, "Republicanism, National Identity, and Europe" at 141.

ly" to make judgements on any political subject, including issues of human rights[447] – *particularly* on issues of human rights, in fact, since rights are said to protect precisely the kind of individual autonomy and responsibility that is expressed in democratic procedures, so that the two may not be separated.[448] Distrusting the majority would, on that view, "imply distrusting the very abilities human rights aim at protecting".[449]

Accordingly, the ethos-focussed view conceptualises the relationship between intra-State majorities and minorities very differently from the perspectives we discussed in the last chapter. The morality-focussed view perceives a tension due to the danger of the "tyranny of the majority" which may encroach on prepolitical rights of the minority. For the ethos-focussed view, however, rights are inherently political: they must be willed into being and fleshed out by joint ethical-political acts. Rather than constricting majoritarian decisions based on prepolitical rights, civil liberty is at once constituted through and limited by the general will.[450] Because the general will is deemed to be impartial and inclusive, minorities will not be discriminated against despite majoritarian decision-making procedures.[451] On the assumption of the majority's good faith, there are no grounds to not let it be "judge in its own cause" – Dworkin's argument to that effect was based on the difficulty of self-reflection with regard to prejudice,[452] but the good faith assumption stands opposed to the very foundation of that argument.[453] There is, then, no reason not to proceed by way of majoritarian decision.[454]

Against that backdrop, the tension between intra-State minorities and majorities takes on a very different form for the ethos-focussed perspective. Since rights are not conceived of as inherently counter-majoritarian, enforcing such rights over the will of the majority becomes problematic. Alexander Bickel famously coined the term "counter-majoritarian *difficul-*

447 Besson, "European Human Rights, Supranational Judicial Review and Democracy - Thinking Outside the Judicial Box" at 125.

448 Waldron, *Law and Disagreement*, at 222.

449 Besson, "European Human Rights, Supranational Judicial Review and Democracy - Thinking Outside the Judicial Box" at 125.

450 See Rousseau, *The Social Contract*, at 29; on Rousseau's political conceptualisation of rights in contrast to natural law, see Besson, *The Morality of Conflict. Reasonable Disagreement and the Law*, at 140-141.

451 See Habermas, "Inklusion - Einbeziehen oder Einschließen? Zum Verhältnis von Nation, Rechtsstaat und Demokratie" at 166.

452 See Chapter 2, II.

453 See Waldron, "The Core of the Case Against Judicial Review" at 1404.

454 Waldron, *Law and Disagreement*, at 297.

ty" to describe this problem,[455] which becomes particularly acute when courts are tasked with delineating the content of human rights in a legally binding fashion. Thus, proponents of the ethos-focussed perspective may not be opposed in principle to weaker (non-binding) forms of judicial review,[456] since such review does not override majority decisions but rather stimulates further discussions on certain issues and redirects public discourse towards new solutions.[457] The overall focus of ethical normativity, however, remains squarely on majoritarian decision-making.

In sum, the ethos-focussed perspective provides a take on counter-majoritarianism which differs radically from that of the morality-focussed perspective discussed in the preceding chapter, and which lays the groundwork for a more positive evaluation of European consensus. Where the morality-focussed perspective aims to protect prepolitical rights, particularly those of intra-State minorities in the face of a "tyranny of the majority", the ethos-focussed perspective questions the claim to truth underlying prepolitical rights and relies instead, having disavowed any connections to national homogeneity, on democratic procedures as the location of ethical normativity. Because democratic procedures are most pronounced within the macrosubject of the State, it is unsurprising that the State has persisted as the primary reference point of the ethos-focussed perspective. Yet this raises the question of how to operationalise the ethos-focussed perspective in the transnational context of the ECtHR: it is to this question that I now turn.

---

455 Alexander Bickel, *The Least Dangerous Branch. The Supreme Court at the Bar of Politics* (New Haven and London: Yale University Press, 1986).

456 Besson, *The Morality of Conflict. Reasonable Disagreement and the Law*, at 333-336, arguing for a "limited model of judicial interpretation" where the "final interpretive competence [...] shifts back to the legislature"; see also Waldron, "The Core of the Case Against Judicial Review" at 1354, clarifying that his "target is strong judicial review".

457 Bellamy, "The Democratic Legitimacy of International Human Rights Conventions: Political Constitutionalism and the European Convention on Human Rights" at 1029; Waldron, "The Core of the Case Against Judicial Review" at 1370; Waldron, "Rights and Majorities: Rousseau Revisited" at 69.

IV. Ethos-focussed Perspectives at the Transnational Level

1. Lack of Regional Democracy and Human Rights as a Cooperative Venture

To round off the tableau within which European consensus becomes relevant on the basis of the ethos-focussed perspective, I would like to briefly consider the institutional context of the ECtHR as a regional human rights court. In light of the tenets of the ethos-focussed perspective as discussed so far, we can easily identify two challenges which it faces.[458] First, as a court it faces the counter-majoritarian difficulty; second, as a *transnational* court, it is institutionally disconnected from any one individual ethos. This latter point is crucial because it implies a disconnect from the democratic procedures which are taken to express ethical normativity. While various organs of the CoE may be considered to fulfil a certain representative function,[459] for example, they are not democratic in the way national institutions – or even those of the European Union (EU) – are, and hence it is commonly assumed that *no form of regional democracy has yet developed.*[460] Accordingly, transnational courts such as the ECtHR are left without a transnational, democratic constituency. Accordingly, the "central problem in the justification of international courts" has been identified by von Bogdandy and Venzke as lurking in the fact that "their public authority is not embedded in a responsive political system".[461]

This clearly poses a problem for the ethos-focussed perspective, for which human rights are seen as binding on a community only when "con-

---

458 See Dzehtsiarou, *European Consensus and the Legitimacy of the European Court of Human Rights*, at 144; his point here and in following references is related to the ECtHR's sociological legitimacy (on which, see Chapter 9), but also stands on directly normative terms.

459 See Chapter 6, IV.3.

460 See Samantha Besson, "Human Rights and Democracy in a Global Context: Decoupling and Recoupling," (2011) 4 *Ethics & Global Politics* 19 at 29; Samantha Besson, "Subsidiarity in International Human Rights Law - What is Subsidiary about Human Rights?," (2016) 61 *The American Journal of Jurisprudence* 69 at 96; see also Wheatley, "The Legitimacy of International Human Rights Regimes" at 85 ("absence of a meaningful political community").

461 Armin von Bogdandy and Ingo Venzke, "In Whose Name? An Investigation of International Courts' Public Authority and Its Democratic Justification," (2012) 23 *European Journal of International Law* 7 at 19; for the ECHR, see Steven Wheatley, "Minorities under the ECHR and the Construction of a 'Democratic Society'," (2007) *Public Law* 770 at 789.

sciously appropriated" by that community as a whole,[462] and for which, if "human rights are to be democratically legitimate, they ought to be the outcome of a legalisation process in which human rights-holders can also be the authors of their own rights".[463] The election of the ECtHR's judges by the CoE's Parliamentary Assembly,[464] from this perspective, carries little weight since it does not constrain the interpretive discretion which those judges later possess. Thus, from the outset, regional (and global) instruments of human rights protection seem more suspect than they do on the morality-focussed view, where they were welcomed as an additional chance at giving individuals' prepolitical rights legal relevance. Rather, the ethos-focussed perspective's reliance on democratic procedures leads to its insistence that human rights are "meant to be fleshed out at [the] domestic level".[465]

Therefore, while the morality-focussed perspective sees regional human rights as a necessary top-down institutionalisation of prepolitical rights, the ethos-focussed perspective must work *bottom-up*, from the individual ethical-political communities embodied in States.[466] Still, a variety of purposes can be imagined for the ECHR and other regional human rights treaties against this backdrop: they can be conceptualised as a guarantee against levelling-down from agreed-upon standards,[467] as protecting minimal requirements for the functioning of democracy at the national level,[468] or as a mechanism to cautiously spark domestic or pan-European debate

462 Habermas, *Between Facts and Norms*, at 100.

463 Besson, "Human Rights and Democracy in a Global Context: Decoupling and Recoupling" at 30.

464 Article 22 ECHR.

465 Besson, "Human Rights: Ethical, Political... or Legal? First Steps in a Legal Theory of Human Rights" at 242.

466 Besson, "Subsidiarity in International Human Rights Law - What is Subsidiary about Human Rights?" at 100; Besson, "Human Rights Adjudication as Transnational Adjudication: A Peripheral Case of Domestic Courts as International Law Adjudicators" at 59.

467 Besson, "Human Rights: Ethical, Political... or Legal? First Steps in a Legal Theory of Human Rights" at 243; Besson, "Human Rights and Democracy in a Global Context: Decoupling and Recoupling" at 30.

468 Zysset, *The ECHR and Human Rights Theory: Reconciling the Moral and Political Conceptions*, at 210; see also, based on reading of Arendt's right to have rights, Besson, "Human Rights and Democracy in a Global Context: Decoupling and Recoupling" at 28.

on certain issues to enhance democratic deliberation.[469] What all these approaches have in common is that, unlike the morality-focussed perspective, they focus primarily on the influence that States should have on regional human rights, not vice versa: regional human rights should be "products of and controlled by an international system of normal democracy grounded in and attuned to the domestic systems of the contracting states".[470]

At the most general level, then, the object and purpose of the ECHR could be described as *cooperation* between those States. Kanstantsin Dzehtsiarou has been very clear on this point, arguing against the approach taken by George Letsas according to which distrust of States is built into the purpose underlying the ECHR. On Dzehtsiarou's account, the "Convention was signed and the Court was created *not to confront the Contracting Parties but to intensify cooperation* and collective protection of human rights":[471] the Convention is seen less as an external constraint and more as a common venture. Or, as Wildhaber, Hjartarson and Donnelly have put it: "the human rights of the ECHR imitate and reinforce those pre-existing in many domestic legal systems, so as to constitute their general principles".[472]

---

469 Bilyana Petkova, "The Notion of Consensus as a Route to Democratic Adjudication," (2011-2012) 14 *Cambridge Yearbook of European Legal Studies* 663 at 671; Thomas Kleinlein, "Consensus and Contestability: The ECtHR and the Combined Potential of European Consensus and Procedural Rationality Control," (2017) 28 *European Journal of International Law* 871 at 888.

470 Bellamy, "The Democratic Legitimacy of International Human Rights Conventions: Political Constitutionalism and the European Convention on Human Rights" at 1030.

471 Dzehtsiarou, *European Consensus and the Legitimacy of the European Court of Human Rights*, at 120 (emphasis added).

472 Wildhaber, Hjartarson, and Donnelly, "No Consensus on Consensus?" at 251; see also Ganshof Van der Meersch, "La référence au droit interne des Etats contractants dans la jurisprudence de la Cour européenne des droits de l'homme" at 319 ("droit commun"); Draghici, "The Strasbourg Court between European and Local Consensus: Anti-democratic or Guardian of Democratic Process?" at 13; Besson, "Human Rights and Democracy in a Global Context: Decoupling and Recoupling" at 31; see also Dzehtsiarou, *European Consensus and the Legitimacy of the European Court of Human Rights*, at 162. A similar way of justifying the bottom-up approach in formal legal terms emphasises the proximity of European consensus to regional customary law: see further Chapter 10, III.2.

2. The Democratic Credentials of European Consensus

On the ethos-focussed perspective, then, regional human rights can be conceptualised as a form of cooperation between the States parties. Yet this approach needs to be translated into more specific terms insofar as the ECtHR is concerned: since its decisions are legally binding, albeit only declaratory (as opposed to some form of direct effect leading to immediate invalidation of national laws),[473] they have a strong effect throughout Europe. Indeed, any standards set by the ECtHR could, in formal legal terms, be overruled only by amending the ECHR which, given the large number of States parties, is hardly a practical option. Because of the ECtHR's competence to deliver binding rulings, then, the ECHR is "largely withdrawn from the grasp of its individual makers", which "profoundly changes the relationship between law and politics".[474]

From an ethos-focussed perspective, this is a suboptimal state of affairs: even at the national level, most of its proponents would advocate at most for weak forms of judicial review, and this holds true all the more so for a transnational court. However, the fact of the matter is that the ECtHR, as a transnational human rights court with legally speaking relatively strong powers of review, *does exist*. Besides noting the possibility of institutional reform, proponents of the ethos-focussed perspective have grappled with this fact by proposing theories of adjudication for the ECtHR. Since the ECtHR itself cannot change its institutional context, the question then becomes how it should incorporate the concerns of the ethos-focussed perspective into its reasoning, so that the justification of its judgments may still proceed in a bottom-up fashion. This is where European consensus once again enters the scene.

---

473 Articles 41 and 46 (1) ECHR; see Zysset, *The ECHR and Human Rights Theory: Reconciling the Moral and Political Conceptions*, at 117; Bellamy, "The Democratic Legitimacy of International Human Rights Conventions: Political Constitutionalism and the European Convention on Human Rights" at 1037.

474 Von Bogdandy and Venzke, "In Whose Name? An Investigation of International Courts' Public Authority and Its Democratic Justification" at 21; see, in more detail, Gerards, "Judicial Deliberations in the European Court of Human Rights" at 414-415; Kleinlein, "Consensus and Contestability: The ECtHR and the Combined Potential of European Consensus and Procedural Rationality Control" at 884; see also Eric A. Posner and John C. Yoo, "Judicial Independence in International Tribunals," (2005) 93 *California Law Review* 1 at 56.

In building a positive argument in favour of European consensus, one might consider it self-evident in "State-centred international law"[475] that sovereignty concerns necessitate reference to the State parties' positions within their domestic legal systems. That is how some critics, perhaps somewhat uncharitably, understand the rationale of European consensus: as subordinating human rights to "the importance of State sovereignty".[476] Few proponents of consensus would unreservedly agree, however.[477] From a normative perspective, the unquestioned formal sovereignty of States has long lost its appeal; it is usually seen instead as a placeholder for more substantive values. Samantha Besson has been particularly clear on this point. She argues that States "are not the bearers of ultimate value" since they "exist for the sake of human individuals".[478] On that premise, it is clear that "the value of state autonomy can only be explained in terms of the autonomy of the individuals constituting it", or more precisely: as "the product of [a State's] subjects' autonomy as a political entity".[479] State sovereignty serves to protect political self-determination.[480]

---

475 Dzehtsiarou, *European Consensus and the Legitimacy of the European Court of Human Rights*, at 150.

476 Benvenisti, "Margin of Appreciation, Consensus, and Universal Standards" at 852; see also Hwang, "Grundrechtsschutz unter der Voraussetzung des europäischen Grundkonsenses?" at 319; Regan, "A Worthy Endeavour?" at 65.

477 See the measured response by Dzehtsiarou, *European Consensus and the Legitimacy of the European Court of Human Rights*, at 149-155; more sweepingly Legg, *The Margin of Appreciation*, at 113; and indeed in favour of relying on State sovereignty Michael R. Hutchinson, "The Margin of Appreciation Doctrine in the European Court of Human Rights," (1999) 48 *International and Comparative Law Quarterly* 638 at 648; Francisco Pascual-Vives, *Consensus-Based Interpretation of Regional Human Rights Treaties* (Leiden and Boston: Brill, 2019), at 95; see also Kapotas and Tzevelekos, "How (Difficult Is It) to Build Consensus on (European) Consensus?" at 13, highlighting state sovereignty not as a matter of principle but in connection with the legitimacy concerns discussed in Chapters 9 and 10.

478 Besson, "The Authority of International Law - Lifting the State Veil" at 361.

479 Ibid., 364; in agreement: Zysset, *The ECHR and Human Rights Theory: Reconciling the Moral and Political Conceptions*, at 100; see also von Bogdandy and Venzke, "In Whose Name? An Investigation of International Courts' Public Authority and Its Democratic Justification" at 41.

480 Besson, "Human Rights: Ethical, Political... or Legal? First Steps in a Legal Theory of Human Rights" at 243; this view is also clear throughout, though implicit, in Shai Dothan, "In Defence of Expansive Interpretation in the European Court of Human Rights," (2014) 3 *Cambridge Journal of International and Comparative Law* 508.

European consensus would be justified, then, because it *refers back to the forms of ethical-volitional self-realisation by means of democratic procedures which are not available at the transnational level.* Fittingly, Besson describes it as "European *democratic* consensus";[481] or, as Frances Hamilton has put it, consensus links the ECtHR's decisions "back to a democratic mandate of the legislatures of Member States".[482] Paul Mahoney has described it as indicative of the "common will of democratic [implied: European] society".[483] The ECtHR itself has taken up this idea: its standard phrase on the ECHR as a "living instrument", according to which it must be "interpreted in the light of present-day conditions",[484] is now sometimes extended. The Convention must be interpreted, according to the more recent formulation, "in the light of present-day conditions and of the ideas prevailing in *democratic* States today",[485] as expressed through vertically comparative law.

What critics see as the most important drawback of European consensus – its reliance on the positions taken by the States parties, and in particular by intra-State majorities – can thus be reconceptualised, by the ethos-focussed perspective, as its greatest strength. As Dzehtsiarou has put it: "The counter-majoritarian difficulty can be confronted by including European consensus" in the Court's reasoning, since the national laws referred to are "linked to democracy and majoritarian decision-making".[486] The democratic credentials of consensus, given its connection to intra-State majorities, are the reason for giving it normative force.

It should be noted that, as already encountered from the opposite perspective in the preceding chapter, the transition from the purely domestic

---

481 Besson, "Subsidiarity in International Human Rights Law - What is Subsidiary about Human Rights?" at 101 (emphasis added); see also Ryan, "Europe's Moral Margin: Parental Aspirations and the European Court of Human Rights" at 480.

482 Hamilton, "Same-Sex Marriage, Consensus, Certainty and the European Court of Human Rights" at 35; Hamilton connects this to the ECtHR's legitimacy, on which see further Chapter 9.

483 Mahoney, "Judicial Activism and Judicial Self-Restraint in the European Court of Human Rights: Two Sides of the Same Coin" at 75.

484 ECtHR, Appl. No. 5856/72 – *Tyrer v. the United Kingdom*, Judgment of 25 April 1978, at para. 31.

485 E.g. ECtHR (GC), Appl. No. 23459/03 – *Bayatyan*, at para. 102; ECtHR (GC), Appl. Nos. 60367/08 and 961/11 – *Khamtokhu and Aksenchik*, at para. 73 (emphasis added).

486 Dzehtsiarou, *European Consensus and the Legitimacy of the European Court of Human Rights*, at 172; see also Kapotas and Tzevelekos, "How (Difficult Is It) to Build Consensus on (European) Consensus?" at 13.

to the transnational vantage point involves a broadening of scope from discussions of the relationship between intra-State majorities and minorities to a more unified view of individual States. The morality-focussed perspective had to explain why it distrusts not only legislative majorities and majority-led governments, but also domestic courts – recall Benvenisti's argument that those courts, too, are liable to be staffed with members of the intra-State majority.[487] Conversely, for the ethos-focussed perspective the reasons for trust must, at least to some extent, be extended from intra-State majorities to national courts. This move is not self-evident: as we saw above, the ethos-focussed perspective sees little cause for embarrassment in the reliance on majority decisions and conceptualises strong judicial review based on rights as problematic by virtue of its counter-majoritarian nature. Some European States do provide for strong judicial review; and, on the ethos-focussed perspective's terms, the democratic credentials of such review, or even of a statute promulgated only in response to it, must be significantly less than those of a legislative decision that was not dictated by judicial involvement.

On the other hand, the potential previous involvement of domestic courts provides the ethos-focussed perspective with a certain claim to reconciliation: for all its emphasis on majoritarian procedures, it can also claim to have integrated the ECtHR's admonition that "democracy does not simply mean that the views of a majority must always prevail".[488] In light of this, the concerns voiced by the morality-focussed perspective – so the argument might go – will already have been considered at the national level.[489] For the ethos-focussed perspective, this would still seem preferable than the interference by the ECtHR on the basis of morality-focussed reasoning. For one thing, even a domestic court with powers of strong judicial review remains – at least in theory – subject to democratic control by a democratic majority or super-majority, and its decisions are thus in princi-

487 Chapter 2, II.2.

488 ECtHR (Plenary), Appl. Nos. 7601/76 and 7806/77 – *Young, James and Webster v. the United Kingdom*, Judgment of 13 August 1981, at para. 63; see recently e.g. ECtHR, Appl. No. 57792/15 – *Hamidović v. Bosnia and Herzegovina*, Judgment of 5 December 2017, at para. 41; see generally Chapter 1, IV.3.

489 See e.g. Dzehtsiarou, *European Consensus and the Legitimacy of the European Court of Human Rights*, at 118-119 (though primarily on non-judicial "systems for checking compatibility with human rights norms").

ple "revisable in the longer term".[490] For another, a domestic court is embedded in the ethical-political culture of its constituency and thereby closer to the democratic majority of that State than the ECtHR is.[491] Echoes of this view may be found in the ECtHR's own argument that national institutions – including the judiciary – may be "better placed" to identify what amounts to a national ethos, somewhat lyrically described by the Court as "the vital forces of their countries" with which national institutions are in "direct and continuous contact".[492] Ultimately, this is the same argument that Benvenisti made – except that, with the shift from the morality-focussed to the ethos-focussed perspective, the domestic context now has a positive connotation. Trust in intra-State majorities is thus expanded to trust in States.

If we connect this back to the institutional context of the ECtHR discussed above, then we may summarise as follows. For lack of transnational democracy, the ECtHR faces two challenges: as a court, it is counter-majoritarian; and as a transnational court, it largely evades the balance of powers otherwise prevalent in various forms at the national level. Insofar as European consensus takes up the majoritarian decisions which are usually reflected in the States parties' legal systems, it mitigates the counter-majoritarian difficulty which the morality-focussed perspective would face in full force. Insofar as the legal systems referred to themselves incorporate counter-majoritarian elements, for example due to the involvement of domestic courts, they still constitute the result of democratic procedures more broadly conceived, and European consensus thus mitigates the lack of democratic control available at the transnational level. The reference back to the States parties' laws as part of the justification of concrete norms of regional human rights law thus seems less paradoxical than it does from

490 Sandra Fredman, "From Dialogue to Deliberation: Human Rights Adjudication and Prisoners' Rights to Vote," (2013) *Public Law* 292 at 298; the details differ, of course, from State to State – though I am not aware of any constitutional practice in which high-profile court judgments are *actually* deliberately reversed on a semi-regular basis.

491 See Besson, "European Human Rights, Supranational Judicial Review and Democracy - Thinking Outside the Judicial Box" at 133. Chambers of the ECtHR include the judge elected in respect of the respondent State (Article 26 (4) ECHR), but this does not lead to a similarly strong level of embeddedness.

492 ECtHR (Plenary), Appl. No. 5493/72 – *Handyside v. the United Kingdom*, Judgment of 7 December 1976, at para. 48.

the morality-focussed perspective,[493] since bottom-up verticality[494] is reconceptualised with a positive connotation.

3. From National Ethe to a Pan-European Ethos

Based on my argument so far, European consensus could be conceived of as a way of giving national ethe prominence in the reasoning of the ECtHR, since it is within these national ethe that democratic procedures are more pronounced. However, the reliance on national ethe cannot, in and of itself, entirely justify the use of European consensus. Simply put, the very notion of a *European* consensus (or lack thereof) goes beyond normativity developed within individual national ethe *even as it builds on them*.[495] Or, to use the terminology introduced in Chapter 1: because European consensus is a vertical form of comparative reasoning, it incorporates reference to national ethe into the ECtHR's reasoning; but because it does so through the lens of commonality, it reinterprets those national ethe as more than the sum of their parts. In this subsection, I will argue that this involves a crucial shift in the macrosubject within which ethical normativity is constituted: while national ethe remain relevant, the primary location of ethical normativity as implied by European consensus *shifts to the pan-European level.*

The spur effect of European consensus makes this particularly clear, since it pits the two different kinds of ethical normativity directly against one another: European consensus in favour of the applicant (pan-European ethos) constitutes an argument *against* the respondent State (national ethos). If one foregrounds individual national ethe, then, the spur effect of European consensus seems rather suspect. John Murray has made this point with particular force. He cautions against a "hegemony of the majority" and questions whether its spur effect is "consistent with respect for diversity among the democratic and sovereign States which are Contracting Parties to the Convention".[496] If ethical normativity is located within individual States, it seems bizarre to not celebrate such diversity among demo-

493 See Dzehtsiarou, *European Consensus and the Legitimacy of the European Court of Human Rights*, at 119 (at footnote 23); see also, more generally, Wheatley, "The Legitimacy of International Human Rights Regimes" at 105.

494 See Chapter 1, III.

495 See also ECtHR (GC), Appl. Nos. 60367/08 and 961/11 – *Khamtokhu and Aksenchik*, dissenting opinion of Judge Pinto de Albuquerque, at para. 35.

496 Murray, "Consensus: Concordance, or Hegemony of the Majority?" at 26.

cratic outcomes, and hence bizarre to accept an argument that is specifically geared at reducing diversity (at the transnational level)[497] by reference only to what *other* States have decided *for themselves*: from the perspective of those States finding themselves in a minority position, there seems to be no good reason to impose the majority position on them.[498] Giving spur effect to European consensus seems like an unjustified transposition of foreign ethe – a form of normativity developed relative to an entirely different context[499] – and thus overriding the respondent State's "own mores, heritage and culture" which constitute its own ethos and are "deeply rooted in the social fabric of its society".[500]

The difference between a pan-European ethos and traditional approaches foregrounding national ethe is less stark in the context of the rein effect since European consensus, in this scenario, argues against finding a violation of the Convention, thus allowing various different national ethe to persist.[501] Nonetheless, it is striking that the force of the argument depends on the lack of consensus among the States parties or the existence of a consensus in favour of the respondent State – in other words, it depends, once again, on the collectivity of States as a whole and not on any one State viewed individually. For example, Wildhaber, Hjartarson and Donnelly de-

---

497 Brems, *Human Rights: Universality and Diversity*, at 420.

498 See Eva Brems, "The Margin of Appreciation Doctrine in the Case-Law of the European Court of Human Rights," (1996) 56 *Zeitschrift für ausländisches öffentliches Recht und Völkerrecht* 240 at 285, echoed by Francisco Javier Mena Parras, "Democracy, Diversity and the Margin of Appreciation: A Theoretical Analysis from the Perspective of the International and Constitutional Functions of the European Court of Human Rights," (2015) 29 *Revista Electrónica de Estudios Internacionales* 1 at 13; Nußberger, "Auf der Suche nach einem europäischen Konsens – zur Rechtsprechung des Europäischen Gerichtshofs für Menschenrechte" at 205; Gerards, "Giving Shape to the Notion of 'Shared Responsibility'" at 44; Carozza, "Uses and Misuses of Comparative Law" at 1228; Shelton, "The Boundaries of Human Rights Jurisdiction in Europe" at 134; von Ungern-Sternberg, "Die Konsensmethode des EGMR. Eine kritische Bewertung mit Blick auf das völkerrechtliche Konsens- und das innerstaatliche Demokratieprinzip" at 334; Daniel Matthias Klocke, "Die dynamische Auslegung der EMRK im Lichte der Dokumente des Europarats," (2015) *Europarecht* 148 at 154; Tzevelekos and Dzehtsiarou, "International Custom Making" at 326; Føllesdal, "A Better Signpost, Not a Better Walking Stick: How to Evaluate the European Consensus Doctrine" at 204.

499 Klocke, "Die dynamische Auslegung der EMRK im Lichte der Dokumente des Europarats" at 150.

500 Murray, "Consensus: Concordance, or Hegemony of the Majority?" at 46.

501 On how consensus and national ethe work together by means of the margin of appreciation, see in more detail Chapter 8, III.1.-2.

fend the use of European consensus by arguing that "genuinely democratic decisions should be treated with due respect" and that, accordingly, the ECtHR should accept "the diversity of responses to human rights issues".[502] The spur effect of European consensus obviously runs counter to such diversity – but in cases involving the rein effect, though the result may cohere with the sentiment expressed by Wildhaber, Hjartarson and Donnelly, the reasoning nonetheless seems slightly mismatched.[503] If democratic decisions should be treated with respect, why compare them to other democratic decisions in the first place? If, as the ECtHR has put it, "it is for each State to mould its own democratic vision",[504] then why make an argument in favour of the respondent State dependent on the democratic decisions of *other* States parties by means of European consensus?

When posed in this stark form, these questions seem almost ludicrous – at least to those with a precommitment to regional or international human rights.[505] It is worth noting, at this point, that consensus-based reasoning first emerged within the ECtHR's case-law, in *Tyrer v. the United Kingdom*, not so much as a counterpoint to the morality-focussed perspective but in explicit juxtaposition to "local circumstances" on the Isle of Man.[506] The ECtHR emphasised that the Isle of Man has, "[h]istorically, geographically and culturally" always been "included in the European family of nations",[507] thus shifting the relevant macrosubject for the establishment of ethical normativity from the local to the European level. It was in this context that it made reference to the laws of "the great majority of the member States of the Council of Europe".[508]

---

502 Wildhaber, Hjartarson, and Donnelly, "No Consensus on Consensus?" at 252; for a similar point in very ethos-steeped language with regard to the margin of appreciation, see Yuval Shany, "All Roads Lead to Strasbourg?: Application of the Margin of Appreciation Doctrine by the European Court of Human Rights and the UN Human Rights Committee," (2018) 9 *Journal of International Dispute Settlement* 180 at 188.

503 See further, on this mismatch between reasoning and result, Chapter 4, III.3.

504 ECtHR (GC), Appl. No. 48876/08 – *Animal Defenders International v. the United Kingdom*, Judgment of 22 April 2013, at para. 111.

505 Moyn has argued that "the central event in human rights history is the recasting of rights as entitlements that might contradict the sovereign nation-state from above and outside rather than serve as its foundation", i.e. precisely such an internationalist commitment: Moyn, *The Last Utopia*, at 13.

506 ECtHR, Appl. No. 5856/72 – *Tyrer*, at para. 37, in the context of then-Article 63 (3), now Article 56 (3) ECHR.

507 Ibid., at para. 38.

508 Ibid.

Such a shift is hardly surprising – for if the focus were indeed laid exclusively on national ethe, then regional human rights protection could play only a very limited role. The ECHR's role would then be limited to a narrow form of cooperation which might be deemed *cooperation as entrenchment* – in that vein, Samantha Besson speaks of international human rights which "rely on national guarantees to formulate a minimal threshold that they reflect and entrench".[509] Given the extremely limited role for regional (and international) human rights which would result from such an approach,[510] few (if any) commentators follow through on this line of argument.[511] Instead, it is generally acknowledged that requiring the consent of all States parties to any given interpretation would lead the judicial review by the ECtHR ad absurdum.[512] The ECtHR itself, too, has long proceeded on the understanding that giving primacy to individual national ethe would undermine its supervisory role – not only in the specific context which characterised its judgment in *Tyrer*, but also in its case-law more generally.[513] From this, there follows what Janneke Gerards has summarised as "an unavoidable tension between the national desire to protect

509 Besson, "Human Rights and Democracy in a Global Context: Decoupling and Recoupling" at 29.

510 At least insofar as challenges to the status quo are concerned; entrenchment clearly fulfils important (though dubious) roles with regard to the perpetuation of the status quo: See more generally Chapter 10, III.2. and IV.

511 Pascual-Vives, *Consensus-Based Interpretation of Regional Human Rights Treaties* comes closest; he treats cases not involving utter unanimity, "when the respondent State does not participate in the consensus" at issue, as "hard cases" in a "grey area" (at 99).

512 See Ost, "The Original Canons of Interpretation" at 305; Marisa Iglesias Vila, "Subsidiarity, Margin of Appreciation and International Adjudication within a Cooperative Conception of Human Rights," (2017) 15 *International Journal of Constitutional Law* 393 at 402; Fiona de Londras, "When the European Court of Human Rights Decides Not to Decide: The Cautionary Tale of *A, B & C* v. *Ireland* and Referendum-Emergent Constitutional Provisions," in *Building Consensus on European Consensus. Judicial Interpretation of Human Rights in Europe and Beyond*, ed. Panos Kapotas and Vassilis Tzevelekos (Cambridge: Cambridge University Press, 2019) at 317; see also Helfer, "Consensus, Coherence and the European Convention on Human Rights" at 142. As Amy Gutmann has put it in a different context, a "human rights regime […] cannot consistently defend […] the absolute sovereignty of a people": Amy Gutmann, "Introduction," in *Michael Ignatieff, Human Rights as Politics and Idolatry*, ed. Amy Gutmann (Princeton and Oxford: Princeton University Press, 2001) at xv.

513 Most clearly in its case-law on autonomous concepts: see Chapter 8, II.; occasional dissenting opinions implying otherwise (e.g. arguing that "[c]hanges which occur in some States can never affect the scope of the other States' en-

fundamental rights in a way the state thinks fit", on the one hand, and "the ECtHR's task to supervise the compliance of national fundamental rights protection with the Convention", on the other.[514]

The use of European consensus, and the notion of a pan-European ethos which undergirds it, can be understood as an attempt to simultaneously retain a meaningful role for regional human rights law *as well as* an ethical-volitional rather than a moral-cognitive form of reasoning. This kind of shift is perhaps best illustrated by Gerald Neuman's argument in favour of increased consensus-based reasoning in the Inter-American system of human rights protection. Seeking to refute the charge of "State voluntarism", he claims that

> To be sure, letting each state be the judge of its own human rights obligations, free to redefine or retract prior commitments, would negate the effect of the American Convention. But that observation does not entail that the substantive evolution of the regional human rights regime must be independent of the regional community of states.[515]

On this line of argument, reference to European consensus would be justified because it constitutes a kind of ethical normativity that can be operationalised in the specifically transnational context in which the ECtHR is situated, and in which ethical normativity based on individual national ethe cannot take centre stage in a transnational setting since it conflicts too directly with the very idea of judicial review by a regional court.

The shift exemplified so clearly in Neuman's argument can also be observed in a similar argumentative move performed by Kanstantsin Dzehtsiarou, who suggests that consensus "can be conceptualised as an up-

---

gagements": ECtHR, Appl. Nos. 26431/12, 26742/12, 44057/12 and 60088/12 – *Orlandi and Others v. Italy*, Judgment of 14 December 2017, dissenting opinion of Judges Pejchal and Wojtyczek, at para. 2) are in clear contradiction of the ECtHR's case-law (and, it may be noted in passing, quite transparently driven by retrogressive agendas).

514 Gerards, "Judicial Deliberations in the European Court of Human Rights" at 20.

515 Neuman, "Import, Export, and Regional Consent in the Inter-American Court of Human Rights" at 115; see also Draghici, "The Strasbourg Court between European and Local Consensus: Anti-democratic or Guardian of Democratic Process?" at 25; de Londras, "When the European Court of Human Rights Decides Not to Decide: The Cautionary Tale of *A, B & C* v. *Ireland* and Referendum-Emergent Constitutional Provisions" at 329-330.

dated consent of the Contracting Parties".[516] Having noted the problem of overriding the consent of those States that find themselves in a minority, Dzehtsiarou is forced to clarify what he means by State consent: it is not, in fact, the consent of individual States as traditional international law would have demanded it, but rather "a collective acceptance of a particular rule or a particular approach – a common European attitude or commonly accepted rules that build up European public order".[517] The register remains that of the ethos-focussed perspective, with its emphasis of collectivity; the focus has shifted, however, from the "collective acceptance" of a rule at the national level (individual State consent in the formal sense) to its collective acceptance *at the European level*.

Antje von Ungern-Sternberg has similarly defended the spur effect of European consensus by arguing that the ECHR should be conceptualised as expressing "European standards for the protection of fundamental rights, based on a European community sharing common values".[518] The "European community sharing common values" mirrors Dzehtsiarou's "common European attitude" or "European public order". The ECtHR itself has used similar language in specifying, for example, that it will "look for any consensus and common values emerging from the practices of European States"[519] or for a "generally shared approach"[520] among them; and several judges have spoken of consensus as "an expression of the common ground required for the collective approach underlying the Conven-

516 Dzehtsiarou, *European Consensus and the Legitimacy of the European Court of Human Rights*, at 149.

517 Ibid., 154; "common attitude" is also used by Mahoney, "Judicial Activism and Judicial Self-Restraint in the European Court of Human Rights: Two Sides of the Same Coin" at 74; see also Sionaidh Douglas-Scott, "A Tale of Two Courts: Luxembourg, Strasbourg and the Growing European Human Rights Acquis," (2006) 43 *Common Market Law Review* 629 at 653 ("common norms of European human rights law").

518 Von Ungern-Sternberg, "Die Konsensmethode des EGMR. Eine kritische Bewertung mit Blick auf das völkerrechtliche Konsens- und das innerstaatliche Demokratieprinzip" at 330 (my translation); see also Ostrovsky, "What's So Funny About Peace, Love, and Understanding?" at 50; Douglas Lee Donoho, "Autonomy, Self-Governance, and the Margin of Appreciation: Developing a Jurisprudence of Diversity Within Universal Human Rights," (2001) 15 *Emory International Law Review* 391 at 455.

519 ECtHR, Appl. No. 33401/02 – *Opuz v. Turkey*, Judgment of 9 June 2009, at para. 164.

520 ECtHR (GC), Appl. No. 21830/93 – *X, Y and Z v. the United Kingdom*, Judgment of 22 April 1997, at para. 44.

tion system".[521] All of these notions are typical of the ethos-focussed perspective in that they are geared towards a form of normativity that is relative to a certain group; they are atypical, however, in that their focus shifts from the individual State to the States parties as a whole, understood as constituting their own ethical collectivity. Rousseau's "morality of a nation"[522] becomes the morality of a continent[523] or "regional standards of justice".[524] What ethos-focussed supporters of European consensus rely on is the notion of *a pan-European ethos*.

In sum, while European consensus may be justified on the basis of the ethos-focussed perspective, it takes the States parties of the ECHR as a collectivity to constitute the relevant macrosubject. It can thus be understood as an attempt to operationalise the merits of the ethos-focussed perspective – attention to disagreement and, though only indirectly, reliance on democratic procedures – in the context of a regional court that is not itself directly embedded within democratic procedures. As Judge Paulo Pinto de Albuquerque recently summarised it, from the ECtHR's use of European consensus there "emanates a vision of an [sic] deliberative, international democracy in which a majority or representative proportion of the Contracting Parties to the Convention is considered to speak in the name of all".[525] The notion of a pan-European ethos transfers the majoritarian approach known from the national level to the transnational level: this also implies that the majority of States parties on the basis of which the pan-European ethos is identified is, in cases involving the spur effect, "entitled

---

521 Anatoly Kovler et al., "The Role of Consensus in the System of the European Court of Human Rights" (Dialogue between judges, European Court of Human Rights, 2008), at 19; see also Wildhaber, Hjartarson, and Donnelly, "No Consensus on Consensus?" at 257 ("general agreement").

522 Rousseau, *The Social Contract*, at 161.

523 Indeed, the French version of ECtHR (GC), Appl. No. 34503/97 – *Demir and Baykara*, at para. 84 speaks, with clear echoes of Rousseau, of the "volonté générale des Etats contractants" (less clear in the English version, which speaks only of the "general wish of Contracting States); ECtHR (GC), Appl. No. 7334/13 – *Muršić v. Croatia*, Judgment of 20 October 2016, partly dissenting opinion of Judge Pinto de Albuquerque, at para. 20, points out the symbolism involved in "this historically and philosophically much charged expression".

524 ECtHR (Plenary), Appl. No. 14038/88 – *Soering v. the United Kingdom*, Judgment of 7 July 1989, at para. 102, citing the amicus curiae brief by Amnesty International.

525 Pinto de Albuquerque, "Plaidoyer for the European Court of Human Rights" at 124; see also his various dissenting opinions, e.g. as cited in the previous footnotes and ECtHR (GC), Appl. Nos. 60367/08 and 961/11 – *Khamtokhu and Aksenchik*, dissenting opinion of Judge Pinto de Albuquerque, at para. 35.

to impose its will on other parties".[526] The next subsection will consider the implications of this aspect of European consensus in more detail.

4. Implications of Harmonisation: Human Rights and European Integration

I have argued that European consensus can be understood as an expression of a pan-European consensus. When approached in this way – rather than merely the combination of various national ethe – the understanding of the ECHR as a form of "cooperation" among the States parties undergoes a subtle transformation. As the citations from the Court and the descriptions by Dzehtsiarou and von Ungern-Sternberg canvassed above demonstrate, reference is still made to commonality ("common values", "common European attitude", "collective acceptance"); but with a focus on Europe as a whole rather than individual States as the relevant collectivity, commonality takes on a more flexible meaning that allows for majoritarian approaches rather than demanding the consent of every individual State.[527] Co-operation is thus understood not merely as *reaffirming* the lowest common denominator but as *developing* a common position based on pre-existing similarities.[528] Elsewhere, this has been described as combining "descriptive" and "prescriptive"[529] or "retrospective" and "prospective"[530] elements: a certain measure of commonality was already present, but it is expanded

---

526 Pinto de Albuquerque, "Plaidoyer for the European Court of Human Rights" at 124.

527 See von Ungern-Sternberg, "Die Konsensmethode des EGMR. Eine kritische Bewertung mit Blick auf das völkerrechtliche Konsens- und das innerstaatliche Demokratieprinzip" at 334.

528 See Dzehtsiarou's position which I have repeatedly cited (e.g. supra, note 471), according to which the ECHR's object and purpose is to *intensify* (!) cooperation; Martens, "Perplexity of the National Judge Faced with the Vagaries of European Consensus" at 54 ("*building* a democratic European society", emphasis added); see also Iglesias Vila, "Subsidiarity, Margin of Appreciation and International Adjudication within a Cooperative Conception of Human Rights" at 405 (connecting cooperation and incrementalism).

529 Gráinne de Búrca, "The Language of Rights and European Integration," in *New Legal Dynamics of European Union*, ed. Josephine Shaw and Gillian More (Oxford: Clarendon Press, 1995) at 43; see also Günter Frankenberg, "Tocqueville's Question. The Role of a Constitution in the Process of Integration," (2000) 13 *Ratio Juris* 1 at 6.

530 Andreas von Arnauld, "Rechtsangleichung durch allgemeine Rechtsgrundsätze? - Europäisches Gemeinschaftsrecht und Völkerrecht im Vergleich," in

and deepened by means of the cooperative venture at issue. Cooperation as entrenchment becomes cooperation as *harmonisation*.[531]

In this subsection, I would like to further dwell on the implications of approaching the spur effect of European consensus as the expression of a pan-European ethos, since the concept of harmonisation which I just invoked requires some clarification. In a broad sense, most cases in which the ECtHR finds a violation of the Convention will constitute a demand for harmonisation: while its judgments technically bind only the parties to the case according to Article 46 (1) ECHR, it is clear that they also have a broader effect. According to the Court itself, its judgments serve "more generally, to elucidate, safeguard and develop the rules instituted by the Convention", thereby "extending human rights jurisprudence throughout the community of the Convention States".[532] Or, as Judge Zupančič has very palpably put it in one of his concurring opinions: a judgment by the Court concerns the interpretation of human rights in the respondent State "and also, after [the] case, elsewhere in Europe".[533]

While it is controversial how it should be conceptualised in detail,[534] it is thus clear that the Court's judgments have an erga omnes effect of *some* sort.[535] With the possible exception of certain cases decided on the basis of

Rechtsangleichung: Grundlagen, Methoden und Inhalte, ed. Karl Riesenhuber and Kanako Takayama (Berlin: de Gruyter, 2006) at 247.

531 Mena Parras, "Democracy, Diversity and the Margin of Appreciation" at 8; Steven Greer, *The Margin of Appreciation: Interpretation and Discretion under the European Convention on Human Rights* (Strasbourg: Council of Europe Publishing, 2000), at 21; contra: Dominic McGoldrick, "A Defence of the Margin of Appreciation and an Argument for its Application by the Human Rights Committee," (2016) 65 *International and Comparative Law Quarterly* 21 at 30.

532 ECtHR, Appl. No. 25965/04 – *Rantsev v. Cyprus and Russia*, Judgment of 7 January 2010, at para. 197; see also e.g. ECtHR (Plenary), Appl. No. 5310/71 – *Ireland v. the United Kingdom*, Judgment of 18 January 1978, at para. 154; ECtHR, Appl. No. 40016/98 – *Karner v. Austria*, Judgment of 24 July 2003, at para. 26; ECtHR (GC), Appl. No. 30078/06 – *Konstantin Markin v. Russia*, Judgment of 22 March 2012, at para. 89.

533 ECtHR (GC), Appl. No. 64569/09 – *Delfi AS v. Estonia*, Judgment of 16 June 2015, concurring opinion of Judge Zupančič.

534 E.g. Samantha Besson, "The 'Erga Omnes' Effect of the European Court of Human Rights," in *The European Court of Human Rights after Protocol 14: Preliminary Assessment and Perspectives*, ed. Samantha Besson (Geneva: Schulthess, 2011).

535 Gerards, *General Principles of the European Convention on Human Rights*, at 44; Theilen, "Levels of Generality in the Comparative Reasoning of the European

very narrow grounds specific to the respondent State,[536] then, any finding of a violation by the Court will have a harmonising effect. This is independent of the broader theoretical framework within which the ECHR is placed. For example, it would hold true when the justification offered for the judgment is based on the morality-focussed perspective. The reasoning would then focus on prepolitical normative standards without paying heed to the legal situation within the States parties: finding a violation of the Convention on those grounds would still have a harmonising effect due to the erga omnes effect of the Court's judgments, but it would be *incidental* to the postulation of a certain human rights standard.

By contrast, giving normative force to the spur effect of European consensus implies a conceptualisation of the ECHR in which harmonisation is tied up with its very object and purpose.[537] This notion of non-incidental harmonisation has been emphasised, in particular, by various dissenting

Court of Human Rights and the European Court of Justice: Towards Judicial Reflective Equilibrium" at 393; Eva Brems, "Human Rights: Minimum and Maximum Perspectives," (2009) 9 *Human Rights Law Review* 349 at 351; Legg, *The Margin of Appreciation*, at 223; Dzehtsiarou, *European Consensus and the Legitimacy of the European Court of Human Rights*, at 102-103; Ingrid Leijten, *Core Socio-Economic Rights and the European Court of Human Rights* (Cambridge: Cambridge University Press, 2018), at 37; more cautiously e.g. Laurence R. Helfer, "Redesigning the European Court of Human Rights: Embeddedness as a Deep Structural Principle of the European Human Rights Regime," (2008) 19 *European Journal of International Law* 125 at 136, citing the "orthodox view" on inter partes effects, but also acknowledging that the "practical effects" of the Court's judgments are "often more extensive"; in more detail on the latter aspect from an empirical perspective Laurence R. Helfer and Erik Voeten, "International Courts as Agents of Legal Change: Evidence from LGBT Rights in Europe," (2014) 68 *International Organization* 1.

536 For example, on a popular (though doubtful) reading: ECtHR, Appl. Nos. 18766/11 and 36030/11 – *Oliari and Others*; see also the cases focussing on democratic procedures in the respondent State discussed in Chapter 8, III.3.

537 For connections between European consensus and harmonisation, see Arai-Takahashi, "The Margin of Appreciation Doctrine: A Theoretical Analysis of Strasbourg's Variable Geometry" at 89; Mena Parras, "Democracy, Diversity and the Margin of Appreciation" at 12; see also Gless and Martin, "The Comparative Method in European Courts" at 40 (on comparative reasoning being applied "in order to unify"); Christos L. Rozakis, "The Accession of the EU to the ECHR and the Charter of Fundamental Rights: Enlarging the Field of Protection of Human Rights in Europe," in *The EU Accession to the ECHR*, ed. Vasiliki Kosta, Nikos Skoutaris, and Vassilis P. Tzevelekos (Oxford and Portland: Hart, 2014) at 330 (consensus as a means of achieving "homogeneity"); for further references to harmonisation, though it is not entirely clear whether they are referring to the strong sense discussed here or the broader sense mentioned above, see Pär

opinions in cases where the majority within the Court avoided giving spur effect to European consensus. For example, in *S.H. v. Austria*, several dissenting judges argue that European consensus should have been accorded greater weight "considering that one of the Court's tasks is precisely to contribute to harmonising across Europe the rights guaranteed by the Convention".[538] More lyrically, dissenting judges in the case of *A, B and C v. Ireland* describe the spur effect of consensus as "commensurate" with "one of the paramount functions" of the Court, which is to "gradually create a harmonious application of human rights protection, cutting across the national boundaries of the Contracting States and allowing the individuals within their jurisdiction to enjoy, without discrimination, equal protection regardless of their place of residence":[539] cooperation as non-incidental harmonisation.

Thinking of the ECHR in these terms has invited comparisons with the other prominent institution concerned with a European conception of human rights: the EU. In fact, the debates surrounding European consensus, on the one hand, and the development of general principles by the European Court of Justice (ECJ) based on "constitutional traditions common to the Member States",[540] on the other, are in some respects strikingly similar;[541] in particular, the shift from a focus on national ethe to the reliance on a European ethos can be traced in much the same way, albeit with dif-

---

Hallström, "Balance or Clash of Legal Orders - Some Notes on Margin of Appreciation," in *Human Rights in Contemporary European Law*, ed. Joakim Nergelius and Eleonor Kristoffersson (Oxford: Hart, 2015) at 73; Vassilis Tzevelekos even says of the ECHR that "the idea of European integration is its *raison d'être*": Vassilis Tzevelekos, "The Use of Article 31(3)(C) of the VCLT in the Case Law of the ECtHR: An Effective Anti-Fragmentation Tool or a Selective Loophole for the Reinforcement of Human Rights Teleology?," (2010) 31 *Michigan Journal of International Law* 621 at 644 (emphasis in original).

538 ECtHR (GC), Appl. No. 57813/00 – *S.H. and Others*, joint dissenting opinion of Judges Tulkens, Hirvelä, Lazarova Trajkovska and Tsotsoria, at para. 10.

539 ECtHR (GC), Appl. No. 25579/05 – *A, B and C v. Ireland*, Judgment of 16 December 2010, joint partly dissenting opinion of Judges Rozakis, Tulkens, Fura, Hirvelä, Malinverni and Poalelungi, at para. 5.

540 ECJ, Case 11/70 – *Internationale Handelsgesellschaft mbH v Einfuhr- und Vorratsstelle für Getreide und Futtermittel*, Judgment of 17 December 1970, ECLI:EU:C:1970:114, at para. 4.

541 Generally on the similarities and differences between the use of comparative reasoning by the ECtHR and the ECJ, see Theilen, "Levels of Generality in the Comparative Reasoning of the European Court of Human Rights and the European Court of Justice: Towards Judicial Reflective Equilibrium"; Senden, *Interpretation of Fundamental Rights*, at 66-69; one crucial difference is the level of

ferent emphases in light of the differing institutional contexts. As with the ECtHR, proposals to restrict vertically comparative law to the "lowest common denominator" never had a significant impact on the ECJ's case-law;[542] and nowadays it is generally acknowledged that the ECJ conducts an "evaluative" or "critical" comparative survey which does not at all depend on unanimity among the Member States.[543]

While this can also be attributed in part to reliance on arguments more typical of the morality-focussed perspective and thus constituting harmonisation only in the broad sense discussed above, it also involves a shift towards reliance on a specifically European ethos. In fact, the ECJ's typically more vague and obscure references to common constitutional traditions among the Member States, without further disclosure of the comparative background,[544] lend themselves to emphasising a unitary European collectivity rather than discussing in detail the similarities or differences among the Member States.[545] The Charter of Fundamental Rights likewise refers to the collective "peoples of Europe" who, "in creating an ever closer union among them, are resolved to share a peaceful future based on common values".[546] The reference to both pre-existing "common values" but also to an "ever closer union" yet to be accomplished epitomises the harmonising approach by way of both descriptive and prescriptive or both ret-

---

generality at which comparative reasoning is usually used, a point to which I will return in Chapter 7.

542 Franz C. Mayer, "Constitutional Comparativism in Action. The Example of General Principles of EU Law and How They Are Made - A German Perspective," (2013) 11 *International Journal of Constitutional Law* 1003 at 1007.

543 E.g. ECJ, Case C-101/08 – *Audiolux SA e.a v Groupe Bruxelles Lambert SA (GBL) and Others*, Opinion of AG Trstenjak, 30 June 2009, ECLI:EU:C:2009:410, at para. 69 (explicitly contrasting this approach with that of using "the lowest common denominator method") and para. 73; ECJ, Case C-550/07 P – *Akzo Nobel Chemicals Ltd and Akcros Chemicals Ltd v European Commission*, Opinion of AG Kokott, 29 April 2010, ECLI:EU:C:2010:229, at para. 94; for an early rebuttal of the "lowest common denominator" approach in the context of then-Article 215 EEC, see ECJ, 5/71 – *Aktien-Zuckerfabrik v Council*, Opinion of AG Roemer, 13 July 1971, ECLI:EU:C:1971:96, at p. 989.

544 Koen Lenaerts, "Interlocking Legal Orders in the European Union and Comparative Law," (2003) 52 *International and Comparative Law Quarterly* 873 at 874; C.N. Kakouris, "Use of the Comparative Method by the Court of Justice of the European Communities," (1994) 6 *Pace International Law Review* 267 at 275-276.

545 Theilen, "Levels of Generality in the Comparative Reasoning of the European Court of Human Rights and the European Court of Justice: Towards Judicial Reflective Equilibrium" at 413.

546 Charter of Fundamental Rights of the European Union, Preamble.

rospective and prospective elements as described above.[547] The form of non-incidental harmonisation which reliance on a European ethos implies can thus be framed as a project of integration which both the ECJ and the ECtHR are involved in. As Sionaidh Douglas-Scott has influentially put it, "these two transnational courts are engaged in a common project of European integration, albeit one which is conducted by different means".[548]

The juxtaposition with the EU has, however, also been the basis for criticism of the harmonising aim which the spur effect of consensus implies. Murray has argued, for example, that while harmonisation is "required by the defined nature and express objectives of the EU itself, i.e. to lay the foundations of an ever closer political union", the "Convention system is evidently of a different nature".[549] The ECJ, in other words is situated in an institutional context within which non-incidental harmonisation may have its place:[550] can the same by said of the ECtHR?

Supporters of the spur effect have attempted to counter such criticism in various ways.[551] For example, Antje von Ungern-Sternberg has clarified that "one can only speak of a community sharing common values when *an*

---

547 See supra, notes 529-530.

548 Douglas-Scott, "A Tale of Two Courts" at 653; Tobias Lock, "The Influence of EU Law on Strasbourg Doctrines," (2016) 41 *European Law Review* 804 at 814; on the ECHR as part of European integration, see also Rozakis, "The European Judge as Comparatist" at 272; Ignacio de la Rasilla del Moral, "The Increasingly Marginal Appreciation of the Margin-of-Appreciation Doctrine," (2006) 7 *German Law Journal* 611 at 622; Mikael Rask Madsen, "The Protracted Institutionalization of the Strasbourg Court: From Legal Diplomacy to Integrationist Jurisprudence," in *The European Court of Human Rights between Law and Politics*, ed. Jonas Christoffersen and Mikael Rask Madsen (Oxford: Oxford University Press, 2011) at 58-59.

549 Murray, "Consensus: Concordance, or Hegemony of the Majority?" at 43; see also Lucas Lixinski, "The Inter-American Court of Human Rights' Tentative Search for Latin American Consensus," in *Building Consensus on European Consensus. Judicial Interpretation of Human Rights in Europe and Beyond*, ed. Panos Kapotas and Vassilis Tzevelekos (Cambridge: Cambridge University Press, 2019) at 339.

550 See generally on the differing institutional contexts Laurence R. Helfer and Anne-Marie Slaughter, "Toward a Theory of Effective Supranational Adjudication," (1997) 107 *Yale Law Journal* 273 at 297; Gerards, "Pluralism, Deference and the Margin of Appreciation Doctrine" at 102-104.

551 E.g. Dzehtsiarou, *European Consensus and the Legitimacy of the European Court of Human Rights*, at 153, arguing that the ECtHR "does not hold that there is a violation of European consensus, but that there is a violation of the Convention"; this is trivially true, but does not redress the deeper issue since consensus forms part of the justification for whether or not such a violation is found.

overwhelming majority of States truly forms part of it, that is when only few States exhibit contradictory values and rules".[552] Such concessions speak to the continued relevance of national ethe even if they are not foregrounded entirely, an issue I will return to in Chapter 5. For now, it suffices to note that while this move may mitigate the criticism based on national ethe somewhat, it cannot undermine it entirely: even if the respondent State is the "lone dissenter"[553] and all other European States are in agreement, the conceptual framework implied by the spur effect of consensus remains that of non-incidental harmonisation by reference to a pan-European ethos. This is, I would suggest, the consequence of applying the ethos-focussed perspective in the transnational context, with the internationalist commitments implied by the very existence of a *regional* system of human rights protection.[554]

V. Interim Reflections: Vestiges of Homogeneity

European consensus can be understood – or so I have been arguing – as an expression of a pan-European ethos, i.e. an application of the ethos-focussed perspective at the transnational level. By contrast to the morality-focussed perspective, it gives more argumentative relevance to factual disagreement, and consequently relies on majoritarian procedures as the fairest way of dealing with such disagreement. This applies, first, with regard to the relation between majorities and minorities at the national level: contrary to morality-focussed concerns that the reference to European consensus perpetuates a tyranny of the majority at the national level, democratic procedures are favoured over prepolitical minority rights given the disagreement surrounding the latter. Because European consensus builds on the positions taken by the legal systems of the States parties but also goes beyond them in applying the lens of commonality, the majoritarian approach also holds true at the transnational level: diversity among States is protected in some cases (rein effect) but specifically reduced in others by

552 Von Ungern-Sternberg, "Die Konsensmethode des EGMR. Eine kritische Bewertung mit Blick auf das völkerrechtliche Konsens- und das innerstaatliche Demokratieprinzip" at 336 (my translation, emphasis added).

553 Carozza, "Uses and Misuses of Comparative Law" at 1228.

554 See also, in that vein, Iglesias Vila, "Subsidiarity, Margin of Appreciation and International Adjudication within a Cooperative Conception of Human Rights" at 405 (referring to the commitment which States made upon becoming members of the CoE as a justification for the spur effect).

means of non-incidental harmonisation (spur effect). In contrast to the universalising angle of the morality-focussed perspective, the notion of a pan-European ethos understands the ECHR as seeking "to protect certain values within a very specific geographic, cultural, social, political, and economic *milieu*, namely the European continent".[555]

An argument can be made that European consensus operationalises the merits of the ethos-focussed perspective imperfectly, but as well as possible in the context of a regional human rights court: given the lack of democratic procedures at the transnational level, indirect reference to the States parties' legal systems is the next best thing, as it were. Yet some doubts remain. While modern iterations of the ethos-focussed perspective typically present themselves as basing ethical normativity on democratic procedures rather than, say, pre-existent traditions or national homogeneity,[556] their orientation towards any given macrosubject as the locus of normativity does carry a certain tendency towards homogeneity. Because European consensus remains focussed on the dominant position within the States parties, as expressed by their legal systems, it is difficult to adequately represent diversity *within* individual States, i.e. at the national level. As Seyla Benhabib has argued, the reference to States as "the relevant units" in this way "reduces peoples and their histories to a *holistic counterfactual*, which then results in the flattening out of the complex history of discourses and contestations within and among peoples".[557] The charge, in other words, is that the very *reference to States as a holistic entity ignores those not part of the intra-State majority and thereby reintroduces homogeneity* through the back door.

---

555 Tzevelekos, "The Use of Article 31(3)(C) of the VCLT in the Case Law of the ECtHR: An Effective Anti-Fragmentation Tool or a Selective Loophole for the Reinforcement of Human Rights Teleology?" at 627 (emphasis in original); see also Kapotas and Tzevelekos, "How (Difficult Is It) to Build Consensus on (European) Consensus?" at 5.

556 Supra, III.

557 Benhabib, "Is There a Human Right to Democracy? Beyond Interventionism and Indifference" at 84 (emphasis added); see also Martha C. Nussbaum, *Frontiers of Justice. Disability, Nationality, Species Membership* (Cambridge, Mass.: Belknap Press of Harvard University Press, 2006), at 245 and 253. These comments are in response to Rawls's approach in Rawls, *The Law of Peoples*; for similar criticism in the context of European consensus, see e.g. Hwang, "Grundrechtsschutz unter der Voraussetzung des europäischen Grundkonsenses?" at 315-316; Lewis, "What not to Wear: Religious Rights, the European Court, and the Margin of Appreciation" at 405.

Interestingly, this issue also arises – even more clearly, in fact – in the relations *between* States, i.e. at the transnational level. In that context, proponents of European consensus *explicitly rely on the supposed homogeneity* of European States to ground the notion of a pan-European ethos: Dzehtsiarou, for example, describes consensus as having "at its heart a strong emphasis on commonality between states"[558] and cites the fact that European States "are much more homogeneous in terms of human rights protection than States worldwide" as a justification for its use.[559] While often only mentioned in passing, others have made similar arguments, stressing the "homogeneous regional setting"[560] or the "homogeneity of the common background of the member states" as "an important element distinguishing regional human rights protection systems" from their counterparts "at the world level".[561]

558 Dzehtsiarou, "European Consensus and the Evolutive Interpretation of the European Convention on Human Rights" at 1745.

559 Dzehtsiarou, *European Consensus and the Legitimacy of the European Court of Human Rights*, at 129.

560 Lize R. Glas, "The European Court of Human Rights' Use of Non-Binding and Standard-Setting Council of Europe Documents," (2017) 17 *Human Rights Law Review* 97 at 99, citing Jörg Polakiewicz, "Alternatives to Treaty-Making and Law-Making by Treaty and Expert Bodies in the Council of Europe," in *Developments of International Law in Treaty Making*, ed. Rüdiger Wolfrum and Volker Röben (Heidelberg et al.: Springer, 2005) at 287.

561 Brems, "The Margin of Appreciation Doctrine in the Case-Law of the European Court of Human Rights" at 301; see also Shany, "All Roads Lead to Strasbourg?: Application of the Margin of Appreciation Doctrine by the European Court of Human Rights and the UN Human Rights Committee" at 189; Nico Krisch, *Beyond Constitutionalism: The Pluralist Structure of Postnational Law* (Oxford: Oxford University Press, 2010), at 144; Donoho, "Autonomy, Self-Governance, and the Margin of Appreciation: Developing a Jurisprudence of Diversity Within Universal Human Rights" at 462-463; Mahoney, "Judicial Activism and Judicial Self-Restraint in the European Court of Human Rights: Two Sides of the Same Coin" at 74; Bates, "Consensus in the Legitimacy-Building Era of the European Court of Human Rights" at 60 with further references; Posner and Yoo, "Judicial Independence in International Tribunals" at 55 go so far as to claim that Europe forms a "political community" whereas "the rest of the world does not"; also on homogeneity, though acknowledging "real" differences, Paolo G. Carozza, "Subsidiarity as a Structural Principle of International Human Rights Law," (2003) 97 *American Journal of International Law* 38 at 75; Dothan, "Judicial Deference Allows European Consensus to Emerge" at 404; Tzevelekos, "The Use of Article 31(3)(C) of the VCLT in the Case Law of the ECtHR: An Effective Anti-Fragmentation Tool or a Selective Loophole for the Reinforcement of Human Rights Teleology?" at 644; see also de la Rasilla del Moral, "The Increasingly Marginal Appreciation of the Margin-of-Appreciation Doctrine" at 623; for the

Statements such as these can claim to build on the Preamble to the ECHR itself, which describes the States parties as "like-minded" and possessing "a common heritage of political traditions, ideals, freedom and the rule of law".[562] The point is not so much to directly challenge this claim by means of a counter-claim geared at postulating general characteristics of sameness or difference, but rather to question the reasons for which the claim is raised at all, specifically in the context of European consensus. Generally speaking, can one meaningfully "divide human reality" into the ostensible homogeneous European States and "others" based on "generalities"?[563] Specifically with regard to European consensus, why does the supposed (relative) homogeneity within Europe supply a reason for further harmonisation – for imposing a certain human rights standard on those States which, by virtue of the fact that the spur effect of consensus is working against them, evidently do *not* form part of a homogeneous position on a certain issue?[564] For all the conceptual differences that might be highlighted between the national and the transnational level, is this not precisely the kind of hegemony that Habermas and Mouffe caution against when they remind us that behind ostensible homogeneity there lurk hegemony and exclusion[565] – now occurring as the "hegemony of the majority" that John Murray criticised in the context of the spur effect of European consensus?[566] Is it not, also, precisely the kind of false unity which critical comparatists have cautioned against?[567]

I would argue that, even if one accepts an ethos-focussed justification of European consensus in principle, the hegemonic potential of these homogenising tendencies needs to be taken seriously. This implies neither European consensus nor the notion of a pan-European ethos which under-

---

opposite perspective emphasising diversity among the States parties, see e.g. Wojciech Sadurski, *Constitutionalism and the Enlargement of Europe* (Oxford: Oxford University Press, 2012), at 2-3 (but see also at 11); Regan, "A Worthy Endeavour?" at 58; more generally Richard H. Pildes, "Supranational Courts and The Law of Democracy: The European Court of Human Rights," (2018) 9 *Journal of International Dispute Settlement* 154 at 160.

562 Preamble to the ECHR, fifth recital.

563 See generally Said, *Orientalism*, at 45.

564 See critically Carozza, "Uses and Misuses of Comparative Law" at 1229; and, though more cautiously, Petkova, "The Notion of Consensus as a Route to Democratic Adjudication" at 693.

565 Supra, notes 431-433.

566 Supra, note 496.

567 E.g. Frankenberg, "Critical Comparisons: Re-thinking Comparative Law" at 453.

girds it should be accepted at face value, but rather placed in a broader context which also recognises their downsides. This, in turn, leads to a more nuanced take on the various kinds of normativity we have been considering so far: in the next chapter, I will suggest that they must be read alongside one another rather than merely opposed to one another.

Chapter 4: Interaction between Morality-focussed and Ethos-focussed Perspectives: Triangular Tensions and Instrumental Allegiances

I. Introduction

Should European consensus be used by the ECtHR? Should agreement or disagreement among the States parties to the Convention play a role in the justification of its decisions, or should they be based on a moral reading of the Convention? Should judgments based on European consensus be allowed to prevail over positions reached within the more developed democratic procedures at the national level? The preceding chapters will have made clear that the answers to these questions depend on the perspective from which one approaches them. The morality-focussed perspective, for example, would focus on substantive normative reasoning and disparage the reliance on European consensus as perpetuating prejudice against intra-State minorities; the ethos-focussed perspective, by contrast, would charge proponents of the morality-focussed perspective with arrogantly substituting their own reasoning for majority opinions as expressed within democratic procedures, be in within individual States (national ethe) or in cumulated form as European consensus (pan-European ethos).

These ideal-type perspectives are helpful for teasing out the way in which European consensus relates to various broader controversies such as the relevance of disagreement to legal argument or the role of the is-ought distinction. Yet in the stark form in which I have been presenting them so far, they leave the interested observer in an overly simplistic normative environment: either one accepts the notion of a pan-European ethos and, accordingly, the ECtHR's use of European consensus – or one does not, either because one favours the morality-focussed perspective or because one does not accept the move to the transnational level within ethical normativity. This would discount the way in which European consensus is situated within a broader context, one of many arguments within the ECtHR's reasoning. To account for this fact, the stark edges of the different kinds of normativity considered thus far need to be softened. Accordingly, this chapter aims to explore the *interaction* between different forms of normativity despite their diametrically opposed starting points, insofar as it relates to European consensus.

These interactions tend to crystallise around certain constellations in which the tensions between the different perspectives become most apparent; they may best be captured by distinguishing between those cases involving the spur effect (in which consensus is at conflict, at a minimum, with the national ethos of the respondent State) and those involving the rein effect (in which consensus is often at conflict with the morality-focussed perspective).[568] I set out to explore these tensions by reference to a framework which might, if it were considered convincing, mitigate them to some extent: the epistemic approach based on the Condorcet Jury Theorem, which has been argued to justify the ECtHR's use of European consensus by Shai Dothan. On this account, majoritarian decision-making constitutes a way of identifying truth, and European consensus – because of its transnational vantage point building on a large number of independent decisions within domestic legal systems – provides a particularly strong instance of such truth-identification (II.1.). If this was uncontroversially the case, then it would both straddle the divide between the morality-focussed and the ethos-focussed perspective by exchanging the focus of the latter on self-government with the logic of truth constituted by aggregated opinions, and it would justify the reference to European consensus in the face of a divergent position by the respondent State. However, I will argue that the tensions just mentioned persist: they are built into the starting assumptions of the Condorcet Jury Theorem and destabilise its claims both in cases involving the spur effect (II.2.) and those involving the rein effect (II.3.).

If this is correct, then it seems more profitable to deal with the tensions between the different forms of normativity head-on. The second half of this chapter therefore aims to provide a broader framework within which to situate the tensions identified while discussing the epistemic approach. I will argue that because they each involve certain idealisations (III.1.), they are always liable to be undermined by criticism from opposing perspectives; and I will illustrate this by reference to the oscillation between the ethos-focussed perspective underlying European consensus, on the one hand, and the morality-focussed perspective, on the other, in cases involving so-called "core rights" (III.2.). Yet while the oscillation between these two perspectives is arguably the most foundational within Western metaphysics, the tableau in the context of regional human rights law contains additional complications. Because the tensions at the transnational level are triangular in the sense that the ethical normativity is further bifurcated

---

568 See generally Chapter 1, III.

according to the relevant macrosubject (national ethe or pan-European ethos), there is room not only for direct tensions between opposing forms of normativity pointing towards different results, but also, in some cases, for instrumental allegiances between them (III.3.).

In light of all this, the overall aim of the chapter is to demonstrate, first, that the tensions between the various forms of normativity discussed so far persist regardless of alternate frameworks such as the epistemic approach; second, that their triangular interrelation leads to different constellations of opposition and allegiance in cases involving the rein effect and the spur effect, respectively; and third, that the idealisations involved in any one form of normativity leads to its susceptibility to challenge by others, which in turn results in the oscillation between different perspectives in the reasoning that sets out to justify concrete norms of regional human rights law. With regard to European consensus, this means that while its use may, in principle, be justified as a variant of the ethos-focussed perspective adapted to the transnational context of the ECtHR, it is by no means "natural" in the sense that it can and should not be challenged. The focus then shifts from the justification of European consensus in the abstract to the specifics of the manner in which it is used (IV.).

II. An Attempt at Reconciliation: The Condorcet Jury Theorem

1. European Consensus as Collective Wisdom

Let me begin, then, by introducing a framework which, if accepted, might mitigate the tensions just mentioned: the epistemic approach, which combines the truth-claims of the morality-focussed perspective with the democracy-based argument of the ethos-focussed perspective and uses the transnational context of the ECtHR to read them together. The argument goes roughly as follows: by basing its judgments on (among other things) the approach taken by the majority of the States parties, itself based on the decisions of democratic intra-State majorities, the ECtHR may learn from their experiences and increase the likelihood of reaching the right decision. Consensus should therefore be accorded normative force – in form of the spur effect when it favours the applicant, and in form of the rein effect when it favours the respondent State.

In its most formal and substantiated form, the argument builds on the so-called Condorcet Jury Theorem, according to which a decision made by a number of independent jurors who are, on average,[569] more likely than not to individually make the correct decision between two options,[570] is more likely to be correct the greater the number of jurors.[571] If applied to large groups of people, accordingly, the statistical likelihood that a majority favours the correct result (under the conditions specified) becomes extremely high. Given the large number of people typically involved in the voting procedures of modern democracy, this insight is sometimes taken to constitute an argument in favour of the results favoured by democratic majorities.

Arguments in favour of democracy based on the Condorcet Jury Theorem are known as *epistemic* arguments,[572] for they see the virtue of democ-

---

569 Condorcet himself assumed that *each* juror is more likely than not to be correct, but see Bernard Grofman, Guillermo Owen, and Scott L. Feld, "Thirteen Theorems in Search of the Truth," (1983) 15 *Theory and Decision* 261.

570 Again, this is the initial formulation; it has since been argued that even if more than two options are admitted, the Condorcet Jury Theorem may hold under certain conditions (see Christian List and Robert E. Goodin, "Epistemic Democracy: Generalizing the Condorcet Jury Theorem," (2001) 9 *The Journal of Political Philosophy* 277 at 286), although it breaks down and indeed transforms into the so-called Condorcet Paradox in others. In human rights law, formulating the issue in binary terms will often be a simplification, but it does relate to the choice ultimately to be made between a finding of a violation and a finding of no violation (on which see Schlüter, "Beweisrechtliche Implikationen der margin of appreciation-Doktrin" at 44), and it resonates with the way in which European consensus is often used (see Chapter 1, III.); more complex approaches to vertically comparative law, however, will encounter problems with this binary structure, as acknowledged in Dothan, "Judicial Deference Allows European Consensus to Emerge" at 414-418; see critically also Føllesdal, "A Better Signpost, Not a Better Walking Stick: How to Evaluate the European Consensus Doctrine" at 207. I will mostly bracket these issues here, but they are worth noting since they constitute yet another reason why the merits of the Condorcet Jury Theorem are likely to be limited in practice (and indeed relate to some of the reasons I will foreground); see further on framing the issue for comparison Chapter 7, I.

571 Originally proposed by Condorcet in *Essai sur l'application de l'analyse à la probabilité des decision rendues à la pluralité des voix* (1785); for a succinct summary, see e.g. Dothan, "The Optimal Use of Comparative Law" at 23 and many of the other works cited in what follows.

572 Cohen, "An Epistemic Conception of Democracy" at 35; List and Goodin, "Epistemic Democracy: Generalizing the Condorcet Jury Theorem" at 277; José Luis Martí, "The Epistemic Conception of Deliberative Democracy Defended: Reasons, Rightness and Equal Political Autonomy," in *Deliberative Democracy and its Discontents*, ed. Samantha Besson and José Luis Martí (Aldershot: Ashgate, 2006) at 38-39.

racy in its assumed tendency to reach correct results, or, perhaps more provocatively formulated: to identify truth.[573] In this, they differ from what I have been calling the ethos-focussed perspective, since on that account, the ethical-volitional aspect of democracy qua self-rule – the authors and addressees of laws being identical – is seen as inherently valuable, an end in itself.[574] Applying the Condorcet Jury Theorem does not necessarily imply self-rule: one might, for example, imagine taking advantage of the epistemic virtues of a certain large group of people but applying the result to a different group of people. If one leaves such scenarios aside, however, then the epistemic approach is congenial to the ethos-focussed perspective, and the two are often combined.[575] In fact, the prototypical ethos-focussed account by Rousseau has increasingly been given an epistemic reading based on Condorcet:[576] in particular, the Jury Theorem supplies mathematical grounding for the claim that a majority decision on the common good constitutes the infallible general will.[577] I will return to the differences and similarities between the epistemic approach and the ethos-focussed perspective in a moment; let me first introduce how the prior relates to European consensus.

The Condorcetian logic has been applied to comparative reasoning by national courts by Eric Posner and Cass Sunstein, who argue in favour of

---

573 See Bernard Grofman and Scott L. Feld, "Rousseau's General Will: A Condorcetian Perspective," (1988) 82 *The American Political Science Review* 567 at 568 (voting as "a process that searches for 'truth.'").

574 Zysset, *The ECHR and Human Rights Theory: Reconciling the Moral and Political Conceptions*, at 218; Besson, "The Authority of International Law - Lifting the State Veil" at 354; see also Habermas, *Between Facts and Norms*, at 100 ("intrinsic, noninstrumentalizable value of civic self-organization").

575 E.g. Waldron, *Law and Disagreement*, at 134-136; see Samantha Besson and José Luis Martí, "Introduction," in *Deliberative Democracy and its Discontents*, ed. Samantha Besson and José Luis Martí (Aldershot: Ashgate, 2006) at xviii ("conceptually compatible").

576 Brian Barry, *Political Argument* (London: Routledge & Kegan Paul, 1965), at 292-293; Grofman and Feld, "Rousseau's General Will: A Condorcetian Perspective", passim; David M. Estlund, "Democratic Theory and the Public Interest: Condorcet and Rousseau Revisited," (1989) 83 *The American Political Science Review* 1317 at 1318; Waldron, "Rights and Majorities: Rousseau Revisited" at 63; Hélène Landemore, *Democratic Reason. Politics, Collective Intelligence, and the Rule of the Many* (Princeton and Oxford: Princeton University Press, 2013), at 69-70 (but also qualifying this reading at 74); Dijn, "Rousseau and Republicanism" at 12; see also Besson, *The Morality of Conflict. Reasonable Disagreement and the Law*, at 218-219.

577 Rousseau, *The Social Contract*, at 39 and 135.

such reasoning based on its informational value.[578] The basic idea, on their account, is that so long as each State, taken individually, is more likely than not to provide a correct answer to any given issue, following the lead of a majority of States drastically increases the overall likelihood of a correct decision.[579] The conditions that Posner and Sunstein identify are that first, States must be making judgments based on private information; second, they must be relevantly similar; and third, they must make decisions independently, rather than following each other's lead.[580]

This last condition leads to the problem of so-called informational cascades: precisely because of the presumed informational benefits of comparative reasoning, States may defer to the judgement of other States in making their own decisions and thus fail to provide their own information, undermining the Condorcet Jury Theorem's premise.[581] If used by national courts, the Theorem would thus turn self-defeating: "courts should learn from each other in order to reach better results; but if all courts learn from each other, their decisions are not independent and other courts should not learn from them".[582] To avoid this problem, Shai Dothan has suggested that instead of applying the Theorem to national courts, one might look instead to regional courts such as the ECtHR.[583] Because of the vertical position of the ECtHR vis-à-vis the States parties, it is placed outside the vicious circle in which they would get caught up.[584] On Dothan's account, the national courts and States more generally should therefore make decisions independently of each other;[585] in this way, the path is freed for the ECtHR to use the Condorcet Jury Theorem and learn from their experi-

578 Eric A. Posner and Cass R. Sunstein, "The Law of Other States," (2006) 59 *Stanford Law Review* 131 at 140.

579 Ibid., 141-143.

580 Ibid., 146 et seqq.

581 Ibid., 160-164; Kai Spiekermann and Robert E. Goodin, "Courts of Many Minds," (2011) 42 *British Journal of Political Science* 555 at 564-565.

582 Dothan, "The Optimal Use of Comparative Law" at 24, building on Posner and Sunstein, "The Law of Other States" at 163.

583 Dothan, "The Optimal Use of Comparative Law" at 22.

584 Ibid., 27.

585 The "should" here makes clear that this is, of course, one of the many counterfactual assumptions on which the epistemic defence of European consensus operates; for, as Føllesdal has noted, "European states do look to each other's jurisprudence in law making": Føllesdal, "A Better Signpost, Not a Better Walking Stick: How to Evaluate the European Consensus Doctrine" at 206; see further Dothan, "The Optimal Use of Comparative Law" at 30-38.

ence. European consensus is the condensed form of that experience and, for that reason, obtains normative force.[586]

This justification of European consensus is thus particularly conscious of the fact that consensus, unlike some forms of comparative reasoning in other contexts, refers to a multiplicity of States rather than to individual legal orders: it not only builds on the verticality of European consensus to avoid informational cascades, but also on its prism of commonality to establish a broader basis on which to build by means of the Condorcet Jury Theorem. Waldron has described comparative references to a large number (or "accumulation") of foreign legal systems as "more than the sum of its parts"[587] since it represents "the accumulated wisdom of the world".[588] The same could be said of European consensus – and indeed, Steven Wheatley has described it, with echoes of Waldron, as the "collective wisdom of the peoples of Europe".[589] This also resonates with those contributions that focus on the informational value of consensus – Dzehtsiarou and Lukashevich, for example, have argued that "the Court is likely to produce a 'good, just, or right decision' if all relevant [comparative] information is duly taken into account".[590] That is precisely the intuition which the approach based on the Condorcet Jury Theorem aims to capture and formalise.[591]

The idea that the positions taken by the States parties' legal systems, when considered through the prism of collectivity, constitute more than the sum of their parts is reminiscent, to some extent, of the notion of a pan-European ethos, as discussed in the preceding chapter. The potential overlap between epistemic and ethical-volitional justifications of democracy which I mentioned above shines through again here, since European consensus is conceptualised as building on democratic decisions. For example, Dothan picks up on the epistemic defence of democracy and argues that reference, by means of European consensus, to States parties' laws is

586 Dothan, "The Optimal Use of Comparative Law" at 26.

587 Jeremy Waldron, "Foreign Law and the Modern Ius Gentium," (2005) 119 *Harvard Law Review* 129 at 145.

588 Ibid., 138.

589 Wheatley, "Minorities under the ECHR and the Construction of a 'Democratic Society'" at 783.

590 Dzehtsiarou and Lukashevich, "Informed Decision-Making" at 277; insofar as they argue that an informed decision also "*present[s]* itself as more fair and better" (ibid., emphasis added), their argument collapses back into the strategic approach based on sociological legitimacy, discussed in the Chapter 9.

591 See Posner and Sunstein, "The Law of Other States" at 136.

particularly apt in the case of democratic States.[592] Samantha Besson, while relying primarily on the volitional, ethos-focussed argument in favour of democracy, notes that majority rule may "in certain deliberative conditions be vested with epistemic qualities".[593] She also notes that justifications for the subsidiarity of international human rights law tend to be both epistemic and democratic and that "the combination is not surprising in the light of the epistemic justifications often put forward for democratic procedures themselves".[594] In principle, epistemic and ethos-focussed justifications of democracy point in the same direction – majority rule – and can provide support for European consensus in tandem.

Nevertheless, the differing justifications of democracy lead to different perspectives from which European consensus is approached. For one thing, the rein effect and spur effect are delineated from one another differently – because of the Condorcet Jury Theorem's focus on majorities above the fifty percent mark, the middle category of a "lack of consensus", normally associated with the rein effect, loses its importance. I will return to this in the next chapter which deals in more detail with numerical issues involved in establishing consensus. For now, the more fundamental difference to the ethos-focussed perspective (which also underlies the numerical issue) is that, because the democratic credentials of consensus are appreciated for different reasons, consensus itself, too, is valued for different reasons. On the epistemic approach, consensus is approached not so much as an expression of the collective will of the peoples of Europe, but rather as a way of identifying the best way to regulate any given issue based on their experience. As Lovett puts it in a discussion of Rousseau, the epistemic reading relies on "a sort of cognitive exercise in discovering what the general will or common good already is".[595] Similarly, Joshua Cohen has described the epistemic approach more generally as involving "a *cognitive* account of voting".[596]

---

592 Dothan, "The Optimal Use of Comparative Law" at 28; see also Posner and Sunstein, "The Law of Other States" at 158-160.

593 Besson, "The Authority of International Law - Lifting the State Veil" at 354; see also on the epistemic qualities of national courts Besson, "Human Rights Adjudication as Transnational Adjudication: A Peripheral Case of Domestic Courts as International Law Adjudicators" at 50.

594 Besson, "Subsidiarity in International Human Rights Law - What is Subsidiary about Human Rights?" at 95.

595 Frank Lovett, "Can Justice Be Based on Consent?," (2004) 12 *The Journal of Political Philosophy* 79 at 83.

596 Cohen, "An Epistemic Conception of Democracy" at 34 (emphasis in original).

The epistemic justification of democracy – and hence of European consensus – thus has a certain affinity to the morality-focussed perspective and its emphasis on moral-cognitive elements. And yet, because it runs in parallel to the ethos-focussed perspective in relying on majoritarian procedures to discover the "truth", it also presents a different, more approving take on the use of consensus than that of the morality-focussed perspective. The reliance on majoritarian procedures and the mathematical grounding given to any truth claims further avoids the problem of disagreement usually associated with substantive moral argument – or so it seems at first. In the following subsections, I would like to test how the epistemic defence of European consensus plays out in more detail, by reference to the spur effect and the rein effect, respectively.

2. The Spur Effect and the Similarity Condition

Shai Dothan, in applying the Condorcet Jury Theorem to European consensus, seems to be concerned primarily with those cases in which European consensus speaks in favour of the applicant. He speaks of "emerging consensus" and introduces it as follows: "if the majority of European states protect a certain human right, the [ECtHR] will read the Convention as ensuring protection of this right and will find states that infringe this right in violation of the Convention".[597] Dothan's focus is thus on the spur effect of consensus: the argument would be that, on statistical grounds, the position taken by a majority of the States parties within Europe is likely to be correct, even if it conflicts with the position taken by the respondent State and a number of other States parties.

Consider, first, the similarities and differences to the morality-focussed perspective. I have argued that while the morality-focussed perspective is less opposed to the spur effect than to the rein effect of European consensus since the prior has a less immediate (or less harmful) impact on diversity management at the national level, consensus nonetheless is not considered to have independent normative force on its own terms: rather, if accepted at all, it merely constitutes an add-on to a result that was already justified by means of normative argument independent of consensus.[598]

597 Dothan, "The Optimal Use of Comparative Law" at 25; a similar formulation is at 22, and the focus on this scenario is clear throughout as well as in other articles.

598 Chapter 2, III.

Dothan's argument, by contrast, *proceeds in the opposite direction*: rather than accepting the argument from consensus if it conforms to independently discovered truth, truth is discovered *by means of* consensus.[599] This reprioritising of consensus as the primary argument brings Dothan closer, in substance, to the ethos-focussed view.

The epistemic approach also reaches similar conclusions to the ethos-focussed perspective as regards the object and purpose of the ECHR. Though it does not use the assumptions underlying the ethos-focussed perspective, it performs a conceptual shift that is similar to the one evidenced in the move from national ethe to a pan-European ethos; for example, in discussing the need for States to decide independently of one another in order for the effects of the Condorcet Jury Theorem to unfold, Dothan juxtaposes profitable choices for individual States with the "European interest".[600] Ultimately, the focus on the collectivity of European States is tied up with the very rationale underpinning the Condorcet Jury Theorem: to make reference to a multiplicity of decision-makers in order to improve the probability of a correct result.

Dothan is also well aware that this means overriding those States that find themselves in a minority position: he very clearly posits that the spur effect of consensus means that "human rights standards that are respected by at least a *majority* of the countries in Europe" are "then required from *all* European countries".[601] The implication is that the ECtHR should "strive to *harmonize* how human rights are protected in different states in Europe"[602] – harmonisation being understood here not in the general sense of setting uniform standards, but in the strict sense of non-incidental harmonisation as part of the very object and purpose of the ECHR, as discussed in Chapter 3.[603] While the underlying motivation, on the epistemic approach, is that such harmonisation will identify and give normative force to the best solution to the issue before the Court, rather than giving expression to a pan-European ethos, the two lines of argument are clearly compatible.

This compatibility is confirmed, in fact, by a glance at Dothan's further writings which go beyond the confines of the Condorcet Jury Theorem.

---

599 Dothan, "The Optimal Use of Comparative Law" at 43.

600 Ibid., 32.

601 Dothan, "Judicial Deference Allows European Consensus to Emerge" at 397 (emphasis in original).

602 Dothan, "The Optimal Use of Comparative Law" at 26 (emphasis added).

603 Chapter 3, IV.4.

His baseline assumption in those writings has been that, insofar as "states represent their citizens", the ECtHR should adopt restrictive rulings so as not to contradict the democratically bolstered "will of the public under the Court's jurisdiction".[604] By contrast, Dothan advocates for more expansive interpretation where it "does not contradict the established will of the citizens of Europe".[605] The language of "will" used here is, of course, volitional and thus wedded to the ethos-focussed perspective. Furthermore, speaking of "the established will of the citizens of Europe" clearly assumes the existence of a pan-European ethos as opposed to merely co-existing national ethe – it mirrors the language of proponents of the ethos-focussed perspective who have spoken, for example, of the "collective will of the community of European states",[606] though Dothan is more resolute in lifting the "State veil"[607] and dealing directly with the political self-determination underlying it.[608]

The main point here, however, is that as with the more cognitively oriented approach underlying the Condorcet Jury Theorem, the relevant collectivity shifts, at least in part,[609] from the individual State to the European community of States as a whole. Dothan does not deal explicitly with the spur effect of European consensus in this context, but his reference to (what amounts to) a pan-European ethos once more confirms the congeniality of the epistemic approach and the ethos-focussed perspective despite their differing theoretical assumptions. The Condorcet Jury Theorem might thus be understood as a further justification for the reference to the States parties as a collectivity and the harmonising purpose which follows from it.

Yet from the perspective of the respondent State – and other States whose position is overruled by decisions of the ECtHR based at least in

604 Dothan, "In Defence of Expansive Interpretation in the European Court of Human Rights" at 516.

605 Ibid., 518.

606 Glas, "The European Court of Human Rights' Use of Non-Binding and Standard-Setting Council of Europe Documents" at 105-106, citing Polakiewicz, "Alternatives to Treaty-Making and Law-Making by Treaty and Expert Bodies in the Council of Europe" at 248; see also, in the Inter-American context, Neuman, "Import, Export, and Regional Consent in the Inter-American Court of Human Rights" at 114 ("the will of OAS member states").

607 Besson, "The Authority of International Law - Lifting the State Veil".

608 See Chapter 3, IV.2.

609 Contrast e.g. Dothan, "In Defence of Expansive Interpretation in the European Court of Human Rights" at 519, speaking of the will of citizens in an individual State.

part on the spur effect of European consensus – the claim that a position contrary to theirs is "better" based on the collective wisdom of other States is bound to appear no more convincing than the claim that it constitutes the will of the majority of States within Europe. Jeremy Waldron has formulated this quite clearly in the context of comparative references by American courts: he argues that they can be justified on epistemic terms so long as one adopts a vision of "law as reason" rather than "law as will".[610] Those who adopt the latter approach "do not see any reason why expressions of will elsewhere in the world should affect [their] expressions of will in America", whereas those who adopt a less volitional approach might rely "not just on [their] own reasoning but on some rational relation between what [they] are wrestling with and what others have figured out".[611] The notion of a pan-European ethos complicates the understanding of law as will by introducing a volitionally conceptualised macrosubject beyond the individual State, but the gist of Waldron's statement remains valid: if one focusses on ethical-volitional normativity by reference to individual States, then the reason-by-majority approach expressed by an epistemic defence of the spur effect will not seem convincing.[612]

To some extent, this is acknowledged within Dothan's framework, though in a manner internal to the Condorcet Jury Theorem. States parties can put forward special justifications to counteract the spur effect of European consensus, in particular, by challenging whether the "similarity condition" is fulfilled in their case. As one of the preconditions for the Condorcet Jury Theorem to apply at all, that criterion demands that the legal orders referred to "must be sufficiently similar to make learning from them useful".[613] With regard to the spur effect of European consensus, this means that "where European states are dissimilar, the adoption of the same policy by the majority of the states in Europe does not necessarily indicate that it is a good policy".[614] This seems intuitively sensible: collective experience should be drawn on only if it is relevant. Indeed, consensus has sometimes been described as "measur[ing] attitudes and legal solutions adopted

---

610 Waldron, "Foreign Law and the Modern Ius Gentium" at 146.

611 Ibid., 146-147; see also Posner and Sunstein, "The Law of Other States" at 149-151.

612 In that vein, see Føllesdal, "A Better Signpost, Not a Better Walking Stick: How to Evaluate the European Consensus Doctrine" at 207.

613 Dothan, "The Optimal Use of Comparative Law" at 23.

614 Ibid., 30.

in respect of *similar* socio-political dilemmas".[615] However, the requirement of similarity departs from the otherwise formal approach of the Condorcet Jury Theorem by opening the door to difficult questions: given that all States are liable to differ from one another in some ways and be similar in others, how should one decide whether the States being referred to by way of comparative reasoning are, as Posner and Sunstein put it, "sufficiently similar *in the right way*"?[616]

Dothan's main example for a case of dissimilarity is the ECtHR's ruling in *Leyla Şahin v. Turkey*, according to which the Turkish ban on religious clothing within universities did not violate the right to freedom of religion (Article 9 ECHR). He points to the ECtHR's focus on the Turkish principle of secularism and the historical context within which it developed[617] and argues that they "set Turkey apart from the rest of Europe", thus justifying a finding of no violation despite the existence of a European consensus in favour of the applicant.[618] The tension at issue here mirrors that which could, in the language of ethical normativity, be described as the tension between a pan-European ethos and the individual national ethos of the respondent State. That tension thus persists in cases involving the spur effect, even when it is framed in terms of the similarity condition within the epistemic approach. For how to decide between relevant similarity and dissimilarity?

Even if we grant that the religious history of Turkey sets it apart from other European States (itself, of course, a matter of interpretation), it remains a clearly normative question whether the claimed dissimilarity is relevant for assessing the ban on religious clothing. Since the application of the Condorcet Jury Theorem depends on the answer to this question, it cannot be answered from within that Theorem, and thus depends on argument external to it. This, in turn, reimports the tensions between different forms of ethical normativity, as well as the kind of substantive moral argu-

---

615 ECtHR, Appl. No. 57792/15 – *Hamidović*, dissenting opinion of Judge Ranzoni, at para. 27 (emphasis added).

616 Posner and Sunstein, "The Law of Other States" at 148 (emphasis in original).

617 ECtHR (GC), Appl. No. 44774/98 – *Leyla Şahin*, at paras. 114-116.

618 Dothan, "The Optimal Use of Comparative Law" at 30; Dothan also points to the general diversity of States parties' approaches to the issue of religious symbols in educational institutions as cited in ECtHR (GC), Appl. No. 44774/98 – *Leyla Şahin*, at para. 109; see further on that aspect of the judgment Chapter 7, III.1. and Chapter 8, III.2. The issue could also be approached through the lens of intransitivity between more than two options: see supra, note 570 and the examples given by Dothan in the passage there cited.

ment favoured by the morality-focussed perspective. Is it sufficient, for example, for Turkey to claim that the principle of secularism is of such importance within its historical context that it establishes sufficient dissimilarity vis-à-vis other European States (national ethos), or does the assessment of the dissimilarity's relevance depend, conversely, on the weight accorded to secularism elsewhere in Europe (pan-European ethos)? Or should one shift perspective entirely and assess the relevance of any given dissimilarity by reference to external standards – which might mean, for example, dismissing the relevance of any potential dissimilarity in the case of *Leyla Şahin* because Turkey's ban on religious clothing might be driven by prejudice (morality-focussed perspective)? In brief: by reference to which kind of normativity should controversies surrounding the relevant similarity condition be resolved? This, in turn, points to deeper questions pertaining to the foundational assumptions of the epistemic approach: what kind of normativity lurks behind its ostensibly formal and mathematical grounding? These issues become even more apparent in cases concerning the rein effect of consensus: it is to these that I now turn.

3. The Rein Effect and Bias Across States

Dothan's main focus, as mentioned above, seems to be on cases involving the spur effect of consensus. One might, however, also apply the epistemic justification of its use to cases involving the rein effect: if there is a consensus among the States parties to the ECHR in favour of the respondent State rather than the individual applicant, then the application of the Condorcet Jury Theorem would lead the ECtHR to believe that the majority position is likely to be correct, and consensus would therefore speak against finding a violation of the Convention.[619] In a sense, this follows as the flip side of applying the Jury Theorem to the spur effect, even if one does not phrase the finding of a non-violation in the strong language of establishing legal or moral truth but rather in more doctrinal and contingent terms such as the granting of a margin of appreciation to the respondent State.[620] Dothan does discuss issues usually connected with the rein effect in his defence of consensus: he notes potential criticism based on the idea that

619 This differs from the way the rein effect is usually approached, by way of a "lack of consensus": for a more detailed juxtaposition, see Chapter 5, III.3.

620 It is in that vein that I read Dothan, "Judicial Deference Allows European Consensus to Emerge" at 398.

there may be "a European consensus that restricts human rights instead of protecting them", and in particular the problem of political majorities and prejudice.[621]

Dothan's discussion of prejudice is telling, since it succinctly encapsulates the way in which the epistemic approach is ambivalently perched between the morality-focussed perspective and the ethos-focussed perspective. I already mentioned above that while its results cohere with the latter, the epistemic approach is, at heart, more cognitive than volitional, and thus seems closer to the outlook of the morality-focussed perspective. The discussion of the similarity condition in the preceding sub-section also showed that, for all its formality and mathematical grounding, the Condorcet Jury Theorem cannot disavow normative assumptions. These are not limited to the similarity condition: ultimately, normative assumptions are built into the foundational claim that any given State is more likely than not to make (legally or morally) *correct* decisions[622] – the standards for that correctness must be identified "along some specified evaluative dimension",[623] which in turn implies "an *independent standard* of correct decisions".[624]

Such standards external to the Condorcet Jury Theorem shine through clearly, for example, when Posner and Sunstein postulate that some States are "better" suited as a source of comparative materials because their "population is heathier, freer, happier, and wealthier".[625] Dothan similarly refers to "the relative success of states" as a potentially relevant criterion, but acknowledges that this involves a choice between what are, in effect, various moral positions – for example, he cites the "happiness of the population", which would imply a utilitarian approach, or "the protection of political rights", which implies a liberal moral theory.[626] Briefly put: "any epistemic justification of democracy" – or, by extension, of the use of European consensus – "is committed to the claim that political questions can

621 Ibid., 402.
622 See Posner and Sunstein, "The Law of Other States" at 149; Dothan, "The Optimal Use of Comparative Law" at 23.
623 Grofman and Feld, "Rousseau's General Will: A Condorcetian Perspective" at 569.
624 Cohen, "An Epistemic Conception of Democracy" at 34 (emphasis in original).
625 Posner and Sunstein, "The Law of Other States" at 174.
626 Dothan, "The Optimal Use of Comparative Law" at 28.

have substantively right or wrong answers",[627] and thus needs to clarify which standards are considered relevant and how they should be justified.

In light of this, the problem of prejudiced external preferences that drove the morality-focussed perspective to argue for anti-majoritarian procedures returns in full force. As we saw in the preceding chapter, the ethos-focussed perspective sidesteps these issues by questioning the concept of prejudice: on a more volitionally oriented epistemology, it becomes unclear and thus subject to majority decision whether a certain position is, in fact, prejudiced.[628] The epistemic approach cannot make use of that argument, however, since it must set up a certain normative standard and substantiate its claim that the decision-makers are, on average, more likely than not to correctly identify that standard.[629] On the other hand, it is "more grounded" than the morality-focussed perspective which looks "just to philosophic reason",[630] referring, as it does, instead to decisions *actually* made by voters and thus including factual elements rather than emphasising the "critical edge" of the is-ought distinction.[631] Measured against the prepolitical normative standard, however, these factual elements may be a vehicle of prejudice.

Condorcet himself regarded prejudice as one of the most serious barriers to achieving that goal in practice: "there must be a reason why [a voter] decides less well than one would at random. The reason can only be found in the prejudices to which this voter is subject".[632] Or, as John Rawls later put it, "clearly society is not a stochastic process" of the type envisaged by the Jury Theorem:[633] discrimination of certain groups, from a morality-focussed perspective, will always distort decision-making on at least some issues, particularly individual rights.[634] It is worth noting that on those

627 Cristina Lafont, "Is the Ideal of a Deliberative Democracy Coherent?," in *Deliberative Democracy and its Discontents*, ed. Samantha Besson and José Luis Martí (Aldershot: Ashgate, 2006) at 11.

628 Chapter 3, II.

629 See Martí, "The Epistemic Conception of Deliberative Democracy Defended: Reasons, Rightness and Equal Political Autonomy" at 41.

630 Waldron, "Foreign Law and the Modern Ius Gentium" at 134.

631 Tellingly, analogies are often drawn in this regard between moral and factual (scientific) knowledge: in that vein ibid., 143; Posner and Sunstein, "The Law of Other States" at 149.

632 Cited from Waldron, "Democratic Theory and the Public Interest: Condorcet and Rousseau Revisited" at 1323.

633 Rawls, *A Theory of Justice*, at 147, contra Edgeworth; directly on the Condorcet Jury Theorem see ibid., 314-315.

634 See Dworkin, "Constitutional Cases" at 176.

premises, the Jury Theorem would actually constitute an argument *against* majoritarian procedures since it works both ways: if decision-makers are more likely than not to reach the correct decision, bundling their votes increases the likelihood of a correct overall decision; but if they are individually more likely than not to reach the wrong decision, then the Jury Theorem teaches us that it becomes extremely likely that the decision made by a great number of them will be wrong.[635] On the Theorem's terms, then, the existence of prejudice might actually constitute an argument in favour of leaving questions of individual rights to individuals or small groups – such as judges.

Dothan is aware of these problems for an epistemic defence of majoritarian democracy at the national level: although he remains optimistic that States' decisions "are probably better than random in most cases", he also acknowledges that in cases of discrimination, States' decisions "may be worse than random".[636] According to him, however, the problem disappears when one introduces the transnational vantage point of the ECtHR in using European consensus – for, qua Dothan, "even if one state discriminates against a certain group, other states may not discriminate against the same group" and therefore "the laws chosen by the majority of the states will not be systematically biased".[637] Here, we have reached a point in the argument which already shone through in earlier chapters.[638] We saw there that minority rights were regarded as necessary by the morality-focussed perspective to counter prejudice, the existence of which was substantiated by an appeal to history. We also noted that given the transnational context, critics of European consensus must argue that prejudice tends to exist with regard to the *same* minorities across the States of Europe: hence Carozza's misgivings since the "history of the human rights movement makes it lamentably obvious that even large groups of states might share internal norms that all violate some basic aspect of human dignity"[639] and Letsas's claim that hostile external preferences will be

635 Waldron, "Democratic Theory and the Public Interest: Condorcet and Rousseau Revisited" at 1322 (also elaborating on the problem of prejudice on the following pages).

636 Dothan, "The Optimal Use of Comparative Law" at 31; see also Dothan, "In Defence of Expansive Interpretation in the European Court of Human Rights" at 520-522.

637 Dothan, "The Optimal Use of Comparative Law" at 31.

638 Particularly Chapter 2, II.2.

639 Carozza, "Uses and Misuses of Comparative Law" at 1228.

found "across Contracting States generally".[640] Dothan opposes such statements in claiming that different States will discriminate against different groups.

That latter claim, however, seems to be somewhat detached from the way in which discrimination works in actual fact: discriminatory practices do not usually end at State borders. For example, Condorcet himself wrote even in 1790 that "*all* races have [...] had a legal inequality between men and women".[641] Today, too, one is likely to encounter discrimination of similar groups across Europe: women and gender non-conforming persons, sexual minorities, disabled persons, ethnic and religious minorities, people of colour, poor persons, immigrants, etc.[642] The discrimination of such groups is social and thus in principle historically contingent rather than natural, so of course counter-examples may be found; but the morality-focussed perspective on European consensus in any case assumes historically similar discrimination of certain minority groups across Europe,[643] and thus would not be deterred by epistemic arguments but rather remain critical of according normative force to European consensus in its rein effect.

Recognising this problem, Dothan has further specified his position in more recent publications and argued that "there is no reason to think that all countries will discriminate against the same minorities *in the same way*".[644] His example goes as follows: a third of the States parties violate the right of minorities to a fair trial, another third their freedom of speech, and yet another third their privacy; since the Condorcet Jury Theorem would always favour the majority position over the third of States violating any given right, "their biases will balance themselves out and the majority's opinion will be optimal".[645]

640 Letsas, *A Theory of Interpretation of the European Convention on Human Rights*, at 121.

641 Marquis de Condorcet, "On the Emancipation of Women. On giving Women the Right of Citizenship," in *Condorcet: Political Writings*, ed. Steven Lukes and Nadia Urbinati (Cambridge: Cambridge University Press, 2012) at 161 (emphasis added).

642 On the "embarrassed 'etc.'", see Judith Butler, *Gender Trouble. Feminism and the Subversion of Identity* (New York and London: Routledge, 1999), at 196.

643 As does the ECtHR: see with regard to the schooling of Roma children ECtHR (GC), Appl. No. 57325/00 – *D.H. and Others v. the Czech Republic*, Judgment of 13 November 2007, at para. 205.

644 Dothan, "Judicial Deference Allows European Consensus to Emerge" at 402.

645 Ibid.

It is true that discrimination of minorities does not always work "in the same way"; in particular, it is experienced differently along different, often intersecting axes of oppression.[646] However, this is not the point Dothan is raising, and I am not convinced that his rather abstract example and the conclusion which he draws capture the issue in a helpful manner. His way of framing discrimination makes it seem as though minorities are discriminated against in different contexts almost at random, with different rights impacted upon in different States, rather than viewing the matter through the lens of complex intersecting structures. In reality, however, structures which marginalise certain groups tend to have broad effects on various aspects of life and thus touch upon many different rights. In addition, and the first point notwithstanding,[647] controversies in human rights law will often crystallise around certain issues relating to the specific group – accessible legal gender recognition and transition-related health care for trans persons, decriminalisation and later access to recognised partnerships and marriage for gay people, permissibility of religious attire for religious minorities, and so on. Both of these points make the neat division into different rights violations in different States rather unlikely.

Dothan's response is that "[e]ven if the European majority cannot be trusted in such issues, any individual country is" – by virtue of the Condorcetian logic that less jurors lead to worse results – "even less trustworthy",[648] thus arguing that the commonality-based approach of European

646 Angela Y. Davis, *Women, Race & Class* (New York: Random House, 1983) remains an absolutely foundational study of these intersections; another account I find helpful is Sara Ahmed, *Queer Phenomenology* (Durham and London: Duke University Press, 2006), at 136-137; particularly in the legal context, the classics (and the origin of the term "intersectionality") are Kimberle Crenshaw, "Demarginalizing the Intersection of Race and Sex: A Black Feminist Critique of Antidiscrimination Doctrine, Feminist Theory and Antiracist Politics," (1989) *University of Chicago Legal Forum* 139 and Kimberle Crenshaw, "Mapping the Margins: Intersectionality, Identity Politics, and Violence Against Women of Color," (1991) 43 *Stanford Law Review* 1241; in the context of the ECHR, the issue is touched upon e.g. by Alexandra Timmer, "Toward an Anti-Stereotyping Approach for the European Court of Human Rights," (2011) 11 *Human Rights Law Review* 707.

647 The disconnect here, I think, arises at least in part because legal discourse tends to *neglect* the intersections just mentioned, particularly insofar as economic disadvantage is at issue: see critically e.g. Hilary Charlesworth, Gina Heathcote, and Emily Jones, "Feminist Scholarship on International Law in the 1990s and Today: An Inter-Generational Conversation," (2019) 27 *Feminist Legal Studies* 79 at 83.

648 Dothan, "Judicial Deference Allows European Consensus to Emerge" at 403.

consensus is preferable to the position of any one State. But this cannot mitigate the criticism of the morality-focussed perspective which would trust neither individual States *nor* the community of European States taken as a whole. Thus, even on the epistemic approach, European consensus remains "an imperfect tool", and Dothan is forced to acknowledge that "in cases that involve a persistent bias against a certain minority", it might be more apt to "rely on abstract moral principles to justify intervention" which, sometimes, "is the only reasonable option".[649]

But if this is the case, then we are left with a similar dilemma to cases involving the similarity condition: by which standard should we evaluate when a "persistent bias against a certain minority" is at issue? I argued in Chapter 2 that this always involves a normative assessment; and, as with the similarity condition, this assessment is prior to the application of the Condorcet Jury Theorem so it cannot be answered by its own logic. The ethos-focussed perspective would avoid the issue: it would consider the examples given over the course of the preceding paragraphs (or similar examples to the same effect) non-conclusive since it would not accept the prepolitical standards against which the political will of a collectivity is measured. If the epistemic perspective were to adopt this stance so as to retain its faith in majoritarian decision-making, however, then it would lose its distinctive claim to supply not just a form of ethical-volitional normativity, but also a substantively correct decision in broader moral terms. If a morality-focussed perspective is retained, by contrast, then the problem of prejudice remains unsolved. The normative presuppositions of the epistemic approach are built into its starting assumptions and thus partially obscured, but no less controversial for it: it cannot, therefore, resolve the tensions between different kinds of normativity nor, in consequence, the controversies surrounding European consensus.

649 Ibid.; to avoid this conclusion, Dothan switches to a legitimacy-based argument (ibid.): on this type of justification for European consensus, see Chapter 9; for morality-focussed elements in his argument, see also Shai Dothan, "Three Interpretive Constraints on the European Court of Human Rights," in *The Rule of Law at the National and International Levels. Contestations and Deference*, ed. Machiko Kanetake and André Nollkaemper (Oxford and Portland: Hart, 2016) at 245.

III. Triangular Tensions and Instrumental Allegiances

1. Persistent Tensions Due to Differing Epistemologies and Idealisations

Since the epistemic approach cannot, as I have argued, mitigate the tensions between the different perspectives discussed over the course of the preceding chapters, these tensions must be grappled with directly. Insofar as the morality-focussed perspective and the ethos-focussed perspective are concerned, this problem is well-known from the national level; as will have become clear at this point, the transnational context of the ECtHR further complicates matters by partitioning ethical normativity according to different macrosubjects within which it is developed: the primary reference point becomes a pan-European ethos so as to enable the ECtHR's supervisory function, even as individual national ethe likewise remain relevant because of their more developed democratic procedures. We are thus faced with what might be deemed a *triangulation* of the tensions familiar from the national level: rather than a mere dichotomy, tensions now persist between moral normativity, ethical normativity coined within individual national ethe, and ethical normativity based on the notion of a pan-European ethos. As the discussion of the epistemic approach showed, these tensions materialise in different ways depending on whether the rein effect or the spur effect of European consensus is at issue.

This section is dedicated to illustrating the way in which the various different perspectives interact with one another in the context of European consensus. I begin by recalling the different epistemologies which underlie the morality-focussed and the ethos-focussed perspective and connecting them to different idealisations (III.1.). Because of the counterfactuality involved in these idealisations, none of the perspectives can claim absolute validity. As a result, the accounts of the various perspectives in their "pure" form given in the preceding chapters need to be complexified by demonstrating the argumentative shifts which occur, in practice, *between* the different perspectives. I demonstrate this by reference to the example of "core rights" which are assumed to carve out a space in which European consensus is irrelevant (III.2.). Finally, I will argue that the triangulation of tensions at the transnational level leads to the possibility of instrumental allegiances between the otherwise opposed perspectives and suggest that the air of compromise which surrounds the notion of a pan-European ethos in that context may have contributed substantially to the popularity of European consensus (III.3.).

To begin, then, with the differing epistemologies and idealisations of the different perspectives involved: the morality-focussed perspective, as argued in Chapter 2, proceeds by side-lining democratic processes and majoritarian decisions and foregrounding the moral-cognitive over the ethical-volitional moment. In so doing, it places a great deal of faith in courts reaching the correct decision on the basis of the judges' substantive reasoning. For example, it is assumed that the ECtHR would adequately enable the moral self-determination of the individual if it did not refer to European consensus. There is a clear potential for judicial hegemony here, with judges deemed competent to disregard State will entirely.[650] It is not for nothing, perhaps, that proponents of the morality-focussed perspective often write in the Dworkinian tradition, treating adjudication as a Herculean task.[651] As Dworkin himself put it: "the institution [of rights] requires an act of faith".[652] Since that faith cannot be placed in States and national laws which are regarded as the most important point of crystallisation of prejudice, faith is placed, instead, in judges[653] – specifically, those that constitute the ECtHR.

The ethos-focussed perspective, discussed in Chapter 3, is quick to point out that assigning Herculean roles to judges involves an idealisation, but its own solution – to instead rely on ethical-volitional normativity as expressed by means of political autonomy – involves the opposite idealisation, as it were. The ethos-focussed perspective avoids the problem of prejudice by virtue of its different epistemological approach: since it disavows reliance on normative claims about prepolitical rights in light of persistent disagreement about them, the very concepts of "minority" and "prejudice" must themselves be specified within the democratic process. Yet, from the perspective of the morality-focussed view, this seems like a weak excuse.

---

650 See Mégret, "The Apology of Utopia" at 487: "hegemony never thrives as much as on utopia" (in the Koskenniemian sense).

651 Critically on the idealisations involved in Dworkin's theory Habermas, *Between Facts and Norms*, at 213 ("The theory requires a Hercules for its author; this ironic attribution makes no secret of the ideal demands the theory is supposed to satisfy.").

652 Dworkin, "Taking Rights Seriously" at 246; for an account of "faith" in human rights in a slightly different sense, critical of "naturalist" accounts of rights reminiscent of the morality-focussed perspective, see Henri Féron, "Human Rights and Faith: A 'World-wide Secular Religion'?," (2014) 7 *Ethics & Global Politics* 181.

653 See in a different context Milanovic, "On Realistic Utopias and Other Oxymorons: An Essay on Antonio Cassese's Last Book" at 1046, criticising that Cassese "puts too much faith in courts and judges".

The fact of disagreement is not considered directly relevant to normative argument in light of the is-ought distinction[654] – all the more so since disagreement between the applicant and the respondent State lies, by definition, at the heart of every proceeding before the ECtHR.[655] To emphasise it as strongly as the ethos-focussed perspective does seems like an epistemological ploy to foreground ethical normativity and deny recourse to normative standards that are independent of the political will of a society. One is then reduced to judging "simply contingently in terms of existing social fact or social power",[656] or, to use the terminology often invoked by the morality-focussed perspective: one paves the way for a tyranny of the majority.

The ethos-focussed perspective's response to this issue is based on the faith it places in democratic structures to prevent the subjugation of intra-State minorities. Faith is now placed not in judges, but in citizens voting in accordance with civic virtues. As Waldron acknowledges, this involves an idealisation: the assumption that votes are conducted in good faith has "an aspirational quality";[657] more critically, Habermas has spoken of an "overexertion of the virtuous citizen".[658] To make this point more generally, one might say that democratic processes as they actually exist are transformed into what Susan Marks calls "venerable fictions" based on "a conception of citizenship and political participation abstracted from informal political processes, socio-economic contexts and membership of particular communities".[659] Thus, where the critics of European consensus idealise

654 Supra, Chapter 2, II.3.

655 Letsas, *A Theory of Interpretation of the European Convention on Human Rights*, at 53-55.

656 Allott and others, "Thinking Another World" at 274; see also Allott, *Eutopia*, at 88.

657 Waldron, *Law and Disagreement*, at 14; see further Chapter 3, III.

658 Habermas, "Volkssouveränität als Verfahren" at 611 (my translation); see also Benvenisti, "The Margin of Appreciation, Subsidiarity and Global Challenges to Democracy" at 241, criticizing the assumptions underlying the margin of appreciation doctrine as "highly optimistic" and "not adequately meet[ing] political reality".

659 Marks, *The Riddle of All Constitutions*, at 51 and 72; see also the important distinction between "the People" as a "rhetorical trope", on the one hand, and an "empirical fact", on the other, drawn by de Londras, "When the European Court of Human Rights Decides Not to Decide: The Cautionary Tale of *A, B & C* v. *Ireland* and Referendum-Emergent Constitutional Provisions" at 327 in the context of referenda.

the ECtHR and its substantive reasoning, the ethos-focussed perspective idealises the democratic process within the States parties.[660]

Insofar as a pan-European ethos is concerned, a further idealisation lies in the fact that the States parties, *as a collectivity*, are taken to constitute the relevant macrosubject within which ethical normativity is developed. In particular, if ethical norms "give objective embodiment to the concrete life of a political community", as Pheng Cheah puts it,[661] then the notion of a pan-European ethos immediately raises the question of how the relevant political community is constituted. At the national level, the ethos-focussed perspective points to democratic procedures. At the transnational level, such procedures are largely absent; hence, as I argued in Chapter 3, the reference to a majority of the States parties by means of European consensus in their stead. Even if one accepts this approach due to the transnational context within which the ECtHR is situated, however, it remains difficult to conceptualise a "European polity" – at most, one might think of "an imbricated polity made of the 47 European national polities".[662] Or, more provocatively in the words of Frédéric Mégret: "the projection of, say, a 'European society' can no more hide that it is a fiction".[663]

Within the triangular tensions between moral normativity, ethical normativity coined within individual national ethe, and ethical normativity based on the notion of a pan-European ethos, we are thus left with differing idealisations for each perspective – one might say, echoing Mary Ann Glendon, that they choose to pin their hopes on different institutions and processes.[664] The controversies surrounding the rein effect of European consensus can be reframed, in other words, as a dispute over *which idealisation is more adequate* – which institutions and processes to pin one's hopes on. In David Luban's words, much depends on "political-philosophical

660 Fredman, "From Dialogue to Deliberation: Human Rights Adjudication and Prisoners' Rights to Vote" at 297-298; this idealisation is increasingly put into question for certain Eastern European States (tending in that direction e.g. Peat, *Comparative Reasoning in International Courts and Tribunals*, at 176-177), but the idealisation as such holds true for all States parties and the answer to the question of when it is appropriate in turn depends on the perspective from which it is approached.

661 Cheah, *Inhuman Conditions. On Cosmopolitanism and Human Rights*, at 150.

662 Besson, "European Human Rights, Supranational Judicial Review and Democracy - Thinking Outside the Judicial Box" at 134; see also Besson, "Subsidiarity in International Human Rights Law - What is Subsidiary about Human Rights?" at 88.

663 Mégret, "The Apology of Utopia" at 482.

664 See Glendon, *Rights Talk*, at 182.

commitments" to, say, nationalism or internationalism, which in turn involves "[t]rust or mistrust" of different institutions.[665]

2. From Tensions to Oscillation: The Example of Core Rights

So, which idealisation *is* more adequate? Since critics and proponents of consensus approach this issue from different Archimedean points, with different epistemological assumptions, it is difficult if not impossible to find common ground from which such a judgement could be made. As Gerard Hauser has described the related opposition between moral universalism and cultural relativism: "Both rely on fundamentally different assumptions that are difficult to translate into the other's perspective".[666] Yet this also points towards the limitations of any one perspective taken on its own – because of the differing idealisations involved, each perspective constantly remains subject to challenge simply by pointing out the counterfactuality involved and approaching the issue from within a different epistemology. As a result, the different perspectives tend to depart from their "pure" form, which I have mostly been taking as the basis of the discussion until now, and integrate elements of one another into their accounts.

This may take place in different ways and between different forms of normativity within the triangular tensions just described – indeed, the following chapters will largely be dedicated to tracing the oscillations which result from the interaction of different forms of normativity. My intention in this subsection is merely to set the scene by providing an example from academic commentary on European consensus – and in so doing, to give additional nuance to the accounts of the morality-focussed and ethos-focussed perspectives in the preceding chapters. For my example, I take the tensions between the European consensus, based on the notion of a pan-European ethos, and the morality-focussed perspective as my starting point; I do so partly because they are, in a sense, more foundational than the tensions between different kinds of ethical normativity (i.e. they not only foreground different macrosubjects but build on different epistemologies altogether), and partly because the differences and tensions be-

665 David Luban, "Human Rights Pragmatism and Human Dignity," in *Philosophical Foundations of Human Rights*, ed. Rowan Cruft, S. Matthew Liao, and Massimo Renzo (Oxford: Oxford University Press, 2015) at 264.
666 Gerard A. Hauser, "The Moral Vernacular of Human Rights Discourse," (2008) 41 *Philosophy & Rhetoric* 440 at 451.

tween different kinds of ethical normativity were already touched upon in the preceding chapter. Moral and ethical normativity, by contrast, have so far been presented independently of one another, albeit engaged in mutual criticism. My aim here is to show how this criticism translates over into an oscillation between the two kinds of normativity.

Some of the authors cited throughout the preceding chapters do adhere quite strictly to one form of normativity, for example to a liberal theory of rights exemplary of the morality-focussed perspective.[667] Many will, however, also acknowledge its limits and hence admit elements of other forms of normativity. For example, given the morality-focussed perspective's concern with protecting the prepolitical rights of intra-State minorities against a tyranny of the majority, its proponents will often be more open to elements of the ethos-focussed perspective where it is not minority rights, but "matters that affect the general population in a given society" that are at stake[668] – hence the importance of specifying what counts as a "minority" matter.[669] In other matters, these commentators would acknowledge the limitations of substantive argument in light of disagreement, and hence be amenable to stronger deference to democratic procedures by way of European consensus.

Conversely, the criticism facing the ethos-focussed perspective – in particular, the charge that it does not adequately confront the problem of prejudice by virtue of its focus on factual disagreement which blunts the critical edge of the is-ought distinction – has led to certain concessions with regard to the role of European consensus. As the above discussion of the epistemic approach has shown, the prism of commonality through which European consensus approaches domestic laws does little to mitigate this kind of criticism: at least in some cases, prejudice will manifest itself in similar ways across Europe, and European consensus hence risks perpetuating such prejudice despite its reliance on a multiplicity of domestic legal systems. Proponents of European consensus have therefore (more or less explicitly) acknowledged the idealisations involved in the ethos-

667 E.g. Letsas, who arguably maintains his anti-consensus stance most consistently and within the most developed and self-aware theoretical framework.

668 Benvenisti, "Margin of Appreciation, Consensus, and Universal Standards" at 847; the strong focus specifically on minority rights is echoed e.g. by Bribosia, Rorive, and Van den Eynde, "Same-Sex Marriage: Building an Argument before the European Court of Human Rights in Light of the US Experience" at 20.

669 See Chapter 2, II.1.

focussed perspective by proposing different ways to mitigate the problem of prejudice.[670]

One of the most popular ways of doing so within academic commentary has been by reference to the notion of "core rights" (or a right's core[671]), which I would like to discuss in this subsection. This notion is often used to demarcate *an area within which European consensus will have no normative relevance*: particularly in those cases which are liable to be marked by prejudice or in which the proper functioning of democratic procedures is otherwise implicated, this kind of caveat mitigates the concerns of the morality-focussed perspective to some extent. There is some resemblance, perhaps, to the way in which human rights have sometimes been conceptualised at the global level when confronted with the debate between universalists and relativists. The core of a right is then seen as a last bastion against relativism while allowing cultural diversity on the periphery. As Eva Brems has put it, "[t]he core is essential and universal, while the periphery should permit cultural variations".[672]

In a similar vein, then, a right's core might be seen as a bastion again the use of consensus, particularly when used in its rein effect. Many proponents of consensus – even those otherwise very strongly insistent on its merits – have advocated for such a "safe zone",[673] although they rarely elaborate further, contenting themselves instead with brief and categorical statements. Thus it has been said that "[i]f a core right is at stake, the Court should not base itself on consensus"[674] or that "a certain 'hard core' of human rights should be defended even against the majority or the consen-

670 Besides the discussion of core rights which follows, see also Chapter 8, III.2.

671 I will leave the distinction between "core rights" and the "core *of* a right" aside here; see generally, on the rhetoric of framing an issue as its own "right to …", Andreas von Arnauld and Jens T. Theilen, "Rhetoric of Rights: A Topical Perspective on the Functions of Claiming a 'Human Right to …'," in *Cambridge Handbook of New Human Rights. Recognition, Novelty, Rhetoric*, ed. Andreas von Arnauld, Kerstin von der Decken, and Mart Susi (Cambridge: Cambridge University Press, 2020).

672 Eva Brems, "Enemies or Allies? Feminism and Cultural Relativism as Dissident Voices in Human Rights Discourse," (1997) 19 *Human Rights Quarterly* 136 at 147.

673 See also Kapotas and Tzevelekos, "How (Difficult Is It) to Build Consensus on (European) Consensus?" at 6 ("consensus exclusion zones").

674 Kleinlein, "Consensus and Contestability: The ECtHR and the Combined Potential of European Consensus and Procedural Rationality Control" at 887.

sus".[675] Some judges at the ECtHR have likewise announced their support for such an approach: Judge Dedov has opined in a concurring opinion that because "the right to life is absolute, and is one of the *fundamental* rights, neither the margin of appreciation nor sovereignty nor consensus is a relevant factor";[676] and former President Wildhaber, writing extra-judicially with Hjartarson and Donnelly, has noted in passing that European consensus should be supported since, "*[a]part from core or elementary rights*, there can be no harm in leaving adequate room for human rights diversity and pluralism".[677]

The silence as to the details is telling, for those who do try to provide further details invariably run into problems stemming from the tension between the morality-focussed and the ethos-focussed perspective. As proponents of consensus, they will usually approach the issue from an ethos-focussed perspective – based on the impossibility of proving strictly normative statements about morality and hence focussing instead on a factually-oriented epistemology that favours volitional elements and reference to democratic procedures. From within that perspective, consensus would itself indicate which aspects of a right should be considered its core. For example, according to Ostrovsky, consensus "aids the court in determining whether [...] a universal (or European) core right is actually being threatened", and thus to "draw a line around core rights".[678] However, on this approach, the notion of a right's core would merely describe the conclusion thus reached rather than claiming independent force as an argument: it would not serve as the kind of "safe zone" in which European consensus plays no role, as envisioned above.

---

675 Péter Paczolay, "Consensus and Discretion: Evolution or Erosion of Human Rights Protection?" (Dialogue between judges, European Court of Human Rights, 2008), at 78.

676 ECtHR (GC), Appl. No. 46470/11 – *Parrillo v. Italy*, Judgment of 27 August 2015, concurring opinion of Judge Dedov, at para. 8 (emphasis added).

677 Wildhaber, Hjartarson, and Donnelly, "No Consensus on Consensus?" at 252 (emphasis added).

678 Ostrovsky, "What's So Funny About Peace, Love, and Understanding?" at 57; Ostrovsky is technically referring here to the margin of appreciation, but the prior pages make it clear that his main focus is its relation to European consensus; see also Donoho, "Autonomy, Self-Governance, and the Margin of Appreciation: Developing a Jurisprudence of Diversity Within Universal Human Rights" at 455 and 458; on consensus-based demarcation of core rights more generally, see also Leijten, *Core Socio-Economic Rights and the European Court of Human Rights*, at 181, and at 218-219 in the context of the ECtHR.

Most commentators therefore take a different approach and simply postulate that certain issues belong to a right's core, independently of the state of European consensus – popular candidates include those rights which are vital for democracy to function and the most important rights for the purposes of protecting intra-State minorities.[679] The mention of intra-State minorities is revealing, for it reflects the concerns of the morality-focussed perspective; and indeed, the reasoning at this point usually switches to substantive normative reasoning of the kind that is likewise typical of the morality-focussed perspective. It is symptomatic when Brems describes a right's core as "essential and universal".[680] As Koskenniemi has rather lyrically put it, in order to uphold the distinction between core rights and other rights we must "fall back on [a] naturalist (or 'mythical') conception of basic rights"[681] – on precisely the kind of purely normative argument, in other words, which the ethos-focussed perspective seeks otherwise to avoid. There is a clear parallel, here, with the way in which Dothan acknowledges that sometimes the epistemic approach may not be able to mitigate the problem of prejudice and that, accordingly, reliance on moral principles would be preferable to reliance on European consensus.[682]

My point is not at all to criticise this argumentative move in substance, but merely to show how it destabilises the overall argument at issue: for if reasoning on the basis of the morality-focussed perspective is admitted here, why not elsewhere? Take Samantha Besson's approach as an example. Although otherwise highly focussed on national ethe and thus a strong

679 Besson, "Subsidiarity in International Human Rights Law - What is Subsidiary about Human Rights?" at 101 ("non-discrimination rights and the fundamental core of human rights"); von Ungern-Sternberg, "Die Konsensmethode des EGMR. Eine kritische Bewertung mit Blick auf das völkerrechtliche Konsens- und das innerstaatliche Demokratieprinzip" at 330 ("those rights particularly endangered in a democracy, e.g. minority rights, and those which are vital for its functioning, e.g. political rights", my translation); Martens, "Perplexity of the National Judge Faced with the Vagaries of European Consensus" at 65 ("discriminatory infringement of a right safeguarded by the Convention or the impairment of the essence of such a right"); see also, though not directly relating to consensus, Gerards, "Pluralism, Deference and the Margin of Appreciation Doctrine" at 112 ("the maintenance and promotion of the ideals and values of a democratic society, and human dignity and human freedom").

680 Supra, note 672.

681 Koskenniemi, "The Effect of Rights on Political Culture" at 148.

682 Supra, II.3.

proponent of giving European consensus normative force,[683] she has recently added a caveat to the effect that "the existence or absence of European democratic consensus only works as a test for human rights substantive subsidiarity within the egalitarian limits of subsidiarity, i.e., provided non-discrimination rights and the fundamental core of human rights are not at stake".[684]

But this seems oddly out of place in an otherwise ethos-focussed account. Echoing Jeremy Waldron,[685] Besson has herself repeatedly emphasised that persistent and reasonable disagreement applies to all issues of morality and justice including human rights, and hence advocated majoritarian solutions rather than strong judicial review, and reliance of European consensus rather than substantive moral argument.[686] Yet the same line of reasoning applies to the limits she now mentions – including the "fundamental core" of human rights, which is bound to be no less subject to reasonable disagreement than human rights in general.[687] In order to defend the "fundamental core" despite such disagreement, even Besson must thus allow elements of the morality-focussed perspective into her reasoning and build a substantive normative argument. This does not emerge more clearly only because she does not further elaborate on which specific (aspects of) rights are considered part of the "fundamental core".

---

683 Particularly clear e.g. in Besson, "Human Rights Adjudication as Transnational Adjudication: A Peripheral Case of Domestic Courts as International Law Adjudicators".

684 Besson, "Subsidiarity in International Human Rights Law - What is Subsidiary about Human Rights?" at 101; see also ibid., 96.

685 Waldron, *Law and Disagreement*, e.g. at 212-213.

686 E.g. Besson, "European Human Rights, Supranational Judicial Review and Democracy - Thinking Outside the Judicial Box" at 125; see in the context of consensus Besson, "Human Rights Adjudication as Transnational Adjudication: A Peripheral Case of Domestic Courts as International Law Adjudicators" at 61, arguing for States' "core duties" to be based on consensus.

687 Brems notes that the ECtHR may not have elaborated on the "substance" or "essence" of rights much because there is widespread agreement on these issues so that not many cases of this kind come before it: Brems, "The Margin of Appreciation Doctrine in the Case-Law of the European Court of Human Rights" at 290; this is probably true, but should be read as a pragmatic rather than a theoretical point; and in any case which *does* come before the Court, disagreement is implied simply by virtue of the fact that the proceedings have reached it (see supra, note 655); since the ethos-focussed perspective makes use of a broad, factual understanding of reasonableness (see further Chapter 5, II.), it is liable to also be considered reasonable disagreement – irrespective of whether that disagreement is framed in terms of a right's "core".

As an example, consider Judge Dedov's claim, mentioned above, according to which the right to life is a core right of such fundamental importance that "neither the margin of appreciation nor sovereignty nor consensus is a relevant factor".[688] Certainly, many would agree in the abstract that the right to life is of particular importance. Judge Dedov's concrete concern in the case at hand, however, was the right to life of *embryos* – and *that*, as the ECtHR itself has noted,[689] is an area which is particularly liable to generate controversy and in which agreement is not even remotely on the cards. Judge Dedov thus inadvertently demonstrates how claims to core or "fundamental" rights sweep controversy under the rug, and how the turn away from consensus in cases involving core rights involves positing a "core" by reference to a morality-focussed epistemology.

The same goes for "non-discrimination rights". The thorny question is precisely which specific (aspects of) rights are included under this heading. Many of the most controversial cases in which the ECtHR used European consensus – particularly its rein effect – involved arguably discriminatory rules or practices vis-à-vis intra-State minorities: that is precisely the criticism made of these cases by the morality-focussed perspective. For example, does the case of *Schalk and Kopf v. Austria* not involve an anti-discrimination right (i.e., not to be excluded from the institution of marriage) which might qualify as a core right?[690] The ethos-focussed perspective would usually express doubt as to the normative assessment involved in the claim that a certain group constitutes a minority subject to prejudice or that a certain practice constitutes discrimination as opposed to merely different treatment, and defer to majoritarian procedures as the best way of arbitrating between opposing claims – hence, for example, the ECtHR's reliance on consensus in *Schalk and Kopf*.[691] The caveat of "non-discrimination rights" as core rights thus again begs the question of how to identify which claims are covered by "non-discrimination rights" and thus remain untouched by the state of European consensus.

In sum, while many proponents of European consensus acknowledge that it should not be used in certain cases – often deemed the "core" of human rights – it is telling that such proposals are not usually fleshed out.

688 Supra, note 676.

689 See Chapter 7, II.

690 See e.g. Lau, "Rewriting Schalk and Kopf: Shifting the Locus of Deference" at 247.

691 See Chapter 1, II.; as usual, an alternate reason for relying on consensus is its ostensible legitimacy-enhancement: see the chapter by Lau just cited and in more detail Chapters 9 and 10.

For if the core is itself specified by reference to consensus, then it cannot fulfil the function assigned to it; but if it is specified in other ways, then the argument is liable to slip into the environs of the morality-focussed perspective and build on precisely the kind of purely normative epistemology which the ethos-focussed perspective would otherwise reject. The difficulty lies in demarcating the boundaries between the differing epistemological perspectives involved without a fixed point from which to do so. The notion of the "core" of a right provides a way of doing so, though without resolving the underlying tensions or providing a clear account of what counts as inside or outside of the core.

3. Instrumental Allegiances

While the preceding subsection has demonstrated the oscillations between different forms of normativity resulting from their respective idealisations by reference to the limitations of European consensus in cases dealing with minority rights, it bears repeating that this is not the only idealisation nor the only tension at issue. In particular, tensions also persist between nationalist and internationalist commitments – for example, between individual national ethe as the primary location of democratic procedures, on the one hand, and the notion of a pan-European ethos with its reliance on an imbricated macrosubject of the States parties to the ECHR viewed as a collectivity, on the other. The triangular tensions described above explain both why counter-arguments to European consensus are always easy to find (its idealisations can be countered) and why they remain difficult to put in reasoned relation with European consensus (they build on other forms of normativity). Given the double idealisation involved in the case of European consensus (first, the faith in democratic procedures that is typical of the ethos-focussed perspective; and second, the shift to the transnational level in which the States parties' legal systems are added up into an idealised form of European macrosubject), it also comes as no surprise its use has remained extremely controversial.

Why, then, has European consensus remained so prevalent in practice and so popular in academic commentary despite these controversies? Part of the answer may be that it has, rightly or wrongly, developed connotations of legitimacy: I deal further with this issue in Chapters 9 and 10. For now, I would hazard a guess that consensus also enjoys the prevalence and popularity it does because of the way it interacts with different forms of normativity within the triangular tensions which I described above. Because they are triangular rather than dichotomous (as the opposition between the morality-focussed and the ethos-focussed perspective would be at the national level), there is room for various interactions along different axes, involving not only tensions but also instrumental allegiances.[692] The easiest way to demonstrate this is to return, once again, to the distinction between the rein effect and the spur effect. The tensions described in the preceding sub-section are operationalised differently depending on which of these is at issue. Since the two scenarios, by definition, reinforce or oppose the national ethos of the respondent State, *different allegiances between the varying perspectives can be formed in either case.*

Consider, first, the rein effect of European consensus. Because it refers to a lack of consensus (or a consensus in favour of the respondent State) *among European States*, it is based on the notion of a pan-European ethos. The core tension here, as the example of core rights shows and the case of *Schalk and Kopf* exemplifies, is with the morality-focussed perspective; because it constitutes an argument in favour of not finding a violation and thus leaving the matter to democratic procedures at the national level, the pan-European ethos works in tandem with national ethe. Still, the two kinds of ethical normativity do stay in tension, even as they also relate to one another: as discussed in Chapter 3, from the perspective of ethical normativity developed at the national level the position of other States parties seems irrelevant. Thus, there remains a disconnect between the two forms of ethical normativity within the *reasoning* employed; however, in cases of the rein effect European consensus constitutes an argument against finding a violation of the Convention and therefore points towards a *result* that is favourable to the respondent State.

A similar structure, though with different allegiances at play, can be observed in cases involving the spur effect. Since it speaks in favour of finding a violation of the ECHR, the primary tension here is between European consensus and the national ethos of the respondent State. In Chapter 2, I noted that the morality-focussed perspective occupies a somewhat ambivalent position in these cases: because the spur effect does not speak against finding a violation of the Convention and is thus regarded as less dangerous to minority rights and more compatible with a critical stance

692 For the traditional binary structure of critical international legal theory within which European consensus would represent an area of middle-ground between utopian and apologetic reasoning, see Chapter 1, IV.3.; the sense of consensus as a compromise would then relate precisely to the notion of a "middle-ground" solution.

vis-à-vis the respondent State, it seems less alarming from a human rights perspective. European consensus is not supported for its own sake – the morality-focussed perspective continues to rely on substantive *reasoning* – but, at least in some cases, it is admitted as a form of concurrent rather than conventional morality since it speaks in favour of a *result* which protects prepolitical minority rights. This allegiance is more brittle than that between European consensus and national ethe in cases involving the rein effect: much depends on the substance of the case at issue and the theory of rights being applied by proponents of the morality-focussed perspective, and not all cases of the spur effect will be supported. Nonetheless, it some cases at least the results achieved by reference to moral normativity and by reference to a pan-European ethos will cohere.

In sum, the triangular tensions between moral normativity, ethical normativity coined within individual national ethe, and ethical normativity based on the notion of a pan-European ethos may play out in different ways depending on whether the rein effect or the spur effect is at issue, with different allegiances being formed. Arguably, one of the reasons why European consensus has become increasingly prominent in the practice of the ECtHR is not so much by virtue of a strong justification on its own terms but *because it can potentially strike up such allegiances with both the morality-focussed perspective and with national ethe, depending on the case at issue* – there is, in other words, an air of compromise surrounding it.[693] Promoting ethical normativity by reference to individual national ethe may run counter to the idea of review by a regional court,[694] but the rein effect of European consensus will achieve the same result. Insisting on normative reasoning independent of will-formation within individual States may seem epistemologically suspect, but the spur effect of European consensus will provide backing for claims otherwise made in the language of prepolitical rights.[695]

One consequence of thinking about European consensus in this way is to highlight the crucial issue of how (a lack of) consensus is established: since this will determine whether the rein effect or the spur effect takes hold, it is clearly of paramount importance.[696] Chapters 5 to 7 will take up

---

693 See Chapter 1, IV.3.; for more on how these allegiances work in practice, see Chapter 8, III.

694 See Chapter 3, IV.2.

695 See Chapter 2, III. and Chapter 5, II.

696 Aalt Willem Heringa, "The 'Consensus Principle': The Role of 'Common Law' in the ECHR Case Law," (1996) 3 *Maastricht Journal of European and Comparative Law* 108 at 130.

the ECtHR's case-law in that regard. Here, I would like to highlight a different (though related) aspect. If we acknowledge that the prominence of European consensus is due in large part to its flexibility in establishing allegiances with other forms of reasoning, then it becomes all the more important to keep in mind that such allegiances do nothing to mitigate the potential for hegemony involved in the idealisations which reliance on a pan-European ethos entails. It is sometimes implied that the rein effect and the spur effect justify one another. For example, the rein effect may run counter to minority rights from the morality-focussed perspective, but the spur effect actually supports such rights, so the use of consensus is considered to be justified.[697] My point here is the opposite: European consensus may strike up allegiances with other forms of reasoning (with the morality-focussed perspective, in the example just given) but this does not defuse the deeper tensions discussed throughout this chapter. Any justification for the use of European consensus in the abstract, I would therefore suggest, needs to be complemented with a more specific account of its use and the way its idealisations are to be mitigated in any given case, regardless of whether it involves the rein effect or the spur effect.[698] In that spirit, forms of normativity which run counter to European consensus remain crucially important.

IV. Interim Reflections: Against Naturalisation

My aim in this chapter has been to move from the static representation of different "pure" types of normativity to the way they interact. I have argued that European consensus might be conceptualised as based on a form of ethical normativity developed within a pan-European macrosubject, but

---

697 This is a sense I often get from reading arguments in favour of European consensus, though seldom made explicit; most clearly Peat, *Comparative Reasoning in International Courts and Tribunals*, at 157-159; Wildhaber, Hjartarson, and Donnelly, "No Consensus on Consensus?" at 251; Dzehtsiarou, *European Consensus and the Legitimacy of the European Court of Human Rights*, at 123 and 142; Robert Wintemute, "Consensus Is the Right Approach for the European Court of Human Rights," *The Guardian*, 12 August 2010. The "overall" evaluation of both rein effect and spur effect also relates to the way in which consensus is conceptualised in the context of legitimacy-enhancement: see Chapter 9, II.4. and Chapter 10, III.2.

698 Of the authors just cited, Dzehtsiarou grapples with this problem most extensively: see Chapter 8, III.2. and III.3.

that it must be viewed in a broader context in which other forms of normativity – specifically, ethical normativity coined within individual national ethe as well as moral normativity – likewise remain relevant. Depending on whether the rein effect or the spur effect is at issue, the triangular tensions between these different kinds of normativity manifest in opposition or in instrumental allegiances; because the idealisations involved in any one perspective can always be challenged by the others, the result is an oscillation between them.

This may seem like a rather mundane conclusion. Despite the occasional argument in favour of relying only on a moral reading of the ECHR or only on the position established by European consensus, the vast majority of commentators takes it as a matter of course that *some* kind of counter-point to the primary form of normativity which they champion should be allowed[699] – the discussion of the notion of core rights in this chapter is merely one particularly tangible example of this. I would nonetheless emphasise the importance of foregrounding the idealisations of any one perspective and the resulting oscillation between them because it *opens up space to challenge whichever form of normativity claims a hegemonic position*. It *denaturalises* static and absolutizing accounts of normativity, in other words.[700] In the context of human rights, this is a well-known response to the morality-focussed perspective. Because of the "moral exigency" it claims for its ostensibly prepolitical positions,[701] it carries a particularly strong tendency to naturalise them: hence the common charge that human rights, understood as innate and inalienable, claim to be "antipolitics".[702]

---

699 As discussed in Chapter 1, IV.1. and V., my descriptions of morality-focussed and ethos-focussed perspectives in the previous chapters are intended merely as ideal-type depictions of certain presumptions and epistemologies, and most commentators in practice incorporate elements of both *with differing points of emphasis*.

700 On naturalisation as a mode through which ideology operates to render social arrangements – or corresponding kinds of reasoning, in this case – "obvious and self-evident", see Marks, *The Riddle of All Constitutions*, at 22; on the aim of denaturalisation, see Chapter 1, IV.5. and Chapter 11, II.

701 Mouffe, *The Democratic Paradox*, at 24.

702 See critically e.g. Wendy Brown, "'The Most We Can Hope For…': Human Rights and the Politics of Fatalism," (2004) 103 *The South Atlantic Quarterly* 451 at 453; Balakrishnan Rajagopal, "International Law and Social Movements: Challenges of Theorizing Resistance," (2003) 41 *Columbia Journal of Transnational Law* 397 at 420; Başak Çalı and Saladin Meckled-García, "Human Rights Legalized - Defining, Interpreting, and Implementing an Ideal," in *The Legalization of Human Rights. Multidisciplinary Perspectives on Human Rights and Human Rights Law*, ed. Saladin Meckled-García and Başak Çalı (London and New York:

A similar though inverted tendency can also be observed with regard to European consensus, however. Because the ethos-focussed perspective underlying it is sceptical of any prepolitical claims to normativity, the political aspect involved is more apparent and naturalisation seems less likely.[703] Nonetheless, by taking the notion of a pan-European ethos to be self-evident, some proponents of consensus do present the use of European consensus as "natural". On these accounts, regional systems of human rights protection *invariably* call for vertically comparative reasoning. For example, Paul Mahoney and Rachael Kondak have stated that European consensus is "not merely a useful interpretative tool to which the Court can choose to have recourse now and again if it so wishes", but that it "is *inherent* in the application and development of the Convention";[704] and Maija Dahlberg has argued that the ECtHR, situated "at the crossroads of the forty-seven Contracting States", is "*by its very nature* a 'comparative' institution" and that the use of consensus "is thus somewhat *natural and obvious*".[705] In fact, according to interviews conducted by Kanstantsin Dzehtsiarou, it is not an uncommon view among the ECtHR's judges that

Routledge, 2006) at 4; critically on the morality-focussed perspective in the ECtHR context in this regard Ben Golder, "On the Varieties of Universalism in Human Rights Discourse," in *Human Rights Between Law and Politics: The Margin of Appreciation in Post-National Contexts*, ed. Petr Agha (London: Hart, 2017) at 49.

703 See Carozza, "Uses and Misuses of Comparative Law" at 1219 and 1236; on which, see further Chapter 11, IV.2.

704 Mahoney and Kondak, "Common Ground" at 119 (emphasis added); see also Zoethout, "The Dilemma of Constitutional Comparativism" at 804; Bates, "Consensus in the Legitimacy-Building Era of the European Court of Human Rights" at 45; the implicit notion of a *duty* to refer to European consensus is also treated, through the lens of treaty interpretation, e.g. by Legg, *The Margin of Appreciation*, at 106; Monica Lugato, "The 'Margin of Appreciation' and Freedom of Religion: Between Treaty Interpretation and Subsidiarity," (2013) 52 *Journal of Catholic Legal Studies* 49 at 64; Besson, "Human Rights Adjudication as Transnational Adjudication: A Peripheral Case of Domestic Courts as International Law Adjudicators" at 59.

705 Dahlberg, "'The Lack of Such a Common Approach' - Comparative Argumentation by the European Court of Human Rights" at 76 (emphasis added); Mahoney and Kondak, "Common Ground" at 120 also speak of European consensus as "natural"; Rozakis, "The European Judge as Comparatist" at 269 mentions the ECHR's "'natural' legal environment"; parallel claims have been made with regard to the European Court of Justice: see e.g. Lenaerts, "Interlocking Legal Orders" at 874 ("As an international institution, the Community judicature is '*naturally*' brought to adopt a comparative approach", emphasis added).

consensus is "simply an inherent and natural argument for the Court as a regional human rights court".[706]

Yet while there is a certain intuitive connection between European consensus and the institutional setting of the ECtHR – and, indeed, this intuition is borne out by the practically oriented justification of European consensus which relies on the transnational context within which the ECtHR operates, as discussed in the previous chapter[707] – it is important to keep in mind that use of consensus appears "natural" *only* on the basis of ethical normativity by reference to a pan-European ethos,[708] and that this sense of self-evidence is potentially dangerous since it leads to the naturalisation of one form of normativity and its idealisations.

This is all the more so in light of the argument made above: that European consensus has gained prominence not so much because of a strong justification for its use on its own terms, but because it is capable of establishing shifting allegiances with other forms of normativity depending on whether the spur effect or the rein effect is at issue. In other words: rather than accepting it as "natural", we must continue to pay attention to *why* European consensus is used so as to create room for questioning the underlying idealisations – be they those of a pan-European ethos or of the other forms of normativity with which European consensus may be temporarily aligned. Quite contrary to suggestions that the judges of the ECtHR should "commit themselves to the outcomes of the consensus research *no matter what*",[709] then, it becomes important to *contextualise* any argument based on European consensus.

---

706 Dzehtsiarou, *European Consensus and the Legitimacy of the European Court of Human Rights*, at 182.

707 Chapter 3, IV.3.

708 Or, on a different plane, by reference to considerations of legitimacy: but see Chapters 9 and 10.

709 Tom Zwart, "More Human Rights Than Court: Why the Legitimacy of the European Court of Human Rights is in Need of Repair and How It Can Be Done," in *The European Court of Human Rights and Its Discontents: Turning Criticism Into Strength*, ed. Spyridon Flogaitis, Tom Zwart, and Julie Fraser (Cheltenham: Edward Elgar, 2013) at 93 (emphasis added).

On this approach, the various perspectives we have been discussing appear less as absolute commitments and more as differing points of emphasis. The crucial question, then, becomes how they are set in relation to one another – which point of emphasis should be used in which context, how this should be determined, and ultimately how European consensus should be operationalised in practice. To come to grips with these questions, the following chapters turn to an examination of the ECtHR's case-law insofar as it relates to European consensus.

Chapter 5: Establishing Consensus (I): Numerical Issues

I. Introduction

In this chapter and some that follow, I will take up a question which I have been deliberately suspending since Chapter 1: when is consensus considered to be established – or, differently put, when does lack of consensus turn into consensus?[710] Considering how crucial a question this is to determine whether consensus unfolds its rein effect or its spur effect, one might expect a relatively clear answer within the ECtHR's case-law, or at least suggestions clearly made in the literature. Yet to the contrary, the debate surrounding European consensus trades in large part on the ambiguities on when and how consensus is established.

Given that consensus (in)famously involves "counting" of States so as to establish whether commonality is present or not,[711] a particularly evident aspect of establishing whether or not consensus exists pertains to the *number of States* required to invoke the rein or spur effect, respectively. The ECtHR has been described as following a "statistical",[712] "mechanical" or "arithmetical" approach,[713] at least in some cases tending towards "a formal approach based purely on numbers".[714] On the other hand, however,

---

710 See Dzehtsiarou, *European Consensus and the Legitimacy of the European Court of Human Rights*, at 24.

711 Ibid., 175; see Chapter 1, III. for the notion of commonality which this involves.

712 Kanstantsin Dzehtsiarou and Pavel Repyeuski, "European Consensus and the EU Accession to the ECHR," in *The EU Accession to the ECHR*, ed. Vasiliki Kosta, Nikos Skoutaris, and Vassilis P. Tzevelekos (Oxford and Portland: Hart, 2014) at 322.

713 Gless and Martin, "The Comparative Method in European Courts" at 40; Nazim Ziyadov, "From Justice to Injustice: Lowering the Threshold of European Consensus in Oliari and Others versus Italy," (2019) 26 *Indiana Journal of Global Legal Studies* 631 at 645; the mathematical connotation also shines through in the denomination as "consensus calculus": de Londras, "When the European Court of Human Rights Decides Not to Decide: The Cautionary Tale of *A, B & C* v. *Ireland* and Referendum-Emergent Constitutional Provisions" at 333.

714 Lock, "The Influence of EU Law on Strasbourg Doctrines" at 823; see also Fenwick and Fenwick, "Finding 'East'/'West' Divisions in Council of Europe States on Treatment of Sexual Minorities: The Response of the Strasbourg Court and the Role of Consensus Analysis" at 271: "crude tallying".

the ECtHR's reluctance to provide a clear indication of when it considers consensus to be established is legendary. As early as 1993, Laurence Helfer summarised the state of affairs by stating that "the Court and the Commission have not specified what percentage of the Contracting States must alter their laws before a right-enhancing norm will achieve consensus status".[715]

Not much has changed, it would seem: despite increasing professionalization of its comparative endeavours and more explicit indications of the comparative materials underlying its analysis,[716] the ECtHR has not indicated with any degree of precision when it interprets those materials as constituting consensus.[717] As Frances Hamilton put it as recently as 2018: the ECtHR "has shown no consistent application as to determine when consensus exists", and "its case-law leaves no clues" as to when it should be considered established.[718] Tzevelekos and Dzehtsiarou conclude that the Court "has preserved flexibility in relation to how many contracting parties should adopt a particular standard to qualify for [European consensus]."[719] In fact, it has become something of a commonplace that whether or not consensus exists is itself open to interpretation – as evidenced, for

715 Helfer, "Consensus, Coherence and the European Convention on Human Rights" at 140; see also Heringa, "The 'Consensus Principle': The Role of 'Common Law' in the ECHR Case Law" at 130.

716 Mahoney and Kondak, "Common Ground" at 119 and 126.

717 Critically e.g. Wildhaber, Hjartarson, and Donnelly, "No Consensus on Consensus?" at 249 and 258; Brauch, "The Margin of Appreciation and the Jurisprudence of the European Court of Human Rights: Threat to the Rule of Law" at 145; McHarg, "Reconciling Human Rights and the Public Interest: Conceptual Problems and Doctrinal Uncertainty in the Jurisprudence of the European Court of Human Rights" at 691; Murray, "Consensus: Concordance, or Hegemony of the Majority?" at 36; Howard Charles Yourow, *The Margin of Appreciation Doctrine in the Dynamics of the European Human Rights Jurisprudence* (The Hague: Martinus Nijhoff Publishers, 1996), at 195; Henrard, "How the ECtHR's Use of European Consensus Considerations Allows Legitimacy Concerns to Delimit Its Mandate" at 150; contra: Peat, *Comparative Reasoning in International Courts and Tribunals*, at 154-155.

718 Hamilton, "Same-Sex Marriage, Consensus, Certainty and the European Court of Human Rights" at 39.

719 Tzevelekos and Dzehtsiarou, "International Custom Making" at 321; see also Kapotas and Tzevelekos, "How (Difficult Is It) to Build Consensus on (European) Consensus?" at 9.

example, in the conflicting takes on the issue sometimes found in majority and minority opinions of the ECtHR.[720]

One reaction to these inconsistencies and ambiguities is to call for greater methodological rigour on the part of the ECtHR. This reaction, too, goes back to early assessments of European consensus and continues until the present day: Helfer, while acknowledging the "inevitable controversies" involved, argued in favour of a more rigorous and consistent approach; and Hamilton devotes a recent article on the topic to arguing that the ECtHR should "outline how many domestic legislatures need to legislate in favour of" any given issue – her focus is on same-gender marriage – "before it will determine that a consensus exists".[721] Calls such as these resonate, in a sense, with the idea that relying on European consensus is or should be "objective". I mentioned this perspective in Chapter 3 as part of the ethos-focussed epistemology which incorporates facts as (ostensibly) less elusive than normative claims;[722] in a related though not identical sense, objectivity based on European consensus also carries connotations of clarity, legal certainty, and non-arbitrariness.[723] For example, Hamilton argues that clarifying the number of States required to establish consensus would have "major advantages of transparency, certainty and predictability".[724]

While I do think that the ECtHR's reasoning surrounding European consensus could be significantly improved, I do not think clarifying a definite number of States required to establish consensus is a particularly helpful starting point in that regard. This assessment builds on the oscillation between different kinds of normativity as discussed in the previous chapter: for one thing, in light of the tensions behind that oscillation, I do not

---

720 See Ambrus, "Comparative Law Method in the Jurisprudence of the European Court of Human Rights in the Light of the Rule of Law" at 369; McGoldrick, "A Defence of the Margin of Appreciation and an Argument for its Application by the Human Rights Committee" at 31, both with further references.

721 Hamilton, "Same-Sex Marriage, Consensus, Certainty and the European Court of Human Rights" at 35.

722 Chapter 3, II.

723 Most vividly in Ambrus's argument that the ECtHR's use of comparative reasoning is subject to the requirements of the rule of law: see Ambrus, "Comparative Law Method in the Jurisprudence of the European Court of Human Rights in the Light of the Rule of Law" at 354-356; see also e.g. Kapotas and Tzevelekos, "How (Difficult Is It) to Build Consensus on (European) Consensus?" at 2.

724 Hamilton, "Same-Sex Marriage, Consensus, Certainty and the European Court of Human Rights" at 42.

think the ECtHR would ever let itself be pinned down to a definite number; and for another, I do not think this would be desirable since it would further consolidate the idea that consensus provides for some kind of pregiven objectivity, thus contributing to the naturalisation of European consensus in whatever numerical shape is proposed.[725]

Against this backdrop, my approach in this chapter (and the following chapters) is to view the ECtHR's case-law through the lens of the morality-focussed perspective and the ethos-focussed perspective, respectively.[726] This theoretical framework provides for a way of structuring the inconsistencies found within the case-law without, on the one hand, understanding them as entirely random while also, on the other hand, not aiming to reinterpret them as departing from some alternative which is posited as objective.[727] I begin by setting the framework developed over the course of the preceding chapters more clearly in relation to the *establishment* of European consensus: My argument, in brief, is that the various critical points raised in relation to using European consensus at all transfer over to the question of how it is operationalised, including the question of how it should be established; differently put, consensus *internalises* the triangular tensions between different forms of normativity. Even the morality-focussed perspective, which eschews reference to consensus in principle, can be reframed as depicting a kind of hypothetical or "reasonable" agreement (II.).

The controversies about the number of States parties required to establish consensus can then be seen as one way in which the internalised tensions between different kinds of normativity resurface. To demonstrate this, I will first give what I call the "conventional account" of European consensus: this is the account on which most commentators implicitly rely, and which I have likewise been assuming over the course of the preceding chapters in equating the use of consensus with the ethos-focussed view. Its hallmark, I will argue, is a focus on *lack* of consensus as an instance of

---

725 See Chapter 4, IV.

726 One might think of this as investigating the "reasons lying outside the exact numbers" involved in consensus, as Djeffal, "Consensus, Stasis, Evolution: Reconstructing Argumentative Patterns in Evolutive ECHR Jurisprudence" at 71 suggests.

727 For a similar point, though with different conclusions, see Jaroslav Větrovský, "Determining the Content of the European Consenus Concept: The Hidden Role of Language," in *Building Consensus on European Consensus. Judicial Interpretation of Human Rights in Europe and Beyond*, ed. Panos Kapotas and Vassilis Tzevelekos (Cambridge: Cambridge University Press, 2019) at 127.

the disagreement which carries such strong epistemological relevance for the ethos-focussed perspective, and which provides grounds for deference to democratic procedures as the best way of resolving it. To put this aspect into sharp relief, I will contrast it with some alternative approaches to European consensus, including the epistemic approach already mentioned in the last chapter (III.).

While there is, in the Court's case-law, considerable support for the conventional account and the ethos-focussed perspective which drives it, there are also several countervailing tendencies which bring the morality-focussed perspective into the picture during the stage of assessment. In this chapter, I will examine one of these tendencies: the flexibility with regard to the number of States needed for consensus – or a "trend", as the Court sometimes puts it in this context – to be established. It will emerge that the Court can reinterpret a lack of consensus as a trend in favour of the applicants, thus foregrounding an evolution in a certain direction rather than the disagreement among the States parties: in so doing, more substantive considerations of directionality enter the picture and thus bring the Court's approach closer to the morality-focussed perspective (IV.). By the end of the chapter, I thus hope to have substantiated my claim that the tension between the ethos-focussed and the morality-focussed perspective is in evidence within the ECtHR's case-law not only when it places consensus-based argument in relation to other forms of reasoning, but even when it establishes whether consensus exists – or not (IV.).

II. Consensus as Reasonable Agreement: But What Is Reasonable?

Kanstantsin Dzehtsiarou has distinguished between procedural and substantive criticism of European consensus.[728] The prior takes issue with the way in which consensus has been applied by the Court – in particular, many claim that it has hitherto been used in a haphazard and unpredictable way.[729] Criticism as to the lack of clarity regarding the number of States required to establish consensus is one instance of this. Substantive

---

728 Dzehtsiarou, "Does Consensus Matter? Legitimacy of European Consensus in the Case Law of the European Court of Human Rights" at 539; Dzehtsiarou, *European Consensus and the Legitimacy of the European Court of Human Rights*, at 115; see also Peat, *Comparative Reasoning in International Courts and Tribunals*, at 154, similarly distinguishing between methodological and principled criticism.

729 E.g. Helfer, "Consensus, Coherence and the European Convention on Human Rights"; Ambrus, "Comparative Law Method in the Jurisprudence of the Euro-

criticism, by contrast, cuts deeper since it rejects the use of consensus on a more conceptual level, not on the grounds of its incoherent application in practice but rather based on theoretical arguments that deny it any normative force in the first place – this is the kind of criticism commonly adduced by the morality-focussed perspective.

While there is some heuristic value in this distinction, my baseline assumption in what follows is that procedural and substantive criticism are not as categorically distinct as it may at first seem. Rather, if we take the *oscillations* between the morality-focussed perspective and the ethos-focussed perspective (with, additionally, the possibility of regarding different macrosubjects as the relevant ethe) as our starting point, then the general (substantive) criticisms made of European consensus will translate over into criticisms of its use in particular ways.[730] But these points of criticism will in turn remain controversial because their normative force depends on the perspective from which they are approached – each perspective, as Koskenniemi famously put it, "remaining open to challenge from the opposite argument".[731] Since the ECtHR gives priority to different kinds of normativity in different cases and there is no independent normative standpoint from which to evaluate this, its case-law is, in a sense, *bound* to seem incoherent. This should not be taken to mean that the justifications offered by the ECtHR cannot or should not be improved – quite the opposite – but merely to underline that substantive and procedural criticism are not entirely distinct, since the prior builds on tensions which will also resurface in considering the latter. Echoing Kapotas and Tzevelekos, we might say that "technical" issues as to how consensus is used are "but the tip of a pretty sizeable iceberg" which involves "the more abstract philosophical difficulties" in situating European consensus within the ECHR system.[732]

The continued presence of the tensions between different forms of normativity is perhaps most clearly in evidence in cases in which European

---

pean Court of Human Rights in the Light of the Rule of Law"; Brauch, "The Margin of Appreciation and the Jurisprudence of the European Court of Human Rights: Threat to the Rule of Law" at 138-145; Ost, "The Original Canons of Interpretation" at 305; a helpful overview is Kukavica, "National Consensus and the Eigth Amendment: Is There Something to Be Learned from the United States Supreme Court?" at 364-365.

730 See Chapter 4, IV. in fine.

731 Koskenniemi, *From Apology to Utopia*, at 60.

732 Kapotas and Tzevelekos, "How (Difficult Is It) to Build Consensus on (European) Consensus?" at 6.

consensus and its counter-arguments are clearly juxtaposed to one another – the notion of "core rights" discussed in the preceding chapter is one register in which this juxtaposition can be conducted,[733] and Chapter 8 will consider other examples from the ECtHR's case-law. However, they can also be internalised in the sense that differing kinds of normativity influence the way in which consensus (or lack thereof) is established in the first place. One way in which this transpires is by shifts in the number of States required to take a certain position for the rein effect or spur effect to be invoked. Before turning to the ECtHR's case-law in that regard, let me briefly connect this issue back more explicitly to the different kinds of normativity at issue, particularly insofar as the differing epistemologies of the morality-focussed and ethos-focussed perspectives are concerned.

The morality-focussed perspective, as I have been presenting it thus far, is focussed on substantive argument independent of facts such as the opinions actually held by people or the positions actually taken by States – as reflected, for example, in its strong emphasis on the is-ought distinction.[734] However, even without any concessions to the ethos-focussed perspective, the morality-focussed perspective can present its conclusions as well as its reasoning as a form of agreement or consensus; in fact, following the work of John Rawls which re-popularised the notion of a social contract by way of his "original position", this way of presentation may even seem to be a matter of course. The very notion of a (social) contract carries connotations of agreement: in that vein, for example, Rawls states that the principles of justice are conceived of as "the object of the original agreement" in which we imagine those engaging in social cooperation as "choos[ing] together, in one joint act", those very principles.[735]

Precisely because the original position is an imaginary exercise,[736] however, the agreement implied by the reference to a contract remains entirely *hypothetical*.[737] It is *reasonable* agreement in a strongly circumscribed sense: the notion of "reasonableness" implies strong normative constraints as to

---

733 Chapter 4, III.2.

734 See Chapter 2, II.3.

735 Rawls, *A Theory of Justice*, at 10.

736 David Lyons, "Nature and Soundness of the Contract and Coherence Arguments," in *Reading Rawls: Critical Studies on Rawls' 'A Theory of Justice'*, ed. Norman Daniels (Stanford: Stanford University Press, 1989) at 150; Nussbaum, *Frontiers of Justice. Disability, Nationality, Species Membership*, at 28.

737 Rawls, *A Theory of Justice*, at 14; Rawls, *Political Liberalism*, at 24-27 and 271-275; see critically e.g. Dworkin, "Justice and Rights" at 186 ("A hypothetical contract [...] is no contract at all").

permissible positions.[738] The ethos-focussed perspective, predictably, would approach the issue from the opposite direction. While its supporters also often make use of the term "reasonableness", they typically understand it in a broader sense which coheres with their general epistemology: because any strong normative constraints based on ostensible reasonableness will themselves be controversial, a more factually oriented understanding is likely to give less space to such constraints and instead understand any positions taken in good faith as reasonable.[739] The focus thus shifts from reasonable (hypothetical, normatively circumscribed) agreement to reasonable (factually oriented, unscrutinised) disagreement.

This factually oriented approach based on (reasonable) disagreement coheres with the epistemology of the ethos-focussed perspective discussed in Chapter 3 and, in particular, with its reliance on European consensus insofar as a form of ethical normativity at the transnational level is at issue.[740] Because the primary reference here is to the position *actually* taken by the States parties within their legal systems, there are few limits set on a numerical establishment of consensus. By contrast, proponents of the morality-focussed perspective may use the notion of a *hypothetical* agreement to pick up on the language of consensus and explain vertically comparative references, but the differing epistemology gives this kind of reference an entirely different meaning. As George Letsas puts it with regard to "hypothetical consensus" in contrast to "actual consensus", the question then is: "how *would* reasonable people agree to apply [the principles underlying the Convention] to concrete human rights cases?"[741]

These differing perspectives lead to differing readings of the ECtHR's case-law. Proponents of the ethos-focussed perspective argue that the

---

738 On the distinction between reasonable and actual agreement, see e.g. T.M. Scanlon, *What We Owe to Each Other* (Cambridge, Mass.: Belknap Press of Harvard University Press, 1998), at 154; critically on the circumscribed notion of "reasonableness" Chantal Mouffe, "The Limits of John Rawls's Pluralism," (2005) 4 *Politics, Philosophy & Economics* 221 at 223.

739 Particularly clear in Devlin, "Morals and the Criminal Law" at 15; for more detail and a juxtaposition with the morality-focussed perspective, see Chapter 2, II.3.; see also the "empirical" account of reasonableness in Besson, *The Morality of Conflict. Reasonable Disagreement and the Law*, at 98, and the connection between "good faith disagreement" and reasonableness in Waldron, *Law and Disagreement*, at 274.

740 See Chapter 3, II.

741 Letsas, "Strasbourg's Interpretive Ethic: Lessons for the International Lawyer" at 531 (emphasis added); see also Letsas, *A Theory of Interpretation of the European Convention on Human Rights*, at 79.

ECtHR operates primarily with a notion of consensus which "must be clearly substantiated", and that cases in which the Court proceeds otherwise are "considered unusual".[742] Proponents of the morality-focussed perspective, by contrast, argue that the Court's references to European consensus are often "altogether independent of the empirical data", "flimsy", or "yet to be rigorously tested", and thus "different from mere numerical majority of the member states".[743] This opens up space for understanding the ECtHR's use of European consensus as more closely related to the notion of hypothetical agreement (reasonable agreement in the normatively circumscribed sense), with only "lip-service" being paid to the positions of the States parties.[744] My point in what follows is not to vindicate either of these readings in the sense it should take clear precedence over the other. Instead, my interest is precisely in the fact that *both* readings can be substantiated to some extent by reference to various elements within the ECtHR's case-law. The tensions between the morality-focussed perspective and the ethos-focussed perspective thus play a role not only when pitting European consensus against other forms of reasoning, but even within the establishment of consensus itself. The following section will trace these tensions by exploring the different ways in which the ECtHR has established (lack of) consensus and connecting them back to the various forms of normativity discussed in the preceding chapters.

III. Factually Oriented Approaches to European Consensus

1. The Conventional Account: Asymmetry in Favour of the Rein Effect

Let me begin by setting out what I think is fair to call the "conventional account" of how European consensus is established. For all the controversies surrounding this issue, the ECtHR *has* indicated how it usually conceives of the establishment of consensus. Whether it follows this approach in any given case – even those in which it has recited its standard formula

742 Dzehtsiarou, *European Consensus and the Legitimacy of the European Court of Human Rights*, at 45.

743 Arai-Takahashi, "The Margin of Appreciation Doctrine: A Theoretical Analysis of Strasbourg's Variable Geometry" at 88.

744 Letsas, "The ECHR as a Living Instrument: Its Meaning and Legitimacy" at 116.

as a matter of general principle[745] – is a different matter, but the formula itself is both well-established in the case-law and commonly accepted in academic commentary.[746] Of crucial importance in that regard is that the options which the Court considers encompass not only consensus in favour of the applicant or the respondent State, but also a *lack* of consensus.[747]

On the Court's conventional account, lack of consensus becomes invested with normative force in a similar fashion to the way a finding of consensus in favour of the respondent State would: it speaks against the finding of a violation, i.e. unfolds the rein effect. As the Court has repeatedly emphasised:

> Where [...] there is *no consensus* within the member States of the Council of Europe, either as to the relative importance of the interest at stake or as to the best means of protecting it, particularly where the case raises sensitive moral or ethical issues, the margin [of appreciation] will be wider [...].[748]

---

745 See generally Janneke Gerards, "Margin of Appreciation and Incrementalism in the Case Law of the European Court of Human Rights," (2018) *Human Rights Law Review* 495 at 509.

746 Ryan, "Europe's Moral Margin: Parental Aspirations and the European Court of Human Rights" at 488 calls it "cited and recited".

747 Dzehtsiarou, *European Consensus and the Legitimacy of the European Court of Human Rights*, at 24; I will leave aside here the fourth option which Dzehtsiarou mentions (establishing neither consensus nor lack thereof), but of course it involves a further element of flexibility.

748 ECtHR (GC), Appl. No. 37359/09 – *Hämäläinen v. Finland*, Judgment of 16 July 2014, at para. 67 (emphasis added); see also with identical or similar formulations (usually pertaining to the right to private life) e.g. ECtHR (GC), Appl. No. 6339/05 – *Evans v. the United Kingdom*, Judgment of 10 April 2007, at para. 77; ECtHR (GC), Appl. No. 44362/04 – *Dickson v. the United Kingdom*, Judgment of 4 December 2007, at para. 78; ECtHR (GC), Appl. Nos. 30562/04 and 30566/04 – *S. and Marper v. the United Kingdom*, Judgment of 4 December 2008, at para. 102; ECtHR, Appl. No. 23338/09 – *Kautzor v. Germany*, Judgment of 22 March 2012, at para. 70; ECtHR, Appl. No. 43547/08 – *Stübing v. Germany*, Judgment of 12 April 2012, at para. 60; ECtHR, Appl. No. 14793/08 – *Y.Y. v. Turkey*, Judgment of 10 March 2015, at para. 101; for other cases in which the lack of consensus (as opposed to a consensus in favour of the respondent State) led to the rein effect, see among many others e.g. ECtHR, Appl. No. 36515/97 – *Fretté*, at para. 41; ECtHR, Appl. No. 34438/04 – *Egeland and Hanseid v. Norway*, Judgment of 16 April 2009, at paras. 54-55; ECtHR (GC), Appl. No. 30814/06 – *Lautsi and Others*, at para. 70; ECtHR (GC), Appl. No. 48876/08 – *Animal Defenders International*, at para. 123.

The establishment of consensus is thus *asymmetrical in favour of the rein effect*: for consensus to unfold the spur effect, there must be consensus – a "super-majority"[749] – in favour of the applicant, but for it to unfold the rein effect, it suffices that there be consensus in favour of the respondent State *or lack of consensus*. Proponents of consensus rarely elaborate on this asymmetry, yet it is consistently acknowledged as a matter of course[750] – in fact, Dzehtsiarou rightly notes that while lack of consensus is a fairly common basis for the rein effect, an established consensus in favour of the respondent State is not very commonly found within the Court's case-law.[751]

The introduction of this "middle ground" as a third category between consensus one way or the other complicates the stage of assessment quite significantly: instead of a clear dividing line at the fifty percent point, distinguishing consensus in favour of the applicant from consensus in favour of the respondent,[752] it becomes necessary to clarify which situations amount to a lack of consensus and how they are demarcated from an established consensus – how far the "middle ground" of "lack of consensus" extends, or when the relevant "super-majority" is reached.[753] Wildhaber, Hjartarson and Donnelly have concluded from their analysis of the ECtHR's case-law that the Court "frequently, but not consistently, opts

749 The term is from ECtHR (GC), Appl. No. 37359/09 – *Hämäläinen*, joint dissenting opinion of Judges Sajó, Keller and Lemmens, at para. 5; differently put, the respondent State must be part of a "distinct" minority: ECtHR, Appl. No. 45245/15 – *Gaughran v. the United Kingdom*, Judgment of 13 February 2020, at para. 82.

750 E.g. Wildhaber, Hjartarson, and Donnelly, "No Consensus on Consensus?" at 249; Arai-Takahashi, "The Margin of Appreciation Doctrine: A Theoretical Analysis of Strasbourg's Variable Geometry" at 87-89; Besson and Graf-Brugère, "Le droit de vote des expatriés, le consensus européen et la marge d'appréciation des États" at 942-943.

751 Dzehtsiarou, *European Consensus and the Legitimacy of the European Court of Human Rights*, at 26.

752 As on Shai Dothan's account: see infra, III.3.

753 Arguably, the Court's occasional equivocation as to the existence of consensus or the extent of its argumentative force could be explained, in part, by the fact that the situation could reasonably be read both as a simple majority (lack of consensus, rein effect) or as a super-majority (existing consensus, spur effect), and it thus awkwardly compromises by acknowledging neither of the two: e.g. ECtHR (GC), Appl. No. 74025/01 – *Hirst v. the United Kingdom (No. 2)*, Judgment of 6 October 2005, at para. 81 ("cannot in itself be determinative"); ECtHR (GC), Appl. No. 27510/08 – *Perinçek v. Switzerland*, Judgment of 15 October 2015, at paras. 256-257 ("cannot play a weighty part in the Court's conclusion"); in this way, however, morality-focussed reasoning gains greater weight: see infra, text to note 758.

against the existence of consensus, as long as some 6 to 10 States adhere to solutions which differ from the majority view", whereas it usually assumes the existence of consensus where it finds that there are "only some 3 or 4 countries in the minority".[754]

Assuming that these numbers refer to the current number of member States within the Council of Europe, this would mean that consensus in favour of the applicant (and thus the spur effect) is established only when around 90% of the member States do not share the position of the respondent State: asymmetric indeed! In fact, even more extreme cases can be adduced: in *S.A.S. v. France*, the ECtHR found no consensus among the States parties on the permissibility of wearing a full-face veil in public although only *two* States – Belgium and the respondent State, France – provided for such a ban.[755] In some cases, the ECtHR finds a lack of consensus, discusses various positions taken by the States parties, and concludes that the respondent State is "not the only member State of the Council of Europe" to take a certain position – a formulation which, if taken seriously, would seem to imply e contrario that the spur effect can only be invoked if the respondent State is the sole outlier.[756]

I do not think too much weight should be given to these occasional formulations, although they do demonstrate the wide range of different ways in which the ECtHR might approach consensus; but even if we leave the more extreme cases aside, the asymmetry in favour of the rein effect remains by virtue of the fact that the "middle ground" – lack of consensus – is connected to the rein effect. My argument in what follows will be that the conventional account of European consensus involving this asymmetry coheres with the main tenets of the ethos-focussed perspective. For one thing, its focus on disagreement keeps it from ceding too much ground to moral normativity (III.2.), and for another, the asymmetry in favour of the

754 Wildhaber, Hjartarson, and Donnelly, "No Consensus on Consensus?" at 259; for a more extensive and nuanced analysis, see Senden, *Interpretation of Fundamental Rights*, at 245-255.

755 ECtHR (GC), Appl. No. 43835/11 – *S.A.S.*, at para. 156; the Court acknowledged that Belgium and France were "very much in a minority position in Europe" yet still found no consensus based, inter alia, on ongoing public debate in other States; this move is generally regarded as a badly reasoned front for the Court's political deferral to France: see critically e.g. Theilen, "Levels of Generality in the Comparative Reasoning of the European Court of Human Rights and the European Court of Justice: Towards Judicial Reflective Equilibrium" at 395; Henrard, "How the ECtHR's Use of European Consensus Considerations Allows Legitimacy Concerns to Delimit Its Mandate" at 156.

756 ECtHR (GC), Appl. No. 46470/11 – *Parrillo*, at paras. 176-179.

rein effect pays homage to the continued relevance of national ethe as the primary location of democratic procedures (III.3.). To bring out these implications, I will juxtapose the conventional account with two alternate conceptualisations of European consensus: Christos Rozakis's suggestion to think of disagreement among the States parties as a kind of consensus-agnostic middle ground, which would provide more space for morality-focussed considerations, and the epistemic approach advocated for by Shai Dothan.

2. The Ethos-focussed Perspective versus Consensus-Agnostic Middle Ground

As a first counterpoint to the conventional account, I would like to contrast the Court's case-law on lack of consensus with an alternative approach proposed extra-judicially by Christos Rozakis. He would continue to uphold both the rein effect and the spur effect where a clear consensus exists one way or the other: where "wide acceptance" of a certain solution is established, the Court should "proceed to the establishment of a new jurisprudential pattern", whereas a consensus against the applicant – "a situation where [...] a matter before [the Court] presents an issue which European States have not touched upon, or in respect of which they are strongly opposed to a particular solution" – the Court should refrain from finding a violation.[757] In between these two situations – that is, when there is a lack of consensus – Rozakis envisages a kind of consensus-agnostic middle ground: "in situations where there is no consensus, the Court is free to undertake its own assessment of the facts and produce its own reasoning".[758] A lack of consensus would thus unfold no normative force at all, freeing up space for other forms of reasoning which, besides references to precedent and the like, will be likely to include substantive reasoning of the

757 Rozakis, "Through the Looking Glass: An "Insider"'s View of the Margin of Appreciation" at 535-536.

758 Ibid., 536; other judges have given indications of similar views: see e.g. ECtHR (GC), Appl. No. 48876/08 – *Animal Defenders International*, joint dissenting opinion of Judges Ziemele, Sajó, Kalaydjieva, Vučinić and de Gaetano, at para. 15, noting that they "do not for a moment believe" that one should "give some weight to the alleged *lack of* consensus" (emphasis in original); similarly ECtHR (GC), Appl. No. 46470/11 – *Parrillo*, dissenting opinion of Judge Sajó, at para. 3 (in footnote 4), who even seems to argue in favour of an asymmetry in favour of the spur effect.

kind advocated for by the morality-focussed perspective[759] – the Court's "own reasoning", as Rozakis puts it.

Yet such a proposal stands in stark contrast with the epistemology advocated for by the ethos-focussed perspective. Recall its main tenets: for lack of an uncontroversial method of demonstrating moral truth, it is regarded as "unpleasantly condescending" to privilege once view over another in light of reasonable disagreement.[760] A morality-focussed reading of the ECHR is therefore rejected precisely because the ECtHR is said to face "an epistemological quandary"[761] due to the fact that "people can disagree about rights".[762] To advocate for a consensus-agnostic middle ground, then, turns the matter entirely on its head: Rozakis advocates for substantive reasoning where there is most disagreement among States, whereas foregrounding disagreement about rights, as the ethos-focussed perspective does, implies that substantive reasoning should be avoided in favour of democratic procedures precisely *because of* disagreement.

The conventional account of European consensus could thus be said to cohere with the ethos-focussed perspective in that the asymmetry in favour of the rein effect foregrounds disagreement about rights in defiance of the morality-focussed perspective.[763] The emphasis on disagreement also serves to explain the second parenthesis in the ECtHR's standard formulation of the rein effect as quoted above: lack of consensus leads to a wide margin of appreciation, "particularly where the case raises sensitive moral or ethical issues".[764] From a morality-focussed perspective, one might expect sensitive moral issues to heighten the ECtHR's scrutiny rather than weaken it: from within that perspective, moral sensitivity would require enhanced protection from majoritarian decisions, reminiscent perhaps of those cases in which the ECtHR deems a particularly important facet of an individual's

---

759 See also, in this vein, the proposal by Henrard, "How the ECtHR's Use of European Consensus Considerations Allows Legitimacy Concerns to Delimit Its Mandate" at 164.

760 Waldron, *Law and Disagreement*, at 303.

761 Legg, *The Margin of Appreciation*, at 115.

762 Dzehtsiarou, *European Consensus and the Legitimacy of the European Court of Human Rights*, at 154.

763 Indeed, in ECtHR (GC), Appl. Nos. 66069/09, 130/10 and 3896/10 – *Vinter and Others v. the United Kingdom*, Judgment of 9 July 2013, at para. 105 the ECtHR connected a broad margin of appreciation to topics which "are the subject of rational debate and civilised [sic!] disagreement".

764 Supra, note 748; on the connection see also Kapotas and Tzevelekos, "How (Difficult Is It) to Build Consensus on (European) Consensus?" at 6.

existence or identity to be at stake.[765] Yet from the context of the phrase referring to "sensitive moral or ethical issues" – or "delicate issues",[766] in some cases – we may deduce that this is not the way in which the Court understands it here. Instead, the notion of sensitivity is introduced to reinforce the relevance of disagreement about moral issues:[767] lack of consensus "reflects" the sensitivity of the issue.[768] Bearing in mind that the ethos-focussed perspective deems it "unpleasantly condescending" to privilege one view over another in light of disagreement, it seems *particularly* condescending – dangerous, even – to overrule the results of democratic procedures concerning issues that are deemed especially important or "sensitive", and to reduce complex issues to the ECtHR's own moral reasoning.[769]

The ethos-focussed perspective also shines through in other formulations used by the Court in relation to the lack of European consensus. In fact, in one of the classic cases to first argue in favour of the rein effect based on a lack of consensus – *Handyside v. the United Kingdom* – the Court noted that "it is not possible to find in the domestic law of the various Contracting States a uniform European conception of morals", but rather that "the requirements of morals" as reflected in the States parties' laws vary "from time to time and from place to place".[770] It thus explicitly made use of a conception of normativity which – far from the universalising beam of the morality-focussed perspective – is temporally and spatially *relative* to individual States and thus constitutes, in the terminology I have been using, a form of *ethical* normativity.[771] Disagreement across Europe

---

765 See Chapter 8, III.2.

766 ECtHR, Appl. No. 36515/97 – *Fretté*, at para. 41; ECtHR (GC), Appl. Nos. 60367/08 and 961/11 – *Khamtokhu and Aksenchik*, at para. 85.

767 Or, perhaps, to hint at strategic concerns: see Chapter 10, III.2.

768 ECtHR, Appl. No. 65192/11 – *Mennesson v. France*, Judgment of 26 June 2014, at para. 79.

769 For the connection between "sensitivity" and "complexity", see ECtHR (GC), Appl. 27238/95 – *Chapman v. the United Kingdom*, Judgment of 18 January 2001, at para. 94; on complexity, see also e.g. ECtHR, Appl. No. 15450/89 – *Casado Coca v. Spain*, Judgment of 24 February 1994, at para. 55; ECtHR (GC), Appl. No. 44362/04 – *Dickson*, at para. 78; ECtHR, Appl. Nos. 48151/11 and 77769/13 – *National Federation of Sportspersons' Associations and Unions (FNASS) and Others v. France*, Judgment of 18 January 2018, at para. 182.

770 ECtHR (Plenary), Appl. No. 5493/72 – *Handyside*, at para. 48.

771 One might also note in passing that the notion of sensitivity, discussed above, is introduced in relation to moral *or ethical* issues; since the adjective "ethical" is

thus served to justify the shift from a moral to an ethical form of normativity.

Finally, I should mention the infamous case of *Vo v. France*, which concerned the lack of criminal sanction of a doctor whose negligence had forced the applicant to undergo a therapeutic abortion. The ECtHR's decision in this case revolved around the assessment of whether harm to a foetus could be treated as relevant for the State's obligations under the right to life (Article 2 ECHR). In the Court's own wording, this issue required "a preliminary examination of whether it is advisable for the Court to intervene in the debate as to who is a person and when life begins"[772] – an interesting formulation which already frames the issue as an ongoing "debate" into which the Court would "intervene", rather than a matter for it to decide. (The language of "sensitivity" was not used in this case, but it would surely have captured the spirit of the Court's approach.) Having then noted the diversity of views and the lack of European consensus on the issue,[773] the Court concluded that "it is neither desirable, *nor even possible* as matters stand, to answer in the abstract the question of whether the unborn child is a person" for the purposes of the right to life.[774]

The Court then attempted to defuse the issue by ruling that in any case, even *assuming* the applicability of Article 2 ECHR in the present case, France would have complied with its positive obligations relating to the preservation of life.[775] Nonetheless, several judges disagreed with the majority's inference from the lack of consensus on the status of the foetus. For example, Judge Costa argued that despite the "present inability of ethics to reach a consensus", it is nonetheless "the task of lawyers, [...] especially human rights judges, to identify the notions [...] that correspond to the words or expressions in the relevant legal instruments", be they philosoph-

often used synonymously with its counterpart "moral", however, I do not think this terminological choice carries much weight. See generally on the terminology Chapter 1, IV.3.; on the ECtHR's use of "moral" in this context, see also Ryan, "Europe's Moral Margin: Parental Aspirations and the European Court of Human Rights" at 486.

772 ECtHR (GC), Appl. No. 53924/00 – *Vo v. France*, Judgment of 8 July 2004, at para. 81.

773 Ibid., at paras. 82-84.

774 Ibid., at para. 85 (emphasis added).

775 Ibid.; the lack of consensus as to "when the right to life begins" made a controversial come-back in ECtHR (GC), Appl. No. 25579/05 – *A, B and C*, at para. 237.

ical or technical concepts.[776] Judge Ress simply held that differences between the embryo and the child after birth do "not justify the conclusion [reached by the majority] that it is not possible to answer in the abstract the question whether the unborn child is a person" under Article 2 ECHR.[777]

My point here is not to resolve this particular controversy one way or the other, but rather to point out that the majority's position in *Vo v. France* is paradigmatic of the ethos-focussed perspective. In many respects, the case constitutes a standard application of the rein effect of consensus, with a lack of consensus among the States parties constituting a reason for the Court to not find a violation of the Convention.[778] It is unusual, above all, for the particularly strong conclusion that it is not "possible" to answer the question whether the right to life applies to the unborn child, given the lack of consensus among the States parties. From the perspective of the morality-focussed view, as evidenced in the separate and dissenting opinions mentioned above, this constitutes an abdication of the judicial function – but from the perspective of the ethos-focussed view, it neatly encapsulates the literal impossibility of demonstrating moral truth given the lack of an epistemology that would allow for the mitigation of disagreement. While the ECtHR is usually more reticent about providing a rationale for its use of the consensus argument, *Vo v. France* thus brings the ethos-focussed perspective which undergirds it to the foreground with refreshing clarity.

All this serves to illustrate that the ethos-focussed perspective coheres with the conventional account of European consensus. However, while the ethos-focussed perspective's emphasis on disagreement to avoid moral normativity explains the absence of a consensus-agnostic middle ground in the conventional account, its epistemological stance does not, in and of itself, explain the asymmetry in favour of the rein effect: moral normativity could also be avoided by conceptualising the rein effect and the spur effect as symmetrical and thus eschewing any kind of middle ground whatsoever in favour of a clear dividing line at fifty percent of the States parties. To explain the asymmetry, it is necessary to return to the ethos-focussed per-

776 ECtHR (GC), Appl. No. 53924/00 – *Vo*, separate opinion of Judge Costa, joined by Judge Traja, at para. 7.

777 Ibid., dissenting opinion of Judge Ress, at para. 3.

778 Although other arguable particularities (use of consensus at the stage of applicability rather than justification, comparative input at a high level of generality) could also be noted: see Chapter 7, II. and Chapter 8, II. for a discussion.

spective's response to the "circumstances of politics", i.e. how it proposes to react to reasonable disagreement.[779] The following sub-section takes up this task by contrasting the conventional account of European consensus with the epistemic approach.

3. The Ethos-focussed Perspective versus the Epistemic Approach

The epistemic approach provides a useful second counterpoint because the question of how many States are required for European consensus to be considered established is precisely the point at which it deviates most clearly from the conventional account of consensus. As I noted when discussing Shai Dothan's epistemic approach in Chapter 4, it often seems to work in parallel to the ethos-focussed perspective and reaches similar conclusions as to the normative force of consensus both in its rein effect and its spur effect, albeit based on a differing rationale. Situations involving a *lack* of consensus, however, bring the differing theoretical assumptions to the fore: on the epistemic approach, they become relevant only if framed as lack of comparability among States or as an intransitive plurality of options to choose from, i.e. as conditions for the applicability of the Condorcet Jury Theorem. With the logic of the Theorem itself once admitted, however, there is no space allotted to situations involving a lack of consensus as the basis for any kind of normative conclusion.

Thus, Dothan introduces what he calls the "Emerging Consensus" doctrine as examining whether "a particular practice has been outlawed by a *critical number* of states".[780] That "critical number" is later specified as "at least a *majority* of the countries in Europe"[781] – in other words, there is a clear cut-off mark at the half-way point, rather than demanding a "supermajority" for the spur effect. If the position of over half the States parties to the ECHR coheres with that of the respondent State, consensus unfolds its rein effect; conversely, if over half of the States parties' legal systems are in accordance with the applicant's position, then consensus unfolds its spur effect: Dothan's approach is *symmetrical* and there is thus no "middle ground" left to be conceptualised as "lack of consensus".

779 Waldron, *Law and Disagreement*, at 102.
780 Dothan, "The Optimal Use of Comparative Law" at 22 (emphasis added).
781 Dothan, "Judicial Deference Allows European Consensus to Emerge" at 397 (emphasis in original); see also ibid. at 399 with a further specification.

If one subscribes to the formality of the Condorcet Jury Theorem, then this approach makes perfect sense: given the comparatively large number of States involved – and the even larger number of people making democratic choices within those States – the statistical probability of even a slim majority reflecting the "correct" choice would be quite high. Stronger majorities both in favour of the respondent State and in favour of the applicant would serve to further heighten that probability and thus strengthen the normative force of consensus in its rein effect and spur effect, respectively[782] – but they would not be necessary to avoid a finding of "lack of consensus". Simple majorities, in principle, suffice.[783]

The ethos-focussed perspective differs from this approach by virtue of its different rationale for giving normative force to European consensus. The democratic procedures underlying it are taken to be relevant not because of their likelihood to produce truth given the large number of people involved, as on the epistemic approach, but because they constitute an expression of the general will of a population expressed in an egalitarian manner.[784] Accordingly, while the epistemic approach sees the move to the transnational level in a positive light (more people, hence a higher statistical likelihood of the correct decision), the volitionally oriented ethos-focussed perspective is more ambivalent given the lack of democratic procedures at the transnational level. This context is crucial for grasping the ethos-focussed perspective's approach to the number of States parties required to establish European consensus, for it takes us back to the continuing tensions between nationalist and internationalist precommitments or, differently put, between national ethe and a pan-European ethos.

At the national level, proponents of ethical normativity tend to advocate for majoritarian decision-making by way of democratic procedures because they view this as the fairest approach in circumstances of politics involving widespread disagreement. European consensus, however, is not itself a democratic procedure but only takes up the democratic credentials of national laws *even as it stands in tension to them* because it shifts from national ethe to a pan-European ethos.[785] These tensions cannot be *avoided* by shifting the number of States parties required to establish consensus: the focus remains on a pan-European ethos which has the potential to overrule at

782 See Dothan, "The Optimal Use of Comparative Law" at 26.

783 But see generally John O. McGinnis and Michael Rappaport, "The Condorcet Case for Supermajority Rules," (2008) 16 *Supreme Court Economic Review* 67.

784 See the juxtaposition in Chapter 4, II.1.

785 Chapter 3, IV.3.

least one national ethos, that of the respondent State. However, the continued importance of national ethe as the primary location of democratic procedures can be *accommodated* within the pan-European ethos by increasing the number of States parties required to establish European consensus in favour of the applicant.[786]

It follows from these considerations that the conventional account of European consensus can be read as a result of the continuing tensions, but also allegiances, between the notion of a pan-European ethos and national ethe. This is all the more so when combined with the emphasis on disagreement among States as discussed in the previous subsection. Since the ethos-focussed perspective conceives of disagreement as best resolved within democratic procedures, it makes sense to regard lack of consensus as a reason for deferral to national ethe, where such procedures exist – and hence to see lack of consensus as a reason for the ECtHR not to interfere with those procedures by finding a violation of the Convention. If anything, lack of consensus makes the concerns of the ethos-focussed perspective even more apparent than consensus in favour of the respondent State would, for it showcases the "diversity of responses to human rights issues"[787] and the "different cultural interpretation[s]"[788] among democratic States in all its force.

In sum, the asymmetry in favour of the rein effect which forms part of the conventional account of European consensus not only prevents morality-focussed considerations from gaining too much ground by avoiding a consensus-agnostic middle ground, it also differs from the cognitively oriented reasoning of the epistemic approach. Where the latter avoids a middle ground altogether in favour of a clear dividing line at fifty percent of the States parties to establish consensus either in favour of the applicant or the respondent State, the continuing tensions between the national ethe and a pan-European ethos point towards deferral to democratic procedures at the national level in cases of disagreement among States – hence the operationalisation of the rein effect in cases involving lack of consensus. By shifting the number of States required between fifty percent and almost-unanimity, the role of national ethe can be decreased or increased.

786 See in particular von Ungern-Sternberg, "Die Konsensmethode des EGMR. Eine kritische Bewertung mit Blick auf das völkerrechtliche Konsens- und das innerstaatliche Demokratieprinzip" at 336.

787 Wildhaber, Hjartarson, and Donnelly, "No Consensus on Consensus?" at 252.

788 Arai-Takahashi, "The Margin of Appreciation Doctrine: A Theoretical Analysis of Strasbourg's Variable Geometry" at 87.

It comes as no surprise, then, that the conventional account of European consensus seems unacceptable to the morality-focussed perspective – on epistemological grounds, for one thing, but also more pragmatically because the asymmetry in favour of the rein effect means that precisely those situations which the morality-focussed perspective is concerned about are given more ground. Yet as the following section will demonstrate, there are also countervailing tendencies within the Court's case-law.

IV. Morality-focussed Elements: Trends and Directionality

There would be a number of ways in which to use vertically comparative reasoning in a manner more amenable to the morality-focussed perspective. One possibility would be to pay less attention to the number of States parties which have adopted a certain solution and instead focus primarily on the reasons which they provide for these solutions.[789] While certainly one attractive option, it is not commonly made use of by the ECtHR: it "more frequently utilizes the results of various legal regulations rather than looking into the reasoning behind them".[790] It is because of this approach to vertically comparative reasoning that European consensus builds on the notion of commonality as described in Chapter 1.

However, as the discussion of reasonable agreement above has shown, substantive reasoning of the kind deployed by the morality-focussed perspective can also be presented as a form of commonality, albeit hypothetical or reasonable in a normatively circumscribed sense. "Hypothetical consensus",[791] of course, stands in a certain tension with the positions *actually* taken by the States parties which European consensus builds on (or at least claims to). Yet there are several ways of approximating the two by shifting the way in which European consensus is approached. For the purposes of the present chapter, I would like to consider how the ECtHR interprets the tableau it finds within the States parties' legal systems by taking a different perspective on the number of States required to establish consensus in favour of the applicant – effectively shifting the boundary between the rein

789 As on the deliberative approach proposed by Fredman, "Foreign Fads or Fashions? The Role of Comparativism in Human Rights Law".

790 Dzehtsiarou, "What Is Law for the European Court of Human Rights?" at 122; see further Chapter 1, III.

791 Supra, note 741.

effect and the spur effect to a more symmetrical picture than the conventional account considered above would offer.

Accordingly, this section will explore some cases in which the Court has dealt with lack of consensus in a way which de-emphasises disagreement among the States parties and instead uses comparative references in a manner more compatible with the morality-focussed perspective – as George Letsas has put it, cases in which "the Court does not consider [...] whether the emerging practice is followed by *all or most* contracting states".[792] I should note at the outside that "comparative references" (or "emerging practice", in Letsas's wording) may, in this context, include both the domestic laws of the States parties and to their international commitments. The particularities of the latter will be treated in more detail in the next chapter. For present purposes, I will include them only insofar as they are of interest specifically because they raise numerical issues as to the establishment of consensus – or lack thereof.

The cases I will examine in this section are perhaps best described as those in which the Court relies on a "trend", since the comparative analysis is usually connected to notions of *movement, evolution and directionality*.[793] Letsas has emphasised this aspect by referring, in a chapter on the Court's "living instrument" approach, to its reliance "on *evolving* trends and *emerging* consensus".[794] As in previous chapters, the terminology should not be taken as gospel. Many commentators refer to consensus as a trend in order to distinguish it from consensus in the sense of unanimity,[795] and some have argued that "trend" would, in fact, be a better designation in general precisely because it does not carry a connotation of unanimity.[796] The Court has sometimes spoken of a "trend" or "general trend" even when a

792 Letsas, "The ECHR as a Living Instrument: Its Meaning and Legitimacy" at 119 (emphasis added); for an overview, see Senden, *Interpretation of Fundamental Rights*, at 245-258.

793 See also Sébastien Van Drooghenbroeck, *La Proportionnalité dans le Droit de la Convention Européenne des Droits de l'Homme* (Bruxelles: Bruylant, 2001), at 533; Djeffal, "Consensus, Stasis, Evolution: Reconstructing Argumentative Patterns in Evolutive ECHR Jurisprudence" at 92; Douglas-Scott, "Borges' *Pierre Menard, Author of the Quixote* and the Idea of a European Consensus" at 171-172.

794 Letsas, "The ECHR as a Living Instrument: Its Meaning and Legitimacy" at 119 (emphasis in original).

795 E.g. Dzehtsiarou, *European Consensus and the Legitimacy of the European Court of Human Rights*, at 12; Mahoney and Kondak, "Common Ground" at 122.

796 ECtHR (GC), Appl. No. 19010/07 – *X and Others v. Austria*, Judgment of 19 February 2013, joint partly dissenting opinion of Judges Casadevall, Ziemele, Kovler, Jočienė, Šikuta, de Gaetano and Sicilianos, at para. 15 ("moving from

large majority of the States parties shared a certain position,[797] i.e. when consensus was clearly established according to the standards of the ethos-focussed perspective. My focus here, by contrast, is on those cases where the numerical basis for a consensus in favour of the applicant is less clear and the Court nonetheless makes use of the spur effect – where lack of consensus was not interpreted in the usual manner as evidencing strong disagreement and thus leading to the rein effect. Conor Gearty memorably described these cases as those of an emerging consensus in which "the birth [of true consensus] needs to be induced, helped on its way by a judicial midwife that is certain of its importance".[798] It is in that sense that I will be using the term "trend".

The locus classicus – and quite probably still the most striking instance – of the Court's reliance on a trend is the early case of *Marckx v. Belgium*. Ruling on the permissibility of distinguishing between "legitimate" and "illegitimate" children, it began by noting that "the domestic law of the great majority of the member States of the Council of Europe has evolved and is continuing to evolve" away from that distinction[799] – it thus established a directionality while referring to the "great majority" of member States without further substantiating this latter claim with comparative references.[800] Instead, it referred to two international instruments (the Brussels Convention on the Establishment of Maternal Affiliation of Natural Children and the European Convention on the Legal Status of Children born out of Wedlock). The ECtHR noted the "currently small number of Contracting States" to have signed and ratified these Conventions, but in-

methodology to terminology, should we always adhere to the somewhat restrictive notion of 'consensus', which is rarely encountered in real life? Would it not be more appropriate and simpler to speak in terms of a 'trend'?").

797 E.g. ECtHR (GC), Appl. No. 36760/06 – *Stanev v. Bulgaria*, Judgment of 17 January 2012, at para. 243; ECtHR, Appl. No. 29865/96 – *Ünal Tekeli v. Turkey*, Judgment of 16 November 2004, at paras. 61-62; sometimes the term "trend" is even used in relation to unanimity: e.g. ECtHR (GC), Appl. No. 24888/94 – *V. v. the United Kingdom*, Judgment of 16 December 1999, at para. 77.

798 Gearty, "Building Consensus on European Consensus" at 459.

799 ECtHR (Plenary), Appl. No. 6833/74 – *Marckx*, at para. 41.

800 Indeed, as Nußberger, "Auf der Suche nach einem europäischen Konsens – zur Rechtsprechung des Europäischen Gerichtshofs für Menschenrechte" at 203 notes, the Court's reference to *continuing* evolution contains a "prognostic element"; this would be difficult if not impossible to substantiate at all, except perhaps by reference on ongoing debates on law reform. The dynamic element is also emphasised by Tzevelekos, "The Use of Article 31(3)(C) of the VCLT in the Case Law of the ECtHR: An Effective Anti-Fragmentation Tool or a Selective Loophole for the Reinforcement of Human Rights Teleology?" at 663.

sisted that in light of the more general "evolution" in standards, their mere "existence" denoted "a clear measure of common ground in this area amongst modern societies", i.e. a form of consensus sufficient to unfold the spur effect.[801]

Marckx is striking because it makes the importance of the notion of "evolution" particularly clear – in light of the directionality which it implies, even treaties *signed and ratified only by a minority of States parties to the ECHR* were used to argue in favour of the existence of "common ground".[802] While the reliance on positions found in *less* than half of the States parties never gained prominence within the ECtHR's later case-law, it is not entirely unheard of:[803] for example, in *Biao v. Denmark*, the Court referred to the Council of Europe's Convention on Nationality, then ratified by only 20 of the 47 States parties, and stated that it nonetheless "suggests a certain trend towards a European standard which must be seen as a relevant consideration".[804] In both these cases, however, the reference to international instruments ratified by less than half of the States parties to the ECHR must be read alongside the ECtHR's reference to their domestic laws: in *Marckx*, the "great majority" of domestic laws were said to align with the applicants' position,[805] and in *Biao*, the Court acknowledged a "degree of variation" regarding the conditions for family reunification, but

---

801 ECtHR (Plenary), Appl. No. 6833/74 – *Marckx*, at para. 41

802 As emphasised by George Letsas, "The Truth in Autonomous Concepts: How To Interpret the ECHR," (2004) 15 *European Journal of International Law* 279 at 300; Nußberger, "Auf der Suche nach einem europäischen Konsens – zur Rechtsprechung des Europäischen Gerichtshofs für Menschenrechte" at 203; both treaties were ratified by only 4 of the then-21 member States of the Council of Europe; for criticism of this approach, see e.g. J.G. Merrills, *The Development of International Law by the European Court of Human Rights* (Manchester: Manchester University Press, 1988), at 225-226; Wildhaber, Hjartarson, and Donnelly, "No Consensus on Consensus?" at 254.

803 A further example, again by reference to the European Convention on the Legal Status of Children born out of Wedlock (then in force for 21 of 47 States parties), is ECtHR, Appl. No. 3545/04 – *Brauer v. Germany*, Judgment of 28 May 2009, at para. 40; see also e.g. ECtHR (GC), Appl. No. 26374/18 – *Guðmundur Andri Ástráðsson v. Iceland*, Judgment of 1 December 2020, at para. 228, speaking of national laws in 19 out of 40 States surveyed as "already a considerable consensus"; in that case, though, the situation in many of the other States was deemed "undetermined", so a less clear counter-consensus than usual was found.

804 ECtHR (GC), Appl. No. 38590/10 – *Biao v. Denmark*, Judgment of 24 May 2016, at para. 132.

805 ECtHR (Plenary), Appl. No. 6833/74 – *Marckx*, at para. 41.

also found that of all the legal systems examined, *only* the respondent State, Denmark, upheld the particular distinction at issue in the case – between "different groups of their own nationals", and specifically between those who are nationals by birth and those who are not.[806] Both cases thus arguably involved a clear consensus in favour of the applicants which underlay the spur effect alongside the reference to a less established international trend.

Other cases have operated on a similar principle although they were concerned primarily with references to the domestic laws of the States parties. The ECtHR's case-law on gay rights is, in some respects, illustrative of this. Take the case of *Vallianatos v. Greece*, in which the applicants argued that the existence of a registered partnership other than marriage was discriminatory in that it was not open to same-gender couples. The ECtHR noted that "there is no consensus among the legal systems of the Council of Europe member States", yet it immediately relativized this statement by adding that "a trend is currently emerging with regard to the introduction of forms of legal recognition of same-sex relationships".[807] While in principle an instance of favouring a trend over a clear consensus, the more decisive point was presumably the States parties' positions as to "the specific issue" which the case raised: out of the 19 States which provided for a registered partnership other than marriage, only two – Lithuania and the respondent State, Greece – reserved it exclusively for different-gender couples.[808] The trend was thus, once again, supported by a clear consensus once the question was framed differently.[809]

---

806 ECtHR (GC), Appl. No. 38590/10 – *Biao*, at para. 133.

807 ECtHR (GC), Appl. Nos. 29381/09 and 32684/09 – *Vallianatos and Others v. Greece*, Judgment of 7 November 2013, at para. 91.

808 Ibid.; see also ECtHR, Appl. No. 14793/08 – *Y.Y.*, noting (at para. 111) that "certain States parties have recently changed their legislation" on access to gender confirmation surgery, but immediately following up (at para. 112) by emphasising the "specificity" of the Turkish law at issue, i.e. implying a consensus of which it does not form part; on the particularity of that law, see also Jens T. Theilen, "The Long Road to Recognition: Transgender Rights and Transgender Reality in Europe," in *Transsexualität in Theologie und Neurowissenschaften. Ergebnisse, Kontroversen, Perspektiven*, ed. Gerhard Schreiber (Berlin, Boston: de Gruyter, 2016) at 384, with further references.

809 For a similar case, also involving Article 14 ECHR, in which the ECtHR took the opposite route, see ECtHR (GC), Appl. Nos. 60367/08 and 961/11 – *Khamtokhu and Aksenchik* and particularly the criticism in the joint partly dissenting opinion of Judges Sicilianos, Møse, Lubarda, Mourou-Vikström and Kucsko-Standlmayer, at para. 19; on the importance of how the question is framed, see further Chapter 7, II.

The case-law on gay rights *also* illustrates, however, that the Court sometimes refers to a trend which *cannot* as easily be supported by a clear consensus in other respects. Helfer and Voeten cite the early report by the European Commission of Human Rights in the case of *Sutherland v. the United Kingdom*, which referred to the equal treatment of gay and straight people in respect of the age of consent as "now recognized by the great majority of Member States of the Council of Europe".[810] They argue that the ostensible "great majority" actually consisted of only around half of the States parties, and therefore that "the European consensus that the ECtHR often cites as a justification for finding a violation of the convention need not be a super-majority of states".[811]

The case of *Oliari v. Italy* provides a more recent example in that regard. In contrast to *Vallianatos*, it concerned not the more circumscribed issue of an existing form of registered partnership which excludes same-gender couples (as a discrimination case), but rather their access to a registered partnership *per se* (as a positive obligation of the State).[812] The consensus as to the "specific issue" in *Vallianatos* thus provided no support for the applicants, and the Court instead acknowledged that only 24 of the 47 States parties provide for some form of registered partnership (whether marriage or otherwise) for same-gender couples.[813] On the conventional account, this would be a clear indication of lack of consensus and thus lead to the rein effect – yet instead, the Court emphasised the "relevance" of "the movement towards legal recognition of same-sex couples which has continued to develop rapidly in Europe".[814] In light of this evolution, lack of consensus was reinterpreted as a "thin majority" which gave rise to the spur effect.[815]

---

810 EComHR, Appl. No. 25186/94 – *Euan Sutherland v. the United Kingdom*, Report of 1 July 1997, at para. 59

811 Helfer and Voeten, "International Courts as Agents of Legal Change: Evidence from LGBT Rights in Europe" at 17.

812 Contrast ECtHR, Appl. Nos. 18766/11 and 36030/11 – *Oliari and Others*, at para. 164 with ECtHR (GC), Appl. Nos. 29381/09 and 32684/09 – *Vallianatos and Others*, at para. 75.

813 ECtHR, Appl. Nos. 18766/11 and 36030/11 – *Oliari and Others*, at para. 55.

814 Ibid., at para. 178; see also ECtHR, Appl. No. 30141/04 – *Schalk and Kopf*, at paras. 93-94.

815 ECtHR, Appl. Nos. 18766/11 and 36030/11 – *Oliari and Others*, at para. 178; besides morality-focussed considerations (infra, note 833) another factor which may well have influenced this reinterpretation was the societal and legal situation within Italy itself, i.e. different elements of the national ethos such as indications by "the general Italian population and the highest judicial authorities in

Similar tendencies are in evidence in some of the Court's judgments on trans rights. *Christine Goodwin v. the United Kingdom* has perhaps becomes as much of a classic as *Marckx*, with many proponents of the morality-focussed perspective enthusiastically endorsing it as an instance of comparative reasoning used in way that reinforces rather than delimits prepolitical rights[816] – and indeed, the Court's ruling that it "attaches less importance to the lack of evidence of a common European approach [...] than to the [...] continuing international trend"[817] in favour of a right to legal gender recognition differs quite strongly from the ethos-focussed perspective's take on the relevance of a lack of consensus. *Goodwin* remains a somewhat special case by virtue of its reliance on comparative developments in States outside Europe: the "international trend" was not, in other words, based on *vertically* comparative law.[818] It should also, I think, be read in the context of a long line of preceding judgments which reached opposing results.[819] I will therefore not consider *Goodwin* in detail here, except to note that the Court *did* make use of the spur effect based on a trend, despite having asserted the lack of consensus.

The reliance on a trend – undeniably European this time, rather than international – comes through even more clearly in the subsequent case of

Italy" that the legislative status quo was insufficient (ibid., at para. 179); see in greater detail Fenwick and Fenwick, "Finding 'East'/'West' Divisions in Council of Europe States on Treatment of Sexual Minorities: The Response of the Strasbourg Court and the Role of Consensus Analysis".

816 E.g. Erdman, "The Deficiency of Consensus in Human Rights Protection: A Case Study of Goodwin v. United Kingdom and I. v. United Kingdom"; Letsas, "The ECHR as a Living Instrument: Its Meaning and Legitimacy" at 116; Radačić, "Rights of the Vulnerable Groups" at 607 and 612.

817 ECtHR (GC), Appl. No. 28957/95 – *Christine Goodwin*, at para. 85.

818 On verticality, see generally Chapter 1, III.; arguably, an "unmistakable trend in the member States of the Council of Europe towards giving full legal recognition to gender re-assignment", i.e. a *European* trend, also existed: see ibid., at para. 55; the ECtHR was, however, prevented from relying on this trend since there had been no development since its preceding judgment in ECtHR (GC), Appl. Nos. 22985/93 and 23390/94 – *Sheffield and Horsham v. the United Kingdom*, Judgment of 30 July 1998; see Alexander Morawa, "The 'Common European Approach', 'International Trends', and the Evolution of Human Rights Law. A Comment on Goodwin and I v. the United Kingdom," (2002) 3 *German Law Journal* at para. 33.

819 Tzevelekos, "The Use of Article 31(3)(C) of the VCLT in the Case Law of the ECtHR: An Effective Anti-Fragmentation Tool or a Selective Loophole for the Reinforcement of Human Rights Teleology?" at 663 aptly speaks of "a fairly maladroit correction of [the ECtHR's] previous case law".

A.P., Garçon and Nicot v. France, in which the Court was called upon to judge, inter alia, the permissibility of sterilisation as a precondition for legal gender recognition. Having initially determined a lack of consensus among the States parties (with 22 of the 40 States providing for legal gender recognition at all retaining the precondition),[820] it noted in favour of the applicants that "this precondition has disappeared from the positive law of eleven States parties between 2009 and 2016", i.e. in the period preceding the judgment, and that there was thus "a tendency to abandon it".[821] While the rein effect due to the lack of consensus was thus initially retained, it was subsequently counterbalanced by the spur effect evidenced by the trend in favour of the applicants – even though the States having abandoned the sterilisation precondition were in the minority.

Having provided examples of the ECtHR relying on trends at some length, I must emphasise once again that it is not my intention to argue that this is the only or even the dominant approach of the Court.[822] Many contrary cases can be adduced in which the ECtHR not only deployed the rein effect based on a lack of consensus,[823] but did so despite explicitly taking note of developments which it *could* have emphasised to precisely the opposite effect.[824] Thus, in *Fretté v. France*, it spoke not of a "trend" but of legal systems "in a transitional stage" leading to a wide margin of appreciation.[825] In the case of *S.H. v. Austria*, concerning the use of ova and sperm from donors for in vitro fertilisation, the Court did acknowledge an "emerging European consensus", but specified that it was "not [...] based on settled and long-standing principles" but rather a mere "stage of devel-

820 ECtHR, Appl. Nos. 79885/12, 52471/13 and 52596/13 – *A.P., Garçon and Nicot*, at paras. 71 and 122.

821 Ibid., at para. 124.

822 Dean Spielmann, "Allowing the Right Margin: The European Court of Human Rights and the National Margin of Appreciation Doctrine. Waiver or Subsidiarity of European Review?," (2012) 14 *Cambridge Yearbook of European Legal Studies* 381 at 406 states that a trend is not enough "most of the time".

823 See supra, in particular the cases cited in note 748.

824 E.g. ECtHR (Plenary), Appl. No. 9532/81 – *Rees v. the United Kingdom*, Judgment of 17 October 1986, at para. 37; ECtHR (Plenary), Appl. No. 10843/84 – *Cossey v. the United Kingdom*, Judgment of 27 September 1990, at para. 40; ECtHR (GC), Appl. No. 37112/97 – *Fogarty v. the United Kingdom*, Judgment of 21 November 2001; ECtHR (GC), Appl. No. 48876/08 – *Animal Defenders International*, at para. 123; ECtHR, Appl. No. 30141/04 – *Schalk and Kopf*, at para. 105; ECtHR (GC), Appl. Nos. 60367/08 and 961/11 – *Khamtokhu and Aksenchik*, at paras. 85-86.

825 ECtHR, Appl. No. 36515/97 – *Fretté*, at para. 41.

opment within a particularly dynamic field".[826] In light of this assessment, it ruled that "there is not yet clear common ground among the member States" and granted a wide margin of appreciation[827] – a standard case of the rein effect based on a lack of consensus.

These cases form part of the point I wish to make just as much as the previously discussed cases emphasising the importance of trends. Taken together, all these cases illustrate that, as a group of dissenting judges once put it in a rather understated manner, "the Court has some discretion regarding its acknowledgment of trends".[828] Sometimes, it will emphasise lack of consensus over any trends or developments which might be said to exist – but sometimes, it will focus on the directionality provided by certain trends rather than the lack of consensus.[829] My point is that the oscillation between these two approaches reflects the deeper tensions between the ethos-focussed perspective and the morality-focussed perspective, respectively. When the Court foregrounds the lack of consensus, it emphasises disagreement and defers to democratic procedures at the national level by means of the rein effect, in line with the ethos-focussed perspective.[830] When relying instead on a trend in a certain direction, the relevance of disagreement is dismissed and the ethos-focussed perspective thus side-lined.

More than that, the reliance on trends arguably connects to concerns which are entirely typical of the morality-focussed perspective. Why refer to trends in the first place? The context of the ECtHR's references may provide some clues: for example, in *A.P., Garçon and Nicot*, the Court refers to the lack of consensus and yet to the tendency among European States to abandon the sterilisation requirement in two separate paragraphs. Con-

826 ECtHR (GC), Appl. No. 57813/00 – *S.H. and Others*, at para. 96.

827 Ibid., at para. 97; see also ECtHR (Plenary), Appl. No. 5493/72 – *Handyside* on a "rapid and far-reaching evolution of opinions"; a summary of this temporal aspect is given by McGoldrick, "A Defence of the Margin of Appreciation and an Argument for its Application by the Human Rights Committee" at 29; on "consistent" trends and *S.H.*, see Anja Seibert-Fohr, "The Effect of Subsequent Practice on the European Convention on Human Rights: Considerations from a General International Law Perspective," in *The European Convention on Human Rights and General International Law*, ed. Anne van Aaken and Iulia Motoc (Oxford: Oxford University Press, 2018) at 72.

828 ECtHR (GC), Appl. No. 37359/09 – *Hämäläinen*, joint dissenting opinion of Judges Sajó, Keller and Lemmens, at para. 5; see also Helfer and Voeten, "International Courts as Agents of Legal Change: Evidence from LGBT Rights in Europe" at 17.

829 See also Senden, *Interpretation of Fundamental Rights*, at 249.

830 Supra, III.

necting them is a further paragraph which emphasises the genital integrity of trans persons as an essential aspect of their identity[831] – an aspect, in other words, which is in principle independent from consensus-related considerations and reminiscent, rather, of the kind of substantive reasoning employed by the morality-focussed perspective.[832] In much the same manner, the paragraph referencing the trend in favour of recognising same-gender partnerships in *Oliari* is immediately preceded by the claim that the case concerns not "supplementary" but rather "core rights".[833] In the preceding chapter, I considered the issue of "core rights" in more detail and connected it to the concerns and epistemology of the morality-focussed perspective. In that context, core rights were mostly used by commentators to described an area immune to consensus-based argument.[834] Here, it seems that they also impact the way in which consensus is operationalised. As Wildhaber, Hjartarson and Donnelly have summarised it: in "situations of core guarantees, [...] the Court proceeded to find a European consensus without establishing a clear quantitative majority of States as punctiliously as in most other cases".[835] The tensions between the ethos-focussed perspective and the morality-focussed perspective thus become internal to the establishment of "consensus" itself.

The implication of cases such as *A.P., Garçon and Nicot* and *Oliari* is that lack of consensus is not decisive in and of itself, but may be reconceptualised as a trend *if there are good reasons to do so*.[836] The ethos-focussed perspective would not accept this references to "good reasons" since they would not be established by reference to ethical normativity: accordingly, when the ethos-focussed perspective is retained, as in *Fretté* or *S.H.*, then

831 ECtHR, Appl. Nos. 79885/12, 52471/13 and 52596/13 – *A.P., Garçon and Nicot*, at para. 123; see also ECtHR, Appl. No. 14793/08 – *Y.Y.*, at para. 109, similarly bringing up the importance of physical integrity in between references to trends à la *Goodwin* and recent changes in the legal systems of the States parties.

832 See further on this aspect (and this case) Chapter 8, III.2.

833 ECtHR, Appl. Nos. 18766/11 and 36030/11 – *Oliari and Others*, at para. 177.

834 Chapter 4, III.2.; see also the discussion of "core rights" or "key rights" within the ECtHR's case-law in Chapter 8, III.2.

835 Wildhaber, Hjartarson, and Donnelly, "No Consensus on Consensus?" at 261; see also Helfer, "Consensus, Coherence and the European Convention on Human Rights" at 161.

836 My point here is, of course, conceptual and not descriptive: I do not claim that the ECtHR's emphasis of lack of consensus in some cases and of trends in others actually reflects (what I take to be) good reasons, but rather that it is rooted in an oscillation between the ethos-focussed and the morality-focussed perspective, respectively.

the reconceptualization does not take hold.[837] The morality-focussed perspective, of course, has no such qualms about assessing the merits of reasons independently from factual disagreement in the form of lack of consensus, and thus more readily embraces the notion of trends. By connecting trends to good reasons for supporting them, however, the morality-focussed perspective also lessens their relevance. This is entirely in line with its general approach to the spur effect of consensus as described in Chapter 2 – the focus is on *better* understanding[838] or *progressive* developments,[839] with the comparative and international materials referred to thus being concurrent to substantive reasoning rather than constitutive of its result.[840]

V. *Interim Reflections: Statistical and Ideal Majorities*

I have argued in this chapter that the controversies surrounding the question of how many States parties are required to establish European consensus can be read as an internalised manifestation of the tensions between the different kinds of normativity discussed in previous chapters. In principle, the use of European consensus is based on ethical normativity established by reference to a pan-European ethos. However, as discussed in Chapter 4, it may strike up instrumental allegiances with both ethical normativity located within individual national ethe and with moral normativity, depending on the case at hand (the prior in cases involving the rein effect, the latter particularly in cases involving the spur effect). By shifting the number of States delineating the boundary between the rein effect and the spur effect, therefore, these allegiances can wax or wane in prominence. The conventional account of European consensus is asymmetrical in favour of the rein effect so as to defer to democratic procedures within individual States in cases of disagreement among the States parties; but lack of consensus can also be reconceptualised as a trend in favour of the applicant if it is approached in light of morality-focussed considerations which it aims to substantiate.

837 Thus Wildhaber, Hjartarson, and Donnelly, "No Consensus on Consensus?" at 257 reject the reliance on trends, arguing that the Court should "wait for further consolidation and corroboration" of a strong consensus.

838 Letsas, *A Theory of Interpretation of the European Convention on Human Rights*, at 79.

839 Radačić, "Rights of the Vulnerable Groups" at 612.

840 Chapter 2, III.

When viewed as an expression of the tensions between different kinds of normativity, it hardly seems surprising that the numerical issues involved in establishing European consensus sometimes appear difficult to grasp, with regard to individual cases but even more so with regard to the ECtHR's case-law as a whole.[841] As Ost has put it, when the Court refers to a "majority" of States, it is sometimes "difficult to decide whether the Court is referring to the statistical majority or an ideal majority of those States with a high level of protection of individual rights".[842] Differently put: sometimes the ECtHR seems to be interested in actual convergence or divergence between the legal systems of the States parties, as suggested by the ethos-focussed perspective; but sometimes it focusses instead on hypothetical or "reasonable" agreement while retaining a (merely) concurrent reference to European consensus or "trends".

As Rietiker has put it: "Taking into consideration the complexity of the questions that the Court has to face, its approach cannot be a mathematically precise one".[843] Interpreting vertically comparative materials through the lens of commonality – deciding, for example, whether to read them as "lack of consensus" or as a "trend" in a certain direction – presupposes a commitment to the morality-focussed or ethos-focussed perspective and hence cannot easily be answered in the abstract. To be sure, one might argue that morality-focussed considerations, in particular, could be incorporated into the ECtHR's reasoning at a later stage, after consensus (or lack thereof) has been established by reference to numerically precise standards.[844] While this is quite true, my impression is nonetheless that calls

---

841 There is perhaps a parallel here to customary international law and the "curiously inconclusive discussion about the generality of a practice to have eligibility for custom": Koskenniemi, *From Apology to Utopia*, at 442.

842 Ost, "The Original Canons of Interpretation" at 305; see also Van Drooghenbroeck, *La Proportionnalité dans le Droit de la Convention Européenne des Droits de l'Homme*, at 533 ("qualitatif ou quantitatif").

843 Daniel Rietiker, "The Principle of 'Effectiveness' in the Recent Jurisprudence of the European Court of Human Rights: Its Different Dimensions and Its Consistency with Public International Law - No Need for the Concept of Treaty Sui Generis," (2010) 79 *Nordic Journal of International Law* 245 at 265; see also Helfer, "Consensus, Coherence and the European Convention on Human Rights" at 159; Senden, *Interpretation of Fundamental Rights*, at 265; Ryan, "Europe's Moral Margin: Parental Aspirations and the European Court of Human Rights" at 495.

844 For doctrinal constellations tending in that direction, see Chapter 8 – although it is worth noting, as argued there, that explicit counter-arguments to already-established (lack of) consensus are relatively rare in practice.

for a certain number of States parties to be clearly fixed as the relevant hurdle to establish consensus[845] implies a level of formal uniformity across cases which not only seems unlikely to transpire in practice, but also undesirable in that it would naturalise the use of European consensus and diminish the impact of other forms of normativity.[846]

We might summarise with Paul Johnson that, in establishing (lack of) consensus, the ECtHR "does not simply assess the existence of an 'objective' reality but actively constructs representations of consensus in particular ways".[847] Yet the idea that consensus does somehow form an "'objective' reality" external to the ECtHR persists, and it contributes to the idea that the ECtHR as comparatist is what Frankenberg describes as a "pure spectator, objective analyst, and disinterested evaluator" merely assessing "objective facts".[848] My worry is that if the ECtHR were to formalise a certain numerical standard as absolute, this would only serve to strengthen and consolidate that line of thinking, thus also lending more credence to the notion that this form of reality should take precedence over other, less "objective" forms of reasoning. Or, in the words of Andrew Legg, for the ECtHR "to prescribe a formulaic role to state practice in [its] reasoning would be for [it] to misrepresent that consensus is merely one factor amongst numerous other reasons, all of which are relevant in resolving the dispute".[849]

Last but not least, it is important to note once more that numerical issues are not the only aspect relevant to the controversies surrounding the establishment of European consensus – a consideration which threatens to be obscured by calls for an ostensible mechanical or arithmetical approach. One particularly important aspect is the way in which the question is framed, for example the level of generality at which the vertically comparative analysis is conducted.[850] Another question is which comparative materials are regarded as relevant in the first place. In line with most academic commentary, I have so far been referring primarily to the domestic legal

---

845 Supra, I., particularly note 721.

846 As when Dzehtsiarou, *European Consensus and the Legitimacy of the European Court of Human Rights*, at 142 deems consensus "one of the most objective criteria" in determining "the 'tipping point' for evolutive interpretation".

847 Johnson, *Homosexuality and the European Court of Human Rights*, at 78-79; see also Henrard, "How the ECtHR's Use of European Consensus Considerations Allows Legitimacy Concerns to Delimit Its Mandate" at 161.

848 Frankenberg, "Critical Comparisons: Re-thinking Comparative Law" at 424.

849 Legg, *The Margin of Appreciation*, at 127.

850 See Chapter 7.

systems of the States parties. But the discussion of trends, in particular, has already demonstrated that the ECtHR's comparative endeavours are of a broader reach: it refers not only to domestic statutes or judgments, but also to international legal materials associated with the States parties. The following chapter will take up this aspect of establishing European consensus in more detail.

Chapter 6: Establishing Consensus (II): International Law as European Consensus

I. Introduction

In the justification of its judgments, the ECtHR routinely refers to norms of international law. These references are manifold and varied. To pick a few almost at random: they include references to the human rights treaties developed within the United Nations as well as their interpretation by the relevant committees on subjects such as conscientious objection[851] and the distinction between torture and inhuman or degrading treatment,[852] as well as general principles of international law on access to courts.[853] They also include reference to regional norms based, for example, on Council of Europe (CoE) materials pertaining to whistleblowing,[854] gay rights and trans rights,[855] and many subjects besides.

An in-depth study of the ECtHR's references to international law would easily fill entire volumes.[856] Their context and purposes are manifold, and it is not my intention to catalogue them exhaustively here: I will leave aside entirely, for example, references to international law that are explicit in certain provisions of the ECHR,[857] references to international law

---

851 ECtHR (GC), Appl. No. 23459/03 – *Bayatyan*, at para. 105.

852 ECtHR (GC), Appl. No. 25803/94 – *Selmouni v. France*, Judgment of 28 July 1999, at para. 97.

853 ECtHR (Plenary), Appl. No. 4451/70 – *Golder v. the United Kingdom*, Judgment of 21 February 1975, at para. 35.

854 ECtHR, Appl. No. 28274/08 – *Heinisch v. Germany*, Judgment of 21 July 2011, at paras. 73 and 80.

855 ECtHR (GC), Appl. Nos. 29381/09 and 32684/09 – *Vallianatos and Others*; ECtHR, Appl. No. 14793/08 – *Y.Y.*, at para. 110; ECtHR, Appl. Nos. 79885/12, 52471/13 and 52596/13 – *A.P., Garçon and Nicot*, at para. 125.

856 See e.g. Forowicz, *The Reception of International Law in the European Court of Human Rights*; Anne van Aaken and Iulia Motoc, eds., *The European Convention on Human Rights and General International Law* (Oxford: Oxford University Press, 2018); for Council of Europe materials, the best overview is Glas, "The European Court of Human Rights' Use of Non-Binding and Standard-Setting Council of Europe Documents".

857 For example, Article 1 of Protocol 1: "No one shall be deprived of his possessions except in the public interest and subject to the conditions provided for by

which are treated as facts of the case rather than (fact-based) legal arguments,[858] and references to international law which are intended specifically to bolster only a historical approach to interpretation.[859] Instead, I will focus exclusively on those cases in which references to international law form part of the ECtHR's justification of its decisions (particularly insofar as substantive rather than procedural aspects are concerned), and specifically on their relation to the establishment of European consensus. As the ECtHR itself put it in *Mosley v. the United Kingdom*, international law is considered "relevant to the interpretation of the guarantees of the Convention and in particular to the identification of any common European standard in the field".[860]

There has been relatively little academic analysis of the role which international law plays in relation to European consensus – sometimes it is ignored altogether, sometimes it is accepted as a matter of course but not further analysed, sometimes it is mentioned in passing as a particularity.[861] One reason why the spotlight has so seldom been directed at references to international law in this context might be that, despite the explicit link made by the ECtHR in cases such as *Mosley*, they are regarded as less relevant to European consensus than to other doctrinal figures such as the systemic integration of international law. Without seeking to diminish the importance of the latter, I therefore begin by substantiating the connection between international law and European consensus, both within the ECtHR's case-law and on a more conceptual level (II.).

---

law and by the general principles of international law"; see Merrills, *The Development of International Law by the European Court of Human Rights*, at 207-217.

858 See Dzehtsiarou, *European Consensus and the Legitimacy of the European Court of Human Rights*, at 46; Dzehtsiarou, "What Is Law for the European Court of Human Rights?" at 112; Lock, "The Influence of EU Law on Strasbourg Doctrines" at 807.

859 See Merrills, *The Development of International Law by the European Court of Human Rights*, at 218.

860 ECtHR, Appl. No. 48009/08 – *Mosley v. the United Kingdom*, Judgment of 10 May 2011, at para. 110.

861 For example, Peat, *Comparative Reasoning in International Courts and Tribunals*, at 143 explicitly excludes references to international law from the scope of his analysis; Nikos Vogiatzis, "The Relationship Between European Consensus, the Margin of Appreciation and the Legitimacy of the Strasbourg Court," (2019) 25 *European Public Law* 445 at 450 claims that only a comparative analysis of domestic laws "can truly be viewed as European consensus", though without explaining why.

If international law is accepted as relevant to European consensus – as a way of establishing "common ground" or lack thereof among the States parties – then it can be understood as a form of ethical normativity giving expression to a pan-European ethos. It is notable, however, that proponents of the morality-focussed perspective often welcome references to international law as preferable to domestic law, though usually without setting out in great detail why this should be the case or what the implications might be.[862] My goal will therefore be to provide a rough overview of the way in which references to international law fit into the tensions between the morality-focussed and the ethos-focussed perspective (III.).

Such an account can only be tentative and fragmented – much depends, inter alia, on the substantive background of any given case, on the way in which both domestic law and international law are approached, and on the kind of international materials referred to. With regard to the latter, I will provide at least a few examples of distinctions between different kinds of international law and the differing approaches to a pan-European ethos which they imply. This also involves revisiting the numerical issues discussed in the previous chapter in light of different procedures within international organisations such as the CoE, which may lead to Europe-wide norms decided upon by only a minority of States parties (IV.). These shifts, in turn, account in part for the possible tensions between consensus established by reference to international law and consensus based on a comparative overview of domestic law: from the perspective of the morality-focussed perspective, the prior is arguably perceived as more "progressive" partly because it sometimes lessens the asymmetry in favour of the rein effect which forms part of the conventional account of consensus (V.). References to international law thus complicate the triangular tensions between individual national ethe, a pan-European ethos, and moral normativity, but it also allows for a form of pragmatic convergence between the two latter kinds of normativity at the expense of the former (VI.).

II. European Consensus and Systemic Integration

To begin with, I must substantiate the connection between the ECtHR's references to international law and European consensus. Against this connection, Andreas Føllesdal has given voice to a common sentiment by ar-

862 Most explicitly Letsas, "The ECHR as a Living Instrument: Its Meaning and Legitimacy".

guing that references to international law should be considered "not part of the consensus practice" but rather "attempts at a systematic integration in accordance with Article 31(3)(c) of the Vienna Convention on the Law of Treaties".[863] On this account, then, any references to international law should not be considered through the lens of European consensus (thus situating them, in particular, in relation to the notion of a pan-European ethos), but rather in the context of the principle of systemic integration of international law. As popularised, in particular, by Martti Koskenniemi's report for the International Law Commission on fragmentation in international law, that principle demands that the interpretation of any given treaty takes into account other norms of international law which constitute its "normative environment".[864] The justification of any interpretative decisions reached thus "refers back to the wider legal environment, indeed the 'system' of international law as a whole".[865]

If the ECtHR's references to international law are approached through the lens of systemic integration, then they are interesting not primarily for epistemological reasons or because of their relation to the States parties, but because they have the potential to introduce "a sense of coherence and meaningfulness" with regard to other norms of international law[866] – for example as part of the attempt to ensure that international human rights law as a whole "develops consistently" so that "it is possible to speak of 'human rights law' at all, and not simply the provisions of particular conventions".[867] The ECHR would then be understood as "part of a broad network of rules and interpretations of international human rights law" as a whole,[868] and this understanding would be reflected in its interpretation. This approach is often connected to Article 31 (3) lit. c VCLT, which supports its pull towards coherence in international law by providing that interpretation of international treaties should take into account any "relevant rules of international law applicable in the relations between the parties".

863 Føllesdal, "A Better Signpost, Not a Better Walking Stick: How to Evaluate the European Consensus Doctrine" at 197.

864 E.g. Martti Koskenniemi, "Fragmentation of International Law: Difficulties Arising From the Diversification and Expansion of International Law" (UN Doc. A/CN.4/L.682, 2006), at paras. 415 and 419.

865 Ibid., para. 479.

866 Ibid., para. 419.

867 Merrills, *The Development of International Law by the European Court of Human Rights*, at 224.

868 Glas, "The European Court of Human Rights' Use of Non-Binding and Standard-Setting Council of Europe Documents" at 115.

While the particulars remain controversial,[869] Koskenniemi's report proposed that Article 31 (3) lit. c VCLT constitutes an "expression" of the principle of systemic integration, and they are now often cited in tandem.[870]

Against this background, it is easy to find traces of systemic integration within the ECtHR's jurisprudence. For one thing, Article 31 (3) lit. c VCLT has been cited in a great variety of cases since its first appearance in the Court's case-law in *Golder v. the United Kingdom*.[871] More specifically, the standard formulation by which it is often introduced carries strong connotations of systemic integration: while it does emphasise the ECHR's "special character as a human rights treaty", it also urges that it "cannot be interpreted in a vacuum" and that the Court must "take the relevant rules of international law into account" and indeed, so far as possible, interpret the Convention "in harmony with other rules of international law of which it forms part".[872] Finally, Koskenniemi's fragmentation report itself has been cited by the ECtHR in the context of its attempts to harmonise

869 See e.g. Tzevelekos, "The Use of Article 31(3)(C) of the VCLT in the Case Law of the ECtHR: An Effective Anti-Fragmentation Tool or a Selective Loophole for the Reinforcement of Human Rights Teleology?" at 632, with further references.

870 Koskenniemi, "Fragmentation of International Law: Difficulties Arising From the Diversification and Expansion of International Law" at para. 423; see also Campbell McLachlan, "The Principle of Systemic Integration and Article 31(3)(C) of the Vienna Convention," (2005) 54 *International and Comparative Law Quarterly* 279 at 280; Panos Merkouris, *Article 31(3)(c) VCLT and the Principle of Systemic Integration* (Leiden and Boston: Brill, 2015), at 4-5; Geir Ulfstein, "Evolutive Interpretation in the Light of Other International Instruments: Law and Legitimacy," in *The European Convention on Human Rights and General International Law*, ed. Anne van Aaken and Iulia Motoc (Oxford: Oxford University Press, 2018) at 83.

871 ECtHR (Plenary), Appl. No. 4451/70 – *Golder*, at para. 35; in that case, it was also noted (at para. 29) that the VCLT, not being retroactive (Article 4 VCLT), does not apply directly to the ECHR, but that "its Articles 31 to 33 enunciate in essence generally accepted principles of international law"; see also ECtHR, Appl. No. 65542/12 – *Stichting Mothers of Srebrenica and Others v. the Netherlands*, Decision of 11 June 2013, at para. 144, specifying that Article 31 (3) lit. c VCLT is one of the provisions which "codify pre-existing international law".

872 ECtHR (GC), Appl. No. 35763/97 – *Al-Adsani v. the United Kingdom*, Judgment of 21 November 2001, at para. 55; see also e.g. ECtHR (GC), Appl. No. 15318/89 – *Loizidou v. Turkey*, Judgment of 18 December 1996, at para. 43; ECtHR, Appl. No. 31045/10 – *National Union of Rail, Maritime and Transport Workers v. the United Kingdom*, Judgment of 8 April 2014, at para. 76; ECtHR (GC), Appl. No. 29750/09 – *Hassan v. the United Kingdom*, Judgment of 16

potentially "diverging commitments" under international law.[873] It comes as no surprise, then, that Article 31 (3) lit. c VCLT is regarded by many as a solid justification for the ECtHR's references to international law,[874] and that these references are conceptualised in relation to systemic integration.[875]

My intention here is not at all to contest this reading of the Court's case-law, but merely to contest the *additional* claim that it *excludes* the conceptualisation of references to international law as part of European consensus – as Føllesdal implies when he suggests viewing them as an attempt at systemic integration *instead* of being "part of the Consensus practice".[876] If this claim were correct, then there would be little sense in further dis-

---

September 2014, at para. 77; particularly strong also in ECtHR (GC), Appl. No. 51357/07 – *Naït-Liman v. Switzerland*, Judgment of 15 March 2018, at paras. 173-204.

873 ECtHR (GC), Appl. No. 10593/08 – *Nada v. Switzerland*, Judgment of 12 September 2012, at para. 170.

874 Most emphatically Forowicz, *The Reception of International Law in the European Court of Human Rights*, at 25, suggesting that "Article 31(3)(c) became an implicit basis of the Strasbourg bodies' reasoning in *all* cases referring to international law" (emphasis added); see also e.g. Rietiker, "The Principle of 'Effectiveness' in the Recent Jurisprudence of the European Court of Human Rights" at 271; Legg, *The Margin of Appreciation*, at 141; Pinto de Albuquerque, "Plaidoyer for the European Court of Human Rights" at 121; Glas, "The European Court of Human Rights' Use of Non-Binding and Standard-Setting Council of Europe Documents" at 114; Klocke, "Die dynamische Auslegung der EMRK im Lichte der Dokumente des Europarats" at 151-152; and in great detail Tzevelekos, "The Use of Article 31(3)(C) of the VCLT in the Case Law of the ECtHR: An Effective Anti-Fragmentation Tool or a Selective Loophole for the Reinforcement of Human Rights Teleology?", passim.

875 Rietiker, "The Principle of 'Effectiveness' in the Recent Jurisprudence of the European Court of Human Rights" at 271-275; Dzehtsiarou, "What Is Law for the European Court of Human Rights?" at 126; Tzevelekos and Dzehtsiarou, "International Custom Making" at 318; see also Çalı, "Specialized Rules of Treaty Interpretation: Human Rights" at 542.

876 Supra, note 863; it is relatively rare that this claim is made explicitly, but the dichotomy between European consensus and systemic integration comes through, for example, in Forowicz, *The Reception of International Law in the European Court of Human Rights*, at 9; Tzevelekos, "The Use of Article 31(3)(C) of the VCLT in the Case Law of the ECtHR: An Effective Anti-Fragmentation Tool or a Selective Loophole for the Reinforcement of Human Rights Teleology?" at 640, 645 and 661; Tzevelekos and Kapotas, "Book review of Dzehtsiarou, 'European Consensus'" at 1147; contrast Glas, "The European Court of Human Rights' Use of Non-Binding and Standard-Setting Council of Europe Documents" at 115, who suggests both rationales for the ECtHR's references to CoE

cussing references to international law in the present context. However, the ECtHR's case-law itself casts doubt on this claim, since the Court has explicitly situated such references in relation to consensus. In the leading case *Demir and Baykara v. Turkey*, for example, it cited domestic and international law side by side and held that it

> can and must take into account elements of international law other than the Convention [...] and the practice of European States reflecting their common values. The *consensus emerging from specialised international instruments and from the practice of Contracting States* may constitute a relevant consideration for the Court when it interprets the provisions of the Convention in specific cases.[877]

As Hanneke Senden has noted, this "probably comes closest to a definition the comparative method in the entire case law of the Court",[878] and indeed it constitutes a rare instance in which the ECtHR, openly and deliberately, sets out its "methodology".[879] *Demir and Baykara* can be backed up with other cases that set its references to international law in relation to European consensus,[880] but as an unusually forthright and unanimous Grand Chamber judgment, it in any case carries significant weight in elucidating the ECtHR's approach.

Reading (some of) the ECtHR's references to international law as part of European consensus also explains its relative lack of interest in whether the respondent State is bound by the norms of international law referred to. In *Demir and Baykara*, the ECtHR ruled that "it is not necessary for the respondent State to have ratified the entire collection of instruments that are applicable in respect of the precise subject matter of the case con-

materials; Gerards, *General Principles of the European Convention on Human Rights*, at 97, who cites Article 31 (3) lit. c VCLT in the context of international law as European consensus.

877 ECtHR (GC), Appl. No. 34503/97 – *Demir and Baykara*, at para. 85 (emphasis added).

878 Senden, *Interpretation of Fundamental Rights*, at 225.

879 ECtHR (GC), Appl. No. 34503/97 – *Demir and Baykara*, at para. 60.

880 E.g. ECtHR (Plenary), Appl. No. 6833/74 – *Marckx*, at para. 41; ECtHR (GC), Appl. Nos. 52562/99 and 525620/99 – *Sørensen and Rasmussen v. Denmark*, Judgment of 11 January 2006, at paras. 70-75; ECtHR (GC), Appl. No. 21906/04 – *Kafkaris*, at para. 101; ECtHR (GC), Appl. No. 7/08 – *Tănase v. Moldova*, Judgment of 27 April 2010, at para. 176; ECtHR (GC), Appl. No. 41615/07 – *Neulinger and Shuruk v. Switzerland*, Judgment of 6 July 2010, at para. 135; ECtHR, Appl. No. 48009/08 – *Mosley*, at para. 110.

cerned".[881] While it does seem to sometimes attach *additional* weight to instruments by which the respondent State is bound,[882] its case-law at large confirms this approach: norms of international law have repeatedly been referred to even when they do not bind the respondent State.[883]

Against the background of the prevailing interpretations of Article 31 (3) lit. c VCLT, this approach seems questionable;[884] in that vein, for example, Turkey argued in *Demir and Baykara* that the ECtHR should refer to international law only "if it complied with the criteria set out in [Article 31 (3) lit. c VCLT], and, in particular, if account was taken only of those instruments by which the State concerned was bound".[885] Whatever one

---

881 ECtHR (GC), Appl. No. 34503/97 – *Demir and Baykara*, at para. 86; see also para. 78.

882 Even in *Demir and Baykara*: See ibid., at paras. 123-124 and 166; see also e.g. ECtHR, Appl. No. 39051/03 – *Emonet and Others v. Switzerland*, Judgment of 13 December 2007, at para. 65; when the ECtHR can point to international legal commitments of the respondent State, it is clearly able to mobilise the argument of self-contradiction: particularly clear e.g. in ECtHR (GC), Appl. No. 7/08 – *Tănase*, at para. 176, where the ECtHR somewhat reproachfully points to obligations under the European Convention on Nationality which Moldova had "freely undertaken"; see generally Djeffal, "Consensus, Stasis, Evolution: Reconstructing Argumentative Patterns in Evolutive ECHR Jurisprudence" at 84.

883 Including the classic case of ECtHR (Plenary), Appl. No. 6833/74 – *Marckx*, at para. 41; quite explicitly e.g. in ECtHR, Appl. No. 35853/04 – *Bajrami v. Albania*, Judgment of 12 December 2006, at paras. 53, 55 and 65-67.

884 Traditionally, it is assumed that either all States parties to a treaty or at least the parties to the dispute (in this case, the respondent State) must be bound by the international norm being referred to: see e.g. Ulf Linderfalk, "Who Are 'the Parties'? Article 31, Paragraph 3(C) of the 1969 Vienna Convention and the 'Principle of Systemic Integration' Revisited," (2008) 55 *Netherlands International Law Review* 343 at 345; Oliver Dörr, "Article 31," in *Vienna Convention on the Law of Treaties. A Commentary*, ed. Oliver Dörr and Kirsten Schmalenbach (Berlin: Springer, 2018) at 610 (all parties); Koskenniemi, "Fragmentation of International Law: Difficulties Arising From the Diversification and Expansion of International Law" at para. 472; Duncan French, "Treaty Interpretation and the Incorporation of Extraneous Legal Rules," (2006) 55 *International and Comparative Law Quarterly* 281 at 305-307 (parties to the dispute); on this basis, it would seem fair to assume that Article 31 (3) lit. c VCLT does *not* cover all the ECtHR's references to international law: in that vein e.g. Senden, *Interpretation of Fundamental Rights*, at 243; and, more critically, von Ungern-Sternberg, "Die Konsensmethode des EGMR. Eine kritische Bewertung mit Blick auf das völkerrechtliche Konsens- und das innerstaatliche Demokratieprinzip" at 333; Wildhaber, Hjartarson, and Donnelly, "No Consensus on Consensus?" at 254.

885 ECtHR (GC), Appl. No. 34503/97 – *Demir and Baykara*, at para. 61.

makes of this approach within the framework of the VCLT,[886] the issue resolves itself into a familiar tension if the references to international law are conceptualised as part of European consensus: for better or for worse, the notion of a pan-European ethos shifts the focus from the position of the individual respondent State to a more general consideration of the *collectivity* of the States parties.[887] This is precisely the point made by the ECtHR in *Demir and Baykara*, where it states that while ratification by the respondent State is not necessary, it will instead pay attention to whether

> the relevant international instruments denote a continuous evolution in the norms and principles applied in international law or in the domestic law of the majority of member States of the Council of Europe and show, in a precise area, that there is common ground in modern societies (see, *mutatis mutandis*, *Marckx*, cited above, § 41).[888]

The connection to European consensus comes through clearly here – in the dual reference to norms of international law and domestic law, but especially in the orientation towards the "majority" of the States parties which is taken to denote "common ground", and not least in the citation of *Marckx*.

On this approach, obligations of the States parties under international law are conceived of, in parallel to the position of their domestic legal systems, as a way of establishing (lack of) European consensus. Just as domestic laws may be tallied up to construct "common ground", so may ratification of treaties, votes cast to create secondary international law, and the like: they, too, create "common ground" or "common international-law standards".[889] The way in which international documents are tied back to the States parties' positions comes through quite clearly, for example, in the case of *M.C. v. Bulgaria*, in which the ECtHR referred to certain standards for the protection of women against violence (specifically, that showing "signs of resistance" against non-consensual sexual acts is not necessary to trigger such protection) as set forth in a recommendation of the CoE's Committee of Ministers (CoM). The ECtHR cited these standards not only

886 For an argument in favour of a more flexible approach than the traditionalist picture sketched in footnote 884, see Rietiker, "The Principle of 'Effectiveness' in the Recent Jurisprudence of the European Court of Human Rights" at 274.

887 Chapter 3, IV.3.

888 ECtHR (GC), Appl. No. 34503/97 – *Demir and Baykara*, at para. 86.

889 Both formulations are used in ECtHR, Appl. Nos. 48151/11 and 77769/13 – *National Federation of Sportspersons' Associations and Unions (FNASS) and Others*, at para. 181.

by direct reference to the CoM itself, but rather, tellingly, as an agreement among "the member States of the Council of Europe, *through* the Committee of Ministers".[890] The international document is thus taken to reflect back on the States parties. In light of all this, then, it would seem that the ECtHR – at least in some contexts – views norms of international law as an indication of the States parties' values,[891] and thus places them in relation to European consensus.[892]

Again, consensus need not be the *only* framework applicable to the ECtHR's references to international law. I have aimed to demonstrate in this section that such references can, rather, be viewed within *different* frameworks. In particular, they can be read as referring back to general international law in the interest of coherence of a larger system (systemic integration) or as part of an assessment as to whether there is common ground on a certain issue among the States parties (European consensus). The framework of systemic integration can be applied, based on dominant interpretations of Article 31 (3) lit. c VCLT, to those cases in which all States parties to the dispute including the respondent State are bound by the international norm at issue; the framework of European consensus, since it builds on "common ground" but not unanimity among the States parties, can be applied in a broader range of cases.

I would suggest that both frameworks are present within the ECtHR's case-law: while the ECtHR sometimes refers to international law without further specifying its rationale for doing so and sometimes – as showcased above – connects it to either consensus or systemic integration, either rationale may be in evidence regardless of whether it was made explicit by

890 ECtHR, Appl. No. 39272/98 – *M.C.*, at para. 162 (emphasis added); see also, e contrario, ECtHR (GC), Appl. No. 34503/97 – *Demir and Baykara*, at para. 75; further on CoM recommendations infra, IV.3.

891 Von Ungern-Sternberg, "Die Konsensmethode des EGMR. Eine kritische Bewertung mit Blick auf das völkerrechtliche Konsens- und das innerstaatliche Demokratieprinzip" at 331.

892 For accounts mentioning international law in relation to European consensus, see e.g. Dzehtsiarou, *European Consensus and the Legitimacy of the European Court of Human Rights*, at 46 and 49; Helfer, "Consensus, Coherence and the European Convention on Human Rights" at 161-162; Ambrus, "Comparative Law Method in the Jurisprudence of the European Court of Human Rights in the Light of the Rule of Law" at 362-363; Koch and Vedsted-Hansen, "International Human Rights and National Legislatures - Conflict or Balance?" at 12; Fenwick, "Same-sex Unions at the Strasbourg Court in a Divided Europe: Driving Forward Reform or Protecting the Court's Authority via Consensus Analysis?" at 251.

the ECtHR, depending on the international norm at issue and whether it binds all States parties to the ECHR or not. Where an analysis based on systemic integration would regard the ECtHR's international law references as evidence of an overarching system of international law (horizontal connections between different treaties, as it were), approaching them through the lens of European consensus connects norms of international law back, vertically, to the States parties to the ECHR. Systemic integration and European consensus thus form different perspectives which often overlap,[893] though they may also conflict with one another.[894] My focus here will be less on the possible tensions between the two frameworks; rather, having established that the ECtHR's references relate, inter alia, to European consensus, I will focus in the following sections on the continuing tensions *within* that framework, particularly those between the morality-focussed and the ethos-focussed perspective.

III. Ethos-focussed and Morality-focussed Perspectives on International Law

The vertical connection of norms of international law to the States parties to the ECHR, I have argued, allows them to be understood as "common ground" and thus supplies the backdrop for inclusion of international law references in the establishment of European consensus. Because international law references are read through the lens of commonality, this approach resonates with the kind of relative normativity undergirding the ethos-focussed perspective. In line with the internationalist precommitment that is typical of European consensus, the search for "common ground" at the transnational level shifts the focus from individual States to the collective will of a majority of the States parties, which builds on individual national ethe but may also stand in conflict with them.[895]

---

893 See Pascual-Vives, *Consensus-Based Interpretation of Regional Human Rights Treaties*, chapter 5, for an analysis of consensus-based reasoning that is also very strongly driven by anti-fragmentation concerns.

894 Tzevelekos, "The Use of Article 31(3)(C) of the VCLT in the Case Law of the ECtHR: An Effective Anti-Fragmentation Tool or a Selective Loophole for the Reinforcement of Human Rights Teleology?" at 664.

895 Hence the criticism by von Ungern-Sternberg, "Die Konsensmethode des EGMR. Eine kritische Bewertung mit Blick auf das völkerrechtliche Konsens- und das innerstaatliche Demokratieprinzip" at 332-334, though framed in more doctrinal terms, coheres with her larger framework based on the principles of sovereignty and democracy; see also Tzevelekos, "The Use of Article 31(3)(C) of

As for the democratic concerns underlying the ethos-focussed perspective, even when developed by reference to a pan-European ethos, there is room for differentiation. Intuitively, international law seems more removed from democratic procedures at the national level than domestic law – accordingly, it comes as no surprise that some proponents of the ethos-focussed perspective are more sceptical of the prior than the latter.[896] We might say that the positions taken by States in international law are *externalised* from their domestic procedures. The details will depend on the kind of international law at issue;[897] but the paradigmatic example of an international treaty demonstrates that this need not necessarily signal a *disconnect* from democratic procedures at the national level, for example in the form of parliamentary assent to treaty ratification.[898]

Even when the connection to democratic procedures at the national level is more tenuous – for example, by virtue of democratic accountability of the executive representatives making decisions at the transnational level – any international norms that can be connected back to the States parties of the ECHR can be considered, in some sense, grounded in State will. They thus represent not only the ethical-volitional orientation of the ethos-focussed perspective, but also its aversion to moral-cognitive reasoning which privileges the views of some over others despite reasonable disagreement.[899] Vestiges of these epistemological concerns can perhaps be found in *Demir and Baykara*, when the ECtHR notes that it relies on the "common international or domestic law standards of European States", i.e. European consensus, when it "is called upon to clarify the scope of a Con-

---

the VCLT in the Case Law of the ECtHR: An Effective Anti-Fragmentation Tool or a Selective Loophole for the Reinforcement of Human Rights Teleology?" at 655, who points out that, for "a traditional international lawyer", *Demir and Baykara* "absolutely neglects states' will": this is true insofar as it refers to *individual* States' will; given the voluntarist element inherent in international law (which I will expand on in a moment), it is less evident with regard to the *community* of States parties; for the parallel to consensus based on domestic law with regard to possible counter-arguments based on "contextual factors" within individual national ethe, see Brems, *Human Rights: Universality and Diversity*, at 421; on that point, see further Chapter 8, III.3.

896 Wildhaber, Hjartarson, and Donnelly, "No Consensus on Consensus?" at 254.

897 See further infra, IV.

898 For a global overview demonstrating the involvement of parliaments in international law-making, see Oona A. Hathaway, "Treaties' End: The Past, Present, and Future of International Lawmaking in the United States," (2008) 117 *Yale Law Journal* 1236 at 1362-1372.

899 See generally Chapter 3, II.

vention provision that more conventional means of interpretation have not enabled it to establish with a sufficient degree of certainty".[900] If one understands the "more conventional means of interpretation" to include the kind of substantive reasoning preferred by the morality-focussed perspective, then European consensus, *including consensus based on international law*, supplies a more ethically grounded counterpoint to its epistemological weaknesses which the ECtHR implicitly admits to. In Geir Ulfstein's words: "One reason for relying on international instruments is that such practice represents objective factors, rather than the Court's subjective assessment or its own 'moral reading' of the Convention".[901]

Conversely, the morality-focussed perspective's epistemology leads it to be wary of the ethical-volitional aspect of international law. International law is no less politically determined than domestic law, and hence stands in tension to the morality-focussed perspective's focus on protecting *prepolitical* rights. It is based, after all, at least in part on the will of States,[902] perhaps most clearly in the case of treaties which showcase "the voluntarist element in international law (the right to decide which treatises to sign up to, pull out of, or enter reservations to)".[903] Even human rights treaties are politically determined in this sense: while they "may be allowed to operate in discreet [legal] regimes, they ultimately do so at the discretion of the very subjects they seek to constrain",[904] and their content is likewise mediated by State consent – thus embodying a paradox very similar to that criti-

900 ECtHR (GC), Appl. No. 34503/97 – *Demir and Baykara*, at para. 76.

901 Ulfstein, "Evolutive Interpretation in the Light of Other International Instruments: Law and Legitimacy" at 92.

902 On the tension between will and knowledge in international law, see generally Chapter 1, IV.3.

903 Saladin Meckled-García and Başak Çalı, "Lost in Translation. The Human Rights Ideal and International Human Rights Law," in *The Legalization of Human Rights. Multidisciplinary Perspectives on Human Rights and Human Rights Law*, ed. Saladin Meckled-García and Başak Çalı (London and New York: Routledge, 2006) at 24; see also Legg, *The Margin of Appreciation*, at 104; see further the volitionally oriented definition of treaties as "contracts between sovereign states" by Wildhaber, Hjartarson, and Donnelly, "No Consensus on Consensus?" at 253; the voluntarist element of international law is (over-)emphasised by Pascual-Vives, *Consensus-Based Interpretation of Regional Human Rights Treaties*, at 14.

904 Mégret, "The Apology of Utopia" at 470; see also Matthew Craven, "Legal Differentiation and the Concept of the Human Rights Treaty in International Law," (2000) 11 *European Journal of International Law* 489 at 493; Martti Koskenniemi, "The Pull of the Mainstream," (1989-1990) 88 *Michigan Law Review* 1946 at 1951.

cised by the morality-focussed perspective in the context of consensus based on domestic law.[905]

Because international law is thus based, at least in part, on the will of States – determined either by the same majoritarian procedures which are criticised in the context of consensus based on domestic law, or otherwise by State elites who are unlikely to be attuned to minority concerns – it is unlikely to be free from moralistic preferences or, more broadly, the perpetuation of various prejudices.[906] Accordingly, proponents of the morality-focussed perspective tend to view references to international law as merely concurrent to substantive normative reasoning, and retain a position from which to criticise international law, including international human rights law.[907]

Like consensus based on domestic law, then, references to international law are viewed, in principle, only as a "secondary source supporting the interpretation already warranted by other sources".[908] However, a brief glance at the primary proponents of the morality-focussed perspective in the academic literature on European consensus also makes it apparent that references to international law are commonly deemed more acceptable than consensus based on domestic law, as when George Letsas approvingly notes the ECtHR's turn to "evidence of common ground and trends of evolution in international law materials".[909] Where reliance on domestic law is read as retroactive, international law is more likely to be read as "progressive".[910] Why?

I would submit that international law is perceived as more "progressive" than domestic law by proponents of the morality-focussed perspective for two interrelated reasons, which we might call *form* and *content*. With regard to form, the *externalisation* of international law from domestic procedures constitutes its key characteristic: because international law is exter-

---

905 See Chapter 2, II.2.

906 See more generally the human rights critiques cited in Chapter 11, II. and III. – although such accounts typically stand diametrically opposed to the morality-focussed view in that they do not seek to establish certain standards as prepolitical, and their critique is accordingly not limited to the voluntarist elements within international law.

907 E.g. very clearly Letsas, "Strasbourg's Interpretive Ethic: Lessons for the International Lawyer" at 539-540; Griffin, *On Human Rights*, at 5 and 192.

908 Koch and Vedsted-Hansen, "International Human Rights and National Legislatures - Conflict or Balance?" at 12 (on international soft law).

909 Letsas, "The ECHR as a Living Instrument: Its Meaning and Legitimacy" at 116.

910 E.g. Radačić, "Rights of the Vulnerable Groups" at 605 and 608; see generally Chapter 2, III.

nalised as a standard which the States parties *should* adhere to – by contrast to their domestic laws *as they stand* – it carries a formally more aspirational quality. Where consensus based on domestic law is perceived as merely rubber-stamping the status quo,[911] international law may form part of the status quo but *also* retains an aspirational quality by virtue of the demands it makes of States. Differently put: although the volitional element inherent in international law connects it back to the States parties, its simultaneous externalisation from them opens up space for scenarios in which "the current domestic practice of states does not yet conform to [its] lofty aspiration".[912]

Because this line of reasoning relates to formal points only, however, its significance remains limited: the depiction of international law as aspirational only holds true so long as the standards set by international norms are also deemed substantively valuable. This is where the *content* of the ECtHR's references to international law enters the picture: while the ECtHR does not always use them to argue in favour of broad interpretations of the ECHR,[913] it does refer most often to other norms of international *human rights* law,[914] and these tend to cohere with the positions advocated for by proponents of the morality-focussed perspective and usually gathered under the banner of "liberalism".[915] So long as this rough coherence in substance persists, the ECtHR's references to international (human rights) law can be deemed both formally and substantively aspirational by proponents of the morality-focussed perspective.

In sum, references to international law as part of European consensus can be understood as a form of ethical normativity by reference to a pan-European ethos – in principle similar to European consensus based on domestic law, but with some measure of caution called for depending on the way in which international law is externalised from democratic procedures

---

911 See Chapter 2, II.3.

912 Helfer, "Consensus, Coherence and the European Convention on Human Rights" at 162.

913 See infra, V.

914 One of its standard introductory formulations (often when citing Article 31 (3) lit. c VCLT) is that it takes into account relevant rules of international law, and "in particular" those of human rights law: see e.g. ECtHR, Appl. No. 31045/10 – *National Union of Rail, Maritime and Transport Workers*, at para. 76; ECtHR, Appl. Nos. 78028/01 and 78030/01 – *Pini and Others v. Romania*, Judgment of 22 June 2004, at para. 138; ECtHR (GC), Appl. No. 51357/07 – *Naït-Liman*, at para. 174.

915 As with Dworkin's theory and its application to the ECHR by Letsas, discussed in Chapter 2.

at the national level. From the morality-focussed perspective, conversely, it is the volitional element contained in international law which calls for caution, whereas its aspirational quality makes it a more acceptable reference point than domestic law; accordingly, allegiances between the morality-focussed perspective and international law are more common than when consensus based on domestic law is at issue.[916]

Gerald Neuman has aptly summarised the resulting ambiguities: on his account, references to international law contain different aspects, including "consensual" aspects – i.e. the consensual acts of State will which give "positive force as international law" to treaties – and "suprapositive" aspects, i.e. the "moral authority" which human rights provisions claim "independent of or prior to their embodiment in positive law".[917] Because norms of international (human rights) law combine these aspects and reference to them may, accordingly, "be justified from any of these […] perspectives, individually or in combination", they perpetuate the tension between what I have been calling the morality-focussed perspective and the ethos-focussed perspective.[918] The following section will delve into this tension in more depth by considering some of various norms of international law which the ECtHR refers to and their different ways of establishing ethical normativity at the pan-European level.

IV. Different Kinds of Regional and International Law

1. Taxonomies of International Law References

The ECtHR refers to a number of different instruments of international law in its efforts to establish European consensus – indeed, it has acknowledged the "[d]iversity of international texts and instruments used for the

916 See generally Chapter 4, III.3.

917 Neuman, "Import, Export, and Regional Consent in the Inter-American Court of Human Rights" at 111; a similar distinction is between the form and function of human rights treaties: see Craven, "Legal Differentiation and the Concept of the Human Rights Treaty in International Law" at 493; Neuman also refers to a third, "institutional" aspect which I leave aside here; it partly overlaps, however, with the argument of consensus as legitimacy-enhancement which I consider in more detail in Chapters 9 and 10.

918 Neuman, "Import, Export, and Regional Consent in the Inter-American Court of Human Rights" at 111.

interpretation of the Convention".[919] Various taxonomies have been proposed: Magdalena Forowicz, for example, has distinguished between legal texts relating to the European Union (EU), the CoE, and the global international legal order.[920] Others have also distinguished between what could loosely be described as different kinds of sources of (primary or secondary) international law[921] – for example, between treaties, customary international law, the decisions of judicial or quasi-judicial bodies, and various declarations or resolutions.

The reason for distinguishing sources along these lines lies in the different ways in which they are established and in the differing number of States parties sharing any given position, which in turn means that they relate in different ways to the triangular tensions between moral normativity and ethical normativity at the national and the pan-European levels. The ECtHR itself does not usually distinguish, at least not explicitly, between different sources of law or the organs, procedures or contexts from which they originate.[922] Yet there are clear differences in the way different kinds of international law can (or cannot) be understood as an expression of a pan-European ethos: for example, in the case of treaties, the measure of "common ground" depends on the number of ratifications, which may vary according to the treaty; and for secondary law of international organisations, it depends on the voting rules and procedures of the organisation at issue.

My intention here is neither to provide any kind of exhaustive taxonomy nor a detailed empirical assessment of the ECtHR's case-law with regard to its manifold references to international law. Instead, I would merely like to briefly discuss some instances so as to consider, by way of example, the conceptual implications for European consensus if different kinds of international law are referred to – in particular, the differing implications for

---

919 ECtHR (GC), Appl. No. 34503/97 – *Demir and Baykara*, chapeau to para. 69.

920 Forowicz, *The Reception of International Law in the European Court of Human Rights*, at 3; echoed e.g. by Klocke, "Die dynamische Auslegung der EMRK im Lichte der Dokumente des Europarats" at 150; similarly Ambrus, "Comparative Law Method in the Jurisprudence of the European Court of Human Rights in the Light of the Rule of Law" at 363.

921 These distinctions are sometimes mentioned in passing, though often entangled with the previously mentioned differences in scope of applicability: see e.g. Legg, *The Margin of Appreciation*, at 130; Senden, *Interpretation of Fundamental Rights*, at 256; Dzehtsiarou, *European Consensus and the Legitimacy of the European Court of Human Rights*, at 48-49.

922 See Glas, "The European Court of Human Rights' Use of Non-Binding and Standard-Setting Council of Europe Documents" at 103-104.

the way in which a pan-European ethos is expressed. I begin by tracing Forowicz's distinction between EU law (2.), materials originating in the CoE (3.), and global international law (4.), in each case discussing the numerical issues involved insofar as generalisations can be made. I then briefly discuss the special case of soft law (5.). For all their differences, I would argue that the comparative materials mentioned thus far can be understood as the basis of a pan-European ethos in some sense, since it is plausible to connect them back to the States parties of the ECHR in such a way that they can be read as vertically established "common ground". I close this section by considering a counter-example (6.): materials such as judgments, quasi-judicial decisions and expert reports do not purport to be representative of the States parties' positions and are therefore less closely related to ethical normativity.

2. Law of the European Union

Let me begin, then, with EU law. It clearly occupies a distinct position on several grounds, the most important of which in the context of European consensus is the fact that it binds, in principle, only 27 of the 47 States parties to the ECtHR.[923] While it has been argued that norms of EU law, *in and of themselves*, suffice to "prove the existence of European consensus" in favour of the applicant and operationalise the spur effect because "the Member States of the EU constitute the majority of the states parties to the ECHR",[924] the discussion of numerical issues involved in establishing consensus casts some doubt on this:[925] while it might be a possible approach on the basis of the morality-focussed perspective emphasising a "trend", the ethos-focussed perspective would usually demand a significantly higher percentage of States parties to establish consensus in favour of the applicant rather than a lack of consensus.[926]

923 I leave aside the complexities of, for example, certain EU norms not applying to all Member States or, conversely, the indirect applicability of certain EU norms to non-Member States via the European Free Trade Association (EFTA).

924 Rozakis, "The Accession of the EU to the ECHR and the Charter of Fundamental Rights: Enlarging the Field of Protection of Human Rights in Europe" at 331.

925 See also Draghici, "The Strasbourg Court between European and Local Consensus: Anti-democratic or Guardian of Democratic Process?" at 19.

926 Chapter 5, III.1.

Furthermore, it should be noted that there is room for further differentiation based on the source within EU law. Whereas primary law such as the Charter of Fundamental Rights (CFR)[927] is, in principle, based on the consent of all Member States, secondary EU law[928] follows different procedures. The implications are manifold and complicated, all the more so when the European Parliament is involved; but their gist can be summarised by Tobias Lock's assessment that "legislation can usually be adopted with a qualified majority of Member States voting in its favour, so that sole reliance on numbers may not even reflect the true consensus among EU Member States"[929] – let alone, it is implied, among CoE Member States.[930] Even though secondary EU law binds *all* Member States (and despite its primacy and direct effect[931]), then, it may be *based* on the preferences of only some of them, thus further weakening any claim to pan-European ethical normativity based on it.

Giving strong weight to consensus in favour of the applicant based only on EU law, then, would amount to a form of ethical normativity which is noticeably disconnected from pan-European ethical normativity understood as relative to (all) the States parties of the ECHR while strongly de-emphasising the importance of national ethe, particularly but not exclusively those of non-EU Member States.[932] Given the rather obvious element of transnational homogenisation at play here, it comes as no surprise that cases in which the ECtHR refers to EU law as the sole or clearly de-

927 Referred to e.g. in ECtHR, Appl. No. 30141/04 – *Schalk and Kopf*, at paras. 60-61; ECtHR (GC), Appl. No. 23459/03 – *Bayatyan*, at para. 106.

928 Referred to e.g. in ECtHR (GC), Appl. No. 30078/06 – *Konstantin Markin*, at paras. 63-64 and 140; ECtHR (GC), Appl. No. 57325/00 – *D.H. and Others*, at para. 187; ECtHR (GC), Appl. Nos. 50541/08, 50571/08, 50573/08 and 40351/09 – *Ibrahim and Others v. the United Kingdom*, Judgment of 13 September 2016, at paras. 259, 261 and 264.

929 Lock, "The Influence of EU Law on Strasbourg Doctrines" at 823.

930 Draghici, "The Strasbourg Court between European and Local Consensus: Anti-democratic or Guardian of Democratic Process?" at 19.

931 Emphasised by Lock, "The Influence of EU Law on Strasbourg Doctrines" at 821; Dzehtsiarou, "What Is Law for the European Court of Human Rights?" at 118.

932 Dzehtsiarou, "What Is Law for the European Court of Human Rights?" at 120 also notes the danger of "marginalis[ing] the legal practices of non-EU members of the Council of Europe", though his concern is primarily with sociological legitimacy; Helfer, "Consensus, Coherence and the European Convention on Human Rights" at 160 notes consensus based on EU (then EC) law as an instance in which national ethe should be given more weight relative to European consensus due to "geo-political distinctions".

cisive element in establishing consensus are relatively rare[933] – often, consensus based on domestic law or on other international norms are cited alongside EU law.[934]

3. Council of Europe Materials

CoE materials, for present purposes, can be understood to include both treaties developed under the auspices of the CoE and resolutions or recommendations decided on by organs of the CoE without need for further ratification by the States parties. There seems to be an intuitive sense of congruence between CoE materials and European consensus. One might argue that the ECHR itself is historically connected to the CoE, having been developed under its auspices; furthermore, all Member States of the CoE are party to the ECHR and vice versa,[935] thus avoiding the numerical issues which, as just discussed, plague EU law from the outset.

More importantly, however, there is a more teleologically loaded sense of kinship: for example, Dzehtsiarou connects the use of CoE materials sensu stricto to the "logic" of the Strasbourg system and suggests that because "the ECHR and other Council of Europe documents are developed by the same international organization and designed to fulfil similar objectives", the latter can be used to inform the interpretation of the prior.[936] Daniel Klocke similarly sees a "connection" between the ECtHR and the CoE with regard to the task of developing human rights standards and

933 Lock, "The Influence of EU Law on Strasbourg Doctrines" at 824; Gerards, *General Principles of the European Convention on Human Rights*, at 102-104.

934 E.g. ECtHR (GC), Appl. No. 23459/03 – *Bayatyan*, at para. 106; there are quite a few borderline cases, however: consider e.g. ECtHR, Appl. No. 30141/04 – *Schalk and Kopf*, at para. 61 where the ECtHR argues that "[r]egard being had to Article 9 [CFR], therefore, the Court would no longer consider that the right to marry enshrined in Article 12 [ECHR] must in all circumstances be limited to marriage between two persons of the opposite sex" – *in spite of* a lack of consensus in domestic law (although the latter was ultimately more decisive in preventing a violation); see in more detail on *Schalk and Kopf* Chapter 1, II.; see also e.g. ECtHR (GC), Appl. No. 41615/07 – *Neulinger and Shuruk*, at para. 135 where the Court refers to different comparative materials but gives particular emphasis to the CFR.

935 As noted in ECtHR (Plenary), Appl. No. 4451/70 – *Golder*, at para. 34.

936 Dzehtsiarou, "What Is Law for the European Court of Human Rights?" at 105-106; see also Pascual-Vives, *Consensus-Based Interpretation of Regional Human Rights Treaties*, at 222-223.

concludes that the prior must take into account standards set by the latter.[937] Notably, the theme of harmonisation, familiar from the spur effect of European consensus,[938] resurfaces here: both the retroactive and the prospective element are captured within Article 1 of the Statute of the Council of Europe (CoE Statute), which establishes as the CoE's aim "to achieve a greater unity between its members for the purpose of safeguarding and realising the ideals and principles which are their common heritage". The provisions on resolutions and recommendations by the CoE organs reflect this aim;[939] the prior, in particular, thus constitute an encouragement to the Member States "to develop harmonious policies on matters of common interest, including human rights".[940]

Traces of the special significance of CoE materials can also be found within the ECtHR's case-law. Not only does it refer to such materials extensively and with great frequency,[941] it sometimes explicitly assigns them particular weight. In that vein, it has stated that it takes into account "relevant international instruments and reports, and *in particular* those of other Council of Europe organs, in order to interpret the guarantees of the Convention and to establish whether there is a common European standard in the field".[942] While confirming the relevance of international instruments more generally, CoE materials are thus deemed particularly relevant in establishing a "common European standard". Although he acknowledges the differing roles assigned to them within the ECtHR's reasoning, Klocke has even gone so far as to compare the relevance of CoE materials to that of the ECtHR's own precedent.[943]

---

937 Klocke, "Die dynamische Auslegung der EMRK im Lichte der Dokumente des Europarats" at 163-164.

938 Chapter 3, IV.4.

939 Articles 15 and 23 lit. (a) CoE Statute, respectively.

940 Helfer, "Consensus, Coherence and the European Convention on Human Rights" at 163; the PACE's recommendations do so less directly since they are addressed to the CoM (see infra, note 960).

941 Just a few examples, all Grand Chamber judgments: ECtHR (GC), Appl. No. 34503/97 – *Demir and Baykara*, at paras. 103-104 and 122; ECtHR (GC), Appl. No. 23459/03 – *Bayatyan*, at para. 107; ECtHR (GC), Appl. No. 57325/00 – *D.H. and Others*, at para. 182; ECtHR (GC), Appl. No. 35810/09 – *O'Keeffe v. Ireland*, Judgment of 28 January 2014, at paras. 92 and 147; ECtHR, Appl. No. 25965/04 – *Rantsev*, at paras. 158-174.

942 ECtHR (GC), Appl. No. 7/08 – *Tănase*, at para. 176 (emphasis added).

943 Klocke, "Die dynamische Auslegung der EMRK im Lichte der Dokumente des Europarats" at 157-158.

Empirical research by Lize Glas has shown that certain CoE materials referred to by the ECtHR become by far the most relevant during the proportionality assessment, particular in cases pertaining to Article 8 ECHR.[944] Glas suggests that this might because the matter of proportionality in these cases is "comparably difficult to resolve in the sense that it is open to interpretation to a great extent"[945] and pertains to "usually sensitive" matters.[946] This reflects the more general rationale mentioned above for references to international law as the alternative to morality-focussed reasoning:[947] given disagreement about the ("sensitive") substantive issues, international law – and, in this case, CoE materials – supply an alternative form of normativity which is more volitionally oriented, grounded in a pan-European ethos instead of substantive reasoning.

It should be noted, however, that the number of States on whose will such a pan-European ethos is based vary widely depending on the CoE materials in question.[948] This is most evidently the case with regard to treaties developed under the auspices of the CoE, since their acceptance by the States parties ultimately hinges on their subsequent ratification. Some treaties, such as the Convention on Action against Trafficking in Human Beings[949] or the Convention for the Protection of Individuals with regard to Automatic Processing of Personal Data,[950] enjoy unanimous or near-unanimous ratification – although this was not necessarily the case when the ECtHR first referred to them in its leading cases.[951] Still, in more recent cases references to treaties such as these can be reconciled with the ap-

944 Glas, "The European Court of Human Rights' Use of Non-Binding and Standard-Setting Council of Europe Documents" at 107.

945 Ibid., 108.

946 Ibid., 111; on sensitivity in the sense of the ethos-focussed perspective, see Chapter 5, III.2.

947 Supra, III.

948 See also Draghici, "The Strasbourg Court between European and Local Consensus: Anti-democratic or Guardian of Democratic Process?" at 19.

949 CETS No. 197, treaty of 16 May 2005, entry into force on 1 February 2008.

950 CETS No. 108, treaty of 28 January 1981, entry into force on 1 October 1985; see also the Protocol recently opened for signature: CETS No. 223 of 10 October 2018.

951 E.g. ECtHR (GC), Appl. No. 27798/95 – *Amann v. Switzerland*, Judgment of 16 February 2000, at para. 65; ECtHR, Appl. No. 25965/04 – *Rantsev*, at para. 160; my impression is that many of the CoE treaties referred to are not all that broadly ratified, at least initially: see the overview provided in the report by the Research Division of the ECtHR, "The use of Council of Europe treaties in the case-law of the European Court of Human Rights", available at <https://www.echr.coe.int/Documents/Research_report_treaties_CoE_ENG.pdf>; contrast later

proach of the ethos-focussed perspective based on a pan-European ethos because it clearly constitutes "common ground" in the sense of (at least) a supermajority of States parties.[952] By contrast, a treaty with significantly fewer ratifications – such as the European Convention on the Legal Status of Children born out of Wedlock referred to in *Marckx* – shifts the focus away from a pan-European ethos and towards a sense of directionality based on morality-focussed considerations,[953] even if "concluded within the Council of Europe".[954]

With regard to resolutions or recommendations by the CoM and the Parliamentary Assembly (PACE), the picture is even more complicated. For one thing, they are not legally binding, an issue I will return to in a moment.[955] For another, they are based on different Member State representatives – the ministers of foreign affairs and their deputies in the CoM, members of national parliaments in the case of the PACE.[956] Finally, the voting procedures leading to the adoption of the relevant materials may involve the endorsement by quite a varying number of States. Recommendations by the CoM, for example, are sometimes said to have a "direct connection" to European consensus and a particularly appropriate basis for pan-European standards, for Article 20 lit. (a)(i) CoE Statute requires unanimity for such resolutions.[957] If this was the case, then CoM recommendations would reflect positions taken by the representatives of all Member States, even the respondent State in any proceedings before the ECtHR. In practice, however, a two thirds majority of those voting and a simple majority of those entitled to vote is sufficient for the unanimity rule not to be invoked,[958] thus introducing the possibility of CoM recommendations

---

citations of e.g. the Anti-Trafficking Convention in ECtHR, Appl. No. 21884/15 – *Chowdury and Others v. Greece*, Judgment of 30 March 2017, at paras. 42, 88, 93, 100, 104 and 126; ECtHR (GC), Appl. No. 60561/14 – *S.M. v. Croatia*, Judgment of 25 June 2020, inter alia at paras. 294-295 (now in force for all States parties except Russia).

952 See generally Chapter 5, III.1. and, for international law, supra, II.

953 See Chapter 5, IV.

954 ECtHR (Plenary), Appl. No. 6833/74 – *Marckx*, at para. 20.

955 Infra, IV.5.

956 Articles 14 and 25 lit. (a) CoE Statute, respectively.

957 Klocke, "Die dynamische Auslegung der EMRK im Lichte der Dokumente des Europarats" at 156.

958 519bis meeting of 4 November 1994; see Marten Breuer, "Establishing Common Standards and Securing the Rule of Law," in *The Council of Europe. Its Laws and Policies*, ed. Stefanie Schmahl and Marten Breuer (Oxford: Oxford University Press, 2017), mn 28.37.

closer to the kind of majority-without-unanimity usually associated with European consensus.

Recommendations by the PACE are usually regarded as a less authoritative base for European consensus than those by the CoM,[959] in large part because they are not directed directly at the Member States, but rather at the CoM.[960] But with regard to their relation to diverse positions among the States parties, there are also significant limitations as to the number of States represented by any given recommendation. The requisite majority is two thirds of the representatives casting a vote (for resolutions, even a simple majority is sufficient).[961] Since the number of representatives differs from State to State (ranging from two e.g. for Andorra and Liechtenstein to eighteen e.g. for Germany and Turkey), the PACE departs from the traditional international law perspective of equality of States.[962] More importantly, the quorum (if it is even invoked) is reached with only one third of the representatives present.[963] Recommendations can therefore be made based on the positions taken by the representatives of only a small minority of States, and indeed some recommendations which the ECtHR has referred to were based on affirmative votes by representatives of less than half the States parties.[964] Of course, in all these cases resolutions and recommendations may also be passed by larger majorities up to and including unanimity, so the evaluation depends on the documents at issue – although the ECtHR rarely mentions the underlying majorities within the CoE when it cites them.[965]

---

959 Helfer, "Consensus, Coherence and the European Convention on Human Rights" at 163; Klocke, "Die dynamische Auslegung der EMRK im Lichte der Dokumente des Europarats" at 161.

960 Article 22 CoE Statute.

961 Article 29 (i) CoE Statute; for resolutions, see Michaela Wittinger, *Der Europarat: Die Entwicklung seines Rechts und der "europäischen Verfassungswerte"* (Baden-Baden: Nomos, 2005), at 142-143.

962 Article 26 CoE Statute.

963 Rule 42.3., Rules of Procedure of the Assembly, originally adopted as Res. 1202 (1999) and subsequently modified; available at <http://assembly.coe.int/nw/xml/RoP/RoP-XML2HTML-EN.asp>.

964 E.g. PACE, "Putting an end to coerced sterilisations and castrations", Resolution 1945 (2013): representatives of 23 States at least partly in favour, cited in ECtHR, Appl. Nos. 79885/12, 52471/13 and 52596/13 – *A.P., Garçon and Nicot*, at paras. 76 and 125.

965 See Breuer, "Impact of the Council of Europe on National Legal Systems", mn 36.92.

In any case, none of this is to say that the ECtHR should not refer to CoE materials within its reasoning, even if one restricts one's assessment to the ethos-focussed perspective. Compared to other vertically comparative references, they carry both advantages and disadvantages. For example, particularly in the case of the PACE as the CoE's "deliberative organ" (Article 22 CoE Statute), one might argue that there is a greater sense of jointly developed ethical normativity for the pan-European level than when the States parties' disparate domestic laws are simply added up to produce (lack of) European consensus.[966] In that sense, CoE materials can indeed be considered "convincing evidence of a developing *regional* perspective on individual rights" and thus emblematic of a pan-European ethos,[967] as opposed to domestic positions which merely happen to overlap.[968] However, this perspective does not negate the disadvantages, including the less direct connection to democratic procedures at the national level and the numerical issues just discussed, which make it more difficult to justify imposing a pan-European ethos on the national ethe of those States parties with differing positions. Therefore, claims that CoE materials may be regarded as "an expression of the collective will of the community of European States",[969] while certainly defensible in a sense, should also be treated with caution.

4. Global International Law

The ECtHR also references international instruments of broader geographical application than the ECHR itself[970] – "texts of universal scope", as it

---

966 But see ibid., mn 36.93; more generally on "deliberation and debate" in "representative fora" such as the General Assembly of the United Nations as the basis for "global public discourses" Wheatley, "The Legitimacy of International Human Rights Regimes" at 108-109.

967 Helfer, "Consensus, Coherence and the European Convention on Human Rights" at 162 (on CoE treaties, emphasis added).

968 See critically Murray, "Consensus: Concordance, or Hegemony of the Majority?" at 34, who notes that in contrast to national Supreme Courts, the ECtHR deals with "forty-seven distinct *demoi*" (emphasis in original).

969 Glas, "The European Court of Human Rights' Use of Non-Binding and Standard-Setting Council of Europe Documents" at 105-106, citing Polakiewicz, "Alternatives to Treaty-Making and Law-Making by Treaty and Expert Bodies in the Council of Europe" at 248.

970 Brems, *Human Rights: Universality and Diversity*, at 414; Brems, "The Margin of Appreciation Doctrine in the Case-Law of the European Court of Human Rights" at 286.

has dubbed them.[971] Here, one might expect to encounter a problem that is diametrically opposed to that described above in the context of EU law: where the latter encompasses "too few" States for the conventional account of European consensus, the prior might be thought to encompass "too many". Differently put: when global rather than European treaties are at issue, it may at first seem somewhat counter-intuitive to establish a *European* consensus by reference to (global) *international* law.[972] One might hypothesise that this intuition is based on the connection between European consensus and the desire for some kind of specifically European identity as reflected within regional human rights law – an identity which would then be derived in part negatively,[973] by virtue of a contrast between "us" Europeans (part of European consensus) and non-Europeans "others" (not part of European consensus, not even indirectly by reference to global international law).

In that vein, for example, Hanneke Senden has classified such references as part of the "*external component* of comparative interpretation" together with references to national jurisdictions outside of Europe, while (only) references to the domestic legal systems of the States parties are seen as the internal component of comparative interpretation.[974] While acknowledging that the boundaries may be blurry, Dzehtsiarou has proposed a very similar distinction, arguing that "only those sources which are directly

971 ECtHR (GC), Appl. No. 34503/97 – *Demir and Baykara*, at para. 72.

972 Although, given the European hegemony in establishing the universal, there is perhaps less of dichotomy here than it may at first seem; see generally Dorothy Makaza, "Towards Afrotopia: The AU Withdrawal Strategy Document, the ICC, and the Possibility of Pluralistic Utopias," (2017) 60 *German Yearbook of International Law* 485 at 488-489 and, in the context of human rights, Golder, "Varieties of Universalism" at 37; Ratna Kapur, "Human Rights in the 21st Century: Take a Walk on the Dark Side," (2006) 28 *Sydney Law Review* 665 at 673-674.

973 See generally Said, *Orientalism*, at 54; see also Chapter 1, IV.3.

974 Senden, *Interpretation of Fundamental Rights*, at 115-116; see also von Ungern-Sternberg, "Die Konsensmethode des EGMR. Eine kritische Bewertung mit Blick auf das völkerrechtliche Konsens- und das innerstaatliche Demokratieprinzip" at 331, who similarly cites references to international law and those to non-European domestic legal systems in tandem and refers to them as "foreign legal orders", and Henrard, "How the ECtHR's Use of European Consensus Considerations Allows Legitimacy Concerns to Delimit Its Mandate" at 154-155, who does the same under the heading of comparative references "beyond Europe"; this resonates, to some extent, with the alternate framework of systemic integration, which could be said to foreground "horizontal" rather than vertical harmonization: see Rietiker, "The Principle of 'Effectiveness' in the Recent Jurisprudence of the European Court of Human Rights" at 271.

connected to the Council of Europe legal order" – understood as including Council of Europe documents and the domestic laws of the States parties – "can be called internal", while "customary and treaty-based international legal norms", so long as they are not implemented in the domestic legal systems of the States parties, are deemed to constitute "[e]xternal legal sources" together with domestic laws of non-States parties and non-European norms of regional law.[975]

Yet from within the framework of European consensus, such an externalisation of international law hardly seems necessary – after all, as Mónika Ambrus has put it, "the member states of the Council of Europe are also part of [the] international legal system" being referred to".[976] References to global international law can thus be thought of as vertical in a similar sense to references to CoE materials since the prior, too, relate to the States parties of the ECHR, regardless of what other States the norms at issue apply to.[977] The ECtHR itself has occasionally used formulations which indicate this kind of perspective on global international law, as when it refers to the Convention on the Rights of the Child in *Hadzhieva v. Bulgaria* and notes that it "has binding force under international law on the Contracting States, *including* all of the member States of the Council of Europe".[978]

In other words, European common ground (or lack thereof) might be discerned even if it is not *particular* to Europe: what matters from within this approach is the number of States parties within Europe which subscribe to any given norm of international law, not necessarily the number of States (if any) outside of Europe who likewise do so. This is not to say that references to CoE materials and to "texts of universal scope" are considered identical within the ECtHR's case-law – as discussed above, the prior are sometimes deemed to be of particular importance.[979] For all the intuitive connections between the notion of a pan-European ethos and CoE

975 Dzehtsiarou, "What Is Law for the European Court of Human Rights?" at 97; this also seems to be the position of McCrudden, "Using Comparative Reasoning in Human Rights Adjudication" at 387.

976 Ambrus, "Comparative Law Method in the Jurisprudence of the European Court of Human Rights in the Light of the Rule of Law" at 365.

977 On verticality, see generally Chapter 1, III.; clearly, this framework brackets as non-vertical any non-European regional treaties such as the Inter-American Convention on Human Rights, though these could still be referred to on other grounds (e.g. based on general arguments in favour of any kind of comparative law, or systemic integration). I will not take up these broader issues here.

978 ECtHR, Appl. No. 45285/12 – *Hadzhieva v. Bulgaria*, Judgment of 1 February 2018, at para. 43 (emphasis added).

979 Supra, IV.3.

materials, however, global international can likewise be connected back to the Member States of the CoE. Even if there are non-negligible differences between the two kinds of norms, then, they do not seem so stark as to render global international law qualitatively different from distinctly European law, as when it is classified as "external" together with the domestic laws of non-European States.

5. Soft Law

Whatever the geographical scope of application of comparative materials referred to, some of them may not, in and of themselves, be considered legally binding. As one dissenting opinion summarised it: "In the Court's jurisprudence, three factors are relevant in order to determine the existence of a European consensus: international treaty law, comparative law and international soft law".[980] The aforementioned resolutions and recommendations by organs of the CoE, in particular, constitute non-binding yet standard-setting documents.[981] Given their classification as "mere" soft law, however, it is sometimes disputed whether such documents should play a role in the establishment of (lack of) European consensus: by transposing the standards set by soft law into the context of interpreting the ECHR, it is argued, originally non-binding standards become indirectly binding, thus subverting States' intentions to avoid legal obligations.[982]

While there is a certain logic to this kind of argument, it is worth noting that it goes well beyond the usual criticisms levelled at soft law, which simply note that resolutions and recommendations "*in themselves* [...] do not

980 ECtHR (GC), Appl. No. 43835/11 – *S.A.S.*, joint partly dissenting opinion of Judges Nussberger and Jäderblom, at para. 19; this taxonomy could be elaborated on (e.g. by reference to other forms of international law besides treaties), but as a rough summary I think it is quite accurate and helpful.

981 See Glas, "The European Court of Human Rights' Use of Non-Binding and Standard-Setting Council of Europe Documents" at 97.

982 Koch and Vedsted-Hansen, "International Human Rights and National Legislatures - Conflict or Balance?" at 12; Christoph Grabenwarter and Katharina Pabel, *Europäische Menschenrechtskonvention*, 6th ed. (München: Beck, 2016), § 5 mn 12; the criticism by Wildhaber, Hjartarson, and Donnelly, "No Consensus on Consensus?" at 256 also seems to go in this direction; see also Glas, "The European Court of Human Rights' Use of Non-Binding and Standard-Setting Council of Europe Documents" at 98-99, although the doubts she mentions are ultimately based more on prudential reasons.

constitute the formal source of new norms".[983] On Jean d'Aspremont's account, this means that soft law documents should be considered legal facts rather than legal acts in the positivist sense.[984] But this does not mean that they are legally irrelevant; indeed, according to d'Aspremont it is "undisputed, even by positivists", that soft law may, for example, "play a role in the internationalization of the subject-matter" or "provide guidelines for the interpretation of other legal acts".[985] Both of these roles are clearly relevant in the case of soft law as European consensus.

The ECtHR, in any case, does not seem bothered by the idea of indirectly transforming soft law into "hard" law. Quite to the contrary, it is unapologetic about doing so,[986] and has repeatedly emphasised that it even "attaches considerable importance" to certain instruments "despite their non-binding character".[987] Judge Pinto de Albuquerque has even gone so far as to describe soft law as "the most important source of crystallization of the European consensus".[988] While I think this is, on the whole, somewhat of an exaggeration, the connection between soft law and European consensus certainly holds true, with the prior sometimes used as "evidence of a common standard" adopted by the States parties.[989]

Within the framework of European consensus, this seems adequate insofar that, "even though an instrument does perhaps not bind the states, it

---

983 Prosper Weil, "Towards Relative Normativity in International Law?," (1983) 77 *American Journal of International Law* 413 at 417 (emphasis omitted and added).

984 Jean d'Aspremont, "Softness in International Law: A Self-Serving Quest for New Legal Materials," (2008) 19 *European Journal of International Law* 1075 at 1083.

985 Ibid., 1082.

986 ECtHR (GC), Appl. No. 34503/97 – *Demir and Baykara*, at para. 74.

987 ECtHR, Appl. Nos. 15018/11 and 61199/12 – *Harakchiev and Tolumov v. Bulgaria*, Judgment of 8 July 2014, at para. 204; see also e.g. ECtHR, Appl. No. 33834/03 – *Riviere v. France*, Judgment of 11 July 2006, at para. 72; ECtHR, Appl. No. 41153/06 – *Dybeku v. Albania*, Judgment of 18 December 2007, at para. 48; ECtHR, Appl. No. 44084/10 – *Gülay Çetin v. Turkey*, Judgment of 5 March 2013, at para. 130.

988 Pinto de Albuquerque, "Plaidoyer for the European Court of Human Rights" at 123; see also in great detail ECtHR (GC), Appl. No. 7334/13 – *Muršić*, partly dissenting opinion of Judge Pinto de Albuquerque, at para. 14 and passim; contrast Nußberger, "Hard Law or Soft Law - Does it Matter? Distinction Between Different Sources of International Law in the Jurisprudence of the ECtHR", emphasising differences between the ECtHR's references to hard and soft international law.

989 Koch and Vedsted-Hansen, "International Human Rights and National Legislatures - Conflict or Balance?" at 12; Gerards, *General Principles of the European Convention on Human Rights*, at 98-99.

can give an indication of their intent and practice".[990] Such instruments may thus be non-binding, but they can be understood as "common actions" by the States parties.[991] From this perspective, the criticism that references to soft law subvert the intention of States to avoid legal obligations seems at least partly off the mark: like references to binding international law, so too can references to soft law avoid substantive reasoning of the kind preferred by the morality-focussed perspective, instead providing a connection to materials based, at least in some sense, on States' will.[992] After all, the connections between the ECtHR's vertically comparative reasoning and the materials it refers to can always be questioned: in the case of soft law due to its lack of legally binding force, but also in the case of international law due to the ECtHR's lack of mandate to enforce it,[993] and even in the paradigmatic case of domestic law since any given position within domestic legal systems does not necessarily imply that it should be internationalised as a human rights obligation.[994]

My point is not to disparage any of these arguments in substance, but merely to suggest that they operate within a different logic to that which drives European consensus, at least if the latter is understood as an expres-

990 Glas, "The European Court of Human Rights' Use of Non-Binding and Standard-Setting Council of Europe Documents" at 111.

991 Pinto de Albuquerque, "Plaidoyer for the European Court of Human Rights" at 125.

992 See Nußberger, "Hard Law or Soft Law - Does it Matter? Distinction Between Different Sources of International Law in the Jurisprudence of the ECtHR" at 49 on the use of soft law as "guidelines for interpretation and filling in gaps in the text of the Convention" where its provisions are "vague and open".

993 As sometimes stressed by the ECtHR when it wishes to distance itself from certain norms of international law: see e.g. ECtHR, Appl. No. 31045/10 – *National Union of Rail, Maritime and Transport Workers*, at para. 106; see also von Ungern-Sternberg, "Die Konsensmethode des EGMR. Eine kritische Bewertung mit Blick auf das völkerrechtliche Konsens- und das innerstaatliche Demokratieprinzip" at 332; for the parallel between soft law and international law sensu stricto in that regard, see Dzehtsiarou, "What Is Law for the European Court of Human Rights?" at 105.

994 Ulfstein, "Evolutive Interpretation in the Light of Other International Instruments: Law and Legitimacy" at 92; this point of criticism is also at least implied by Murray, "Consensus: Concordance, or Hegemony of the Majority?" at 43, who cautions that national legislation (as opposed to constitutional law or international treaties) "may reflect no more than local compromises"; see also Djeffal, "Consensus, Stasis, Evolution: Reconstructing Argumentative Patterns in Evolutive ECHR Jurisprudence" at 88; for a defence, see Seibert-Fohr, "The Effect of Subsequent Practice on the European Convention on Human Rights: Considerations from a General International Law Perspective" at 74.

sion of a pan-European ethos. On that account, the crucial aspect is simply to identify European positions which are in some sense – however imperfectly – "shared" rather than arrived at by virtue of substantive reasoning open to the charge of paying insufficient attention to disagreement about moral matters. This does not imply that distinctions cannot be made between soft law and international law sensu stricto (by assigning them differing argumentative weight within the ECtHR's reasoning); for example, given the democratic concerns which ultimately underlie the ethos-focussed perspective's interest in State will,[995] one might argue that treaty ratifications are more likely to be democratically bolstered than soft law documents.[996] So long as soft law instruments are in some way supported by a super-majority of the States parties, however, it seems to me that their inclusion in the establishment of (lack of) European consensus is not per se contrary to the logic of ethical normativity developed within a pan-European ethos – it merely demonstrates that ethical normativity can be established in different ways.

6. Non-Representative Documents

The ECtHR goes even further: as it summarised its approach in *Demir and Baykara*, its references to soft law, particularly in the context of the CoE, have led it "to support its reasoning by reference to norms emanating from other Council of Europe organs, *even though those organs have no function of representing States Parties* to the Convention, whether supervisory mechanisms or expert bodies", including e.g. the Venice Commission or the European Commission against Racism and Intolerance.[997] The same is true at the global level, with references to the supervisory bodies of the various global human rights treaties being particularly common.[998] Furthermore, such non-representative materials need not be limited to soft law: they also

995 See Chapter 3, IV.2.

996 Jan Klabbers, *The Concept of Treaty in International Law* (The Hague et al.: Kluwer, 1996), at 160; see also Nußberger, "Hard Law or Soft Law - Does it Matter? Distinction Between Different Sources of International Law in the Jurisprudence of the ECtHR" at 43.

997 ECtHR (GC), Appl. No. 34503/97 – *Demir and Baykara*, at para. 75 (emphasis added); see e.g. ECtHR (GC), Appl. No. 310/15 – *Mugemangango v. Belgium*, Judgment of 10 July 2020, at paras. 32-34 and 106-107 for references to the Venice Commission.

998 See e.g. supra, note 851.

encompass, for example, legally binding judgments by other European or international courts. While emphasising the "distinct character" of its own judicial review compared to other supervisory procedures,[999] the ECtHR regularly takes them into account.

What all these various documents (judgments, quasi-judicial decisions, expert reports, and many more) have in common is the lack of direct connection to positions taken by the States parties in a way which can be considered in some sense part of their democratic process: instead, like judgments of the ECtHR itself, they are the product of only a few individuals' reasoning.[1000] As such, they are open to the general criticism made by the ethos-focussed perspective of the morality-focussed perspective's epistemology: in light of reasonable disagreement, individual views should not be preferred over the outcome of a democratic process, even those views are put forward as interpretations of e.g. a treaty signed by a super-majority of the States parties.[1001] Whatever one makes of this criticism in substance, I would submit that it shows a certain disconnect between non-representative materials and ethical normativity: the prior are relatively far removed from the positions developed by the States parties themselves,[1002] even if they may apply to them as a matter of international law or soft law.

This is not to say, of course, that other potential rationales for reference to non-representative materials cannot be adduced. The principle of systemic integration discussed above, for example, provides one rationale for such references – if one aims to achieve a harmonious system of international (human rights) law, then at least legally binding norms should be taken into account regardless of whether they are representative of the States parties or not.[1003] For both supervisory mechanisms and other reports, deference on the basis of "expertise" may also play a role, as when the ECtHR deems the Committee of Independent Experts established by

999 ECtHR, Appl. No. 31045/10 – *National Union of Rail, Maritime and Transport Workers*, at para. 98.

1000 Of course, they may in turn employ consensus-based reasoning, but the level of scrutiny required to establish whether this is the case is rarely if ever performed by the ECtHR.

1001 Chapter 3, II.

1002 See also Pascual-Vives, *Consensus-Based Interpretation of Regional Human Rights Treaties*, at 123; see generally Chapter 1, III.

1003 This rationale seems to be motivating e.g. Legg, *The Margin of Appreciation*, at 130-135; Wildhaber, Hjartarson, and Donnelly, "No Consensus on Consensus?" at 255 insofar as references to other international courts or tribunals are at issue.

the European Social Charter to be a "particularly well-qualified" body in the area of labour rights.[1004] Finally, as with any more representative form of consensus, non-representative documents may be referred to concurrently to other forms of argument, as when the morality-focussed perspective uses it to bolster results already reached by way of independent reasoning.[1005]

V. Consensus based on International Law versus Consensus based on Domestic Law

My argument thus far has been that various kinds of international law (with the exception of the non-representative documents just discussed) can be considered a kind of ethical normativity developed within a pan-European ethos. The preceding section considered some of the different procedures which might lead to the expression of such a pan-European ethos: for example, the ratification of treaties tends to remain relatively close to democratic procedures within individual States parties, whereas the secondary law of international organisations such as the CoE is more disconnected from them but also involves more active deliberation and decision-making by the States parties as a whole, as opposed to disparate domestic laws. Needless to say, different norms of international law may provide conflicting guidance on any given issue before the ECtHR, and in such cases different kinds of ethical normativity at the pan-European level may be considered in conflict. Any kind of (lack of) consensus based on international law can, furthermore, potentially point in a different direction than (lack of) consensus based on domestic law. In this section, I will consider the ECtHR's case-law on this latter issue, which will shed further light on the way in which references to international law relate to the tensions between the morality-focussed and the ethos-focussed perspective.

Before turning to the relation between consensus based on international and domestic law, respectively, let me briefly provide some examples of the latter fulfilling the typically Janus-faced function of consensus – what I have been treating under the headings of "rein effect" and "spur effect".[1006]

1004 ECtHR, Appl. No 28602/95 – *Tüm Haber Sen and Çinar v. Turkey*, Judgment of 21 February 2006, at para. 39; see also Gerards, *General Principles of the European Convention on Human Rights*, at 97.

1005 See generally Chapter 2, III.

1006 Chapter 1, III.

The spur effect appears to be the most prominent within the ECtHR's case-law: These are the paradigmatic cases such as *Demir and Baykara* in which the ECtHR considers international law to demonstrate common ground among the States parties in favour of the applicant's position, and privileges this super-majoritarian commonality over the national ethos of the respondent State.[1007] Conversely, there may be common ground in favour of the respondent State when international law is geared at allowing a certain practice,[1008] or even *prohibits* States from taking an expansive approach to human rights of the kind demanded by the applicants before the ECtHR, as was the case (on the ECtHR's reading of international law) in a number of high-profile judgments concerning State immunity from civil suits. In these cases, the ECtHR held that "measures taken by a High Contracting Party which reflect generally recognised rules of public international law on State immunity cannot in principle be regarded as imposing a disproportionate restriction on the right of access to a court",[1009] thus making the normative effect of international law in favour of the respondent State particularly clear.[1010]

Finally, there are cases involving a *lack* of consensus within international law, i.e. those in which international law is in some way equivocal about the issue before the ECtHR. This issue is even more complex than when lack of consensus within the States parties' domestic legal systems is at issue, and there are several different situations which the ECtHR might describe as lack of consensus. For example, ratification by only a small number of the States parties can be interpreted as lack of consensus,[1011] as can the fact that treaties on a similar subject-matter "are silent" on the matter

1007 ECtHR (GC), Appl. No. 34503/97 – *Demir and Baykara*, at paras. 85-86.

1008 E.g. unannounced doping tests based on a duty to disclose sportspersons' whereabouts: ECtHR, Appl. Nos. 48151/11 and 77769/13 – *National Federation of Sportspersons' Associations and Unions (FNASS) and Others*, at para. 184.

1009 ECtHR (GC), Appl. No. 35763/97 – *Al-Adsani*, at para. 56; ECtHR (GC), Appl. No. 37112/97 – *Fogarty*, at para. 36; ECtHR (GC), Appl. No. 31253/96 – *McElhinney v. Ireland*, Judgment of 21 November 2001, at para. 37.

1010 The ECtHR itself framed the issue primarily as one of systemic integration (unsurprisingly, given the possibility of a direct norm conflict with other areas of international law if it had found a violation of the Convention). As argued above (II.), however, there is an overlap between the frameworks of European consensus and systemic integration; and thus I would argue that the international law of State immunity can *also* be considered common ground among the States parties and read through the prism of verticality.

1011 See e.g. ECtHR, Appl. No. 39051/03 – *Emonet and Others*, at para. 84; but see also ECtHR (GC), Appl. No. 19010/07 – *X and Others*, at paras. 50 and 149-150

at issue.[1012] The most common occurrence of lack of consensus based on (lack of) international law within the ECtHR's case-law seems to be that an issue was in some way debated within international fora *and yet* no agreement was reached – somewhat unsurprisingly, perhaps, because these cases make the disagreement among States more explicit than those previously mentioned. For example, in *Chapman v. the United Kingdom*, the ECtHR interpreted the lack of precise standards in the various international instruments cited by the applicant as showing that "the signatory States *were unable to agree* on means of implementation" of the general goal to protect minorities – there was, in other words, a lack of consensus – which reinforced the Court's view that "the complexity and sensitivity of the issues" involved should lead to its supervisory role being largely reduced.[1013] A similar approach is in evidence in the more recent case of *Animal Defenders v. the United Kingdom*: here, the ECtHR noted that "[s]uch is the lack of consensus" with regard to the regulation of paid advertising that the CoM repeatedly "declined to recommend a common position on the issue", which led to a broad margin of appreciation for the respondent State.[1014]

In principle, then, international law in favour of the applicant leads to the spur effect and international law in favour of the respondent State or lack of consensus in international law leads to the rein effect. This mirrors the conventional account of consensus based on domestic law, including,

---

for a case in which few ratifications were associated with lack of common ground, yet the "narrowness of [the] sample" prompted the ECtHR to not draw any normative conclusions from this; contrast the joint partly dissenting opinion of Judges Casadevall, Ziemele, Kovler, Jočienė, Šikuta, de Gaetano and Sicilianos, at para. 18.

1012 ECtHR (GC), Appl. No. 57813/00 – *S.H. and Others*, at para. 107 (with regard to CoE conventions); see also ECtHR (GC), Appl. No. 61827/00 – *Glass v. the United Kingdom*, Judgment of 9 March 2004, at para. 75; ECtHR (GC), Appl. No. 57592/08 – *Hutchinson v. the United Kingdom*, Judgment of 17 January 2017, at para. 49; finally, see ECtHR (GC), Appl. No. 51357/07 – *Naït-Liman*, at para. 178, relying on the relative *ambiguity* of certain provisions.

1013 ECtHR (GC), Appl. 27238/95 – *Chapman*, at para. 94; the ECtHR later changed its interpretation of this passage in *D.H.*: see infra, note 1022; on the switch between levels of generality within its comparative reasoning, see further Chapter 7, III.2.

1014 ECtHR (GC), Appl. No. 48876/08 – *Animal Defenders International*, at para. 123; the explanatory memoranda to the relevant CoM recommendations explicitly mentioned the lack of a common standard based on "the different positions on this matter": see ibid., at paras. 74-75; see also ECtHR (GC), Appl. No. 57813/00 – *S.H. and Others*, at para. 107 (with regard to Directive 2004/23/EC).

in principle, the asymmetry in favour of the rein effect.[1015] However, the two types of consensus need not necessarily point in the same direction. Cases of conflict between them are seldom made explicit within the ECtHR's reasoning[1016] – somewhat unsurprisingly, both because one can expect at least a rough coherence between the States parties' positions in domestic and international law and because the flexibility in determining whether there is a consensus or lack of consensus allows the ECtHR to iron out any incoherence if it so wishes. Nonetheless, different implications of consensus based on international law and domestic law, respectively, sometimes shine through; and especially if one reads various majority opinions against submissions by the applicants, the respondent State and intervening parties or in contrast to dissenting opinions, it becomes clear that either domestic law or international law may be prioritised depending on the case at issue.

The ECtHR itself has simply stated that it is "for the Court to decide [...] how much weight to attribute" to various international instruments[1017] – a statement that is self-evidently true in the sense that the ECtHR itself decides on the judicial reasoning it will deploy,[1018] but of little help if one is looking for guidance as to general standards on how European consensus is established at the interface between domestic and international law. In some cases, the majority ruling quite clearly gives priority to consensus (or lack thereof) in domestic law, while consensus based on international law is either not mentioned or quickly passed over.[1019] For example, in the case of *A.P., Garçon and Nicot v. France*, the ECtHR glossed

1015 See generally Chapter 5, III.1.

1016 See e.g. ECtHR (GC), Appl. No. 34503/97 – *Demir and Baykara*, at para. 98; ECtHR (GC), Appl. Nos. 52562/99 and 525620/99 – *Sørensen and Rasmussen*, at paras. 70-75; ECtHR (GC), Appl. Nos. 66069/09, 130/10 and 3896/10 – *Vinter and Others*, at paras. 114-118; ECtHR, Appl. No. 16130/90 – *Sigurdur A. Sigurjónsson v. Iceland*, Judgment of 30 June 1993, at para. 35.

1017 ECtHR (GC), Appl. No. 7/08 – *Tănase*, at para. 176; see also ECtHR (GC), Appl. No. 310/15 – *Mugemangango*, at para. 99 (not "decisive"); contrast ECtHR (GC), Appl. No. 60561/14 – *S.M.*, at para. 290.

1018 Emphasised by Tzevelekos and Dzehtsiarou, "International Custom Making" at 325.

1019 E.g. ECtHR (Plenary), Appl. No. 10843/84 – *Cossey*, at para. 40 (contrast with the dissenting opinion of Judge Martens, at paras. 5.5. and 5.6.2.; see also similarly ECtHR (GC), Appl. Nos. 22985/93 and 23390/94 – *Sheffield and Horsham*, dissenting opinion of Judge van Dijk, at para. 3); ECtHR (GC), Appl. No. 42326/98 – *Odièvre v. France*, Judgment of 13 February 2003, at para. 47 (contrast with the joint dissenting opinion of Judges Wildhaber, Sir Nicolas Bratza, Bonello, Loucaides, Cabral Barreto, Tulkens and Pellonpää, at para. 15);

over international materials in favour of the depathologisation of trans identities, despite having applied some of them in an earlier part of the judgment dealing with other issues.[1020] Accordingly, there is some support for Koch and Vedsted-Hansen's statement that the ECtHR "usually" examines domestic law as the "primary source of reference", only taking international treaties into account "[i]n addition" to this primary source.[1021]

Yet, conversely, a number of cases may be identified in which more weight was attached to international law than to consensus based on domestic law.[1022] The case of *D.H. and Others v. the Czech Republic* makes this particularly clear, for different passages in the judgment give different weight to different types of consensus: the respondent State built its case based in part on lack of consensus in domestic legislation,[1023] the majority judgment instead relied on consensus in favour of the applicant based on international law,[1024] and the dissenting opinion of Judge Jungwiert in turn criticised the majority's reliance on international texts.[1025] As Føllesdal has summarised it: the ECtHR "sometimes, but not always, seems to put greater weight on [international law] than on a consensus among European states".[1026]

ECtHR (GC), Appl. No. 21906/04 – *Kafkaris*, at para. 104 (contrast with the joint partly dissenting opinion of Judges Tulkens, Cabral Barreto, Fura-Sandström, Spielmann and Jebens, at para. 4).

1020 ECtHR, Appl. Nos. 79885/12, 52471/13 and 52596/13 – *A.P., Garçon and Nicot*, at para. 139; see critically Damian A. Gonzalez-Salzberg, "An Improved Protection for the (Mentally Ill) Trans Parent: A Queer Reading of AP, Garçon and Nicot v France," (2018) 81 *Modern Law Review* 526 at 534; on this case, see also Chapter 5, IV. and Chapter 7, III.2.

1021 Koch and Vedsted-Hansen, "International Human Rights and National Legislatures - Conflict or Balance?" at 12.

1022 See e.g. Radačić, "Rights of the Vulnerable Groups" at 605, citing ECtHR, Appl. No. 73316/01 – *Siliadin v. France*, Judgment of 26 July 2005 and highlighting the tension between international materials referred to by the ECtHR and the domestic legal orders of the States parties at the time.

1023 ECtHR (GC), Appl. No. 57325/00 – *D.H. and Others*, at para. 155.

1024 Ibid., at para. 181.

1025 ECtHR (GC), Appl. No. 57325/00 – *D.H. and Others*, dissenting opinion of Judge Jungwiert, at para. 5; see also Dzehtsiarou, *European Consensus and the Legitimacy of the European Court of Human Rights*, at 58-59 and, for more detail on *D.H.*, see Chapter 7, III.2.

1026 Føllesdal, "A Better Signpost, Not a Better Walking Stick: How to Evaluate the European Consensus Doctrine" at 197.

It thus becomes clear that the multiplicity of potential sources for establishing European consensus further contributes to its malleability.[1027] Mónika Ambrus, for example, has argued that "the choice of the concrete source is decisive for the result of comparison" and that "the application of the sources of comparison" should therefore be "consistent across the cases".[1028] In a similar vein, Kanstantsin Dzehtsiarou has urged the ECtHR to "clarify its methodology for deciding between consensus based on international treaties", on the one hand, and "European consensus based on a comparative analysis of laws and practices of the Contracting Parties", on the other, when they "point in different directions".[1029] He admits, however, that the question of which source should take priority is "nearly impossible to answer [...] in the abstract" and that its answer "may depend on the facts and context of the case, clarity of the trend of rules and applicability of the principles to the case".[1030]

Based on the analysis above and the framework which I introduced over the course of the preceding chapters, I would suggest that it further depends on whether the ECtHR foregrounds the ethos-focussed perspective or the morality-focussed perspective within its reasoning. These two perspectives may conflict or intermingle with one another in complex ways, and I argued above that consensus based on international law occupies an ambivalent position within these tensions since it is grounded in volitional elements yet also read as carrying a more aspirational quality.[1031] We might also consider international law as a specific instance of the numerical issues discussed in the last chapter. Most straight-forwardly, as the example of *Marckx* has shown,[1032] the influence of the morality-focussed perspective may lead to shifts in the number of States required to establish consensus in favour of the applicant: notions of directionality such as a

---

1027 Fenwick, "Same-sex Unions at the Strasbourg Court in a Divided Europe: Driving Forward Reform or Protecting the Court's Authority via Consensus Analysis?" at 251.

1028 Ambrus, "Comparative Law Method in the Jurisprudence of the European Court of Human Rights in the Light of the Rule of Law" at 365; on consistency, see also Nußberger, "Hard Law or Soft Law - Does it Matter? Distinction Between Different Sources of International Law in the Jurisprudence of the ECtHR" at 50.

1029 Dzehtsiarou, *European Consensus and the Legitimacy of the European Court of Human Rights*, at 57.

1030 Ibid., 58-59.

1031 Supra, III.

1032 Chapter 5, IV., and supra, IV.3.

"continuous evolution" of norms[1033] or a "growing measure" of common ground[1034] can be and have been applied to international law as well as to domestic law, providing for a morality-focussed element in the very establishment of consensus.

More interestingly, however, in some cases these numerical shifts are already woven into the procedures leading to the establishment of international norms. As discussed above, PACE recommendations may be decided upon with the support of less than half the States parties to the ECHR, let alone a supermajority.[1035] One might nonetheless take them to be an expression of a pan-European ethos because they were decided by the deliberative organ of the CoE, and thus as a volitionally grounded alternative to the morality-focussed perspective.[1036] But one might also regard them as too fragile a base for ethical normativity at the pan-European level, too easily setting aside the national ethe of those States who did not support them. In this case, the invocation of such recommendations would be more likely to also be based on morality-focussed considerations, as a way of bolstering normative results reached by way of moral-cognitive reasoning rather than an expression of ethical normativity worth supporting.

The choice between this kind of consensus based on international law and an antithetical lack of consensus based on domestic law, then, turns out to be a choice between different kinds of normativity – and it comes as no surprise that lack of consensus based on domestic law, in this kind of case, is sometimes re-interpreted as a "trend" so as to smooth away the conflict.[1037] This is not to say that the ECtHR should not provide "reasons for preferring one [type of consensus] over the other"[1038] and thus "clarify why it has chosen a particular source of comparison";[1039] but since the choice of such reasons itself depends on the kind of normativity undergirding them,

1033 ECtHR (GC), Appl. No. 34503/97 – *Demir and Baykara*, at para. 86.

1034 ECtHR, Appl. No. 16130/90 – *Sigurdur A. Sigurjónsson*, at para. 35.

1035 Supra, IV.3.

1036 Supra, text to notes 944-947.

1037 E.g. ECtHR (GC), Appl. Nos. 29381/09 and 32684/09 – *Vallianatos and Others*, at para. 91; conversely, international law may also push the ECtHR to favour the rein effect, finding "no common approach" among domestic legal systems despite a "significant" majority in favour of the applicant: ECtHR, Appl. No. 19840/09 – *Shindler v. the United Kingdom*, Judgment of 7 May 2013, at para. 115 (and paras. 110-114 for international law).

1038 Dzehtsiarou, *European Consensus and the Legitimacy of the European Court of Human Rights*, at 59.

1039 Ambrus, "Comparative Law Method in the Jurisprudence of the European Court of Human Rights in the Light of the Rule of Law" at 365.

the more foundational tension between the morality-focussed perspective and the ethos-focussed perspective, as well as different approaches to the latter, in any case persists.

The scenario just described and the numerical issues it involves also help to further explain the relative lack of hostility towards international law references among proponents of the morality-focussed perspective:[1040] because of the procedures involved, international law can sometimes (but by no means always) be used to *lessen the asymmetry in favour of the rein effect*, thus making "progressive" positions more easily available. These procedures may, in a sense, also be defensible as an expression of a pan-European ethos; but they certainly shift the focus away from individual national ethe, i.e. the reason why the ethos-focussed perspective would usually demand a supermajority rather than (at the very least) a simple majority at the transnational level.

VI. Interim Reflections: International Law as Grounded Yet Aspirational

We are left with a complex picture. References to international law may support both the rein effect and the spur effect, with shifting boundaries between the two depending on angle from which it is approached, the kind of international norm at issue, and the procedures behind it. So long as it can be considered in some way representative of the States parties to the ECHR, it represents a form of ethical normativity; but differences remain, for example with regard to the level of democratic accountability within individual States, the amount of joint deliberation and decision-making at the transnational level, and the number of States behind any given norm of international law. Some rough hierarchies between different kinds of international law have been proposed in response – hard law over soft law, CoM resolutions over PACE recommendations – but they remain tentative and dependent on the case and the precise materials at issue. Furthermore, while international law references are often accepted as a concurrent form of reasoning by proponents of the morality-focussed perspective, the volitional elements involved ultimately remain secondary to independent, moral-cognitive reasoning, and as such support for any given norm of international law may depend simply on its substantive content.

1040 Supra, III.

Many of these distinctions have not been discussed at length until now, at least within the framework of European consensus. This may be in part because the ECtHR's references to international law are read instead as (exclusively) an instance of systemic integration, setting aside the vertical connection to the States parties' positions; it may also be because the ECtHR itself does not usually comment on the "character, tasks or compositions" of the organs from which international documents referred to originate, nor "on the character of a document which it mentions",[1041] nor yet on its deeper rationale for referring to international law in the first place.

I also suspect that the role of international law within European consensus has so far escaped critical scrutiny because it performs a delicate balancing function between the ethos-focussed perspective (by reference to a pan-European ethos) and the morality-focussed perspective. From the perspective of the prior, reasoning grounded in State-made international law seems preferably to purely moral-cognitive reasoning. It may even provide a pragmatic short-cut to ascertaining the States parties' positions since norms of international law are often easier to identify than the domestic law of 47 different States parties.[1042] From the perspective of liberal proponents of the latter, references to international human rights law, in particular, seem a helpful resource to prod the ECtHR in the "right" direction. Within the progress narrative of international human rights law,[1043] the States parties are deemed to have externalised aspirational standards which

---

1041 Glas, "The European Court of Human Rights' Use of Non-Binding and Standard-Setting Council of Europe Documents" at 103-104

1042 Von Ungern-Sternberg, "Die Konsensmethode des EGMR. Eine kritische Bewertung mit Blick auf das völkerrechtliche Konsens- und das innerstaatliche Demokratieprinzip" at 331; Dzehtsiarou, *European Consensus and the Legitimacy of the European Court of Human Rights*, at 95; Dzehtsiarou, "What Is Law for the European Court of Human Rights?" at 114; Lock, "The Influence of EU Law on Strasbourg Doctrines" at 821; Laura Van den Eynde, "The Consensus Argument in NGOs' *Amicus Curiae* Briefs: Defending Minorities through a Creatively Used Majoritarian Argument," in *Building Consensus on European Consensus. Judicial Interpretation of Human Rights in Europe and Beyond*, ed. Panos Kapotas and Vassilis Tzevelekos (Cambridge: Cambridge University Press, 2019) at 110; see also Pascual-Vives, *Consensus-Based Interpretation of Regional Human Rights Treaties*, at 109; for an example from the ECtHR's case-law, see e.g. ECtHR, Appl. No. 37222/04 – *Altinay v. Turkey*, Judgment of 9 July 2013, at para. 43, in which international materials seem to be used to substantiate a trend within domestic law.

1043 See generally Authers and Charlesworth, "The Crisis and the Quotidian in International Human Rights Law" at 26; Kapur, "Human Rights in the 21st Century: Take a Walk on the Dark Side" at 668-673.

they do not yet live up to, and reference to these standards rather than the domestic laws of the States parties thus constitutes a step forward. In particular, certain kinds of international law may be viewed as an expression of "modern European society",[1044] with the implication that those States not part of the consensus it establishes are less developed, less progressive, and must change their policies accordingly to "catch up".[1045] Thus, the perception of international law as both grounded and aspirational caters, to some extent, to the concerns of both the ethos-focussed and the morality-focussed perspective – with the prior focussing on a pan-European ethos in such a way that it side-lines individual national ethe, arguably more so than consensus based on domestic law usually does.

For all these pragmatic convergences between ethical normativity developed by reference to a pan-European ethos, on the one hand, and moral normativity, on the other, international law should not be understood as supplying a straight-forward solution to the problem of how concrete norms set by the ECtHR can be justified: instead, the multiplicity of international norms and the different procedures underlying them as well as the possibility of conflict with consensus based on domestic laws all contribute to the further malleability of establishing (lack of) consensus, in addition to the more general numerical issues discussed in the previous chapter. The triangular tensions between ethical normativity by reference to a pan-European ethos and individual ethe as well as moral normativity are not solved by international law, but rather complicated further by introducing different procedures which can be taken to express a pan-European ethos. To further destabilise the notion of a pan-European ethos, the following chapter discusses another crucial aspect of how consensus is established: its level of generality.

1044 ECtHR (GC), Appl. No. 23459/03 – *Bayatyan*, at para. 106 (in the context of "the unanimous recognition of the right to conscientious objection by the member States of the European Union": see supra, IV.2.), invoking the idea of "modern societies" already present in ECtHR (Plenary), Appl. No. 6833/74 – *Marckx*, at para. 41; the designation as "modern" could be seen as fulfilling a similar function as the reference to "progressive" consensus: see Chapter 2, III.

1045 See generally on this dynamic in connection with European progress narratives David Kennedy, "Turning to Market Democracy: A Tale of Two Architectures," (1991) 32 *Harvard International Law Journal* 373.

Chapter 7: Establishing Consensus (III): Different Levels of Generality

I. Introduction

Establishing whether or not a consensus among the States parties can be made out, I have argued, is no easy matter. I pointed out, in Chapters 5 and 6, several ways in which the tensions between the morality-focussed perspective and the ethos-focussed perspective influence this assessment – in particular, by virtue of the shifting boundary between the rein effect and the spur effect (lack of consensus or trend in favour of the applicant), as well as the choice of sources (consensus based primarily on domestic or international law). The notion of commonality introduced in Chapter 1, it transpires, is hardly ideologically neutral.

A further, perhaps even more foundational way in which accounts of commonality and difference across the States parties to the ECHR may differ is by virtue of their orientation towards different questions: which issues within the legal systems of the States parties, precisely, are investigated with a view to establishing (lack of) European consensus? One of the ECtHR's standard formulations on the role of consensus in determining the margin of appreciation makes the possibility of different approaches particularly explicit: the Court speaks of lack of consensus "either as to the relative importance of the interest at stake or as to the best means of protecting it" as a relevant factor.[1046] It specifies, in other words, at least two different issues which might be considered through the lens of vertically comparative law: the relatively general issue of how important a certain interest is considered to be, on the one hand, and the more specific issue of which means are adopted to protect it, on the other. This formulation thus makes clear that one can conceive of different objects to which (lack of)

1046 ECtHR (GC), Appl. No. 37359/09 – *Hämäläinen*, at para. 67; for further cases involving this formulation, as well as the connection to the margin of appreciation more generally, see Chapter 8, III.2.

consensus pertains.[1047] Differently put, it matters *how the issue is framed* since it will influence what exactly to compare.[1048]

It will usually be "possible to trace as many similarities as differences [between the States parties], depending on the precise criterion chosen for comparison"[1049] – therefore, the criterion chosen may have a crucial and often decisive impact on whether commonality among the States parties is discovered and whether the rein effect or the spur effect of consensus is operationalised. This remains a somewhat underappreciated issue in general,[1050] but I will focus, for present purposes, on only one aspect of it: the fact that the vertically comparative analysis which forms the basis of European consensus can be conducted *at different levels of generality*. I will mostly leave aside, therefore, discussions as to the appropriate way of framing the issue in non-discrimination cases involving Article 14 ECHR, or cases in which there is debate as to whether the comparative materials relied on by the ECtHR cover the topics it claims they do.[1051]

With regard to the level of generality at which consensus is approached, a common approach in the ECtHR's case-law – and often the unspoken premise underlying accounts of European consensus by academic commentators[1052] – is to identify the issue before the Court[1053] in binary terms (e.g., does sterilisation as a precondition of legal gender recognition violate the right to private life or not) and, with a certain sense of self-evidence, to

---

1047 Føllesdal, "A Better Signpost, Not a Better Walking Stick: How to Evaluate the European Consensus Doctrine" at 196.

1048 Ryan, "Europe's Moral Margin: Parental Aspirations and the European Court of Human Rights" at 496; Senden, *Interpretation of Fundamental Rights*, at 130; Henrard, "How the ECtHR's Use of European Consensus Considerations Allows Legitimacy Concerns to Delimit Its Mandate" at 152.

1049 Gerards, "Giving Shape to the Notion of 'Shared Responsibility'" at 45.

1050 Although one of the merits of the recent edited volume on European consensus has been to put more of a spotlight on it: see the summary in Gearty, "Building Consensus on European Consensus" at 460-461.

1051 Both of these issues are well illustrated in ECtHR (GC), Appl. Nos. 60367/08 and 961/11 – *Khamtokhu and Aksenchik*, joint partly dissenting opinion of Judges Sicilianos, Møse, Lubarda, Mourou-Vikström and Kucsko-Standlmayer; for the prior point, see also briefly Chapter 5, IV.

1052 See Chapter 1, III.

1053 This issue might itself be identified in different ways, e.g. from different angles or at different levels of generality. I will mostly bracket this question for present purposes, but see Chapter 5, IV. for a discussion of ECtHR (GC), Appl. Nos. 29381/09 and 32684/09 – *Vallianatos and Others* which clearly indicates how a non-discrimination perspective may change the way in which the issue before the Court is framed.

then tailor the level of generality of the comparative materials so that it coheres with this issue (e.g., do the States parties retain sterilisation as a precondition of legal gender recognition or not).[1054] One might think of it as a Goldilocks level of generality: neither too general nor too specific, but "just right" for the case at issue. Sometimes this element of "just right" shines through in the ECtHR's formulations. For example, in *De Tommaso v. Italy*, the Court provided a comparative overview which aims to ascertain whether or not the States parties' laws make provision for "measures comparable to those applied in Italy in the present case".[1055]

Yet while this is a common approach, probably even the dominant approach within the ECtHR's case-law, it by no means exhausts the possibilities and it is certainly not the only way in which the ECtHR conducts its vertically comparative analysis; indeed, the ECtHR itself seems well aware of the fact that it can tailor its comparative analysis towards different objects.[1056] I will begin this chapter, therefore, by demonstrating the Court's use, within its processes of justification,[1057] of European consensus at various different levels of generality (II.). This overview also shows how the different levels of generality may relate in different ways to various sources of consensus, particularly to consensus based on domestic law and consensus based on international law.

It quickly becomes apparent that the possibility of moving between different levels of generality contributes massively to the malleability of estab-

---

1054 The example is from ECtHR, Appl. Nos. 79885/12, 52471/13 and 52596/13 – *A.P., Garçon and Nicot*, at para. 122.

1055 ECtHR (GC), Appl. No. 43395/09 – *De Tommaso v. Italy*, Judgment of 23 February 2017, at para. 69; the Goldilocks element also comes through quite clearly in ECtHR (GC), Appl. No. 26374/18 – *Guðmundur Andri Ástráðsson*, at para. 151, where the Court examines the States parties' laws at different levels of generality but notes that the comparative survey of the specific requirement at issue (compare at para. 224) is "particularly relevant to the present case".

1056 See e.g. ECtHR (GC), Appl. No. 35289/11 – *Regner v. the Czech Republic*, Judgment of 19 September 2017, at para. 70, where the Court discusses various aspects of national security and classified access to information before turning "*more specifically* to the refusal or the withdrawal of security clearance granting courts access to confidential documents" (emphasis added).

1057 For the distinction between processes of discovery and justification, see generally Chapter 1, IV.5.; for an argument that, in some cases at least, "the actual margin of appreciation is determined at a more concrete level [of generality with regard to (lack of) consensus] than is explained in the Court's reasoning", see Henrard, "How the European Court of Human Rights' Concern Regarding European Consensus Tempers the Effective Protection of Freedom of Religion" at 400.

lishing (lack of) consensus which preceding chapters have already touched upon. As in those chapters, I want to argue that the ECtHR's use of European consensus at different levels of generality need not necessarily be aleatory, but can rather be understood as an expression of the triangular tensions between different kinds of normativity. The second half of this chapter is dedicated to exploring this connection. I begin by showing how the move to a higher level of generality as the basis for the consensus enquiry may either create space for morality-focussed reasoning or, conversely, for emphasis on the national ethos of the respondent State (III.1.). I then consider the prior possibility in more detail by discussing ways in which consensus might be referred to at different levels of generality within the Rawlsian framework of reflective equilibrium (III.2.). The merit of such a framework, I suggest, is that it moves away from the unquestioning reliance on consensus at the Goldilocks level of generality; but the coherentist orientation of frameworks such as reflective equilibrium also threatens to underestimate and hence obscure the contradictory nature of the patterns of argument involved (IV.).

II. Levels of Generality in the Court's Use of European Consensus

I have already mentioned the assumption of a Goldilocks level of generality underlying many accounts of European consensus. But for all that the ECtHR often does tailor its use of consensus to the level of generality of whatever it takes to be the relevant issue in the case before it, there are also numerous instances of comparative surveys being conducted or analysed at different levels of generality,[1058] sometimes within the same judgment. For example, in *Bărbulescu v. Romania*, the ECtHR mentioned, first, European consensus as to the right to secrecy of correspondence "in general terms";[1059] second, lack of consensus as to how the specific issue of monitoring employees at their workplace should be regulated;[1060] but, third, a trend to require that the data subject be informed before any monitoring

1058 Van Drooghenbroeck, *La Proportionnalité dans le Droit de la Convention Européenne des Droits de l'Homme*, at 533; Gerards, *General Principles of the European Convention on Human Rights*, at 105 speaks of "uncertainty regarding the level of abstraction".

1059 ECtHR (GC), Appl. No. 61496/08 – *Bărbulescu v. Romania*, Judgment of 5 September 2017, at para. 52.

1060 Ibid., at para. 118.

activities are carried out.[1061] In *Opuz v. Turkey*, the Court noted that "there seems to be no general consensus among States Parties regarding the pursuance of the criminal prosecution against perpetrators of domestic violence when the victim withdraws her complaints", but it did draw on vertically comparative law to establish "certain factors that can be taken into account in deciding to pursue the prosecution".[1062]

In some cases, the ECtHR builds on aspects which are *more specific* than (what was arguably) the primary issue before it. To stay with the example of trans rights mentioned above: in earlier cases, the focus was not yet whether certain preconditions of legal gender recognition are permissible or not, but rather whether there is a right to such recognition *at all*. In the case of *Sheffield and Horsham v. the United Kingdom*, the ECtHR had argued that there was a lack of consensus "as to how to address the repercussions" of legal gender recognition, for example with regard to areas of law "such as marriage, filiation, privacy or data protection" or with regard to situations in which trans people might be obliged to reveal their previously assigned legal gender.[1063] The comparative analysis was thus conducted at a rather specific level relative to the question before the Court (i.e. the right to legal gender recognition as such, not its specific repercussions),[1064] but nonetheless served to establish a lack of consensus and led to the rein effect: no violation of the Convention was found.

This conclusion was famously reversed four years later in *Christine Goodwin v. the United Kingdom*, which exemplifies the different levels of generality available to the ECtHR in its comparative endeavours. It now left aside the lack of European consensus regarding "the resolution of the legal and

---

1061 Ibid., at para. 132.

1062 ECtHR, Appl. No. 33401/02 – *Opuz*, at para. 138; the ECtHR went on to argue (at para. 143) that the Turkish authorities had taken too one-sided an approach in light of the variety of factors identified; for use of consensus with regard to different factors within proportionality and balancing, see e.g. ECtHR (GC), Appl. Nos. 40660/08 and 60641/08 – *von Hannover v. Germany (No. 2)*, Judgment of 7 February 2012, at paras. 106 and 110; ECtHR (GC), Appl. No. 80982/12 – *Muhammad and Muhammad v. Romania*, Judgment of 15 October 2020, at paras. 148-150.

1063 ECtHR (GC), Appl. Nos. 22985/93 and 23390/94 – *Sheffield and Horsham*, at para. 57; in a similar vein, see e.g. ECtHR (GC), Appl. No. 42202/07 – *Sitaropoulos and Giakoumopoulos v. Greece*, Judgment of 15 March 2012, at paras. 74-75, discussing different "arrangements" for voting from abroad; similarly ECtHR, Appl. No. 19840/09 – *Shindler*, at para. 115.

1064 See critically Ambrus, "Comparative Law Method in the Jurisprudence of the European Court of Human Rights in the Light of the Rule of Law" at 365-367.

practical problems posed" (the "repercussions" of *Sheffield and Horsham*, one surmises) and relied instead on international trends in favour of "increased social acceptance" of trans persons (very high level of generality) and of their "legal recognition" (mid-level generality, precisely the question at issue).[1065] While the judgment in *Christine Goodwin* is somewhat unusual in that it relied primarily on trends outside Europe,[1066] other cases also refer to *vertically* comparative materials which are *more general* than (what was arguably) the issue before the ECtHR. For example, a number of cases establish the great importance of the best interests of the child in custody cases by reference to European consensus, thus taking a principle of a relatively high level of generality as a "common point of departure" among the States parties which then also constitutes the starting point for the ECtHR's consideration of the more specific issue before it.[1067]

A number of cases involving consensus at a relatively high level of generality have gained notoriety in part because of just how general the lack of consensus identified by the ECtHR was. Thus, in the case of *Vo v. France*, the Court held that "there is no European consensus on the scientific and legal definition of the beginning of life",[1068] a point later echoed in *A, B and C v. Ireland*.[1069] Despite being anchored in the kind of vertically comparative legal reference to "[e]xisting legislation in the Member States"

1065 ECtHR (GC), Appl. No. 28957/95 – *Christine Goodwin*, at para. 85.

1066 See Chapter 5, IV.

1067 ECtHR, Appl. No. 22028/04 – *Zaunegger v. Germany*, Judgment of 3 December 2009, at para. 60 which also, however, refers to the more specific aspect of "scrutiny by the national courts" in that regard, which was crucial in the case at issue; see similarly ECtHR, Appl. No. 35637/03 – *Sporer v. Austria*, Judgment of 3 February 2011, at para. 87; the Court has repeatedly noted the "broad consensus" that the best interests of the child are paramount: see e.g. ECtHR (GC), Appl. No. 41615/07 – *Neulinger and Shuruk*, at para. 135; ECtHR, Appl. No. 27496/15 – *Mohamed Hasan v. Norway*, Judgment of 26 April 2018, at paras. 123 and 149; ECtHR, Appl. No. 70879/11 – *Ilya Lyapin v. Russia*, Judgment of 30 June 2020, at para. 44; somewhat more specifically see also ECtHR (GC), Appl. No. 37283/13 – *Strand Lobben and Others v. Norway*, Judgment of 10 September 2019, at para. 207; children's rights have also been emphasised based on consensus in other contexts, see e.g. ECtHR (GC), Appl. No. 36391/02 – *Salduz v. Turkey*, Judgment of 27 November 2008, at para. 60 on "the fundamental importance of providing access to a lawyer where the person in custody is a minor" based on the "relevant international law materials".

1068 ECtHR (GC), Appl. No. 53924/00 – *Vo*, at para. 82; see further on this case Chapter 5, III.2. and Chapter 8, II.

1069 ECtHR (GC), Appl. No. 25579/05 – *A, B and C*, at para. 237; see further infra, notes 1110-1120.

which is typical of European consensus,[1070] this claim is made at such a high level of generality as to have been described as relating to the "philosophical premises" of the case.[1071]

In these cases as in some others which I will mention below, the turn to lack of consensus at a high level of generality served to operationalise the rein effect and thus favoured the respondent State. Conversely, however, in some judgments the reliance on consensus at a high level of generality established principles which, as in *Christine Goodwin*, mitigated in favour of the applicant – e.g., "consensus among Contracting States to promote economic and social rights"[1072] or "the equality of the sexes" as "a major goal in the member States of the Council of Europe"[1073] – and the ECtHR found a violation of the Convention.

The possibility of approaching vertically comparative reasoning at different levels of generality also lends additional complexity to the tensions which may exist between consensus established primarily by reference to domestic law and consensus established primarily by reference to *international law*, as discussed in the previous chapter. Depending on the kind of materials which are available or which the ECtHR chooses to rely on, several different constellations may occur. On the one hand, international law is sometimes linked to consensus at the level of principles rather than rules, i.e. supplying only "general concepts which underpin legal standards" but no "specific implementing measures".[1074] This seems intuitively plausible in many cases, since norms of international law (like the Convention itself) will often leave States a margin of appreciation in deciding the

---

1070 See ECtHR (GC), Appl. No. 53924/00 – *Vo*, at para. 40, citing from an opinion of the European Group on Ethics in Science and New Technologies at the European Commission.

1071 Føllesdal, "A Better Signpost, Not a Better Walking Stick: How to Evaluate the European Consensus Doctrine" at 196.

1072 ECtHR (GC), Appl. No. 34503/97 – *Demir and Baykara*, at para. 84.

1073 ECtHR (Plenary), Appl. Nos. 9214/80, 9473/81 and 9474/81 – *Abdulaziz, Cabales and Balkandali v. the United Kingdom*, Judgment of 28 May 1985, at para. 78; see also e.g. ECtHR (GC), Appl. No. 30078/06 – *Konstantin Markin*, at para. 127.

1074 Dzehtsiarou, *European Consensus and the Legitimacy of the European Court of Human Rights*, at 13 (for the citation distinguishing rules from principles) and 59 (for the connection between international law and principles, on the one hand, and domestic law and rules, on the other); see also Dzehtsiarou, "What Is Law for the European Court of Human Rights?" at 132.

specifics of implementation.[1075] Thus, the ECtHR has sometimes referred to consensus established by reference to international law at a very high level of generality, for example to establish that compliance with Article 4 ECHR (freedom from slavery and forced labour) involves positive as well as negative obligations for the States parties,[1076] or that the protection of health constitutes a legitimate aim in the context of doping controls.[1077]

On the other hand, particularly within human rights law, the question may be whether a certain manner of implementation still falls within that margin or not,[1078] and the requirements of international law may become rather specific – one need only think, for example, of some conventions of the International Labour Organization (ILO) or of the various specialised United Nations treaties such as the Convention on the Elimination of All Forms of Discrimination Against Women or the Convention on the Rights of Persons with Disabilities. In that vein, the ECtHR relied, inter alia, on ILO Convention No. 87 on Freedom of Association and Protection of the Right to Organise and on ILO Convention No. 151 concerning Protection of the right to Organise and Procedures for Determining Conditions of Employment in the Public Service in the case of *Demir and Baykara v. Turkey*.[1079] In cases such as this, consensus based on international law has the ring of a *lex specialis* to it: the ECtHR itself has on occasion referred to the "consensus emerging from *specialised* international instruments".[1080] More specialised need not necessarily mean more specific, but there is certainly an area of overlap: as Eva Brems has put it, "if a State has underwritten certain detailed obligations in one text, the interpretation of a more

1075 I am referring here to a substantive, not a structural margin; see Chapter 8, III.1.

1076 ECtHR, Appl. No. 73316/01 – *Siliadin*, at paras. 85-89; see also on Art. 4 ECHR and norms of international law ECtHR (GC), Appl. No. 60561/14 – *S.M.*, at paras. 279 et seqq.

1077 ECtHR, Appl. Nos. 48151/11 and 77769/13 – *National Federation of Sportspersons' Associations and Unions (FNASS) and Others*, at para. 165.

1078 The development of the case-law on trans rights exemplifies this: having initially acknowledged only a right to legal gender recognition as such, with the "appropriate means of achieving recognition" falling within the States parties' substantive margin (ECtHR (GC), Appl. No. 28957/95 – *Christine Goodwin*, at para. 93), subsequent case-law has scrutinised various preconditions for legal gender recognition and thus narrowed the substantive margin left to the States parties; see further Theilen, "The Long Road to Recognition: Transgender Rights and Transgender Reality in Europe" at 378.

1079 ECtHR (GC), Appl. No. 34503/97 – *Demir and Baykara*, at paras. 37, 44, 100, 122, 148 and 165.

1080 ECtHR (GC), Appl. No. 23459/03 – *Bayatyan*, at para. 102 (emphasis added).

general text can be oriented in that sense".[1081] This kind of reliance on consensus established by reference to fairly specific norms of international law has played a role in a number of cases before the ECtHR.[1082]

These examples should suffice to illustrate the malleability of the ECtHR's consensus enquiry with regard to the level(s) of generality at which it is conducted. Some of these examples also indicate very clearly that the conclusions drawn from European consensus may differ quite drastically depending on the level of generality which is deemed relevant:[1083] depending on how it frames the issue, the ECtHR may discover anything from a "spectrum of national positions" indicating a lack of consensus, to common ground with the respondent State left sequestered "at one end of the comparative spectrum", and tend towards the rein effect or the spur effect accordingly.[1084] Yet, as several commentators have noted, the ECtHR rarely specifies why it chooses any given level of generality to base its analysis on.[1085] In what follows, I would like to suggest that this

1081 Brems, *Human Rights: Universality and Diversity*, at 421; echoed by Dzehtsiarou, *European Consensus and the Legitimacy of the European Court of Human Rights*, at 46; see also Rietiker, "The Principle of 'Effectiveness' in the Recent Jurisprudence of the European Court of Human Rights" at 274; finally, see also ECtHR (Plenary), Appl. No. 14038/88 – *Soering*, at para. 88, dismissing an *e contrario* argument to the effect that specifically explicated obligations in other treaties should not be interpreted into the ECHR; but see also ECtHR, Appl. No. 31045/10 – *National Union of Rail, Maritime and Transport Workers*, at para. 106, in which the ECtHR distanced itself from the "more specific and exacting norm regarding industrial action" contained in the European Social Charter.

1082 Senden, *Interpretation of Fundamental Rights*, at 258.

1083 Ambrus, "Comparative Law Method in the Jurisprudence of the European Court of Human Rights in the Light of the Rule of Law" at 366; Ryan, "Europe's Moral Margin: Parental Aspirations and the European Court of Human Rights" at 496; Senden, *Interpretation of Fundamental Rights*, at 129-130; Dzehtsiarou, *European Consensus and the Legitimacy of the European Court of Human Rights*, at 15; Henrard, "How the ECtHR's Use of European Consensus Considerations Allows Legitimacy Concerns to Delimit Its Mandate" at 151.

1084 Both citations are from ECtHR, Appl. No. 31045/10 – *National Union of Rail, Maritime and Transport Workers*, at para. 91; see also the oscillations e.g. in ECtHR (GC), Appl. No. 74025/01 – *Hirst*, at para. 81.

1085 Janneke Gerards, "Diverging Fundamental Rights Standards and the Role of the European Court of Human Rights," in *Constructing European Constitutional Law*, ed. M. Claes and M. De Visser (Oxford: Hart), available at <https://papers.ssrn.com/sol3/papers.cfm?abstract_id=2344626>, at 9; Ambrus, "Comparative Law Method in the Jurisprudence of the European Court of Human Rights in the Light of the Rule of Law" at 366; see Dzehtsiarou, *European Consensus and the Legitimacy of the European Court of Human Rights*, at 16-17.

choice relates at least in part to the triangular tensions between the kind of ethical normativity associated with consensus itself (i.e. a pan-European ethos), on the one hand, and individual national ethe as well as moral normativity, on the other.

III. The Implications of Shifting Levels of Generality

1. Different Constellations within Triangular Tensions

One way to approach the implications of shifting levels of generality for these triangular tensions is to discuss how different levels of generality at which European consensus is discussed relate to the ECtHR's conclusions as to the issue before it, and how this in turn bears on other forms of reasoning independent of European consensus. Cases in which consensus is established in such a way that it relates directly to the ECtHR's conclusions are relatively straight-forward, at least when viewed from the ethos-focussed perspective: ethical normativity developed at the level of a pan-European ethos provides an immediate response to the question at hand.[1086] Thus Mónika Ambrus has argued that "the level of abstraction [for the comparison] should defer to the level at which the concrete rights or interests have been formulated",[1087] and Kristin Henrard has similarly held that "the appropriate level to measure consensus is the one that connects most directly to the central matter of a case".[1088]

For example, if the question at issue is deemed to be whether a complete lack of legal gender recognition for trans persons violates human rights, then the comparative analysis would investigate neither the importance accorded to gender identity within law (too general) nor the different preconditions and procedures attached to gender recognition (too specific), but whether or not a possibility of legal gender recognition exists at all within the States parties' legal systems.[1089] This is what I referred to above

1086 By saying this, I do *not* mean to imply that this way of using consensus could predetermine outcomes: at a minimum, the tensions discussed in the preceding chapters would continue to necessitate a variety of choices as to its application.

1087 Ambrus, "Comparative Law Method in the Jurisprudence of the European Court of Human Rights in the Light of the Rule of Law" at 367.

1088 Henrard, "How the ECtHR's Use of European Consensus Considerations Allows Legitimacy Concerns to Delimit Its Mandate" at 151.

1089 See supra, notes 1063-1065.

as the Goldilocks level of generality: neither too general nor too specific, but "just right" for the case at issue, and hence understood as being of most direct relevance for it. This sense of immediate relevance no doubt accounts in part for the sense of self-evidence with which the level of generality of the consensus analysis is often tailored towards whatever the issue before the Court is construed as being.

By contrast, when consensus is approached at a relatively high level of generality, then there is a certain disconnect between the claims that can be made on that basis and the more specific conclusions which the ECtHR must ultimately reach. As Rachovitsa has put it in the context of systemic integration, "[t]he higher the degree of abstraction, the lower the impact on the interpretation of the treaty in dispute".[1090] In the spectrum between "the uselessly general and the controversially specific", as Ely memorably put it,[1091] the move from consensus at a general level to more specific conclusions "entails a value judgment" which cannot be justified by reference to the comparative materials themselves.[1092] On the basis of the ethos-focussed perspective, consensus at a high level of generality cannot, therefore, "claim the same degree of persuasive value" as consensus relating directly to the specific issue before the ECtHR.[1093] Though commentators on consensus rarely write from within the tradition of legal realism, it is to the typically realist "distrust of abstraction" that this attitude is indebted.[1094]

1090 Adamantia Rachovitsa, "Fragmentation of International Law Revisited: Insights, Good Practices, and Lessons to be Learned from the Case Law of the European Court of Human Rights," (2015) 28 *Leiden Journal of International Law* 863 at 878.

1091 Ely, *Democracy and Distrust. A Theory of Judicial Review*, at 64 (on ostensible societal consensus in the national context).

1092 ECJ, C-411/05 – *Félix Palacios de la Villa v Cortefiel Servicios SA*, Opinion of AG Mazák, 15 February 2007, ECLI:EU:C:2007:106, at para. 91; for a positioning of this citation in relation to consensus-based reasoning, see Theilen, "Levels of Generality in the Comparative Reasoning of the European Court of Human Rights and the European Court of Justice: Towards Judicial Reflective Equilibrium" at 408-409.

1093 Dzehtsiarou, *European Consensus and the Legitimacy of the European Court of Human Rights*, at 17; this point is also implied in Glas, "The European Court of Human Rights' Use of Non-Binding and Standard-Setting Council of Europe Documents" at 117.

1094 Kennedy, *A Critique of Adjudication (fin de siècle)*, at 106. The most famous version is probably Holmes's phrasing that "general propositions do not decide concrete cases" (Supreme Court of the United States, *Lochner v. New York*, 198 U.S. 45, 76 (1905) (Holmes, J., dissenting)); more generally, this approach can

Conversely, proponents of the morality-focussed perspective are likely to welcome assessments of European consensus at a higher level of generality *precisely because* it leaves space for a value judgement in the course of moving from consensus at a general level to more specific conclusions, and therefore leaves a space undetermined by ethical normativity. Daniel Regan has been the most explicit on this point: while he opposes the use of European consensus in its currently predominant form as "incompatible with the Convention's aim of providing protection of certain fundamental rights" by stifling its "normative development",[1095] he suggests that the ECtHR could be "inspired by the general principles of laws of the Contracting States".[1096] Such an approach would be reminiscent of the way in which the European Court of Justice deploys vertically comparative reasoning in its case-law on general principles, with vertically comparative analysis usually restricted to broad principles at a high level of generality, thus leaving ample space for substantive reasoning of the kind preferred by the morality-focussed perspective.[1097] European consensus, in this scenario, provides only a "starting point" for further reasoning based on moral rather than ethical normativity.[1098]

Other commentators have welcomed the use of consensus at high levels of generality less explicitly; but given the space it opens up for the morality-focussed perspective, it nonetheless seems compatible – or, at the very least, *more* compatible – with their approach than consensus geared specifically at the case at hand. For example, George Letsas juxtaposes the use of European consensus (which he opposes) with a "search for 'common values' in international human rights materials".[1099] There are several ele-

be traced back to the Kantian insight that "rules do not spell out the conditions of their own application": see Martti Koskenniemi, "Constitutionalism as Mindset: Reflections on Kantian Themes About International Law and Globalization," (2006) 8 *Theoretical Inquiries in Law* 9.

1095 Regan, "A Worthy Endeavour?" at 52.

1096 Ibid., 75.

1097 Theilen, "Levels of Generality in the Comparative Reasoning of the European Court of Human Rights and the European Court of Justice: Towards Judicial Reflective Equilibrium" at 402-403; see also Gerard Conway, "Levels of Generality in the Legal Reasoning of the European Court of Justice," (2008) 14 *European Law Journal* 787.

1098 Regan, "A Worthy Endeavour?" at 76; see also supra, note 1067.

1099 Letsas, "Strasbourg's Interpretive Ethic: Lessons for the International Lawyer" at 523; see also Letsas, "The ECHR as a Living Instrument: Its Meaning and Legitimacy" at 115 and 122; the phrasing "common values" is taken from ECtHR (GC), Appl. No. 34503/97 – *Demir and Baykara*, at para. 85.

ments at play here, many of which (such as the numerical issues and sources of consensus involved) have been treated over the course of the preceding chapters. But there is also, arguably, an implicit acknowledgement of the permissibility of referring to European consensus *provided that this is done at a high level of generality*. While Letsas's focus is elsewhere, and he styles the reference to "common values" as "common *values*",[1100] one could also emphasise it differently: *common* values.

Within this debate, then, those who favour a strong place for the notion of a pan-European ethos within regional human rights adjudication tend to advocate the use of European consensus in such a way that the level of generality at which the vertically comparative analysis is conducted coheres with whatever is taken to be the main question before the ECtHR: in this way, European consensus gains the most immediate relevance for the outcome of the case. Conversely, proponents of the morality-focussed perspective favour the use of consensus at higher levels of generality since this creates a disconnect between the consensus analysis and the question at issue, creating more space for other kinds of normativity. Both sides of the debate thus commonly assume that consensus, particularly consensus in favour of the applicant, will be "easy to discover at a high level of abstraction" but quickly dissipate with regard to more specific issues:[1101] hence why Letsas, for example, can talk of *common* values at a high level of generality.

In many cases, this assumption of greater agreement at higher levels of abstraction may hold, but it is by no means universally valid. Certain propositions may be consensual only so long as one does scrutinise their underlying, more general rationale too deeply. This scenario is often said to apply, at least to some extent, to the human rights project as a whole: "Yes, we agree on the rights, but on condition that no one asks us

1100 Letsas, "Strasbourg's Interpretive Ethic: Lessons for the International Lawyer" at 523.

1101 Gerards, "Giving Shape to the Notion of 'Shared Responsibility'" at 45; see also Dzehtsiarou, *European Consensus and the Legitimacy of the European Court of Human Rights*, at 16; Tzevelekos and Dzehtsiarou, "International Custom Making" at 323; I have also previously emphasised this scenario in Theilen, "Levels of Generality in the Comparative Reasoning of the European Court of Human Rights and the European Court of Justice: Towards Judicial Reflective Equilibrium" at 408; in the context of the European Union, see de Búrca, "The Language of Rights and European Integration" at 46; and see generally Besson, *The Morality of Conflict. Reasonable Disagreement and the Law*, at 156.

why".[1102] In a similar vein, one might say that European consensus at a relatively specific level might be based on more general concepts on which there is *less* agreement.

One area within which lack of consensus among the States parties at a high level of generality has often been emphasised by the ECtHR is that of freedom of religion, especially religious attire. For example, the case of *Leyla Şahin v. Turkey* concerned a Turkish ban on religious clothing within universities, which the ECtHR deemed compatible with the right to freedom of religion. The majority opinion argued that a wide margin of appreciation must be accorded where "the relationship between State and religions are at stake", and notably "when it comes to regulating the wearing of religious symbols in educational institutions, especially" – as the comparative legal materials adduced in that case were deemed to illustrate – "in view of the diversity of the approaches taken by national authorities on the issue".[1103] The majority thus focussed on the lack of consensus on religious attire in educational institutions in general, and even connected this issue to the extremely general proposition that it is "not possible to discern throughout Europe a uniform conception of *the significance of religion in society*".[1104] By way of contrast, Judge Tulkens in her dissenting opinion applied a vertically comparative analysis more specifically to the States parties' laws on religious attire *in universities*, and found a consensus in favour

---

1102 As related by Jacques Maritain in UNESCO, "Human Rights. Comments and Interpretations", UN Doc. UNESCO/PHS/3 (rev.), 25 July 1948, available at <https://unesdoc.unesco.org/ark:/48223/pf0000155042>, at p. I; my reading here is that notions even more general than the already-general formulations of human rights at issue are controversial (e.g. human dignity, the meaning of life, etc.); one might, conversely, also frame this as the general concept of human rights being relatively consensual, with more specific conceptions of human rights being more controversial; since I think my argument in this section holds true in substance regardless of what is regarded as relatively abstract and what as relatively specific, I leave aside any attempt at a clear delineation of whether and how one could or should decide between these different perspectives.

1103 ECtHR (GC), Appl. No. 44774/98 – *Leyla Şahin*, at para. 109; see also e.g. ECtHR, Appl. No. 27058/05 – *Dogru v. France*, Judgment of 4 December 2008, at para. 63.

1104 ECtHR (GC), Appl. No. 44774/98 – *Leyla Şahin*, at para. 109; though the ECtHR does not invoke the phrasing in this case, this could be connected back to lack of consensus on "the relative importance of the interest at stake": see supra, note 1046; critically on this approach as involving "too high a level of abstraction" Henrard, "How the ECtHR's Use of European Consensus Considerations Allows Legitimacy Concerns to Delimit Its Mandate" at 152.

of the applicant: "in none of the member States has the ban on wearing religious symbols extended to university education, which is intended for young adults".[1105]

Since the move to a more general level for the vertically comparative analysis in this case led to a finding of *lack* of consensus, thus invoking the rein effect by way of a broad margin of appreciation, the effect was to provide more space to the national ethos of the respondent State:[1106] because of the broad margin of appreciation, "the role of the national decision-making body must be given special importance".[1107] Far from using consensus at a high level of generality to find an area of common ground and create space for morality-focussed considerations in its further reasoning, then, the ECtHR here uses lack of consensus at a high level of generality to give more weight to national ethe, specifically the national ethos of the respondent State.

It is notable that the case of *Leyla Şahin* concerned religious freedom in a country which raises strong exceptionalist claims as to its traditional understanding of the principle of secularism,[1108] and it is likely that this context motivated the direction which the ECtHR's judgment took. My point here is that the strong emphasis on national ethe which results comes at the expense of a pan-European ethos in one sense (i.e. relatively specific rules on religious attire) but, crucially, it is also in line with it in a different sense (i.e. lack of consensus on the appropriate relationship between State and church, or on the significance of religion in society). Indeed, if we take the ECtHR's reasoning at its word, then it is lack of consensus at a high level of generality, not the national ethos and a possible claim to exceptionalism, which constitutes the starting point of its justification: in a formulation which strongly foregrounds the ethos-focussed perspective's emphasis on reasonable disagreement about moral matters, the Court notes that when "opinion in a democratic society may reasonably differ widely", *then* the role of the national decision-making body attains particular im-

1105 ECtHR (GC), Appl. No. 44774/98 – *Leyla Şahin*, dissenting opinion of Judge Tulkens, at para. 3; see also ECtHR, Appl. No. 64846/11 – *Ebrahimian v. France*, Judgment of 26 November 2015, at para. 65, where the ECtHR came close to admitting a consensus against the respondent State at relatively specific levels of generality but posited a narrow margin of appreciation by reference to *Leyla Şahin* and the "national context of State-Church relations".

1106 On such allegiances in general see Chapter 4, III.3.; on this constellation in relation to the margin of appreciation, see especially Chapter 8, III.1. and III.2.

1107 ECtHR (GC), Appl. No. 44774/98 – *Leyla Şahin*, at para. 109.

1108 See Chapter 4, II.2. in fine.

portance – and the lack of consensus as to the relationship between the State and religions is used to illustrate that opinion may indeed reasonably differ.[1109]

An example already cited in the previous section, the infamous case of *A, B and C* in which the applicants challenged Ireland's (then) highly restrictive abortion regime, may demonstrate the way in which this dynamic unfolds. The first point which this case demonstrates is how lack of consensus at a general level can be operationalised despite consensus at the more specific level. In *A, B and C*, the Court was compelled to accept that "there is indeed a consensus amongst a substantial majority of the Contracting States of the Council of Europe towards allowing abortion on broader grounds than accorded under Irish law" – yet it held that this did not decisively narrow the margin of appreciation.[1110] "Of central importance" for this conclusion was the fact that, as established in the prior judgment in *Vo*,[1111] the Court can establish "no European consensus on the scientific and legal definition of the beginning of life".[1112] Because of this lack of consensus *as to a general issue, the importance of unborn life*, the margin remained broad – and, as in *Leyla Şahin*, no violation of the Convention was found.

The second point of note in this case is the way in which lack of consensus worked alongside but also *preceded*, within the ECtHR's reasoning, what was presented as Ireland's national ethos. Because the ECtHR, in *A, B and C*, gave strong weight to (what it took to be) the Irish national ethos in the form of the "profound moral views of the Irish people",[1113] it is sometimes said that the respondent State's national ethos "trumped" the spur effect of European consensus,[1114] that the ECtHR allowed said national ethos "as a counter-argument to European consensus",[1115] or that "the

1109 ECtHR (GC), Appl. No. 44774/98 – *Leyla Şahin*, at para. 109.
1110 ECtHR (GC), Appl. No. 25579/05 – *A, B and C*, at paras. 235-236.
1111 See supra, note 1068.
1112 ECtHR (GC), Appl. No. 25579/05 – *A, B and C*, at para. 237.
1113 Ibid., at para. 241; see also paras. 222-227 in the context of a "legitimate aim".
1114 See in that vein de Londras and Dzehtsiarou, "Grand Chamber of the European Court of Human Rights: A, B & C v Ireland, Decision of 17 December 2010" at 256 ("the limited availability of abortion in Ireland was said to be based on the 'profound moral views' of the Irish people, which constituted a trumping internal consensus").
1115 Draghici, "The Strasbourg Court between European and Local Consensus: Anti-democratic or Guardian of Democratic Process?" at 24.

Court went against [European consensus]".[1116] Framing the issue in this way,[1117] I think, underestimates the malleability of consensus itself: the immediate counter-argument to the consensus in favour of the applicant was *itself based on European consensus*, namely the lack of consensus at higher levels of generality.[1118] It was in light of the broad margin which followed from this and which the ECtHR continued to emphasise[1119] that the "profound moral views of the Irish people" appeared, later on in the judgment, as part of the Court's (very limited) substantive assessment.[1120]

I will consider the connection between European consensus and the margin of appreciation in more detail in the next chapter.[1121] For present purposes, the conclusion I wish to draw is that shifting between different levels of generality within the consensus analysis can not only be of crucial import for the establishment of either consensus or lack thereof, but also, relatedly, has implications for the role consensus plays within the triangular tensions which I have been discussing throughout. In particular, emphasis on consensus at high levels of generality may allow it to function as a "starting point"[1122] – but also *no more* than a starting point – for the ECtHR's reasoning, creating a disconnect between the general consensus analysis and the more specific conclusions which the ECtHR must reach and thus opening up space for morality-focussed reasoning. Conversely – and in that regard the concerns aired by commentators on *A, B and C* ultimately ring true – the emphasis on lack of consensus at high levels of generality points towards giving significant argumentative weight to the na-

1116 Kapotas and Tzevelekos, "How (Difficult Is It) to Build Consensus on (European) Consensus?" at 7 in footnote 25; see also Peat, *Comparative Reasoning in International Courts and Tribunals*, at 145-146.

1117 A tendency which originates, I suspect, in ECtHR (GC), Appl. No. 25579/05 – *A, B and C*, joint partly dissenting opinion of Judges Rozakis, Tulkens, Fura, Hirvelä, Malinverni and Poalelungi, at para. 6; see also the government's argument summarised in para. 186 of the majority opinion.

1118 See also Henrard, "How the ECtHR's Use of European Consensus Considerations Allows Legitimacy Concerns to Delimit Its Mandate" at 156, noting how "a strong consensus [...], in other respect" is balanced out "by lack of consensus, in another respect".

1119 ECtHR (GC), Appl. No. 25579/05 – *A, B and C*, at paras. 238 and 240.

1120 Ibid., at para. 241; see also Dzehtsiarou, *European Consensus and the Legitimacy of the European Court of Human Rights*, at 60-61, where he acknowledges that the Court "avoided juxtaposing European consensus and internal consensus" yet still upholds the idea that the latter trumped the former.

1121 Chapter 8, III.; see in particular III.3. for the point at issue here.

1122 Supra, note 1098.

tional ethos of the respondent State.[1123] In the following subsection, I would like to build on the possibility of shifting between different levels of generality to explore the way in which different kinds of normativity are set in relation to one another.

2. Shifting Levels of Generality as a Search for Reflective Equilibrium

The preceding subsection has shed some light on why the ECtHR invokes (lack of) European consensus at different levels of generality in different cases: doing so allows it to shift its point of emphasis within the triangular tensions between different kinds of normativity according to the case at issue and the solution it seeks to justify. If we accept this connection, then it also provides a partial explanation for the ECtHR's reluctance to specify *why* it approaches consensus at a certain level of generality:[1124] such a specification lies implicit in the kind of reasoning it otherwise employs (i.e. giving more weight to morality-focussed reasoning or to the national ethos of the respondent State), but accordingly also depends on the internal logic of that form of normativity and can always be undermined from different perspectives. In this subsection, I would like to further develop this insight by exploring some ways in which the shift between different levels of generality has been deliberately operationalised within commentary on the ECtHR's use of consensus in particular and liberal political philosophy more broadly. I do so by considering a proposal by Kanstantsin Dzehtsiarou for the use of consensus in cases involving minority rights and further developing this proposal within the Rawlsian framework of reflective equilibrium. My point will be to show that, whatever the heuristic merits of such frameworks, they cannot resolve the triangular tensions at issue – although, as I discuss in this chapter's final section, they may obscure them.

Let me begin, then, by describing Dzehtsiarou's proposal for the use of consensus in cases concerning minority rights – one of the few proposals which explicitly relies on the use of consensus at *different* levels of generality. As briefly indicated above, Dzehtsiarou distinguishes between consensus at the level of principles ("general concepts which underpin legal stan-

---

1123 See de Londras, "When the European Court of Human Rights Decides Not to Decide: The Cautionary Tale of *A, B & C* v. *Ireland* and Referendum-Emergent Constitutional Provisions" at 321-323.

1124 See supra, note 1085.

dards") and consensus at the level of rules ("specific implementing measures which are undertaken to give effect to a legal principle in a particular system").[1125] His underlying assumption is that, all else being equal, the ECtHR's consensus analysis should be conducted at the level of rules[1126] – this part of his argument, I would suggest, broadly follows the Goldilocks approach common in academic commentary on consensus. Yet in cases concerning minority rights, Dzehtsiarou suggests, "the Court can be satisfied with the existence of consensus at the level of principles, without requiring the existence of consensus at the level of rules".[1127] This chimes with the possibility of creating space for morality-focussed considerations as mentioned above: shifting to a higher level of generality within ethical normativity creates a disconnect between consensus and the issue before the Court. In light of the morality-focussed perspective's focus on protecting minority rights, it comes as no surprise that Dzehtsiarou suggests this approach in cases dealing with minority rights, while retaining a more ethos-focussed perspective for other cases.

One might further develop this way of shifting between different levels of generality as one aspect of trying to achieve *reflective equilibrium* within the ECtHR's reasoning. The notion of reflective equilibrium was popularised by John Rawls in the realm of political morality and has since also been applied to legal reasoning.[1128] Simply put, it constitutes a method of interpretation and justification by means of which "one tries to find a scheme of principles that match people's considered judgments and general convictions" by going to and fro between them, retaining some and altering others along the way.[1129] Reflective equilibrium thus takes a *coherentist* and *anti-foundationalist* approach. The prior indicates that justification

---

1125 Supra, note 1074.

1126 Dzehtsiarou, "What Is Law for the European Court of Human Rights?" at 132; see also supra, note 1093.

1127 Dzehtsiarou, *European Consensus and the Legitimacy of the European Court of Human Rights*, at 124. This point is complicated, however, by Dzehtsiarou's preoccupation with the ECtHR's sociological legitimacy: see further Chapter 10, III.1.

1128 See e.g. Dworkin, "Justice and Rights" at 197; MacCormick, *Legal Reasoning and Legal Theory*, at 245-246; D.W. Haslett, "What Is Wrong with Reflective Equilibria?," (1987) 37 *The Philosophical Quarterly* 305 at 309.

1129 John Rawls, "The Independence of Moral Theory," in *John Rawls: Collected Papers*, ed. Samuel Freeman (Cambridge, Mass.: Harvard University Press, 1999) at 288; the "to and fro" movement is particularly clear e.g. at Rawls, *A Theory of Justice*, at 18. By referring broadly to interpretation and justification, I mean to draw attention to the fact that reflective equilibrium can be considered rele-

is seen as "a matter of the mutual support of many considerations, of everything fitting together into one coherent view".[1130] The latter, relatedly, means that a conception of justice "cannot be deduced from self-evident premises or conditions on principles", and accordingly any normative principles are proposed not as "necessary truths or derivable from such truths" but rather, more contingently, as provisional, revisable conclusions.[1131] As a consequence, reflective equilibrium in a strict sense is "a point at infinity that we can never reach", though we can strive towards it[1132] – but any point that we take to constitute reflective equilibrium in practice must be regarded as unstable and "liable to be upset by further examination".[1133]

A key point in this process of constant re-examination (of making "adjustment decisions", as Haslett calls them[1134]) is the potential relevance of normative principles and considered judgements *at all levels of generality*.[1135] Rawls notes that "considered judgments at all levels of generality" are considered relevant, "from those about particular situations and institutions up through broad standards and first principles to formal and abstract conditions on moral conceptions",[1136] and including "intermediate levels of generality".[1137] Each "considered conviction whatever its level" is

---

vant within both processes of discovery and processes of justification as discussed in Chapter 1, IV.5. The aspect of justification is perhaps more prominent in Rawls (e.g. Ibid., 15, 18-19 and 507); for the connection to processes of discovery, see e.g. T.M. Scanlon, "Rawls on Justification," in *The Cambridge Companion to Rawls*, ed. Samuel Freeman (Cambridge: Cambridge University Press, 2003) at 149; Kai Nielsen, "Grounding Rights and a Method of Reflective Equilibrium," (1982) 25 *Inquiry* 277 at 291.

1130 Rawls, *A Theory of Justice*, at 19.

1131 Ibid.; the typically constructivist disconnect of moral theory from metaphysics and claims of "moral truth" – in Rawls's case, by depending on reflective equilibrium – is also the main point of Rawls, "The Independence of Moral Theory" at 286-291; see also, very clearly, Nielsen, "Grounding Rights and a Method of Reflective Equilibrium" at 292.

1132 Rawls, *Political Liberalism*, at 385; see also Rawls, "The Independence of Moral Theory" at 289.

1133 Rawls, *A Theory of Justice*, at 18.

1134 Haslett, "What Is Wrong with Reflective Equilibria?" at 306.

1135 Besides the citations that follow, see also Rawls, *Political Liberalism*, at 381; Rawls, *The Law of Peoples*, at 58; for an overview of Rawls's development in this regard, see Scanlon, "Rawls on Justification" at 141.

1136 Rawls, "The Independence of Moral Theory" at 289.

1137 Rawls, *Political Liberalism*, at 45.

seen as "having a certain initial credibility", but "there are no judgments on any level of generality that are in principle immune to revision".[1138]

This explicit reliance on shifting levels of generality provides one reason why reflective equilibrium might be set in relation to the ECtHR's case-law involving European consensus, as described above. In Rawls's later works (following his so-called "political turn"), he takes the "public culture" of a democratic society as "the shared fund of implicitly recognized basic ideas and principles".[1139] This public culture is said to comprise "the political institutions of a constitutional regime and the public traditions of their interpretation (including those of the judiciary), as well as historic texts and documents that are common knowledge".[1140] In the transnational context of the ECtHR, one might thus interpret vertically comparative references as a way of grappling with the notion of a *European public culture* as part of a search for reflective equilibrium.[1141]

Understanding European consensus as part of a search for reflective equilibrium in this way might bolster Dzehtsiarou's take on cases involving minority rights. The move to a higher level of generality to avoid reliance on presumably prejudiced laws at the more specific level mirrors Rawls's response to claims that reflective equilibrium might be too "conservative",[1142] in which he emphasised that "one does not count people's more particular considered judgments, say those about particular actions

1138 Rawls, "The Independence of Moral Theory" at 289.

1139 Rawls, *Political Liberalism*, at 8.

1140 Ibid., 13-14.

1141 I first drew this connection in Theilen, "Levels of Generality in the Comparative Reasoning of the European Court of Human Rights and the European Court of Justice: Towards Judicial Reflective Equilibrium" at 416; but see infra, IV.; see also Gerards, *General Principles of the European Convention on Human Rights*, at 44 for an account of the ECtHR as searching for reflective equilibrium, although geared not at consensus but rather at the move between general principles and individual cases within the ECtHR's case-law itself.

1142 The phrasing is from Rawls himself at Rawls, "The Independence of Moral Theory" at 288; for a variety of criticisms of reflective equilibrium, see e.g. Haslett, "What Is Wrong with Reflective Equilibria?" at 311; R.M. Hare, "Rawls' Theory of Justice," in *Reading Rawls: Critical Studies on Rawls' 'A Theory of Justice'*, ed. Norman Daniels (Stanford: Stanford University Press, 1989) at 82-83; Simon Blackburn, "Can Philosophy Exist?," in *Méta-Philosophie: Reconstructing Philosophy?*, ed. Jocelyne Couture and Kai Nielsen (Calgary: University of Calgary Press, 1993) at 91; Peter Singer, "Sidgwick and Reflective Equilibrium," (1974) 58 *The Monist* 490 at 516; Daniel Little, "Reflective Equilibrium and Justification," (1984) 22 *The Southern Journal of Philosophy* 373 at 379.

and institutions, as exhausting the relevant information".[1143] Rather, more general judgments – or, in the case of consensus, more general aspects of European public culture – can be understood to point towards an adjustment decision which leads to the reconsideration of more specific (lack of) consensus.

An earlier essay of Rawls's even mirrors the morality-focussed elements in Dzehtsiarou's motivation for avoiding reliance on consensus at a more specific level: he deemed it "desirable, although not essential" that "some convincing reason can be found" to account for those instances in which adjustment decisions are made in the quest for coherence, and names convictions dropped because they are realised to have been "fostered by what is admittedly a narrow bias of some kind" as an example.[1144] As commentators on Rawls have suggested, "one can carefully analyse which biases are likely to occur under specific circumstances and design methodological devices or include specific elements in the process to counter these biases most effectively".[1145] Setting different accounts of (lack of) consensus at different levels of generality in relation to one another within the framework of reflective equilibrium might be understood as one such "methodological device" – an attempt at evening out the biases involved in both morality-focussed and ethos-focussed perspectives.

An example from the ECtHR's case-law may illustrate this approach. Dzehtsiarou cites the case-law on ethnic minorities,[1146] which is a particularly useful case-study since it demonstrates, in its development over time and by virtue of differences between majority opinions and dissents, the differing perspectives involved. We might begin with the case of *Chapman v. the United Kingdom*, which concerned the refusal of planning permission to station caravans on the applicant's land and ensuing enforcement measures. The applicant based her argument, in part, on the Council of Europe Framework Convention for the Protection of National Minorities.[1147] The ECtHR admitted that the Framework Convention could be seen as "an emerging international consensus amongst the Contracting States of the Council of Europe recognising the special needs of minorities and an

1143 Rawls, "The Independence of Moral Theory" at 288-289.

1144 Rawls, "Outline of a Decision Procedure for Ethics" at 11-12.

1145 Wibren van der Burg and Theo van Willigenburg, "Introduction," in *Reflective Equilibrium: Essays in Honour of Robert Heeger*, ed. Wibren van der Burg and Theo van Willigenburg (Dordrecht: Springer, 1998) at 12.

1146 Dzehtsiarou, *European Consensus and the Legitimacy of the European Court of Human Rights*, at 16 and 124-125.

1147 ECtHR (GC), Appl. 27238/95 – *Chapman*, at para. 83.

obligation to protect their security, identity and lifestyle".[1148] *However*, it refused to draw any conclusions from this fact, deeming the consensus thus identified *too general* – the Framework Convention was considered not "sufficiently concrete for [the Court] to derive any guidance" from it, as it merely "sets out general principles and goals but the signatory States were unable to agree on means of implementation";[1149] the respondent State was accorded a wide margin of appreciation and no violation was found. This form of argument mirrors the ethos-focussed perspective's criticism of the use of consensus at high levels of generality, given the disconnect between the comparative materials themselves and the more specific conclusions which might be drawn from them.[1150]

In later cases, however, the ECtHR changed its approach, though without openly admitting as much. In particular, in the famous case of *D.H. and Others v. the Czech Republic*, the ECtHR once again had to consider consensus in relation to the protection of ethnic minorities at relatively high levels of generality, this time in a case concerning the education of Roma children. Implicitly building on the judgment in *Chapman*, the respondent State argued that "neither the Convention nor any other international instrument contained a general definition of the State's positive obligations concerning the education of Roma pupils", nor was there any European consensus within domestic law as to whether special schools are acceptable, i.e. no consensus at the more specific level.[1151]

The ECtHR, by contrast, explicitly relied on *Chapman* to substantiate an "emerging international consensus" in favour of the protection of national minorities, conveniently failing to mention that it had previously deemed this consensus too general to provide any normative guidance.[1152] Instead, it now relied on the consensus as identified in *Chapman* as well as a number of other international instruments and recommendations to establish that "the Roma have become a specific type of disadvantaged and vulnerable minority" deserving of "special protection", particularly in the field of

1148 Ibid., at para. 93.
1149 Ibid., at para. 94; see critically Henrard, "How the ECtHR's Use of European Consensus Considerations Allows Legitimacy Concerns to Delimit Its Mandate" at 152.
1150 Supra, notes 1090-1093.
1151 ECtHR (GC), Appl. No. 57325/00 – *D.H. and Others*, at para. 155.
1152 Ibid., at para. 181; see also ECtHR (GC), Appl. No. 15766/03 – *Oršuš and Others v. Croatia*, Judgment of 16 March 2010, at para. 148.

education.[1153] Consensus at more specific levels did not play a major role;[1154] indeed, when the ECtHR noted that "other European States have had similar difficulties" in providing schooling for Roma children, it is more related to an acknowledgment of the (albeit insufficient) efforts of the Czech Republic than as an indication that the rein effect of European consensus might be at issue.[1155]

The shift is significant:[1156] *D.H.* presents a picture-book example of the deliberate use of consensus at high levels of generality to create space for morality-focussed considerations. Reconstructing the judgment within the framework of reflective equilibrium, one might say that the ECtHR considered the lack of consensus as to whether special schools are acceptable (as proposed by the government), but refused to give normative force to

---

1153 ECtHR (GC), Appl. No. 57325/00 – *D.H. and Others*, at para. 182; for the many international materials cited, see further paras. 54-107; see also ECtHR (GC), Appl. No. 15766/03 – *Oršuš and Others*, at para. 147; on "taking the human rights corpus as [the ECtHR's] reference point for determining group vulnerability", see also Peroni and Timmer, "Vulnerable Groups: The Promise of an Emerging Concept in European Human Rights Convention Law" at 1084. While Peroni and Timmer advocate for such an approach, primarily on the basis of legitimacy concerns (on which, see Chapter 9) they also rightly note the danger of reifying the vulnerability of certain groups (and, for that matter, the groups themselves) if the socially and historically constructed power structures leading to vulnerability are not rendered visible: ibid., 1073-1074; see also, critically on *D.H.* on similar grounds relating to homogenisation of minority groups, Roberta Medda-Windischer, "Dismantling Segregating Education and the European Court of Human Rights. *D.H. and Others vs. Czech Republic*: Towards an Inclusive Education?," (2007/8) 7 *European Yearbook of Minority Issues* 19 at 38-39; and generally Lourdes Peroni, "Religion and Culture in the Discourse of the European Court of Human Rights: The Risks of Stereotyping and Naturalising," (2014) 10 *International Journal of Law in Context* 195; for suggestions on how vertically comparative law could be used to denaturalise rather than naturalise, see Chapter 11, IV.4.

1154 It was used e.g. to introduce the notion of indirect discrimination, i.e. still at a relatively high level of generality: ECtHR (GC), Appl. No. 57325/00 – *D.H. and Others*, at para. 184; with regard to more specific issues, the focus was less on European consensus than on reports pertaining to the Czech Republic itself: ibid., at para. 200, and see Chapter 6, IV. (especially IV.6.) for the different sources at issue.

1155 Ibid., at para. 205.

1156 See also Kagiaros, "When to Use European Consensus: Assessing the Differential Treatment of Minority Groups by the European Court of Human Rights" at 294.

this understanding of consensus at a specific level "no matter what",[1157] and indeed refused to see it as the only approach to constructing consensus or lack thereof. Instead, the ECtHR looked to other elements within European public culture (other sources of European consensus and consensus at different levels of generality), concluded that "biases are likely to occur" if lack of consensus at a more specific level was followed,[1158] made adjustment decisions within its reasoning accordingly and reached a result based on general consensus, though contrary to lack of consensus at a more specific level.

As a counter-example, consider the case of *A.P., Garçon and Nicot v. France*, in which the ECtHR was called upon to consider whether it constitutes a violation of Article 8 ECHR to make legal gender recognition conditional on proof that the person at issue suffers from a gender identity disorder.[1159] Trans persons and non-governmental organisations working on trans rights have, for some time now, been arguing against this precondition:[1160] not only does it position the medical profession as gatekeepers of legal gender recognition,[1161] it also contributes to the stigmatisation of trans identities by reinforcing the notion that trans people are objects of medicine rather than subjects of rights.[1162] The ECtHR stated that it "is mindful" of the prominence of these arguments in pro-trans advocacy, and aware "that addressing gender identities from the perspective of a psychological disorder adds to the stigmatisation of transgender persons".[1163]

1157 As Zwart, "More Human Rights Than Court: Why the Legitimacy of the European Court of Human Rights is in Need of Repair and How It Can Be Done" at 93 suggests the ECtHR should; see Chapter 4, IV.

1158 Supra, note 1145.

1159 ECtHR, Appl. Nos. 79885/12, 52471/13 and 52596/13 – *A.P., Garçon and Nicot*, at para. 136.

1160 For an overview, see <http://stp2012.info/>; in the context of human rights law, see generally Jens T. Theilen, "Depathologisation of Transgenderism and International Human Rights Law," (2014) 14 *Human Rights Law Review* 327.

1161 See, in the context of access to health care, David Valentine, *Imagining Transgender. An Ethnography of a Category* (Durham and London: Duke University Press, 2007), at 58; Chris Dietz, "Governing Legal Embodiment: On the Limits of Self-Declaration," (2018) 26 *Feminist Legal Studies* 185 at 190.

1162 Gonzalez-Salzberg, "An Improved Protection for the (Mentally Ill) Trans Parent: A Queer Reading of AP, Garçon and Nicot v France" at 535.

1163 ECtHR, Appl. Nos. 79885/12, 52471/13 and 52596/13 – *A.P., Garçon and Nicot*, at para. 138; a caveat must be made to the effect that this kind of argument should not be taken to rubber-stamp stigmatisation of mental illnesses more generally: see Transgender Europe, "Anti-Activity Report" (2018), available at

However, it immediately juxtaposed this argument with the European consensus among the domestic laws of the States parties with regard to the specific issue of a psychiatric diagnosis as a precondition of legal gender recognition, noting that this precondition is featured "in the vast majority" of the States parties (only four of them having omitted it) and that there is, therefore, "currently near-unanimity" in favour of the position of the respondent State.[1164] Despite "an important aspect of the identity of transgender persons" being at stake, the ECtHR took this as the basis for leaving the States parties "wide discretion", and concluded without significant further argument that there was no violation of the Convention.[1165] Its brevity was arguably due, at least in part, to the relatively unusual situation of a consensus in favour of the respondent State, rather than a lack of consensus among the States parties;[1166] but regardless of the numerical issues involved, my point here is the way in which consensus is introduced with regard to a specific source (domestic law) at a specific level of generality (psychiatric diagnosis as a precondition for legal gender recognition), without the least attempt to question or re-examine it in the way which reflective equilibrium would require.

There are other cases in which the ECtHR arguably proceeds in this manner.[1167] What makes the judgment in *A.P., Garçon and Nicot v. France* seem particularly callous is that the ECtHR *acknowledged* the stigmatisation involved in the pathologisation of trans identities,[1168] yet still made no attempt to question its reliance on (a specific form of) European consensus which perpetuated such pathologisation.[1169] Had it looked to different aspects of European public culture – resolutions of the CoE's Parliamentary Assembly, for example – it would have found reason for re-examination in the form of statements against trans pathologisation at various

<https://tgeu.org/wp-content/uploads/2018/06/TGEU_Anti-ActvityReport_16-18.pdf>, at p. 13.

1164 ECtHR, Appl. Nos. 79885/12, 52471/13 and 52596/13 – *A.P., Garçon and Nicot*, at para. 139.

1165 Ibid., at paras. 140 and 144.

1166 See generally Chapter 5, III.1.

1167 Most famously in ECtHR, Appl. No. 30141/04 – *Schalk and Kopf*, at para. 106.

1168 Supra, note 1163.

1169 See critically Theilen, "Beyond the Gender Binary: Rethinking the Right to Legal Gender Recognition" at 256-257.

levels of generality.[1170] In accordance with the idea of not accepting any one element of European public culture at face value but rather making constant adjustment decisions, these documents in turn would not, in and of themselves, be decisive within the quest for reflective equilibrium. Simply adopting one particular understanding of consensus and assigning it strong normative force without further question or any attempt to destabilise it by considering the biases it might carry, however, runs counter to the idea of reflective equilibrium.

These brief examples could be further expanded on by providing more detailed accounts of the different elements of European public culture at issue and how they might be set in relation to one another. For present purposes, however, I would instead like to note that while the framework of reflective equilibrium provides a means by which to set morality-focussed and ethos-focussed considerations in relation to one another, it *by no means resolves the triangular tensions at issue*. The above-cited case-law on ethnic minorities exemplifies this: while *Chapman* was open to criticism from the morality-focussed perspective, the comparative materials relied on in *D.H.* were deemed "relatively vague [and] largely theoretical" by a dissenting opinion,[1171] thus pointing back to the ECtHR's earlier stance in *Chapman* and to the ethos-focussed criticism of relying on consensus (only) at high levels of generality.

After all, that Roma constitute a disenfranchised minority facing prejudice is hardly a revolutionary insight (controversial as it may nonetheless

1170 See in particular Parliamentary Assembly of the Council of Europe, Resolution 2048 (2015) of 22 April 2015, "Discrimination against transgender people in Europe", at paras. 1 and 6.2.2 which notes that trans persons face "widespread discrimination", deems pathologisation of trans persons "disrespectful of their human dignity and an additional obstacle to social inclusion", and calls on States to "abolish [...] a mental health diagnosis as a necessary legal requirement to recognise a person's gender identity"; the ECtHR mentions this document as part of its list of international materials at ECtHR, Appl. Nos. 79885/12, 52471/13 and 52596/13 – *A.P., Garçon and Nicot*, at para. 77, but does not bring it up within its reasoning on the matter. For further comparative materials pointing in similar directions, see Gonzalez-Salzberg, "An Improved Protection for the (Mentally Ill) Trans Parent: A Queer Reading of AP, Garçon and Nicot v France" at 534; it should be noted, though, that the representative character of at least some of these documents can in turn be questioned, depending on one's approach to a pan-European ethos: see generally Chapter 6, IV.3.

1171 ECtHR (GC), Appl. No. 57325/00 – *D.H. and Others*, dissenting opinion of Judge Jungwiert, at para. 5.

be in some quarters).[1172] But, as discussed in previous chapters, acknowledging the disenfranchisement of a minority group does not imply agreement on whether, when and how to empower that group by means of transnational human rights, so the ECtHR's conclusion can always be challenged on the basis of lack of consensus at a more specific level,[1173] to say nothing of the national ethos of the respondent State. The framework of reflective equilibrium, while it would encourage to-and-fro movement between different levels of generality and thus add additional complexity – perhaps avoiding too strong a focus on (lack of) consensus at the Goldilocks level of generality, perhaps also avoiding too quick a reliance on general principles by problematising the binary distinctions between e.g. rules and principles or between minority cases and others[1174] – could never point towards any one solution. There can, as critics of Rawls have long since emphasised, be many different reflective equilibria.[1175]

IV. Interim Reflections: Beyond the Goldilocks Level of Generality

In sum, the ECtHR makes use of European consensus at different levels of generality. While it often relies on comparative materials at a Goldilocks level of generality in relation to what it takes to be the main issue of the case, it also regularly refers to comparative materials which are more specific or, in particular, more general. This kind of shift has implications for the way in which the ECtHR situates itself within the triangular tensions between moral normativity, ethical normativity by reference to a pan-European ethos, and ethical normativity by reference to national ethe; approaching the notion of a pan-European ethos in different ways – e.g. by switching to (lack of) consensus at higher levels of generality – may have significant consequences for the instrumental allegiances formed with other kinds of normativity. One way of structuring the ECtHR's reasoning

1172 See e.g. James A. Goldston, "The Struggle for Roma Rights: Arguments that Have Worked," (2010) 32 *Human Rights Quarterly* 311 (Roma as "the quintessential pan-European ethnic minority").

1173 See e.g. Chapter 3, II and Chapter 4, III.2.

1174 See supra, particularly notes 1074 and 1127.

1175 Haslett, "What Is Wrong with Reflective Equilibria?" at 307 and 310; Nielsen, "Grounding Rights and a Method of Reflective Equilibrium" at 294; on the "relativist implications" of this point, see Little, "Reflective Equilibrium and Justification" at 384; for a defence of Rawls, see Scanlon, "Rawls on Justification" at 151-153.

against this backdrop might be to conceptualise it as searching for reflective equilibrium, with the to-and-fro movement between different levels of generality understood as an attempt to set different kinds of normativity in relation to one another and even out biases as far as possible, even though the underlying tensions could never be fully resolved.

I have previously argued that seeing European consensus as the basis of a European public culture which forms part of the search for reflective equilibrium provides a helpful way of conceptualising it.[1176] I continue to see certain advantages to this framework: in particular, while the notion of a European public culture of course mirrors that of a pan-European ethos which I have been referring to throughout, it differs insofar as its introduction *as part of the process of reaching towards reflective equilibrium* means that it would be geared, from the very beginning and in its various elements at different levels of generality, as "liable to be upset by further examination".[1177] The anti-foundationalist character of reflective equilibrium and the acknowledgment of different ways of using European consensus point away from an understanding of consensus which regards it as an "objective element" external to the Court:[1178] different understandings of consensus – and for that matter other forms of normativity – are all part of, but all *only* part of, the search for reflective equilibrium and may be used to unsettle one another. Accordingly, the "outcome of the case is […] not tied to [European consensus] *on the impugned measure*"[1179] because that (lack of) consensus is understood to be only one of several levels of generality which might be relevant within the ECtHR's reasoning.

Contrary to the intuitive sense that consensus should be used at a Goldilocks level of generality which is "just right" for the issue at hand, then, I would suggest that different levels of generality should be taken into account. Restricting vertically comparative legal reasoning to just one issue creates the impression that a pan-European ethos can be clearly and uncontroversially defined and obscures the choice that was made in defining what "the issue" is. Such an approach to consensus thus carries the same danger as advocating for a fixed number of States parties to consti-

1176 Theilen, "Levels of Generality in the Comparative Reasoning of the European Court of Human Rights and the European Court of Justice: Towards Judicial Reflective Equilibrium".

1177 Supra, note 1133.

1178 See Chapter 1, IV.5. and Chapter 3, II.

1179 Kagiaros, "When to Use European Consensus: Assessing the Differential Treatment of Minority Groups by the European Court of Human Rights" at 306 (emphasis added).

tute "consensus" or "lack of consensus", or of setting up a fixed hierarchy between consensus based on national laws and consensus based on (various elements within) international law:[1180] it tends to naturalise a certain understanding of European consensus without sufficient regard to countervailing elements within European public culture, let alone other forms of normativity.

Approaching European consensus as an aspect of the search for reflective equilibrium points away from its use only at a Goldilocks level of generality. But reflective equilibrium is not only anti-foundationalist but also, as mentioned above, coherentist. It is for this reason that I am now less inclined to advocate for it as a way of approaching the ECtHR's reasoning, since I have come to share the critical mistrust of coherentist theories in favour of those which foreground contradiction and paradox. On the basis of more critically minded approaches, the coherentist approach associated (for example) with reflective equilibrium is seen as too reconciliatory in the face of conflicting logics such as those of the morality-focussed and the ethos-focussed perspective,[1181] and the resulting denial of paradox, as Chantal Mouffe argues, makes it more difficult to grasp the hegemonic aspects of any particular arrangement[1182] – or, as Martti Koskenniemi puts it in the legal context, "the competition of opposite interests that are the flesh and blood of the legal everyday".[1183]

There *is* an interesting discussion to be had, I think, about the relationship between these two approaches (coherentist and paradoxicalist) in turn, which perhaps need not only be one of opposition but could also have symbiotic elements.[1184] After all, the very idea of establishing coherence can be taken to imply an underlying contradiction, so one might conceive of reflective equilibrium, for example, as a structuring device for establishing contingent coherence in the form of a judicial decision,[1185]

1180 See Chapter 5, V. and Chapter 6, VI.

1181 Mouffe, *The Democratic Paradox*, at 29; Koskenniemi, *From Apology to Utopia*, at 65.

1182 Mouffe, *The Democratic Paradox*, at 45.

1183 Koskenniemi, "An Essay in Counterdisciplinarity" at 19.

1184 Jeffrey Edward Green, "On the Co-originality of Liberalism and Democracy: Rationalist vs. Paradoxicalist Perspectives," (2015) 11 *Law, Culture and the Humanities* 198 at 215 rather charmingly speaks of rationalist and paradoxicalist understandings of co-originality which are themselves co-original.

1185 The element of contingency of judgments, i.e. their place within a broader discursive process, comes through e.g. in Kleinlein, "Consensus and Contestability: The ECtHR and the Combined Potential of European Consensus and Procedural Rationality Control"; see also Chapter 11, III. and IV.3.

without *necessarily* denying the underlying contradictions. If one looks for it, then, one may find some measure of overlap between coherentist and paradoxicalist approaches,[1186] and the framework sketched above may still be of interest in the context of judicial processes of justification (and, for that matter, of interpretation). However, the emphasis of coherentist and paradoxicalist approaches is clearly different; and to my mind that is far from irrelevant. Because reflective equilibrium emphasises coherence over paradox, it ends up downplaying not only the differences between different kinds of normativity but also the opposition between different substantive positions underlying conflicts before the ECtHR, which remains an important aspect mitigating against its use at least without further incorporation of paradoxicalist elements.

Consider, for example, the notion of "bias" referred to above as part of the justification for making adjustment decisions within the search for reflective equilibrium. On some level, I take this to be a helpful notion, especially in contrast to universalising approaches such as the morality-focussed perspective, which "attempts to understand itself as if it were free of all bias" although it clearly represents particular interests[1187] – but also in contrast to use of European consensus which does not acknowledge the idealisations of the ethos-focussed perspective. The move between different levels of generality within reflective equilibrium can be thought of as a way of self-reflectively trying to grapple with the problem of bias, regardless of whether morality-focussed or ethos-focussed considerations are at issue.[1188] But this also makes particularly clear how reflective equilibrium is implicated in a coherentist approach: the notion of bias serves not only to explain different perspectives but also to *position some as preferable to others*

1186 For example, Mouffe's point that no "final resolution or equilibrium" between the "conflicting logics" of (what I have been calling) the morality-focussed and ethos-focussed perspective is "ever possible" (Mouffe, *The Democratic Paradox*, at 45) is echoed in Rawls's admission that reflective equilibrium is a "point at infinity that we can never reach" (supra, note 1132) – *but* I would argue that the focus on hegemonic articulations which results from Mouffe's different priorities nonetheless gives her approach a very different flavour.

1187 Cynthia Weber, *Queer International Relations. Sovereignty, Sexuality and the Will to Knowledge* (Oxford: Oxford University Press, 2016), at 137 (on ostensibly "universal figures").

1188 With regard to gender stereotypes, this is reflected e.g. in Timmer, "Toward an Anti-Stereotyping Approach for the European Court of Human Rights" at 717 (arguing for an anti-stereotyping approach both with regard to the national level and the ECtHR's "own reasoning"); see Chapter 2, II.1. and Chapter 3, II., and generally on different idealisations Chapter 4, III.1.

so as to make a coherent result possible. The attempt to even out biases thus aims to mitigate the differences between what would otherwise be seen as "logics which are incompatible in the last instance",[1189] thereby denying or at least distracting from that incompatibility.

Several points follow from this. Practically speaking, there is the danger of slipping into a position of comfortable self-affirmation in which bias is always attributed to whichever form of normativity is opposed[1190] – proponents of the morality-focussed perspective are quick to point out that democratic procedures underlying European consensus are flawed, proponents of the ethos-focussed perspective are just as quick to point out how condescending it is to place one's own opinion above that of others as expressed by those very democratic procedures, and so on. A related point is the overall bias of reflective equilibrium itself: the focus on achieving an overall coherent position based on adjustment decisions within European public culture tends to be oriented (only) towards relatively marginal change, although more radical positions are not theoretically excluded. Even if applied self-reflectively, reflective equilibrium may thus "cause our imaginative space to become stagnant"[1191] by simply reproducing dominant aspects within European public culture.

This is perhaps particularly true insofar as reflective equilibrium is associated primarily with the use of consensus at higher levels of generality in cases concerning minority rights, as discussed above. By way of contrast, consider again cases such as *A, B and C* or *Leyla Şahin*: while I disagree emphatically with the outcome of these cases, the move to a *lack* of consensus at higher levels of generality is interesting because it shows how easily consensus can be destabilised by pointing to divergence and disagreement within European public culture. I will sketch a similar approach in the final chapter of this study by exploring the ways in which vertically compar-

---

1189 Mouffe, *The Democratic Paradox*, at 5.

1190 See generally on the limits of self-reflectivity Tzouvala, *Capitalism as Civilisation. A History of International Law*, at 38-39 and 216; Jean d'Aspremont, "Martti Koskenniemi, the Mainstream, and Self-Reflectivity," (2016) 29 *Leiden Journal of International Law* 625; for (what I read as) a more positive rendition of self-reflexivity, however, see Jean d'Aspremont, "Three international lawyers in a hall of mirrors," (2019) 32 *Leiden Journal of International Law* 367; see also Chapter 11, IV.1. for discussion of the implications of centring a reflective subject in this way.

1191 Adamantia Rachovitsa, "The Principle of Systemic Integration in Human Rights Law," (2017) 66 *International and Comparative Law Quarterly* 557 at 573 (on systemic integration).

ative legal reasoning might be used to emphasise *contradictions* within European public culture rather than consensus. For now, I propose to consider European consensus in its broader doctrinal context within the ECtHR's reasoning: turning from the establishment to the deployment of consensus might teach us more about the way in which the ECtHR situates itself within the underlying triangular tensions.

Chapter 8: Consensus in Context: Autonomous Concepts, the Margin of Appreciation, and Tensions within the Court's Doctrines

"In modern life, margin is everything."[1192]

I. Introduction

Over the course of the three preceding chapters, I have considered how the tensions between the morality-focussed and ethos-focussed perspectives play out with regard to the question of how (lack of) consensus is established – differently put, with regard to the question of whether and how (in the form of the rein effect or the spur effect) consensus is invested with normative force. However, this is not the only area in which these tensions emerge: because European consensus is usually not considered binding in the sense that it *wholly* predetermines the ECtHR's conclusions,[1193] it takes its place within the Court's reasoning *alongside other forms of argument*. Accordingly, in this chapter I would like to re-contextualise consensus to some extent by considering its connection to various doctrinal figures within the ECtHR's case-law, in order to show that the conflicting background assumptions of different kinds of normativity resurface even when consensus is not analysed in isolation.

It is clear that the Court has a plentiful array of varying arguments at its disposal, and I cannot here do justice to all of them. I would like to focus specifically on the kind of substantive argument foregrounded by the morality-focussed perspective, and to show how the interaction between such arguments and European consensus unfolds within the Court's case-law. In a sense, these are the paradigmatic cases of tensions between morality-focussed and ethos-focussed considerations – in contrast to the establishment of consensus where the morality-focussed perspective could be accused of "sneaking in" e.g. by framing its claims as reasonable agree-

1192 As Mrs. Erlynne quite rightly noted, albeit in an entirely different context, in the Second Act of *Lady Windermere's Fan* by Oscar Wilde.

1193 Wildhaber, Hjartarson, and Donnelly, "No Consensus on Consensus?" at 256.

ment,[1194] the cases I now have in mind involve a heads-on juxtaposition of different kinds of normativity. My main claim will be that while morality-focussed reasoning and ethos-focussed reasoning can be placed in proximity and connected by doctrinal figures such as autonomous concepts or the margin of appreciation, their epistemological differences persist and render any such combination inherently unstable. In that vein, any use of consensus-based argument can be unsettled by refusing to trust the States parties, emphasising the is-ought distinction and giving more prominence to substantive reasoning which puts their position into question – while any substantive argument can be unsettled by foregrounding reasonable disagreement about the question at issue and hence reverting back to ethical rather than moral normativity.

These tensions play out differently in various doctrinal contexts. As a general caveat, I should note that while the central tenets of the ECtHR's main doctrines seem to be well-established at first glance, scratching the surface often reveals uncertainties as to both their use and their rationales. My purpose here is not to give a comprehensive overview of either the doctrines at issue or the various analyses and assessments of them offered by academic commentators, but merely to introduce them insofar as they relate to European consensus and serve to underline the tensions that arise when it is used alongside other forms of reasoning. I shall consider two main doctrines which I take to be paradigmatically connected to different kinds of normativity: autonomous concepts (II.) and the margin of appreciation (III.). In the case of the first, the tendency is to give stronger weight to the morality-focussed perspective, although this does not fully resolve the tensions mentioned above. In the case of the margin of appreciation, the tendency is to give more weight to the ethos-focussed perspective – hence why use of European consensus has become so strongly associated with the margin of appreciation. In fact, the ethos-focussed perspective helps to explain some of the conceptual difficulties surrounding the margin of appreciation (III.1.). Nonetheless, tensions with the morality-focussed perspective persist here as well, particularly insofar as the rein effect of consensus is at issue (III.2.). In addition, in cases of the spur effect there is a secondary line of tension *within* the ethos-focussed perspective, depending on whether ethical normativity is located at the pan-European level or within the traditions or democratic procedures of the respondent State (III.3.).

1194 See Chapter 5, II.

Particularly in the context of the margin of appreciation, the tensions under discussion often arise in the form of counter-arguments to European consensus – at least this is how academic commentary approaches the case-law. When turning to the case-law itself, however, an analytical difficulty presents itself: it is relatively rare that the ECtHR itself presents European consensus as providing an argument in a certain direction (whether in its rein effect to argue against a violation of the Convention, or in its spur effect to argue in favour of a violation) but nonetheless reaches a contrary conclusion[1195] – in other words, it rarely presents explicit and "successful" counter-arguments to consensus. This fact may not be without significance, and I return to it at the end of the chapter (IV.). Until then, I will discuss a variety of cases which nonetheless demonstrate the triangular tensions at issue in some way, and occasionally refer at length to academic commentary in order to provide a clearer example of the tensions left implicit within the Court's judgments.

II. Autonomous Concepts

I would like to begin by taking up the notion of "autonomous concepts" within the Court's case-law. It captures the Court's approach to the interpretation of certain key terms contained in the Convention – such as "civil rights and obligations" or "criminal charge", the meaning of which is crucial for determining the scope of the right to a fair trial (Article 6 (1) ECHR). I will be fairly brief, for while autonomous concepts had a "tremendous impact" on the scope of Convention rights when they were

1195 See Douglas-Scott, "Borges' *Pierre Menard, Author of the Quixote* and the Idea of a European Consensus" at 176-177; Glas, "The European Court of Human Rights' Use of Non-Binding and Standard-Setting Council of Europe Documents" at 113; contra Peat, *Comparative Reasoning in International Courts and Tribunals*, at 145-146 who claims that "the Court has ruled contrary to the consensus approach on a number of occasions" but cites only *A, B and C* (in which the ECtHR relied on lack of consensus at a high level of generality, see Chapter 7, III.1.) and *Christine Goodwin* (in which the ECtHR relied on an international trend, see Chapter 5, IV.); similarly, Vogiatzis, "The Relationship Between European Consensus, the Margin of Appreciation and the Legitimacy of the Strasbourg Court" at 453 et seqq. discusses a number of cases, most of which involve various complications at the level of establishing European consensus (as he notes at 459); at any rate, he does conclude that such cases are "not the norm" (at 460).

first proclaimed,[1196] the notion now seems almost *passé* – after all, there is a limited number of terms contained in the Convention to which it might apply, and the Court has, at this point, established a fairly consistent case-law on most of them. While it still makes reference to autonomous concepts, it usually does so only to then refer to its settled case-law on the interpretation of the term at issue, and goes on to apply the standards set out in prior judgments.[1197] Yet of course, the understanding of these terms is settled only so long as it is not challenged. I will come back to this aspect below; let me first briefly set out the case-law on autonomous concepts and their relation to European consensus, and to the morality-focussed perspective and the ethos-focussed perspective more generally.

A classic and much-cited phrasing is that of the European Commission of Human Rights in an early case. Interpreting the term "civil rights and obligations", it stated that it

> cannot be construed as a mere reference to the domestic law of the High Contracting Party concerned but relates to an autonomous concept which must be interpreted independently, even though the general principles of the domestic law of the High Contracting Parties must necessarily be taken into consideration in any such interpretation.[1198]

The Court took a very similar approach in the leading case of *Engel and Others v. the Netherlands*, in which it was confronted with the question whether proceedings classified as merely disciplinary under Dutch law could nonetheless constitute a "criminal charge" for the purposes of Arti-

1196 Brems, "The Margin of Appreciation Doctrine in the Case-Law of the European Court of Human Rights" at 304.

1197 E.g. on the established meaning of "home" in Article 8 ECHR as an autonomous concept: ECtHR, Appl. No. 3572/06 – *Paulić v. Croatia*, Judgment of 22 October 2009, at para. 33; ECtHR, Appl. No. 15729/07 – *Globa v. Ukraine*, Judgment of 5 July 2012, at para. 37; ECtHR, Appl. No. 7177/10 – *Brežec v. Croatia*, Judgment of 18 July 2013, at para. 35; ECtHR, Appl. No. 27013/07 – *Winterstein and Others v. France*, Judgment of 17 October 2013, at para. 69; ECtHR, Appl. No. 66610/10 – *Yevgeniy Zakharov v. Russia*, Judgment of 14 March 2017, at para. 30; on the autonomous concept "criminal charge" or "criminal offence" and the *Engel* criteria (see infra, notes 1199-1201), e.g. ECtHR, Appl. No. 46998/08 – *Mikhaylova v. Russia*, Judgment of 19 November 2015, at para. 51; for the notion of "penalty" in Article 7 see e.g. ECtHR (GC), Appl. Nos. 1828/06 et al. – *G.I.E.M. S.R.L. and Others v. Italy*, Judgment of 28 June 2018, at paras. 210-211.

1198 EComHR, Appl. Nos 3134/67 et al. – *Twenty-One Detained Persons v. Germany*, Decision of 6 April 1968, at II.4.

cle 6 ECHR. It ruled very emphatically that the classification exhibited by the respondent State, though not entirely irrelevant, plays only a minimal role in the justification of its decision: it "provides no more than a starting point" and has "only a formal and relative value".[1199] Instead, the Court proposed two substantive criteria which, as it later specified, are "of greater importance" for its conclusions:[1200] the nature of the offence and the severity of the penalty. Crucially for our purposes, it stated in *Engel* that they should "be examined in the light of the common denominator of the respective legislation of the various Contracting States".[1201]

The impression which these statements all give is that the notion of "autonomy" is intended primarily to establish the Court's interpretive freedom to discount classifications made by the legal system of the respondent State: as it later summarised, the terms contained in the Convention "cannot be interpreted solely by reference to the domestic law of the respondent State".[1202] Comparative references to the States parties seen collectively – the "common denominator" or what would now usually be termed common ground or consensus – are, by contrast, presented as significantly more important, and did indeed appear in several subsequent judgments involving autonomous concepts.[1203] The Convention would thus be autonomous vis-à-vis the respondent State, but not vis-à-vis the *collectivity* of

1199 ECtHR (Plenary), Appl. Nos. 5100-5102/71, 5354/72 and 5370/72 – *Engel and Others v. the Netherlands*, Judgment of 8 June 1976, at para. 82; see also e.g. ECtHR (Plenary), Appl. No. 8562/79 – *Feldbrugge v. the Netherlands*, Judgment of 29 May 1986, at para. 28; ECtHR (Plenary), Appl. No. 9384/81 – *Deumeland v. Germany*, Judgment of 29 May 1986, at para. 62.

1200 ECtHR, Appl. No. 13057/87 – *Demicoli v. Malta*, Judgment of 27 August 1991, at para. 33.

1201 ECtHR (Plenary), Appl. Nos. 5100-5102/71, 5354/72 and 5370/72 – *Engel and Others*, at para. 82; see also ECtHR (Plenary), Appl. No. 8544/79 – *Öztürk v. Germany*, Judgment of 21 February 1984, at para. 50.

1202 ECtHR (Plenary), Appl. No. 6232/73 – *König v. Germany*, Judgment of 28 June 1978, at para. 88.

1203 ECtHR (Plenary), Appl. No. 8544/79 – *Öztürk*, at paras. 50 and 53; see also the dissenting opinion of Judge Matscher in that case, arguing for a different interpretation of the vertically comparative references (at para. 2); ECtHR (Plenary), Appl. No. 8562/79 – *Feldbrugge*, at para. 29; ECtHR (Plenary), Appl. No. 9384/81 – *Deumeland*, at para. 63; ECtHR (GC), Appl. No. 63235/00 – *Vilho Eskelinen and Others v. Finland*, Judgment of 19 April 2007, at paras. 57 and 60; ECtHR (GC), Appl. Nos. 68273/14 and 68271/14 – *Gestur Jónsson and Ragnar Halldór Hall v. Iceland*, Judgment of 22 December 2020, at paras. 54-60 and 89; see generally Ambrus, "Comparative Law Method in the Jurisprudence of the European Court of Human Rights in the Light of the Rule of Law" at 359.

States parties. This precisely mirrors the position taken by many proponents of European consensus:[1204] recall, for example, Neuman's argument that "letting each state be the judge of its own human rights obligations" would negate their effect, but that this "does not entail that the [...] regional human rights regime must be independent of the regional *community of states*".[1205] On this account, autonomous concepts would, like consensus-based reasoning more generally, amount to an expression of a pan-European ethos.

Yet there are strong countervailing tendencies in the ECtHR's case-law on autonomous concepts. Consider again the reasons for proclaiming autonomy from the legal order of the respondent State: the most obvious reason is that, as Legg has put it, "states cannot merely attach their own labels to squirm out of their treaty obligations",[1206] which would be the consequence of deferring to the classifications made within the legal order of the respondent State – the effect of the Convention would otherwise "potentially be reduced to vanishing point".[1207] The Court itself made a similar point in *Engel*, stating that if "the Contracting States were able at their discretion to classify an offence as disciplinary instead of criminal", then "the operation of the fundamental clauses of Articles 6 and 7 [...] *would be subordinated to their sovereign will*", which "might lead to results *incompatible with the purpose and object of the Convention*".[1208] In another leading case on autonomous concepts, *Chassagnou and Others v. France*, the Court later reiterated this rationale, this time with reference to the term "association" contained in Article 11 ECHR. It pointed out that

> [i]f Contracting States were able, at their discretion, by classifying an association as 'public' or 'para-administrative', to remove it from the scope of Article 11, that would give them such latitude that it might lead to results incompatible with the object and purpose of the Con-

1204 See in more detail Chapter 3, IV.3.

1205 Neuman, "Import, Export, and Regional Consent in the Inter-American Court of Human Rights" at 115 (emphasis in original).

1206 Legg, *The Margin of Appreciation*, at 111.

1207 Eirik Bjorge, *Domestic Application of the ECHR: Courts as Faithful Trustees* (Oxford: Oxford University Press, 2015), at 203.

1208 ECtHR (Plenary), Appl. Nos. 5100-5102/71, 5354/72 and 5370/72 – *Engel and Others*, at para. 81 (emphasis added); see also e.g. ECtHR (GC), Appl. Nos. 68273/14 and 68271/14 – *Gestur Jónsson and Ragnar Halldór Hall*, at para. 76.

vention, which is to protect rights that are not theoretical or illusory but practical and effective.[1209]

It is interesting to note that in both these instances, the "Contracting States" are referred to in the *plural* form – while context may point towards the respective respondent State as the primary target of these remarks, they are thus also geared, in a sense, towards the States parties as a whole. One may likewise note the reference to the object and purpose of the Convention and, in *Chassagnou*, the insistence that rights should be "practical and effective". All of this sounds much less ethos-focussed, and rather more reminiscent of the kind of reasoning deployed by the morality-focussed perspective: the Court foregrounds the rights contained in the Convention as independent of the "sovereign will" of the States parties and instead nods towards substantive reasoning – "its own assessment"[1210] – which would give rise to prepolitical human rights. By formulating the distrust of the respondent State's classifications in the plural form, it in fact mirrors a rhetorical strategy often employed by critics of consensus:[1211] it draws attention to the fact that all States parties are *potential respondents*, and thus conceptualises their legal systems as objects of its own judgments rather than a potentially influential factor in justifying them.

On its own, pointing out the use of the plural form in these instances might well be considered something of an overinterpretation; yet it combines with other factors which likewise indicate that the ECtHR might, in cases concerning autonomous concepts, be operating on the basis of the morality-focussed perspective. For one thing, the reasoning just discussed was combined in other cases with an acknowledgment of "the moves towards 'decriminalisation' which are taking place – in extremely varied forms – in the member States of the Council of Europe".[1212] The refusal to subordinate the interpretation of terms contained in the Convention to the States parties' sovereign will, as cited above, followed this acknowledgment and was thus an *explicit response to an argument based on the lack of consensus* – a situation which would usually constitute a strong argument

1209 ECtHR (GC), Appl. Nos. 25088/94, 28331/95 and 28443/95 – *Chassagnou and Others v. France*, Judgment of 29 April 1999, at para. 100.

1210 ECtHR, Appl. No. 19359/04 – *M. v. Germany*, Judgment of 17 December 2009, at para. 133; ECtHR (GC), Appl. Nos. 10211/12 and 27505/14 – *Ilnseher v. Germany*, Judgment of 4 December 2018, at para. 236.

1211 See Chapter 2, II.3.

1212 ECtHR (Plenary), Appl. No. 8544/79 – *Öztürk*, at para. 49; see also ECtHR, Appl. No. 46998/08 – *Mikhaylova*, at para. 53.

in favour of deferral. Similar argumentative patterns may be discerned in yet other cases dealing with autonomous concepts. For example, in *Pellegrin v. France*, the Court claimed that it must establish an autonomous interpretation so as to avoid, inter alia, "inequality of treatment from one State to another".[1213] Its mission here seems to be precisely to *prevent* divergence among the States parties rather than giving deference to lack of consensus among them – indeed, Janneke Gerards has noted that "[t]he existence of diverging practices here provided an important motive for the Court to offer strong and autonomous protection, rather than a reason to step back and refuse to give a uniform interpretation".[1214] Such an approach is, of course antithetical to the ethos-focussed perspective's insistence on the importance of democratic procedures and the diversity among States which follows from them.

My main point here is to demonstrate the difficulties in combining the morality-focussed and the ethos-focussed perspective. Formally, they are easy to place in juxtaposition, as when the Court states that it must "take account of the object and purpose of the Convention and of the national legal systems of the other Contracting States"[1215] – the former, in light of the citations discussed above, implies substantive reasoning of the kind deployed by the morality-focussed perspective, whereas the latter implies an ethos-focussed scepticism of moral argument and the reliance, instead, on ethical normativity developed at the pan-European level. Yet it is difficult to relate these different forms of normativity to one another in the course of the further reasoning: it is difficult, in other words, to see the States parties *simultaneously* as the location of democratic procedures worthy of deference *and* as potential respondents whose legal systems should be subjected to scrutiny, not given normative force in justifying the ECtHR's judgments. It is entirely in line with this dilemma, for example, when Steven

---

1213 ECtHR (GC), Appl. No. 28541/95 – *Pellegrin v. France*, Judgment of 8 December 1999, at paras. 62-63; see also ECtHR (GC), Appl. No. 37575/04 – *Boulois v. Luxembourg*, Judgment of 3 April 2012, joint dissenting opinion of Judges Tulkens and Yudkivska, at para. 10; though in a different way, a similarly unusual use of vertically comparative law can be found in ECtHR (GC), Appl. Nos. 65731/01 and 65900/01 – *Stec and Others v. the United Kingdom (Admissibility)*, Decision of 6 July 2005, at para. 50.

1214 Gerards, "Judicial Deliberations in the European Court of Human Rights" at 433; note that the subsequent judgment in ECtHR (GC), Appl. No. 63235/00 – *Vilho Eskelinen and Others*, which overruled *Pellegrin*, seems somewhat more open to consensus-based argument: see ibid., at paras. 57 and 60; see also Gerards, *General Principles of the European Convention on Human Rights*, at 73-74.

1215 ECtHR (Plenary), Appl. No. 6232/73 – *König*, at para. 89.

Greer describes the "principle of autonomous interpretation" as maintaining that "some of the Convention's key terms should be defined authoritatively by the Court independently of how they may be understood by member states" – but then immediately goes on to acknowledge that this principle is, "in its turn, [...] constrained by the principle of commonality" which *does* refer to the States parties' understanding of certain terms.[1216] As Janneke Gerards has put it, the one seems "hardly reconcilable" with the other.[1217]

On the whole, my impression is that the morality-focussed perspective has carried more sway in cases dealing with autonomous concepts.[1218] Any statement as broad as this must of course make certain generalisations, and counter-examples can no doubt be found; yet on the whole, it seems to me that even in those judgments which paid lip service to vertically comparative references, consensus did not play a significant role.[1219] For example, Judge Matscher criticised the majority's approach in *König v. Germany* for

---

1216 Greer, *The Margin of Appreciation: Interpretation and Discretion under the European Convention on Human Rights*, at 18-19.

1217 Gerards, "Judicial Deliberations in the European Court of Human Rights" at 432.

1218 Though with a slightly different focus, this is also the main analytic claim in Letsas, "The Truth in Autonomous Concepts: How To Interpret the ECHR"; Letsas, *A Theory of Interpretation of the European Convention on Human Rights*, chapter 2; see also Bjorge, *Domestic Application of the ECHR: Courts as Faithful Trustees*, at 203.

1219 Even in the leading cases: *Engel*, although it established the relevance of consensus for autonomous interpretation in theory, contained no comparative references itself on this issue – despite giving them strong argumentative weight with regard to a different aspect: ECtHR (Plenary), Appl. Nos. 5100-5102/71, 5354/72 and 5370/72 – *Engel and Others*, at para. 72; the other leading case, *Chassagnou*, does not mention consensus at all; and even insofar as it might be said to have considered "arguments about deference" (Legg, *The Margin of Appreciation*, at 111), these are found in a different section of the judgment, while the section on autonomous interpretation contains only substantive argument: ECtHR (GC), Appl. Nos. 25088/94, 28331/95 and 28443/95 – *Chassagnou and Others*, at para. 101; similarly in the recent case of ECtHR (GC), Appl. No. 19867/12 – *Moreira Ferreira v. Portugal (no. 2)*, Judgment of 11 July 2017, which does contain references to consensus (at paras. 34-39 and 91), but again not in relation to autonomous interpretation; the high-profile case of ECtHR, Appl. No. 19359/04 – *M.* includes a section on comparative law (at paras. 69-75) but makes no reference to it when discussing autonomous concepts (at paras. 120 and 126) or, for that matter, elsewhere in the judgment; the later case of ECtHR (GC), Appl. Nos. 10211/12 and 27505/14 – *Ilnseher* contains a comparative overview (at para. 98) and mentions the relevance of vertically compara-

giving too much weight to a "teleological interpretation" and thus "venturing into the field of legislative policy", when it should instead have established its "autonomous" interpretation by reference to the "common denominator" as "found through a comparative analysis of the domestic law of the Contracting States".[1220] My hunch is that, given the rhetoric of preventing subordination of the Convention to the will of the States parties – in the plural form, as discussed above – and its importance as the driving rationale behind the ECtHR's case-law on autonomous concepts, that line of case-law became associated with the morality-focussed perspective's distrust of not only the respondent State, but also the States parties as a whole. The ECtHR's classifications thus became, for the most part, autonomous from both, to the point that it is now argued that "it seems conceptually incorrect to carry out comparative exercises in combination with the principle of autonomous interpretation".[1221]

---

tive law in the abstract (at para. 210), but makes no use of it and reverts back to the Court's "own assessment" (see supra, note 1210); ECtHR (GC), Appl. Nos. 68273/14 and 68271/14 – *Gestur Jónsson and Ragnar Halldór Hall* also contains relatively detailed comparative references, but refers to them only in passing later on (in the abstract at para. 77 and specifically at para. 89); finally, even cases with unusually detailed vertically comparative references in the context of autonomous concepts often end up being decided on substantive grounds which overrule a lack of consensus: e.g. ECtHR (Plenary), Appl. No. 8562/79 – *Feldbrugge*, at paras. 29-40; ECtHR (Plenary), Appl. No. 9384/81 – *Deumeland*, at paras. 63-74. See also Gerards, *General Principles of the European Convention on Human Rights*, at 71, who speaks of "a very limited number of cases" in which controversy among the States parties negated an autonomous interpretation.

1220 ECtHR (Plenary), Appl. No. 6232/73 – *König*, separate opinion of Judge Matscher.

1221 Ambrus, "Comparative Law Method in the Jurisprudence of the European Court of Human Rights in the Light of the Rule of Law" at 361; see also e.g. Douglas-Scott, "Borges' *Pierre Menard, Author of the Quixote* and the Idea of a European Consensus" at 179, citing autonomous interpretation as an "obvious alternative" to consensus; Peat, *Comparative Reasoning in International Courts and Tribunals*, at 144, who juxtaposes consensus with autonomous interpretation, the latter "understood in isolation from domestic legal systems"; Tzevelekos, "The Use of Article 31(3)(C) of the VCLT in the Case Law of the ECtHR: An Effective Anti-Fragmentation Tool or a Selective Loophole for the Reinforcement of Human Rights Teleology?" at 639, associating autonomous interpretation with the ECtHR providing "one single pan-European definition" so as to prevent "cultural diversity and polyphony" from turning into "Babel"; Dzehtsiarou, *European Consensus and the Legitimacy of the European Court of Human Rights*, at 24, who seems to conceptualise consensus-based argument and autonomous interpretation as separate from one another, al-

This claim remains entirely speculative, of course. I bring it up only because it relates to the observation with which I began this subsection: the relative negligibility of references to autonomous concepts in the Court's more recent judgments. In part, this can no doubt be attributed to the existence of settled case-law on formerly controversial issues – yet, as suggested above, challenges to that case-law are constantly underfoot and new interpretative controversies thus continue to abound.[1222] Perhaps the difference is that the Court now operates increasingly from within the ethos-focussed perspective and therefore *avoids the language of autonomous concepts and its morality-focussed connotations* when adjudicating on these issues.

Consider, for example, the case of *Vo v. France* on how negligent harm to a foetus should be treated. The Court held that its decision required a "preliminary examination" of "when life begins, in so far as Article 2 provides that the law must protect 'everyone's right to life'".[1223] This is precisely the kind of issue discussed in the various cases above – the interpretation of a term contained in the Convention (in this case, the term "life" in Article 2 ECHR) and its relation to classifications established by the States parties (in this case, whether unborn life is covered by the term). Yet the majority made no reference to the notion of autonomous concepts, instead stating that "the issue of when the right to life begins comes within the margin of appreciation", based in particular on the vertically comparative argument that "there is no European consensus on the scientific and legal definition of the beginning of life".[1224] The majority thus adopted a strongly ethos-focussed perspective, foregrounding disagreement among the

---

though he later views them in tandem: Kanstantsin Dzehtsiarou, "European Consensus: New Horizons," in *Building Consensus on European Consensus. Judicial Interpretation of Human Rights in Europe and Beyond*, ed. Panos Kapotas and Vassilis Tzevelekos (Cambridge: Cambridge University Press, 2019) at 39-40.

1222 Compare e.g. ECtHR (GC), Appl. No. 33804/96 – *Mennitto v. Italy*, Judgment of 5 October 2000, at para. 27 with the dissenting opinion of Judge Ferrari Bravo, joined by Judge Butkevych, in that case. For another recent case of controversy, see ECtHR, Appl. Nos. 12096/14 and 39335/16 – *Rola v. Slovenia*, Judgment of 4 June 2019, as well as the comment by Bas van Bockel, "A Court Divided: Discord and Disagreement in Rola v. Slovenia" (Strasbourg Observers, 2019), available at <https://strasbourgobservers.com/2019/07/09/a-court-divided-discord-and-disagreement-in-rola-v-slovenia/#more-4365>.

1223 ECtHR (GC), Appl. No. 53924/00 – *Vo*, at para. 81.

1224 Ibid., at para. 82.

States parties rather than establishing standards independently of their views.[1225]

Judge Costa, in his separate opinion, adopted a different approach and gave less weight to the lack of consensus: he argued that the Court should instead have been prepared to "identify the *notions* – which may, if necessary, be the *autonomous notions* the Court has always been prepared to use – that correspond to the words or expressions" used in the Convention, and recalled the Court's prior rulings on terms such as "civil rights and obligations" and "criminal charges".[1226] The notion of autonomous concepts thus becomes associated with a morality-focussed approach critical of consensus-based argument,[1227] whereas the majority in *Vo* made use of European consensus but dropped the language of autonomous concepts. A similar structure can arguably be made out in the more recent case of *Boulois v. Luxembourg*: the majority relied, inter alia, on the rein effect of European consensus to establish that prison leave should not be considered a "right" in the sense of Article 6 ECHR.[1228] It made no mention of autonomous concepts, although it was considering the applicability of Article 6 ECHR based on the interpretation of the phrase "civil rights and obligations" – as Judges Tulkens and Yudkivska, writing in dissent, pointed out.[1229]

If my speculative reading of these cases – against the backdrop of the older cases on autonomous concepts – is correct, then it provides a further explanation for the dearth of recent references to autonomous concepts in recent judgments: the notion has simply been displaced in favour of other interpretive and doctrinal figures which are taken to be more open to the ethos-focussed perspective. One move which might be considered a partial "replacement" of the notion of autonomous concepts is the increasing ref-

---

1225 In more detail on *Vo* as exemplary of the ethos-focussed perspective, see Chapter 5, III.2.

1226 ECtHR (GC), Appl. No. 53924/00 – *Vo*, separate opinion of Judge Costa joined by Judge Traja, at para. 7 (second emphasis added).

1227 See also ECtHR (GC), Appl. No. 46470/11 – *Parrillo*, dissenting opinion of Judge Sajó, at para. 3 (in footnote 4), where the term "autonomous concept" seems to be used in a non-technical sense precisely to argue against the rein effect of (lack of) European consensus.

1228 ECtHR (GC), Appl. No. 37575/04 – *Boulois*, at para. 102.

1229 Ibid., joint dissenting opinion of Judges Tulkens and Yudkivska, at para. 10; the case is less thorny than *Vo* in relation to consensus, since the disagreement between the majority and the dissenting judges primarily concerns, I think, the weight given to the law of the respondent State.

erence to the Vienna Convention on the Law of Treaties,[1230] which itself reproduces the tensions between the morality-focussed and the ethos-focussed perspective in its own way.[1231] More importantly however, the use of consensus has become associated with the margin of appreciation. Autonomous concepts and the margin of appreciation have long been regarded as "opposites on the same line",[1232] and indeed, the latter has gained increasing prominence even as references to the prior have dwindled – *Vo* provides only one example of this. It is, therefore, to the margin of appreciation that I now turn.

III. The Margin of Appreciation and Convention Standards

1. Two Concepts of the Margin of Appreciation – and of Consensus?

The margin of appreciation is, without a doubt, one of the most important and yet most controversial doctrines developed by the ECtHR. To describe it in brief terms is well-nigh impossible, given how its use has not only evolved over time,[1233] but also varies from case to case within the same period.[1234] Assessing these varying uses and their differing conceptualisations within the academic literature comprehensively is well beyond the scope

1230 For example, in ECtHR, Appl. No. 26629/95 – *Witold Litwa v. Poland*, Judgment of 4 April 2000, the Court relied primarily on the VCLT (at para. 57) and only subsequently referred, in passing, to the "autonomous meaning" thus established (at para. 76).

1231 I cannot discuss the VCLT in detail here, but see Chapter 6, II. on its Article 31 (3) lit. c and Chapter 10, III.2. on its Article 31 (3) lit. b.

1232 Brems, "The Margin of Appreciation Doctrine in the Case-Law of the European Court of Human Rights" at 306; see also Bjorge, *Domestic Application of the ECHR: Courts as Faithful Trustees*, at 204-205, arguing that autonomous concepts and the margin of appreciation should be considered two "disaggregated" elements.

1233 For an overview, see Bates, "Activism and Self-Restraint: The Margin of Appreciation's Strasbourg Career... Its 'Coming of Age'?"; analyses of the recent case-law are e.g. Madsen, "Rebalancing European Human Rights: Has the Brighton Declaration Engendered a New Deal on Human Rights in Europe?"; Gerards, "Margin of Appreciation and Incrementalism in the Case Law of the European Court of Human Rights".

1234 Critically e.g. Greer, *The Margin of Appreciation: Interpretation and Discretion under the European Convention on Human Rights*, at 5; Kratochvíl, "The Inflation of the Margin of Appreciation by the European Court of Human Rights" at 325; Patricia Popelier and Catherine Van de Heyning, "Procedural Rational-

of the present study, yet I will give a rough overview insofar as the underlying issues pertain to European consensus. I also leave aside, for the time being, those approaches to the margin of appreciation which emphasise its strategic use, concentrating instead on the principled tensions between the morality-focussed and ethos-focussed perspectives.[1235]

To provide for more analytic clarity in the Court's references to the respondent State's "margin of appreciation", George Letsas has proposed a distinction between what he calls the "structural" and the "substantive" margin. The distinction turns on the reasons given by the ECtHR for its conclusion in a certain case.[1236] Under the structural concept of the margin of appreciation, it establishes "the limits or intensity of [its] review [...] in view of its status as an international tribunal";[1237] thus, this concept is at play, in particular, when the Court *defers* to the respondent State without scrutinising the matter at issue in substance[1238] – or applies standards of scrutiny of varying strictness.[1239] The structural margin thus deals with the relationship between the ECtHR, as a regional court, and the national authorities.

By contrast, when the Court rules directly on whether a right was violated in light of a theory of political morality, then the substantive margin is at play.[1240] Ultimately, the Court's references to a margin of appreciation in this sense are intended, qua Letsas, merely to reiterate that (most) Convention rights are not absolute; because the balance between individual rights and the public interest that follows from this limitability will be struck in light of substantive theories of political morality, reference to the margin of appreciation is "superfluous" and "misleading".[1241]

While the ECtHR has never formally ceded Letsas's point and continues to use the language of the margin of appreciation in those situations he deems "superfluous", it must also be noted that most references to the

---

ity: Giving Teeth to the Proportionality Analysis," (2013) 9 *European Constitutional Law Review* 230 at 243-244.

1235 For strategic considerations, see Chapters 9 and 10.

1236 Letsas, *A Theory of Interpretation of the European Convention on Human Rights*, at 82.

1237 Ibid., 81.

1238 Ibid., 90.

1239 This aspect of "partial deference" is emphasised in Arnardóttir's response to Letsas's account: Oddný Mjöll Arnardóttir, "Rethinking the Two Margins of Appreciation," (2016) 12 *European Constitutional Law Review* 27 at 47.

1240 Letsas, *A Theory of Interpretation of the European Convention on Human Rights*, at 84.

1241 Ibid., 86 and 88.

margin, both in the Court's case-law and in academic commentary, are more concerned with what Letsas calls the *structural* concept.[1242] This is reflected in the commonly acknowledged connection between the margin of appreciation and the ECtHR's varying standards of scrutiny or intensity of review.[1243] It is also the usual understanding when different factors – such as European consensus – influencing the "width" or "breadth" of the margin of appreciation are discussed,[1244] the latter serving to indicate whether the Court's scrutiny will be strict (narrow margin) or lenient (wide margin). In accordance with Letsas's claim that the "margin of appreciation in itself clearly lacks any normative force that can help us strike a balance between individual rights and public interest",[1245] the *substantive* concept of the margin of appreciation is usually discussed instead by reference to notions such as proportionality or a "fair balance" between competing interests. Accordingly, when I speak without further specification of the margin of appreciation in what follows, then I am referring to ideas of deference and standards of review rather than to the Court's substantive proportionality analysis.

This clarification is important because European consensus has become associated with the margin of appreciation (in the sense of a structural margin determining the Court's intensity of review), to the point that they

1242 See explicitly ECtHR (GC), Appl. No. 3455/05 – *A. and Others v. the United Kingdom*, Judgment of 19 February 2009, at para. 184: "the margin of appreciation has always been meant as a tool to define relations between the domestic authorities and the Court".

1243 E.g. Arai-Takahashi, *The Margin of Appreciation Doctrine and the Principle of Proportionality in the Jurisprudence of the ECHR*, at 204; Oddný Mjöll Arnardóttir, *Equality and Non-Discrimination under the European Convention on Human Rights* (The Hague: Martinus Nijhoff, 2003), at 60; Gerards, "Pluralism, Deference and the Margin of Appreciation Doctrine" at 105-106; Gerards, *General Principles of the European Convention on Human Rights*, at 196; Kratochvíl, "The Inflation of the Margin of Appreciation by the European Court of Human Rights" at 344; Henrard, "How the ECtHR's Use of European Consensus Considerations Allows Legitimacy Concerns to Delimit Its Mandate" at 145.

1244 E.g. recently Popelier and Van de Heyning, "Procedural Rationality: Giving Teeth to the Proportionality Analysis" at 241-244; McGoldrick, "A Defence of the Margin of Appreciation and an Argument for its Application by the Human Rights Committee" at 24-25; though very dated, the overview by Brems, "The Margin of Appreciation Doctrine in the Case-Law of the European Court of Human Rights" also still proves helpful.

1245 Letsas, *A Theory of Interpretation of the European Convention on Human Rights*, at 86.

have arguably become *overly* intertwined in many accounts.[1246] To be sure, the margin of appreciation is deeply implicated in the ECtHR's use of consensus, and the two are cited alongside one another in an enormous number of cases. In one standard formulation:

> The scope of the margin of appreciation will vary according to the circumstances, the subject-matter and its background; in this respect, one of the relevant factors may be the existence or non-existence of common ground between the laws of the Contracting States.[1247]

Thus, a common rendition of the way in which consensus functions holds that a lack of consensus or a consensus against the applicant will broaden the margin of appreciation, while a consensus in favour of the applicant will restrict it[1248] – in fact, the terminology of a "rein effect" and a "spur effect" that I have been using was developed by reference to the margin, with the authors stating that the vertically comparative analysis "helps to interpret Convention notions and to decide *whether a State's margin of appreciation should be wide or narrow*".[1249]

Yet this is not all that consensus does. In some cases, it is deployed without reference to the margin of appreciation[1250] – and in such a manner that it seems unrelated to the Court's intensity of review regardless of the language used – and occasionally, it is even used in a way that is explicitly *set apart* from the operation of the margin of appreciation. For example, in the case of *Şükran Aydin and Others v. Turkey*, the Court examined the proportionality of criminal sanctions for the use of minority languages during election campaigns. Having emphasised the importance of the free circulation of political opinions, especially in the context of elections, the Court

---

1246 See e.g. ECtHR, Appl. No. 57792/15 – *Hamidović*, dissenting opinion of Judge Ranzoni, at para. 29, laying a strong emphasis on the connection between consensus and the breadth of the respondent State's margin with no mention of other uses of consensus.

1247 ECtHR, Appl. No. 8777/79 – *Rasmussen v. Denmark*, Judgment of 28 November 1984, at para. 40; see also e.g. ECtHR, Appl. No. 36515/97 – *Fretté*, at para. 40; ECtHR, Appl. No. 30141/04 – *Schalk and Kopf*, at para. 98; ECtHR, Appl. No. 22028/04 – *Zaunegger*, at para. 50.

1248 Mahoney and Kondak, "Common Ground" at 127; Popelier and Van de Heyning, "Procedural Rationality: Giving Teeth to the Proportionality Analysis" at 243; Dothan, "Judicial Deference Allows European Consensus to Emerge" at 400.

1249 Wildhaber, Hjartarson, and Donnelly, "No Consensus on Consensus?" at 251 (emphasis added).

1250 See the cases cited infra, note 1268.

noted that "Turkey stood apart from all of the twenty-two Contracting States surveyed" in the comparative material available to it, and that there was thus a consensus in favour of the applicants.[1251] In light of these arguments and "*notwithstanding* the national authorities' margin of appreciation", it found the Turkish ban to be disproportionate.[1252] Use of the term "notwithstanding", here, seems to me to indicate that consensus constituted an argument *in spite of* the (structural) margin of appreciation, and not as a factor indicating its breadth.[1253] It is thus important to keep in mind that while consensus is often used as a factor determining the ECtHR's intensity of review, this is not its only use and it may also be deployed as part of the Court's substantive argument once the intensity of review has already been established.[1254]

In fact, I would argue that the use of consensus in different, though related, doctrinal contexts within the Court's reasoning reflects the tensions between the various forms of normativity discussed in the preceding chapters, and specifically the way in which these tensions shift depending on whether the spur effect or the rein effect of European consensus is deployed. This claim is based on the observation that *the context in which consensus is most frequently invoked differs according to whether the rein effect or the spur effect is at play*: in cases involving the rein effect, lack of consensus is usually invoked as a factor broadening the (structural) margin of appreciation, which gives more space to the national ethos of the respondent State by lowering the ECtHR's intensity of review and renders further invocation of European consensus during the following substantive assessment largely obsolete. In cases involving the spur effect, by contrast, consensus may be invoked to narrow the margin of appreciation, but it is also and even primarily used to set standards in the substantive assessment which follows by reference to ethical normativity – an aspect of its use which those accounts that link consensus exclusively to the width of the structural margin of appreciation miss. The margin of appreciation thus provides the doctrinal backdrop for the notion of a pan-European ethos to

1251 ECtHR, Appl. Nos. 49197/06, 23196/07, 50242/08, 60912/08 and 14871/09 – *Şükran Aydin and Others v. Turkey*, Judgment of 22 January 2013, at para. 55.

1252 Ibid., at para. 56.

1253 Contrast the way a lack of consensus (on linguistic policies more generally) is directly connected to the margin of appreciation in the same judgment: ibid., at para. 51.

1254 A similar point is made by Ambrus, "Comparative Law Method in the Jurisprudence of the European Court of Human Rights in the Light of the Rule of Law" at 364.

both *set* certain normative standards at the transnational level in cases of the spur effect of consensus, and to *refrain* from setting such standards in cases involving the rein effect. Let me now develop this argument in slightly more detail.

When the Court identifies a lack of consensus among the States parties (or a consensus in favour of the respondent State) and thus deploys the rein effect, it usually does so in connection to the margin of appreciation: "lack of consensus [...] broadens the margin of appreciation".[1255] In cases involving the rein effect, as discussed in Chapters 2 to 4, the main tensions are between the morality-focussed perspective and the ethos-focussed perspective: the prior opposes the use of consensus because it is liable to contain prejudices or moralistic preferences which endanger prepolitical human rights, particularly those of minorities, whereas the latter has no such qualms since it trusts in the democratic procedures within the States parties. Instead, based on a more volitional approach foregrounding political self-determination, it regards the rein effect of consensus as an appropriate safeguard against the external imposition of alleged moral standards, and as an expression of the fact that the ECHR is an instrument of cooperation between the States parties. Because arguments based on the lack of European consensus refer to the States parties as a whole, they make use of the notion of a pan-European ethos; but because they work in favour of the respondent State, they are also compatible with accounts of ethical normativity developed at the national level.

The idea that the ECtHR's intensity of review should be reduced in favour of deferring to the respondent State's democratic choice resonates very strongly with the ethos-focussed perspective in this regard, for it expresses the idea that, at least in some cases, it is "not appropriate for the Court to substitute its judgment on a particular matter for the judgment of the challenged [national] authority".[1256] In other words, it is designed to

1255 ECtHR (GC), Appl. No. 48876/08 – *Animal Defenders International*, at para. 123; see also the cases cited infra, note 1308; note that Letsas primarily connects the ECtHR's references to a *lack* of consensus to the structural margin: Letsas, *A Theory of Interpretation of the European Convention on Human Rights*, at 91.

1256 Macdonald, "The Margin of Appreciation" at 85; Macdonald is here describing a distinction very similar to the one later used by Letsas, and this phrase describes what the latter would then call the structural concept of the margin of appreciation.

prevent the ECtHR from relying on its own moral theory of rights,[1257] as the morality-focussed perspective would have it do. The implication, as Kratochvíl has described it, is that the ECtHR "places a certain amount of *trust* in States to correctly apply the proportionality test in the concrete set of circumstances of the case".[1258] Trusting States in this way is, of course, a hallmark of the ethos-focussed perspective,[1259] and using consensus to limit the intensity of the ECtHR's review gives it a particularly prominent role.[1260] Indeed, any attempt to apply a lack of consensus as a substantive argument must, from within the ethos-focussed perspective and its focus on reasonable disagreement, collapse into a *lack* of substance and thus lead back to the position taken by the national authorities as expressed in the accordance of a wide (structural) margin.[1261] Applying the rein effect of European consensus within the margin of appreciation thus constitutes an interplay between two kinds of ethical normativity working in tandem: because of the lack of consensus, no pan-European ethos can be identified,

1257 George Letsas, "Two Concepts of the Margin of Appreciation," (2006) 26 *Oxford Journal of Legal Studies* 705 at 721; see also Iglesias Vila, "Subsidiarity, Margin of Appreciation and International Adjudication within a Cooperative Conception of Human Rights" at 407.

1258 Kratochvíl, "The Inflation of the Margin of Appreciation by the European Court of Human Rights" at 329 (emphasis added), on norm application, which he describes as "similar to Letsas's structural use" (at 328); on the connection between the margin and trust and States, see also McGoldrick, "A Defence of the Margin of Appreciation and an Argument for its Application by the Human Rights Committee" at 57; and see Yuval Shany, "Toward a General Margin of Appreciation Doctrine in International Law?," (2006) 16 *European Journal of International Law* 907, arguing that a limit to the margin is that "states must always exercise their discretion in good faith"; Gerards, "Pluralism, Deference and the Margin of Appreciation Doctrine" at 87 states that deference is based on the "premise" that national procedures are working "faultlessly".

1259 Chapter 3, III. and IV.2. and Chapter 4, III.1.

1260 For this reason, Hutchinson, "The Margin of Appreciation Doctrine in the European Court of Human Rights" at 648 opposes its use in this context, though he sees it as an acceptable argument within the Court's substantive assessment.

1261 As Letsas acknowledges by citing Waldron's theory foregrounding reasonable disagreement as an instance of strong interaction between the substantive and the structural concept of the margin: Letsas, "Two Concepts of the Margin of Appreciation" at 730; see also Bates, "Activism and Self-Restraint: The Margin of Appreciation's Strasbourg Career… Its 'Coming of Age'?" at 275.

and it thus willingly cedes the ground to the national ethos of the respondent State in a particularly effective way.[1262]

When the spur effect of consensus is deployed, by contrast, there are different tensions involved. As described in Chapters 3 and 4, the pan-European ethos based on a consensus in favour of the applicant now *conflicts* with the national ethos of the respondent State. In some cases, this tension is mentioned by the ECtHR within the margin of appreciation, as when it stated in *S and Marper v. the United Kingdom* that "the strong consensus existing among the Contracting States [...] narrows the margin of appreciation left to the respondent State".[1263] Yet if a narrow margin is identified, then the Court cannot content itself with assessing whether the respondent State's position is "manifestly without reasonable foundation"[1264] – one of its standard formulations for cases involving a wide margin – and must instead set out in detail the Convention standard against which to measure that position. The question then arises how that standard is to be justified.

The morality-focussed perspective would simply invite the ECtHR to develop a substantive theory of rights and proceed in its justification on that basis – using what Arnardóttir calls "merits reasons" or, pragmatically speaking, the ECtHR's "own assessments".[1265] Yet from the ethos-focussed perspective, any standards set by the Court should not be based primarily on moral normativity or its "own assessments", given that they would always be subject to reasonable disagreement.[1266] How, then, to justify standards which are external to the respondent State's ethos – since that is under strict scrutiny – but nonetheless ethos-based? Precisely by reference to European consensus and the pan-European ethos that undergirds it.[1267] It is thus unsurprising that consensus in its spur effect should consistently be

1262 See Kagiaros, "When to Use European Consensus: Assessing the Differential Treatment of Minority Groups by the European Court of Human Rights" at 306.

1263 ECtHR (GC), Appl. Nos. 30562/04 and 30566/04 – *S. and Marper*, at para. 112; see also ECtHR, Appl. No. 45245/15 – *Gaughran*, at para. 84.

1264 E.g. ECtHR (GC), Appl. No. 44362/04 – *Dickson*, at para. 78.

1265 Arnardóttir, "Rethinking the Two Margins of Appreciation" at 47; see also supra, note 1210.

1266 See generally Chapter 3, II.

1267 See Nozawa, "Drawing the Line: Same-sex adoption and the jurisprudence of the ECtHR on the application of the "European consensus" standard under Article 14" at 73 in fine; Niamh Nic Shuibhne, "Consensus as Challenge and Retraction of Rights: Can Lessons Be Drawns from - and for - EU Citizenship Law?," in *Building Consensus on European Consensus. Judicial Interpretation of*

invoked, not only in the context of the margin of appreciation, but also *in direct support of the substantive standards set by the Court* as a result of its proportionality analysis or balancing test.[1268]

On the epistemic account of consensus based on the Condorcet Jury Theorem, this aspect becomes even more clear: if one believes that truth can be established by reference to the position taken by the majority of European States, then it seems more appropriate to regard consensus as establishing the correct human rights standard in substance, not merely a

---

Human Rights in Europe and Beyond, ed. Panos Kapotas and Vassilis Tzevelekos (Cambridge: Cambridge University Press, 2019) at 426 and 442.

1268 E.g. ECtHR, Appl. Nos. 49197/06, 23196/07, 50242/08, 60912/08 and 14871/09 – *Şükran Aydin and Others*, at paras. 55-56 (see supra, text to notes 1250-1253); ECtHR, Appl. Nos. 33985/96 and 33986/96 – *Smith and Grady v. the United Kingdom*, Judgment of 27 September 1999, at para. 104 (consensus connected to the Court's substantive conclusion at para. 105; contrast the prior determination of the margin of appreciation, at paras. 88-89 and 94); ECtHR (GC), Appl. No. 36760/06 – *Stanev*, at para. 243 (margin of appreciation mentioned at para. 241, but consensus explicitly connected to the Court's conclusion in substance at para. 245); similarly ECtHR, Appl. No. 49069/11 – *Nataliya Mikhaylenko v. Ukraine*, Judgment of 30 May 2013, at para. 38; ECtHR (GC), Appl. No. 30078/06 – *Konstantin Markin*, at para. 140 (in reaction to substantive arguments advanced by the Government, see para. 138; intensity of review established beforehand, at para. 137); ECtHR (GC), Appl. No. 34503/97 – *Demir and Baykara*, at paras. 121-122 (citing consensus as an argument that Turkish law "did not correspond to a 'necessity'" under Article 11 (2) ECHR, rather than in the context of the margin of appreciation at para. 119); see similarly paras. 164-165 on the right for civil servants to bargain collectively; ECtHR (GC), Appl. Nos. 29381/09 and 32684/09 – *Vallianatos and Others*, at para. 91 (connecting consensus to the conclusion of a violation at para. 92; margin of appreciation already identified as narrow beforehand, at paras. 77 and 85); ECtHR (GC), Appl. Nos. 66069/09, 130/10 and 3896/10 – *Vinter and Others*, at paras. 114-118 (consensus cited as a reason for the substantive assessment that "there must be both a prospect of release and a possibility of review" in cases of life sentences, see paras. 110 and 119); ECtHR (GC), Appl. Nos. 52562/99 and 525620/99 – *Sørensen and Rasmussen*, at para. 75 (consensus used to argue that closed-shop agreements are not indispensable, wide margin of appreciation mentioned without reference to consensus at para. 58); it is telling, perhaps, that some commentators refer to consensus as "a means of mediation between dynamic interpretation and the margin of appreciation" (Dzehtsiarou, *European Consensus and the Legitimacy of the European Court of Human Rights*, at 23) – thus emphasising the connection between consensus and the margin only in cases concerning the rein effect; see e.g. Peters, "The Rule of Law Dimensions of Dialogues Between National Courts and Strasbourg" at 219-220; Kapotas and Tzevelekos, "How (Difficult Is It) to Build Consensus on (European) Consensus?" at 7.

strong standard of review by the ECtHR.[1269] The ethos-focussed perspective, of course, approaches the issue on less cognitive and more volitional grounds, but it reaches similar conclusions as to substantive human rights standards developed within a pan-European ethos – in contrast to the national ethos of the respondent State.

The differing doctrinal context in which consensus is predominantly used can thus be explained, in part, by connecting it back to the notion of a pan-European ethos and the ensuing tensions with the morality-focussed perspective (in cases concerning the rein effect, where lack of consensus leads to a lenient standard of review and thus privileges the national ethos of the respondent State over moral argument made by the ECtHR itself) and with ethical normativity developed at the national level (in cases concerning the spur effect, where consensus among the States parties establishes not only a strict standard of review, but also the substantive standards against which the respondent State's position is measured). To be clear, however, this analysis is based on an overall impression of the ECtHR's case-law, and by no means applies in every judgment. For one thing, the case-law is simply not always consistent,[1270] and for another, there are still a large number of judgments which fail to clearly uphold the doctrinal distinctions introduced by the Court itself, even the most fundamental distinction between the intensity of review and the substantive assessment that follows from it. Thus, in some cases the ECtHR structures its reasoning along separate sections entitled "margin of appreciation" and "fair balance",[1271] or discusses these issues separately within the same section[1272] – yet in other judgments, it combines various different considerations under the overall title of "necessity in a democratic society" (or similar catch-all phrases) without providing further guidance,[1273] and it is well-nigh impossible to figure out which aspects of its reasoning, if any, pertain to the (structural) margin of appreciation and which to the substantive assessment.

1269 Shai Dothan does connect consensus to the margin of appreciation, however: see supra, note 1248.

1270 See generally supra, note 1234.

1271 E.g. ECtHR, Appl. Nos. 79885/12, 52471/13 and 52596/13 – *A.P., Garçon and Nicot*: see the headings to paras. 121 and 126.

1272 See many of the cases cited in note 1268.

1273 For example, I find it difficult to place the reference in ECtHR (GC), Appl. No. 16574/08 – *Fabris v. France (Merits)*, Judgment of 7 February 2013, at para. 69 (although consensus is clearly connected to the structural concept of the margin at paras. 58-59).

In those cases, it is difficult to describe the doctrinal context of European consensus, and I will thus revert back to the general notion that it is, in some sense, given normative force.[1274] The following sub-sections will consider consensus within the general context of the margin of appreciation and the proportionality analysis in this sense – paying attention not primarily to its precise doctrinal context (structural or substantive) but rather to the way it interacts with other reasons offered by the Court to justify its conclusions in either case. As in the preceding section, my focus will be on foregrounding the difficulties that arise from the combination of different kinds of normativity – moral normativity, ethical normativity at the pan-European level, and ethical normativity at the national level. These distinctions cut across the doctrinal placement of the arguments at issue: for whether we distinguish between "the *reason* for which the Court reaches the conclusion that there was no violation" (structural or substantive à la Letsas),[1275] or between "non-merits" and "merits" reasons à la Arnardóttir,[1276] the shift between moral normativity and different kinds of ethical normativity will determine how the very notion of a "reason" is understood. The following subsections will trace the tensions between these different kinds of normativity, first for cases involving the rein effect of consensus, and then for those involving the spur effect.

2. Contextualising the Rein Effect

The rein effect of European consensus, I have argued, is most commonly deployed within the *structural* margin of appreciation (as opposed to the substantive assessment which follows it), so it is in that context that I will examine the interaction of the various factors, including consensus, which determine the margin's breadth. A general difficulty in doing so is that the ECtHR does not, usually, provide a theoretical justification for the kind of reasons it deems influential in doing so, instead placing a vast array of different arguments in proximity to one another, often without much guid-

1274 See generally Chapter 1, IV.5.

1275 Letsas, *A Theory of Interpretation of the European Convention on Human Rights*, at 82.

1276 Arnardóttir, "Rethinking the Two Margins of Appreciation" at 29.

ance as to their interrelation.[1277] Even identifying the role played by European consensus in any given case has been described as "sheer guesswork".[1278] Yet generally speaking, we may at least note that the argumentative weight accorded to European consensus within the margin of appreciation seems to differ from case to case.[1279] In some cases, the Court only mentions lack of consensus in passing, or even states explicitly that it does not "play a weighty part in the Court's conclusion".[1280] In other cases, it clearly carries more weight – to the point that it may, though rarely, be the only argument offered within a certain section of the Court's reasoning.[1281]

Many commentators have concluded that, by and large, consensus plays a "key role" in determining the margin of appreciation[1282] – indeed, were it not for the argument's prominence within the Court's reasoning, it

---

1277 See Brems, "The Margin of Appreciation Doctrine in the Case-Law of the European Court of Human Rights" at 242; Hutchinson, "The Margin of Appreciation Doctrine in the European Court of Human Rights" at 641; Ryan, "Europe's Moral Margin: Parental Aspirations and the European Court of Human Rights" at 492; Henrard, "How the ECtHR's Use of European Consensus Considerations Allows Legitimacy Concerns to Delimit Its Mandate" at 146; see generally Tzevelekos, "The Use of Article 31(3)(C) of the VCLT in the Case Law of the ECtHR: An Effective Anti-Fragmentation Tool or a Selective Loophole for the Reinforcement of Human Rights Teleology?" at 638; Dzehtsiarou, "What Is Law for the European Court of Human Rights?" at 99.

1278 Wildhaber, Hjartarson, and Donnelly, "No Consensus on Consensus?" at 356.

1279 Dahlberg, "'The Lack of Such a Common Approach' - Comparative Argumentation by the European Court of Human Rights" has made this point at length and distinguishes between a cognitive, decorative, directional and decisive function (e.g. at 76); Wildhaber, Hjartarson, and Donnelly, "No Consensus on Consensus?" at 256 conclude that the Court considers consensus to be "of indicative, persuasive, in some cases probably decisive value"; see also Mahoney and Kondak, "Common Ground" at 139.

1280 ECtHR (GC), Appl. No. 27510/08 – *Perinçek*, at para. 257; for context on this particular instance, see Chapter 5, III.1.

1281 ECtHR, Appl. No. 30141/04 – *Schalk and Kopf*, at paras. 104-106; see Kagiaros, "When to Use European Consensus: Assessing the Differential Treatment of Minority Groups by the European Court of Human Rights" at 292 and 298.

1282 Onder Bakircioglu, "The Application of the Margin of Appreciation Doctrine in Freedom of Expression and Public Morality Cases," (2007) 8 *German Law Journal* 711 at 722 (and see also at 712); de la Rasilla del Moral, "The Increasingly Marginal Appreciation of the Margin-of-Appreciation Doctrine" at 617; Hamilton, "Same-Sex Marriage, Consensus, Certainty and the European Court of Human Rights" at 36; see also Letsas, *A Theory of Interpretation of the European Convention on Human Rights*, at 92 and 95-96; Radačić, "Rights of the Vulnerable Groups" at 604; Dean Spielmann, "Whither the Margin of Apprecia-

would hardly have become as controversial as it has. Broadly speaking, this points to the prevalence of the ethos-focussed perspective in the case-law on the margin of appreciation, especially when contrasted to the somewhat tentative references to (lack of) consensus in the case-law on autonomous concepts as described above. But the differing argumentative weight given to consensus in some cases, and the fact that is usually not on its own considered decisive for the margin's breadth, also makes it clear that other forms of reasoning likewise play a role. For example, Samantha Besson has expressed regret that consensus "is not the sole criterion or test at play in the Court's reasoning when setting the margin of appreciation"[1283] – since she is a firm proponent of the ethos-focussed perspective, it comes as no surprise that she deplores the inclusion of other forms of argument which may open the door to morality-focussed considerations.[1284]

Similarly, Andrew Legg has attempted to keep the margin of appreciation free of considerations with morality-focussed connotations, such as the "nature of the right".[1285] Yet this is in clear contradiction of the ECtHR's case-law.[1286] Thus the Court has stated that "in delimiting the extent of the margin of appreciation in a given case, the Court must also have regard to what is at stake therein"[1287] – the nature of the right being one such aspect of "what is at stake". Another standard formulation of the Court, insofar as the rein effect of consensus is concerned, goes as follows:

> A number of factors must be taken into account when determining the breadth of [the margin of appreciation]. Where a particularly important facet of an individual's existence or identity is at stake, the margin allowed to the State will be restricted [...]. Where, however,

---

tion?," (2014) 67 *Current Legal Problems* 49 at 53; Hallström, "Balance of Clash of Legal Orders" at 62; Mena Parras, "Democracy, Diversity and the Margin of Appreciation" at 11; Popelier and Van de Heyning, "Procedural Rationality: Giving Teeth to the Proportionality Analysis" at 244; Henrard, "How the ECtHR's Use of European Consensus Considerations Allows Legitimacy Concerns to Delimit Its Mandate" at 149; Nussberger, *The European Court of Human Rights*, at 87.

1283 Besson, "Subsidiarity in International Human Rights Law - What is Subsidiary about Human Rights?" at 100.

1284 But see Chapter 4, III.2.

1285 Legg, *The Margin of Appreciation*, at 200.

1286 Arnardóttir, "Rethinking the Two Margins of Appreciation" at 44; the nature of the right may still be determined by the Court from within the ethos-focussed perspective, however: see infra, text to notes 1306-1309.

1287 ECtHR (GC), Appl. No. 43835/11 – *S.A.S.*, at para. 129.

there is no consensus within the member States of the Council of Europe, either as to the relative importance of the interest at stake or as to the best means of protecting it, [...] the margin will be wider.[1288]

Needless to say, the Court often names other factors, or makes use of them in its reasoning without explicitly introducing them in the section in which it sets forth its "general principles" of justification.[1289] I will nonetheless focus here on the juxtaposition of these two factors – lack of consensus and the "particularly important facet of an individual's existence or identity" – for one thing because they constitute a recurring theme, particularly in cases concerning the right to private life, and for another because they showcase the tension between the morality-focussed perspective and the ethos-focussed perspective particularly well. It will quickly emerge that, as the discussion of core rights in Chapter 4 already indicated, this tension is difficult to resolve.

Assessing how the Court places the two factors just mentioned in relation to one another is rendered somewhat difficult by the fact that, as mentioned above, it rarely notes a lack of consensus only to then overrule it by means of other arguments and find a violation of the Convention. Some cases of that kind do exist, however.[1290] Consider, for example, the case of *A.P., Garçon and Nicot v. France*, in which the trans applicants challenged, inter alia, the requirement of sterilisation (or medical treatment with a high probability of entailing sterilisation) as a precondition for legal gen-

---

1288 ECtHR (GC), Appl. No. 37359/09 – *Hämäläinen*, at para. 67; see also e.g. ECtHR (GC), Appl. No. 57813/00 – *S.H. and Others*, at para. 94; ECtHR (GC), Appl. No. 6339/05 – *Evans*, at para. 77; ECtHR (GC), Appl. Nos. 30562/04 and 30566/04 – *S. and Marper*, at para. 102; ECtHR, Appl. No. 23338/09 – *Kautzor*, at para. 70; ECtHR, Appl. No. 14793/08 – *Y.Y.*, at para. 101; ECtHR (GC), Appl. No. 25579/05 – *A, B and C*, at para. 232; ECtHR, Appl. No. 48009/08 – *Mosley*, at paras. 109-110; on this formulation with regard to numerical issues implied by the reference to lack of consensus ("no consensus"), see Chapter 5, III.1.

1289 For a recent overview of some of these, see Pascual-Vives, *Consensus-Based Interpretation of Regional Human Rights Treaties*, chapter 7; an excellent overview is Gerards, *General Principles of the European Convention on Human Rights*, 172 et seqq.

1290 A rare example is ECtHR, Appl. No. 65192/11 – *Mennesson*, at paras. 77-81; sometimes, the Court also mentions comparative materials which might be construed as a (lack of) consensus arguably contrary to its own conclusions, but does not refer to them as part of its reasoning beyond the initial mention in the section on "comparative law materials": see e.g. ECtHR (GC), Appl. No. 78117/13 – *Fábián v. Hungary*, Judgment of 5 September 2017, at para. 43.

der recognition.[1291] Considering the breadth of the margin of appreciation, the Court first acknowledged the lack of consensus among the States parties on this issue: more than half of them retained the sterilisation requirement.[1292] It went on to note, however, that "an essential aspect of a person's intimate identity, or even of their existence, is at the heart of the case" and, on that ground, found that the respondent State's margin of appreciation was restricted[1293] – and, ultimately, that the sterilisation requirement constitutes a violation of the right to private life.

In light of cases such as these, Kanstantsin Dzehtsiarou has suggested that the normative force of European consensus should be conceptualised as a "rebuttable presumption"[1294] – in the case of its rein effect, it establishes a presumption the respondent State enjoys a wide margin of appreciation.[1295] The Court may still argue in favour of a narrow margin despite the lack of consensus, and indeed ultimately rule in favour of the applicants – as it did in *A.P., Garçon and Nicot* – but it "has to justify the rebuttal of such a presumption".[1296] Based on his interviews with numerous judges of the ECtHR, Dzehtsiarou has suggested that many of them take a similar approach and "follow European consensus unless there [are] convincing reasons against it"[1297] – that is, unless counterarguments may be found. Dzehtsiarou has made use of this framework, in particular, to argue that the ECtHR's use of European consensus in its rein effect need not present a danger to the rights of intra-State minorities. As he puts it, if European consensus establishes a rebuttable presumption, then the Court "can disre-

---

1291 This is a different strand of the case than the part relating (directly) to trans pathologisation, discussed in the previous chapter.

1292 ECtHR, Appl. Nos. 79885/12, 52471/13 and 52596/13 – *A.P., Garçon and Nicot*, at paras. 71 and 122; but see also paras. 124-125 on recent trends and international pronouncements in favour of a consensus. These aspects are considered in Chapter 5, IV.

1293 Ibid., at para. 123 (my translation).

1294 Dzehtsiarou, *European Consensus and the Legitimacy of the European Court of Human Rights*, at 27; Tzevelekos and Dzehtsiarou, "International Custom Making" at 322; see also Peters, "The Rule of Law Dimensions of Dialogues Between National Courts and Strasbourg" at 220.

1295 Dzehtsiarou, *European Consensus and the Legitimacy of the European Court of Human Rights*, at 28.

1296 Ibid., 29-30.

1297 Ibid., 190.

gard [it] if justification is provided, and the fact that the case concerns minority rights can be seen as such a justification".[1298]

If one reads this account of consensus as a rebuttable presumption within the margin of appreciation in light of the framework developed over the course of the preceding chapters, then it becomes clear that it involves tensions between the morality-focussed perspective and the ethos-focussed perspective. As with the notion of "core rights", morality-focussed considerations are introduced despite an ethos-focussed starting point. In fact, the ECtHR sometimes refers to "core rights" or "key rights" within its reasoning, sometimes connecting this notion to the more general formulation relating to a "particularly important facet of an individual's existence".[1299] When it is only "'supplementary' (as opposed to core) rights" that are at issue, the margin of appreciation is broad;[1300] conversely, when the case is deemed to concern a core right or key right, then "the margin will tend to be narrower".[1301] As with the more general phrase referring to important facets of an individual's existence, the notion of "key rights" has repeatedly been juxtaposed with a lack of European consensus as a countervailing factor within the margin of appreciation.[1302]

In Chapter 4, I noted that when morality-focussed and ethos-focussed considerations are placed in juxtaposition in this way, the question in-

---

1298 Ibid., 123-124; Dzehtsiarou also points out the flexibility of European consensus, which accords with the ECtHR's use of it – though not necessarily in favour of minority rights; see the remainder of this subsection, as well as Chapter 7, III.1.

1299 ECtHR, Appl. No. 14793/08 – *Y.Y.*, at para. 101 ("accordingly").

1300 The citation is from ECtHR, Appl. Nos. 18766/11 and 36030/11 – *Oliari and Others*, at para. 177, where the ECtHR held that core rights were at stake; on that case, see further Chapter 5, IV.; for a case explicitly *not* involving core rights, see ECtHR (GC), Appl. No. 46470/11 – *Parrillo*, at para. 174 (on the right to donate embryos to scientific research, in contrast to cases concerning prospective parenthood); the juxtaposition between core and periphery is also reflected in ECtHR (GC), Appl. No. 42326/98 – *Odièvre*, joint dissenting opinion of Judges Wildhaber, Sir Nicolas Bratza, Bonello, Loucaides, Cabral Barreto, Tulkens and Pellonpää, at para. 11.

1301 ECtHR, Appl. No. 66746/01 – *Connors v. the United Kingdom*, Judgment of 27 May 2004, at para. 82.

1302 ECtHR (GC), Appl. Nos. 30562/04 and 30566/04 – *S. and Marper*, at para. 102; ECtHR (GC), Appl. No. 42857/05 – *van der Heijden v. the Netherlands*, Judgment of 3 April 2012, at paras. 59-60; ECtHR, Appl. No. 14793/08 – *Y.Y.*, at para. 101; ECtHR (GC), Appl. No. 56030/07 – *Fernández Martínez v. Spain*, Judgment of 12 June 2014, at para. 124; ECtHR, Appl. No. 50001/12 – *Breyer v. Germany*, Judgment of 30 January 2020, at para. 80.

evitably arises in which cases the presumption established by consensus should be rebutted, and on which grounds – or, differently put, how to distinguish between key or core rights, on the one hand, and "supplementary rights", on the other. As Janneke Gerards has stated, the ECtHR itself has, so far, "omitted to provide clear and general criteria to determine which elements of rights belong to the core and which elements should be considered rather peripheral in nature".[1303]

Dzehtsiarou's proposal runs as follows: after initially speaking of any case which "concerns" minority rights – which would cast a fairly broad net, though still dependent on one's understanding of "minority rights" – Dzehtsiarou specifies that the presumption established by consensus should be considered rebutted in those cases which "unreasonably limit" minority rights.[1304] The issue then turns on how he understands *reasonableness*, a controversy familiar from Chapter 5. Since Dzehtsiarou is building an argument that serves to *rebut* the argumentative force initially attributed to consensus, his approach here seems to be based on the more circumscribed sense of "reasonableness" which excludes certain positions from consideration on the basis of morality-focussed considerations – but such an approach stands in contradiction to the emphasis on reasonable disagreement which forms part of the argument for according European consensus normative force in the first place.[1305]

A different approach is possible, and indeed shines through in the way in which the ECtHR sometimes frames the issue. When, according to the Court, is a "key right" or a "particularly important facet of an individual's existence or identity" at stake, pointing to a narrow margin of appreciation? According to the standard formulation cited above, it seems that this question would be answered by European consensus: note that the Court states it will grant a wide margin where there is a lack of consensus, inter alia, "as to the relative importance of the interest at stake",[1306] so that the consensus enquiry could be understood as determining whether a particu-

1303 Gerards, "Pluralism, Deference and the Margin of Appreciation Doctrine" at 112.

1304 Dzehtsiarou, *European Consensus and the Legitimacy of the European Court of Human Rights*, at 125.

1305 Again, this chimes with the discussion of core rights in Chapter 4, III.2.; for another example, see Vogiatzis, "The Relationship Between European Consensus, the Margin of Appreciation and the Legitimacy of the Strasbourg Court" at 475, where everything turn on how one understands the phrase "where appropriate".

1306 Supra, note 1288.

lar facet of an individual's existence or identity *is*, in fact, "particularly important" – or not.[1307]

This would point to a prevalence of the ethos-focussed perspective, and indeed – contrary to Dzehtsiarou's morality-focussed suggestion of overruling lack of consensus in cases concerning minority rights – the Court often seems to have taken this approach. For one thing, there is a large number of cases in which the rein effect of European consensus seems to have been crucial in establishing the respondent State's wide margin of appreciation (and thus, ultimately, a finding of no violation) despite the subject-matter relating to minority rights.[1308] For another, some of these cases seem to make use of an ethos-focussed argument based on lack of consensus precisely *in order to dispute the importance of the interest at stake*. This brings us back to the level of generality at which consensus is used, as discussed in the previous chapter. In *Leyla Şahin v. Turkey*, for example, the ECtHR noted the lack of European consensus on the "significance of religion in soci-

---

1307 In the language of "core rights", this would mean that consensus is used to "draw a line around core rights", as argued by Ostrovsky, "What's So Funny About Peace, Love, and Understanding?" at 57; see further Chapter 4, III.2.; the ECtHR has similarly used the spur effect of consensus to "support" its argument as to the "very essence of the right to organise" for public servants: ECtHR (GC), Appl. No. 34503/97 – *Demir and Baykara*, at paras. 97-98; for a case concerning the rein effect, see e.g. ECtHR, Appl. No. 45892/09 – *Junta Rectora del Ertzainen Nazional Elkartasuna v. Spain*, Judgment of 21 April 2015, at paras. 39-40; for a morality-focussed approach to the notion of a right's "essence", see Greer, *The Margin of Appreciation: Interpretation and Discretion under the European Convention on Human Rights*, at 15.

1308 Some of the most obvious cases concerning minority groups are e.g. ECtHR, Appl. No. 36515/97 – *Fretté*, at para. 41; ECtHR, Appl. No. 30141/04 – *Schalk and Kopf*, at para. 105; ECtHR (GC), Appl. No. 43835/11 – *S.A.S.*, at para. 156; ECtHR, Appl. Nos. 79885/12, 52471/13 and 52596/13 – *A.P., Garçon and Nicot*, at para. 139; see also ECtHR (GC), Appl. No. 37359/09 – *Hämäläinen*, at para. 74, where the Court referred to a lack of consensus but made no mention of its acknowledgment, in an earlier case on a similar issue, of the "direct and invasive effect on the applicants' enjoyment of their right to respect for their private and family life" which was at stake: for the latter, see ECtHR, Appl. No. 42971/05 – *Parry v. the United Kingdom*, Decision of 28 November 2006, p. 10; if the ambit is broadened to include minorities in the sense discussed in Chapter 2, II.1., the number of examples amplifies even more: see e.g. ECtHR (Plenary), Appl. No. 5493/72 – *Handyside*, at paras. 48, 53 and 57; ECtHR, Appl. No. 13470/87 – *Otto-Preminger-Institut v. Austria*, Judgment of 20 September 1994, at para. 50; ECtHR (GC), Appl. No. 42326/98 – *Odièvre*, at para. 47; ECtHR (GC), Appl. No. 30814/06 – *Lautsi and Others*, at para. 70; ECtHR (GC), Appl. No. 46470/11 – *Parrillo*, at paras. 175-182.

ety":[1309] this led to deference to the respondent State as to the significance accorded to religion, whereas the importance which the applicant herself attached to wearing the headscarf was side-lined entirely. A more morality-focussed approach would instead have picked up on the Court's dictum that freedom of religion makes up "one of the most vital elements that go to make up the identity of believers"[1310] and applied it more specifically to religious attire; yet by taking an ethos-focussed approach also to the question of the "relative importance of the interest at stake", though not in those words, the Court avoided this inconvenience.

Besides demonstrating the use of consensus at different levels of generality, then, cases such as *Leyla Şahin* also show that whether a case concerns a "particularly important facet of an individual's existence or identity" and the respondent State's margin of appreciation is therefore narrowed *can* be determined from an ethos-focussed perspective – but the important point is that this is by no means *necessary*.[1311] In other cases – as in the above-mentioned case of *A.P., Garçon and Nicot*, insofar as the sterilisation requirement is concerned – the argument that the case concerns "an essential aspect of a person's intimate identity", is introduced as a *counterargument* to the lack of consensus and thus relies instead on substantive reasoning of the kind preferred by the morality-focussed perspective.[1312] In *Perinçek v. Switzerland*, the Court even noted explicitly that, since "there are other factors which have a significant bearing on the breadth of the applicable margin of appreciation" – which included, inter alia, precisely such substantive reasoning – "the comparative law position cannot play a weighty part in the Court's conclusion".[1313] The structure of the Court's reasoning, in such cases, coheres neatly with Dzehtsiarou's account of consensus as a rebuttable presumption within the margin of appreciation – and thus also replicates the tensions inherent within it.

In sum, my argument is that while the margin of appreciation provides the doctrinal framework within which differing arguments can be brought together and juxtaposed by the ECtHR, it does not resolve the underlying tensions produced, in particular, by the differing epistemological assump-

1309 ECtHR (GC), Appl. No. 44774/98 – *Leyla Şahin*, at para. 109; see further Chapter 7, III.1.

1310 Ibid., at para. 104.

1311 A case for the "important facet" argument as a *counter* to lack of consensus is made by ECtHR (GC), Appl. No. 37359/09 – *Hämäläinen*, joint dissenting opinion of Judges Sajó, Keller and Lemmens, at para. 5.

1312 Supra, note 1293.

1313 ECtHR (GC), Appl. No. 27510/08 – *Perinçek*, at para. 257.

tions of the morality-focussed and the ethos-focussed perspective. As Janneke Gerards has put it, there "does not seem to be a single standard that helps the court decide if intensity-determining factors pull in different directions",[1314] and the ECtHR is thus reduced to solving such dilemmas "by simply stopping short of making a real choice".[1315] Steven Greer has likewise noted that it is "impossible to set out in the abstract" how the different "principles of interpretation" which he identifies in connection with the margin of appreciation "interact with each other";[1316] and Samantha Besson has opined that the margin's application "remains largely unpredictable" specifically because factors other than European consensus are included within it.[1317] In part, such statements echo the vast swaths of commentators criticising the Court for its lack of clarity and consistence in applying the margin of appreciation[1318] – but there is also a sense that the criticism goes deeper, and that the tension between the morality-focussed and the ethos-focussed perspective makes it difficult to develop a clear standard at all. After all, any such unifying standard would be based, prima facie, in either moral or ethical normativity and thus favour one of the competing factors from the outset.

3. Contextualising the Spur Effect

As repeatedly touched upon over the course of the preceding chapters, the spur effect of European consensus involves somewhat different tensions: for while the differing approaches of the morality-focussed perspective and the ethos-focussed perspective persist – the prior more cognitive and the latter more volitional – and they may reach different conclusions accordingly, they are generally seen as less drastically opposed given that the spur effect speaks in favour of a broad understanding of human rights and thus presents less of a danger to individuals, particularly those belonging to intra-State minorities. This alignment is perhaps heightened even further in the context of the (structural) margin of appreciation. Whatever the moral-

1314 Gerards, "Pluralism, Deference and the Margin of Appreciation Doctrine" at 114.

1315 Ibid., 115.

1316 Greer, *The Margin of Appreciation: Interpretation and Discretion under the European Convention on Human Rights*, at 22.

1317 Besson, "Subsidiarity in International Human Rights Law - What is Subsidiary about Human Rights?" at 100.

1318 See supra, notes 1234 and 1277; and more generally Chapter 5, II.

ity-focussed perspective's take on the substantive issue at hand, it will be sceptical of trusting the respondent State by deferring to its judgment in light of a broad margin of appreciation,[1319] and thus work in tandem with the spur effect of consensus in that regard.

By contrast, insofar as the substantive assessment by the Court is concerned, conflict is more likely. Recall, in particular, that the morality-focussed perspective need not always be in favour of a broad understanding of human rights, for example to prevent their devaluation by means of "inflation".[1320] In such cases,[1321] the spur effect of consensus might speak in favour of a violation while the morality-focussed perspective demurs. Yet in practice, even when the spur effect of consensus is deployed as part of the Court's substantive assessment, the tension is not usually between the morality-focussed and the ethos-focussed perspective, respectively – rather, it is between different forms of ethical normativity, depending on whether it is located at the pan-European or at the national level. Giving spur effect to European consensus relies on the prior, since it takes the position of a majority of States parties to the ECHR to express a pan-European ethos – which then constitutes an argument *against* the respondent State and its national ethos.[1322] For example, in *Ebrahimian v. France*, the Court made this tension explicit by first implying that France was one of only five States parties identified "as prohibiting completely the wearing of religious signs by civil servants" (spur effect of consensus, leading to a narrow margin), but immediately juxtaposing this finding to the "*national context* of State-Church relations" within France (leading to a broad margin).[1323]

1319 See supra, III.1.

1320 See Chapter 2, III.

1321 Letsas cites the ECtHR's Chamber judgment in ECtHR (Third Section), Appl. No. 36022/97 – *Hatton and Others v. the United Kingdom*, Judgment of 2 October 2001 (the "right to sleep well") as an example of dangerous inflation: Letsas, *A Theory of Interpretation of the European Convention on Human Rights*, at 127; contrast the dissenting opinion arguing in favour of a violation of Article 8 ECHR in the subsequent Grand Chamber judgment, relying in part on consensus-based reasoning: ECtHR (GC), Appl. No. 36022/97 – *Hatton and Others v. the United Kingdom*, Judgment of 8 July 2003, joint dissenting opinion of Judges Costa, Ress, Türmen, Zupančič and Steiner, at para. 1.

1322 See in more detail Chapter 3, IV.3.

1323 ECtHR, Appl. No. 64846/11 – *Ebrahimian*, at para. 65 (emphasis added); see further Chapter 7, III.1.: the ECtHR also made implicit reference to lack of consensus at higher levels of generality, by virtue of its reference to *Leyla Şahin*.

In this subsection, I would like to explore how these various tensions play out within the Court's case-law.

One of the clearest statements in favour of the spur effect of European consensus as an important factor in determining the breadth of the margin of appreciation was given in the case of *S and Marper v. the United Kingdom*, where the Court held that "the strong consensus existing among the Contracting States [...] is of considerable importance and narrows the margin of appreciation left to the respondent State".[1324] In that case, European consensus very much took centre-stage in the determination of the margin's breadth. In other judgments, it explicitly worked alongside more morality-focussed forms of reasoning. Take the case of *Glor v. Switzerland*, which concerned the forced payment of a tax as a substitute for military service for persons with disabilities. The ECtHR again invoked the spur effect of consensus, stating that it "must have regard to the changing conditions [...] within Contracting States" and respond to "any emerging consensus as to the standards to be achieved", which forms "one of the relevant factors in determining the scope of the authorities' margin of appreciation".[1325] The Court noted that this type of tax levied against the applicant in Switzerland "does not seem to exist in other countries, at least in Europe"[1326] – that there was, in other words, a consensus against the respondent State. In a more morality-focussed vein, it also noted that the tax posed a risk of discriminating against persons with disabilities, before concluding *in light of both these factors* that the margin of appreciation was "considerably reduced",[1327] and going on to find a violation of the Convention. Both the morality-focussed and the ethos-focussed reasons considered by the Court thus pointed in favour of a narrow margin – the latter being based on a pan-European ethos, with the national ethos of the respondent State receiving no specific mention.

Indeed, the national ethos of the respondent State has not traditionally been accorded a strong presence in determining the breadth of the margin of appreciation – instead, it usually makes its appearance during the substantive assessment once the appropriate level of scrutiny has been deter-

---

1324 ECtHR (GC), Appl. Nos. 30562/04 and 30566/04 – *S. and Marper*, at para. 112.

1325 ECtHR, Appl. No. 13444/04 – *Glor v. Switzerland*, Judgment of 30 April 2009, at para. 75; see also e.g. ECtHR (GC), Appl. No. 42202/07 – *Sitaropoulos and Giakoumopoulos*, at para. 66.

1326 ECtHR, Appl. No. 13444/04 – *Glor*, at para. 83.

1327 Ibid., at para. 84.

mined.[1328] Yet one countervailing tendency, in which aspects of the respondent State's national ethos are referred to as an element within the structural margin of appreciation, should be noted: these are cases in which the Court refers to the *quality of the democratic procedures within the respondent State*. Several commentators have noted that "the Strasbourg Court is currently in the process of reformulating the substantive and procedural criteria that regulate the appropriate level of deference to be afforded to the Member States",[1329] and giving greater weight to the quality of democratic procedures in the respondent State is a major aspect of this reformulation. The paradigmatic example is the judgment in *Animal Defenders v. the United Kingdom*, in which the Court held that "[t]he quality of the parliamentary and judicial review of the necessity of [the legislative measure at issue] is of particular importance [...], including to the operation of the relevant margin of appreciation".[1330] In cases in which the quality of democratic procedures within the respondent State was high – so the argument goes – the Court has more reason to trust the result they reached, and therefore to reduce the intensity of its review by allowing a wide (structural) margin of appreciation.[1331]

1328 See infra, text following note 1337, for cases involving the spur effect; in relation to the rein effect, the discussion of cases involving lack of consensus at high levels of generality (leading to a broad margin of appreciation) in relation to the resulting (though doctrinally distinct) focus on the national ethos of the respondent State in Chapter 7, III.1. also exemplifies this scenario.

1329 Spano, "Universality or Diversity of Human Rights? Strasbourg in the Age of Subsidiarity" at 498.

1330 ECtHR (GC), Appl. No. 48876/08 – *Animal Defenders International*, at para. 108; see also e.g. ECtHR (GC), Appl. No. 74025/01 – *Hirst*, at para. 79.

1331 The connection to the structural margin of appreciation is made explicit e.g. by Matthew Saul, "The European Court of Human Rights' Margin of Appreciation and the Processes of National Parliaments," (2015) 15 *Human Rights Law Review* 745 at 750; see also, though within her slightly different framework, Oddný Mjöll Arnardóttir, "The 'Procedural Turn' under the European Convention on Human Rights and Presumptions of Convention Compliance," (2017) 15 *International Journal of Constitutional Law* 9 at 11; in that vein, see also Kleinlein, "Consensus and Contestability: The ECtHR and the Combined Potential of European Consensus and Procedural Rationality Control" at 872 (in footnote 2); critically: Popelier and Van de Heyning, "Procedural Rationality: Giving Teeth to the Proportionality Analysis" at 243; for an overview of cases in which national procedures played a role not in determining the width of the margin, but as the object of scrutiny within the substantive assessment in light of it, see Eva Brems and Laurens Lavrysen, "Procedural Justice in Human Rights Adjudication: The European Court of Human Rights," (2013) 35 *Human Rights Quarterly* 176 at 195-198; contrast ibid., 200.

This clearly constitutes an argument steeped in ethical normativity developed at the national level, since it is precisely in democratic procedures that national ethe are commonly located nowadays.[1332] While the national ethos of the respondent State is not given free rein entirely – both because it must conform to certain standards in order to broaden rather than narrow the margin of appreciation, and because it continues to be subject to review by the ECtHR, albeit in limited form if the margin is broad – such an argument must perforce seem out of place from the morality-focussed perspective. As Tom Lewis has put it, "[i]t is difficult to see, from the rights-holder's perspective" – i.e. when foregrounding the individual rather than the political collectivity of the State, thus reflecting the concerns of the morality-focussed perspective – "why the quality and quantity of debate should have a determinative impact on whether there has been a violation of his or her rights".[1333]

But insofar as a high-quality process in the respondent State speaks in favour of a broad margin of appreciation, the national ethos of the respondent State is also set to conflict with the spur effect of European consensus as an expression of a pan-European ethos. Thomas Kleinlein has raised this issue most explicitly, while acknowledging that the Court's case-law thus far provides no answer as to how such cases should be handled.[1334] Yet he suggests that "[h]igh standards in domestic procedures can possibly rebut the presumption in favour of the solution adopted by the majority of Convention states".[1335] Kleinlein thus makes use of the notion of consensus as a rebuttable presumption in determining the breadth of the margin of ap-

---

1332 See Chapter 3, III.

1333 Tom Lewis, "*Animal Defenders International* v *United Kingdom*: Sensible Dialogue or a Bad Case of Strasbourg Jitters?," (2014) 77 *Modern Law Review* 460 at 469; see also Saul, "The European Court of Human Rights' Margin of Appreciation and the Processes of National Parliaments" at 760; Eva Brems, "Procedural Protection. An Examination of Procedural Safeguards Read into Substantive Convention Rights," in *Shaping Rights in the ECHR. The Role of the European Court of Human Rights in Determining the Scope of Human Rights*, ed. Eva Brems and Janneke Gerards (Cambridge: Cambridge University Press, 2013) at 159; the more cognitive and outcome-based concerns of the morality-focussed perspective also comes through quite clearly in the position of several dissenting judges: see ECtHR (GC), Appl. No. 48876/08 – *Animal Defenders International*, joint dissenting opinion of Judges Ziemele, Sajó, Kalaydjieva, Vučinić and de Gaetano, at paras. 9-10.

1334 Kleinlein, "Consensus and Contestability: The ECtHR and the Combined Potential of European Consensus and Procedural Rationality Control" at 878.

1335 Ibid., 871.

preciation, as discussed above by reference to the rein effect.[1336] The tensions arising in the present context are similar, albeit perhaps somewhat less stark: while the reasoning remains rooted in the epistemology of the ethos-focussed perspective throughout, the presumption and its rebuttal locate ethical normativity in different macrosubjects (the collectivity of European States and the individual respondent State, respectively), thus making it difficult to mediate between them by reference to a form of normativity shared by both. Kleinlein's caveat that high democratic standards can "possibly" rebut the presumption established by consensus might, perhaps, be read as a concession to this difficulty.

The idea of consensus as a rebuttable presumption has carried some sway with regard to the spur effect of consensus more generally, not just as a factor within the structural margin of appreciation but also when applied within the Court's substantive reasoning (or, for that matter, in cases in which its doctrinal context remains somewhat unclear).[1337] Thus, Dzehtsiarou argues that the "presence of European consensus", like its lack, "also establishes a presumption" – this time "in favour of the solution adopted in the majority of the Contracting Parties".[1338] Despite this presumption, the State(s) in the minority position may prevent a violation of the Convention if they can offer "a particularly strong justification for the law in question even if this law is different to [the] common European trend".[1339] Hutchinson has similarly suggested that the Court must "take seriously any arguments laid out by a defendant State which suggested that, in its case, the general presumption [established by the spur effect of consensus] should not apply".[1340]

Though they have not usually been successful,[1341] counter-arguments to the spur effect of consensus based on the national ethos of the respondent State remain a distinct possibility within the Court's case-law, at least in

1336 Supra, III.2.

1337 See generally on these distinctions supra, III.1.

1338 Dzehtsiarou, *European Consensus and the Legitimacy of the European Court of Human Rights*, at 29; critically on the merits of establishing presumptions within the ECtHR's balancing test Djeffal, "Consensus, Stasis, Evolution: Reconstructing Argumentative Patterns in Evolutive ECHR Jurisprudence" at 89.

1339 Dzehtsiarou, "European Consensus and the Evolutive Interpretation of the European Convention on Human Rights" at 1733.

1340 Hutchinson, "The Margin of Appreciation Doctrine in the European Court of Human Rights" at 648.

1341 See Draghici, "The Strasbourg Court between European and Local Consensus: Anti-democratic or Guardian of Democratic Process?" at 22.

some scenarios.[1342] The case of *F. v. Switzerland*, while somewhat dated, makes this aspect particularly explicit. The applicant complained about a waiting period which prevented him from remarrying at the time of his choice. The ECtHR noted the existence of a European consensus against the respondent State: a waiting period akin to that found in Swiss law "no longer exists under the laws of other Contracting States".[1343] It recalled that the Convention must be interpreted in the light of present-day conditions and went on to find a violation – yet with regard to the spur effect of consensus, it nonetheless cautioned that the "isolated position" of one State "does not necessarily imply that that aspect offends the Convention, particularly in a field – matrimony – which is so closely bound up with the cultural and historical traditions of each society and its deep-rooted ideas about the family unit".[1344] In other words, it juxtaposed the notion of a pan-European ethos with the national ethos of the respondent State, the latter not even based on democratic procedures but on the older notion of "cultural and historical traditions". It did not make clear how it would adjudicate between these two different forms of ethical normativity.

Another instance of these tensions – and one of the potential counterarguments to the spur effect of consensus cited by Dzehtsiarou[1345] – is the Court's reference to special historical or political considerations within the respondent State. For example, in the case of *The Republican Party of Russia v. Russia*, it was called upon to consider the dissolution of a political party because, inter alia, it did not have a sufficient number of regional branch-

---

1342 In cases involving difference of treatment on certain grounds (gender, ethnicity, etc.), the ECtHR has held that prevailing social attitudes in a particular country cannot, by themselves, serve as justification: see e.g. ECtHR (GC), Appl. No. 30078/06 – *Konstantin Markin*, at para. 127; ECtHR (GC), Appl. Nos. 60367/08 and 961/11 – *Khamtokhu and Aksenchik*, at para. 78.

1343 ECtHR (Plenary), Appl. No. 11329/85 – *F. v. Switzerland*, Judgment of 18 December 1987, at para. 33.

1344 Ibid.; contrast ECtHR (GC), Appl. No. 30814/06 – *Lautsi and Others*, at para. 68 – though the Court found no violation in that case (based in part on the rein effect of consensus), it emphasised that "the reference to a tradition cannot relieve a Contracting State of its obligation to respect the rights and freedoms enshrined in the Convention and its Protocols".

1345 Dzehtsiarou, "European Consensus and the Evolutive Interpretation of the European Convention on Human Rights" at 1733; Dzehtsiarou, *European Consensus and the Legitimacy of the European Court of Human Rights*, at 32-34; see also Helfer, "Consensus, Coherence and the European Convention on Human Rights" at 160 ("unique circumstances"); Brems, *Human Rights: Universality and Diversity*, at 419-420 ("cultural, economic or other contextual factors"); see also Chapter 4, II.2.

es. The Court considered that "a review of practice across Council of Europe member States reveals a consensus that regional parties should be allowed to be established", yet emphasised that "notwithstanding this consensus, a different approach may be justified where special historical or political considerations exist which render a more restrictive practice necessary".[1346] This form of reasoning quite clearly makes reference both to the historical particularity of the respondent State's national ethos and to the democratic procedures within which ethical normativity at the national level is now commonly located, and thus seems to indicate that a national ethos may take precedence over ethical normativity developed at the pan-European level in some situations.[1347] Yet contrast the Court's position in *Tănase v. Moldova*, where it likewise indicated that special historical or political considerations might justify departure from a European consensus,[1348] but then went on to note that "historico-political considerations should be viewed in the broader context of the obligations which Moldova has freely undertaken" under international law.[1349] While still somewhat focussed on the respondent State and its ratification of the relevant treaties, the Court also referred to the latter as part of European consensus,[1350] as an aspect of "establish[ing] whether there is a common European standard in the field".[1351] It thus oscillated between ethical normativity developed at the national and at the pan-European level, once more without a clear indication of how to adjudicate between them.

Throughout all these oscillations between the two kinds of ethical normativity considered here, the continuing tensions with the morality-focussed perspective must not be forgotten. Its universalising normativity would be well-suited to adjudicate between the pan-European ethos underlying the spur effect of consensus and the national ethos of the respondent State, since it remains unmoved by both; yet from within the ethos-focussed perspective, that solution must remain unconvincing in light of

1346 ECtHR, Appl. No. 12976/07 – *Republican Party of Russia v. Russia*, Judgment of 12 April 2011, at para. 126; in that case, that necessity was deemed to not be demonstrated (see paras. 127-130).

1347 See also ECtHR (Plenary), Appl. No. 5493/72 – *Handyside*, at para. 57, where the Court countered the spur effect of consensus by noting that the States parties "have each fashioned their approach in the light of the situation obtaining in their respective territories".

1348 ECtHR (GC), Appl. No. 7/08 – *Tănase*, at para. 172.

1349 Ibid., at para. 176.

1350 See generally, on international law as part of European consensus, Chapter 6.

1351 ECtHR (GC), Appl. No. 7/08 – *Tănase*, at para. 176.

reasonable disagreement. Furthermore, if the morality-focussed perspective did take centre-stage, then it would be open to question what role the spur effect of European consensus truly plays in the Court's reasoning: as argued in Chapter 2, it would then merely be concurrent to the conclusion reached independently, rather than unfolding normative force of its own accord. In other cases, ethical normativity developed at the national level might likewise be concurrent to morality-focussed reasoning – yet as soon as the conclusions reached differ, the tensions resurface.

These three-way tensions are reflected in differing conceptualisations of the spur effect of consensus within academic commentary. For example, Dzehtsiarou demands a "strong justification for divergence" to counter it, and emphasises this aspect of justification, i.e. *reason-giving*, as an advantage of other conceptualisations which merely speak of an "exception".[1352] While this does not resolve the question of how "reasons" should be understood, the sense is that, although the national ethos of the respondent State may play a role, it will be subject to significant scrutiny in light of other forms of normativity, particularly the morality-focussed perspective.[1353] By contrast, Samantha Besson speaks of "the possibility of a persistent objection to the transnational practice of states and their consensus".[1354] While the notion of a "persistent objector" is itself controversial and unstable,[1355] the connotations here would seem to be that the demand for reason-giving made by Dzehtsiarou is lessened: the respondent State

1352 Dzehtsiarou, *European Consensus and the Legitimacy of the European Court of Human Rights*, at 29-30; on the inverse relation between the margin of appreciation and the demand for reason-giving, see generally Eirik Bjorge, "Been There, Done That: The Margin of Appreciation and International Law," (2015) 4 *Cambridge Journal of International and Comparative Law* 181 at 188.

1353 For example, Dzehtsiarou refers – as he does in the context of the rein effect – to "reasonable" justification – Dzehtsiarou, "European Consensus and the Evolutive Interpretation of the European Convention on Human Rights" at 1733 – which I take to be a concession to the morality-focussed perspective; see supra, text to note 1305.

1354 Besson, "Human Rights Adjudication as Transnational Adjudication: A Peripheral Case of Domestic Courts as International Law Adjudicators" at 61; for other mentions of the "persistent objector" topos, see Wildhaber, Hjartarson, and Donnelly, "No Consensus on Consensus?" at 259; Tzevelekos and Dzehts 8288iarou, "International Custom Making" at 321; see also Draghici, "The Strasbourg Court between European and Local Consensus: Anti-democratic or Guardian of Democratic Process?" at 25 who, dissatisfied with the possibility of persistent objection but caught in the framework of customary international law, proclaims the relevance (only) of a "collective persistent objector".

1355 See Koskenniemi, *From Apology to Utopia*, at 443-445.

can develop its own reasons internally, based on its national ethos; but externally, the mere fact of its persistent objection is considered sufficient and it need not justify itself within the framework of ethical normativity developed at the pan-European level, or of the morality-focussed perspective.[1356]

My point here, as before, is not to criticise any of these argumentative moves in and of themselves, but merely to showcase the tensions which inevitably emerge in the reasoning surrounding European consensus. In discussing counter-arguments to the spur effect of consensus, whether within the margin of appreciation or the Court's substantive assessment of the issue before it, the focus generally shifts from the pan-European ethos back to giving priority to the national ethos of the respondent State; yet the national ethos is rarely given free rein, but rather constrained in turn by either moral normativity or a shift back to the pan-European ethos. As Greer has summarised it: "the principle of commonality may argue in favour of harmonisation, while the principles of democracy and subsidiarity may pull in the opposite direction".[1357]

Caught between these different kinds of arguments, it becomes necessary for the ECtHR to clarify when the one or the other takes priority (e.g. when the presumption established by consensus should be rebutted) and, crucially, on which grounds. The form of argument used to establish this must in turn refer to either the pan-European ethos or the national ethos of the respondent State, or to moral normativity; while some of them may at times align in their conclusions, any reasons given will be open to challenge from the opposing perspectives when they do not. Carozza has stated that "inter-state comparison will not itself give us the reasons to choose in any instance whether to affirm a uniform international standard of human rights or whether to allow the play of difference and discretion among states".[1358] Within the framework I have been using here, one could subscribe to this claim and further specify that the abeyance which Carozza

1356 See the brief but factually oriented comments in the classic cases of ICJ, *Asylum Case (Colombia v. Peru)*, Judgment of 20 November 1950, ICJ Rep. 1950, pp. 277-278; ICJ, *Fisheries Case (United Kingdom v. Norway)*, Judgment of 18 December 1951, ICJ Rep. 1951, p. 131, as well as Besson's own description in Samantha Besson, "State Consent and Disagreement in International Law-Making. Dissolving the Paradox," (2016) 29 *Leiden Journal of International Law* 289 at 315.

1357 Greer, *The Margin of Appreciation: Interpretation and Discretion under the European Convention on Human Rights*, at 21.

1358 Carozza, "Uses and Misuses of Comparative Law" at 1233.

mentions is due to different kinds of normativity pulling the conclusion in different directions.

IV. Interim Reflections: Instable Oscillations and Doctrinal Connotations

In this chapter, I hope to have made the case that, in examining the way consensus is contextualised within the ECtHR's broader reasoning by its proponents, we come across much the same tensions which we previously identified in arguments between proponents and critics of consensus more generally, and within the establishment of consensus itself. For example, in the case-law on autonomous concepts we find both references to the importance of incorporating vertically comparative references to identify the general principles of the legal systems of the States parties (ethos-focussed perspective), and a deep distrust of those very States parties, leading to a strong focus on substantive reasoning by the Court itself rather than giving weight to European consensus (morality-focussed perspective).

When determining the breadth of the respondent State's margin of appreciation and during the Court's substantive assessment which follows it, these tensions emerge in particularly complicated ways, and European consensus is arguably deployed somewhat differently depending on whether the rein effect or the spur effect is at issue. In both cases, however, it has been suggested that consensus is best conceptualised as a rebuttable presumption. On that account, the reasoning which counter-arguments are based on will usually switch once more from ethical normativity located at the pan-European level to either the morality-focussed perspective (especially when the rein effect is at issue) or to ethical normativity focussing on the national ethos of the respondent State (when the spur effect is at issue) – yet in both cases, the Court may also switch back the notion of a pan-European ethos. These argumentative shifts are emblematic of the Court's reasoning, yet they also render it unstable since there is no common standard connecting the different forms of normativity.

Thus, the triangular tensions between different kinds of normativity previously discussed as internal to the establishment of consensus re-emerge here in the form of counter-arguments to consensus, once it is contextualised within the Court's broader reasoning. The margin of appreciation, in particular, is well-known as the location of precisely these tensions: McGoldrick has described it, for example as "mediat[ing] between the idea of universal human rights and leaving space for reasonable disagreement, legitimate differences, and national or local cultural diversity".[1359] The same is true for the principle of subsidiarity which is often said to underlie the concept of the margin of appreciation:[1360] Carozza famously described it as "a somewhat paradoxical principle" because it expresses – in the context of the ECHR – both the idea that it is primarily the responsibility of the States parties to safeguard human rights (thus limiting the role of the ECtHR) while also justifying external intervention when they do not do so appropriately (thus empowering the ECtHR).[1361] Many will accept this double-edged account of subsidiarity in the abstract, yet the difficulties lie in managing the tensions resulting from it when faced with particular cases. Moving between the two poles of subsidiarity will then require moving between the ethos-focussed perspective and the morality-focussed perspective, and hence lead back to the difficulties described throughout this chapter. It is precisely because of the mediating role assigned to doctrines such as the margin of appreciation that they end up caught between opposed epistemologies and become as unstable as many commentators charge them with being.[1362]

Yet the analysis of various different doctrinal contexts has also served to indicate that a limited form of stability may emerge, as certain doctrines become more associated with a particular role or perspective.[1363] For example, I argued above that autonomous concepts became associated with the morality-focussed perspective in this way, whereas the margin of appreciation is more strongly connected to the ethos-focussed perspective. I hope to have made it clear that such connotations are always contingent rather

1359 McGoldrick, "A Defence of the Margin of Appreciation and an Argument for its Application by the Human Rights Committee" at 41; there is a veritable multitude of similar formulations, see e.g. Macdonald, "The Margin of Appreciation" at 83 and 122-123; Mena Parras, "Democracy, Diversity and the Margin of Appreciation" at 3; Donoho, "Autonomy, Self-Governance, and the Margin of Appreciation: Developing a Jurisprudence of Diversity Within Universal Human Rights" at 451; Pascual-Vives, *Consensus-Based Interpretation of Regional Human Rights Treaties*, at 230; see also the excellent summary of differing positions of the margin of appreciation and their connection to the role assigned to the ECtHR by Bates, "Activism and Self-Restraint: The Margin of Appreciation's Strasbourg Career… Its 'Coming of Age'?" at 276.

1360 E.g. Arnardóttir, "Rethinking the Two Margins of Appreciation" at 38, with further references.

1361 Carozza, "Subsidiarity as a Structural Principle" at 44; see also e.g. Spielmann, "Whither the Margin of Appreciation?" at 63-64.

1362 See supra, note 1234.

1363 See generally Martti Koskenniemi, "International Law and Hegemony: A Reconfiguration," (2004) 17 *Cambridge Review of International Affairs* 197 at 202.

than necessary, since any demarcation is always open to challenge on the basis of a differing epistemology. In a sense, they also serve merely to relocate and perhaps even to obfuscate the problem:[1364] for it needs to be established in any given case which doctrine is applicable and why, thus reintroducing any tensions that might have been temporarily suspended *within* the application of that doctrine.

Let me end this chapter by again pointing to an aspect of the case-law already mentioned in its introduction: it is noticeable how rarely the ECtHR presents European consensus as providing an argument in a certain direction but nonetheless reaches a contrary conclusion on the basis of explicit counter-arguments. I would suggest that this may relate, in part, to the flexibility inherent to the establishment of (lack of) consensus, and to the way in which the triangular tensions between different kinds of normativity are internalised before the rein effect or spur effect of consensus are even deployed: it is not by accident that the chapters analysing the establishment of consensus within the ECtHR's case-law took up more space than the chapter dealing with its deployment once established. However, the lack of successful counter-arguments to consensus within the ECtHR's processes of justification *also* serves to position it as a powerful argument in its own right, once (lack of) consensus has been established. This prominence has been defended on the basis of the notion of a pan-European ethos, as previous chapters have shown. However, there is also a different line of argument undergirding the ECtHR's use of consensus: many commentators emphasise the importance of using consensus to bolster the ECtHR's legitimacy. That line of argument will be the subject of the following chapters.

1364 See e.g. the criticism made by Lewis, "*Animal Defenders International* v *United Kingdom*: Sensible Dialogue or a Bad Case of Strasbourg Jitters?" at 470 of the ECtHR's shifting approach depending on whether a measure is conceptualised as a "general measure" or a "blanket ban", without further justification of one or the other.

Chapter 9: The Strategic Approach: Consensus as Legitimacy-Enhancement

I. Introduction

"The key rationale behind the ECtHR's consensus method is legitimacy".[1365] This statement by Tobias Lock succinctly puts forward a sentiment that is extremely widespread in the academic literature on European consensus[1366] – to the point that its popularity has long since surpassed the defence of consensus based on its (indirectly) democratic credentials or its contribution to an ethos-focussed jurisprudence. Any justification or critique of the use of European consensus must therefore grapple with the idea of consensus as legitimacy-enhancement.

The use of the term "legitimacy" (and indeed its recurring and insistent use[1367]) is quite interesting, since it is notoriously ambiguous: I will therefore begin this chapter by recalling the basic distinction between normative and sociological legitimacy, which one might parse (very roughly) as investigating whether an object of legitimacy is *justifiable* within a certain institutional context, on the one hand, and whether it is *perceived as justified* by certain actors, on the other. My argument is that (in contrast to the lines of reasoning canvassed so far) legitimacy-based defences of European consensus commonly refer to the latter notion, but they do so in a way that invests the initially empirical perspective of sociological legitimacy with normativity: in other words, sociological legitimacy *should* be nour-

1365 Lock, "The Influence of EU Law on Strasbourg Doctrines" at 817.

1366 See in particular Dzehtsiarou, "Does Consensus Matter? Legitimacy of European Consensus in the Case Law of the European Court of Human Rights"; Draghici, "The Strasbourg Court between European and Local Consensus: Anti-democratic or Guardian of Democratic Process?" at 14; Henrard, "How the ECtHR's Use of European Consensus Considerations Allows Legitimacy Concerns to Delimit Its Mandate" at 143; Hamilton, "Same-Sex Marriage, Consensus, Certainty and the European Court of Human Rights" at 35; Lixinski, "The Inter-American Court of Human Rights' Tentative Search for Latin American Consensus" at 340, as well as infra, note 1410; see also, with a primarily historical ambit, Bates, "Consensus in the Legitimacy-Building Era of the European Court of Human Rights".

1367 Pildes, "Supranational Courts and The Law of Democracy: The European Court of Human Rights" at 160 calls it "overused".

ished so as the generate support for the ECtHR, European consensus helps to do so, and hence European consensus *should* form part of the ECtHR's reasoning (II.1.).

This idea that consensus should be used so as to ensure support for the ECtHR deeply resonates with the political situation within which the ECtHR finds itself – as Clare Ryan has vividly put it, "[g]iven the challenges that the ECtHR faces in a Europe that is pulling apart at the seams", a pragmatic approach to adjudication is regarded as indispensable.[1368] I will therefore spend some time specifying the background assumptions as to why a pragmatic approach based on sociological legitimacy matters, particularly the sense that the ECtHR is facing a "legitimacy crisis" which needs to be mitigated (II.2.). It is in this context that the idea of consensus as legitimacy-enhancement needs to be understood: this becomes particularly clear when considering the way in which the States parties to the ECHR are framed as the most important agents of legitimacy, since it is their support of the ECtHR which is deemed most crucial (II.3.). Since European consensus refers back to the legal systems of the States parties, it is assumed to cater towards them. This argument may assume a number of different forms; in what I take to be its most important version, which I will primarily foreground in this chapter, it holds that consensus sets the pace for an incremental development of the ECtHR's case-law which is acceptable to the States parties (II.4.).

When introduced under the heading of "legitimacy-enhancement", the implications of this approach do not necessarily become clear. Given the "twofold coding of the concept" of legitimacy as both normative and sociological,[1369] arguing the European consensus increases the ECtHR's legitimacy has a rather pleasant ring to it and thus covers up, to some extent, the normative tensions involved in justifying consensus in this way.[1370] I will argue that it is important to realise that consensus as legitimacy-enhancement proposes a particular form of *strategy* to enable the ECtHR to retain the support of the States parties to the ECHR and set increasingly higher human rights standards. Such a strategic approach to adjudication

---

1368 Ryan, "Europe's Moral Margin: Parental Aspirations and the European Court of Human Rights" at 521.

1369 Michael Zürn, "Perspektiven des demokratischen Regierens und die Rolle der Politikwissenschaft im 21. Jahrhundert," (2011) 52 *Politische Vierteljahresschrift* 603 at 606 ("*doppelte Kodierung des Konzepts (normative und empirisch)*").

1370 On similar dynamics in the use of the notion of legitimacy more generally, see Koskenniemi, "Legitimacy, Rights and Ideology: Notes Towards a Critique of the New Moral Internationalism" at 371.

resonates with the perceived need for pragmatism in light of a "legitimacy crisis", but it also means that the focus of the argument shifts away from a consideration of individual judgments to a long-term view of the ECtHR as an institution (II.5.).

If we thus take the argument in favour of consensus based on legitimacy-enhancement to be a strategic argument based on the recurring reliance of consensus to set the pace for an incremental development of the ECtHR's case-law, then there are (at least) two lines of questioning to which it is exposed. The first is principled and takes issue with the very notion of a strategic approach to the reasoning of a human rights court: I will turn to this criticism in the following chapter. The second line of questioning is more practically oriented and relates specifically to the viability of using consensus as the basis for an incremental development which boosts the ECtHR's sociological legitimacy. After all, if the motivation for justifying the use of consensus in this way comes from the assumed need to mitigate the ECtHR's "legitimacy crisis", then it is important to assess whether consensus is up to the task.

I approach this difficult question by recalling some general characteristics of consensus touched upon throughout this and previous chapters – its use of the notion of commonality, its relative formality, and its reliance on incremental development over time – and setting these in relation to certain patterns of opposition to the ECtHR. My argument is that European consensus may not be well-suited to form the basis of a strategic approach which aims to prevent the most relevant and high-profile forms of opposition to the ECtHR, and hence its role in mitigating an assumed "legitimacy crisis" is fairly limited (III.). Yet this limitation might itself be construed as a strength, since unmitigated strategy need not be normatively desirable. I therefore conclude by situating consensus as legitimacy-enhancement as a *less starkly* strategic approach than some other proposals (IV.). This classification will form the basis of its further evaluation in the following chapter.

II. European Consensus as Legitimacy-Enhancement

1. Investing Sociological Legitimacy with Normativity

If the key rationale behind European consensus is indeed legitimacy-enhancement, as many academic commentators claim, then it is crucial to grasp precisely in which sense the term "legitimacy" is being used. It is, Richard Fallon wrote in 2005, "a term much invoked but little analysed in constitutional debates".[1371] Over a decade later, the same could be said of debates concerning international law and human rights law – as Samantha Besson has noted, for example, different understandings of legitimacy continue to be used and intermingled without much clarification.[1372]

The most foundational distinction is that between *normative* and *sociological* legitimacy. The denominations make their differing perspectives clear: while the prior implies a normative assessment of a certain issue, the latter takes a sociological approach and investigates certain actors' positions, *in fact*, on that issue. In a sense, it adds an additional layer, since it does not deal with (normative) legitimacy head-on but rather with other peoples' takes on it. Accordingly, we might say that sociological legitimacy is acquired not by means of justification according to a certain normative standard, but rather by being *perceived* as justified.[1373] Perhaps the most famous example of a sociological account is that of Max Weber, who spoke of "Legitimitätsglauben", i.e. the *belief in* legitimacy.[1374]

While it is seldom made explicit, most legitimacy-based defences of European consensus refer (at least primarily) to a *sociological* notion of legitimacy.[1375] This becomes quite clear, for example, from the chapter on

1371 Richard H. Fallon, Jr., "Legitimacy and the Constitution," (2005) 118 *Harvard Law Review* 1789 at 1789; see also e.g. Lovett, "Can Justice Be Based on Consent?" at 80 (in footnote 3).

1372 Samantha Besson, "The Legitimate Authority of International Human Rights. On the Reciprocal Legitimation of Domestic and International Human Rights," in *The Legitimacy of International Human Rights Regimes. Legal, Political and Philosophical Perspectives*, ed. Andreas Føllesdal, Johan Karlsson Schaffer, and Geir Ulfstein (Cambridge: Cambridge University Press, 2013) at 69; see also Zysset, *The ECHR and Human Rights Theory: Reconciling the Moral and Political Conceptions*, at 103; Andreas Føllesdal, "The Legitimacy Deficits of the Human Rights Judiciary: Elements and Implications of a Normative Theory," (2013) 14 *Theoretical Inquiries in Law* 339 at 341.

1373 Nienke Grossman, "Legitimacy and International Adjudicative Bodies," (2009) 41 *George Washington International Law Review* 107 at 110 and 115; Thomas M. Franck, "Legitimacy in the International System," (1988) 82 *American Journal of International Law* 705 at 706; see also Daniel M. Bodansky, "The Legitimacy of International Governance: A Coming Challenge for International Environmental Law?," (1999) 93 *American Journal of International Law* 596 at 600-602.

1374 E.g. Max Weber, *Wirtschaft und Gesellschaft. Grundriss der verstehenden Soziologie*, 5th ed. (Tübingen: Mohr Siebeck, 1972), at 450.

1375 Explicitly (though critically) see Føllesdal, "A Better Signpost, Not a Better Walking Stick: How to Evaluate the European Consensus Doctrine" at 200, who calls it "social legitimacy"; contrast e.g. the explicit use of *normative* legitimacy by Letsas, "The ECHR as a Living Instrument: Its Meaning and Legitimacy" at 127 (in footnote 68).

legitimacy in Kanstantsin Dzehtsiarou's monograph, *European Consensus and the Legitimacy of the European Court of Human Rights*. The "legitimacy challenges" he identifies there are well-known controversies of substantive political morality which we have considered, in various forms, over the course of the previous chapters: for example, is it desirable (or, one might say, normatively legitimate) for international courts to make important decisions, considering that such decisions may conflict with States' sovereign and democratic choices? Yet this is not the perspective from which Dzehtsiarou considers these questions. His definition of legitimacy takes it to mean

> the *respect and support* for the Court that emanates *from stakeholders' conviction* that the Court will decide cases consistently and in a manner that respects the nature of both the European Convention on Human Rights [...] (as a human rights instrument) and its jurisdiction (as subsidiary and limited), as well as by reference to clear and transparent evidence.[1376]

Dzehtsiarou's reference to support emanating from stakeholders' convictions adds the empirical layer of sociological legitimacy to the "legitimacy challenges" he considers. Despite the thematic overlap with the normative questions, considered directly, the entire chapter thereby takes on a different, more empirically oriented meaning:[1377] the question is no longer what the proper place of an international court should be, but what the States parties' stances on the issue are.

This shift is emblematic of the differences between normative and sociological legitimacy. Whatever manifold connections can be drawn between them, particularly in the legal context,[1378] they nonetheless imply fundamentally different perspectives.[1379] Because one is normative and the other empirical, they are kept apart by the age-old distinction between the *ought*

1376 Dzehtsiarou, *European Consensus and the Legitimacy of the European Court of Human Rights*, at 143 (emphases added).

1377 E.g. "the Court creates an *impression* that it is constrained by a legal argument" (at 164) or "counting does create an *impression*, if not of a real acceptance, at least of a perceived acceptance of a particular rule" (at 175), emphases added.

1378 For a succinct but informative overview, see Johan Karlsson Schaffer, Andreas Føllesdal, and Geir Ulfstein, "International Human Rights and the Challenge of Legitimacy," in *The Legitimacy of International Human Rights Regimes*, ed. Andreas Føllesdal, Johan Karlsson Schaffer, and Geir Ulfstein (Cambridge: Cambridge University Press, 2014) at 13-14.

1379 This is strongly emphasised by Habermas, *Between Facts and Norms*, at 69-70.

and the *is*. So long as this separation is indeed upheld, there is logically no possibility of conflict between normative and sociological legitimacy: they operate on different planes, as it were. As always, however, this separation can be bridged by providing reasons for referring to facts so as to conjoin the is and the ought,[1380] as when (factual) acceptance is regarded as part of (normative) legitimacy because it provides for a form of output-based feedback from the governed to the governing.[1381]

In a similar vein, when legitimacy is referred to in discussions of European consensus, its proponents do not content themselves with the empirical insights which accounts of sociological legitimacy offer, but rather *invest their initially empirical approach with normativity*.[1382] As Tom Franck put it: "If legitimacy can be studied, it can also be deliberately nourished."[1383] Proponents of European consensus as legitimacy-enhancement further make the (normative) claim that sociological legitimacy *should* be deliberately nourished, and that European consensus can assist in doing so. In other words, European consensus is introduced as a partial solution to the empirically understood "legitimacy challenges" which the ECtHR is said to face[1384] and, conversely, its use is considered to be justified because of this. Increasing sociological legitimacy becomes a normatively acknowledged goal. Why?

1380 See generally Chapter 2, II.3.

1381 See Utz Schliesky, *Souveränität und Legitimität von Herrschaftsgewalt. Die Weiterentwicklung von Begriffen der Staatslehre und des Staatsrechts im europäischen Mehrebenensystem* (Tübingen: Mohr Siebeck, 2004), at 179 ("*Akzeptanz als Rückkoppelung der Legitimität zu den Herrschaftsunterworfenen*").

1382 Mann, "Non-ideal Theory of Constitutional Adjudication" at 20 makes this shift particularly clear; see also e.g. Dzehtsiarou, "What Is Law for the European Court of Human Rights?" at 92.

1383 Franck, "Legitimacy in the International System" at 711; on legitimacy as a mechanism for increasing compliance, see Ian Hurd, "Torture and the Politics of Legitimation in International Law," in *The Legitimacy of International Human Rights Regimes. Legal, Political and Philosophical Perspectives*, ed. Andreas Føllesdal, Johan Karlsson Schaffer, and Geir Ulfstein (Cambridge: Cambridge University Press, 2013) at 166-173; critically Koskenniemi, "An Essay in Counterdisciplinarity" at 18.

1384 Dzehtsiarou, *European Consensus and the Legitimacy of the European Court of Human Rights*, at 143 and 175-176; see also Merris Amos, "Can European Consensus Encourage Acceptance of the European Convention on Human Rights in the United Kingdom?," in *Building Consensus on European Consensus: Judicial Interpretation of Human Rights in Europe and Beyond*, ed. Panos Kapotas and Vassilis Tzevelekos (Cambridge: Cambridge University Press, 2019) at 258-259.

2. The Background Assumption: Overcoming a "Legitimacy Crisis"

To understand the strong pull which this approach is currently exerting on academic commentators, it is important to explicate the background assumptions against which it is set: the focus on nourishing sociological legitimacy can best be explained by worries about (allegedly) increasing criticism of the ECtHR and the sense that such criticism must be mitigated. Again, Dzehtsiarou's account offers the clearest example of this, though it is by no means idiosyncratic. It is telling that his monograph opens by asking whether the ECtHR has "lost its legitimacy" – and while the answer is given in the negative, it is somewhat tentative (softened by the caveat of a "perhaps") and discussion immediately turns to the importance of nourishing sociological legitimacy to ensure enforcement of the ECtHR's judgments.[1385] When discussing the ECtHR's legitimacy in more detail later on, Dzehtsiarou notes that "[i]n recent years, the Court has been widely criticised by nearly all stakeholders – national governments, local judges, the media, Convention commentators and even the Pope";[1386] and he conjures up the image of a Court no longer "able to set standards in the area of human rights protection" if its sociological legitimacy were to lessen further, or indeed of the utter "collapse of the Strasbourg system".[1387] Accordingly, before taking up the "legitimacy challenges" he identifies, Dzehtsiarou adds a chapeau section on the importance of being perceived as legitimate.[1388] In this way, he sets the scene for the claim that legitimacy-enhancement is necessary: sociological legitimacy invested with normativity.

It is worth nothing that this focus within the literature on European consensus is hardly surprising in light of the discourse surrounding human rights law in general and the ECtHR in particular in recent years. Jean-Paul Costa, then President of the ECtHR, summarised the Court's situation in 2011 as follows:

> [I]n certain states, including some of those who founded the system and who ratified the European Convention on Human Rights at the outset, very strong criticism of the Court was voiced in the press as

1385 Dzehtsiarou, *European Consensus and the Legitimacy of the European Court of Human Rights*, at 1.

1386 Ibid., 147 (footnotes omitted, though it is worth noting that they are numerous and of above-average length).

1387 Ibid., 146 and 147.

1388 Ibid., 145.

well as by public representatives, calling its legitimacy or its putative 'activism' into question. Some of the Court's judgments have met with strongly negative reactions.[1389]

Or, as Michael O'Boyle has somewhat wryly put it: one could be "forgiven for believing that the Court is about to be towed into the middle of the Rhine and scuppered by a coalition of unhappy State Parties".[1390]

Such criticism has been connected to the (implicitly: sociological) legitimacy of the ECtHR by various commentators. Nils Muižnieks, the Council of Europe's Commissioner for Human Rights, warned in 2016 that "[i]n recent years direct challenges to the authority of the Court within a handful of member states have [...] become more explicit and vocal" and that such challenges are "of particular concern because the integrity and *legitimacy* of the Convention system is at stake".[1391] Colm O'Cinneide has recently posited with regard to human rights law in general that it "has entered stormy waters", its "scope and content is increasingly contested", and it is facing "a full-blown *legitimacy crisis*".[1392] Faced with such a diagnosis, it seems eminently sensible to emphasise the importance of winning back sociological legitimacy. Enter European consensus as "an important legit-

1389 Jean-Paul Costa, "On the Legitimacy of the European Court of Human Rights' Judgments," (2011) 7 *European Constitutional Law Review* 173 at 174; for similar sentiments, see e.g. Thorbjørn Jagland, "Communication on the Occasion of the First Part of the 2016 Parliamentary Assembly Session," available at <https://www.coe.int/en/web/secretary-general/speeches/-/asset_publisher/gFMvl0SKOUrv/content/communication-on-the-occasion-of-the-first-part-of-the-2016-parliamentary-assembly-session>; Parliamentary Assembly of the Council of Europe, "The Implementation of Judgments of the European Court of Human Rights," Resolution 2178 (2017) of 29 June 2017, at para. 8.

1390 O'Boyle, "The Future of the European Court of Human Rights" at 1862.

1391 Nils Muižnieks, "Non-implementation of the Court's Judgments: Our Shared Responsibility," available at <https://www.coe.int/en/web/commissioner/-/non-implementation-of-the-court-s-judgments-our-shared-responsibility> (emphasis added).

1392 Colm O'Cinneide, "Rights under Pressure," (2017) *European Human Rights Law Review* 43 at 43-44 (emphasis added); see also Kanstantsin Dzehtsiarou and Alan Greene, "Legitimacy and the Future of the European Court of Human Rights: Critical Perspectives from Academia and Practitioners," (2011) 12 *German Law Journal* 1707 at 1707; Dzehtsiarou, "What Is Law for the European Court of Human Rights?" at 129; B.M. Oomen, "A Serious Case of Strasbourg-Bashing? An Evaluation of the Debates on the Legitimacy of the European Court of Human Rights in the Netherlands," (2016) 20 *International Journal of Human Rights* 407 at 409.

imising tool" which is said to be particularly "useful at a time when certain political factions are discussing leaving the Council of Europe".[1393]

3. The States Parties as Agents of Legitimacy

If the goal is to nourish sociological legitimacy, however, then it becomes crucial to identify the *agents* of legitimacy, by which I mean those actors (or "stakeholders"[1394]) whose beliefs are regarded as relevant in establishing the measure of respect and support which the institution enjoys. Whose support actually matters – whose criticism is supposed to be mitigated? Needless to say, one's take on sociological legitimacy depends decisively on the actors selected as relevant agents, since their perspectives, though potentially interlinked, may differ greatly[1395] – Nienke Grossman calls this the "agent-relative" nature of sociological legitimacy.[1396] There is a multitude of options:[1397] the general public, the public in a certain State, or individual applicants; the States under a Court's jurisdiction, collectively or individually; certain State organs such as national courts; international organisations or foreign States; non-governmental organisations or the academic community; the list goes on.

In the literature on international courts in general, the tendency seems to be to acknowledge the multiplicity of relevant stakeholders, but to nonetheless focus primarily on the States under the jurisdiction of the court at issue.[1398] This approach has been mirrored with regard to the ECtHR, with commentators noting, for example, the potential relevance of the positions taken by "applicants, non-governmental organisations (NGOs) or the academic community", but nonetheless arguing that "the Court has a particular need to maintain functioning relationships with

1393 Hamilton, "Same-Sex Marriage, Consensus, Certainty and the European Court of Human Rights" at 38; see also at 42.

1394 Supra, note 1376.

1395 Costa, "On the Legitimacy of the European Court of Human Rights' Judgments" at 178.

1396 Grossman, "Legitimacy and International Adjudicative Bodies" at 116.

1397 Føllesdal, "The Legitimacy Deficits of the Human Rights Judiciary: Elements and Implications of a Normative Theory" at 342-343.

1398 See e.g., with different points of emphasis, Shai Dothan, "How International Courts Enhance Their Legitimacy," (2013) 14 *Theoretical Inquiries in Law* 455 at 457; Grossman, "Legitimacy and International Adjudicative Bodies" at 116; Yuval Shany, "Assessing the Effectiveness of International Courts: A Goal-Based Approach," (2012) 106 *American Journal of International Law* 225 at 267.

contracting parties, i.e. states".[1399] The focus on the States parties goes some way toward explaining the connection to European consensus – after all, consensus refers, by definition, to the legal systems of the States parties to the Convention, rather than integrating the position of other stakeholders into the ECtHR's reasoning.[1400]

The importance of the States parties as agents of legitimacy is usually explained, above all, by their "power to affect the court's interests".[1401] For one thing, any individual Member State might, if it does not perceive the Court and its judgments as legitimate, refuse to implement said judgments (whether when directly concerned as respondent State or proactively based on rulings against other States) or even denounce the Convention entirely (Article 58 ECHR).[1402] Collectively,[1403] the Member States might refuse to enforce certain judgments (in their role as members of the Committee of

---

1399 Dzehtsiarou, *European Consensus and the Legitimacy of the European Court of Human Rights*, at 145-146, citing de Londras and Dzehtsiarou, "Managing Judicial Innovation in the European Court of Human Rights" at 527 (but see 545); see also Dzehtsiarou, "What Is Law for the European Court of Human Rights?" at 131; Gerards, "Judicial Deliberations in the European Court of Human Rights" at 412; for an emphatic counter-point, see Amos, "Can European Consensus Encourage Acceptance of the European Convention on Human Rights in the United Kingdom?" at 273 (focussing on non-governmental organisations); see also Wayne Sandholtz, "Expanding Rights: Norm Innovation in the European and Inter-American Courts," in *Expanding Human Rights. 21st Century Norms and Governance*, ed. Alison Brysk and Michael Stohl (Cheltenham: Edward Elgar, 2017) at 169; and, more generally, Mikael Rask Madsen, Pola Cebulak, and Micha Wiebusch, "Backlash Against International Courts: Explaining the Forms and Patterns of Resistance to International Courts," (2018) 14 *International Journal of Law in Context* 197 at 204, criticising a "state-centric approach to backlash".

1400 At least in the sense in which I understand it for present purposes: see Chapter 1, III.

1401 Dothan, "How International Courts Enhance Their Legitimacy" at 457.

1402 It is worth noting in passing that, besides passing over the role of civil society (supra, note 1399), the conceptualisation of the States parties as unitary actors (rather than distinguishing e.g. between the executive, legislative, and judiciary) leads the strategic approach to a somewhat simplistic notion of implementation; contrast e.g. Dia Anagnostou and Alina Mungiu-Pippidi, "Domestic Implementation of Human Rights Judgments in Europe: Legal Infrastructure and Government Effectiveness Matter," (2014) 25 *European Journal of International Law* 205 at 207. For one example of how this impacts European consensus in particular, see infra, III.

1403 On the distinction between individual and collective action by States, see further infra, note 1499.

Ministers[1404]), withdraw funding from the Court, reform it in such a way as to suit their preferences or, at the extreme, give up the Convention system as a whole – recall the worry about the "collapse of the Strasbourg system".[1405]

While these very different worries are often jumbled together without further specification, the overall impression is that the ECtHR's position as an *international* court – in light of States' "fierce protection of [their] sovereignty" – makes it particularly precarious.[1406] Since "there is no democratic 'State' at the Convention-wide level within which those judges are embedded" and the ECtHR's judges are hence "considerably more distant from the domestic systems" than national judges would be, they are assumed to be "more likely to be viewed as lacking legitimacy than their domestic counterparts"[1407] – the focus on their *perception* as lacking legitimacy making it clear that the issue here is one of sociological, not (only) normative legitimacy. Simultaneously, they are thought of as *more in need* of such sociological legitimacy – especially so in the light of the "legitimacy crisis", but again also by reference to their position as judges of an international court. In particular, national courts are said to profit from "a better infrastructure ensuring execution of their judgments than the judgments of international tribunals".[1408] With its relatively weak enforcement mechanisms, the ECtHR is, by contrast, considered to face a "substantial

1404 For the composition of the Committee of Ministers, see Article 14 Statute of the Council of Europe; for its role in the execution of the ECtHR's judgments, see Article 46 ECHR; see further the Rules of the Committee of Ministers for the supervision of the execution of judgments and of the terms of friendly settlements; and, on the more complex realities, e.g. Elisabeth Lambert Abdelgawad, "The Execution of the Judgments of the European Court of Human Rights: Towards a Non-coercive and Participatory Model of Accountability," (2009) 69 *Zeitschrift für ausländisches öffentliches Recht und Völkerrecht* 471. Perhaps noteworthy is that the Committee of Ministers has recently made use of Article 46 (4) ECHR for the first time: see Interim Resolution CM/ResDH(2017)429 of 5 December 2017.

1405 Supra, note 1387.

1406 Dzehtsiarou, *European Consensus and the Legitimacy of the European Court of Human Rights*, at 144 (and from 149 on "international constitutional challenges").

1407 Pildes, "Supranational Courts and The Law of Democracy: The European Court of Human Rights" at 161.

1408 Kanstantsin Dzehtsiarou, "Book Review of Shai Dothan, Reputation and Judicial Tactics. A Theory of National and International Courts," (2015) 15 *Human Rights Law Review* 391 at 394-395; see also Lau, "Rewriting Schalk and Kopf: Shifting the Locus of Deference" at 257; Posner and Yoo, "Judicial Independence in International Tribunals" at 56; it is open to doubt, however, whether

structural deficiency" – in other words, a particular need to nourish sociological legitimacy as an alternative to coercive enforcement of its judgments, so as to ensure their implementation.[1409]

In this way, the focus on the States parties as agents of legitimacy (and hence the reference to their positions by way of European consensus) is introduced as a way of placating the most powerful stakeholders and thus mitigating the ECtHR's "legitimacy crisis" to enable its proper functioning despite a myriad of obstacles and threats following from its position as an international court. It is difficult to overstate the importance of this point. While the notion of European consensus as legitimacy-enhancement has become increasingly popular, some proponents of consensus do not explicitly frame their argument in those terms, much less specify that it is sociological rather than normative legitimacy that they are concerned with. Yet concerns about a potential lack of cooperation by the States parties are found, in one way or the other, at the heart of the overwhelming majority of arguments in favour of European consensus.[1410] By conceptualising consensus as a way of retaining or regaining the States parties' support and en-

---

this line of reasoning holds up to scrutiny: see Yonatan Lupu, "International Judicial Legitimacy: Lessons from National Courts," (2013) 14 *Theoretical Inquiries in Law* 437 at 439-440.

1409 Dzehtsiarou, *European Consensus and the Legitimacy of the European Court of Human Rights*, at 1; Dzehtsiarou, "What Is Law for the European Court of Human Rights?" at 129; echoed by Hamilton, "Same-Sex Marriage, Consensus, Certainty and the European Court of Human Rights" at 43; see also de Londras and Dzehtsiarou, "Managing Judicial Innovation in the European Court of Human Rights" at 544; Başak Çalı, Anne Koch, and Nicola Bruch, "The Legitimacy of the European Court of Human Rights: The View from the Ground" (2011), at 5; Fenwick, "Same-sex Unions at the Strasbourg Court in a Divided Europe: Driving Forward Reform or Protecting the Court's Authority via Consensus Analysis?" at 249; Ryan, "Europe's Moral Margin: Parental Aspirations and the European Court of Human Rights" at 478; more generally on the lack of enforcement mechanisms and the importance of legitimacy for international courts e.g. Clifford James Carrubba and Matthew Joseph Gabel, "Courts, Compliance, and the Quest for Legitimacy in International Law," (2013) 14 *Theoretical Inquiries in Law* 505 at 509.

1410 In order to drive home the popularity of this line of reasoning, I would like to cite its proponents extensively (though by no means exhaustively): Bribosia, Rorive, and Van den Eynde, "Same-Sex Marriage: Building an Argument before the European Court of Human Rights in Light of the US Experience" at 19; Mike Burstein, "The Will to Enforce: An Examination of the Political Constraints upon a Regional Court of Human Rights," (2006) 24 *Berkeley Journal of International Law* 423 at 438-439; Dahlberg, "'The Lack of Such a Common Approach' - Comparative Argumentation by the European Court of Human

dorsing its use for this very reason, reference is unavoidably, if sometimes

Rights" at 82; Draghici, "The Strasbourg Court between European and Local Consensus: Anti-democratic or Guardian of Democratic Process?" at 14-15; Dzehtsiarou, *European Consensus and the Legitimacy of the European Court of Human Rights*, at 154; Dzehtsiarou, "What Is Law for the European Court of Human Rights?" at 129; Dzehtsiarou and Lukashevich, "Informed Decision-Making" at 275; Fenwick, "Same-sex Unions at the Strasbourg Court in a Divided Europe: Driving Forward Reform or Protecting the Court's Authority via Consensus Analysis?" at 249; Forowicz, *The Reception of International Law in the European Court of Human Rights*, at 9; Gerards, "Judicial Deliberations in the European Court of Human Rights" at 432; Gerards, "Pluralism, Deference and the Margin of Appreciation Doctrine" at 108-109; Hamilton, "Same-Sex Marriage, Consensus, Certainty and the European Court of Human Rights" at 35 and 42-43; Helfer, "Consensus, Coherence and the European Convention on Human Rights" at 137; Helfer and Slaughter, "Toward a Theory of Effective Supranational Adjudication" at 315-317; Henrard, "How the European Court of Human Rights' Concern Regarding European Consensus Tempers the Effective Protection of Freedom of Religion" at 414; Kagiaros, "When to Use European Consensus: Assessing the Differential Treatment of Minority Groups by the European Court of Human Rights" at 288; Krisch, *Beyond Constitutionalism: The Pluralist Structure of Postnational Law*, at 139-140; Lau, "Rewriting Schalk and Kopf: Shifting the Locus of Deference" at 253-257; Lock, "The Influence of EU Law on Strasbourg Doctrines" at 808 and 818; Mahoney and Kondak, "Common Ground" at 121; McGoldrick, "A Defence of the Margin of Appreciation and an Argument for its Application by the Human Rights Committee" at 30; Nussberger, *The European Court of Human Rights*, at 88; Ostrovsky, "What's So Funny About Peace, Love, and Understanding?" at 59; Pascual-Vives, *Consensus-Based Interpretation of Regional Human Rights Treaties*, at 230; Roberto Perrone, "Public Morals and the European Convention on Human Rights," (2014) 47 *Israel Law Review* 361 at 370; Cesare Pitea, "Interpretation and Application of the European Convention on Human Right[s] in the Broader Context of International Law: Myth or Reality?," in *Human Rights and Civil Liberties in the 21st Century*, ed. Yves Haeck and Eva Brems (Dordrecht: Springer, 2014) at 6; Ryan, "Europe's Moral Margin: Parental Aspirations and the European Court of Human Rights" at 472-474; Schlüter, "Beweisrechtliche Implikationen der margin of appreciation-Doktrin" at 58; Senden, *Interpretation of Fundamental Rights*, at 121; Wildhaber, Hjartarson, and Donnelly, "No Consensus on Consensus?" at 251; Wintemute, "Consensus Is the Right Approach for the European Court of Human Rights"; see also, summarising such arguments without necessarily agreeing, Carozza, "Uses and Misuses of Comparative Law" at 1227; critically also Letsas, *A Theory of Interpretation of the European Convention on Human Rights*, at 124; Erdman, "The Deficiency of Consensus in Human Rights Protection: A Case Study of Goodwin v. United Kingdom and I. v. United Kingdom" at 333; Henrard, "How the ECtHR's Use of European Consensus Considerations Allows Legitimacy Concerns to Delimit Its Mandate" at 159 and 162-163; Shahid, "The Right to Same-Sex Marriage: Assessing the European Court of Human Rights' Consensus-Based Analysis in

implicitly, made to a sociological notion of legitimacy invested with normativity as discussed above.

4. European Consensus as the Basis of Incremental Development

The fact that the States parties are foregrounded as the relevant agents of legitimacy thus sheds further light on the motivation behind legitimacy-enhancement as the rationale for using European consensus: safeguarding the interests of the Court in the face of a "legitimacy crisis". One might imagine many different ways of attempting to enhance the ECtHR's sociological legitimacy, including what Madsen, Cebulak and Wiebusch call "out-of-court judicial diplomacy":[1411] informal dialogue with national judges[1412] and education on or public discussion of human rights[1413] are just two examples. For present purposes, however, I am interested in accounts of legitimacy-enhancement which are "in-court" rather than "out-of-court", i.e. which relate directly to the ECtHR's reasoning and its decisions and in particular to the use of European consensus. Even if there is an intuitive connection between the States parties to the Convention as agents of legitimacy and the reference to their legal systems by way of European consensus, it remains to be explained more precisely *how* consensus is said to contribute to an increase in legitimacy.

While this part of the case in favour of consensus as legitimacy-enhancement is not often made explicit, quite a few different yet overlapping

Recent Judgments Concerning Equal Marriage Rights" at 195; for a similar rationale with regard to vertically comparative references within the Inter-American system, see Neuman, "Import, Export, and Regional Consent in the Inter-American Court of Human Rights" at 115; and for the European Court of Justice, see Lenaerts, "Interlocking Legal Orders" at 879; Koen Lenaerts and José A. Gutiérrez-Fons, "The Constitutional Allocation of Powers and General Principles of EU Law," (2010) 47 *Common Market Law Review* 1629 at 1636; Sibylle Seyr, "Verfassungsgerichte und Verfassungsvergleichung. Der EuGH," (2010) 18 *Journal für Rechtspolitik* 230 at 233.

1411 Madsen, Cebulak, and Wiebusch, "Backlash Against International Courts: Explaining the Forms and Patterns of Resistance to International Courts" at 214.

1412 See Jean-Paul Costa, "The Relationship between the European Court of Human Rights and the National Courts," (2013) *European Human Rights Law Review* 264 at 272.

1413 On the crucial importance of this approach, see Anagnostou and Mungiu-Pippidi, "Domestic Implementation of Human Rights Judgments in Europe: Legal Infrastructure and Government Effectiveness Matter" at 221 and 227.

strands of reasoning have by now been offered.[1414] My intention here is not to examine them exhaustively,[1415] but merely to identify some common themes so as to lay the groundwork for discussing the merits and limits of consensus as legitimacy-enhancement. I will therefore focus on those arguments which relate most specifically to European consensus by building on its core characteristics as identified in Chapter 1. The first such characteristic is its *verticality* which, of course, supplies the connection between the ECtHR and the States parties to the ECHR as the relevant agents of legitimacy.

The second characteristic is that European consensus regards the legal orders of the States parties through the prism of *collectivity* – is there "common ground" between them or not? I argued in Chapter 3 that this aspect is closely connected to the ECtHR's institutional context as a transnational institution: foregrounding the individual national ethos of the respondent State would run danger of negating the ECtHR's judicial function, but ethical normativity can be retained by focussing instead on the notion of a pan-European ethos as identified through the States parties' legal systems viewed collectively.[1416] The argument there was not concerned with sociological legitimacy,[1417] but a similar point can be made in that regard by switching from the consideration of the States parties' collective will as an expression of ethical normativity to the States parties' preferences as the basis of sociological legitimacy. For example, Kanstantsin Dzehtsiarou at one point takes as his starting assumption that the States parties "wish to be condemned for human rights violations as rarely as possible (preferably

1414 In particular by Dzehtsiarou, *European Consensus and the Legitimacy of the European Court of Human Rights*, Chapter 6.

1415 Besides the focus on incrementalism in this chapter, some further strands of reasoning are considered in Chapter 10.

1416 See Chapter 3, IV.3.

1417 In Chapter 3, I cited Neuman, "Import, Export, and Regional Consent in the Inter-American Court of Human Rights" at 115, arguing that "letting each state be the judge of its own human rights obligations" would negate the effect of human rights, but that this "does not entail that the substantive evolution of the regional human rights regime must be independent of the regional *community of states*" (emphasis in original); I read Neuman's point as principled (he speaks of "legitimation" in a way which seems to refer primarily to *normative* legitimacy since it builds on ideas of self-commitment and collective self-determination), but it *also* contains an element of (sociological) legitimacy-enhancement in its reference to ensuring the "effectiveness" of human rights, for example by making "national enforcement more feasible".

never)".[1418] However, he hastens to add, "giving the Contracting Parties *carte blanche* would probably undermine the whole idea behind the ECtHR as an effective international human rights arbiter", so reference should instead be made to "commonly accepted rules that build up European public order as reflected by European consensus".[1419] Because of the prism of collectivity, in other words, the States parties' preferences can be taken as the basis of the ECtHR's decision so as to ensure its sociological legitimacy without undermining its supervisory role entirely.

This approach to European consensus as legitimacy-enhancement places a strong emphasis on the connection between (lack of) consensus and the outcome of any given case: the idea is that consensus allows the ECtHR to develop its case-law in such a way that it keeps pace with, but does not surpass, the stance taken by the majority of the States parties. Dzehtsiarou again: European consensus "positively impacts the legitimacy of the ECtHR as it *prevents the Court from going beyond those developments that the Contracting Parties are able to accept*".[1420] Or, as Holning Lau has put it, "the Court needs to defer to Contracting States to elicit their cooperation" and consensus "is a means through which the Court achieves such deference",[1421] because it only requires States "to implement legal standards that a critical mass of Contracting States has already adopted".[1422] More generally, this approach is commonly dubbed *incrementalism*: the ECtHR only incrementally develops its case-law, with European consensus setting the pace.[1423] Since the focus is on incrementally developing human rights

1418 Dzehtsiarou, *European Consensus and the Legitimacy of the European Court of Human Rights*, at 153.

1419 Ibid., 153-154 (emphasis in original); see also Ryan, "Europe's Moral Margin: Parental Aspirations and the European Court of Human Rights" at 494.

1420 Dzehtsiarou, *European Consensus and the Legitimacy of the European Court of Human Rights*, at 150 (emphasis added); see also Senden, *Interpretation of Fundamental Rights*, at 67.

1421 Lau, "Rewriting Schalk and Kopf: Shifting the Locus of Deference" at 257.

1422 Ibid., 254.

1423 For various connections between incrementalism and European consensus, see e.g. Helfer and Slaughter, "Toward a Theory of Effective Supranational Adjudication" at 314-317; de Londras and Dzehtsiarou, "Managing Judicial Innovation in the European Court of Human Rights" at 544; Yourow, *The Margin of Appreciation Doctrine*, at 196; Ed Bates, "Analysing the Prisoner Voting Saga and the British Challenge to Strasbourg," (2014) 14 *Human Rights Law Review* 503 at 536-537; Lau, "Rewriting Schalk and Kopf: Shifting the Locus of Deference" at 253-256; Draghici, "The Strasbourg Court between European and Local Consensus: Anti-democratic or Guardian of Democratic Process?" at 20; see

standards by reference to European consensus, its connection to the *outcome* of the ECtHR's judgments is crucial.

As I mentioned above, further arguments may be made to explain why consensus contributes to the ECtHR's sociological legitimacy[1424] – indeed, different arguments are sometimes cited alongside one another and might be seen as mutually reinforcing. Regarding consensus as the basis for an incremental development of the ECtHR's case-law is of particular interest, however, not only because it seems to have been the most influential understanding of consensus as legitimacy-enhancement but also because of the conceptualisation of consensus which it implies. If consensus is seen as an indicator of whether or not the ECtHR should find a violation of the Convention while incrementally developing its case-law, then its use is quite strictly prescribed: for the incremental build-up to be successful, consensus would have to be deployed in such a way that it forms a stabilising and predictable element within the ECtHR's reasoning which clearly influences the ECtHR's conclusion in a significant number of cases.[1425]

This points towards a relatively formulaic approach to consensus – e.g. constructed by reference to domestic law rather than international law,[1426] geared at a specific issue rather than involving different levels of generali-

---

also Shany, "Assessing the Effectiveness of International Courts: A Goal-Based Approach" at 268-269.

1424 In particular, other strands of argument are more focussed on the legitimacy-enhancing merits of consensus as a form of reasoning *mentioned* in processes of justification, regardless of the outcome of the case, arguing e.g. that consensus makes the ECtHR seem well-informed (Dzehtsiarou and Lukashevich, "Informed Decision-Making" at 274) and presents it as willing to engage in judicial dialogue (Dzehtsiarou, *European Consensus and the Legitimacy of the European Court of Human Rights*, at 157; see generally on strategic use of judicial dialogue Krisch, *Beyond Constitutionalism: The Pluralist Structure of Postnational Law*, at 126). I focus instead on consensus in relation to outcomes, partly because this line of argument seems more relevant in generating legitimacy (see generally Madsen, Cebulak, and Wiebusch, "Backlash Against International Courts: Explaining the Forms and Patterns of Resistance to International Courts" at 212) and partly because its focus on determinate outcomes contrasts more strongly with the framework which I have been advocating for.

1425 Although this approach is self-described as a "moderate" view: Dzehtsiarou, "European Consensus and the Evolutive Interpretation of the European Convention on Human Rights" at 1740; but see Chapter 10, III.1. for its implications.

1426 Indeed, the main claim of Dzehtsiarou, "What Is Law for the European Court of Human Rights?" at 127-133 is that international law (with the exception of Council of Europe materials) is less suited to increasing the ECtHR's legitimacy, even going so far as to claim a causal relation between reliance on "exter-

ty,[1427] and endowed with strong normative force, making counter-arguments the exception rather than the rule.[1428] Accepting an account of consensus as legitimacy-enhancement which focusses on its connections to the outcome of any given case so as to allow for the incremental development of the ECtHR's case-law would, in brief, serve to reinstate consensus as an "objective element" external to the ECtHR – precisely the understanding which I have been arguing against throughout. In light of this tension, it is this kind of argument in favour of consensus as legitimacy-enhancement based on incrementalism which I primarily focus on in what follows.

5. The Court as the Object of Legitimacy: Strategic Implications

The notion of incrementalism brings us to a consideration of the *object* of legitimacy, in other words: the legitimacy of who or what is being considered? This could be, for example, a regime, a constitution, an institution, a norm, or a judgment. Since European consensus forms part of the ECtHR's reasoning which aims to justify its decision in a certain case, as mandated by the Convention (Article 45 (1) ECHR),[1429] one might assume that the primary reference is *to that decision or judgment*. However, on an account of consensus as legitimacy-enhancement which emphasises the *incremental development of the ECtHR's case-law*, the idea is that consensus should influence the ECtHR's conclusions in such a way that its case-law develops in a manner acceptable to the States parties *over time*.

The implication is that the scope of enquiry should be broadened to include not just individual judgments, but rather the overall performance of the Court: what accounts of consensus as legitimacy-enhancement based on the notion of incrementalism arguably have in common is a normative commitment to the human rights project *as a whole*, and hence to the ECtHR *as an institution* rather than its individual judgments. At the same time, however, the latter remains connected to the former. In the vocabulary of legitimacy, this is often reflected in a certain oscillation between

nal" sources and the ECtHR's "legitimacy crisis" (at 117-118 and 129); for conceptual criticism of his distinction between "internal" and "external" sources, see Chapter 6, IV.4.

1427 See explicitly ibid., 132.

1428 Ibid., 130; on the preponderance of reliance on consensus in the ECtHR's case-law, particularly when the margin of appreciation is concerned, see Chapter 8, IV.

1429 See also Rule 74 (1) h Rules of the Court.

two objects of legitimacy: individual judgments (and the concrete norm they set) and the ECtHR itself (as an institution).[1430]

A popular way to refine this framework is by reference to David Easton's distinction between diffuse and specific support.[1431] Specific support relates to the content of an institution's output – an example would be support for a certain judgment because one agrees with its result. Diffuse support means support for an institution that is, to the contrary, not contingent on satisfaction with the content of particular results – for example, continued support of the ECtHR and implementation of its judgments even when a State does not agree with the concrete norm at issue. Diffuse support is needed to maintain a system in force permanently,[1432] but it depends in part on the generation of specific support.[1433]

In light of the distinction between diffuse and specific support, an account of consensus as legitimacy-enhancement focussing on the incremental development of the ECtHR's case-law could be specified roughly as follows. While individual States' stances may be overruled in particular judgments, their position will usually influence the conclusions reached by the Court since it forms part of European consensus. Assuming that the State parties will support those judgments which cohere with the position of

1430 Most clearly: Dzehtsiarou, *European Consensus and the Legitimacy of the European Court of Human Rights*, chapter 6 ("Legitimacy of the Court and legitimacy of its judgments" and mostly focussing on the prior, e.g. at 145; the title of this book also refers to the legitimacy of the ECtHR as a whole); Costa, "On the Legitimacy of the European Court of Human Rights' Judgments" (referring to judgments in its title but mostly to the Court in its content, e.g. at 174); see also Dzehtsiarou, "Does Consensus Matter? Legitimacy of European Consensus in the Case Law of the European Court of Human Rights" at 536; generally on legitimacy "of institutions – rather than […] actors or decisions": Çalı, Koch, and Bruch, "The Legitimacy of the European Court of Human Rights: The View from the Ground" at 4; in their terminology, I am concerned here with social legitimacy insofar as it relates to performance dimension of the ECtHR (see ibid. at 9-10).

1431 David Easton, *A Systems Analysis of Political Life* (New York: Wiley, 1965), at 273; see e.g. de Londras and Dzehtsiarou, "Managing Judicial Innovation in the European Court of Human Rights" at 526; Zwart, "More Human Rights Than Court: Why the Legitimacy of the European Court of Human Rights is in Need of Repair and How It Can Be Done" at 81; Dothan, "How International Courts Enhance Their Legitimacy" at 456.

1432 Easton, *A Systems Analysis of Political Life*, at 269.

1433 Dothan, "How International Courts Enhance Their Legitimacy" at 456; Lupu, "International Judicial Legitimacy: Lessons from National Courts" at 441.

their legal system and take a critical stance towards those that do not,[1434] giving strong weight to European consensus and deciding cases accordingly will, on this account, ensure specific support often enough to generate diffuse support – the cases in which a State either forms part of the inter-State majority (spur effect) or there is no violation of the Convention (rein effect), and it thus does not have to adapt its legal system to newly set standards, will outweigh the cases in which it has to do so because it forms part of the inter-State minority (spur effect). These assumptions, it seems to me, underlie proposals of incrementalism based on European consensus, since they specify why consensus could be said to prevent the Court from "going beyond those developments that the Contracting Parties are able to accept".[1435]

This reconstruction of consensus as legitimacy-enhancement resonates with approaches that see the use of consensus as a "strategy of majoritarian activism",[1436] meaning that the Court is constrained by the States parties' preferences but has an important role both in extending progressive standards accepted by the majority to laggard States and in preventing regression from common standards, thus contributing to the overall improvement of human rights standards.[1437] Beyond the substantive argument at issue, this denomination ("strategy of majoritarian activism") is interesting because it makes explicit a point which is not often acknowledged in accounts of consensus as legitimacy-enhancement: they are, at heart, *strategic* accounts.[1438] Helen Fenwick, for example, has acknowledged this while discussing the role of consensus in cases relating to same-gender marriage.

1434 Supra, note 1418.

1435 Supra, note 1420.

1436 Alec Stone Sweet and Thomas L. Brunell, "Trustee Courts and the Judicialization of International Regimes: The Politics of Majoritarian Activism in the European Convention on Human Rights, the European Union, and the World Trade Organization," (2013) 1 *Journal of Law and Courts* 61 at 78; Helfer and Voeten, "International Courts as Agents of Legal Change: Evidence from LGBT Rights in Europe" at 4; Ryan, "Europe's Moral Margin: Parental Aspirations and the European Court of Human Rights" at 494; the term was coined in the context of EU law: see Miguel Poiares Maduro, *We The Court: The European Court of Justice and The European Economic Constitution. A Critical Reading of Article 30 of the EC Treaty* (Oxford: Hart, 1998), at 11.

1437 Burstein, "The Will to Enforce: An Examination of the Political Constraints upon a Regional Court of Human Rights" at 425.

1438 See supra, I. for comments on the vocabulary of "legitimacy"; for acknowledgements of the strategic aspect, see e.g. Gerards, "Giving Shape to the Notion of 'Shared Responsibility'" at 40; Kleinlein, "Consensus and Contestability: The ECtHR and the Combined Potential of European Consensus and Pro-

She concludes that its use is "*strategically understandable* at the present time when a number of states have taken the step of enshrining their opposition to same-sex marriage in recent amendments to the Constitutions".[1439]

We are faced, then, with a strategic approach which aims to maintain the sociological legitimacy of the ECtHR (as the object of legitimacy) vis-à-vis the States parties (the agents of legitimacy) over time. The deeper assumption underlying the strategic approach – the "ultimate end" of its strategy[1440] – lies in the postulation of a better future. As Benvenisti has rather lyrically put it in describing (and criticising) the use of European consensus, the ECtHR is conceptualised as "guiding the communal ship towards more enlightened standards, yet taking into account the prevailing winds and sea conditions".[1441] The notion of "prevailing winds" perhaps harkens back to a piece of advice to princes given by Machiavelli, which contains similar language (in some translations, at least): "To preserve the state", Machiavelli opines, the prince "often has to do things [...] against humanity" because "he has to have a mind ready to shift as the winds of fortune and varying circumstances of life may dictate".[1442] The proximity to Machiavelli is telling, but it need not necessarily be read as negative. The suspicion that the ECtHR's institutional power is being preserved for its own sake is, of course, ever present, and realist accounts would be quick to foreground it.[1443] But at least on a benevolent reading of the notions of incrementalism and majoritarian activism, the strategic approach is primarily about enhancing the ECtHR's sociological legitimacy so that it may continue to effectively set human rights standards in the

---

cedural Rationality Control" at 880; Krisch, *Beyond Constitutionalism: The Pluralist Structure of Postnational Law*, at 139-140; see also Nic Shuibhne, "Consensus as Challenge and Retraction of Rights: Can Lessons Be Drawns from - and for - EU Citizenship Law?" at 441 who speaks of "appropriate deference to and respect for (or even, more cynically, strategic appeasement of) the relevant states parties".

1439 Fenwick, "Same-sex Unions at the Strasbourg Court in a Divided Europe: Driving Forward Reform or Protecting the Court's Authority via Consensus Analysis?" at 269 (emphasis added).

1440 In the terminology of Shany, "Assessing the Effectiveness of International Courts: A Goal-Based Approach" at 232.

1441 Benvenisti, "Margin of Appreciation, Consensus, and Universal Standards" at 852.

1442 Niccolò Machiavelli, *The Prince*, section XVIII.

1443 See André Nollkaemper, "International Adjudication of Global Public Goods: The Intersection of Substance and Procedure," (2012) 23 *European Journal of International Law* 769 at 783 (in footnote 92), noting "the tendency of all organizations to see themselves as indispensable".

long run.[1444] These long-term implications are crucial, however: Benvenisti's naval metaphor is spatial, but the strategic approach in fact contains a *temporal* element.

This temporal element has shone through at several points – for example, in the notion of incremental development over time or in Fenwick's admission that the ECtHR's take on same-gender marriage is "strategically understandable *at the present time*"[1445] – and is largely considered self-evident, yet it is important to note that the presumed benefits of the strategic approach are *removed from the present*. The notion of European consensus as the basis of an incremental or slow-and-steady build-up not for normative, but for strategic reasons ("cautiously",[1446] with an "awareness of political boundaries"[1447]) implies that while adequate human rights standards may not be attainable at present, they will be at a later point in time.[1448] As Nico Krisch has put it, incrementalism "helps to avoid clashes with member states and their courts while keeping alive the promise of a more effective human rights protection in the future".[1449] The present is thus operationalised strategically in the service of the future.

III. *The Practical Limitations of Consensus as Legitimacy-Enhancement*

The strategic approach is concerned, as explored over the course of the preceding section, with nourishing the ECtHR's sociological legitimacy in order to mitigate criticism by the States parties, with the ultimate end of securing their support for the Court so that it may set higher human rights standards in the long term. With regard to European consensus, this ap-

---

1444 This focus is established as a normative demand by Mann, "Non-ideal Theory of Constitutional Adjudication" at 21 and 42.

1445 Supra, note 1439.

1446 Yourow, *The Margin of Appreciation Doctrine*, at 196.

1447 Helfer and Slaughter, "Toward a Theory of Effective Supranational Adjudication" at 314.

1448 Janneke Gerards has explicated the strategic approach and long-term implications of incrementalism with particular force: see Gerards, "Margin of Appreciation and Incrementalism in the Case Law of the European Court of Human Rights"; see also, more generally on strategy as the basis for "effectiveness and compliance *in the long term*" (emphasis added), Jed Odermatt, "Patterns of Avoidance: Political Questions Before International Courts," (2018) 14 *International Journal of Law in Context* 221 at 222.

1449 Krisch, *Beyond Constitutionalism: The Pluralist Structure of Postnational Law*, at 140 and 150 on incrementalism, and at 141 for the quote.

proach is combined with the claim that use of consensus will indeed help to boost the ECtHR's sociological legitimacy by pointing the Court towards decisions which the majority of the States parties will be ready to honour. Accepting, for present purposes, the normative premises of the strategic approach, one might nonetheless inquire whether European consensus can, in fact, fulfil the role assigned to it in boosting the ECtHR's sociological legitimacy. Given the sense of urgency underlying accounts of a "legitimacy crisis" and the need to respond to it, this is a crucial issue. It is this aspect that I will explore in the present section.

A sceptical take on the practical aspects of operationalising European consensus strategically would hold that there is simply not sufficient evidence that consensus plays a role in nourishing the sociological legitimacy of the ECtHR and its judgments – as Merris Amos has put it, "there has been very little assessment of the validity of the [...] assumption that this method [i.e. European consensus] enhances the legitimacy of judgments".[1450] Further, it seems quite difficult to make such an assessment since consensus is not only used differently in different cases,[1451] but also embedded in a complicated socio-political context which renders generalisations difficult.[1452] My aim here is therefore not to provide an empirical assessment of the effectiveness of consensus as legitimacy-enhancement in practice, but rather to provide a conceptual account of how use of consensus relates to some prominent forms of criticism directed at the ECtHR.

To this end, I suggest recalling, once more, some characteristics of European consensus which *set consensus as legitimacy-enhancement apart from other strategic approaches*. One might imagine, for example, a strategy which approaches each judgment of the ECtHR in a highly contextualised manner, assessing the strategic merits of finding a violation or non-violation by reference to the subject-matter of the case, the political climate in the respondent State, and other factors.[1453] This is not the approach taken by

1450 Amos, "Can European Consensus Encourage Acceptance of the European Convention on Human Rights in the United Kingdom?" at 259; see also Peat, *Comparative Reasoning in International Courts and Tribunals*, at 163.

1451 See Chapters 5 to 8.

1452 See Dzehtsiarou, "What Is Law for the European Court of Human Rights?" at 123.

1453 I am thinking, for example, of Dothan's approach based on a calculation of material and reputational costs of compliance in any given case: see Shai Dothan, "Judicial Tactics in the European Court of Human Rights," (2011-2012) 12 *Chicago Journal of International Law* 115; for the interplay be-

those who see consensus as the basis for strategic incrementalism.[1454] For one thing, the *prism of collectivity*[1455] means that the focus is on the community of States parties as a whole, not primarily on the position of the respondent State. The reliance on *incremental development* of the case-law points away from an individualised consideration of the case at issue and its subject-matter, instead placing its hopes on the aggregation of diffuse support over time. A similar effect is also achieved by the *relative formality* of European consensus: as discussed in Chapter 1, I understand it as a form of vertically comparative law, i.e. referring to formal legal acts rather than, for example, to public opinion.[1456] European consensus may be considered "evidence" of the States parties' preferences,[1457] but its relative formality due to its legal nature means that it does not attempt to capture the broader political discourse surrounding any given issue.

The merits and limits of this particular kind of strategic approach should be considered specifically in light of the ECtHR's situation as a regional court. Even in the best of cases, it is difficult to gauge how judgments will impact on a court's sociological legitimacy since the "social consequences, especially the long-term social consequences, of adopting

---

tween such a more individualised strategic approach and European consensus, see Dothan, "Judicial Deference Allows European Consensus to Emerge"; but note also that Dothan now also places consensus in relation to legitimacy-enhancement (ibid. at 403); for his take on European consensus more generally, see Chapter 4, II.

1454 I continue to focus on the particular strategic account of consensus as described above (II.4.-5.), i.e. consensus setting the pace for incremental development of the ECtHR's case-law. Given the malleability of consensus, there are clearly "opportunities for strategic definitions" (Føllesdal, "A Better Signpost, Not a Better Walking Stick: How to Evaluate the European Consensus Doctrine" at 196) which may lead to strategic approaches different from the one I am foregrounding. But since *any* kind of judicial reasoning may hide strategic considerations (see e.g. Mann, "Non-ideal Theory of Constitutional Adjudication" at 24), this kind of strategy would not be specific to consensus and therefore would have no added value in justifying its use. I therefore leave it aside here; but see Chapter 10, III.1. on how these questions re-emerge in practice.

1455 See supra, II.4.

1456 See Chapter 1, III.

1457 Dzehtsiarou, "European Consensus and the Evolutive Interpretation of the European Convention on Human Rights" at 1743; Helfer, "Consensus, Coherence and the European Convention on Human Rights" at 139; see also Nußberger, "Auf der Suche nach einem europäischen Konsens – zur Rechtsprechung des Europäischen Gerichtshofs für Menschenrechte" at 200-201.

one legal rule rather than another are notoriously difficult to calculate".[1458] As Simmons has put it, determining the political possibility and likely effectiveness of various strategies "will require reasonably specialized knowledge of the structure and workings of [...] particular societies".[1459] Such determinations are likely to be even more difficult for the ECtHR as a transnational court. Dzehtsiarou, for example, has argued that "national constitutional courts always face only one possible respondent and, therefore, they can predict the reaction to their judgment better than their international counterparts".[1460] Lupu makes a similar point regarding the "larger audiences" of international courts, leading to "a constituency with sharply divided preferences".[1461] He argues that this makes controversy more likely but also, relatedly, that it is more difficult for international courts to gauge the preferences of the States parties: "Especially with a diverse audience, it is often difficult for international courts to discern the preferences of the public and of the political actors in the applicable states".[1462]

There are, in other words, (at least) two related difficulties at play in specifying a strategic approach for the ECtHR: identifying the preferences of the States parties and taking into account that these preferences are likely to be diverse and sometimes conflicting. An approach based on European consensus as the basis for incremental development of the ECtHR's case-law could be considered a response to these difficulties in light of some of the characteristics of consensus identified above. Comparative reasoning carries its own methodological and epistemological difficulties

1458 Neil MacCormick, *Rhetoric and the Rule of Law. A Theory of Legal Reasoning* (Oxford: Oxford University Press, 2005), at 103 (on consequentialist arguments in general).

1459 Simmons, "Ideal and Nonideal Theory" at 19; accordingly, one of Roni Mann's criteria for the admission of strategic considerations into constitutional adjudication is that there be "*sociologically-grounded evidence* that the social backlash of an ideal decision would be counterproductive": Mann, "Non-ideal Theory of Constitutional Adjudication" at 45 (emphasis added); see also Pablo Gilabert and Holly Lawford-Smith, "Political Feasibility: A Conceptual Exploration," (2012) 60 *Political Studies* 809 at 823 ("best available evidence").

1460 Dzehtsiarou, "Book Review of Shai Dothan, Reputation and Judicial Tactics. A Theory of National and International Courts" at 394.

1461 Lupu, "International Judicial Legitimacy: Lessons from National Courts" at 452; see also Pildes, "Supranational Courts and The Law of Democracy: The European Court of Human Rights" at 160.

1462 Lupu, "International Judicial Legitimacy: Lessons from National Courts" at 453.

(and indeed European consensus is hardly a form of comparative reasoning which owns up to these difficulties),[1463] but its relative formality could be regarded as providing the ECtHR with a kind of shortcut to assessing the preferences and possible reactions of the States parties in more detail.[1464] Furthermore, the reference to the legal orders of the States parties through the prism of collectivity, rather than focussing primarily on the respondent State, attempts to grapple with the conflicting preferences as reflected in the differences among the legal orders. It thus takes into account that, although the ECtHR's judgments are formally binding only inter partes (Article 46 (1) ECHR), they also have broader effects erga omnes, i.e. for the States parties other than the respondent State.[1465] The possibility of conflicting preferences also explains why consensus relies on incremental development of the ECtHR's case-law *over time*, thus aiming to generate sufficient diffuse support for the ECtHR to overcome the inevitable lack of specific support by some States in some cases.

Basing a strategic approach on European consensus thus has certain advantages; but the very features of consensus on which these advantages are based also point to significant limitations. In essence, it seems to me that they combine in such a way as to create a curious disconnect from the kind of criticism and political pressure facing the ECtHR – from the very "legitimacy crisis" which motivates the turn to a strategic approach in the first place.[1466] Because the strategic approach to consensus which I have been considering relies on its relative formality, on the prism of collectivity, and on the generation of diffuse support over time it does not take into account, for example, for States' unusually strong reactions to the finding of a violation in politically sensitive cases[1467] – or in any case that can be

---

1463 See Chapter 1, III.

1464 All the more so in cases involving international law as consensus: see Chapter 6, VI.

1465 See Chapter 3, IV.4. for further references.

1466 Supra, II.2.

1467 The general gist of my argument thus resonates with Helfer's and Alter's suggestion that international courts may "spark controversy due to the domestic political consequences of their rulings" rather than generalist considerations of an ostensible "legitimacy crisis" or specifically expansionist rulings per se: Laurence R. Helfer and Karen J. Alter, "Legitimacy and Lawmaking: A Tale of Three International Courts," (2013) 14 *Theoretical Inquiries in Law* 479 at 502; see also Ximena Soley and Silvia Steininger, "Parting Ways or Lashing Back? Withdrawals, Backlash and the Inter-American Court of Human Rights," (2018) 14 *International Journal of Law in Context* 237 at 242. Dzehtsiarou,

politicised if the general political climate in the respondent State is such that there is a tendency to criticise the ECtHR.[1468]

To underline the kinds of political discourse which lie outside the conceptual ambit of this kind of strategic approach based specifically on European consensus, I would like to cite some examples of criticism which the ECtHR has faced in practice, focussing on criticism emanating from the United Kingdom and Russia as two cases often cited as emblematic of the ECtHR's "legitimacy crisis". Of course, on some level these examples are bound to appear disingenuous: no strategy could ever prevent criticism in all cases (nor would such a strategy be normatively desirable[1469]) and European consensus is clearly no panacea, so it is easy to point at instances in which criticism was levelled at the ECtHR despite its use. Perhaps, after all, they would be harsher or more numerous or if the Court had not relied on consensus and reached other conclusions?[1470] But my point is not simply to draw attention to criticism of the ECtHR in and of itself, but to sketch how the form which such criticism takes makes it difficult to account for within the conceptual framework of a strategic approach based specifically on European consensus.

Consider, then, the political climate in the United Kingdom. Merris Amos has recently conducted a thorough survey of various high-profile judgments, their use of European consensus, and the political reactions to these judgments within the United Kingdom. The focus on high-profile judgments is already telling, since their notoriety is hardly politically innocent: as Amos puts it, the heated criticism of the ECtHR "centres very much on a limited selection of case law from an earlier era".[1471] For example, a key policy paper by the Conservative Party expresses "mounting concern at Strasbourg's attempts to overrule decisions of our democratically elected Parliament".[1472] It mentions four areas of concern which the

---

"What Is Law for the European Court of Human Rights?" at 123 admits that, "[v]ery often, effective implementation of judgments depends on the political will of the Contracting Parties".

1468 See generally Madsen, Cebulak, and Wiebusch, "Backlash Against International Courts: Explaining the Forms and Patterns of Resistance to International Courts" at 201.

1469 See Chapter 10, II.

1470 In Clare Ryan's words, "it is impossible to know what would have happened had the Court ruled otherwise": Ryan, "Europe's Moral Margin: Parental Aspirations and the European Court of Human Rights" at 512-513.

1471 Amos, "Can European Consensus Encourage Acceptance of the European Convention on Human Rights in the United Kingdom?" at 267.

1472 Conservative Party, "Protecting Human Rights in the UK" (2014), at p. 3.

ECtHR has ruled on: voting rights for prisoners, prisoners' right to go through artificial insemination with their partners, non-refoulement of foreign nationals who have committed crimes, and "banning whole life sentences even for the gravest crimes" (a misrepresentation of *Vinter v. the United Kingdom*, which in fact concerned the need for review of whole life tariffs rather than whole life tariffs per se).[1473] Based on this very limited and inaccurate overview, the Conservative Party proposes a number of reform objectives which essentially aim to greatly restrict the role of the ECtHR; otherwise, the paper notes in a thinly veiled threat, there would be "no alternative but to withdraw from the European Convention on Human Rights".[1474] This exemplifies the kind of political sentiment which is somewhat disconnected from the framework of consensus as legitimacy-enhancement, since it demonstrates that findings of a violation in some cases cannot necessarily be counter-balanced by other cases with results more acceptable to a State party. Rather, the focus remains exclusively on a limited number of politicised cases which are presented as sufficient evidence that the Convention system as a whole lacks legitimacy.

Beyond such general criticism, another form of negative reaction by States parties which the strategic approach aims to mitigate is non-compliance.[1475] The United Kingdom fares somewhat better in this regard, usually implementing controversial judgments despite its threatening political gestures. The ECtHR's judgment in *Hirst v. the United Kingdom (No. 2)* on

---

1473 Ibid.; see ECtHR (GC), Appl. Nos. 66069/09, 130/10 and 3896/10 – *Vinter and Others*; for the other issues, see ECtHR (GC), Appl. No. 44362/04 – *Dickson*; ECtHR, Appl. No. 8139/09 – *Othman (Abu Qatada) v. the United Kingdom*, Judgment of 17 January 2012; and infra, note 1476, on prisoners' voting rights.

1474 Conservative Party, "Protecting Human Rights in the UK" at p. 8; Brexit has since distracted somewhat from foundational criticism of the ECtHR, but the Conservative Party's more recent manifesto stating that the United Kingdom will remain a signatory of the ECHR "for the duration of the next parliament" still carries a threatening undercurrent for the future: Conservative Party, "Forward, Together. Our Plan for a Stronger Britain and a Prosperous Future" (2017), available at <https://www.conservatives.com/manifesto>, p. 37. Under Boris Johnson, too, there have been repeated squabbles over opting out of (parts of) the Convention, especially insofar as it prevents certain deportations of foreign nationals, although these have been more focussed on amendments to domestic legislation.

1475 See e.g. Dzehtsiarou, *European Consensus and the Legitimacy of the European Court of Human Rights*, at 145, as well as supra, text to notes 1401-1405.

prisoners' voting rights is, of course, the infamous counter-example.[1476] Its conclusion that the United Kingdom's blanket ban on prisoners voting violates Article 3 of Protocol No. 1 has not only been subject to a barrage of criticism within the United Kingdom, but was also repeatedly rejected politically.[1477] Accordingly, proponents of consensus as legitimacy-enhancement often point to this judgment and the reaction to it to underline the need for a strategic approach so as to avoid a "legitimacy crisis".[1478] Yet while *Hirst* certainly exemplifies a certain form of backlash against judgments of the ECtHR, it seems somewhat ironic to cite it in favour of a strategic approach based specifically on European consensus, since the ECtHR's reasoning did make reference to consensus: while it acknowledged that "the United Kingdom is not alone among Convention countries in depriving all convicted prisoners of the right to vote", it nonetheless held that "it is a minority of Contracting States in which a blanket re-

---

1476 ECtHR (GC), Appl. No. 74025/01 – *Hirst*; see also ECtHR, Appl. Nos. 60041/08 and 60054/08 – *Greens and M.T. v. the United Kingdom*, Judgment of 23 November 2010; confirmed in: ECtHR, Appl. Nos. 47784/09 et al. – *Firth and Others v. the United Kingdom*, Judgment of 12 August 2014; ECtHR, Appl. No. 51987/08 and 1,014 others – *McHugh and Others v. the United Kingdom*, Judgment of 10 February 2015; ECtHR, Appl. Nos. 44473/14 et al. – *Millbank and Others v. the United Kingdom*, Judgment of 30 June 2016; see also, with different respondent States but nonetheless closely connected to the (arguably varying) standards set by Strasbourg: ECtHR, Appl. No. 20201/04 – *Frodl v. Austria*, Judgment of 8 April 2010; ECtHR (GC), Appl. No. 126/05 – *Scoppola v. Italy (No. 3)*, Judgment of 22 May 2012; ECtHR, Appl. Nos. 11157/04 and 15162/05 – *Anchugov and Gladkov v. Russia*, Judgment of 4 July 2013 (see further infra, text to note 1487); ECtHR, Appl. No. 29411/07 – *Söyler v. Turkey*, Judgment of 17 September 2013; ECtHR, Appl. No. 9540/07 – *Murat Vural v. Turkey*, Judgment of 21 October 2014; ECtHR, Appl. No. 63849/09 – *Kulinski and Sabev v. Bulgaria*, Judgment of 21 July 2016.

1477 For an overview, see Bates, "Analysing the Prisoner Voting Saga and the British Challenge to Strasbourg"; most recently, a compromise has been reached. See CM/Del/Dec(2017)1302/H46-39: The Ministers' Deputies consider, "in light of the wide margin of appreciation in this area", that the (very minimal) measures proposed by the United Kingdom "respond to the European Court's judgments in this group of cases". The examination was officially closed by CM/ResDH(2018)467 of 6 December 2018.

1478 E.g. Hamilton, "Same-Sex Marriage, Consensus, Certainty and the European Court of Human Rights" at 43; Dzehtsiarou, *European Consensus and the Legitimacy of the European Court of Human Rights*, at 147.

striction on the right of convicted prisoners to vote is imposed or in which there is no provision allowing prisoners to vote".[1479]

As Amos has summarised it: "What the reaction to *Hirst* indicates is that consensus based reasoning is no match for a highly politicised issue resulting in an adverse judgment"; rather, in such instances, "the Court's use of consensus seems to add nothing at all".[1480] Neither, one might add, did the ECtHR's use of consensus in cases preceding and succeeding *Hirst* – including the operationalisation of its rein effect in favour of the United Kingdom in high-profile cases like *Animal Defenders International v. the United Kingdom*[1481] – lead to results generating sufficient diffuse support to overcome the lack of specific support in *Hirst* itself. Instead, the issue was presented as one of heightened political and emotional stakes, perhaps exemplified by David Cameron's declaration that giving prisoners the right to vote makes him feel "physically ill".[1482] Again, this kind of rhetoric is conceptually difficult to set in relation to the aggregate-type and relatively formal framework of consensus as legitimacy-enhancement as described above.

As a further example, consider Russia – one of the "most vocal criticizers" of the ECtHR along with the United Kingdom.[1483] Russia's recent resistance must be seen in the context of "a significant worsening of political

1479 ECtHR (GC), Appl. No. 74025/01 – *Hirst*, at para. 81; the tendency was thus towards the spur effect, with reference to a lack of consensus being phrased as a hypothetical ("even if"); however, *Hirst* also very clearly exemplifies the malleability of consensus (see e.g. Chapter 5, III.1. on numerical issues and Chapter 7, II. on the level of generality used, both of which are relevant here); see further e.g. Pildes, "Supranational Courts and The Law of Democracy: The European Court of Human Rights"; Shai Dothan, "Comparative Views on the Right to Vote in International Law: The Case of Prisoners' Disenfranchisement," in *Comparative International Law*, ed. Anthea Roberts, et al. (Oxford: Oxford University Press, 2018).

1480 Amos, "Can European Consensus Encourage Acceptance of the European Convention on Human Rights in the United Kingdom?" at 268.

1481 ECtHR (GC), Appl. No. 48876/08 – *Animal Defenders International*, at para. 123.

1482 HC Deb., Vol. 517, Col. 921 (3 November 2010).

1483 Lauri Mälksoo, "Concluding Observations. Russia and European Human-Rights Law: Margins of the Margin of Appreciation," in *Russia and European Human-Rights Law: The Rise of the Civlizational Argument*, ed. Lauri Mälksoo (Leiden: Brill, 2014) at 222; see also e.g. Pinto de Albuquerque, "Plaidoyer for the European Court of Human Rights" at 126-128.

and economic relations between Russia and the West",[1484] so that the ECtHR's own jurisprudence in any case can only form part of a bigger picture.[1485] Nonetheless, it is easy to identify a number of areas in which the ECtHR's stance has led to particular opposition: they span from discrimination based on sex in the Russian army,[1486] over the right of prisoners to vote (in conflict with an explicit provision in the Russian constitution),[1487] to gay rights with regard to freedom of assembly and expression,[1488] as well as a number of other controversial judgments.[1489] As in the case of the United Kingdom, it seems unlikely that the criticism of these highly politicised cases would abate because of the ECtHR's position in other cases, rendering it difficult to imagine how the use of European consensus over time would generate sufficient diffuse support to overcome the lack of specific support in these cases.

A formalised critical stance on the ECtHR in juridical terms has since been provided by the Russian Constitutional Court in a judgment which emphasised the primacy of the Russian Constitution and derived therefrom a right not to implement judgments of the ECtHR insofar as they are in conflict with it.[1490] This was swiftly followed by the passing of a law for-

---

1484 Lauri Mälksoo, "Russia's Constitutional Court Defies the European Court of Human Rights," (2016) 12 *European Constitutional Law Review* 377.

1485 This kind of political backdrop may be what Dzehtsiarou has in mind when he mentions challenges to the ECtHR which "are linked to profound disagreement with the European project and cannot be changed by any means" – at least not by European consensus; Dzehtsiarou, *European Consensus and the Legitimacy of the European Court of Human Rights*, at 147-148.

1486 ECtHR (GC), Appl. No. 30078/06 – *Konstantin Markin*.

1487 ECtHR, Appl. Nos. 11157/04 and 15162/05 – *Anchugov and Gladkov*.

1488 ECtHR, Appl. Nos. 4916/07, 25924/08 and 14599/09 – *Alekseyev v. Russia*, Judgment of 21 October 2010; ECtHR, Appl. Nos. 67667/09 et al. – *Bayev and Others*; see also, on broadly similar themes with different respondent States, e.g. ECtHR, Appl. No. 1543/06 – *Bączkowski and Others v. Poland*, Judgment of 3 May 2007; ECtHR, Appl. No. 1813/07 – *Vejdeland and Others v. Sweden*, Judgment of 9 February 2012; ECtHR, Appl. No. 9106/06 – *Genderdoc-M v. Moldova*, Judgment of 12 June 2012; ECtHR, Appl. No. 20981/10 – *Mladina D.D. Ljubljana v. Slovenia*, Judgment of 17 April 2014; ECtHR, Appl. No. 73235/12 – *Identoba and Others v. Georgia*, Judgment of 12 May 2015.

1489 E.g.: ECtHR (GC), Appl. No. 36376/04 – *Kononov v. Latvia*, Judgment of 17 May 2010 (indirectly dealing with war crimes of a Soviet partisan); ECtHR, Appl. No. 14902/04 – *OAO Neftyanaya Kompaniya Yukos v. Russia (Just Satisfaction)*, Judgment of 31 July 2014 (compensation of almost two billion euros in a highly politicised case).

1490 Constitutional Court of the Russian Federation, Judgment No. 21-P of 14 July 2015.

mally establishing a procedure to obtain the Constitutional Court's judgment in this regard,[1491] a procedure which has since been used to declare the implementation of *Anchugov and Gladkov v. Russia* as well as *Yukos v. Russia* unconstitutional.[1492] The effect of judicialising opposition to the ECtHR by basing it on a review of constitutionality by the Constitutional Court is quite interesting for present purposes. It need not depoliticise the issue – to the contrary, the Constitutional Court's Chairman, Valery Zorkin, is one of the most vocal critics of the ECtHR – but it leads to each controversial case being considered *individually* and, at least formally, on the basis of its legal merits.

In other words, where the conceptual framework of consensus as the basis for incremental development of the ECtHR's case-law depends on generating diffuse support by obtaining specific support for *a number of judgments over time*, the Constitutional Court's perspective formally considers *only one case at a time* and thus operates in a rather different framework. Again, this points to a form of non-implementation which European consensus seems unsuited to mitigate since its aggregate-type approach puts it on a different level. Of course, the primacy of a national constitution over international obligations of the State, in and of itself, is hardly unusual (in fact, the Russian Constitutional Court builds on similar, albeit less far-reaching judgments in other States parties), and if sufficient diffuse support for the ECtHR had been generated in Russia, then some form of adjustment to accommodate obligations under the ECHR would no doubt have been possible. The issue must, therefore, be read against the backdrop of the more generally critical Russian position as mentioned above. It exemplifies how general political opposition and formal legal responses can work together in the context of non-implementation in way that European consensus is ill equipped to counter.

1491 "On amendments to the Federal Constitutional Law 'On the Constitutional Court of the Russian Federation'", Law No. 7-FKZ of 14 December 2015.

1492 For an overview, see Rachel M. Fleig-Goldstein, "The Russian Constitutional Court versus the European Court of Human Rights: How the Strasbourg Court Should Respond to Russia's Refusal to Execute ECtHR Judgments," (2017) 56 *Columbia Journal of Transnational Law* 172 at 207; for a somewhat different perspective, see Bill Bowring, "Russia and the European Convention (or Court) of Human Rights: The End?," (2020) *Revue québécoise de droit international* 201 (and see also ibid. at 217-218 for further constitutional amendments pertaining to the enforceability of decisions made by international institutions in mid-2020).

In sum, the core characteristics of European consensus make it difficult to relate its use to the mitigation of some of those forms of strong opposition which are commonly cited as the basis for the ECtHR's "legitimacy crisis" and hence motivated the turn to a strategic approach. Its focus on collectivity contrasts with the way in which certain issues become particularly controversial within individual political systems.[1493] The hope for the States parties' collective acquiescence to an incremental development of the ECtHR's case-law *over time* likewise contrasts with the politicisation of certain substantive issues (or, to put it in more explicitly temporal terms: the "short time horizons" of many political actors which lead to a focus on "the material or political impact of legal decisions"[1494]) as well as, potentially, the individual consideration of certain issues by national constitutional courts. Finally, the politically and emotionally charged responses to the ECtHR's rulings on certain issues cannot be accounted for within the relatively formal purview of European consensus: the assumed rationality of "counting"[1495] pales in the face of political rhetoric.

I would emphasise again that my point here is not to claim that a strategy based on European consensus *should have* prevented the examples of criticism given above or that it *cannot at all* contribute to enhancing the ECtHR's sociological legitimacy, but merely to suggest that, conceptually, a strategic account based on consensus must acknowledge the limitations which follow from its focus on collectivity, its aggregate-type approach with long-term temporal horizons, and its relative formality. These limitations are somewhat obscured by presenting European consensus as a response to the ECtHR's (ostensible) "legitimacy crisis", the depiction of which builds, in turn, on forms of high-profile opposition to the ECtHR which *European consensus is not necessarily well-suited to mitigate*. Incrementalism based on consensus may ensure that the ECtHR "moves as Europe

---

1493 Accordingly, Andreas Føllesdal criticises reliance of European consensus in the context of legitimacy-enhancement because "the most important target constituency in the short term is the violating government and the population in that state": Føllesdal, "A Better Signpost, Not a Better Walking Stick: How to Evaluate the European Consensus Doctrine" at 200.

1494 Karen J. Alter, *Establishing the Supremacy of European Law. The Making of an International Rule of Law in Europe* (Oxford: Oxford University Press, 2001), at 186.

1495 Dzehtsiarou, *European Consensus and the Legitimacy of the European Court of Human Rights*, at 175.

moves",[1496] but keeping pace with European developments is hardly the primary concern of most critics of the Court.[1497]

One might argue that the kind of worst-case scenarios which are commonly cited as potential consequences of the "legitimacy crisis" – withdrawal of funding, reforms of the ECtHR curtailing its competences, or even dismantling the Convention system entirely[1498] – are more liable to be prevented by the use of European consensus since they rely on forms of *collective* rather than *individual* action by the States parties.[1499] In that vein, Sandholtz has argued that a strategy of majoritarian activism (such as a strategic account of European consensus as the basis for incremental development of the ECtHR's case-law) "protects the court from *generalized* backlash because a majority of the states would support the court's interpretation".[1500] One might certainly argue that mitigating "generalized backlash" is a worthy goal, and one need only point to the controversies surrounding the Brighton reform process and the recent Copenhagen Declaration to substantiate that collective action by the States parties could have restrictive effects for the ECtHR.[1501]

Still, these processes *also* exemplify that the reaction of individual States to certain politicised issues, as well as their general scepticism towards ex-

---

1496 Ryan, "Europe's Moral Margin: Parental Aspirations and the European Court of Human Rights" at 497.

1497 For example, Ryan argues that consensus is pragmatically helpful to appease the States parties since it refers to "the very terms established *collectively* by the Member States" (ibid., 494; emphasis added), yet herself repeatedly cites *nationalism* as a major factor propelling backlash against the Court (ibid., 472-473, 490 and 522); see also on this tension Douglas-Scott, "Borges' *Pierre Menard, Author of the Quixote* and the Idea of a European Consensus" at 167; see further on consensus not (only) in the sense of vertically comparative law, but (also) in the sense of general political will towards "the idea of the European human rights supervision project" Bates, "Consensus in the Legitimacy-Building Era of the European Court of Human Rights" at 42. Of course, the ECtHR only has limited influence over such factors (see supra, note 1485), but the fact remains that other kinds of strategy could (for better or worse) respond to them more fully.

1498 See supra, II.3.

1499 For the distinction, see Madsen, Cebulak, and Wiebusch, "Backlash Against International Courts: Explaining the Forms and Patterns of Resistance to International Courts" at 204.

1500 Sandholtz, "Expanding Rights: Norm Innovation in the European and Inter-American Courts" at 159.

1501 For an overview, see Madsen, "Rebalancing European Human Rights: Has the Brighton Declaration Engendered a New Deal on Human Rights in Europe?" at 204; see also Chapter 1, IV.4.

ternal scrutiny by the ECtHR, cannot be discounted even within the context of collective action by the States parties: it is arguably because of this that the most restrictive proposals were put forward by certain States.[1502] One particularly transparent example is the Danish Draft Copenhagen Declaration, which bluntly stated that, in "cases related to asylum and immigration", the ECtHR should "assess and take full account of the effectiveness of domestic procedures and, where these procedures are seen to operate fairly and with respect for human rights, avoid intervening except in the most exceptional circumstances".[1503] Since the ECtHR's case-law on asylum and immigration is known to have caused significant concern in Denmark (and, for that matter, in some other States parties to the ECHR),[1504] this speaks volumes as to (part of) the overall motivation for drafting the Copenhagen Declaration in a manner unfavourable to the ECtHR.

1502 See e.g. Laurence R. Helfer, "The Burdens and Benefits of Brighton," ESIL Reflections Vol. 1, issue 1 (2012), available at <http://esil-sedi.eu/node/138>, at 1 (on *Hirst* and the political atmosphere in the United Kingdom as a backdrop to the Brighton Conference).

1503 Draft Copenhagen Declaration, para. 26; see critically on this point e.g. the Joint NGO Response to the Draft Copenhagen Declaration of 13 February 2018 at 6-7, available at <http://www.omct.org/files/2018/02/24721/joint_ngo_response_to_the_copenhagen_declaration___13_february_2018.pdf>: "This paragraph [...] seeks, without justification, to single out asylum and immigration cases as meriting a lesser and inadequate standard of review by the Court"; even the ECtHR's very diplomatic and measured response to the Draft Declaration contained the telling caveat "Insofar as it is appropriate to single out one particular aspect of the Court's case-law" before commenting on this point: Opinion on the draft Copenhagen Declaration, adopted by the Bureau in light of the discussion in the Plenary Court on 19 February 2018, available at <https://www.echr.coe.int/Documents/Opinion_draft_Declaration_Copenhague%20ENG.pdf>.

1504 For Denmark, see Jacques Hartmann, "A Danish Crusade for the Reform of the European Court of Human Rights," available at <https://www.ejiltalk.org/a-danish-crusade-for-the-reform-of-the-european-court-of-human-rights/>; Silvia Adamo, "Protecting International Civil Rights in a National Context: Danish Law and Its Discontents," (2016) 85 *Nordic Journal of International Law* 119 at 139 and 142; for some other examples, see e.g. the United Kingdom, supra, notes 1472-1473; as well as, infamously, Nicolas Bratza, "The Relationship between the UK Courts and Strasbourg," (2011) *European Human Rights Law Review* 505 at 505 (on "xenophobic" opposition to the ECtHR); or the Netherlands: Oomen, "A Serious Case of Strasbourg-Bashing? An Evaluation of the Debates on the Legitimacy of the European Court of Human Rights in the Netherlands", throughout but especially at 418.

Of course, after an outpouring of protest from various quarters including academia and non-governmental organisations,[1505] the form in which the Copenhagen Declaration was finally adopted dropped not only the express reference to "cases related to asylum and immigration", but also many other restrictive formulations.[1506] One might read this as a confirmation of European consensus as legitimacy-enhancement, since there seems to have been sufficient diffuse support for the ECtHR from a sufficient number of States parties to mitigate generalised backlash. There may be some truth to this, although I would suggest that the process leading up to the Copenhagen Declaration also points towards the importance of *counter-resistance*,[1507] as well as the relevance of manifold actors other than the States parties who are side-lined in accounts of consensus as legitimacy-enhancement.[1508] In the end, Merris Amos's assessment stands as true as ever: the connection between European consensus and the ECtHR's legitimacy remains rather nebulous.[1509]

IV. Interim Reflections: Abstract Strategizing

In this chapter, I have aimed to elaborate upon and critically assess the popular argument that European consensus should be used by the ECtHR so as to enhance its legitimacy. I have argued that the kind of legitimacy at play here is sociological rather than normative – the point is to increase actual support for the ECtHR, not to justify its role by reference to normative standards – but that the notion of European consensus as legitimacy-enhancement does not retain the empirical perspective which this implies.

1505 E.g. Joint NGO Response to the Draft Copenhagen (supra, note 1503); Response by the Danish Helsinki-Committee of Human Rights of 16 February 2018, available at <http://helsinkicommittee.dk/6957-2/>; for academic criticism, see e.g. the blog posts on StrasbourgObservers, available at <https://strasbourgobservers.com/category/by-topic/copenhagen-declaration/>, or on EJIL:Talk!, available at <https://www.ejiltalk.org/?s=copenhagen+declaration>.

1506 Janneke Gerards and Sarah Lambrecht, "The Final Copenhagen Declaration: Fundamentally Improved With a Few Remaining Caveats," available at <https://strasbourgobservers.com/2018/04/18/the-final-copenhagen-declaration-fundamentally-improved-with-a-few-remaining-caveats/>.

1507 See generally Madsen, Cebulak, and Wiebusch, "Backlash Against International Courts: Explaining the Forms and Patterns of Resistance to International Courts" at 205-206 and 217.

1508 Supra, note 1399.

1509 Supra, note 1450.

Instead, it invests the initially sociological approach with normativity: the ECtHR's sociological legitimacy *should* be nourished to mitigate its presumed "legitimacy crisis". Allen Buchanan's description of the connection between sociological legitimacy and normativity more generally sums up the dynamic quite succinctly: "Sociological legitimacy is [considered to be] normatively important, to the extent that an institution's ability to perform its functions depends on whether it is perceived to have authority or warrant respect".[1510]

The primary agents of legitimacy are assumed to be the States parties to the ECHR, since it is they who are seen as having the power to affect the Court's interests. To retain or regain their support for the ECtHR is therefore seen as crucial so as to allow it to incrementally but effectively set human rights standards in the long term (the ECtHR's main "function", if we apply Buchanan's phrasing). This motivation explains, in turn, why the object of legitimacy shifts from individual judgments of the ECtHR to encompass also the ECtHR itself as an institution. European consensus is said to assist in nourishing the ECtHR's sociological legitimacy vis-à-vis the States parties: because it refers back to their legal orders and thus provides "evidence" of their take on a certain issue, it is assumed to promote decisions which are, by and large, acceptable to them.

I have argued that the use of European consensus in order to nourish the ECtHR's legitimacy is *strategic*: it operationalises the case before the Court in the service of assumed future chances to set higher human rights standards. I have also, however, pointed out some limitations of a strategic approach based on European consensus. While there may be an intuitive connection between the position taken by the legal orders of the States parties and their support for similar positions taken by the ECtHR, there is arguably a disconnect between European consensus (referring to legal orders and focussing only on the collective of the States parties with a long-term outlook) and the way in which support for or criticism of the ECtHR is actually generated (in a more political and emotionally charged forum, geared towards substantive issues on the basis of a short time horizon, as well as within individual States rather than a European collective).

Against this backdrop, one might simply discount European consensus as an inadequate reference point for a strategic approach to adjudication. While this is correct on some level, I would argue that there is more to it. The characteristics of European consensus which have guided my conceptual exploration in this chapter – its relatively formal, collectivity-oriented

1510 Buchanan, *The Heart of Human Rights*, at 112.

and aggregate-type approach – share a common feature: they all point *away from strategic considerations that are specific to any given case*. In light of this, it seems that consensus as legitimacy-enhancement constitutes what one might call a form of *abstract strategizing*: it is driven by strategic concerns, but because the way in which these are operationalised do not take into account of the specifics of individual cases, it is *less starkly strategic* than some other approaches.[1511] Instead, my impression is that it operates as a kind of barely tangible background strategy – an impression which resonates with the difficulties encountered in attempting to specify more precisely *how* the use of consensus enhances the ECtHR's legitimacy.

On the basis of a resolutely strategic approach, this kind of abstract strategizing is bound to appear deficient. But larger questions need to be considered. Should strategy be the starting point of a human rights court in the first place? How do strategic considerations relate to the more principled arguments discussed over the course of the preceding chapters? From a more normatively probing perspective, reliance on incremental development based on European consensus might have significant advantages over other forms of strategy. For example, its focus on collectivity makes it less likely to privilege certain powerful (or "high-reputation") States than more individualised forms of strategy would, hence retaining a more principled stance in the face of the divided preferences of its audience.[1512] Because of its relative formality, European consensus is also less liable to allow the ECtHR's more principled stances to be watered down by deliberate threats of non-compliance or restrictive reform.[1513]

Yet, simultaneously, consensus as legitimacy-enhancement does remain a strategic approach itself, however abstract. Like other strategic approaches, it therefore has to face up to the difficult questions which follow from the inclusion of strategic considerations in the jurisprudence of a human rights court. Branding the strategic approach to consensus as "legitimacy-enhancement" makes these questions seem less pressing, but the potential conflicts between principled and strategic approaches to consensus must nonetheless be addressed. This is the task of the next chapter.

1511 Although the specifics of individual cases may reemerge in deciding how to apply consensus: see Chapter 10, III.1.

1512 See Dothan, "How International Courts Enhance Their Legitimacy" at 461.

1513 See generally Mann, "Non-ideal Theory of Constitutional Adjudication" at 42 on the "problem of reflectivity".

Chapter 10: Of Conflation and Normalisation: European Consensus between Strategy and Principle

I. Introduction

If different rationales undergird the use of consensus, then it becomes important to discuss how they relate to one another. In this chapter, I would like to approach this task by bringing together several different strands of argument commonly adduced in defence of European consensus. In particular, if the use of consensus is commonly justified on grounds of legitimacy enhancement which, as I argued in the preceding chapter, constitutes a form of strategic justification, then the question arises how this form of justification relates to its defence on democratic grounds as explored in earlier chapters.

This question has mostly been side-lined in debates on European consensus, and understandably so: it is a difficult question to grapple with because it is difficult to disentangle different rationales for the use of consensus. First, given the indeterminacy of human rights law, the counter-position to strategy can seem fleeting and intangible; accordingly, I will simply denote this position as "principle" so as to capture a position against which to evaluate the use of strategy while retaining the open-endedness of that position.[1514] Second, strategy itself depends on a multitude of both normative and empirical assessments and ultimately presents a bouquet of possible approaches no less diverse than assessments of principle. Strategic approaches to European consensus also prove elusive: I argued in the preceding chapter that conceptualising consensus as a stepping stone for the incremental development of the ECtHR's case-law constitutes a form of abstract strategizing – but that abstractness does not resolve questions as to how consensus should be applied in specific cases.[1515]

Finally, disentangling different rationales for the use of consensus must face the difficulty that these rationales are *not always made explicit*. This holds true, in particular, for the use of consensus by the ECtHR itself: the

1514 See further Chapter 1, IV.4.
1515 See infra, III.1.

Court "eschews abstract theorising"[1516] and seldom offers meta-justifications for the kind of reasoning it applies within its processes of justification;[1517] and on the rare occasion that it does so, it does not make explicit reference to *strategic* considerations. I therefore refer primarily to academic accounts of consensus, which do distinguish between principled and strategic rationales for its use although they rarely deal with the possible tensions between them. The picture I will paint aims to take into account the overall impression which results from this state of affairs: the conceptualisation of consensus as a fulcrum of both strategy and principle without sufficient attention to the implications of this conflation.[1518]

To introduce the interplay between strategy and principle, I begin by setting out what I call the "dilemma of strategic concessions" as part of non-ideal theory (II.). My aim in this section is twofold. First, to show that strategy is not in and of itself problematic, but rather a helpful perspective which focusses on the realisation of human rights in social life instead of autarkic judicial pronouncements. Second, that strategic concessions nonetheless come at a high cost since the deviation from principle implies that justice is subordinated to power. It is precisely because of this cost that the dilemma of strategic concessions needs to be faced head-on, rather than obscured by conflating strategy and principle, as it currently is in the context of European consensus – or so I will argue.

To tease out the implications of this conflation, I first discuss various perspectives on consensus in both ideal and non-ideal theory to underline that different rationales for the use of consensus need not always be in sync. It matters, in other words, *for which reasons* the use of consensus is supported or on which grounds it is justified (III.1.); I then show how the conflation of strategy and principle is celebrated because it is assumed to create an impression of objectivity – for example by setting consensus in relation to formal sources of international law – and discuss possible disadvantages to this approach such as the dilution of principled standards when indistinguishable from strategy (III.2.); and I argue, finally, that conflating strategy and principle within the fulcrum of European consensus contributes to a normalisation of strategy which makes the use of consen-

1516 Mowbray, "The Creativity of the European Court of Human Rights" at 61.

1517 See Chapter 1, IV.1.

1518 See also Or Bassok, "The European Consensus Doctrine and the ECtHR Quest for Public Confidence," in *Building Consensus on European Consensus. Judicial Interpretation of Human Rights in Europe and Beyond*, ed. Panos Kapotas and Vassilis Tzevelekos (Cambridge: Cambridge University Press, 2019) at 252.

sus more difficult to challenge, hence impeding contestation on principled terms (III.3.). I conclude with some reflections on the role of the ECtHR vis-à-vis the States parties to the ECHR, and on how certain images of its role might influence its desire to stay in strategic proximity to the States parties by means of European consensus (IV.).

II. Non-Ideal Theory: The Dilemma of Strategic Concessions

One way of approaching the dilemma of strategic concessions is through the lens of so-called "non-ideal theory" (although, as I mentioned in Chapter 1, strategy forms only one prong of non-ideal theory).[1519] Vast swaths of political morality and constitutional theory are concerned with ideal theory which, as Rawls put it, deals with "the principles of justice that would regulate a well-ordered society" in which everyone "is presumed to act justly and to do his part in upholding just institutions".[1520] These presumptions, as Rawls admits, are clearly "highly idealized".[1521] Non-ideal theory loosens them and, accordingly, concerns "how we are to deal with injustice" of the kind "that we are faced with in everyday life" rather than an idealised, "well-ordered" society.[1522]

The Rawlsian framework seems helpful to me in approaching the dilemma of strategic concessions in the context of consensus as legitimacy-enhancement, for his approach to non-ideal theory is inextricably connected to "questions of transition".[1523] With the goal of ideal theory in mind, non-ideal theory "asks how this long-term goal might be achieved, or worked toward, usually in gradual steps", thus seeking transitional "policies and courses of action that are morally permissible and politically possible as well as likely to be effective".[1524] This resonates with the aim which I ascribed to the strategic approach to consensus in the preceding chapter: if we assume it to maintain a benevolent aim that goes beyond the mere accumulation of institutional power, then its goal is to enhance the sociological legitimacy of the ECtHR *so that it may set higher human rights standards*

1519 See Chapter 1, IV.4.

1520 Rawls, *A Theory of Justice*, at 8.

1521 Rawls, *Political Liberalism*, at 35; see further Marcus Arvan, "First Steps Toward a Nonideal Theory of Justice," (2014) 7 *Ethics & Global Politics* 95 at 98-99.

1522 Rawls, *A Theory of Justice*, at 8.

1523 Rawls, *The Law of Peoples*, at 90; strongly emphasised by Simmons, "Ideal and Nonideal Theory" at 20-23.

1524 Rawls, *The Law of Peoples*, at 89.

in the long run.[1525] We could frame this as an instance of working towards ideal theory by means of non-ideal theory.

Roni Mann has recently elaborated on this way of approaching the issue by building on Rawls to develop a *non-ideal theory of constitutional adjudication.*[1526] In line with the general approach on non-ideal theory, she presents the problem at issue as a conflict between the demands of ideal theory and non-ideal circumstances:

> The dilemma of institutionally-hard cases arises [...] where there is a significant tension or conflict between what the court would hold to be right *constitutionally* (in ideal circumstances) and what seems wise or prudent *institutionally*, given the actually existing non-ideal circumstances.[1527]

Part of Mann's argument is that we need to acknowledge that such cases *do present a dilemma*[1528] – in other words, neither pure principle nor pure strategy would provide a satisfactory answer across the board.

Framing this dilemma in reconciliatory terms, one might emphasise that strategy and principle require one another in order to function in a meaningful way. First, strategy needs principle. Indeed, on the Rawlsian approach, its transitional character means that non-ideal theory is inherently oriented towards ideal theory: "For until the ideal is identified [...] nonideal theory lacks an objective, an aim, by reference to which its queries can be answered".[1529] Values cannot be meaningfully realised unless we have a stance on what those values are.[1530] Yet the very notion of realisation also points principle towards strategy. As I mentioned above, Rawls himself admits that ideal theory is "highly idealized"[1531] – and accordingly, a court that approaches its task of interpretation without any awareness of the non-ideal circumstances surrounding it whatsoever risks making grand pronouncements at the cost of their effectiveness in prac-

---

1525 See Chapter 9, II.5.

1526 Mann, "Non-ideal Theory of Constitutional Adjudication", on Rawls at 38.

1527 Ibid., 16 (emphasis in original).

1528 See ibid., 21.

1529 Rawls, *The Law of Peoples*, at 90; see also Rawls, *A Theory of Justice*, at 8, 215-218 and 343; Rawls, *Political Liberalism*, at 285; Simmons, "Ideal and Nonideal Theory" at 34.

1530 This does not, I think, imply any particular grounding for those values, i.e. the distinction holds even if we accept the indeterminacy critique and do not see them as somehow already contained "in" law; see supra, I.

1531 Supra, note 1521.

tice.[1532] It seems more desirable, following Mann, to require courts to be concerned with both the "pronouncement of ideal constitutional values, and with the meaningful and sustainable *realisation* of these values in actual social and political life".[1533]

The need for some kind of strategy can be found, though often more latent than explicit, in many accounts of international adjudication. As at the national level,[1534] many commentators make primarily descriptive claims (i.e., courts *do* act strategically) rather than normative claims (i.e., courts *should* act strategically).[1535] Yet the prior tends to imply the latter by virtue of a certain sense of necessity, as when Shai Dothan claims that "[c]ourts that do not learn to act strategically will lose relevance or cease to function, leaving in operation only good strategists".[1536] From that perspective – similar to the talk of a "legitimacy crisis" of the ECtHR[1537] – any approach that leaves aside strategic considerations seems undesirable as it would, sooner or later, lead to States parties categorically refusing to comply with the ECtHR's judgments, withdrawing from the Convention system, or dismantling it entirely.[1538] In a colourful phrase of Frédéric

---

1532 Accordingly, the notions of (sociological) legitimacy and effectiveness are often linked in accounts of European consensus: see e.g. Helfer and Slaughter, "Toward a Theory of Effective Supranational Adjudication" at e.g. 290 and 316, read together; Dahlberg, "'The Lack of Such a Common Approach' - Comparative Argumentation by the European Court of Human Rights" at 82; Dzehtsiarou, *European Consensus and the Legitimacy of the European Court of Human Rights*, at 118; Krisch, *Beyond Constitutionalism: The Pluralist Structure of Postnational Law*, at 140-141; see generally Helfer and Alter, "Legitimacy and Lawmaking: A Tale of Three International Courts" at 483.

1533 Mann, "Non-ideal Theory of Constitutional Adjudication" at 38 (emphasis in original).

1534 For an overview, see Lee Epstein and Jack Knight, "Toward a Strategic Revolution in Judicial Politics: A Look Back, A Look Ahead," (2000) 53 *Political Research Quarterly* 625.

1535 E.g. Dothan, "How International Courts Enhance Their Legitimacy" at 456 ("International courts try to enhance their legitimacy and behave strategically to pursue this goal"); see also Lupu, "International Judicial Legitimacy: Lessons from National Courts" at 448-449.

1536 Dothan, "Judicial Tactics in the European Court of Human Rights" at 124 (in footnote 22).

1537 See Chapter 9, II.2. and infra, III.3.

1538 Of course, the less one is invested in the ECtHR as a helpful institution, the less this would seem bothersome. For present purposes, I assume that the ECtHR is worth retaining, and focus more on how this might be achieved in light of opposition and, crucially, *at what cost*; for some thoughts on how to decenter the ECtHR, see Chapter 11.

Mégret's, it would resemble an "unyielding deontological line" with "the morbid, cultish feel of an absolutist's death wish".[1539]

Even if such extreme images are avoided, there is an awareness that practical relevance matters more than mere pronouncements. Françoise Tulkens has (extra-judicially) made this point most emphatically:

> To have any meaning in the lives of individuals and communities, [human rights] *must be embedded in practice*. A judgment of the European Court of Human Rights is not an end in itself, but a promise of future change, the starting-point of a process which should enable rights and freedoms to be made effective.[1540]

In other words, the ECtHR's judgments, like those of national constitutional courts, are proclaimed with the aim of *being realised*,[1541] thus potentially bringing strategy – including strategic concessions – into the equation to grapple with the question of how that goal can best be achieved.

Despite these convergences, it is clear that strategy and principle may also point in different directions in the non-ideal circumstances in which we often find ourselves, and in that sense be fundamentally irreconcilable – hence Mann's insistence on acknowledging the dilemma involved in institutionally-hard cases, and the admission that such cases are likely to involve a "'dirty hands' situation" when strategic concessions are at issue.[1542] It might well be argued that prioritising strategy in the context of human rights adjudication constitutes what Habermas has called a the subtle redefinition of a moral or ethical question as strategic.[1543] In other words: by focussing on the goal of upholding support for the ECtHR, the individual case – and the individual applicant – at issue are side-lined. One hesitates

1539 Mégret, "The Apology of Utopia" at 478 (on lack of ascending argument in human rights law and the risk that it will not "be taken very seriously by states"); the notion of deontological suicide is also used by Mann, "Non-ideal Theory of Constitutional Adjudication" at 24 and 48.

1540 Françoise Tulkens, "Execution and Effects of the Judgments of the European Court of Human Rights. The Role of the Judiciary" (Dialogue between judges, European Court of Human Rights, 2006), at 9-10 (emphasis in original).

1541 On realisation of rights in the (Inter-American) regional context, see e.g. Neuman, "Import, Export, and Regional Consent in the Inter-American Court of Human Rights" at 115; on the link between legitimacy and realisation, see critically Koskenniemi, "Legitimacy, Rights and Ideology: Notes Towards a Critique of the New Moral Internationalism" at 369-370.

1542 Mann, "Non-ideal Theory of Constitutional Adjudication" at 37.

1543 Habermas, *Between Facts and Norms*, at 177; see also Dworkin, "Liberty and Moralism" at 305.

to wield the heavy cudgel of Kant,[1544] yet there is a sense in which the applicant is objectified as merely a means to further the ECtHR as an institution, rather than taking seriously the potential human rights violation that is being asserted. As Koskenniemi has put it discussing the "political moralist" disparaged by Kant, it will always be possible to "find a strategic consideration to justify putting other people into harm's way".[1545]

Accordingly, it is acknowledged even by those approaching the ECtHR (or other regional or international courts) from a strategic angle that strategy should not always carry the day. Fiona de Londras and Kanstantsin Dzehtsiarou, although strongly focussed on the need for strategic awareness, admit that it leads to the ECtHR becoming "susceptible to being captured by states' interests", and to the "possible negative implications" that follow from this.[1546] Helen Fenwick has made the dilemma in what Roni Mann would deem institutionally-hard cases particularly clear. Describing the ECtHR's exclusion of same-gender couples from the right to marry, she argues that "its reliance on one version of consensus analysis to take that stance is defensible" since "a degree of self-restraint based partly on such analysis allows the Court to maintain its legitimacy in positivist terms", i.e. to maintain its sociological legitimacy as part of a strategic approach.[1547] But while "defensible", such a strategy comes at a cost: "in taking this stance the Court is opposing a number of core Convention values", i.e. principled considerations such as non-discrimination.[1548] The core tension – in Fenwick's terms, the "struggle to maintain a balance"[1549] – between strategy and principle thus persists.

1544 E.g. Immanuel Kant, "Grundlegung zur Metaphysik der Sitten," in *Die Kritiken* (Frankfurt a.M.: Zweitausendeins, 2008) at 677.

1545 Koskenniemi, "Constitutionalism as Mindset" at 30; for a similar point with regard to the International Court of Justice, see Nollkaemper, "International Adjudication of Global Public Goods: The Intersection of Substance and Procedure" at 783.

1546 De Londras and Dzehtsiarou, "Managing Judicial Innovation in the European Court of Human Rights" at 544 and 547.

1547 Fenwick, "Same-sex Unions at the Strasbourg Court in a Divided Europe: Driving Forward Reform or Protecting the Court's Authority via Consensus Analysis?" at 271.

1548 Ibid.

1549 Ibid.; see also Hamilton, "Same-Sex Marriage, Consensus, Certainty and the European Court of Human Rights" at 36, arguing that there "needs to be a compromise between the competing interests at stake" (i.e. setting principled standards and retaining sociological legitimacy); Lau, "Rewriting Schalk and Kopf: Shifting the Locus of Deference" at 257-258, juxtaposing "normative

In sum, taking note of strategic concerns in one sense provides a helpful departure from a purely principled stance which would focus only on the judgment at issue without any awareness of how power operates in the environs of a court; but on the other hand, taking a strategic approach carries the very real danger of giving too much normative force to such power within the court's reasoning, and hence leaving too little room to question it. As Gilabert and Lawford-Smith have put it with regard to the incorporation of certain feasibility constraints into political theory:

> [I]ncluding them risks a cynical realism capitulating to injustices that could be superseded. But [...] not including them leads to impotent idealism seeking desirable but extremely improbable outcomes, or to irresponsible risk taking that is likely to involve great costs in the face of dim prospects for major gains.[1550]

This is what I take to constitute the dilemma of strategic concessions. The subsequent section will explore how it plays out in the context of European consensus.

III. European Consensus as a Conflation of Strategy and Principle

1. Different Perspectives on Consensus within Non-Ideal Theory

The justification of consensus on strategic grounds which I explored in Chapter 9 adopts long-term support for human rights protection by the ECtHR as its goal, and regards the incremental development of the ECtHR's case-law based on European consensus as the appropriate path towards that goal. Use of European consensus is thus conceptualised as a "pragmatic"[1551] or "expedient tool"[1552] to ensure that the ECtHR does not incur the wrath of the States parties and thus retains sufficient sociological legitimacy to uphold human rights in the future. The emphasis on this

---

problems" with the ECtHR's "institutional constraints" and seeking to "balance" them.

1550 Gilabert and Lawford-Smith, "Political Feasibility: A Conceptual Exploration" at 815.

1551 Macdonald, "The Margin of Appreciation" at 123; see also Lau, "Rewriting Schalk and Kopf: Shifting the Locus of Deference" at 253; Ryan, "Europe's Moral Margin: Parental Aspirations and the European Court of Human Rights" at 471.

1552 Yourow, *The Margin of Appreciation Doctrine*, at 195.

strategic aspect explains, perhaps, why European consensus is sometimes seen less as a way of legally justifying a certain concrete norm and more as an "extra-legal" argument.[1553] The interesting twist to this kind of admission is that consensus is clearly *also* considered a legal argument.[1554] This bifurcation is possible because the gist of the matter lies not so much in the form of vertically comparative reasoning itself but in the rationale for its use:[1555] insofar as that rationale is strategic, it may be considered "extra-legal"; but because European consensus can also be defended on principled terms which are understood as "legal", it becomes the fulcrum in which strategy and principle meet. This section is dedicated to disentangling the various different perspectives on consensus which result from this amalgamation.

I would begin by emphasising that the different rationales for supporting or opposing the use of consensus *can be distinguished*. It may seem, at first, that there is significant overlap between support of or opposition to the use of consensus, no matter for which reason. Both ideal and non-ideal theory build on and construct certain images of the judicial role,[1556] and these may resonate with one another in different ways in practice. For example, the morality-focussed perspective tends to be critical of the States parties in an effort to protect the prepolitical rights of intra-State minorities; and this vision of the ECtHR as deliberately counter-majoritarian makes it seem problematic if the States parties' positions are taken into ac-

1553 Burstein, "The Will to Enforce: An Examination of the Political Constraints upon a Regional Court of Human Rights" at 439; Petkova, "The Notion of Consensus as a Route to Democratic Adjudication" at 675; see also de Londras and Dzehtsiarou, "Managing Judicial Innovation in the European Court of Human Rights" at 524.

1554 Explicitly Dzehtsiarou, "What Is Law for the European Court of Human Rights?"; see also Nussberger, *The European Court of Human Rights*, at 84 ("European consensus as a legal term").

1555 See Chapter 1, IV.2.

1556 For ideal theory, this is most immediately evident; for the ECtHR, see with particular clarity Bates, "Activism and Self-Restraint: The Margin of Appreciation's Strasbourg Career… Its 'Coming of Age'?" at 275-276; Kleinlein, "Consensus and Contestability: The ECtHR and the Combined Potential of European Consensus and Procedural Rationality Control" at 881; for non-ideal theory, see Mann, "Non-ideal Theory of Constitutional Adjudication" at 43; see also the discussion of different judicial "characters" in Ezgi Yildiz, "A Court with Many Faces: Judicial Characters and Modes of Norm Development in the European Court of Human Rights," (2020) 31 *European Journal of International Law* 73; see further infra, IV.

count, whether for idealised democratic or non-ideal strategic reasons.[1557] Most often, proponents of the morality-focussed perspective therefore simply criticise the use of European consensus in and of itself, without any further specification along principled or strategic lines.[1558]

Conversely, many academic commentators support European consensus both for principled and for strategic reasons. Andrew Legg has summed up this approach most succinctly: on his conceptualisation of European consensus, it "furnishes [principled] substantive guidance about the content of moral norms, but also [strategically] addresses the legitimacy problems raised by interpretations of the Treaties that result in new moral guidelines for signatory states".[1559] Others have more or less explicitly taken a similarly conjunctive approach,[1560] often without further clarifying the relationship between the two different strands of argument. The underlying assumption seems to be that the fact of moral disagreement not only points towards ethical normativity as a matter of principle, but also makes it difficult for a (regional) court to retain its sociological legitimacy if it were to adopt the morality-focussed approach.[1561]

1557 See Kagiaros, "When to Use European Consensus: Assessing the Differential Treatment of Minority Groups by the European Court of Human Rights" at 288; Bassok, "The European Consensus Doctrine and the ECtHR Quest for Public Confidence" at 254; more generally Mann, "Non-ideal Theory of Constitutional Adjudication" at 23.

1558 Letsas and Benvenisti are among the few to make this dual opposition to consensus explicit: see Letsas, *A Theory of Interpretation of the European Convention on Human Rights*, arguing against the use of consensus on principled (at 121) and strategic (at 124-125) grounds; Benvenisti, "Margin of Appreciation, Consensus, and Universal Standards", arguing against the use of consensus on principled (at 847, via the margin of appreciation) and strategic (at 851-853) grounds, although he also acknowledges strategic use of the margin of appreciation (see note 1562).

1559 Legg, *The Margin of Appreciation*, at 115.

1560 E.g. Wildhaber, Hjartarson, and Donnelly, "No Consensus on Consensus?" at 251; Lock, "The Influence of EU Law on Strasbourg Doctrines" at 817-818; Hamilton, "Same-Sex Marriage, Consensus, Certainty and the European Court of Human Rights" at 35-36; McGoldrick, "A Defence of the Margin of Appreciation and an Argument for its Application by the Human Rights Committee" at 30-31 also combines "instrumental" and "normative" arguments, although it seems to me that, on his reading, the latter retain a strong strategic element.

1561 This seems to be Dzehtsiarou's main point: while he does not explicitly relate the respective chapters on principle and strategy in his monograph on European consensus to one another, the strategic criticism of the morality-focussed perspective shines through in both chapters; see in particular Dzehtsiarou,

Yet this kind of overlap between principle and strategy is by no means logically necessary. For example, it is possible to oppose the use of consensus on principled grounds such as those associated with the morality-focussed perspective, yet still support it on strategic grounds as necessary for an effective realisation of minority rights.[1562] Holning Lau has elaborated on this position at length in his rewriting of the ECtHR's judgment of *Schalk and Kopf v. Austria*.[1563] In terms of ideal theory, his argument paradigmatically reflects the concerns of the morality-focussed perspective. He argues that the national laws which form the basis of consensus may "often reflect flawed democratic deliberations" impaired by "entrenched stereotypes", and that the States parties are therefore "not particularly well positioned to determine whether sexual-orientation-based differentiation is justified".[1564] In principle, then, Lau is opposed to consensus. Yet he supports its use as a matter of non-ideal theory: for "pragmatic reasons", specifically to prevent "enforcement problems", he suggests that the ECtHR should require the States parties to only "implement legal standards that a critical mass of Contracting States has already adopted".[1565] The dilemma of strategic concessions is rendered explicit, on Lau's account, because he only "begrudgingly" accepts deference to the States parties in response to non-ideal conditions.[1566]

One might think that it makes little difference whether the use of consensus is supported for strategic or principled reasons: some commentators, like Lau, do only the prior; others, like Samantha Besson, do only the latter;[1567] and many others besides do both or do not distinguish clearly

---

European Consensus and the Legitimacy of the European Court of Human Rights, at 117-118 and 154; see also Wildhaber, Hjartarson, and Donnelly, "No Consensus on Consensus?" at 251; Legg, *The Margin of Appreciation*, at 115.

1562 As acknowledged by Benvenisti, "The Margin of Appreciation, Subsidiarity and Global Challenges to Democracy" at 252-253.

1563 On that case, see generally Chapter 1, II.

1564 Lau, "Rewriting Schalk and Kopf: Shifting the Locus of Deference" at 248-249.

1565 Ibid., 253-254.

1566 Ibid., 257; see also Fenwick and Fenwick, "Finding 'East'/'West' Divisions in Council of Europe States on Treatment of Sexual Minorities: The Response of the Strasbourg Court and the Role of Consensus Analysis" at 273, "unpalatably" concluding that consensus should not be abandoned.

1567 Besson, "Human Rights Adjudication as Transnational Adjudication: A Peripheral Case of Domestic Courts as International Law Adjudicators" at 63; see also Henrard, "How the ECtHR's Use of European Consensus Considerations Allows Legitimacy Concerns to Delimit Its Mandate" at 160-161, acknowledg-

between support of consensus for principled or strategic reasons.[1568] One reason why it does not seem necessary to distinguish between principled or strategic elements in justifications of European consensus might be that the strategic approach, as described in Chapter 9, constitutes what I there called a form of abstract strategizing:[1569] its focus on the incremental development of the ECtHR's case-law by reference to developing standards within the community of the States parties points away from the specifics of individual cases, thus making it seem more compatible with a principled approach based on a pan-European ethos.

But proclaiming support of consensus in the abstract leaves open an entire host of questions as to its application in practice because, as I have been arguing throughout, consensus is not an "objective" method. In any given case, the ECtHR must face these questions in applying the framework of consensus to vertically comparative materials: how many States parties are needed to establish (lack of) consensus? Which sources should be regarded as decisive? What level of generality should the comparative analysis be conducted at, and which conclusions should be drawn from it? Are counter-arguments to consensus permissible and how can they be established? In answering these questions, tensions between different perspectives immediately re-emerge – not only between different perspectives within ideal theory but also between principled and strategic considerations. With regard to the *way in which consensus is used*, then, it is highly relevant whether its use is considered justified (primarily) on principled or strategic grounds.[1570]

This becomes particularly clear when considering in which cases consensus might *not* have normative weight or might be outweighed by other arguments, for example because elements of the morality-focussed perspective are introduced to counteract the idealisations involved in the reference to a pan-European ethos. The most widely discussed case to which I have made reference throughout concerns the adequate protection of minority rights: within ideal theory, some kind of caveat is commonly introduced even by proponents of European consensus to prevent a "tyranny of the

---

ing epistemological advantages to consensus but sceptical of its use since she regards it as driven primarily by misguided legitimacy concerns; see generally, on sensitivity to institutional context within (only) ideal theory, Mann, "Non-ideal Theory of Constitutional Adjudication" at 23.

1568 Supra, notes 1559-1561.

1569 Chapter 9, IV.

1570 The possibility of a stark divergence is illustrated by Bassok, "The European Consensus Doctrine and the ECtHR Quest for Public Confidence" at 250.

majority", be it the notion of "core rights" or the rebuttal of a presumption established by consensus.[1571] Simultaneously, however, the overwhelming, structural force of prejudice and the interest dominant groups have in retaining their privilege make cases concerning minority rights liable to generate considerable controversy,[1572] and a primarily strategic defence of European consensus would thus mitigate *against* any form of counter-argument that defends minority rights at the expense of endangering the ECtHR's sociological legitimacy.[1573]

Similarly, rights which are vital for democracy to function are often singled out as necessitating particular protection within ideal theory, even by those favouring the ethos-focussed perspective[1574] – since the ethos-focussed perspective relies on trust of democratic procedures, it becomes crucial to ensure that such procedures can run their course smoothly. Yet the case-law of the ECtHR provides manifold examples that "judicial intervention into the way the democratic processes of democratic states are designed can trigger some of the most significant domestic political backlash against a supranational court like the ECtHR" since national polities "experience perhaps the most powerful sense of moral ownership over the terms of their own systems of democratic self-governance".[1575] Again, there is a tension between principle and strategy,[1576] and the way in which European consensus is operationalised in cases concerning the democratic process – for example, the way it is established, the argumentative weight ac-

1571 See Chapter 2, II.1. for the morality-focussed criticism, Chapter 4, III.2. for the notion of core rights, Chapter 7, III. for use of different levels of generality in this context, and Chapter 8, III.2. for consensus as a rebuttable presumption.

1572 Henrard, "How the ECtHR's Use of European Consensus Considerations Allows Legitimacy Concerns to Delimit Its Mandate" at 159.

1573 See generally Chapter 9, II.4. for the kind of approach to consensus usually associated with consensus as legitimacy-enhancement.

1574 Von Ungern-Sternberg, "Die Konsensmethode des EGMR. Eine kritische Bewertung mit Blick auf das völkerrechtliche Konsens- und das innerstaatliche Demokratieprinzip" at 330; see also Cram, "Protocol 15 and Articles 10 and 11 ECHR - The Partial Triumph of Political Incumbency Post-Brighton?" (explicitly speaking of "principled" arguments at 484).

1575 Pildes, "Supranational Courts and The Law of Democracy: The European Court of Human Rights" at 157.

1576 See Shai Dothan, "Margin of Appreciation and Democracy: Human Rights and Deference to Political Bodies," (2018) 9 *Journal of International Dispute Settlement* 145 at 150.

corded to it or the kind of counter-argument that is allowed – depends on what is considered the primary justification for its use.[1577]

In other words, for all the connections that can be drawn between strategy and principle,[1578] combining them to justify the use of European consensus without further discussion of their interrelation seems somewhat misleading because it covers up persistent tensions between ideal and non-ideal theory. Neither the structural similarity between principled and strategic arguments in favour of European consensus nor its relative formality serve to resolve these tensions, and hence standards of some kind for approaching institutionally-hard cases would be necessary if an abstract justification of European consensus is to translate over into a justification of its use in practice.[1579] If consensus is conceptualised as necessary to maintain support for the ECtHR (strategic element) and yet easily discarded in controversial cases such as those concerning minority rights (principled element), then there is a sense of having the cake and eating it.[1580]

2. Consensus and an Impression of Objectivity

If academic commentary provides little guidance on how the use of European consensus relates to the dilemma of strategic concessions, then the ECtHR's case-law is even less clear. Like most other courts, the ECtHR rarely admits to the reliance on strategic considerations in its judg-

1577 In both cases, of course, there is ample room for disagreement; the examples serve merely to illustrate the potential tensions between strategy and principle: see supra, I.

1578 For example, by virtue of connections between normative and sociological legitimacy: see Chapter 9, II.1.

1579 See generally on the tendency to eschew such standards Mann, "Non-ideal Theory of Constitutional Adjudication" at 32-37.

1580 See e.g. Dzehtsiarou, *European Consensus and the Legitimacy of the European Court of Human Rights*, at 117-119 and 123-124, moving from the importance of consensus as legitimacy-enhancement to its rebuttal in cases concerning minority rights; see also Dzehtsiarou, "What Is Law for the European Court of Human Rights?" at 130, claiming that "[t]he departure from the solutions supported by internal legal sources [i.e. some forms of consensus] is profoundly problematic" without a minority-related caveat; elsewhere, Dzehtsiarou has suggested with Fiona de Londras that the ECtHR follows strategic considerations unless a case is of "sufficient constitutionalist significance": de Londras and Dzehtsiarou, "Managing Judicial Innovation in the European Court of Human Rights" at 545, though without (at least on my reading of the passage) endorsing this empirical-analytical claim normatively.

ments.[1581] At most, it might use certain wordings – such as the reference to "sensitive" or "delicate" matters[1582] – which hint at what Clare Ryan calls "obscured justifications" including strategy.[1583] Despite this reluctance to admit to the relevance of strategic concerns, however, it seems likely that they were behind the Court's conclusions in quite a few cases, including some in which consensus was referred to: its convoluted treatment of consensus in *S.A.S. v. France*,[1584] its reliance on lack of consensus without any further argument in *Schalk and Kopf*,[1585] and its about-face in *Lautsi v. Italy* following criticism of the preceding chamber judgment[1586] come to mind as possible examples. Yet even if a strategic approach to consensus may, to some extent, constitute a relevant factor within the ECtHR's processes of discovery,[1587] then it is not usually made explicit within its processes of justification.[1588] This further reinforces the idea of European consensus as a fulcrum of strategy and principle by making different rationales for its use indistinguishable ("obscured", as Ryan puts it[1589]) in practice. In what follows, I would like to discuss the advantages and disadvantages of conflating strategy and principle in this way.

1581 Hence why I analysed its case-law, in Chapters 5 to 8, primarily through the lens of ideal theory.

1582 Both adjectives could be read as "likely to engender criticism"; but see also Chapter 5, III.2. for a reading relating them to moral complexity and the ethos-focussed perspective.

1583 Ryan, "Europe's Moral Margin: Parental Aspirations and the European Court of Human Rights" at 487 (and e.g. 488 on avoiding backlash); see also Henrard, "How the ECtHR's Use of European Consensus Considerations Allows Legitimacy Concerns to Delimit Its Mandate" at 161-162. Tellingly, former Judge and Vice President of the ECtHR Angelika Nussberger also speaks of a "more hidden" purpose of consensus in that it serves to predict the acceptability of the Court's judgments: Nussberger, *The European Court of Human Rights*, at 88.

1584 ECtHR (GC), Appl. No. 43835/11 – *S.A.S.*, at para. 156; see Chapter 5, III.1.

1585 ECtHR, Appl. No. 30141/04 – *Schalk and Kopf*, at para. 105; see Chapter 1, II.

1586 ECtHR (GC), Appl. No. 30814/06 – *Lautsi and Others*, at paras. 68 and 70; see Henrard, "How the ECtHR's Use of European Consensus Considerations Allows Legitimacy Concerns to Delimit Its Mandate" at 162, citing this case as "an attempt [by the Court] to win back its political legitimacy", although Henrard is sceptical of this approach.

1587 See Dzehtsiarou, *European Consensus and the Legitimacy of the European Court of Human Rights*, at 184-186 for more detail, based on interviews with ECtHR judges.

1588 For the distinction between processes of discovery and justification, see Chapter 1, IV.5.

1589 Supra, note 1583.

The general sentiment in academic commentary (and, one may surmise from the relative lack of reference to strategic considerations in processes of justification, also the putative position of most judges) seems to be that strategy should not be made explicit. There are many good reasons to substantiate this position – for example, admitting to strategic concessions might exacerbate problems of reflectivity (i.e. the court might increasingly be criticised or threatened so as to achieve renewed concessions).[1590] Many commentators also assume that mentions of strategy rather than principle would impact negatively on a court's sociological legitimacy by tarnishing its image as an impartial arbiter of law,[1591] thus jeopardising at least in part the very aim of turning to strategy in the first place. This tendency is mirrored in the literature on European consensus as legitimacy-enhancement, where it is often taken as given that the strategic responsiveness of consensus to the States parties' positions "in a doctrinal, *not openly political* framework" is a *positive* aspect.[1592]

Given the underlying ideas of courts as forums of principle rather than strategy,[1593] the idea that courts should avoid becoming entangled (or admitting to being entangled) in "issues of political power"[1594] is widespread. Accordingly, the commonly drawn conclusion that strategic considerations should be hidden within processes of justification is hardly specific to European consensus. It nonetheless becomes particularly relevant in the present context, I think, mainly for two reasons. First, it is striking how widespread the justification of the use of consensus on primarily strategic grounds, i.e. as the basis for legitimacy-enhancement, has become.[1595] The

1590 See generally Mann, "Non-ideal Theory of Constitutional Adjudication" at 42.

1591 Lupu, "International Judicial Legitimacy: Lessons from National Courts" at 444; Odermatt, "Patterns of Avoidance: Political Questions Before International Courts" at 227; Helfer and Slaughter, "Toward a Theory of Effective Supranational Adjudication" at 313; and, more generally on themes of judicial independence, Laurence R. Helfer and Anne-Marie Slaughter, "Why States Create International Tribunals: A Response to Professors Posner and Yoo," (2005) 93 *California Law Review* 899.

1592 Krisch, *Beyond Constitutionalism: The Pluralist Structure of Postnational Law*, at 140 (emphasis added).

1593 See Mann, "Non-ideal Theory of Constitutional Adjudication" at 43, building on Ronald Dworkin, "The Forum of Principle," (1981) 56 *New York University Law Review* 469.

1594 Dworkin, "The Forum of Principle" at 517.

1595 See Chapter 9, I.; the vocabulary of "legitimacy" with its potentially normative implications (see ibid.) further reinforces the conflation of strategy and principle.

unspoken disconnect between its (allegedly principled) use in the judgments of the ECtHR and the (primarily strategic) underlying rationale thus becomes particular noticeable. Second, it is noteworthy that consensus is not only conceptualised as conveniently "doctrinal, not openly political" but that the associated connotation of legal "objectivity" is *itself taken as a positive aspect in terms of legitimacy-enhancement*. In that vein, it has been argued that the ECtHR "enhances its legitimacy if it is seen to be constrained by objectively verified legal arguments" and European consensus "creates an impression that it is", in fact, "constrained" by such a legal argument.[1596] Differently put, it the words of Daniel Peat, "consensus may shield the Court from criticisms of subjectivity".[1597]

I have been arguing against the conceptualisation of consensus as an "objective" argument throughout, but the point here is subtly different: the point is not (necessarily) that consensus *is* objective, but that it gives off an *impression* of objectivity. This is complicated terrain, for much nuance depends on how one understands the basic terms of debate such as "objective",[1598] "political", "strategic", and so on.[1599] Objectivity might be challenged in different ways, and these would usually be geared also at challenging the widespread impression of objectivity among legal actors – where else, if not in their perceptions, would objectivity reside? Critical international legal theory, for example, often aims to disrupt the "illusion" of objectivity in precisely this way,[1600] and it has occasionally been discussed whether this is a helpful move in particular contexts but not in oth-

1596 Dzehtsiarou, *European Consensus and the Legitimacy of the European Court of Human Rights*, at 164; see also Dzehtsiarou, "What Is Law for the European Court of Human Rights?" at 90.

1597 Peat, *Comparative Reasoning in International Courts and Tribunals*, at 170.

1598 See e.g. the slightly different senses used in Chapter 1, IV.5., Chapter 3, II., and Chapter 5, I. and V.

1599 See Chapter 1, IV.4.

1600 Koskenniemi, *From Apology to Utopia*, at 536.

ers,[1601] or with regard to the perception of objectivity *by certain actors but not others*.[1602]

The debate about admitting to strategic considerations is also geared towards the perception of certain actors, primarily the States parties,[1603] but it is aimed at a slightly different, though not unrelated issue. Roughly speaking, I would suggest that strategic considerations constitute *one of many* considerations lurking behind an ostensible objectivity (alongside e.g. principled moral-political considerations). The key point for present purposes, however, is that because legal objectivity is commonly understood to exclude strategic considerations, admitting to strategic concessions is regarded as an "extra-legal" argument[1604] – hence the celebration of consensus as a form of reasoning which is said to seem legal while incorporating strategic concerns, indeed even urged to seem legal *because of* strategic concerns.

One way in which consensus is often connected to legal objectivity is by situating it in relation to customary international law (or, less commonly, general principles of international law).[1605] This connection was popularised, in particular, by Judge Ineta Ziemele – although she initially seemed to equate only a subset of cases involving European consensus with regional custom and argued that reliance exclusively on the latter might have provided greater clarity for the ECtHR's case-law.[1606] In a subsequent concurring opinion, her position seems to have changed to a more general equation of the two concepts: discussing European consensus, she holds that "the Court, when it examines domestic laws and practices [...] is in

---

1601 E.g. famously Matthew Craven et al., "We Are Teachers of International Law," (2004) 17 *Leiden Journal of International Law* 363 at 374; see Robert Knox, "Strategy and Tactics," (2010) 21 *Finnish Yearbook of International Law* 193 for a critical response; see also Kennedy, *A Critique of Adjudication (fin de siècle)*, at 246 on the possibility of different effects of critique in different "social milieus".

1602 E.g. Severin Meier, "The Influence of Utopian Projects on the Interpretation of International Law and the Healthy Myth of Objectivity," (2017) 60 *German Yearbook of International Law* 519 at 536.

1603 See Chapter 9, II.3.

1604 Supra, note 1553.

1605 For the latter, see briefly Chapter 3, IV.1.

1606 Ineta Ziemele, "Customary International Law in the Case Law of the European Court of Human Rights - The Method," (2013) 12 *The Law and Practice of International Courts and Tribunals* 243 at 250-251.

fact looking for [...] regional custom".[1607] Other judges[1608] and academic commentators[1609] have voiced similar sentiments, although often without further elaboration. Most recently, Vassilis Tzevelekos and Kanstantsin Dzehtsiarou have analysed the connection in detail and concluded that while there are "sonorous parallels", the Court does not currently conceptualise European consensus as custom and would face significant challenges were it to do so – although such an approach would be possible in theory.[1610]

The gist of this debate does not, I think, lie in confirming or disputing the doctrinal classification of consensus as custom, but rather in the connotations of legal objectivity crafted onto European consensus by virtue of its proximity to the sources of international law.[1611] As Dzehtsiarou has put it, regardless of the precise classification "the Court's approach to consensus can be located within the structure of the sources of international

1607 ECtHR (GC), Appl. No. 59552/08 – *Rohlena v. the Czech Republic*, Judgment of 27 January 2015, concurring opinion of Judge Ziemele, para. 2; see also more recently Ineta Ziemele, "European Consensus and International Law," in *The European Convention on Human Rights and General International Law*, ed. Anne van Aaken and Iulia Motoc (Oxford: Oxford University Press, 2018).

1608 ECtHR (GC), Appl. No. 18030/11 – *Magyar Helsinki Bizottság v. Hungary*, Judgment of 8 November 2016, concurring opinion of Judge Sicilianos, joined by Judge Raimondi, para. 16.

1609 Besson, "Human Rights Adjudication as Transnational Adjudication: A Peripheral Case of Domestic Courts as International Law Adjudicators" at 58; Draghici, "The Strasbourg Court between European and Local Consensus: Anti-democratic or Guardian of Democratic Process?" at 15-16; Rietiker, "The Principle of 'Effectiveness' in the Recent Jurisprudence of the European Court of Human Rights" at 275; more cautiously e.g. Dzehtsiarou, *European Consensus and the Legitimacy of the European Court of Human Rights*, at 163; Legg, *The Margin of Appreciation*, at 116 and 119; Wildhaber, Hjartarson, and Donnelly, "No Consensus on Consensus?" at 256; Tzevelekos, "The Use of Article 31(3)(C) of the VCLT in the Case Law of the ECtHR: An Effective Anti-Fragmentation Tool or a Selective Loophole for the Reinforcement of Human Rights Teleology?" at 654 and 662.

1610 Tzevelekos and Dzehtsiarou, "International Custom Making" at 336.

1611 Of course, this assumes in turn that international custom as one of these sources is (perceived as) objective: contrast Koskenniemi, *From Apology to Utopia*, chapter 6.

law"[1612] – and this makes the use of consensus seem appropriate.[1613] A similar motivation can be assumed for those commentators who relate the ECtHR's use of consensus to "subsequent practice" in the sense of Article 31 (3) lit. b VCLT, thus investing it with the authority of international law's "toolkit on treaty interpretation".[1614] All these frameworks serve to situate consensus as a form of reasoning which shows that the ECtHR is not "making political decisions"[1615] including (but not restricted to) the obfuscation of a strategic rationale for using consensus.

Practically speaking, one might question whether the use of European consensus truly does promote an impression of objectivity, even when connected to sources of international law in this way.[1616] Doubts might be raised, first and foremost, with regard to those States already liable to criti-

---

1612 Dzehtsiarou, *European Consensus and the Legitimacy of the European Court of Human Rights*, at 163.

1613 See Větrovský, "Determining the Content of the European Consenus Concept: The Hidden Role of Language" at 134; Lixinski, "The Inter-American Court of Human Rights' Tentative Search for Latin American Consensus" at 349-350.

1614 Dzehtsiarou, "What Is Law for the European Court of Human Rights?" at 125; see also on consensus and Article 31 (3) lit. b VCLT in different ways Lugato, "The 'Margin of Appreciation' and Freedom of Religion: Between Treaty Interpretation and Subsidiarity" at 62; Legg, *The Margin of Appreciation*, at 106; Georg Nolte, "Jurisprudence under Special Regimes Relating to Subsequent Agreements and Subsequent Practice," in *Treaties and Subsequent Practice*, ed. Georg Nolte (Oxford: Oxford University Press, 2013) at 256; Djeffal, "Consensus, Stasis, Evolution: Reconstructing Argumentative Patterns in Evolutive ECHR Jurisprudence" at 81; Karl Zemanek, "Court Generated State Practice?," (2015) 20 *Austrian Review of International and European Law* 3 as well as the commentaries on that article in the same volume; more critically Peat, *Comparative Reasoning in International Courts and Tribunals*, at 47-48 and 165-166; on Article 31 (3) lit. c VCLT, see Chapter 6, II.

1615 Dzehtsiarou, *European Consensus and the Legitimacy of the European Court of Human Rights*, at 164.

1616 With regard to the international legal sources, one might also note that the connections are primarily drawn in separate opinions or academic commentary, seldom in the ECtHR's majority opinions; especially Article 31 (3) lit. b VCLT is rarely referred to at all (with its absence all the more striking compared to frequent reliance on lit. c), and usually only in the context of formal or procedural issues: see e.g. ECtHR (Plenary), Appl. No. 15576/89 – *Cruz Varas and Others v. Sweden*, Judgment of 20 March 1991, at para. 100; ECtHR (GC), Appl. No. 15318/89 – *Loizidou v. Turkey (Preliminary Objections)*, Judgment of 23 March 1995, at para. 73; ECtHR (GC), Appl. No. 52207/99 – *Banković and Others v. Belgium and Others*, Decision of 12 December 2001, at paras. 56 and 62; ECtHR (GC), Appl. No. 29750/09 – *Hassan*, at para. 101.

cise the ECtHR.[1617] In the context of Russia "'erecting walls' of sovereignty"[1618] or the United Kingdom emphasising its position as an "independent nation",[1619] a form of reasoning *based on other States' positions* may not only further fuel antagonism towards the ECtHR,[1620] it also seems likely to be immediately politicised rather than being viewed as "objective".

One might argue that the situation is at least different with regard to those States in which there is already a higher level of diffuse support for the ECtHR. There may be some truth to this – the impression of consensus as "objective evidence"[1621] of how human rights should be approached is widespread in academic commentary, so it might be similar among State officials[1622] – but it is also worth remembering that even those who support the use of European consensus have long criticised its inconsistent and incoherent use within the ECtHR's case-law.[1623] This hardly creates an impression of objectivity, so that any defence of consensus on these grounds involves an extremely stark idealisation.[1624] And here we come back to the broader critique of objectivity, i.e. the claim of legal indeterminacy even insofar as principled arguments are at issue. If my argument in previous chapters is correct – if consensus is implicated in the triangular tensions underlying a regional system of human rights protection – then it

1617 See also Chapter 9, III. for more background on these cases.

1618 Sergei Yu. Marochkin, "A Russian Approach to International Law in the Domestic Legal Order: Basics, Development and Perspectives," (2016) XXVI *Italian Yearbook of International Law* 15 at 40.

1619 Leonard Hoffmann, "The Universality of Human Rights," (2009) 125 *Law Quarterly Review* 416 at 430.

1620 Amos, "Can European Consensus Encourage Acceptance of the European Convention on Human Rights in the United Kingdom?" at 267; Senden, *Interpretation of Fundamental Rights*, at 130; for a similar point in the context of EU law, see de Búrca, "The Language of Rights and European Integration" at 46.

1621 Mahoney, "Judicial Activism and Judicial Self-Restraint in the European Court of Human Rights: Two Sides of the Same Coin" at 74; for further references, see Chapter 3, II.

1622 Empirical research would be needed to back up this assumption, analogous to the more general research on legitimacy by Çalı, Koch, and Bruch, "The Legitimacy of the European Court of Human Rights: The View from the Ground".

1623 See e.g. the references in Chapter 5, II.

1624 See e.g. the caveat by Dzehtsiarou, "European Consensus and the Evolutive Interpretation of the European Convention on Human Rights" at 1736: "*If* European consensus is deployed consistently", then it prevents arbitrariness (emphasis added); or Dzehtsiarou, *European Consensus and the Legitimacy of the European Court of Human Rights*, at 172: consensus as an "objectively verified argument", but only "in theory".

seems highly unlikely that it could be used to strengthen an impression of objectivity, for its application always depends on how the ECtHR situates itself within those tensions. If the impression of objectivity were to be heightened, this would involve giving consensus an extremely formulistic and pivotal role in the ECtHR's reasoning[1625] – which would imply significant trade-offs with issues of principle and thus bring us back to the dilemma of strategic concessions.

More specifically with regard to the *obfuscation* of that dilemma within processes of justification, it is also worth raising the question whether an impression of objectivity despite a primarily strategic rationale for the use of consensus is truly desirable. Roni Mann's non-ideal theory of adjudication is once more helpful here as a counter-point, for she argues that, in light of the dilemma of strategic concessions, a consciously non-ideal theory "implies a distinctness of the ideal from the non-ideal, and a requirement to work with this distinctness", hence suggesting a two-phase deliberation and *also* a "two-tiered justification".[1626] Accordingly, Mann posits that decisions justified on strategic grounds should be identifiable as such: where non-ideal considerations form part of their justification, this "should be reflected in the language of the decision and in the effect it would have for the future, when circumstances change".[1627]

This is clearly a controversial proposal, but I would like to foreground one particular argument adduced by Mann to shake up the received wisdom that hiding strategic considerations is the preferable approach. If strategy is not made explicit as separate from principle, Mann argues, there

---

1625 See Chapter 9, II.4. in fine.

1626 Mann, "Non-ideal Theory of Constitutional Adjudication" at 40; Gilabert and Lawford-Smith, "Political Feasibility: A Conceptual Exploration" similarly suggest a conceptual distinction between desirability and feasibility (at 818), leading to "all-things-considered" judgments when both are taken into account (at 822).

1627 Mann, "Non-ideal Theory of Constitutional Adjudication" at 52 (emphasis in original); a rare instance of such an approach in the context of European consensus (or, for that matter, the ECtHR more generally) can be found in Holning Lau's rewriting of *Schalk and Kopf* (see already supra, text to notes 1563-1566), which declares a right to same-gender marriage (thus seeking to retain the judgment's "expressive power") even as it abstains from finding a violation of the ECHR based on the rein effect of consensus (due to the ECtHR's "institutional constraints"): Lau, "Rewriting Schalk and Kopf: Shifting the Locus of Deference" at 257; see also the two-tiered approach in Wintemute's take on *Schalk and Kopf*: Wintemute, "Consensus Is the Right Approach for the European Court of Human Rights".

is a danger of *dilution*: "as non-ideal decisions are idealised, they create diluted or eroded ideal precedent",[1628] thereby "distorting the elaboration of constitutional doctrine (first-order) and the evolving understanding of the role of the court in the constitutional system (second-order)".[1629] What was in fact a reaction to contingent non-ideal circumstances will subsequently be read, if not identifiable as such, as a point of principle. As David Hollinger has put it with regard to strategic minimalism, it may fulfil a certain purpose, but "it carries the same risk carried by its famous sibling, strategic essentialism: the risk that it shall deceive its own advocates".[1630]

This kind of consequence is arguably in evidence with regard to the conflation of strategy and principle as the relevant rationale(s) for the use of European consensus, with different implications depending on whether the rein effect or the spur effect is at issue and mirroring the criticisms made of European consensus within ideal theory as discussed in previous chapters.[1631] With regard to the rein effect, my sense is that the amalgamation of ideal and non-ideal theory may contribute to the idealisation of theories that emphasise judicial deference and restraint. This is what Roni Mann calls the erosion of second-order ideal theory: yielding to pressure by the States parties without making the strategic element involved identifiable "supports ideal constitutional theories that seek generally to curb the role of courts and the scope of judicial review, leading to gradual erosion which is unintended and perhaps imperceptible".[1632] If such a develop-

1628 Mann, "Non-ideal Theory of Constitutional Adjudication" at 22 (emphases omitted).

1629 Ibid., 25; for a similar point, though not specifically on courts, see Simmons, "Ideal and Nonideal Theory" at 29.

1630 David A. Hollinger, "Debates with the PTA and Others," in *Michael Ignatieff: Human Rights as Politics and Idolatry*, ed. Amy Gutmann (Princeton: Princeton University Press, 2001) at 122; for strategic essentialism, see Gayatri Chakravorty Spivak, *In Other Worlds. Essays in Cultural Politics* (Abingdon: Routledge, 1998), chapter 12; Sarah Harasym, ed. *Gayatri Chakravorty Spivak: The Post-Colonial Critic. Interviews, Strategies, Dialogues* (New York and London: Routledge, 1990), chapter 1 (interview with Elizabeth Grosz); Spivak later disavowed the term (while remaining ambiguous as to the underlying project) precisely because it "became the union ticket for essentialism" without sufficient regard to the strategic aspect: Sara Danius, Stefan Jonsson, and Gayatri Chakravorty Spivak, "An Interview with Gayatri Chakravorty Spivak," (1993) 20 *boundary 2* 24 at 35; for reflections on strategic essentialism in the context of human rights, see Theilen, "Pre-existing Rights and Future Articulations: Temporal Rhetoric in the Struggle for Trans Rights", at 212.

1631 See Chapter 3, V. for an overview.

1632 Mann, "Non-ideal Theory of Constitutional Adjudication" at 27.

ment is indeed "imperceptible", it is difficult if not impossible to prove; and in any case, it is not my goal here to provide a genealogy of strategic and principled approaches to European consensus and to the ECtHR's role more generally. The suspicion that human rights are being drained of their transformative potential, however, remains – particularly in light of the strong emphasis that has recently been placed on the need for judicial deference (or, conversely, lack of "judicial activism") both in academic commentary[1633] and particularly in political discourse[1634] surrounding the ECtHR.

Simultaneously (and somewhat paradoxically), the danger involved in conflating strategy and principle with regard to the spur effect is that it normalises what one might call a maximalist conception of human rights, according to which a higher level of human rights protection is self-evidently accepted as an improvement. Differently put: if consensus is understood as the prudential base for incremental development of the ECtHR's case-law, there is an underlying sense that while the rein effect signifies wise restraint (perhaps welcomed,[1635] perhaps regrettable[1636]) in the face of controversial issues, the spur effect signifies a positive development to be pursued when it becomes possible.[1637] The spur effect becomes associated with a desirable level of increased human rights protection in "modern

1633 See e.g. Bates, "Activism and Self-Restraint: The Margin of Appreciation's Strasbourg Career… Its 'Coming of Age'?" at 276, who also provides a historical overview through this lens; very starkly Pascual-Vives, *Consensus-Based Interpretation of Regional Human Rights Treaties*, at 3: "judicial activism is incompatible with the rule of law and often generates legal uncertainty".

1634 See generally Chapter 1, IV.4.; as Dothan has summarised it, "Brighton crystalized a political atmosphere that is hostile to excessive ECHR intervention": Dothan, "Margin of Appreciation and Democracy: Human Rights and Deference to Political Bodies" at 150; on the effects of such an atmosphere regardless of formal legal changes, see Madsen, "Rebalancing European Human Rights: Has the Brighton Declaration Engendered a New Deal on Human Rights in Europe?"; generally speaking, I find the description of a "mantra of judicial activism", raised against any case which a government disagrees with regardless of the underlying reasons, to be quite fitting in many cases: see Helfer and Alter, "Legitimacy and Lawmaking: A Tale of Three International Courts" at 502.

1635 Particularly in light of conflation of ideal and non-ideal theory also with regard to the rein effect, discussed in the previous paragraph.

1636 Supra, note 1566.

1637 See also Chapter 4, III.3. on approaches to the rein and spur effect which imply that the latter justifies the former, with the further implication being that results achieved by reference to the spur effect are desirable.

European societies"[1638] and thus *shifts the focus away from the foundational question of which direction the ECtHR's case-law should develop in* and whether "higher" human rights protection actually fulfils an emancipatory purpose. In this way, the strategic approach to consensus bleeds into the justification of the spur effect in ideal theory, making its potentially hegemonic idealisations shift into the background. If ideal and non-ideal theory are conjoined in this way, it becomes increasingly difficult to "know how to measure success"[1639] other than mere maximisation of human rights standards.

Such an approach is potentially problematic, it seems to me, not only because it reinforces harmonisation within Europe at the expense of minority positions among States, but also more generally in terms of the logic of maximisation. Even if one does not subscribe to the idea that more human rights necessarily lead to harmful "inflation" by devaluing other human rights,[1640] their thoughtless maximisation will lead to some measure of depoliticization[1641] and, relatedly, to a reinforcement of the status quo across Europe by elevating it to the transnational level and cloaking it in the language of human rights. The critical potential of human rights thus threatens to be transformed into its opposite – not only because the rein effect of consensus (potentially) makes the emancipatory use of human rights more difficult but also because the spur effect (potentially) narrows down the field within which new human rights standards are constituted[1642] in such a way that they tend to reinforce the status quo rather

---

1638 ECtHR (GC), Appl. No. 23459/03 – *Bayatyan*, at para. 106; on the implications of temporal standards of "progress", see Chapter 2, III. and Chapter 6, VI.

1639 Simmons, "Ideal and Nonideal Theory" at 34.

1640 See Chapter 2, III. on inflation in the context of the morality-focussed perspective; more generally on worries about inflation e.g. Stephen Bouwhuis, "Revisiting Philip Alston's Human Rights and Quality Control," (2016) *European Human Rights Law Review* 475; Dominique Clément, "Human Rights or Social Justice? The Problem of Rights Inflation," (2018) 22 *International Journal of Human Rights* 155; James W. Nickel, *Making Sense of Human Rights* (Malden: Blackwell, 2007), at 96; Michael Ignatieff, *Human Rights as Politics and Idolatry* (Princeton: Princeton University Press, 2001), at 90; critically von Arnauld and Theilen, "Rhetoric of Rights: A Topical Perspective on the Functions of Claiming a 'Human Right to …'", at 49; Jens T. Theilen, "The Inflation of Human Rights: A Deconstruction," (2021) *Leiden Journal of International Law*, forthcoming.

1641 See generally Chapter 3, IV.1., Chapter 4, IV. and in more detail on possible implications Chapter 11.

1642 On field constitution, see Koskenniemi, "The Effect of Rights on Political Culture" at 140-142.

than challenging it. Both points can be raised as downsides of the use of European consensus in ideal theory, but if Mann's argument pertaining to the "gradual erosion" of ideal theory based on strategic considerations is correct, then conflating strategy and principle within the fulcrum of European consensus may well serve to intensify these effects.

3. The Normalisation of a Strategic Approach to Consensus

Even as the conflation of strategy and principle serves to obfuscate strategic considerations within the ECtHR's processes of justification, it also *normalises* them as a relevant background rationale by connecting them to a frequently-used, "well-established",[1643] and ostensibly principled way of reasoning. Normalisation has been described by Susan Marks as one of the ways in which ideology operates to make authority "seem valid and appropriate" by making "a particular set of arrangements [...] seem normal" and, accordingly, making different arrangements "come to appear as deviations from the proper state of things".[1644] With regard to the ECtHR, I would suggest that this mode of normalisation applies both to the use of European consensus and to the relevance of strategy as "normal".

By way of contrast, consider once again what I called the dilemma of strategic concessions.[1645] Building on Roni Mann, I argued that it is important to recognise that whether or not to give weight to non-ideal considerations which deviate from ideal standards *does constitute a dilemma*. We may well grant that strategic concerns can be a helpful counterbalance to pure ideal theory so as to foreground the realisation of ideal principles rather than their mere proclamation, but their simultaneous tension with those very ideal principles makes strategic concessions problematic. Even when an argument can be made that strategy should trump principle in a certain case, and the strategic approach thus considered the "right" approach – even then, "this does not mean that there is *nothing wrong* with the outcome", since the non-ideal decision "remains at some level *not* a right deci-

1643 Dzehtsiarou, "What Is Law for the European Court of Human Rights?" at 131; see also Senden, *Interpretation of Fundamental Rights*, at 264.
1644 Marks, *The Riddle of All Constitutions*, at 19.
1645 Supra, II.

sion".[1646] There is, as Laurence Helfer has acknowledged, a "price to pay" for focussing on the sociological legitimacy of a court.[1647]

If strategy and principle are conflated within the fulcrum of European consensus, however, then not only does this potentially lead to the dilution of ideal standards as discussed in the previous sub-section, it also distracts from the "price to pay" for strategic concessions given the constant reliance on a kind of reasoning which, by virtue of the popularity of legitimacy-enhancement as the rationale for the use of consensus, is understood to be (at least in part) strategically motivated. The fact that consensus constitutes a form of abstract strategizing based on incremental development of the ECtHR's case-law is also relevant here:[1648] this makes the strategic element less stark and less visible, but also *ubiquitous within the ECtHR's reasoning* since consensus as legitimacy-enhancement relies on the *consistent use of consensus over time*. This in turn exacerbates the problem of dilution since strategic considerations will consistently water down ideal standards which the ECtHR might otherwise have set. It comes as no surprise that ubiquitous strategy can easily make a court "lose sight of a truly transformative vision".[1649]

Normalising the strategic element involved in European consensus as legitimacy-enhancement further makes it more difficult to challenge its implications in any given case since it will increasingly be taken for granted.[1650] Indeed, there is a tendency to discount any opposition to European consensus as "unrealistic": setting aside European consensus has been said to "lose touch with reality",[1651] whereas its use, by contrast, is "solidly an-

---

1646 Mann, "Non-ideal Theory of Constitutional Adjudication" at 52 (emphases in original).

1647 Although his point is that it is a "modest" price to pay; I am not so sure. See Laurence R. Helfer, "Populism and International Human Rights Institutions: A Survival Guide" (iCourts Working Paper Series, No. 133, 2018), available at <https://papers.ssrn.com/sol3/papers.cfm?abstract_id=3202633>, at p. 19; see also Gearty, "Building Consensus on European Consensus" at 453, arguing against "disregarding the politics of the day" via consensus but also acknowledging that it is "dangerous".

1648 See Chapter 9, IV.

1649 Mann, "Non-ideal Theory of Constitutional Adjudication" at 43.

1650 See generally e.g. Supreme Court of the United States, *Mathews v. Lucas*, 427 U.S. 495, 520 (1976) (Stevens, J., dissenting): "Habit, rather than analysis, makes [traditional legal justifications] seem acceptable and natural".

1651 Dzehtsiarou, *European Consensus and the Legitimacy of the European Court of Human Rights*, at 117-118; see also Legg, *The Margin of Appreciation*, at 114 ("not

chored in reality".[1652] Consensus is "essential" in light of "the world in which we actually happen to find ourselves, as opposed to that of our imagining or our dreams".[1653] Robert Wintemute has used particularly dramatic terms: European consensus "serves to anchor the court in legal, political and social reality on the ground", whereas human rights law at the global level "often loses all contact with Earth, and floats off into the stratosphere".[1654] The ECtHR itself has taken on board this kind of rhetoric by holding, in *Demir and Baykara v. Turkey*, that "the common international or domestic law standards of European States reflect a reality that the Court cannot disregard".[1655]

Statements such as these are telling. They demonstrate, first, that normalisation works dialectically to undergird both the use of European consensus and the reliance on strategic considerations in the form of legitimacy-enhancement.[1656] The reference to a harsh "reality" external to the ECtHR takes it as a given that strategic concessions are preferable to taking a principled stance; discounting results which do not cohere with (whatever is interpreted to constitute) European consensus as "unrealistic" simultaneously positions the use of consensus as the appropriate way of making these strategic concessions. The reference to a reality that the Court *cannot*

consonant with international legal reality"); Wildhaber, Hjartarson, and Donnelly, "No Consensus on Consensus?" at 251 ("amazingly distant from the realities of democratic politics"); less critically Ost, "The Original Canons of Interpretation" at 308 ("fear of detaching [the Court] from legal reality"); Lau, "Rewriting Schalk and Kopf: Shifting the Locus of Deference" at 257 (a "realist perspective as opposed to utopianism").

1652 Wildhaber, Hjartarson, and Donnelly, "No Consensus on Consensus?" at 262; see also Petkova, "The Notion of Consensus as a Route to Democratic Adjudication" at 695 ("the notion of consensus provides the Court with a link to [...] empirical realities").

1653 Gearty, "Building Consensus on European Consensus" at 453 and 449-451; the juxtaposition with imagination and dreams invokes airy utopianism as an unsatisfactory contrast to realism, as Lau does more explicitly (supra, note 1651); contrast Theilen, Hassfurther, and Staff, "Towards Utopia - Rethinking International Law" for a more positive spin on utopianism.

1654 Wintemute, "Consensus Is the Right Approach for the European Court of Human Rights".

1655 ECtHR (GC), Appl. No. 34503/97 – *Demir and Baykara*, at para. 76; but see also the less drastic re-renderings of this passage e.g. in ECtHR (GC), Appl. No. 72508/13 – *Merabishvili v. Georgia*, Judgment of 28 November 2017, at para. 306.

1656 On the latter, see generally Koskenniemi, "Legitimacy, Rights and Ideology: Notes Towards a Critique of the New Moral Internationalism" at 367.

disregard demonstrates, second, how normalisation makes both the use of consensus and the reliance on strategic considerations seem *necessary*. Echoing Susan Marks, we might say that disregarding them is made to appear like a deviation from the "proper state of things":[1657] reference to consensus in the interest of legitimacy-enhancement is presented as "*in the design* of the Convention".[1658] Incrementalism based on consensus thus becomes the only possible option.

An alternative approach would not necessarily posit that "realism" of some kind should be avoided entirely – indeed, in a sense references to the circumstances at any given time and place which can be called "reality" is inherent in the very notion of non-ideal theory.[1659] Disregarding alternatives to consensus as "unrealistic", however, not only naturalises the use of consensus, but also implies a static notion of reality which takes no account, for example, of the ECtHR's power to influence the circumstances in which it finds itself. Mann calls this the problem of endogeneity, describing it as an over-emphasis on strategy which "does not take into account the role of the court in influencing preferences: the court is a player, the material is given".[1660] Instead of fatalistically approaching non-ideal theory through the lens of such a static notion of reality, one might make reference to what Ernst Bloch calls those "elements of reality geared towards the future",[1661] hence implying a procedural conception of reality as open-ended and evolving.[1662] Or, to return to Rawls: "the limits of the possible are not given by the actual, for we can to a greater or lesser extent change political and social institutions, and much else".[1663]

1657 Supra, note 1644.

1658 Bates, "Consensus in the Legitimacy-Building Era of the European Court of Human Rights" at 63 (emphasis in original).

1659 See e.g. Mann, "Non-ideal Theory of Constitutional Adjudication" at 38 ("reality as it happens to be at the moment from which we begin acting, with the limitations of existing practices, institutions, convictions").

1660 Ibid., 42.

1661 Ernst Bloch, *Das Prinzip Hoffnung*, 10th ed. (Frankfurt a.M.: Suhrkamp, 2016), at 165 (my translation).

1662 Ibid., 226; see also Jens T. Theilen, "Of Wonder and Changing the World: Philip Allott's Legal Utopianism," (2017) 60 *German Yearbook of International Law* 337 at 350.

1663 John Rawls, *Justice as Fairness: A Restatement* (Cambridge, MA: Harvard University Press, 2001), at 5; see also Gilabert and Lawford-Smith, "Political Feasibility: A Conceptual Exploration" at 813-814; in the context of adjudication, see Mann, "Non-ideal Theory of Constitutional Adjudication" at 42 ("a court's position affects the way others think").

A somewhat more nuanced version of the above-mentioned claims might posit that it is "unrealistic", for strategic reasons, to set aside European consensus *at the current point in time*. This point is at least implied by those who invoke a "legitimacy crisis" of the ECtHR to promote the use of consensus:[1664] there is a sense of periodisation, with strategy being more or less necessary depending on the level of diffuse support for the ECtHR[1665] and, accordingly, with the ECtHR having more leeway to deviate from European consensus in some phases of general contentment or "serendipitous governance".[1666] Yet the implication remains that, at the current point in time, the use of consensus is necessary to counter the assumed "legitimacy crisis", leading to the normalisation of strategy at least for the time being. It is worth keeping in mind, in that regard, that the "legitimacy crisis" is no less constructed than the notion of a "reality" ostensibly disconnected from the ECtHR. Crises "are produced: they are negotiable narratives that can mask as well as reveal".[1667]

Even if we were to accept that the ECtHR currently faces more challenges to its authority than at other times, then, this does not mean that we must normalise the prioritisation of strategy across the board; rather, we can deconstruct the narrative of crisis to *also* take into account elements of

---

1664 See in more detail Chapter 9, II.2., as well as supra, note 1634 on the current atmosphere.

1665 See in particular Spano, "Universality or Diversity of Human Rights? Strasbourg in the Age of Subsidiarity" at 487-488 on "highs and lows" with regard to "approval ratings", also holding that current criticism is "unprecedented"; the very phrase "*age* of subsidiarity", coined by Spano, implies periodisation; Jörg Polakiewicz and Irene Suominen-Picht, "Aktuelle Herausforderungen für Europarat und EMRK: Die Erklärung von Kopenhagen (April 2018), das Spannungsverhältnis zwischen EMRK und nationalen Verfassungen und die Beteiligung der EU an dem europäischen Menschenrechtskontrollmechanismus," (2018) *Europäische Grundrechte-Zeitschrift* 383 at 383 also note that the Council of Europe is currently facing "unprecedented" (*beispiellos*) institutional challenges; see also e.g. Ralph Janik, "How Many Divisions Does the European Court of Human Rights Have? Compliance and Legitimacy in Times of Crisis," (2015) 20 *Austrian Review of International and European Law* 125.

1666 Schliesky, *Souveränität und Legitimität von Herrschaftsgewalt. Die Weiterentwicklung von Begriffen der Staatslehre und des Staatsrechts im europäischen Mehrebenensystem*, at 172 (*glückliche Herrschaft*, on times in which acceptance and legitimacy come together unnoticed).

1667 Authers and Charlesworth, "The Crisis and the Quotidian in International Human Rights Law" at 38; for a similar point with regard to "reality", see Orna Ben-Naftali, "Sentiment, Sense and Sensibility in the Genesis of Utopian Traditions," (2012) 23 *European Journal of International Law* 1133 at 1141.

reality which resonate with more optimistic visions.[1668] Criticism may fade.[1669] The States parties' governments and legislatures may refuse to implement judgments in some cases, but States are not unitary actors: non-governmental organisations or grassroots movements may nonetheless use the judgments to drive and support their activism;[1670] national courts may refer to them,[1671] particularly if prompted by activists;[1672] in brief – all those actors side-lined as agents of legitimacy in accounts of European consensus may yet play a role,[1673] and resistance to the ECtHR may face counter-resistance.[1674]

My point here is not that we should naively assume that all these things will come to pass,[1675] but simply that we should also be wary of leaving them out of our accounts of "crisis" or "reality" which serve to normalise strategic concessions and to position European consensus as an inevitable

1668 For such more optimistic visions in general, by reference to the use of European consensus, see Benvenisti, "Margin of Appreciation, Consensus, and Universal Standards" at 852-853; Letsas, *A Theory of Interpretation of the European Convention on Human Rights*, at 124-125; see also, more generally, e.g. O'Boyle, "The Future of the European Court of Human Rights" at 1866 and 1868.

1669 Costa, "On the Legitimacy of the European Court of Human Rights' Judgments" at 174 (in footnote 2).

1670 Bill Bowring, "Does Russia Have a Human Rights Future in the Council of Europe and OSCE?," in *Shifting Power and Human Rights Diplomacy: Russia*, ed. Doutje Lettinga and Lars van Troost (Amnesty International Netherlands, 2017) at 53 sees "grounds for optimism" in the case of Russia based on a "new generation of activists"; on the importance of local activism for human rights in general, see Beth A. Simmons, *Mobilizing for Human Rights. International Law in Domestic Politics* (Cambridge: Cambridge University Press, 2009), at 371-373; see also Martha Finnemore and Kathryn Sikkink, "International Norm Dynamics and Political Change," (1998) 52 *International Organization* 887 at 893.

1671 Helfer and Voeten, "International Courts as Agents of Legal Change: Evidence from LGBT Rights in Europe" at 13; Anagnostou and Mungiu-Pippidi, "Domestic Implementation of Human Rights Judgments in Europe: Legal Infrastructure and Government Effectiveness Matter" at 225.

1672 Simmons, *Mobilizing for Human Rights*, at 362.

1673 See Chapter 9, II.3.

1674 As mentioned in Chapter 9, III. in fine; see generally Madsen, Cebulak, and Wiebusch, "Backlash Against International Courts: Explaining the Forms and Patterns of Resistance to International Courts" at 205-206; on the role of civil society in that regard (in the context of the IACtHR), see Soley and Steininger, "Parting Ways or Lashing Back? Withdrawals, Backlash and the Inter-American Court of Human Rights" at 254.

1675 See Theilen, Hassfurther, and Staff, "Towards Utopia - Rethinking International Law" at 331-332.

part of the ECtHR's reasoning. Doing so would contribute to the normalisation of strategy to the point that only (a certain kind of) consensus-based reasoning is accepted as "realistic", which severely limits the imaginative space which human rights might otherwise open up.[1676] If one accepts the realisation of certain values as the ultimate goal for regional human rights, then strategy cannot be discounted entirely; but this should not lead to its normalisation to such an extent that a principled stance is indefinitely postponed.[1677]

IV. Interim Reflections: Rethinking the Role of the Court

My goal in this chapter has been to question the position of European consensus as a fulcrum of strategy and principle. Even if we accept connections between these different modes of argument (e.g. strategy geared towards a principled goal, principle dependent on strategy for its realisation), they may nonetheless point in different directions in practice; I have called this the dilemma of strategic concessions. It is important to recognise, I have suggested, that cases in which strategic concessions are considered do constitute a dilemma: while strategic and principles justifications of consensus are often advanced alongside one another and may indeed have a significant area of overlap, they are not identical and foregrounding one or the other will have implications for the way in which consensus is applied. Sweeping these tensions under the rug may lead to the dilution of ideal theory, in the sense that principled and strategic considerations become indistinguishable and the latter increasingly seep into the prior. Si-

1676 See generally Chapter 1, IV.5., and in more detail Chapter 11.

1677 See Marks, *The Riddle of All Constitutions*, at 60, citing William I. Robinson, *Promoting Polyarchy: Globalization, US Intervention and Hegemony* (Cambridge: Cambridge University Press, 1996), at 65, on how "supposedly 'transitional' trade-offs tend to 'become a structural feature [...]'", leading to the "postponement of social justice"; see also ECtHR (GC), Appl. Nos. 60367/08 and 961/11 – *Khamtokhu and Aksenchik*, dissenting opinion of Judge Pinto de Albuquerque, at para. 49, holding (though without specific reference to non-ideal theory) that a "wait-and-see position does not correspond to the role and vocation of the Court"; by contrast, Bates, "Consensus in the Legitimacy-Building Era of the European Court of Human Rights" at 67 deems criticism of consensus to imply "a type of impatience"; such a perspective underestimates, I think, the element of power which waiting implies: see Pierre Bourdieu, *Pascalian Meditations*, trans. Richard Nice (Stanford: Stanford University Press, 2000), at 228.

multaneously (and somewhat paradoxically), the constant background presence of a strategic rationale within academic discourse leads to the normalisation of both strategic considerations and European consensus as the appropriate way of integrating them into the ECtHR's reasoning, to the point that other approaches are discounted as "unrealistic".

I have already indicated some elements within "reality" which might counteract such claims. In the end, though, I suspect that the reluctance to question how "realistic" it would be to not use consensus – or to use it differently from the way in which proponents of consensus as legitimacy-enhancement conceive of it – relates primarily to underlying images as to the appropriate role of the ECtHR vis-à-vis the States parties.[1678] The intuitive connection between European consensus as a form of vertically comparative reasoning and the positions of the States parties resurfaces once again here, for it conjures an image of the ECtHR in which the Court is closely connected to, indeed *responsive* to the States parties.[1679] I would like to end this chapter, therefore, by briefly reflecting on different roles or figures which the ECtHR might inhabit and how these relate to the position of the Court in the area of tensions between strategy and principle.

In evaluating the role of the ECtHR in this context a crucial point to note, I think, that it *does not have the choice of remaining neutral*. If it chooses to "abstain" from intervening in the political struggle underlying certain human rights claims by not finding a violation of the ECHR, then this does not imply, as Article 53 ECHR would have it on formal legal terms, that "the situation after a 'no violation' finding [is] the same as without an intervention" by the ECtHR.[1680] Rather, as Eva Brems has put it, "the public and political perception of such an ECtHR judgment in practice is that of a Court clearance of a restrictive practice as such"[1681] – in other words, where a finding of a violation challenges the status quo, a finding of no vi-

1678 See supra, note 1556.

1679 I would emphasise that the counter-image here need not be that of an autarkic court; see further Chapter 11, III. and IV.3.

1680 Brems, "Human Rights: Minimum and Maximum Perspectives" at 353.

1681 Ibid.; for a recent example, see the responses to the judgment in ECtHR, Appl. No. 62007/17 – *L.F. v. Ireland*, Decision of 10 November 2020; e.g. Máiréad Enright, "Symphysiotomies and an Overlooked Violation of Article 3 ECHR" (2021), available at <https://ichrgalway.wordpress.com/2020/12/21/symphysiotomies-and-an-overlooked-violation-of-article-3-echr/>: "the judgment will be read in Ireland as endorsing the continuing marginalisation of women wounded by symphysiotomy" and "legitimates" the omission of symphysiotomy from apologies for historical gender-based violence.

olation reinforces it.[1682] In fact, the ECtHR itself has implicitly acknowledged as much by claiming that an evolutive approach to its case-law is necessary so as not to become "a bar to reform or improvement".[1683]

I would submit that this effect of reinforcing the status quo needs to be kept in mind when considering the role which the ECtHR should inhabit vis-à-vis the States parties on strategic grounds. Seeking proximity to the States parties positions it as a respected institution which, in a broad sense, might be regarded as part of the legal and administrative procedures of the States parties since its judgments are regularly followed.[1684] The clear advantage is the realisation, at least usually, of the standards which the ECtHR sets – but the price to pay is that those standards will be less oriented at social transformation and thus not only ignore but *reinforce* some forms of injustice rather than challenging them.

In a sense, this is a broader reformulation of the dilemma of strategic concessions, geared at the institutional level rather than at individual judgments – a fundamental question of "political action and strategy", as Koskenniemi has put it in the context of human rights mainstreaming.[1685] He describes the dilemma involved as follows:

> The more 'revolutionary' one is, the more difficult it is to occupy those administrative positions in which the main lines of policy are being set. The more influential one is as an administrative or regulatory agent, the less 'revolutionary' one's policies can be.[1686]

There is something to be said for a human rights court which maintains a high level of legal authority vis-à-vis the States parties and can thus be considered a "policy-setter"; and the reliance on European consensus may be

---

1682 See also Mégret, "The Apology of Utopia" at 488; and more generally Koskenniemi, "The Effect of Rights on Political Culture" at 134; Koskenniemi, *From Apology to Utopia*, at 614. I would add a caveat that findings of a violation may in some scenarios also serve to reinforce the status quo: see briefly supra, III.2. in fine.

1683 ECtHR (GC), Appl. No. 46295/99 – *Stafford v. the United Kingdom*, Judgment of 28 May 2002, at para. 68; ECtHR (GC), Appl. No. 28957/95 – *Christine Goodwin*, at para. 74; ECtHR (GC), Appl. No. 63235/00 – *Vilho Eskelinen and Others*, at para. 56; ECtHR (GC), Appl. No. 34503/97 – *Demir and Baykara*, at para. 153; ECtHR (GC), Appl. No. 23459/03 – *Bayatyan*, at para. 98.

1684 There is, of course, also an element of accumulating institutional power at play here, as noted in Chapter 9, II.5.

1685 Martti Koskenniemi, "Human Rights Mainstreaming as a Strategy for Institutional Power," (2010) 1 *Humanity* 47 at 55.

1686 Ibid.

one way of achieving this.[1687] But, conversely, this implies that it is (a certain interpretation of) European consensus which determines, at least in large part, the content of those very policies. The important point to underline once again is, therefore, that nothing about this is inevitable. The ECtHR is not inextricably bound to one side of the spectrum that unfolds between the administrative and the revolutionary agent. Courts are hardly known for being revolutionary, but that does not mean that they cannot at least tend in that direction. In considering the merits and disadvantages of (only) incrementally developing standards based on a strategic account of European consensus, we might borrow from Sara Ahmed and keep in mind that "if we proceed along a path in order to disrupt it, we can end up not disrupting it in order to proceed".[1688]

1687 Subject to the practical doubts raised in Chapter 9, III.

1688 Ahmed, "Uses of Use. Diversity, Utility and the University", available at <https://www.youtube.com/watch?v=avKJ2w1mhng>, at 1:01:50.

Chapter 11: Engaging with Indeterminacy: Imagining Different Uses for Vertically Comparative Legal Reasoning

I. Pulling Together the Threads: Beyond Consensus as Compromise

I announced in Chapter 1 that part of my overall goal throughout this study on European consensus would be to demonstrate and criticise how, in at least two ways, it can be seen as a kind of *compromise*. The sense of compromise arose, first, with regard to the relationship between different kinds of normativity: because of its Janus-faced nature involving both the rein effect and the spur effect, consensus may seem an appropriate compromise between more stark positions such as the morality-focussed perspective (easily qualified as utopian, or not sufficiently democratic) and the ethos-focussed perspective insofar as it refers to individual national ethe (too apologetic, or not sufficiently internationalist to chime with a regional system of human rights protection). The notion of a pan-European ethos, so intuitively apt in the context of regional human rights law, makes the clash of incompatible epistemologies, idealisations, and positions underlying it disappear behind the compromise of consensus.

The preceding chapter explored the second sense in which consensus can be conceived of as a kind of compromise: it is regarded as the embodiment of both strategy and principle, thus making it seem like it is the appropriate way to accommodate non-ideal circumstances without losing too much ground in ideal theory. Indeed, at least in some cases one suspects that the ECtHR's judges might, in theory, have preferred to argue for a different outcome; perhaps they did not do so "out of a maxim of *strategic* action that suggests that it is almost always useful to compromise".[1689] The reference to European consensus provides one way of taking strategic action geared at compromise – making strategic concessions while rationalising them (and publicly justifying them) as part of an incremental development which respects the States parties' democratic processes. It can thus be thought of as "a way of finding acceptable compromises between the

1689 Koskenniemi, *From Apology to Utopia*, at 598 (emphasis added).

sovereign will of the ECHR signatories", to which the ECtHR must "show appropriate respect", and "the decision-making power of the Court".[1690]

While I have been making use of a heuristic distinction between ideal and non-ideal theory,[1691] the two kinds of compromise are related. Together, they chime with Frédéric Mégret's point that "international law naturally veers towards the mid-stream": compromises "may not in the end be logically sustainable within the liberal canon", but they "will at least appear to navigate these waters in a way that is more savvy and sustainable" than other positions.[1692] Taking both forms of compromise together, and situating them in relation to the kind of position which the ECtHR tends to take in substance, one might consider the use of European consensus one of the "compromises of left liberalism",[1693] or at least a centrist, sometimes vaguely left-leaning liberalism. The sense of objectivity or naturalness which often accompanies the use of consensus further entrenches this compromise as a form of legal or strategic rationality.

In the imperfect world we live in, and within human rights institutions such as the ECtHR as they currently exist, compromises are no doubt ubiquitous – we might even speak of a "world of compromises"[1694] – and they need not be injurious.[1695] They do, however, almost by definition detract attention from potentially more transformative alternatives – they orient us towards certain options and away from others, one might say.[1696] What I have been trying to emphasise throughout is that, because we thus become oriented one way or another, we need to retain the awareness that this orientation is not necessary and there *are*, in fact, alternatives. We should not, in other words, lose sight of the potentially critical and eman-

1690 Kapotas and Tzevelekos, "How (Difficult Is It) to Build Consensus on (European) Consensus?" at 13; on "compromise" in this context, see also Hamilton, "Same-Sex Marriage, Consensus, Certainty and the European Court of Human Rights" at 36.

1691 See in more detail Chapter 1, IV.4.

1692 Mégret, "The Apology of Utopia" at 460; see also Koskenniemi, *From Apology to Utopia*, at 597.

1693 Kennedy, *A Critique of Adjudication (fin de siècle)*, at 339.

1694 Koskenniemi, "What is Critical Research in International Law? Celebrating Structuralism" at 734; see also Ben Golder, "Beyond Redemption? Problematising the Critique of Human Rights in Contemporary International Legal Thought," (2014) 2 *London Review of International Law* 77 at 113.

1695 For a positive notion of compromise, see Mégret, "Where Does the Critique of International Human Rights Stand? An Exploration in 18 Vignettes" at 29.

1696 Phrasing this (and other points) as an issue of orientation owes much to Ahmed, *Queer Phenomenology*.

cipatory force of human rights by turning all too quickly towards European consensus.

Rather than concluding by way of a summary of previous chapters, in this chapter I aim to investigate how the potentially critical force of human rights could be developed rather than suppressed in the context of the ECtHR, and how this relates to the argument made over the course of this study. To approach this task, I begin by revisiting the framework of critical international legal theory already discussed in Chapter 1, and in particular by situating consensus in relation to the so-called "indeterminacy thesis".[1697] I have argued that, although it is often claimed to provide some form of "objectivity" which might mitigate the "vagueness" of the ECHR, European consensus forms part of the very structures of argument which render regional human rights law indeterminate. I will now aim to provide an account of why it is worth foregrounding indeterminacy in this way and how it relates to broader critiques of human rights, especially in their judicial form.

It goes without saying that the various forms of critique and the related yet distinct critical traditions which I will refer to so as to build my argument in these sections are by no means monolithic but rather much more diverse and internally contradictory than what I can present here. As Fleur Johns has very aptly summarised it, "it is far from clear that [critical international legal theory] exists in any consistently recognizable form", let alone under any particular label, and "[t]o the extent that it does, it is better grasped in the doing than in the description".[1698] My own "doing" in this chapter, then, borrows from different, partly contradictory traditions (and may indeed not be without its own contradictions[1699]) without any claim to comprehensiveness, let alone absoluteness.

A rough summary of the approach I will sketch might go as follows. Critique in the sense I am considering aims to denaturalise current social arrangements so as to open up imaginative space for social transformation, specifically social transformation that is relatively far-reaching compared to what seems possible within the dominant ideological framework of current arrangements or institutions. Highlighting the indeterminacy of re-

---

1697 See Chapter 1, IV.5. and V.

1698 Fleur Johns, "Critical International Legal Theory," in *International Legal Theory: Foundations and Frontiers*, ed. Jeffrey L. Dunoff and Mark A. Pollack (Cambridge: Cambridge University Press, forthcoming), available at <https://papers.ssrn.com/sol3/papers.cfm?abstract_id=3224013>.

1699 See also Kennedy, *A Critique of Adjudication (fin de siècle)*, at 6.

gional human rights law forms part of such an approach by insisting on a disconnect between legal reasoning and the decisions which it is assumed to justify, hence opening up space to question prevalent understandings of what the law "says" and provide a point of entry for political critique (II.). This also chimes with those critiques of human rights which emphasise the limitations of human rights *law*, pointing out the way in which legal reasoning tends to depoliticise debates on how human rights could be understood and thus restrict rather than expand imaginative space. For all that human rights courts' judgments can and sometimes do provide helpful resources within broader political struggles, then, their role within processes of social transformation is ambivalent at best for those fundamentally dissatisfied with the status quo (III.).

One consequence of this is that the aim of this chapter which I mentioned above – to investigate how the potentially critical force of human rights could be developed rather than suppressed *in the context of the ECtHR* – is itself limited in that the ECtHR, qua human rights court tasked with legal interpretation, is hardly an institution on which we should place our hopes if the goal is far-reaching social transformation. Still, there might be value in reflecting on the role of the ECtHR against the backdrop of critical approaches, not only to identify aspects of its reasoning and broader adjudicatory culture which may be more or less amenable to political projects of social transformation, but also to explore whether it might be possible to rethink our understandings of law, courts, and judgment-giving in ways which render them more open-ended. While such an exploratory project points far beyond the scope of the present study, I will offer some tentative suggestions, particularly insofar as they relate to the use of European consensus and vertically comparative legal reasoning more broadly (IV.). I conclude with a brief outlook on the ECtHR in relation to future articulations of human rights (V.).

II. Indeterminacy and the Motivation for Critique

Besides intervening in relatively specialised debates on European consensus, the discussion of different kinds of normativity in the preceding chapters aimed to substantiate the claim I made in Chapter 1: that regional human rights law is indeterminate not only in the trite sense of containing "vague" language, but more radically in the sense that different perspectives on how human rights should be understood are based on diametrically opposed assumptions and idealisations and can consistently be used to undermine each other. One can relate this claim to the formal structure of international legal argument more generally by describing it as a contradictory combination of ascending and descending argument, i.e. arguments based on or geared at overriding State will.[1700]

In terms of what I gathered under the banner of "ideal theory", I connected this framework to more substantively loaded positions, distinguishing between conceptions of human rights which see them as prepolitical, aiming to protect moral self-determination (morality-focussed perspective) and those which foreground civic self-organisation and political participation as the basis of shared interpretations of human rights (ethos-focussed perspective). Given the idealisations involved in both these conceptions, neither seems particularly attractive in its pure form – and in light of this, I argued, each seeks to incorporate elements of the other, thus introducing conflicting epistemologies and leading to the indeterminacy of legal reasoning of the ECtHR because any outcome it reaches can be challenged on the basis of morality-focussed or ethos-focussed considerations on the basis of their paradoxical relationship to one another.[1701]

The most basic point that follows from highlighting the paradoxes involved in and hence the indeterminacy of the ECtHR's reasoning is what Martti Koskenniemi has called "the 'gap' between the available legal materials (rules, principles, precedents, doctrines) and the legal decision".[1702] This in turn draws attention to the "political nature" of international law, in this case regional human rights law.[1703] One of the core tenets of critical legal studies and related traditions such as the New Approaches to International Law or critical international legal theory has long since been precisely this point: that law is "political" in the sense that it underdetermines results in individual cases,[1704] and hence that no legal decision or interpretation is inevitable since it would, in principle, always be possible to justify diametrically opposed results within the argumentative structures provided by (international) law.[1705] My argument has been that this point holds

1700 See Chapter 1, IV.2.
1701 See in particular Chapter 4, III. and Chapter 7, IV.
1702 Koskenniemi, *From Apology to Utopia*, at 601.
1703 Ibid.
1704 See Duncan Kennedy, "A Semiotics of Critique," (2001) 22 *Cardozo Law Review* 1147 at 1162-1163; for an overview of both critical legal studies and critical international legal theory, see Johns, "Critical International Legal Theory".
1705 In Koskenniemi's iconic wording, "international law is singularly useless as a means for justifying or criticizing international behaviour": Koskenniemi, *From Apology to Utopia*, at 67.

true in the context of regional human rights law as well, and that the paradoxical elements which generate law's indeterminacy not only form part of a formal argumentative structure but can be connected to underlying, contradictory values such as moral and ethical self-determination.

This paradoxical relationship between moral and ethical normativity, well-known in principle from the national level, acquires additional complexity in the transnational context of the ECtHR, where democratic structures as a way of expressing ethical normativity are largely lacking – hence the prominence of European consensus as a way of compensating, at least to some extent, for this fact. The vertically comparative reference to the legal systems of the States parties, viewed through the prism of collectivity, thus provides for a specifically regional form of ethical normativity which I dubbed a pan-European ethos. But this form of normativity forms part of the tensions within the argumentative structures of regional human rights law rather than resolving them. As a form of ethical normativity, it clearly involves idealisations diametrically opposed to those of the morality-focussed perspective and its focus on moral self-determination, and as a form of ethical normativity developed at the regional level it stands in contrast to national ethe, the traditional locus of ethical self-determination. Accordingly, while it may strike up allegiances with these forms of normativity due to its Janus-faced nature (in doctrinal terms: the invocation of the rein effect and the spur effect of European consensus), it can also be challenged by them and does not resolve the indeterminacy of regional human rights law. Indeed, I have argued that the tensions between the different forms of normativity involved are evident even in the way in which (lack of) European consensus is established in the first place and thus unsettle the very notion of what European consensus *is*.

In light of all this, my core argument is that European consensus cannot be detached from the tensions underlying the European project of regional human rights as a whole (and liberalism more broadly). Its Janus-faced nature gives it the appearance of an appropriate compromise between morality-focussed considerations and overly strong reliance on national ethe, but whether or not this compromise is accepted is a *political* decision in the sense just mentioned, i.e. underdetermined by pre-existing legal materials. European consensus, therefore, is "not an objective 'method' that yields clear conclusions about the proper scope of uniform international standards".[1706]

1706 Carozza, "Uses and Misuses of Comparative Law" at 1219.

It seems important to me to challenge the claims to objectivity of consensus – or related claims such as its "natural" application which is "inherent" to a system of human rights protection – not only because such claims are increasingly being made, but also because consensus is discursively constructed as a form of reasoning with a particularly strong claim to objectivity. Its relative formality and the way it can be presented as a form of "mere" counting or as a "mechanical" approach gives it a veneer of objectivity which would nowadays seem naïve to posit for other kinds of legal reasoning.[1707] The epistemic approach drives this point home with particular fervour by basing truth on consensus interpreted as statistical evidence,[1708] but the general sense of objectivity-through-formality is present in other arguments in favour of consensus as well.[1709] Emphasising the indeterminacy of regional human rights law because of the paradoxical nature of legal argument, *including* European consensus, points in precisely the opposite direction: the "gap" between legal materials (vertically comparative legal materials, in the case of consensus) and the ECtHR's decisions makes the latter political whether or not consensus is used.

This also means, however, that there is no *more* objective form of reasoning available as an alternative:[1710] while consensus forms part of the argumentative structures which render regional human rights law indeterminate, so do other forms of reasoning. The point of underlining the indeterminacy of regional human rights law is not – at least not at this stage of the argument[1711] – to establish any particular form of reasoning as preferable but simply to showcase the form legal argument takes and the disconnect between legal materials and legal decisions which follows from it. In and of itself, this is a largely descriptive exercise[1712] – it simply describes the structure of legal argument.[1713] If nothing else, one might consider this

---

1707 For the way in which connections are drawn between consensus and numbers, see Chapter 5, I.

1708 See Chapter 4, II.

1709 Besides Chapter 5, I. and V., see in particular Chapter 3, II. and Chapter 10, II.; see also O'Hara, "Consensus, Difference and Sexuality: Que(e)rying the European Court of Human Rights' Concept of 'European Consensus'" for an account of how consensus assumes the appearance of truth.

1710 See generally Martti Koskenniemi, "Letter to the Editors of the Symposium," (1999) 93 *American Journal of International Law* 351.

1711 But see infra, IV.2.

1712 Explicitly Koskenniemi, *From Apology to Utopia*, at 563-564.

1713 As the subtitle of *From Apology to Utopia* ("The Structure of International Legal Argument") indicates.

helpful as professional knowledge indicating how to use legal language so as to appear as a savvier lawyer.[1714]

What I am more interested in, however, and what I also take to be the underlying motivation in most critical projects, is the more normative and indeed self-avowedly political aspect of highlighting legal indeterminacy. As Susan Marks has summarised it, "the issue is not just whether we perceive indeterminacy, but what we do with it".[1715] Emphasising indeterminacy, in other words, is only ever a first step. It represents, in Koskenniemi's words, "a rather classical form of ideology critique whose point is to undermine the feeling of naturalness we associate with our institutional practices"[1716] – it denaturalises dominant interpretations and understandings of law and thereby makes law seem less "natural and inevitable" and more "contingent and contestable".[1717] The point of the indeterminacy thesis is thus not to claim that international law does not seem determinate in its "day-to-day reality",[1718] but precisely to open up space for questioning the positions which are projected onto law within that reality. Having established that legal decisions are political rather than predetermined by the law itself, it becomes possible to ask – and therein lies the second step of the argument – why they nonetheless were made the way they were. Differently put: the focus shifts from establishing truth (or some derivative of it, e.g. legal "correctness" or objectivity) to the power structures which shape what we understand to be true (legally correct, objective, etc.) in the first place – and, in consequence, whether and how we can challenge these power structures and change such understandings.[1719]

This is why, in Chapter 1, I described my argument as critical only in a weak sense.[1720] My primary focus throughout has been on the argumentative structures of regional human rights law with specific reference to European consensus, aiming to substantiate their indeterminacy. I have

1714 See Jack M. Balkin, "A Night in the Topics: The Reason of Legal Rhetoric and the Rhetoric of Legal Reason," in *From Law's Stories: Narrative and Rhetoric in the Law*, ed. Peter Brooks and Paul Gewirtz (New Haven: Yale University Press, 1996) at 218; see also supra, note 1692.

1715 Marks, *The Riddle of All Constitutions*, at 144.

1716 Koskenniemi, *From Apology to Utopia*, at 601.

1717 Ibid., 538.

1718 Miles, "Indeterminacy" at 458 (arguing that this poses a "difficulty" to arguments based on structural indeterminacy).

1719 For an example attempting this shift from establishing truth to investigating how truth is established, see Theilen, "Pre-existing Rights and Future Articulations: Temporal Rhetoric in the Struggle for Trans Rights", at 208.

1720 Chapter 1, IV.2.

not, except occasionally in passing, put a spotlight on the structural biases which undergird the system as a whole. Koskenniemi once again: "For the 'weak' indeterminacy thesis to turn into a 'strong' one, it needs to be supplemented by an empirical argument, namely that irrespective of indeterminacy, *the system still de facto prefers some outcomes or distributive choices to other outcomes or choices*".[1721] It is resistance to this kind of structural bias which drives critique, because "something we feel that is politically wrong in the world is produced or supported by that bias" and the indeterminacy claim can be considered "a prologue to a political critique" of the status quo.[1722] At the risk of taking it out of context (as it so often is), a riff on Marx's eleventh thesis on Feuerbach perhaps most succinctly encapsulates the motivation for critique which I am endeavouring to describe here: the point is not only to interpret the world – or law as a part of our social world – but to *change* it.[1723]

Critique in this sense is driven, then, by the desire to denaturalise current social arrangements so as to open up imaginative space for social transformation, specifically *social transformation that is relatively far-reaching compared to what seems possible within the dominant ideological framework of current arrangements or institutions*.[1724] Using the example of human rights and specifically the ECHR in its interpretation by the ECtHR: I think it is fair to assume that nobody, whether conservative, liberal, radical, or otherwise, agrees with the ECtHR's case-law on each and every point. Many observers, however, would express overall satisfaction with that case-law; whatever relatively minor amendments they wish to propose could be easily accommodated within the system, by arguing on its own terms, as it

1721 Koskenniemi, *From Apology to Utopia*, at 606-607 (emphasis in original); for an argument that connects this point directly to "the particular form indeterminacy assumes", rather than a second argumentative step relatively independent from it, see Tzouvala, *Capitalism as Civilisation. A History of International Law*, at 215.

1722 Koskenniemi, *From Apology to Utopia*, at 607 and 609.

1723 For the original, see Karl Marx, "Thesen über Feuerbach," in *Karl Marx: Thesen über Feuerbach*, ed. Georges Labica (Hamburg and Berlin: Argument-Verlag, 1998) at 15; for a connection of this point to denaturalisation and wonder as a first step, see Theilen, "Of Wonder and Changing the World: Philip Allott's Legal Utopianism" at 345-346; on context for Marx's quote in relation to "critical knowledge", see Marks, *The Riddle of All Constitutions*, at 123-125.

1724 On the element of imagination in contrast to current orthodoxies, see Gerry Simpson, "Imagination," in *Concepts for International Law. Contributions to Disciplinary Thought*, ed. Jean d'Aspremont and Sahib Singh (Cheltenham: Edward Elgar, 2019) at 414.

were.[1725] When one perceives a more fundamental disconnect between the status quo and one's political commitments, however, critique enters the picture since it becomes necessary to "call the system into question"[1726] by emphasising its contingency and its structural biases so as to make certain outcomes imaginable, much less potentially realisable.

I consider the structural biases underlying human rights law to have been convincingly established elsewhere, driven by political commitments which I largely share: although this kind of feminist, queer, Marxist or postcolonial critique often does not deal specifically with the ECHR,[1727] the points it makes are broadly transferable from the project of legal human rights as a whole to the ECHR in particular. If anything, some points of critique may be *more* applicable, for example in light of the way in which the ECHR largely neglects socio-economic rights,[1728] while giving particularly strong expression to the (supposed) human rights of corporations.[1729] The preceding chapters could thus be considered a retroactive

1725 See Kennedy, *A Critique of Adjudication (fin de siècle)*, at 245.

1726 Knox, "Strategy and Tactics" at 200.

1727 See e.g. Hilary Charlesworth, Christine Chinkin, and Shelley Wright, "Feminist Approaches to International Law," (1991) 85 *American Journal of International Law* 613; Karen Engle, "International Human Rights and Feminism: When Discourses Meet," (1992) 13 *Michigan Journal of International Law* 517; Makau Mutua, "Savages, Victims, and Saviors: The Metaphor of Human Rights," (2001) 42 *Harvard International Law Journal* 201; Balakrishnan Rajagopal, *International Law from Below. Development, Social Movements and Third World Resistance* (Cambridge: Cambridge University Press, 2003), chapter 7; Brown, "'The Most We Can Hope For…': Human Rights and the Politics of Fatalism"; Dianne Otto, "Lost in Translation: Re-scripting the Sexed Subjects of International Human Rights Law," in *International Law and its Others*, ed. Anne Orford (Cambridge: Cambridge University Press, 2006); Upendra Baxi, *The Future of Human Rights*, 3rd ed. (New Delhi: Oxford University Press, 2008); Dianne Otto, "Queering Gender [Identity] in International Law," (2015) 33 *Nordic Journal of Human Rights* 299; Paul O'Connell, "On the Human Rights Question," (2018) 40 *Human Rights Quarterly* 962; Kapur, *Gender, Alterity and Human Rights*; in the context of the ECtHR, see e.g. Marie-Benedicte Dembour, *Who Believes in Human Rights? Reflections on the European Convention* (Cambridge: Cambridge University Press, 2006); Damian A. Gonzalez-Salzberg, "The Accepted Transsexual and the Absent Transgender: A Queer Reading of the Regulation of Sex/Gender by the European Court of Human Rights," (2014) 29 *American University International Law Review* 797.

1728 See Samuel Moyn, *Not Enough. Human rights in an Unequal World* (Cambridge, Mass.: Belknap Press of Harvard University Press, 2018), at 189.

1729 Anna Grear, "Challenging Corporate 'Humanity': Legal Disembodiment, Embodiment and Human Rights," (2007) 7 *Human Rights Law Review* 511 at 535.

prologue to these forms of critique – a denaturalisation of the way in which legal argument is used by the ECtHR so as to provide for a point of entry for political critique.

III. The Role of Human Rights Courts

The moment of disorientation which follows from denaturalising existing social arrangements – for example by insisting on the indeterminacy of law and thus unsettling the feeling of necessity associated with dominant legal doctrines – is arguably particularly relevant in the context of international law and human rights. Perhaps because of a sense of enthusiasm for "the international", perhaps – relatedly – because of the way in which these areas of law are often discursively produced as morally favourable compared to, say, contract law or company law,[1730] the image of international law "as always already containing [an] ideal of the good society" persists.[1731] Similarly, human rights tend to be perceived in mainstream discourse as a good in and of themselves – mankind's last utopia, our "highest moral precepts and political ideals".[1732] In this context even more so than elsewhere, then, critique takes on a killjoy function[1733] precisely by aiming to disenchant human rights, to present them not as part of some kind of progress narrative,[1734] always already pointing towards a better world, but rather as "an arena where different visions of the world are fought out"[1735] – and thus to open up space for questioning whether human rights are quite as emancipatory as they are made out to be.

1730 See e.g. David Kennedy, "A New World Order: Yesterday, Today, and Tomorrow," (1994) 4 *Transnational Law and Contemporary Problems* 329; Anne Orford, "Embodying Internationalism: The Making of International Lawyers," (1998) 19 *Australian Yearbook of International Law* 1.

1731 Koskenniemi, *From Apology to Utopia*, at 613.

1732 Moyn, *The Last Utopia*, at 1; see Chapter 1, I.1.

1733 On the feminist killjoy, see Sara Ahmed, *Living a Feminist Life* (Durham and London: Duke University Press, 2017); and e.g. Sara Ahmed, *The Promise of Happiness* (Durham and London: Duke University Press, 2010), at 66: "Feminists do kill joy in a certain sense: they disturb the very fantasy that happiness can be found in certain places"; human rights might be considered one of those places.

1734 See Chapter 6, VI.

1735 Kapur, "Human Rights in the 21st Century: Take a Walk on the Dark Side" at 671.

Highlighting the "dark sides"[1736] of human rights and their use as an instrument of power and governmentality need not imply that they cannot *also* have emancipatory potential. There has been much debate in recent years as to whether human rights can be reimagined in a way compatible with political claims for radical social transformation in the wake of the various critiques mentioned above[1737] – a kind of "critical redemption of human rights"[1738] or "rights revisionism".[1739] Some see little to no value in this, insisting that the emancipatory potential of human rights has always been or has become so limited compared to their "dark sides" that it is not worth engaging with them and other languages of resistance should be found.[1740] Others emphasise instead that, for all their failings, human rights "hold possibilities to be used to gesture towards a future that is better than the present and the current oppressive use of power within it",[1741] and hence that the vocabulary of human rights remains useful for those interested in transformative politics.[1742]

Framing the debate as a dichotomy in this way, of course, involves a significant degree of oversimplification. For one thing, there is a broad spectrum of positions ranging from relatively enthusiastic reengagement with human rights while incorporating points of critique to wholesale rejection of any engagement, with various intermediate positions proposing, for example, different ways of engaging strategically with human rights given

1736 David Kennedy, *The Dark Sides of Virtue. Reassessing International Humanitarianism* (Princeton and Oxford: Princeton University Press, 2004).

1737 Mégret, "Where Does the Critique of International Human Rights Stand? An Exploration in 18 Vignettes" at 25.

1738 Golder, "Beyond Redemption? Problematising the Critique of Human Rights in Contemporary International Legal Thought" at 79.

1739 Costas Douzinas, "Adikia: On Communism and Rights", available at <http://criticallegalthinking.com/2010/11/30/adikia-on-communism-and-rights/>.

1740 Very clearly Golder, "Beyond Redemption? Problematising the Critique of Human Rights in Contemporary International Legal Thought" at 113-114; tending in this direction also e.g. David Kennedy, "The International Human Rights Regime: Still Part of the Problem," in *Examining Critical Perspectives on Human Rights*, ed. Rob Dickinson, et al. (Cambridge: Cambridge University Press, 2013) at 34.

1741 Kathryn McNeilly, *Human Rights and Radical Social Transformation: Futurity, Alterity, Power* (London and New York: Routledge, 2018), at 6.

1742 E.g. O'Connell, "On the Human Rights Question" at 964; Grear, "Challenging Corporate 'Humanity': Legal Disembodiment, Embodiment and Human Rights" at 516; see also Kapur, "Human Rights in the 21st Century: Take a Walk on the Dark Side" at 682, though now much more cautious e.g. in Kapur, *Gender, Alterity and Human Rights*, at 152.

their prominence within current global discourses.[1743] For another thing, and more importantly for present purposes, the language of human rights is clearly used in a myriad different ways by different actors in different contexts, and for all the connections that can be drawn between these different uses, it seems counterproductive to lump them all together without further consideration.[1744] It is this latter point which I would like to briefly dwell on in this section, with particular reference to the engagement with human rights in their *judicialized* form.

This is not a common area of critical reengagement of human rights, to say the least. Courts, as I noted at the end of the previous chapter, are hardly known for being revolutionary. Hopes for far-reaching social transformation are typically placed, accordingly, on social movements which make more radical political claims phrased, for example, as peasant rights or decommodification rights. Not only does this shift in focus allow for discussion of normative claims that imply more meaningful social transformation than those typically raised before courts, it also changes the way in which we think of both human rights and our own position within the struggle for social change. In this way, it becomes possible to stress, as Paul O'Connell has put it, "the centrality of social and political struggle in the formulation and defense of human rights".[1745] Legal interpretations of human rights by courts form an explicit counter-point to this way of engaging with human rights: "narrow, formalistic, and overly juridical concepts of what human rights are" need to be overcome so as to enable productive reengagement with the notion of human rights elsewhere.[1746] Or, to make a similar point from within a different framework: foregrounding different interpretations and understandings of human rights by social movements could be thought to support what Robert Cover calls "the jurisgenerative principle by which legal meaning proliferates"[1747] and which, in the words

1743 See McNeilly, *Human Rights and Radical Social Transformation: Futurity, Alterity, Power*, at 4; on strategy more generally, see Knox, "Strategy and Tactics"; and on the prominence of the language of human rights through the topical lens of habituality, see von Arnauld and Theilen, "Rhetoric of Rights: A Topical Perspective on the Functions of Claiming a 'Human Right to …'", at 44-45.

1744 For a similar point in a different context, see Paul O'Connell, "Human Rights: Contesting the Displacement Thesis," (2018) 69 *Northern Ireland Legal Quarterly* 19 at 24.

1745 O'Connell, "On the Human Rights Question" at 964.

1746 Ibid.

1747 Robert M. Cover, "The Supreme Court 1982 Term. Foreword: Nomos and Narrative," (1983) 97 *Harvard Law Review* 4 at 40.

of Seyla Benhabib, "anticipates new forms of justice to come".[1748] Courts, however, are "jurispathic": their legal interpretation does not serve to generate new meanings but rather shrouds other understandings of human rights.[1749]

Having thus, albeit very roughly, situated human rights in their judicialized form against the backdrop of critical discussions of human rights more generally, it becomes possible to further flesh out the theme of indeterminacy and its connection to a quest for far-reaching social transformation, as sketched in the preceding section. The emphasis on legal indeterminacy, I argued there, appears important so as to denaturalise dominant legal narratives and thus provide a point of entry for political critique. It is precisely these legal narratives which also account in large part for the scepticism surrounding the judicialization of human rights in critical quarters. As Duncan Kennedy summarises the way in which judicialization functions to legitimate the status quo: "alternative ways of understanding are rendered invisible or marginal or seemingly irrational by the practice of withdrawing a large part of the law-making function into a domain governed by the convention of legal correctness and the denial of ideological choice",[1750] i.e. professional legal vocabulary. In a similar vein, many critical thinkers have criticised the increasing (jurispathic) judicialization of human rights as contributing to their depoliticization[1751] which, in turn, makes it more difficult to use them in such a way as to challenge current power structures.[1752] Emphasising the indeterminacy of legal argument aims to break open legal discourse to reveal the ideological choices it contains and allow for political contestation – which may, for example, take the form of foregrounding alternative uses of human rights by radical social movements.

1748 Benhabib, "Introduction: Cosmopolitanism without Illusions" at 15; see also Baxi, *The Future of Human Rights*, at 206; von Arnauld and Theilen, "Rhetoric of Rights: A Topical Perspective on the Functions of Claiming a 'Human Right to …'", at 47.

1749 Cover, "Nomos and Narrative" at 40.

1750 Kennedy, *A Critique of Adjudication (fin de siècle)*, at 236; see also Grear, "Challenging Corporate 'Humanity': Legal Disembodiment, Embodiment and Human Rights" at 529.

1751 Mouffe, *The Democratic Paradox*, at 115.

1752 McNeilly, *Human Rights and Radical Social Transformation: Futurity, Alterity, Power*, at 80; Mégret, "Where Does the Critique of International Human Rights Stand? An Exploration in 18 Vignettes" at 15 and 33.

This need not necessarily imply that human rights courts such as the ECtHR cannot be mobilized as part of a strategy for social transformation at all. Contestation always takes place in contexts which are already structured, albeit differently, by various power relations, so in a sense there is nothing unusual about this. Beth Simmons has argued that "[i]n the struggle against oppression from whatever source, it can be quite useful for one hegemony to be used to challenge another".[1753] Transposing this approach to the ECtHR, one might try to conceive of the ECtHR less as an institution providing fixed answers to the interpretation of human rights and rather as an institution which can be "triggered" by activists into providing judgments as resources for further activism at the national level,[1754] thus contributing to contestation of current power structures without itself setting the agenda for social transformation. From within this perspective, courts are perhaps best conceptualised as "marginal actors" in a broader "political struggle" for rights[1755] – marginal in a sense, but nonetheless potentially important given the practical import which the ECtHR's judgments, as statements with significant "expressive power",[1756] for better or worse, may have *in the context of a broader political struggle*.

A number of proposals have been made with regard to the ECtHR which could be read as tending in this direction, including some which make explicit reference to European consensus. In that vein, Thomas Kleinlein has argued for "a vision of the role of the Court"[1757] in which European consensus and the "procedural" approach to the margin of appreciation[1758] are combined in such a way as to generate judgments which "do not represent 'the last word' but can provide a trigger for democratic contestation and deliberation".[1759] Kleinlein is primarily concerned with the democratic legitimacy of the ECtHR, not with its role within processes

---

1753 Simmons, *Mobilizing for Human Rights*, at 371.

1754 See in more detail on the "triggering function" of human rights von Arnauld and Theilen, "Rhetoric of Rights: A Topical Perspective on the Functions of Claiming a 'Human Right to …'", at 45-47.

1755 Henry Steiner and Philip Alston, *International Human Rights in Context: Law, Politics, and Morals*, 1st ed. (Oxford: Oxford University Press, 1996), at vi, cited from Rajagopal, *International Law from Below. Development, Social Movements and Third World Resistance*, at 207.

1756 Lau, "Rewriting Schalk and Kopf: Shifting the Locus of Deference" at 257.

1757 Kleinlein, "Consensus and Contestability: The ECtHR and the Combined Potential of European Consensus and Procedural Rationality Control" at 881.

1758 See Chapter 8, III.3.

1759 Kleinlein, "Consensus and Contestability: The ECtHR and the Combined Potential of European Consensus and Procedural Rationality Control" at 888.

of social transformation; but his approach nonetheless implies a conceptualisation of the ECtHR which sees it not as an autarkic court with unquestioned authority, but embedded within broader political processes in which contestation – including contestation of (what the ECtHR interprets as) European consensus[1760] – plays a vital role. The emphasis, as Conor Gearty has summarised it, is ultimately less on the Court itself and rather on "a rationally based local engagement with rights".[1761]

There is something to be said for such an approach, particularly in light of the fact that many (though of course by no means all) social movements do engage with courts in some way in practice. For those interested in far-reaching social transformation, however, it is also important to appreciate its limits. This goes back to the motivation for critique which I suggested in the previous section: if critique is aimed at opening up imaginative space for social transformation more far-reaching than what currently seems possible within a certain institution – such as the ECtHR – then the conceptualisation of the ECtHR's judgments as useful within a broader political struggle, and thus a tool for contestation, should not distract from what is *not* made available for contestation within the institutional setting of the ECtHR,[1762] nor from the way in which legal discourse tends to restrict rather than expand imaginative space.

IV. Justifying Concrete Norms in Regional Human Rights Law, Revisited

1. The Indeterminacy Thesis in the Judicial Context

I have so far said very little about how the ECtHR *should* decide the cases before it or justify the decisions it reaches. Given the rough overview of critical international legal theory and critical perspectives on human rights in the preceding sections, it becomes clear that this is hardly accidental. One might perhaps describe the difference between a structural critique of judicialized human rights and the question of how the ECtHR should de-

1760 Ibid., 881 and 893.

1761 Gearty, "Building Consensus on European Consensus" at 467.

1762 In that vein, I think there is much to be said for O'Hara's assessment that "queer freedom" (and other kinds of freedom) "may be better sought away from the European Court of Human Rights and its insistence on consensus": O'Hara, "Consensus, Difference and Sexuality: Que(e)rying the European Court of Human Rights' Concept of 'European Consensus'".

cide as a difference in emphasis[1763] – or, perhaps, as differently oriented.[1764] Critique operates on the meta-level:[1765] as Robert Knox has summarised critical international legal theory, it is "about the *structure* of law and legal argument, which is not concerned with [how] specific legal rules should be deployed or the outcomes of specific legal decisions, but is rather about the broader […] relationship between law and social phenomena".[1766] Differently put, where traditional legal scholarship is oriented "inwards" in an attempt at "problem-solving" from within the perspective of the conventions of legal discourse, critique aims to work "outwards" and provide different perspectives on how the problem is framed in the first place.[1767]

Unsurprisingly, this often seems unsatisfying or evasive to those engaging directly in legal debates in the context of particular institutions.[1768] This is perhaps particularly so in the case of courts such the ECtHR: after all, our starting point in Chapter 1 was that the ECtHR's judges are bound to provide an interpretation of the ECHR and, ultimately, either confirm or deny a human rights violation in any given case. If the goal is to justify such an interpretation, then the focus clearly lies on precisely the kind of "problem-solving" for which critique offers little guidance. The question thus remains, from this inwards-oriented perspective, what the implications of critique are for the way in which the ECtHR's judgments should be reached and justified, since the ECtHR does not have the academic privilege of restricting itself to a meta-level analysis without some concrete decision as to the cases before it.[1769]

The obvious starting point, particularly in light of the discussion of the indeterminacy of regional human rights law above, is that the law itself underdetermines the results which the ECtHR's judges can or should reach. As Jan Klabbers has put it, "critical legal studies is not the most ap-

1763 See Marks, *The Riddle of All Constitutions*, at 132 and 138.

1764 Supra, note 1696.

1765 See also Chapter 1, IV. on structuralism.

1766 Knox, "Strategy and Tactics" at 203.

1767 See Marks, *The Riddle of All Constitutions*, at 131-132, building on Robert W. Cox, "Social Forces, States and World Orders: Beyond International Relations Theory," (1981) 10 *Millennium: Journal of International Studies* 126.

1768 On the politics involved in demanding different kinds of answers, see Pierre Schlag, "'Le hors de texte, c'est moi' - The Politics of Form and the Domestication of Deconstruction," (1990) 11 *Cardozo Law Review* 1631 at 1632.

1769 See also the distinction drawn by Kennedy, "A Semiotics of Critique" at 1163 between the decisionist as "responsible actor" (problem-solving) and the "decisionist as analyst" (critique).

propriate tool for analysing what the law says".[1770] Indeed, this is precisely the point, since critical international legal theory – as the indeterminacy thesis makes particularly clear – aims to shift the understanding of law *away* from the idea that the law "says" anything in particular, and to instead draw attention to the power structures which exclude certain positions from the scope of what it is commonly thought to say. Any suggestions as to how the ECtHR should proceed are thus, it bears repeating, *political* in the sense that they entail an element of decisionism rather than following from legal materials.

Aiming to open up legal decisions in this way carries both potential advantages and significant risks in the context of the judicial decision. Optimistically, one might argue that although critical international legal theory provides no "immediate solutions" to the "problems on which practicing lawyers are requested to give advice" – or judges to decide – it nonetheless "serves practice by producing critical reflection and self-awareness".[1771] I mentioned above that one implication of the indeterminacy thesis is that, by descriptively engaging with the structure of legal argument, it provides a resource for how professional legal vocabulary might be used in different ways.[1772] Once normatively saturated, this implies that it might "provide resources for the use of international law's professional vocabulary *for critical or emancipatory causes*".[1773] Taking these statements together, one might hope that the ECtHR's judges, having reflected on the structural biases underpinning legal argument in the context of the ECtHR, make use of their mastery of the language of regional human rights law to support such previously, perhaps inadvertently, disavowed causes.

But there is a difficulty here, most succinctly and rather self-evidently captured by the question of what constitutes "critical or emancipatory causes". The law cannot, in light of its indeterminacy, be regarded as providing answers to this question – and for good reason, since moving beyond the idea that it contains the "ideal of the good society" was part of the reason for critique in the first place.[1774] This also means, however, that we are thrown back to disagreement about moral matters or differences in

1770 Klabbers, *The Concept of Treaty in International Law*, at 11.

1771 Remarks by Martti Koskenniemi, cited from David Kennedy and Chris Tennant, "New Approaches to International Law: A Bibliography," (1994) 35 *Harvard International Law Journal* 417 at 427; on the limits of self-reflectivity, see Chapter 7, IV.

1772 Supra, note 1714.

1773 Koskenniemi, *From Apology to Utopia*, at 581 (emphasis added).

1774 Supra, note 1731.

"political preference".[1775] Since the indeterminacy of regional human rights law means that the outcomes of cases before the ECtHR cannot be crafted onto some understanding of law (or consensus[1776]) external to the Court,[1777] it underlines their responsibility for the decisions which they reach[1778] – but the flipside of this is a strongly subjectified framing of how the ECtHR should decide. The "personal perspective"[1779] of the judges gains immense weight – hence the repeated classification of critical international legal theory as "perspectivism",[1780] "virtue ethics"[1781] or, more pejoratively, "nihilism".[1782]

1775 Kennedy and Tennant, "New Approaches to International Law: A Bibliography" at 427.

1776 In academic commentary, this is sometimes (especially in the context of legitimacy-enhancement) expressed through the description of consensus as a "distancing device", building on Joseph Raz, "On the Authority and Interpretation of Cosntitutions: Some Preliminaries," in *Constitutionalism: Philosophical Foundations*, ed. Larry Alexander (Cambridge: Cambridge University Press, 1998) at 190; see e.g. Senden, *Interpretation of Fundamental Rights*, at 118 (tellingly in the context of "increas[ing] the objectivity of a particular decision"); Legg, *The Margin of Appreciation*, at 134.

1777 See Chapter 1, IV.5. and Chapter 5, V.

1778 See Chapter 1, I. and IV.5., and generally on human responsibility for law Koskenniemi, *From Apology to Utopia*, at 536-537 and 615; Jan Klabbers, "Towards a Culture of Formalism? Martti Koskenniemi and the Virtues," (2013) 27 *Temple International and Comparative Law Journal* 417 at 420; Philip Allott, "The Will to Know and the Will to Power. Theory and Moral Responsibility," in *The Health of Nations. Society and Law beyond the State* (Cambridge: Cambridge University Press, 2002) at 33; Theilen, "Of Wonder and Changing the World: Philip Allott's Legal Utopianism" at 364-365; see also Sahib Singh, "Koskenniemi's Images of the International Lawyer," (2016) 29 *Leiden Journal of International Law* 699 at 709 for a productive probing of critical notions of responsibility.

1779 Korhonen, "New International Law: Silence, Defence or Deliverance?" at 24; see also Paavo Kotiaho, "A Return to Koskenniemi, or the Disconcerting Cooptation of Rupture," (2012) 13 *German Law Journal* 483 at 490: "jurists rather than positive rules become the law's nucleus".

1780 Korhonen, "New International Law: Silence, Defence or Deliverance?" at 24.

1781 Klabbers, "Towards a Culture of Formalism? Martti Koskenniemi and the Virtues" at 422; see also Singh, "Koskenniemi's Images of the International Lawyer" at 725 on "virtue as the last refuge against false promises and possibilities", and passim on the way in which critical international legal theory tends to invest in specific images of the (lawyerly) subject as the basis of its emancipatory politics; on this, see also Tzouvala, *Capitalism as Civilisation. A History of International Law*, at 216-217.

1782 See the discussion in Koskenniemi, *From Apology to Utopia*, at 535-536 and 539; see also Kennedy, *A Critique of Adjudication (fin de siècle)*, at 361.

Generally speaking, my sense is that the charge of nihilism reveals more about those who raise it than about critical international legal theory:[1783] we would live in an impoverished normative universe indeed if questioning legal normativity led directly to nihilism. For those interested in critique in the sense I outlined earlier in this chapter, of course, moving beyond the ideological baggage contained in legal discourse is precisely the point, so worries about legal normativity collapsing, in principle, fall flat. And yet, one might raise doubts about the implications of championing legal indeterminacy in the specific context of human rights courts such as the ECtHR.[1784] To be sure, highlighting indeterminacy in this context seems particularly necessary to open up imaginative space geared at understandings of human rights which differ from dominant judicial approaches and thus to support to kind of critical perspective on human rights sketched in the previous section. The implications of indeterminacy and the perspectivism which comes with it *within the institutional practice of courts as they currently stand*, however, are less clear.

Consider again the question of what counts as "critical or emancipatory causes". Within the ambit of critical international legal theory as a more or less consistently left-wing academic project,[1785] this question could no doubt be answered,[1786] albeit in broad strokes and with many differences in emphasis and indeed plenty of outright disagreement.[1787] Here, the imaginative space opened up by the indeterminacy thesis can be used for the kind of structural critique mentioned above. The ECtHR's judges, however, make their decisions in a very different institutional context and, given the various personal and procedural constraints which that context involves,[1788] are likely to approach their judgments from entirely different,

---

1783 Just as the question of "What would you put in its place?" (i.e., in place of the rule of law or other objects of critique) reveals more about those who ask it than about those it is aimed at: see Richard Michael Fischl, "The Question that Killed Critical Legal Studies," (1992) 17 *Law and Social Inquiry* 779.

1784 For a brief discussion of the indeterminacy thesis with regard to specific contexts, see also Chapter 10, II.2.

1785 See Kennedy, *A Critique of Adjudication (fin de siècle)*, at 246 (primarily in the American context, but I think the point holds more generally).

1786 See also Mégret, "Where Does the Critique of International Human Rights Stand? An Exploration in 18 Vignettes" at 6-7.

1787 For some of these broad strokes, see the critiques cited supra, note 1727.

1788 One obvious point (especially in contrast e.g. with social movements or other less institutionalised actors as mentioned above) is the nomination of the ECtHR's judges by representatives of the States parties in the CoE's Parliamen-

more conservative perspectives.[1789] There are no guarantees that increasing imaginative space in this context will lead to results considered beneficial by those who, like me, emphasise legal indeterminacy in an effort to further what we perceive as critical or emancipatory causes.[1790] Furthermore, one might question whether the subjectification of legal decisions and the de facto empowerment of judges which results from the lack of legal constraints once indeterminacy is acknowledged does not run counter to the spirit of critical perspectives on human rights discussed in the preceding section – an inadvertent invitation for judges to expand their jurispathic activities and pull ever-increasing subject-matters into the ambit of legal discourse.[1791]

Against this rather ambivalent backdrop, I would like to use the remainder of this chapter to make some tentative suggestions as to how the ECtHR's reasoning might be improved with an eye on legal indeterminacy and the Court's position in processes of social transformation. In light of all that I have said so far, it should have become amply clear that there are significant risks associated with this endeavour, and that it is not intended to counteract the well-founded scepticism about the role of courts within transformative politics as sketched in the previous section but rather, a cer-

---

tary Assembly (Article 22 ECHR), which creates an easy way to filter out those with radical views from the outset. Another important point orienting the ECtHR towards conservatism may well be the focus on preserving its own institutional power (see Chapter 9, II.5.), which is part of why I think it is important to de-emphasise (sociological) legitimacy as a value in human rights adjudication (infra, IV.3.). However, ultimately none of the suggestions that follow can counteract the important insight that "possibilities are framed by circumstances", that "change unfolds within a context that includes systematic constraints and pressures" (Marks, "False Contingency" at 2) and that these constraints are particularly pronounced in the judicial context.

1789 See also Mégret, "The Apology of Utopia" at 495 on the difference between judges and litigators; for the related (though not identical) distinction between observers' and judges' standpoints, see Chapter 2, IV.; in that terminology, my point here is that from an observers' standpoint, the judicial context cannot be removed from the limits discussed above.

1790 Kennedy, *A Critique of Adjudication (fin de siècle)*, at 136-137; Tzouvala, *Capitalism as Civilisation. A History of International Law*, at 37-38.

1791 Ibid., 206-207, on the possibility that judges who embrace critique might "tyrannize us worse than they do already" but also making the more fundamental point that fear of this (hypothetical) consequence motivates the denial of critique; see also Mégret, "Where Does the Critique of International Human Rights Stand? An Exploration in 18 Vignettes" at 8, more generally on the connection between indeterminacy and "the discretion of the judge or the technocrat".

tain tension notwithstanding, to complement it. My motivation for this part of the argument is twofold. For one thing, having argued that law is political, it seems all the more important to engage in political debate, which then includes debate as to how human rights in their legal form (e.g. as codified in the ECHR) should be interpreted – even if our expectations for truly transformative potential emanating from the ECtHR's judgements are very much muted. While this relates in large part to substantive debates on the interpretation of different rights which I must bracket here for lack of space, some general observations about different kinds of reasoning in relation to current power structures and the possibilities for social change might be made. Given the overall focus of this study, I will approach this task by putting European consensus back into the spotlight and questioning its merits with regard to a transformative politics (2.).

For another thing, and more foundationally, I think it is worth reflecting on how we think about the ECtHR's reasoning qua legal reasoning. After all, the difficulty in reengaging with the ECtHR or other courts following critique pertains not only to the substantive positions which they are likely to take, but also to the form of reasoning they deploy. If we accept that legal discourse with its tendency towards naturalisation and depoliticization constitutes an obstacle to transformative politics, as those who propose reengagement with human rights in their non-juridical form argue, then the subsequent reengagement with courts as potential enablers of social change may easily be liable to negate the effect of critique, *even if consensus was no longer accorded a prominent place within the ECtHR's reasoning*. But legal reasoning is itself neither monolithic nor set in stone[1792] – so perhaps we might start thinking about how to reimagine the very notions of law, courts, and judgment-giving[1793] in such a way as to make them less inimical to struggles for far-reaching social transformation (3.). As one pos-

1792 See Kennedy, *A Critique of Adjudication (fin de siècle)*, at 14: "We might have the benefits of judiciality without its current drawbacks".

1793 One source of inspiration here (and one which is well aware of the dangers of complicity in engaging reconstructively with judicial pronouncements) are the numerous feminist judgment projects which have been blossoming over the last few years – although, by and large, they do tend to focus on showing how decisions could have been made differently (which chimes with the indeterminacy thesis) but without being "overly experimental with the *form* of the rewritten judgments" in the interest of practical impact (Sharon Cowan, "The Scottish Feminist Judgments Project: A New Frontier" (Oñati Socio-legal Series, v. 8, n. 9 - Feminist Judgments: Comparative Socio-Legal Perspectives on

sible avenue to approaching this task, I propose we might return to the notion of vertically comparative legal reasoning – but we might use it, not as the basis for establishing European consensus or lack thereof, but rather to unsettle dominant concepts within European public culture and thus to contribute, in a sense, to the openness of regional human rights adjudication (4.).

2. European Consensus and the Perpetuation of Current Power Structures

Let me begin, then, by drawing together some themes from the previous chapters on European consensus in relation to what I have said above. The starting point must be to acknowledge that, if consensus does indeed form part of the argumentative structures which render human rights law indeterminate and there is, accordingly, a "gap" between the reference to both European consensus and other forms of reasoning, on the one hand, and the legal decision, on the other,[1794] then consensus *can be used in different ways*[1795] and there is no *necessary* connection between consensus as a form of reasoning and the outcomes which it is used to justify. Not only can it be given more or less weight within the overall reasoning of the ECtHR, it also incorporates the tension between moral and ethical normativity in such a way that whether consensus or lack of consensus is established depends in large part on how the issue is framed and from which angle the vertically comparative legal analysis is approached. I treated these issues by reference, in particular, to numerical issues involved in establishing (lack of) consensus, to the different sources of consensus such as domestic or (different kinds of) international law, and to the level of generality at which consensus is approached.[1796]

Drawing attention to the disconnect between argumentative structures within regional human rights law and the results they are used to justify, however, does not mean that certain forms of reasoning, *if their use in a certain way becomes prevalent*, cannot orient the ECtHR towards certain out-

Judicial Decision Making and Gender Justice, 2018), at 1395, emphasis added; available at <https://papers.ssrn.com/sol3/papers.cfm?abstract_id=3249609>); my approach here is to put the focus on practical impact aside in favour of voicing some more disruptive suggestions.

1794 Supra, note 1702.

1795 See Chapter 1, IV.2. and IV.5.

1796 See in particular Chapters 5 to 7.

comes.[1797] In that vein, although the manifold issues involved in establishing (lack of) European consensus involve a much greater amount of malleability than is commonly acknowledged, the key characteristics of consensus which I posited in Chapter 1 nonetheless give it some shape and render it intelligible as a form of argument the frequent use of which can be politically evaluated.[1798] For another thing, a certain rather formulaic way of using consensus not only appears in some of the ECtHR's judgments, but is also increasingly being advocated for by academic observers of the ECtHR and thus constructed as the paradigmatic case of "European consensus":[1799] based in large part on concerns about the ECtHR's legitimacy, a picture of consensus emerges in which it is constructed primarily by reference to domestic law, ideally to a large number of States parties, approached at what I dubbed the "Goldilocks level of generality", and endowed with strong normative force.[1800] Such an approach chimes with calls that consensus should be used more consistently and predictably,[1801] and would, accordingly, make the notion of consensus more tangible still. It is this restricted conception of consensus which will form the primary subject of my evaluation in this subsection, though I would posit that the gist of my remarks also applies, albeit less starkly, to European consensus as an expression of a pan-European ethos more generally.

How, then, might one evaluate the ECtHR's use of European consensus from the perspective of a politics oriented towards social transformation? To my mind, one might summarise as follows. By virtue of the way European consensus assigns normative force to the legal systems of the States parties as they currently stand, foregrounding it within the ECtHR's reasoning not only carries a noticeable *conservative lilt*[1802] but also *points away from critical engagement with current power structures* both intra-nationally and transnationally within Europe. Let me develop both of these points in slightly more detail by contrasting the implications of foregrounding European consensus with the critical reengagements with human rights mentioned above.

1797 See Chapter 8, IV.

1798 Chapter 1, III.

1799 See the dynamic described by Větrovský, "Determining the Content of the European Consenus Concept: The Hidden Role of Language" at 127-128.

1800 See Chapter 9, II.4.; for the Goldilocks level of generality, see Chapter 7, I.

1801 See Chapter 5, I.

1802 Mégret, "Where Does the Critique of International Human Rights Stand? An Exploration in 18 Vignettes" at 15.

I have already cited Kathryn McNeilly's argument that, once reimagined in a different form from currently dominant understandings, human rights "hold possibilities to be used to gesture towards a future that is better than the present and the current oppressive use of power within it".[1803] She develops the notion of "human rights to come" – a "fundamentally *futural* conception of human rights" linked to alterity and aiming to disrupt current understandings of human rights.[1804] McNeilly's framework is particularly explicit on this point, but other critical scholars have made similar proposals: Costas Douzinas, for example, builds on Ernst Bloch's notion of the "not yet" to conceptualise human rights as "future looking".[1805] Upendra Baxi foregrounds the "extraordinarily complex constitutive notion of *potentiality*" of human rights.[1806] He emphasises both the exclusionary aspects of the currently "existing world of human rights" and the "possibility of decreating this world in the process of recreating new worlds for human rights" so as to give voice to "the stateless, the refugee, the massively impoverished human beings, the indigenous peoples of the world, and peoples living with disabilities".[1807]

There are two related aspects in these reimagined conceptualisations of human rights I would like to foreground here in contrast to European consensus.[1808] The first lies in the temporal mode from within which human rights are approached. The critical engagements just quoted are oriented towards the future, always seeking to keep human rights open for different

1803 Supra, note 1741.

1804 McNeilly, *Human Rights and Radical Social Transformation: Futurity, Alterity, Power*, at 26 (emphasis in original).

1805 Costas Douzinas, *The End of Human Rights* (Oxford: Hart, 2000), at 145 and 245; for Bloch's notion of the "not yet", see Bloch, *Hoffnung*, e.g. at 83; Theilen, "Of Wonder and Changing the World: Philip Allott's Legal Utopianism" at 341.

1806 Baxi, *The Future of Human Rights*, at 2 (emphasis added), building on Giorgio Agamben, *Potentialities. Collected Essays in Philosophy*, trans. Daniel Heller-Roazen (Stanford: Stanford University Press, 2000).

1807 Baxi, *The Future of Human Rights*, at 2.

1808 The points raised here bear some resemblance to criticism made from within the morality-focussed perspective (for which, see Chapter 2, II.), which perhaps attests to how uncomfortably close critical accounts can inadvertently be to the liberal frameworks they aim to contest. However, I do think that the critical mindset sketched above implies a fundamentally different perspective, motivated by different concerns and aiming to ask entirely different questions. Accordingly, as the further argument will make clear, the point of criticising consensus cannot simply be to switch to the morality-focussed perspective and call it a day.

interpretations and engagements yet "to come".[1809] If one subscribes to the critique of human rights which regards them as implicated in power structures and not inherently emancipatory,[1810] then this kind of open, futural approach seems important so to gain the "promise of a better future" not from human rights law as such, let alone in its current form, but from the "sense that it is possible to do things *differently*".[1811] European consensus, by contrast, is oriented backwards, towards the way things *actually are in the present* – specifically, by virtue of its vertically comparative approach, towards the shape the States parties' legal systems currently take. This element of "conservatism"[1812] inherent in consensus has long since been noted, of course: as Paul Martens has put it, European consensus "appears to favour the status quo".[1813]

The second aspect I would like to emphasise is the focus on alterity in the critical conceptualisations of human rights cited above. This clearly relates to the previous point in that the futural mode of human rights serves to promote an openness towards precisely those who cannot yet articulate their claims within human rights as they are currently understood:[1814] as Ratna Kapur has put it, human rights are "radical tools for those who have never had them".[1815] The examples which Baxi provides of those currently given insufficient voice highlights the importance of this point.[1816] Yet once again, European consensus points us in the opposite direction: because the ECtHR tends to establish (lack of) consensus by applying a prism of commonality to vertically comparative legal reasoning "without examining the reasons for the consensus" which it thus constructs,[1817] there is a

1809 See also supra, note 1748.

1810 Supra, III.

1811 McNeilly, *Human Rights and Radical Social Transformation: Futurity, Alterity, Power*, at 40 (emphasis in original).

1812 Brems, "The Margin of Appreciation Doctrine in the Case-Law of the European Court of Human Rights" at 285; James A. Sweeney, "A 'Margin of Appreciation' in the Internal Market: Lessons from the European Court of Human Rights," (2007) 34 *Legal Issues of Economic Integration* 27 at 48.

1813 Martens, "Perplexity of the National Judge Faced with the Vagaries of European Consensus" at 57.

1814 McNeilly would dub this an "excess linked to alterity": McNeilly, *Human Rights and Radical Social Transformation: Futurity, Alterity, Power*, at 25.

1815 Kapur, "Human Rights in the 21st Century: Take a Walk on the Dark Side" at 682.

1816 Supra, note 1807.

1817 Martens, "Perplexity of the National Judge Faced with the Vagaries of European Consensus".

lack of critical engagement with the power structures which lead to exclusion, marginalisation and oppression in the present and hence a lack of engagement with voices who fall outside the current understandings of human rights. If consensus forms a dominant part of the ECtHR's reasoning, it becomes more difficult for the ECtHR to use its position as an authoritative player within European human rights law to "support preferences that are not normally heard"[1818] since such preferences, almost by definition, do not form part of the dominant consensus.[1819]

Based on all this, the compatibility of European consensus with critical perspectives on human rights seems rather minimal. It is also important to keep in mind, however, that alternative forms of reasoning – at least those associated with the conventions of legal argument before the ECtHR – may fare only marginally better. Reliance on national ethe rather than a pan-European ethos, while potentially pointing towards "local engagement with rights",[1820] also makes it even more difficult to question the status quo within the respondent State than reliance on European consensus does.[1821] Turning instead to the morality-focussed perspective may involve more of a "critical edge" vis-à-vis the respondent State and the other States parties,[1822] but it runs the risk of entrenching a view of human rights as moral-cum-legal truth which naturalises current understandings of human rights[1823] and is thus liable to inhibit far-reaching social transformation by presenting human rights as "antipolitics".[1824]

One aspect which has repeatedly come up in previous chapters is that, given the differing idealisations involved in any one of these various forms

1818 Koskenniemi, *From Apology to Utopia*, at 602.

1819 See O'Hara, "Consensus, Difference and Sexuality: Que(e)rying the European Court of Human Rights' Concept of 'European Consensus'"; see also Chapter 3, V. on the tendency of consensus towards homogenisation.

1820 Supra, note 1761.

1821 On both aspects, see Mégret, "Where Does the Critique of International Human Rights Stand? An Exploration in 18 Vignettes" at 29.

1822 See Chapter 2, II.3.

1823 These understandings may also to a significant extent be tied up with the more substantive aspects of the morality-focussed perspective. For example, its focus on moral self-determination of the individual chimes neatly with the liberal subject of human rights – a rational unitary being with the capacity to choose (and to consume); see Grear, "Challenging Corporate 'Humanity': Legal Disembodiment, Embodiment and Human Rights" at 522-523; see also infra, note 1908.

1824 See Chapter 4, IV.

of normativity, there may be a benefit to the oscillation between them.[1825] In light of the ever-present possibility of challenging any position by reverting to a different perspective, the structure of legal argument might be considered to provide "a sort of natural system of checks and balances as it were on others and even on itself".[1826] Unrelated to the context of legal argument, Chantal Mouffe has argued that the interaction between morality-focussed and ethos-focussed perspectives, although or rather precisely because it is paradoxical, results in an "important dynamic" with potentially "positive consequences".[1827]

In that vein, a rather counter-intuitive advantage of including European consensus in the ECtHR's processes of justification might be that, by providing a way of challenging the universalising approach of the morality-focussed perspective and by referring back to the political decisions which shaped the States parties' legal systems, it at least helps to reveal, as Carozza has argued, "the contingency and particularity of the political and moral choices inherent in the specification and expansion of international human rights norms that are sometimes too facilely assumed to be 'universal'".[1828] There is something to be said for this (and I will return to the underlying idea of rendering human rights law more openly political in a moment), but I am sceptical whether European consensus can be thought to fulfil this role in a manner beneficial to transformative politics. For one thing, there is the sense of consensus as compromise which I have repeatedly referred to.[1829] Because its Janus-faced nature allows it to mediate between the morality-focussed perspective and the reliance on national ethe and thus to seem more "savvy and sustainable" than other forms of reasoning,[1830] giving prominence to European consensus within the ECtHR's reasoning runs the risk of *preventing* the dynamic which might otherwise re-

1825 Ibid.

1826 Mégret, "The Apology of Utopia" at 460.

1827 Mouffe, *The Democratic Paradox*, at 44-45; see also on human rights and agonism, building on Laclau and Mouffe, McNeilly, *Human Rights and Radical Social Transformation: Futurity, Alterity, Power*, Chapter 5; Kathryn McNeilly, "After the Critique of Rights: For a Radical Democratic Theory and Practice of Human Rights," (2016) 27 *Law and Critique* 269 at 277-278; see Chapter 1, IV.3.

1828 Carozza, "Uses and Misuses of Comparative Law" at 1219; on the oscillation between universalism and particularism in human rights, see also Dembour, *Who Believes in Human Rights? Reflections on the European Convention*, at 178-179.

1829 See in particular supra, I. as well as Chapter 1.

1830 Supra, note 1692.

sult more fully between different forms of reasoning, and thus depoliticise rather than politicise.

For another thing, the more general downsides of consensus noted above – its conservative lilt and its lack of critical engagement with current power structures – remain relevant. Thus, even if consensus is used to challenge, say, the morality-focussed perspective, it remains a rather bland way of doing so because little transformative momentum can be gained by foregrounding European consensus. Even in cases involving the ostensibly "progressive" spur effect,[1831] consensus merely reproduces the dominant position at the pan-European level rather than providing a counter-hegemonic rationale for the ECtHR's decision; and the premise of grouping together the States parties' legal principles to establish commonality makes it difficult to use consensus for anything else.

The ECtHR's case-law holds manifold examples of this kind of acritically progressive judgment based (at least in part) on consensus. The Court might establish, for example, a right to legal gender recognition,[1832] but subject to certain preconditions,[1833] and without truly challenging dominant gender norms;[1834] a right to same-gender partnerships,[1835] but no same-gender marriage,[1836] and no serious questioning of how and why the law tends to privilege some kinds of partnership over others;[1837] a right to choice of religious attire in some situations,[1838] but not in many others,[1839] and insufficient attention to (or indeed perpetuation of) anti-Muslim

1831 See Chapter 2, III.

1832 ECtHR (GC), Appl. No. 28957/95 – *Christine Goodwin*.

1833 ECtHR (GC), Appl. No. 37359/09 – *Hämäläinen*; ECtHR, Appl. Nos. 79885/12, 52471/13 and 52596/13 – *A.P., Garçon and Nicot*.

1834 See Theilen, "Beyond the Gender Binary: Rethinking the Right to Legal Gender Recognition" at 254; Gonzalez-Salzberg, "The Accepted Transsexual and the Absent Transgender" at 826; Ralph Sandland, "Crossing and Not Crossing: Gender, Sexuality and Melancholy in the European Court of Human Rights," (2003) 11 *Feminist Legal Studies* 191 at 201.

1835 ECtHR (GC), Appl. Nos. 29381/09 and 32684/09 – *Vallianatos and Others*; ECtHR, Appl. Nos. 18766/11 and 36030/11 – *Oliari and Others*.

1836 ECtHR, Appl. Nos. 18766/11 and 36030/11 – *Oliari and Others*, at para. 194; ECtHR, Appl. No. 30141/04 – *Schalk and Kopf*.

1837 See e.g. Aeyal Gross, "Sex, Love, and Marriage: Questioning Gender and Sexuality Rights in International Law," (2008) 21 *Leiden Journal of International Law* 235 at 246-247; Kapur, *Gender, Alterity and Human Rights*, chapter 2.

1838 ECtHR, Appl. No. 41135/98 – *Ahmet Arslan and Others v. Turkey*, Judgment of 23 February 2010; ECtHR, Appl. No. 57792/15 – *Hamidović*.

1839 ECtHR (GC), Appl. No. 44774/98 – *Leyla Şahin*; ECtHR (GC), Appl. No. 43835/11 – *S.A.S.*; ECtHR, Appl. No. 64846/11 – *Ebrahimian*.

stereotypes;[1840] rights which mitigate some extreme forms of punishment like life imprisonment,[1841] but no abolition of life imprisonment as such,[1842] to say nothing of challenging the prison-industrial complex on a more fundamental level;[1843] and so on. Both the sense of consensus as compromise and the limited critical engagement which goes hand in hand with it come through very clearly here.

To conclude: in light of the flexibility of European consensus and the "gap" between legal materials – of which consensus forms part – and the legal decision, I do not think there is much sense in arguing that European consensus should not be used at all. In light of its conservative lilt and its fundamentally acritical stance vis-à-vis current power structures, however, I believe it is fair to claim that giving strong weight to European consensus limits the potentiality of human rights and, as such, is inimical to a transformative politics. As Kathryn McNeilly has summarised it, "an approach to human rights which aims towards consensus cuts off the promise of the 'to come' and is incapable of facilitating conflictual engagements with the alterity constitutive of current rights concepts and regimes of power more generally".[1844]

1840 See generally e.g. Peroni, "Religion and Culture in the Discourse of the European Court of Human Rights: The Risks of Stereotyping and Naturalising"; Kapur, *Gender, Alterity and Human Rights*, chapter 4.

1841 ECtHR (GC), Appl. No. 74025/01 – *Hirst*; ECtHR (GC), Appl. Nos. 66069/09, 130/10 and 3896/10 – *Vinter and Others*.

1842 Confirmed e.g. in ECtHR (GC), Appl. Nos. 60367/08 and 961/11 – *Khamtokhu and Aksenchik*, at para. 74.

1843 See critically on the "alignment of human rights advocates with the carceral state" Karen Engle, "Anti-Impunity and the Turn to Criminal Law in Human Rights," (2015) 100 *Cornell Law Review* 1069 at 1126; in the context of the ECtHR's case-law, the danger of "coercive overreach" through such an alignment has increasingly been noted: see e.g. Natasa Mavronicola, "Taking Life and Liberty Seriously: Reconsidering Criminal Liability Under Article 2 of the ECHR," (2017) 80 *Modern Law Review* 1026 at 1037.

1844 McNeilly, *Human Rights and Radical Social Transformation: Futurity, Alterity, Power*, at 76, on consensual approaches to human rights in general, not specifically on European consensus; on the latter, see O'Hara, "Consensus, Difference and Sexuality: Que(e)rying the European Court of Human Rights' Concept of 'European Consensus'".

3. A More Openly Political Court?

Suppose, then, that the ECtHR were to give less weight to European consensus and to attempt instead, with an awareness of the responsibility which follows from the indeterminacy of regional human rights law, to orient its case-law towards support for "critical or emancipatory causes" and to question current power structures. As noted above, it is by no means clear in which direction this would take the ECtHR's judges in practice, since their understandings of what constitutes "critical or emancipatory causes" surely differ both among themselves and from the (likewise diverse) understandings prevalent in (certain parts of) legal academia.[1845] It is likely, however, that at least some of their judgments would become more experimental, less oriented towards the "middle-ground"[1846] of consensus as compromise.

If we accept, as argued above, that human rights are already deeply implicated in current power structures, then taking a critical stance by no means always speaks in favour of finding a violation of human rights: more human rights may well entrench rather than challenge power structures.[1847] Simultaneously, however, it follows from the discussion of alterity and potentiality in the preceding subsection that, if human rights are to gain critical force, they need to constantly be developed and rethought. As Koskenniemi has put it, "[w]e need new rights, [or] new interpretations of old rights. Routine kills […] rights-regimes".[1848] Assuming, then, that the ECtHR were to take this approach to heart when moving away from European consensus, it would imply that it should, at least in some cases, find human rights violations where it previously saw none.[1849]

But this brings us back to the problem already alluded to above: by encouraging far-reaching judicial decisions, are we not also encouraging precisely the kind of legal expansionism and depoliticization which we previ-

---

1845 Supra, notes 1785-1790.

1846 See Koskenniemi, *From Apology to Utopia*, at 597.

1847 Von Arnauld and Theilen, "Rhetoric of Rights: A Topical Perspective on the Functions of Claiming a 'Human Right to …'", at 43.

1848 Koskenniemi, "Human Rights, Politics and Love" at 153; see also Koskenniemi, *From Apology to Utopia*, at 550 on the connection between routine and roles, which brings us back to the need to rethink not only rights themselves, but the roles of actors such as the ECtHR: hence the ruminations which follow, and those at the end of the preceding chapter.

1849 See Kennedy, *A Critique of Adjudication (fin de siècle)*, at 334; for examples, see the cases cited above, notes 1832-1843.

ously took to task as presenting a "narrow, formalistic, and overly juridical [understanding] of what human rights are"?[1850] I take this to be the central dilemma for any attempt to make use of regional or international human rights law for critically informed projects of social transformation, especially in the context of judicial interpretations of human rights: on the one hand, if human rights law is to do more than legitimate the status quo by means of non-intervention,[1851] then there is a need for far-reaching findings of human rights violations in at least some cases to challenge current power structures and the myriad forms of injustice which they perpetuate. On the other hand, it is precisely such far-reaching findings of human rights violations which will further strengthen the reach of legal discourse and judicial power, thus drawing an ever-increasing range of subject-matters into a domain in which ideological choice is blanketed by the law's supposed objectivity and impeding future contestation of dominant positions.

Perhaps one way of approaching this dilemma (without denying that it *is* a dilemma) would be to consider ways in which human rights courts such as the ECtHR could be rendered *more openly political* as a way of counteracting or at least mitigating the tendency of legal discourse to naturalise dominant ideologies. This opens up a huge host of issues of which I can only touch upon all too few in the present context, but I would like to foreground two aspects. First, mostly for the avoidance of misunderstandings, I will briefly sketch how this proposal relates to the indeterminacy thesis and, second, I will provide a few indications of how it would impact on the (self-)image and reasoning of the ECtHR.

With regard to the first aspect, the main point to note is that openly politicising the ECtHR by no means follows inevitably from the indeterminacy thesis. The latter, as part of its descriptive claims, shows that legal argument *is* indeterminate and hence that law *is* political. As Koskenniemi has argued, "[i]f the law is already, in its core, irreducibly 'political', then the call for political jurisprudence simply fails to make sense".[1852] It seems to me, however, that this question is distinct from how any given decision is *presented* by legal actors, i.e. as more or less *openly* political. In a sense, this is the flip side of the distinction made in Chapter 10 between objectivity and an *impression* of objectivity in the ECtHR's processes of justifica-

1850 Supra, note 1746.
1851 See Chapter 10, IV.
1852 Koskenniemi, *From Apology to Utopia*, at 601-602.

tion.[1853] Where many academic commentators argue that such an impression of objectivity is a worthwhile goal (and that use of European consensus can help to achieve it), my point here is precisely the opposite: what would happen if the ECtHR deliberately eschewed and even counteracted efforts at creating an impression of objectivity?

The much-feared consequence – what those who argue in favour of consensus as legitimacy-enhancement seek to avoid – may well be, of course, an increase in "backlash", i.e. criticism of and opposition to the ECtHR and its decisions.[1854] A substantial part of the criticism geared at the ECtHR already accuses it of "judicial activism", understood as a derogatory term.[1855] More experimental and potentially far-reaching judgments would do little to attenuate such criticism, and representing the ECtHR's judgments in anything other than the language of "formal authority, defined by its claim to universality and neutrality" which we expect from courts would no doubt seem like "a professional mistake"[1856] and fan the flames of backlash, as it were.

If the goal is to prevent a hegemony of legal discourse and the increasing depoliticization which tends to go with it, however, then this need not be a bad thing. Consider again Thomas Kleinlein's conceptualisation of the ECtHR as part of broader democratic processes in which its judgments which "do not represent 'the last word' but can provide a trigger for democratic contestation and deliberation".[1857] Against this backdrop, he argues that there may be benefits to backlash: "backlash provoked by progressive judgments – a phenomenon feared by many liberal scholars – is a welcome means of maintaining the democratic responsiveness of constitutional meaning".[1858] In brief, resistance by the States parties can also be under-

1853 Chapter 10, II.2.

1854 I use the term here as an informal umbrella term for resistance to the ECtHR and its decisions; contrast Madsen, Cebulak, and Wiebusch, "Backlash Against International Courts: Explaining the Forms and Patterns of Resistance to International Courts" at 198.

1855 See again Chapter 10, II.2., and in summary e.g. Peat, *Comparative Reasoning in International Courts and Tribunals*, at 141.

1856 Koskenniemi, "Letter to the Editors of the Symposium" at 358 and 360; see also Koskenniemi, *From Apology to Utopia*, at 550.

1857 Supra, note 1759.

1858 Kleinlein, "Consensus and Contestability: The ECtHR and the Combined Potential of European Consensus and Procedural Rationality Control" at 888.

stood as part of democratic discourse in the absence (mostly) of transnational deliberative fora.[1859]

From this perspective, then, the negative connotation associated with backlash in the context of debates on the ECtHR's legitimacy is overblown.[1860] Indeed, it is precisely the focus on the ECtHR's *legitimacy* which, by aiming to *pre-empt* criticism of the Court, saps emancipatory potential from both the ECtHR's judgments and potential backlash since it prevents critical engagement with power structures. As Koskenniemi has put it, legitimacy is "not a standard external to power, against which power might be assessed but a vocabulary produced and reproduced by power itself through its institutionalised mechanisms of self-validation".[1861] Foregrounding consensus as legitimacy-enhancement based on incrementalism thus not only makes the ECtHR less likely to engage critically with the status quo, as I argued in Chapter 10, it also seeks to bolster the ECtHR's *own* power rather than opening the Court up to resistance which might prompt critical self-reflection. It would be more productive, then, to engage with backlash without the mediation of legitimacy-enhancement.

But perhaps all this is in any case an exaggerated picture of what more openly political processes of justification might entail. Some of the ECtHR's judgments already cause controversy and the reasoning seems a less likely cause than the result.[1862] Conversely, the depoliticization involved in judicial pronouncements on human rights may well be so institutionally entrenched that the ECtHR's reasoning makes little difference.

1859 See also Mikael Rask Madsen, Pola Cebulak, and Micha Wiebusch, "Resistance to International Courts. Introduction and Conclusion," (2018) 14 *International Journal of Law in Context* 193 at 195; Petkova, "The Notion of Consensus as a Route to Democratic Adjudication"; see also more generally Douglas-Scott, "Borges' *Pierre Menard, Author of the Quixote* and the Idea of a European Consensus" at 169-170 on human rights law as "an ongoing conversation".

1860 It goes without saying that some of the current backlash against the ECtHR is based on xenophobia and racism (see e.g. some of the examples mentioned in Chapter 9, III.) and, as such, not in the least worthy of support. Reducing backlash to these instances, however, paints a too one-sided picture: see in the context of populist resistance to international law Christine Schwöbel-Patel, "Populism, International Law and the End of Keep Calm and Carry on Lawyering," (2018) *Netherlands Yearbook of International Law* 97; a less narrow approach would go hand in hand with a focus on actors other than States understood as monolithic and represented by their government: see also Chapter 10, III.3.

1861 Koskenniemi, "Legitimacy, Rights and Ideology: Notes Towards a Critique of the New Moral Internationalism" at 373.

1862 See in more detail Chapter 9, II.4. and III.

Indeed, for all the differences among courts in terms of their style of reasoning or adjudicatory culture,[1863] the underlying Western image of courts is so fixed and the distinction between law and politics so entrenched that it is difficult to imagine what "more openly political" legal reasoning might look like.[1864]

One possible starting point might be to consider once again the critical reconceptualisations of human rights discussed above, specifically the way in which they are future-oriented and seek to be as open-ended as possible.[1865] Such approaches stand in stark contrast to the way in which we think about legal and especially judicial iterations of human rights. Thus, Costas Douzinas contrasts "the messy and open practice of human rights" with "the juridification and internationalisation of human rights" which "has led to attempts to impose a logic of closure",[1866] and Kathryn McNeilly describes her conceptualisation of human rights as "futural, unsettled and always resisting conclusion" as offering "important possibilities to move human rights and their politics away from the structures and thinkabilities of law".[1867]

These "thinkabilities of law" tend to include not only a sense of closure, paradigmatically in evidence in the case of judgments which settle what the law "says", but also a coherentist form of reasoning geared at the justification of precisely that moment of closure. I touched on the downsides of coherentist approaches in Chapter 7, arguing that they tend to underestimate and hence obscure the tensions and paradoxes involved in legal reasoning – in a sense, yet another kind of compromise. Koskenniemi sug-

---

1863 See Theilen, "Levels of Generality in the Comparative Reasoning of the European Court of Human Rights and the European Court of Justice: Towards Judicial Reflective Equilibrium".

1864 It is perhaps easier to specify what I do *not* mean, e.g. not "more openly political" understood (only) as anti-formalism (see Koskenniemi, *From Apology to Utopia*, at 601); rather, I am interested in how one might begin to think beyond "the traditional structure of international legal argumentation" which "stay[s] embedded within the same liberal theory of politics" (Kotiaho, "A Return to Koskenniemi, or the Disconcerting Co-optation of Rupture" at 494) – although the radical potential of such an approach is very much limited by the judicial context in which I am discussing it here (see supra, IV.1.).

1865 Supra, notes 1803-1811.

1866 Douzinas, *The End of Human Rights*, at 175; see also Grear, "Challenging Corporate 'Humanity': Legal Disembodiment, Embodiment and Human Rights" at 523.

1867 McNeilly, *Human Rights and Radical Social Transformation: Futurity, Alterity, Power*, at 159.

gests the following: "A better view [than coherence] is to take one step backwards, accept the irreducible indeterminacy of interpretation and the contradictoriness of legal argument [...], and build on the way legal argument brings out into the open the contradictions of the society" – or societies, in the case of regional courts such as the ECtHR – "in which it operates".[1868]

This brings us back to the distinction between critique and problem-solving[1869] – the prior analyses the relationship between law and broader societal structures (paradoxical, outwards-oriented), the latter provides legal interpretations and justifications within the dominant discursive framework and hence normative solutions to individual cases (coherentist, inwards-looking). Indeed, it has sometimes been suggested that coherentist and paradoxicalist approaches involve "divergent practical perspectives", with paradoxicalist approaches well-suited to describe "the outlook of ordinary citizens" (or, one might add, social movements and academics engaging with them) and coherentist approaches being more suited to capture "the outlook of judges".[1870] This is surely an accurate description of the distribution of these different approaches in practice, especially insofar as the coherentist approach is concerned: as Duncan Kennedy has put it, we might "interpret the social construction of the figure of the Judge as the place where we most clearly develop the collective fantasy of overcoming the endless sense of internal doubleness or contradiction" by seeking coherence.[1871] In terms of how things *could be*, however, I think it also lets judges off the paradoxicalist hook a tad too easily – after all, if there are good reasons to be sceptical of coherentist approaches, then it makes little sense to succumb to them simply because we are used to judges justifying their decisions in a certain way.

There might be value, then, in bringing an explicit awareness of the paradoxicalist elements of legal reasoning into the ECtHR's processes of justification so as to denaturalise the logic of closure involved in the act of judgment-giving – to achieve what Carozza suggests consensus might do, but which I have argued it does not, and "reveal the contingency and particularity of the political and moral choices inherent in the specification

1868 Koskenniemi, "An Essay in Counterdisciplinarity" at 19.

1869 Supra, note 1767.

1870 Green, "On the Co-originality of Liberalism and Democracy: Rationalist vs. Paradoxicalist Perspectives" at 216 (emphasis omitted); for a traditional account of the "judicial perspective" which makes the connection to "problem-solving" very clear, see e.g. Alexy, *Theorie der Grundrechte*, at 26-27.

1871 Kennedy, *A Critique of Adjudication (fin de siècle)*, at 208.

and expansion of international human rights norms".[1872] Attempting to create an open-endedness by emphasising paradox and contradiction would not form a justification of the ECtHR's decision in a strict sense since it would not point towards any particular conclusion, but that might be its very strength: it might lead to a form of reasoning which aims to open up imaginative space not only for the judges making a decision in the case at hand, but also makes the move from interpretation to imagination[1873] explicit, renders the judgment more openly political, and thus carries the challenge of imagination forward into the processes of contestation which follow the judgment.

4. Vertically Comparative Law as a Reflective Disruption of Equilibrium

All this is not only highly hypothetical and of uncertain consequence, but also very abstract. The prior points are, I think, unavoidable in the kind of exploratory approach taken in this chapter;[1874] but in the remainder of this section, I would like to render the suggestions made above somewhat more tangible by way of an example which also relates to previous chapters. To do so, I will discuss a way of using vertically comparative legal reasoning which distances itself from the closure-oriented notion of European consensus and instead aims to highlight contradictions within and among the legal systems of the States parties and thereby bring elements of open-endedness into the ECtHR's processes of justification.

One way of developing the way of using vertically comparative legal reasoning which I have in mind is to revisit the notion of reflective equilibrium and its limitations. I noted in Chapter 7 that reflective equilibrium runs the risk of simply reproducing dominant aspects within European public culture.[1875] This does not mean that it precludes any kind of change: to the contrary, given the constant adjustment decisions made in the process of searching for reflective equilibrium, it "combines conservatism with reform".[1876] Given this combination, however, the kind of reform associated with reflective equilibrium tends to be relatively marginal;

1872 Supra, note 1828.
1873 As Koskenniemi, *From Apology to Utopia*, at 557 puts it.
1874 Supra, I. and IV.1.
1875 Chapter 7, IV.
1876 Joseph Raz, "The Claims of Reflective Equilibrium," (1982) 25 *Inquiry* 307 at 329.

the way in which reflective equilibrium remains stuck in "the way things are" makes it of limited use for transformative politics, or even hostile to them.[1877]

Davina Cooper has described this problem through a conceptual lens: "Trying to build progressive normative concepts out of dominant social practices remains mired in the effects such practices have on the concepts generated – a stuckness that may prove as hard to identify as it is to remove."[1878] One way of trying to work towards social transformation, then, might be to rethink concepts. Cooper does so by focussing on the "small-scale progressive social sites" which she calls everyday utopias.[1879] Others have similarly moved beyond reflective equilibrium by turning away from dominant social practices towards the views and practices which they exclude.[1880] My complementary suggestion here is to further interrogate dominant social practices themselves – but rather than aiming to build on them with only minor modifications, as a coherentist approach would do, one might *foreground their internal inconsistencies so as to unsettle the concepts which they generate*. This would not only point away from the kind of "stuckness" which Cooper identifies, it would also serve to generate the kind of open-endedness which might politicise legal reasoning by subverting expectations of closure.

In the context of the ECtHR, this would mean using vertically comparative law as a way of unearthing contradictions within European public culture.[1881] As mentioned above, this would be a use of vertically comparative law which moves away from European consensus, particularly from the way in which a prism of commonality is applied to comparative materials so as to establish either consensus or lack of consensus, leading to the rein or spur effect.[1882] It moves away, in other words, from the connection between European consensus and ethical normativity in the form of a pan-European ethos, because it is aimed at exposing the contradictions inher-

1877 Davina Cooper, *Everyday Utopias. The Conceptual Life of Promising Spaces* (Durham and London: Duke University Press, 2014), at 28.

1878 Ibid., 29.

1879 Ibid., 30.

1880 E.g. Brooke A. Ackerly, *Universal Human Rights in a World of Difference* (Cambridge: Cambridge University Press, 2008), at 59-60.

1881 For the notion of European public culture, see Chapter 7, III.2.

1882 As Føllesdal notes, "this is not the ordinary way that [consensus-based reasoning is] used": Føllesdal, "A Better Signpost, Not a Better Walking Stick: How to Evaluate the European Consensus Doctrine" at 208; on characteristics of European consensus, see Chapter 1, III.; and on its "use", see Chapter 1, IV.2.

ent in concepts within European public culture without necessarily pointing towards a certain substantive outcome. If then applied in the service of certain transformative political agendas,[1883] one might think of this as a way of mobilising the status quo against itself;[1884] but at a minimum, the idea would be to put into question concepts otherwise left unexamined, and thus set the scene for more imaginative and transformative agendas regardless of the ECtHR's own decision by creating a sense of openness rather than closure. To highlight the contrast to the coherentist approach of reflective equilibrium, we might think of this as a reflective *disruption* of equilibrium.

Let me work towards an example of this way of using vertically comparative law by building on several statements from within the ECtHR's case-law and academic commentary. These examples are not oriented towards disruption and openness in the strong sense just outlined, but they do serve to demonstrate that the discourse surrounding vertically comparative reasoning is not *entirely* taken up by narrow understandings of European consensus and that there is, rather, a sliding scale of approaches which range from only slight modifications of the way in which we think of European consensus to the use of vertically comparative law in a way which leaves the idea of "consensus" behind. The latter, I suggest, could be further developed in an attempt to render them more disruptive.

A relatively minor amendment to dominant notions of European consensus can be found in the occasional suggestion that vertically comparative law might be operationalised in such a way as to "refut[e] claims that certain social arrangements are inevitable".[1885] This approach questions current social arrangements by using vertically comparative law to denatu-

---

1883 On the importance of this point, i.e. moving beyond *only* showcasing inconsistencies, see e.g. Crenshaw, "Mapping the Margins: Intersectionality, Identity Politics, and Violence Against Women of Color" at 1297-1299.

1884 I am taking inspiration here, albeit loosely, from an aspect of the (related) traditions of Marxism, ideology critique and utopianism: see e.g. Bloch, *Hoffnung*, at 168-169; Marks, "International Judicial Activism and the Commodity-Form Theory of International Law"; Carol J. Greenhouse, *A Moment's Notice. Time Politics across Cultures* (Ithaca: Cornell University Press, 1996), at 99; Theilen, "Of Wonder and Changing the World: Philip Allott's Legal Utopianism" at 350-351; see also B.S. Chimni, "Third World Approaches to International Law: A Manifesto," (2006) 8 *International Community Law Review* 3 at 26 on "exploiting the contradictions that mark the international legal system" as part of "[i]maginative solutions" and reconstruction following critique.

1885 Shany, "Toward a General Margin of Appreciation Doctrine in International Law?" at 927 (in footnote 121).

ralise them – to show that they are not inevitable – but its purview is quite limited. In *Sørensen and Rasmussen v. Denmark*, for example, the ECtHR found that "only a very limited number of Contracting States [...] continue to permit the conclusion of closed-shop agreements",[1886] and used this fact to argue that "their use in the labour market is not an indispensable tool for the effective enjoyment of trade union freedoms".[1887] While the wording does indicate a certain sensitivity to denaturalisation of the social arrangements within the respondent State, the thrust of this argument remains quite close to the usual use of consensus in favour of the applicant as an indicator of the spur effect, in which a pan-European ethos trumps the national ethos of the respondent State. There is perhaps a slight difference in emphasis, then, but vertically comparative law continues to be used by reference to European consensus and the prism of commonality that comes with it.

Other examples retain the dynamic underlying the ECtHR's reasoning in *Sørensen and Rasmussen* even if they move away, to some extent, from necessarily requiring a supra-majoritarian consensus in favour of the applicant. In the case of *Cossey v. the United Kingdom*, Judge Martens opined in a dissenting opinion that (what the ECtHR interpreted as) *lack* of consensus among the States parties should not necessarily lead to a wide margin of appreciation. Instead, responding to the United Kingdom's argument that "technical difficulties" stood in the way of a right to legal gender recognition, he argued, inter alia, that "other legislatures had shown that in a democratic society this problem can be regulated".[1888] Ian Cram has recently made a similar point even more explicitly: arguing against the ECtHR's use of the rein effect of consensus in *Animal Defenders International v. the United Kingdom*, based on a lack of consensus in the area of paid political advertising,[1889] he holds that "the very lack of consensus on politi-

---

1886 ECtHR (GC), Appl. Nos. 52562/99 and 525620/99 – *Sørensen and Rasmussen*, at para. 70.

1887 Ibid., at para. 75; see also ECtHR (GC), Appl. Nos. 60367/08 and 961/11 – *Khamtokhu and Aksenchik*, dissenting opinion of Judge Pinto de Albuquerque, at para. 32, where he substantiates at length an "international trend" in favour of abolishing life imprisonment and holds that "[n]one of those systems has collapsed or experienced a marked increase in crime, showing *de facto* [...] that this type of punishment is unnecessary in a democratic society" (emphasis in original).

1888 ECtHR (Plenary), Appl. No. 10843/84 – *Cossey*, dissenting opinion of Judge Martens, at paras. 3.6.1. and 3.7.

1889 ECtHR (GC), Appl. No. 48876/08 – *Animal Defenders International*, at para. 123.

cal advertising could have been deployed as the basis of a proportionality argument *against* the UK's position by evidencing that other 'well-functioning' democracies in Europe had managed to uphold the integrity of their political systems without resort to such draconian bans on political expression".[1890]

This way of using vertically comparative reasoning is helpful in that it problematises the stark distinction between the rein effect and the spur effect by inverting the usual consequences of lack of consensus, and thus alerts us to the possibility of using vertically comparative law in ways which go beyond (and indeed stand in contrast to) European consensus. I would sound two notes of caution with regard to the examples just cited, however. First, differing implications can be drawn from this use of vertically comparative reasoning. One might simply see it as a counter-argument to claims of inevitability raised by the respondent State, without further normative force of its own in any given direction.[1891] One might also view it as a strong argument in favour of the applicant,[1892] or at least as placing a burden on the respondent State to show otherwise.[1893] Especially in the latter case, it is important to note that this kind of argument is very much implicated in the triangular tensions discussed throughout: in particular, (normatively speaking) its over-use could easily lead to the kind of inter-State homogenisation which I have already criticised in the context of European consensus,[1894] and (descriptively speaking) the respondent State will usually try to shift the focus back to its national ethos by arguing that its situation or political choices are distinct from other European States.[1895] Differently put, even when vertically comparative legal reasoning is used in this way, it all too easily collapses back into reasoning geared at normativity rather than disruption, at closure rather than openness.

1890 Cram, "Protocol 15 and Articles 10 and 11 ECHR - The Partial Triumph of Political Incumbency Post-Brighton?" at 494 (emphasis in original).

1891 Shany, for example, merely speaks of "refuting claims": Shany, "Toward a General Margin of Appreciation Doctrine in International Law?" at 927.

1892 Most explicitly Cram, "Protocol 15 and Articles 10 and 11 ECHR - The Partial Triumph of Political Incumbency Post-Brighton?" at 494.

1893 As also mentioned ibid., referring to ECtHR (GC), Appl. No. 48876/08 – *Animal Defenders International*, dissenting opinion of Judge Tulkens, joined by Judges Spielmann and Laffranque, at paras. 15-17 (connecting the different regulations in other States parties to the less restrictive means test within proportionality).

1894 Chapter 3, IV.4. and V.

1895 See e.g. Chapter 8, III.3.

The second point relates to the scope of what is potentially denaturalised by this use of vertically comparative law. In the examples just given, this is limited to a certain social arrangement within the respondent State (e.g. allowing closed-shop agreements, a strict ban on paid political advertising, a complete lack of legal gender recognition). I would argue that this relatively limited scope follows not only from the overall focus of the ECtHR on the issue before it,[1896] but also from the use of vertically comparative law – as on the standard account of European consensus – at the same level of generality as that issue (the "Goldilocks level of generality"). Hence my above suggestion that we might approach the issue through a *conceptual* lens: concepts tend to be of relatively broad reach, and unsettling them therefore does more to open up possibilities and potentialities of human rights than a focus on the more specific issue at hand does.[1897]

I am not aware of any example for the kind of argument I have in mind from within the ECtHR's case-law, but let me attempt to give an example from a different context so as to make this more tangible. I am thinking of Dean Spade's study of the possibilities and preconditions for gender reclassification across jurisdictions and agencies within the United States, which revealed policies varying extensively on several points such as the degree of self-identification or deference to medical authority, or the differing demands made in relation to bodily modification:[1898] a distinct lack of consensus with regard to relatively specific regulations, one might say. Spade suggests that "an examination of this rule matrix shows that the assumption of gender cohesiveness and stability is mythical", that "legal uses of gender distinctions are built upon inconsistent foundations", and that this "reveals the way that the administrative classification of identities does invisible work of naturalizing categories of classification".[1899] In other words, the use of vertically comparative law at relatively specific levels of generali-

1896 See e.g. ECtHR (GC), Appl. No. 57813/00 – *S.H. and Others*, at para. 92: "In cases arising from individual applications the Court's task is not to review the relevant legislation or practice in the abstract; it must as far as possible confine itself, without overlooking the general context, to examining the issues raised by the case before it"; similarly e.g. ECtHR (Plenary), Appl. No. 4451/70 – *Golder*, at para. 39; ECtHR (GC), Appl. No. 43494/09 – *Garib v. the Netherlands*, Judgment of 6 November 2017, at para. 136.

1897 On reimagining concepts, see also Simpson, "Imagination" at 415.

1898 Dean Spade, "Documenting Gender," (2008) 59 *Hastings Law Journal* 731 at 734-735 for a summary.

1899 Ibid., 738; see also Toby Beauchamp, "Artful Concealment and Strategic Visibility: Transgender Bodies and U.S. State Surveillance After 9/11," (2009) 6 *Surveillance & Society* 356 at 361.

ty puts into question the much more general concept of gender and its commonly assumed stability, thus opening up space for contestation.

Spade's study, of course, makes use of comparative reasoning which, though arguably vertical at least in part, is conducted within the context of a federal State rather than focussed on the comparison of different States within a continent, as in the case of the ECtHR's vertically comparative reasoning.[1900] Still, a similar approach might be conceived of in that context, too: when faced with a lack of consensus pertaining to legal gender recognition, the ECtHR need not (necessarily) see this as a trigger for invoking the rein effect and shifting to a deferential stance, nor (necessarily) as a sign that the respondent State's position should be changed to adhere to other States' positions, but simply as an occasion to reflect on the contradictory assumptions underlying the concept of gender (and, for that matter, on the law's role in reaffirming it[1901]).

The ECtHR would ultimately still reach a decision on the facts of the case, but it would – or so one might hope – differ in several respects from a decision reached on the basis of European consensus or other forms of more traditional legal rationality. First, the destabilisation already during the ECtHR's processes of discovery[1902] might influence the judges' decision by virtue of disrupting the sense of self-evidence with which the status quo is so often approached, and thereby rendering transformative judgments more likely. Engaging with vertically comparative law in the way suggested, in other words, may constitute a "learning experience" which in turn may demand "a change in a person's cognitive status quo",[1903] thus prompting the kind of self-reflectivity or "stepping back" which critique seeks to instil.[1904] More importantly, the inclusion of this moment of "stepping back" within the ECtHR's processes of justification might mitigate the depoliticization involved in legal discourse. For one thing, the moment of openness or disruption created by unsettling concepts otherwise left unquestioned could be of use in processes of contestation following the ECtHR's judgments, regardless of the substantive position taken by the Court. And for another, that position would itself be more open to question because the ECtHR's decision to support it would be rendered

---

1900 See generally Chapter 1, III.

1901 See e.g. Judith Butler, "Gender Regulations," in *Undoing Gender* (New York and London: Routledge, 2004) at 40.

1902 See Chapter 1, IV.5.

1903 Frankenberg, "Critical Comparisons: Re-thinking Comparative Law" at 413; see also at 446-447.

1904 Supra, notes 1771 and 1868; but see note 1190 on its limits.

more openly political: unsettling foundational concepts, after all, brings the element of decisionism involved in then interpreting them in any given way to the foreground.

My example has focussed on the concept of gender, but a similar dynamic could be achieved with regard to a variety of other concepts that hold relevance for the ECtHR's case-law: marriage,[1905] family,[1906] or religion, secularism, and public order,[1907] to name but a few. Ultimately, different aspects of European public culture might even be used to challenge the very notion of the "human" underlying human rights – another "largely taken-for-granted concept" within human rights law, the ostensible self-evidence of which belies the fact that notions of subjectivity and individuality are themselves produced in ways which "cohere with liberal, capitalist regimes".[1908] Again, this need not point towards a particular outcome in any given case, at least not without further political commitments – but it might broaden the open-endedness and hence the potentiality of human rights as much as possible in the context of regional human rights adjudication.

1905 See Damian A. Gonzalez-Salzberg, "Confirming (the Illusion of) Heterosexual Marriage: *Hämäläinen v Finland*," (2015) 2 *Journal of International and Comparative Law* 173 (though more in relation to the ECtHR's own case-law than vertically comparative law).

1906 See e.g. Lourdes Peroni, "Challenging Culturally Dominant Conceptions in Human Rights Law: The Cases of Property and Family," (2010) 4 *Human Rights and International Legal Discourse* 241 at 261-262 on how "a world of divorce and remarriage, single parenting, and opposite- and same-sex partnerships" has "increasingly undermined" the concept of family implying (only) a nuclear family model.

1907 The ECtHR itself has laid the groundwork for this approach, though it sees the contradictions within European public culture as a reason to operationalise the rein effect: see Chapter 7, IV.; see more generally e.g. Nehal Bhuta, "Two Concepts of Religious Freedom in the European Court of Human Rights," (2014) 113 *The South Atlantic Quarterly* 9 at 11, discussing "how diverging histories and theories of state and subject coexist within the capacious language of freedom of conscience" and how one might read this as "an unsteady and unstable circumstantial casuistry of historically embedded political concepts such as democracy, secularism, freedom of conscience, and public order".

1908 McNeilly, "After the Critique of Rights: For a Radical Democratic Theory and Practice of Human Rights" at 271.

V. Outlook: Future Articulations of Human Rights

In this chapter, I have examined how the potentially critical force of human rights could be developed rather than suppressed in the context of the ECtHR, specifically by reference to European consensus and other uses of vertically comparative legal reasoning. Within critical traditions, this focus is well-known (although not usually directed at courts, except insofar as it pertains to their role in suppressing far-reaching social transformation). Within the academic discourse surrounding the ECtHR, by contrast, it is far from self-evident: indeed, it remains a matter of controversy whether facilitating social transformation could and should be a purpose of the Court at all, or whether its primary purpose lies elsewhere (in providing a safeguard against authoritarianism,[1909] for example, or more generally in entrenching certain normative standards rather than developing them[1910]). If one adopts a different starting point, then the above suggestions to politicise the Court will likely seem curious or even dangerous.

Regardless of the purpose(s) one assigns to the ECtHR, however, I would suggest that it is of crucial importance to foster an awareness not only of the potentially emancipatory aspects of human rights, but also of how they in many ways legitimate an unjust status quo by *not* critically engaging with it – and hence to gain a sense of what we lose by not considering them in relation to social transformation. Strongly foregrounding European consensus, I have argued, is one way in which this sense of what we lose is rendered more difficult to grasp, especially when (certain understandings of) consensus are normalised as the most appropriate approach to human rights by presenting them as "objective" or "natural", or by deriding alternative approaches as "unrealistic". The use of European consensus in this way orients us towards certain compromises but away from meaningful social transformation. Its prominence is, perhaps, partly a result of and partly productive of the fact that the ECtHR "is not willing to

1909 See Andrew Moravcsik, "The Origins of Human Rights Regimes: Democratic Delegation in Postwar Europe," (2000) 54 *International Organization* 217.

1910 Besson, "Human Rights and Democracy in a Global Context: Decoupling and Recoupling" at 29; for a positive spin on the ECtHR maintaining the status quo without negating "dynamic value", see also Merris Amos, "The Value of the European Court of Human Rights to the United Kingdom," (2017) 28 *European Journal of International Law* 763 at 783.

be the catalyst for change",[1911] and the Court "us[es] consensus reasoning to avoid imposing radical change".[1912]

At the same time, however, I think it is important to keep in mind the more general scepticism about judicialized human rights in relation to far-reaching social transformation, as sketched above, and hence to not over-emphasise the importance of any one form of reasoning. Since consensus is not the only way in which human rights are implicated in current power structures nor the only way in which the status quo is or can be reaffirmed within human rights law, putting into question the use of European consensus and only European consensus would, in a sense, present a distorted and misleading picture. Rather, there is a need to rethink human rights on a more fundamental level, perhaps to shift dominant understandings away from what Arabella Lyon calls "human rights as law, a textual truth" – or consensual truth, or other kinds of legal rationality – towards human rights as "performative deliberative practices leading to the constitution of a new form of life".[1913] Or, as Frédéric Mégret has put it, we need to "dissociat[e] the aspiration to human rights from the strict legal forms that purport to constrain it"[1914] – to realise the openness and emancipatory potential of human rights which far surpasses what can be achieved within legal discourse and current regional and international institutions.

To foreground such emancipatory potential, Judith Butler has argued that "keeping our notion of the human open to a future articulation is essential to the project of international human rights discourse and politics".[1915] Given the way our image of the role of courts tends to be oriented towards closure rather than openness, this is particularly difficult in the context of judicialized human rights.[1916] Courts in general, and regional human rights courts such as the ECtHR in particular, are of course situated in certain contexts, implicated in power structures, and faced with expectations as to the kind of decisions they should reach, the kind of justifi-

---

1911 Amos, "Can European Consensus Encourage Acceptance of the European Convention on Human Rights in the United Kingdom?" at 279.

1912 Ibid., 280.

1913 Arabella Lyon, *Deliberative Acts. Democracy, Rhetoric, and Rights* (University Park, PA: Pennsylvania State University Press, 2013), at 5.

1914 Mégret, "Where Does the Critique of International Human Rights Stand? An Exploration in 18 Vignettes" at 31.

1915 Butler, "On the Limits of Sexual Autonomy" at 36; see also supra, note 1908; I have tentatively developed this line of thought in Theilen, "Pre-existing Rights and Future Articulations: Temporal Rhetoric in the Struggle for Trans Rights".

1916 On the importance of roles, see supra, note 1848.

cation they should offer, and the kind of image of a human rights court they should live up to.[1917] The enthusiastic support of European consensus as legitimacy-enhancement within academic commentary puts the anxieties involved in (openly) moving "beyond objectivism"[1918] into stark relief and highlights the difficulty of even imagining law, courts and judgment-giving in a way which subverts such expectations.[1919]

I have attempted to sketch a use of vertically comparative legal reasoning which might help to create at least brief moments of openness by deliberately creating a reflective disruption of equilibrium. Such an approach would stand in direct contrast to European consensus: where the latter reinforces or only incrementally develops the status quo, the prior showcases its contradictions; where the latter pulls the past into the present by giving normative force to the legal systems of the States parties as they currently stand, the latter aims to open up space for future articulations of human rights; and where the latter aims for (an impression of) legal objectivity, the prior aims to politicise. But a reflective disruption of equilibrium also stands in contrast to other forms of legal reasoning currently used by the ECtHR, for legal reasoning as we traditionally conceive of it is geared at closure rather than at creating moments of disorientation and the "hope of new directions" which comes with them.[1920]

Risking what we have so far achieved within the legal European human rights regime in the face of an uncertain future is no doubt a "terrifying process".[1921] Judith Butler has stated of unknowable futures that many people "recoil" from them, "fearing that the new which is not predictable will lead to a full-scale nihilism".[1922] Indeed, she acknowledges that this is a "risky moment in politics" and that what follows "will not be necessarily good or desirable" – but she immediately goes on to remind us that "it is equally true that nothing good or desirable will arrive without the

1917 See Chapter 10, IV.

1918 Koskenniemi, *From Apology to Utopia*, at 513.

1919 See Chapter 10, III.2.

1920 Ahmed, *Queer Phenomenology*, at 158.

1921 Kay Lalor, "Making Different Differences: Representation and Rights in Sexuality Activism," (2015) 23 *Feminist Legal Studies* 7 at 22 (on embracing uncertainty and unknowability in rights activism more generally, not specifically in the judicial context).

1922 In Judith Butler and William Connolly, "Politics, Power and Ethics: A Discussion Between Judith Butler and William Connolly," (2000) 4 *Theory & Event* (n.p.); the parallel to anxieties about legal nihilism in the context of critical international legal theory (supra, IV.1.) are immediately apparent.

new".[1923] If human rights do indeed constitute humankind's "last utopia",[1924] then we owe it to those whose oppression and marginalisation is not yet intelligible within that utopia to look forwards, to future articulations of human rights, rather than backwards – even in the judicial context.

1923 Ibid.
1924 Moyn, *The Last Utopia*, at 1.

Table of Cases

Constitutional Court of the Russian Federation, Judgment No. 21-P of 14 July 2015.

ECJ, Case 5/71 – *Aktien-Zuckerfabrik v Case Name Part Two*, Opinion of AG Roemer, 13 July 1971, ECLI:EU:C:1971:96.

ECJ, Case C-550/07 P – *Akzo Nobel Chemicals Ltd and Akcros Chemicals Ltd v Case Name Part Two*, Opinion of AG Kokott, 29 April 2010, ECLI:EU:C:2010:229.

ECJ, Case C-101/08 – *Audiolux SA e.a v Case Name Part Two*, Opinion of AG Trstenjak, 30 June 2009, ECLI:EU:C:2009:410.

ECJ, Case C-411/05 – *Félix Palacios de la Villa v Case Name Part Two*, Opinion of AG Mazák, 15 February 2007, ECLI:EU:C:2007:106.

ECJ, Case 11/70 – *Internationale Handelsgesellschaft mbH v Einfuhr- und Vorratsstelle für Getreide und Futtermittel*, Judgment of 17 December 1970, ECLI:EU:C:1970:114.

EComHR, *Euan Sutherland v. the United Kingdom*, Application No. 25186/94, Report of 1 July 1997.

EComHR, *Twenty-One Detained Persons v. Germany*, Application Nos 3134/67 et al., Decision of 6 April 1968.

ECtHR, *Abdulaziz, Cabales and Balkandali v. the United Kingdom*, Application Nos. 9214/80, 9473/81 and 9474/81, Judgment of 28 May 1985.

ECtHR, *Ahmet Arslan and Others v. Turkey*, Application No. 41135/98, Judgment of 23 February 2010.

ECtHR, *Al-Adsani v. the United Kingdom*, Application No. 35763/97, Judgment of 21 November 2001.

ECtHR, *Alekseyev v. Russia*, Application Nos. 4916/07, 25924/08 and 14599/09, Judgment of 21 October 2010.

ECtHR, *Altinay v. Turkey*, Application No. 37222/04, Judgment of 9 July 2013.

ECtHR, *Amann v. Switzerland*, Application No. 27798/95, Judgment of 16 February 2000.

ECtHR, *Anchugov and Gladkov v. Russia*, Application Nos. 11157/04 and 15162/05, Judgment of 4 July 2013.

ECtHR, *A. and Others v. the United Kingdom*, Application No. 3455/05, Judgment of 19 February 2009.

ECtHR, *Animal Defenders International v. the United Kingdom*, Application No. 48876/08, Judgment of 22 April 2013.

ECtHR, *A, B and C v. Ireland*, Application No. 25579/05, Judgment of 16 December 2010.

ECtHR, *Bączkowski and Others v. Poland*, Application No. 1543/06, Judgment of 3 May 2007.

ECtHR, *Bajrami v. Albania*, Application No. 35853/04, Judgment of 12 December 2006.

ECtHR, *Banković and Others v. Belgium and Others*, Application No. 52207/99, Decision of 12 December 2001.

ECtHR, *Bărbulescu v. Romania*, Application No. 61496/08, Judgment of 5 September 2017.

ECtHR, *Bayatyan v. Armenia*, Application No. 23459/03, Judgment of 7 July 2011.

ECtHR, *Bayev and Others v. Russia*, Application Nos. 67667/09 et al., Judgment of 20 June 2017.

ECtHR, *Belgian Linguistics Case (Merits) v.* Application Nos. 1474/62 et al., Judgment of 23 July 1968.

ECtHR, *Biao v. Denmark*, Application No. 38590/10, Judgment of 24 May 2016.

ECtHR, *Big Brother Watch and Others v. the United Kingdom*, Application Nos. 58170/13, 62322/14 and 24960/15, Judgment of 13 September 2018.

ECtHR, *Boulois v. Luxembourg*, Application No. 37575/04, Judgment of 3 April 2012.

ECtHR, *Brauer v. Germany*, Application No. 3545/04, Judgment of 28 May 2009.

ECtHR, *Breyer v. Germany*, Application No. 50001/12, Judgment of 30 January 2020.

ECtHR, *Brežec v. Croatia*, Application No. 7177/10, Judgment of 18 July 2013.

ECtHR, *Casado Coca v. Spain*, Application No. 15450/89, Judgment of 24 February 1994.

ECtHR, *Chapman v. the United Kingdom*, Application 27238/95, Judgment of 18 January 2001.

ECtHR, *Chassagnou and Others v. France*, Application Nos. 25088/94, 28331/95 and 28443/95, Judgment of 29 April 1999.

ECtHR, *Chowdury and Others v. Greece*, Application No. 21884/15, Judgment of 30 March 2017.

ECtHR, *Christine Goodwin v. the United Kingdom*, Application No. 28957/95, Judgment of 11 July 2002.

ECtHR, *Connors v. the United Kingdom*, Application No. 66746/01, Judgment of 27 May 2004.

ECtHR, *Cossey v. the United Kingdom*, Application No. 10843/84, Judgment of 27 September 1990.

ECtHR, *Cruz Varas and Others v. Sweden*, Application No. 15576/89, Judgment of 20 March 1991.

ECtHR, *D.H. and Others v. the Czech Republic*, Application No. 57325/00, Judgment of 13 November 2007.

ECtHR, *Dahlab v. Switzerland*, Application No. 42393/98, Decision of 15 February 2001.

ECtHR, *De Tommaso v. Italy*, Application No. 43395/09, Judgment of 23 February 2017.

ECtHR, *Delfi AS v. Estonia*, Application No. 64569/09, Judgment of 16 June 2015.

ECtHR, *Demicoli v. Malta*, Application No. 13057/87, Judgment of 27 August 1991.

ECtHR, *Demir and Baykara v. Turkey*, Application No. 34503/97, Judgment of 12 November 2008.

ECtHR, *Deumeland v. Germany*, Application No. 9384/81, Judgment of 29 May 1986.

ECtHR, *Dickson v. the United Kingdom*, Application No. 44362/04, Judgment of 4 December 2007.

ECtHR, *Dogru v. France*, Application No. 27058/05, Judgment of 4 December 2008.

ECtHR, *Dudgeon v. the United Kingdom*, Application No. 7525/76, Judgment of 22 October 1981.

ECtHR, *Dybeku v. Albania*, Application No. 41153/06, Judgment of 18 December 2007.

ECtHR, *E.B. v. France*, Application No. 43546/02, Judgment of 22 January 2008.

ECtHR, *Ebrahimian v. France*, Application No. 64846/11, Judgment of 26 November 2015.

ECtHR, *Egeland and Hanseid v. Norway*, Application No. 34438/04, Judgment of 16 April 2009.

ECtHR, *Emonet and Others v. Switzerland*, Application No. 39051/03, Judgment of 13 December 2007.

ECtHR, *Engel and Others v. the Netherlands*, Application Nos. 5100-5102/71, 5354/72 and 5370/72, Judgment of 8 June 1976.

ECtHR, *Evans v. the United Kingdom*, Application No. 6339/05, Judgment of 10 April 2007.

ECtHR, *Eweida and Others v. the United Kingdom*, Application Nos. 48420/10, 36516/10, 51671/10 and 59842/10, Judgment of 15 January 2013.

ECtHR, *F. v. Switzerland*, Application No. 11329/85, Judgment of 18 December 1987.

ECtHR, *Fábián v. Hungary*, Application No. 78117/13, Judgment of 5 September 2017.

ECtHR, *Fabris v. France (Merits)*, Application No. 16574/08, Judgment of 7 February 2013.

ECtHR, *Feldbrugge v. the Netherlands*, Application No. 8562/79, Judgment of 29 May 1986.

ECtHR, *Fernández Martínez v. Spain*, Application No. 56030/07, Judgment of 12 June 2014.

ECtHR, *Firth and Others v. the United Kingdom*, Application Nos. 47784/09 et al., Judgment of 12 August 2014.

ECtHR, *Fogarty v. the United Kingdom*, Application No. 37112/97, Judgment of 21 November 2001.

ECtHR, *Fretté v. France*, Application No. 36515/97, Judgment of 26 February 2002.

ECtHR, *Frodl v. Austria*, Application No. 20201/04, Judgment of 8 April 2010.

ECtHR, *G.I.E.M. S.R.L. and Others v. Italy*, Application Nos. 1828/06 et al., Judgment of 28 June 2018.

ECtHR, *Garib v. the Netherlands*, Application No. 43494/09, Judgment of 6 November 2017.

ECtHR, *Gaughran v. the United Kingdom*, Application No. 45245/15, Judgment of 13 February 2020.

ECtHR, *Genderdoc-M v. Moldova*, Application No. 9106/06, Judgment of 12 June 2012.

ECtHR, *Gestur Jónsson and Ragnar Halldór Hall v. Iceland*, Application Nos. 68273/14 and 68271/14, Judgment of 22 December 2020.

ECtHR, *Glass v. the United Kingdom*, Application No. 61827/00, Judgment of 9 March 2004.

ECtHR, *Globa v. Ukraine*, Application No. 15729/07, Judgment of 5 July 2012.

ECtHR, *Glor v. Switzerland*, Application No. 13444/04, Judgment of 30 April 2009.

ECtHR, *Golder v. the United Kingdom*, Application No. 4451/70, Judgment of 21 February 1975.

ECtHR, *Greens and M.T. v. the United Kingdom*, Application Nos. 60041/08 and 60054/08, Judgment of 23 November 2010.

ECtHR, *Guðmundur Andri Ástráðsson v. Iceland*, Application No. 26374/18, Judgment of 1 December 2020.

ECtHR, *Gülay Çetin v. Turkey*, Application No. 44084/10, Judgment of 5 March 2013.

ECtHR, *Hadzhieva v. Bulgaria*, Application No. 45285/12, Judgment of 1 February 2018.

ECtHR, *Hämäläinen v. Finland*, Application No. 37359/09, Judgment of 16 July 2014.

ECtHR, *Hamidović v. Bosnia and Herzegovina*, Application No. 57792/15, Judgment of 5 December 2017.

ECtHR, *Handyside v. the United Kingdom*, Application No. 5493/72, Judgment of 7 December 1976.

ECtHR, *Harakchiev and Tolumov v. Bulgaria*, Application Nos. 15018/11 and 61199/12, Judgment of 8 July 2014.

ECtHR, *Hassan v. the United Kingdom*, Application No. 29750/09, Judgment of 16 September 2014.

ECtHR, *Hatton and Others v. the United Kingdom*, Application No. 36022/97, Judgment of 8 July 2003.

ECtHR, *Hatton and Others v. the United Kingdom*, Application No. 36022/97, Judgment of 2 October 2001.

ECtHR, *Heinisch v. Germany*, Application No. 28274/08, Judgment of 21 July 2011.

ECtHR, *Hirst v. the United Kingdom (No. 2)*, Application No. 74025/01, Judgment of 6 October 2005.

ECtHR, *Hutchinson v. the United Kingdom*, Application No. 57592/08, Judgment of 17 January 2017.

ECtHR, *Ibrahim and Others v. the United Kingdom*, Application Nos. 50541/08, 50571/08, 50573/08 and 40351/09, Judgment of 13 September 2016.

ECtHR, *Identoba and Others v. Georgia*, Application No. 73235/12, Judgment of 12 May 2015.

ECtHR, *Ilnseher v. Germany*, Application Nos. 10211/12 and 27505/14, Judgment of 4 December 2018.

ECtHR, *Ilya Lyapin v. Russia*, Application No. 70879/11, Judgment of 30 June 2020.

ECtHR, *Ireland v. the United Kingdom*, Application No. 5310/71, Judgment of 18 January 1978.

ECtHR, *Junta Rectora del Ertzainen Nazional Elkartasuna v. Spain*, Application No. 45892/09, Judgment of 21 April 2015.

ECtHR, *Kafkaris v. Cyprus*, Application No. 21906/04, Judgment of 12 February 2008.

ECtHR, *Karner v. Austria*, Application No. 40016/98, Judgment of 24 July 2003.

ECtHR, *Kautzor v. Germany*, Application No. 23338/09, Judgment of 22 March 2012.

ECtHR, *Khamtokhu and Aksenchik v. Russia*, Application Nos. 60367/08 and 961/11, Judgment of 24 January 2017.

ECtHR, *König v. Germany*, Application No. 6232/73, Judgment of 28 June 1978.

ECtHR, *Kononov v. Latvia*, Application No. 36376/04, Judgment of 17 May 2010.

ECtHR, *Konstantin Markin v. Russia*, Application No. 30078/06, Judgment of 22 March 2012.

ECtHR, *Kulinski and Sabev v. Bulgaria*, Application No. 63849/09, Judgment of 21 July 2016.

ECtHR, *L. v. Lithuania*, Application No. 27527/03, Judgment of 11 September 2007.

ECtHR, *L.F. v. Ireland*, Application No. 62007/17, Decision of 10 November 2020.

ECtHR, *Lautsi v. Italy*, Application No. 30814/06, Judgment of 3 November 2009.

ECtHR, *Lautsi and Others v. Italy*, Application No. 30814/06, Judgment of 18 March 2011.

ECtHR, *Leyla Şahin v. Turkey*, Application No. 44774/98, Judgment of 10 November 2005.

ECtHR, *Loizidou v. Turkey*, Application No. 15318/89, Judgment of 18 December 1996.

ECtHR, *Loizidou v. Turkey (Preliminary Objections)*, Application No. 15318/89, Judgment of 23 March 1995.

ECtHR, *Lopes de Sousa Fernandes v. Portugal*, Application No. 56080/13, Judgment of 19 December 2017.

ECtHR, *M. v. Germany*, Application No. 19359/04, Judgment of 17 December 2009.

ECtHR, *M.C. v. Bulgaria*, Application No. 39272/98, Judgment of 4 December 2003.

ECtHR, *Magyar Helsinki Bizottság v. Hungary*, Application No. 18030/11, Judgment of 8 November 2016.

ECtHR, *Marckx v. Belgium*, Application No. 6833/74, Judgment of 13 June 1979.

ECtHR, *Mata Estevez v. Spain*, Application No. 56501/00, Decision of 10 May 2001.

ECtHR, *McElhinney v. Ireland*, Application No. 31253/96, Judgment of 21 November 2001.

ECtHR, *McHugh and Others v. the United Kingdom*, Application No. 51987/08 and 1,014 others, Judgment of 10 February 2015.

ECtHR, *Mennesson v. France*, Application No. 65192/11, Judgment of 26 June 2014.

ECtHR, *Mennitto v. Italy*, Application No. 33804/96, Judgment of 5 October 2000.

ECtHR, *Merabishvili v. Georgia*, Application No. 72508/13, Judgment of 28 November 2017.

ECtHR, *Mihalache v. Romania*, Application No. 54012/10, Judgment of 8 July 2019.

ECtHR, *Mikhaylova v. Russia*, Application No. 46998/08, Judgment of 19 November 2015.

ECtHR, *Millbank and Others v. the United Kingdom*, Application Nos. 44473/14 et al., Judgment of 30 June 2016.

ECtHR, *Mladina D.D. Ljubljana v. Slovenia*, Application No. 20981/10, Judgment of 17 April 2014.

ECtHR, *Mohamed Hasan v. Norway*, Application No. 27496/15, Judgment of 26 April 2018.

ECtHR, *Moreira Ferreira v. Portugal (no. 2)*, Application No. 19867/12, Judgment of 11 July 2017.

ECtHR, *Mosley v. the United Kingdom*, Application No. 48009/08, Judgment of 10 May 2011.

ECtHR, *Mugemangango v. Belgium*, Application No. 310/15, Judgment of 10 July 2020.

ECtHR, *Muhammad and Muhammad v. Romania*, Application No. 80982/12, Judgment of 15 October 2020.

ECtHR, *Murat Vural v. Turkey*, Application No. 9540/07, Judgment of 21 October 2014.

ECtHR, *Muršić v. Croatia*, Application No. 7334/13, Judgment of 20 October 2016.

ECtHR, *Nada v. Switzerland*, Application No. 10593/08, Judgment of 12 September 2012.

ECtHR, *Naït-Liman v. Switzerland*, Application No. 51357/07, Judgment of 15 March 2018.

ECtHR, *Nataliya Mikhaylenko v. Ukraine*, Application No. 49069/11, Judgment of 30 May 2013.

ECtHR, *National Federation of Sportspersons' Associations and Unions (FNASS) and Others v. France*, Application Nos. 48151/11 and 77769/13, Judgment of 18 January 2018.

ECtHR, *National Union of Rail, Maritime and Transport Workers v. the United Kingdom*, Application No. 31045/10, Judgment of 8 April 2014.

ECtHR, *Neulinger and Shuruk v. Switzerland*, Application No. 41615/07, Judgment of 6 July 2010.

ECtHR, *O'Keeffe v. Ireland*, Application No. 35810/09, Judgment of 28 January 2014.

ECtHR, *OAO Neftyanaya Kompaniya Yukos v. Russia (Just Satisfaction)*, Application No. 14902/04, Judgment of 31 July 2014.

ECtHR, *Odièvre v. France*, Application No. 42326/98, Judgment of 13 February 2003.

ECtHR, *Oliari and Others v. Italy*, Application Nos. 18766/11 and 36030/11, Judgment of 21 July 2015.

ECtHR, *Opuz v. Turkey*, Application No. 33401/02, Judgment of 9 June 2009.

ECtHR, *Orlandi and Others v. Italy*, Application Nos. 26431/12, 26742/12, 44057/12 and 60088/12, Judgment of 14 December 2017.

ECtHR, *Oršuš and Others v. Croatia*, Application No. 15766/03, Judgment of 16 March 2010.

ECtHR, *Othman (Abu Qatada) v. the United Kingdom*, Application No. 8139/09, Judgment of 17 January 2012.

ECtHR, *Otto-Preminger-Institut v. Austria*, Application No. 13470/87, Judgment of 20 September 1994.

ECtHR, *Öztürk v. Germany*, Application No. 8544/79, Judgment of 21 February 1984.

ECtHR, *A.P., Garçon and Nicot v. France*, Application Nos. 79885/12, 52471/13 and 52596/13, Judgment of 6 April 2017.

ECtHR, *Parrillo v. Italy*, Application No. 46470/11, Judgment of 27 August 2015.

ECtHR, *Parry v. the United Kingdom*, Application No. 42971/05, Decision of 28 November 2006.

ECtHR, *Paulić v. Croatia*, Application No. 3572/06, Judgment of 22 October 2009.

ECtHR, *Pellegrin v. France*, Application No. 28541/95, Judgment of 8 December 1999.

ECtHR, *Perinçek v. Switzerland*, Application No. 27510/08, Judgment of 15 October 2015.

ECtHR, *Pini and Others v. Romania*, Application Nos. 78028/01 and 78030/01, Judgment of 22 June 2004.

ECtHR, *Rantsev v. Cyprus and Russia*, Application No. 25965/04, Judgment of 7 January 2010.

ECtHR, *Rasmussen v. Denmark*, Application No. 8777/79, Judgment of 28 November 1984.

ECtHR, *Rees v. the United Kingdom*, Application No. 9532/81, Judgment of 17 October 1986.

ECtHR, *Regner v. the Czech Republic*, Application No. 35289/11, Judgment of 19 September 2017.

ECtHR, *Republican Party of Russia v. Russia*, Application No. 12976/07, Judgment of 12 April 2011.

ECtHR, *Riviere v. France*, Application No. 33834/03, Judgment of 11 July 2006.

ECtHR, *Rohlena v. the Czech Republic*, Application No. 59552/08, Judgment of 27 January 2015.

ECtHR, *Rola v. Slovenia*, Application Nos. 12096/14 and 39335/16, Judgment of 4 June 2019.

ECtHR, *S. and Marper v. the United Kingdom*, Application Nos. 30562/04 and 30566/04, Judgment of 4 December 2008.

ECtHR, *S.A.S. v. France*, Application No. 43835/11, Judgment of 1 July 2014.

ECtHR, *S.H. and Others v. Austria*, Application No. 57813/00, Judgment of 3 November 2011.

ECtHR, *S.M. v. Croatia*, Application No. 60561/14, Judgment of 25 June 2020.

ECtHR, *Salduz v. Turkey*, Application No. 36391/02, Judgment of 27 November 2008.

ECtHR, *Schalk and Kopf v. Austria*, Application No. 30141/04, Judgment of 24 June 2010.

ECtHR, *Scoppola v. Italy (No. 3)*, Application No. 126/05, Judgment of 22 May 2012.

ECtHR, *Selmouni v. France*, Application No. 25803/94, Judgment of 28 July 1999.

ECtHR, *Sheffield and Horsham v. the United Kingdom*, Application Nos. 22985/93 and 23390/94, Judgment of 30 July 1998.

ECtHR, *Shindler v. the United Kingdom*, Application No. 19840/09, Judgment of 7 May 2013.

ECtHR, *Sigurdur A. Sigurjónsson v. Iceland*, Application No. 16130/90, Judgment of 30 June 1993.

ECtHR, *Siliadin v. France*, Application No. 73316/01, Judgment of 26 July 2005.

ECtHR, *Sitaropoulos and Giakoumopoulos v. Greece*, Application No. 42202/07, Judgment of 15 March 2012.

ECtHR, *Smith and Grady v. the United Kingdom*, Application Nos. 33985/96 and 33986/96, Judgment of 27 September 1999.

ECtHR, *Soering v. the United Kingdom*, Application No. 14038/88, Judgment of 7 July 1989.

ECtHR, *Sørensen and Rasmussen v. Denmark*, Application Nos. 52562/99 and 525620/99, Judgment of 11 January 2006.

ECtHR, *Söyler v. Turkey*, Application No. 29411/07, Judgment of 17 September 2013.

ECtHR, *Sporer v. Austria*, Application No. 35637/03, Judgment of 3 February 2011.

ECtHR, *Stafford v. the United Kingdom*, Application No. 46295/99, Judgment of 28 May 2002.

ECtHR, *Stanev v. Bulgaria*, Application No. 36760/06, Judgment of 17 January 2012.

ECtHR, *Stec and Others v. the United Kingdom (Admissibility)*, Application Nos. 65731/01 and 65900/01, Decision of 6 July 2005.

ECtHR, *Stichting Mothers of Srebrenica and Others v. the Netherlands*, Application No. 65542/12, Decision of 11 June 2013.

ECtHR, *Stoll v. Switzerland*, Application No. 69698/01, Judgment of 10 December 2007.

ECtHR, *Strand Lobben and Others v. Norway*, Application No. 37283/13, Judgment of 10 September 2019.

ECtHR, *Stübing v. Germany*, Application No. 43547/08, Judgment of 12 April 2012.

ECtHR, *Şükran Aydin and Others v. Turkey*, Application Nos. 49197/06, 23196/07, 50242/08, 60912/08 and 14871/09, Judgment of 22 January 2013.

ECtHR, *Tănase v. Moldova*, Application No. 7/08, Judgment of 27 April 2010.

ECtHR, *Tüm Haber Sen and Çinar v. Turkey*, Application No 28602/95, Judgment of 21 February 2006.

ECtHR, *Tyrer v. the United Kingdom*, Application No. 5856/72, Judgment of 25 April 1978.

ECtHR, *Ünal Tekeli v. Turkey*, Application No. 29865/96, Judgment of 16 November 2004.

ECtHR, *V. v. the United Kingdom*, Application No. 24888/94, Judgment of 16 December 1999.

ECtHR, *Vallianatos and Others v. Greece*, Application Nos. 29381/09 and 32684/09, Judgment of 7 November 2013.

ECtHR, *van der Heijden v. the Netherlands*, Application No. 42857/05, Judgment of 3 April 2012.

ECtHR, *Vejdeland and Others v. Sweden*, Application No. 1813/07, Judgment of 9 February 2012.

ECtHR, *Vilho Eskelinen and Others v. Finland*, Application No. 63235/00, Judgment of 19 April 2007.

ECtHR, *Vinter and Others v. the United Kingdom*, Application Nos. 66069/09, 130/10 and 3896/10, Judgment of 9 July 2013.

ECtHR, *Vo v. France*, Application No. 53924/00, Judgment of 8 July 2004.

ECtHR, *von Hannover v. Germany (No. 2)*, Application Nos. 40660/08 and 60641/08, Judgment of 7 February 2012.

ECtHR, *Winterstein and Others v. France*, Application No. 27013/07, Judgment of 17 October 2013.

ECtHR, *Witold Litwa v. Poland*, Application No. 26629/95, Judgment of 4 April 2000.

ECtHR, *X and Others v. Austria*, Application No. 19010/07, Judgment of 19 February 2013.

ECtHR, *X, Y and Z v. the United Kingdom*, Application No. 21830/93, Judgment of 22 April 1997.

ECtHR, *Y.Y. v. Turkey*, Application No. 14793/08, Judgment of 10 March 2015.

ECtHR, *Yevgeniy Zakharov v. Russia*, Application No. 66610/10, Judgment of 14 March 2017.

ECtHR, *Young, James and Webster v. the United Kingdom*, Application Nos. 7601/76 and 7806/77, Judgment of 13 August 1981.

ECtHR, *Zaunegger v. Germany*, Application No. 22028/04, Judgment of 3 December 2009.

ICJ, "Asylum Case" (*Colombia v. Peru*), Judgment of 20 November 1950, ICJ Reports 1950, p. 266.

ICJ, "Fisheries Case" (*United Kingdom v. Norway*), Judgment of 18 December 1951, ICJ Reports 1951, p. 116.

Supreme Court of the United States, *Lochner v. New York*, Judgment of 18 April 1905, 198 U.S. 45, 76 (1905).

Supreme Court of the United States, *Mathews v. Lucas*, Judgment of 29 June 1976, 427 U.S. 495, 520 (1976).

Supreme Court of the United States, *Roper v. Simmons*, Judgment of 1 March 2005, 543 U.S. 551 (2005).

Bibliography

Van Aaken, Anne, and Iulia Motoc, eds. *The European Convention on Human Rights and General International Law*. Oxford: Oxford University Press, 2018.

Ackerly, Brooke A. *Universal Human Rights in a World of Difference*. Cambridge: Cambridge University Press, 2008.

Adamo, Silvia. "Protecting International Civil Rights in a National Context: Danish Law and Its Discontents." *Nordic Journal of International Law* 85 (2016): 119-145.

Agamben, Giorgio. *Potentialities. Collected Essays in Philosophy*. Translated by Daniel Heller-Roazen. Stanford: Stanford University Press, 2000.

Ahmed, Sara. *Living a Feminist Life*. Durham and London: Duke University Press, 2017.

Ahmed, Sara. *The Promise of Happiness*. Durham and London: Duke University Press, 2010.

Ahmed, Sara. *Queer Phenomenology*. Durham and London: Duke University Press, 2006.

Ahmed, Sara. "Uses of Use. Diversity, Utility and the University." 2018. Available at <https://www.youtube.com/watch?v=avKJ2w1mhng>.

Alexy, Robert. *Theorie der Grundrechte*. Frankfurt: Suhrkamp, 1994.

Alexy, Robert. *Theorie der juristischen Argumentation*. 7th ed. Frankfurt a.M.: Suhrkamp, 2012.

Allott, Philip. *Eutopia. New Philosophy and New Law for a Troubled World*. Cheltenham: Edward Elgar, 2016.

Allott, Philip. "The Will to Know and the Will to Power. Theory and Moral Responsibility." In *The Health of Nations. Society and Law beyond the State*, 3-35. Cambridge: Cambridge University Press, 2002.

Allott, Philip, and others. "Thinking Another World: 'This Cannot Be How the World Was Meant to Be'." *European Journal of International Law* 16 (2005): 255-297.

Alter, Karen J. *Establishing the Supremacy of European Law. The Making of an International Rule of Law in Europe*. Oxford: Oxford University Press, 2001.

Altwicker, Tilmann, and Oliver Diggelmann. "How is Progress Constructed in International Legal Scholarship?". *European Journal of International Law* 25 (2014): 425-444.

Ambrus, Mónika. "Comparative Law Method in the Jurisprudence of the European Court of Human Rights in the Light of the Rule of Law." *Erasmus Law Review* 2 (2009): 353-371.

Amos, Merris. "Can European Consensus Encourage Acceptance of the European Convention on Human Rights in the United Kingdom?". In *Building Consensus on European Consensus: Judicial Interpretation of Human Rights in Europe and Beyond*, edited by Panos Kapotas and Vassilis Tzevelekos, 258-282. Cambridge: Cambridge University Press, 2019.

Amos, Merris. "The Value of the European Court of Human Rights to the United Kingdom." *European Journal of International Law* 28 (2017): 763-785.

Anagnostou, Dia, and Alina Mungiu-Pippidi. "Domestic Implementation of Human Rights Judgments in Europe: Legal Infrastructure and Government Effectiveness Matter." *European Journal of International Law* 25 (2014): 205-227.

Arai-Takahashi, Yutaka. *The Margin of Appreciation Doctrine and the Principle of Proportionality in the Jurisprudence of the ECHR*. Antwerp et al.: Intersentia, 2002.

Arai-Takahashi, Yutaka. "The Margin of Appreciation Doctrine: A Theoretical Analysis of Strasbourg's Variable Geometry." In *Constituting Europe. The European Court of Human Rights in a National, European and Global Context*, edited by Andreas Føllesdal, Birgit Peters and Geir Ulfstein, 62-105. Cambridge: Cambridge University Press, 2013.

Arnardóttir, Oddný Mjöll. *Equality and Non-Discrimination under the European Convention on Human Rights*. The Hague: Martinus Nijhoff, 2003.

Arnardóttir, Oddný Mjöll. "The 'Procedural Turn' under the European Convention on Human Rights and Presumptions of Convention Compliance." *International Journal of Constitutional Law* 15 (2017): 9-35.

Arnardóttir, Oddný Mjöll. "Rethinking the Two Margins of Appreciation." *European Constitutional Law Review* 12 (2016): 27-53.

Von Arnauld, Andreas. "Rechtsangleichung durch allgemeine Rechtsgrundsätze? - Europäisches Gemeinschaftsrecht und Völkerrecht im Vergleich." In *Rechtsangleichung: Grundlagen, Methoden und Inhalte*, edited by Karl Riesenhuber and Kanako Takayama, 247-262. Berlin: de Gruyter, 2006.

Von Arnauld, Andreas. *Rechtssicherheit: Perspektivische Annäherungen an eine "idée directrice" des Rechts*. Tübingen: Mohr Siebeck, 2006.

Von Arnauld, Andreas. "Zur Rhetorik der Verhältnismäßigkeit." In *Verhältnismäßigkeit*, edited by Matthias Jestaedt and Oliver Lepsius, 276-292. Tübingen: Mohr Siebeck, 2015.

Von Arnauld, Andreas, and Jens T. Theilen. "Rhetoric of Rights: A Topical Perspective on the Functions of Claiming a 'Human Right to …'." In *Cambridge Handbook of New Human Rights. Recognition, Novelty, Rhetoric*, edited by Andreas von Arnauld, Kerstin von der Decken and Mart Susi, 34-49. Cambridge: Cambridge University Press, 2020.

Arvan, Marcus. "First Steps Toward a Nonideal Theory of Justice." *Ethics & Global Politics* 7 (2014): 95-117.

D'Aspremont, Jean. "Martti Koskenniemi, the Mainstream, and Self-Reflectivity." *Leiden Journal of International Law* 29 (2016): 625-639.

D'Aspremont, Jean. "Softness in International Law: A Self-Serving Quest for New Legal Materials." *European Journal of International Law* 19, no. 5 (2008): 1075-1093.

D'Aspremont, Jean. "Three international lawyers in a hall of mirrors." *Leiden Journal of International Law* 32, no. 3 (2019): 367-381.

Authers, Benjamin, and Hilary Charlesworth. "The Crisis and the Quotidian in International Human Rights Law." *Netherlands Yearbook of International Law* 44 (2013): 19-39.

Bakircioglu, Onder. "The Application of the Margin of Appreciation Doctrine in Freedom of Expression and Public Morality Cases." *German Law Journal* 8 (2007): 711-734.

Balkin, Jack M. "A Night in the Topics: The Reason of Legal Rhetoric and the Rhetoric of Legal Reason." In *From Law's Stories: Narrative and Rhetoric in the Law*, edited by Peter Brooks and Paul Gewirtz, 211-224. New Haven: Yale University Press, 1996.

Barry, Brian. *Political Argument*. London: Routledge & Kegan Paul, 1965.

Bassok, Or. "The European Consensus Doctrine and the ECtHR Quest for Public Confidence." In *Building Consensus on European Consensus. Judicial Interpretation of Human Rights in Europe and Beyond*, edited by Panos Kapotas and Vassilis Tzevelekos, 236-257. Cambridge: Cambridge University Press, 2019.

Bates, Ed. "Activism and Self-Restraint: The Margin of Appreciation's Strasbourg Career… Its 'Coming of Age'?". *Human Rights Law Journal* 36 (2016): 261-276.

Bates, Ed. "Analysing the Prisoner Voting Saga and the British Challenge to Strasbourg." *Human Rights Law Review* 14 (2014): 503-540.

Bates, Ed. "Consensus in the Legitimacy-Building Era of the European Court of Human Rights." In *Building Consensus on European Consensus. Judicial Interpretation of Human Rights in Europe and Beyond*, edited by Panos Kapotas and Vassilis Tzevelekos, 42-70. Cambridge: Cambridge University Press, 2019.

Baxi, Upendra. *The Future of Human Rights*. 3rd ed. New Delhi: Oxford University Press, 2008.

Beauchamp, Toby. "Artful Concealment and Strategic Visibility: Transgender Bodies and U.S. State Surveillance After 9/11." *Surveillance & Society* 6, no. 4 (2009): 356-366.

Beitz, Charles R. *The Idea of Human Rights*. Oxford: Oxford University Press, 2009.

Bellamy, Richard. "The Democratic Legitimacy of International Human Rights Conventions: Political Constitutionalism and the European Convention on Human Rights." *European Journal of International Law* 25 (2014): 1019-1042.

Bellamy, Richard. "Republicanism, Democracy, and Constitutionalism." In *Republicanism and Political Theory*, edited by Cécile Laborde and John Maynor, 159-189. Malden, Mass.: Blackwell, 2008.

Ben-Naftali, Orna. "Sentiment, Sense and Sensibility in the Genesis of Utopian Traditions." *European Journal of International Law* 23, no. 4 (2012): 1133-1142.

Bengoetxea, Joxerramon, Neil MacCormick, and Leonor Moral Soriano. "Integration and Integrity in the Legal Reasoning of the European Court of Justice." In *The European Court of Justice*, edited by Gráinne de Búrca and J.H.H. Weiler, 43-85. Oxford: Oxford University Press, 2001.

Benhabib, Seyla. "Another Universalism: On the Unity and Diversity of Human Rights." In *Dignity in Adversity: Human Rights in Troubled Times*, 57-76. Cambridge: Polity Press, 2011.

Benhabib, Seyla. "Introduction: Cosmopolitanism without Illusions." In *Dignity in Adversity: Human Rights in Troubled Times*, 1-19. Cambridge: Polity Press, 2011.

Benhabib, Seyla. "Is There a Human Right to Democracy? Beyond Interventionism and Indifference." In *Dignity in Adversity: Human Rights in Troubled Times*, 77-93. Cambridge: Polity Press, 2011.

Bentham, Jeremy. "Nonsense upon Stilts, or Pandora's Box Opened." In *The Collected Works of Jeremy Bentham*, edited by Philip Schofield, Catherine Pease-Watkins and Cyprian Blamires. Oxford: Oxford University Press, 2002.

Benvenisti, Eyal. "Margin of Appreciation, Consensus, and Universal Standards." *New York University Journal of International Law and Politics* 31 (1999): 843-854.

Benvenisti, Eyal. "The Margin of Appreciation, Subsidiarity and Global Challenges to Democracy." *Journal of International Dispute Settlement* 9 (2018): 240-253.

Besson, Samantha. "The Authority of International Law - Lifting the State Veil." *Sydney Law Review* 31 (2009): 343-380.

Besson, Samantha. "The 'Erga Omnes' Effect of the European Court of Human Rights." In *The European Court of Human Rights after Protocol 14: Preliminary Assessment and Perspectives*, edited by Samantha Besson, 125-175. Geneva: Schulthess, 2011.

Besson, Samantha. "European Human Rights, Supranational Judicial Review and Democracy - Thinking Outside the Judicial Box." In *Human Rights Protection in the European Legal Orders: Interaction Between European Courts and National Courts*, edited by Patricia Popelier, Catherine Van de Heyning and Piet Van Nuffel, 97-145. Cambridge: Intersentia, 2011.

Besson, Samantha. "Human Rights Adjudication as Transnational Adjudication: A Peripheral Case of Domestic Courts as International Law Adjudicators." In *International Law and... Select Proceedings of the European Society of International Law, Vol. 5*, edited by August Reinisch, Mary E. Footer and Christina Binder, 43-65. Oxford: Hart, 2016.

Besson, Samantha. "Human Rights and Democracy in a Global Context: Decoupling and Recoupling." *Ethics & Global Politics* 4 (2011): 19-50.

Besson, Samantha. "Human Rights: Ethical, Political... or Legal? First Steps in a Legal Theory of Human Rights." In *The Role of Ethics in International Law*, edited by Donald Earl Childress, 211-245. Cambridge: Cambridge University Press, 2012.

Besson, Samantha. “The Legitimate Authority of International Human Rights. On the Reciprocal Legitimation of Domestic and International Human Rights.” In *The Legitimacy of International Human Rights Regimes. Legal, Political and Philosophical Perspectives*, edited by Andreas Føllesdal, Johan Karlsson Schaffer and Geir Ulfstein, 32-83. Cambridge: Cambridge University Press, 2013.

Besson, Samantha. *The Morality of Conflict. Reasonable Disagreement and the Law.* Oxford: Hart, 2005.

Besson, Samantha. “State Consent and Disagreement in International Law-Making. Dissolving the Paradox.” *Leiden Journal of International Law* 29 (2016): 289-316.

Besson, Samantha. “Subsidiarity in International Human Rights Law - What is Subsidiary about Human Rights?”. *The American Journal of Jurisprudence* 61 (2016): 69-107.

Besson, Samantha, and Anne-Laurence Graf-Brugère. “Le droit de vote des expatriés, le consensus européen et la marge d’appréciation des États.” *Revue Trimestrielle des Droits de l’Homme* 25 (2014): 937-958.

Besson, Samantha, and José Luis Martí. “Introduction.” In *Deliberative Democracy and its Discontents*, edited by Samantha Besson and José Luis Martí, xiii-xxxi. Aldershot: Ashgate, 2006.

Besson, Samantha, and José Luis Martí. “Law and Republicanism: Mapping the Issues.” In *Legal Republicanism: National and International Perspectives*, edited by Samantha Besson and José Luis Martí, 3-36. Oxford: Oxford University Press, 2009.

Besson, Samantha, and Alain Zysset. “Human Rights Theory and Human Rights History: A Tale of Two Odd Bedfellows.” *Ancilla Iuris* (2012): 204-219.

Bhuta, Nehal. “Two Concepts of Religious Freedom in the European Court of Human Rights.” *The South Atlantic Quarterly* 113, no. 1 (2014): 9-35.

Bickel, Alexander. *The Least Dangerous Branch. The Supreme Court at the Bar of Politics.* New Haven and London: Yale University Press, 1986.

Bjorge, Eirik. “Been There, Done That: The Margin of Appreciation and International Law.” *Cambridge Journal of International and Comparative Law* 4, no. 1 (2015): 181-190.

Bjorge, Eirik. *Domestic Application of the ECHR: Courts as Faithful Trustees*. Oxford: Oxford University Press, 2015.

Blackburn, Simon. “Can Philosophy Exist?”. In *Méta-Philosophie: Reconstructing Philosophy?*, edited by Jocelyne Couture and Kai Nielsen, 83-105. Calgary: University of Calgary Press, 1993.

Bloch, Ernst. *Das Prinzip Hoffnung*. 10th ed. Frankfurt a.M.: Suhrkamp, 2016.

Van Bockel, Bas. “A Court Divided: Discord and Disagreement in Rola v. Slovenia”. Strasbourg Observers, 2019. Available at <https://strasbourgobservers.com/2019/07/09/a-court-divided-discord-and-disagreement-in-rola-v-slovenia/#more-4365>.

Bodansky, Daniel M. “The Legitimacy of International Governance: A Coming Challenge for International Environmental Law?”. *American Journal of International Law* 93 (1999): 596-624.

Von Bogdandy, Armin, and Ingo Venzke. "In Whose Name? An Investigation of International Courts' Public Authority and Its Democratic Justification." *European Journal of International Law* 23 (2012): 7-41.

Bothe, Michael. "Die Bedeutung der Rechtsvergleichung in der Praxis internationaler Gerichte." *Zeitschrift für ausländisches öffentliches Recht und Völkerrecht* 36 (1976): 280-299.

Bourdieu, Pierre. *Pascalian Meditations*. Translated by Richard Nice. Stanford: Stanford University Press, 2000.

Bouwhuis, Stephen. "Revisiting Philip Alston's Human Rights and Quality Control." *European Human Rights Law Review*, no. 5 (2016): 475-483.

Bowring, Bill. "Does Russia Have a Human Rights Future in the Council of Europe and OSCE?". In *Shifting Power and Human Rights Diplomacy: Russia*, edited by Doutje Lettinga and Lars van Troost: Amnesty International Netherlands, 2017.

Bowring, Bill. "Russia and the European Convention (or Court) of Human Rights: The End?". *Revue québécoise de droit international* hors-série (2020): 201-218.

Boylan, Michael. *Natural Human Rights. A Theory*. Cambridge: Cambridge University Press, 2014.

Bratza, Nicolas. "The Relationship between the UK Courts and Strasbourg." *European Human Rights Law Review* (2011): 505-512.

Brauch, Jeffrey A. "The Dangerous Search for an Elusive Consensus: What the Supreme Court Should Learn from the European Court of Human Rights." *Howard Law Journal* 52 (2009): 277-318.

Brauch, Jeffrey A. "The Margin of Appreciation and the Jurisprudence of the European Court of Human Rights: Threat to the Rule of Law." *Columbia Journal of European Law* 11 (2004-2005): 113-150.

Brems, Eva. "Enemies or Allies? Feminism and Cultural Relativism as Dissident Voices in Human Rights Discourse." *Human Rights Quarterly* 19 (1997): 136-164.

Brems, Eva. "Human Rights: Minimum and Maximum Perspectives." *Human Rights Law Review* 9 (2009): 349-372.

Brems, Eva. *Human Rights: Universality and Diversity*. The Hague et al.: Martinus Nijhoff, 2001.

Brems, Eva. "The Margin of Appreciation Doctrine in the Case-Law of the European Court of Human Rights." *Zeitschrift für ausländisches öffentliches Recht und Völkerrecht* 56 (1996): 240-314.

Brems, Eva. "Procedural Protection. An Examination of Procedural Safeguards Read into Substantive Convention Rights." In *Shaping Rights in the ECHR. The Role of the European Court of Human Rights in Determining the Scope of Human Rights*, edited by Eva Brems and Janneke Gerards, 137-161. Cambridge: Cambridge University Press, 2013.

Brems, Eva, and Laurens Lavrysen. "Procedural Justice in Human Rights Adjudication: The European Court of Human Rights." *Human Rights Quarterly* 35 (2013): 176-200.

Brest, Paul. "The Substance of Process." *Ohio State Law Journal* 42 (1981): 131-142.

Breuer, Marten. "Establishing Common Standards and Securing the Rule of Law." In *The Council of Europe. Its Laws and Policies*, edited by Stefanie Schmahl and Marten Breuer, 639-670. Oxford: Oxford University Press, 2017.

Breuer, Marten. "Impact of the Council of Europe on National Legal Systems." In *The Council of Europe. Its Laws and Policies*, edited by Stefanie Schmahl and Marten Breuer, 801-873. Oxford: Oxford University Press, 2017.

Bribosia, Emmanuelle, Isabelle Rorive, and Laura Van den Eynde. "Same-Sex Marriage: Building an Argument before the European Court of Human Rights in Light of the US Experience." *Berkeley Journal of International Law* 32 (2014): 1-43.

Brown, Wendy. "'The Most We Can Hope For…': Human Rights and the Politics of Fatalism." *The South Atlantic Quarterly* 103 (2004): 451-463.

Buchanan, Allen. *The Heart of Human Rights*. Oxford: Oxford University Press, 2013.

De Búrca, Gráinne. "The Language of Rights and European Integration." In *New Legal Dynamics of European Union*, edited by Josephine Shaw and Gillian More. Oxford: Clarendon Press, 1995.

Van der Burg, Wibren, and Theo van Willigenburg. "Introduction." In *Reflective Equilibrium: Essays in Honour of Robert Heeger*, edited by Wibren van der Burg and Theo van Willigenburg, 1-25. Dordrecht: Springer, 1998.

Burke, Karen C. "Secret Surveillance and the European Convention on Human Rights." *Stanford Law Review* 33 (1980-1981): 1113-1140.

Burstein, Mike. "The Will to Enforce: An Examination of the Political Constraints upon a Regional Court of Human Rights." *Berkeley Journal of International Law* 24 (2006): 423-443.

Butler, Judith. "Beside Oneself: On the Limits of Sexual Autonomy." In *Undoing Gender*, 17-39. New York and London: Routledge, 2004.

Butler, Judith. "Gender Regulations." In *Undoing Gender*, 40-56. New York and London: Routledge, 2004.

Butler, Judith. *Gender Trouble. Feminism and the Subversion of Identity*. New York and London: Routledge, 1999.

Butler, Judith, and William Connolly. "Politics, Power and Ethics: A Discussion Between Judith Butler and William Connolly." *Theory & Event* 4, no. 2 (2000).

Çalı, Başak. "Specialized Rules of Treaty Interpretation: Human Rights." In *The Oxford Guide to Treaties*, edited by Duncan B. Hollis, 525-548. Oxford: Oxford University Press, 2012.

Çalı, Başak, Anne Koch, and Nicola Bruch. "The Legitimacy of the European Court of Human Rights: The View from the Ground." Strasbourg, 2011.

Çalı, Başak, and Saladin Meckled-García. "Human Rights Legalized - Defining, Interpreting, and Implementing an Ideal." In *The Legalization of Human Rights. Multidisciplinary Perspectives on Human Rights and Human Rights Law*, edited by Saladin Meckled-García and Başak Çalı, 1-8. London and New York: Routledge, 2006.

Carothers, Thomas. "Empirical Perspectives on the Emerging Norm of Democracy in International Law." *Proceedings of the American Society of International Law* (1992): 261-267.

Carozza, Paolo G. "Subsidiarity as a Structural Principle of International Human Rights Law." *American Journal of International Law* 97 (2003): 38-79.

Carozza, Paolo G. "Uses and Misuses of Comparative Law in International Human Rights: Some Reflections on the Jurisprudence of the European Court of Human Rights." *Notre Dame Law Review* 73 (1998): 1217-1237.

Carrubba, Clifford James, and Matthew Joseph Gabel. "Courts, Compliance, and the Quest for Legitimacy in International Law." *Theoretical Inquiries in Law* 14 (2013): 505-541.

Cebada Romero, Alicia. "The European Court of Human Rights and Religion: Between Christian Neutrality and the Fear of Islam." *New Zealand Journal of Public and International Law* 11 (2013): 75-101.

Charlesworth, Hilary, Christine Chinkin, and Shelley Wright. "Feminist Approaches to International Law." *American Journal of International Law* 85, no. 4 (1991): 613-645.

Charlesworth, Hilary, Gina Heathcote, and Emily Jones. "Feminist Scholarship on International Law in the 1990s and Today: An Inter-Generational Conversation." *Feminist Legal Studies* 27 (2019): 79-93.

Cheah, Pheng. *Inhuman Conditions. On Cosmopolitanism and Human Rights*. Cambridge, Mass.: Harvard University Press, 2006.

Chimni, B.S. "Third World Approaches to International Law: A Manifesto." *International Community Law Review* 8 (2006): 3-27.

Clément, Dominique. "Human Rights or Social Justice? The Problem of Rights Inflation." *International Journal of Human Rights* 22, no. 2 (2018): 155-169.

Cohen, Joshua. "An Epistemic Conception of Democracy." *Ethics* 97 (1986): 26-38.

Condorcet, Marquis de. "On the Emancipation of Women. On giving Women the Right of Citizenship." In *Condorcet: Political Writings*, edited by Steven Lukes and Nadia Urbinati, 156-162. Cambridge: Cambridge University Press, 2012.

Conway, Gerard. "Levels of Generality in the Legal Reasoning of the European Court of Justice." *European Law Journal* 14 (2008): 787-805.

Cooper, Davina. *Everyday Utopias. The Conceptual Life of Promising Spaces*. Durham and London: Duke University Press, 2014.

Cooper, Sarah Lucy. "Marriage, Family, Discrimination & Contradiction: An Evaluation of the Legacy and Future of the European Court of Human Rights' Jurisprudence on LGBT Rights." *German Law Journal* 12 (2011): 1746-1763.

Costa, Jean-Paul. "On the Legitimacy of the European Court of Human Rights' Judgments." *European Constitutional Law Review* 7 (2011): 173-182.

Costa, Jean-Paul. "The Relationship between the European Court of Human Rights and the National Courts." *European Human Rights Law Review* (2013): 264-274.

Cover, Robert M. "The Supreme Court 1982 Term. Foreword: Nomos and Narrative." *Harvard Law Review* 97 (1983): 4-68.

Cover, Robert M. "Violence and the Word." *Yale Law Journal* 95 (1986): 1601-1629.

Cowan, Sharon. "The Scottish Feminist Judgments Project: A New Frontier." In *Oñati Socio-legal Series, v. 8, n. 9 - Feminist Judgments: Comparative Socio-Legal Perspectives on Judicial Decision Making and Gender Justice*, 2018. Available at <https://papers.ssrn.com/sol3/papers.cfm?abstract_id=3249609>.

Cox, Robert W. "Social Forces, States and World Orders: Beyond International Relations Theory." *Millennium: Journal of International Studies* 10, no. 2 (1981): 126-155.

Cram, Ian. "Protocol 15 and Articles 10 and 11 ECHR - The Partial Triumph of Political Incumbency Post-Brighton?". *International and Comparative Law Quarterly* 67 (2018): 477-503.

Craven, Matthew. "Legal Differentiation and the Concept of the Human Rights Treaty in International Law." *European Journal of International Law* 11, no. 3 (2000): 489-519.

Craven, Matthew, Gerry Simpson, Susan Marks, and Ralph Wilde. "We Are Teachers of International Law." *Leiden Journal of International Law* 17, no. 2 (2004): 363-374.

Crenshaw, Kimberle. "Demarginalizing the Intersection of Race and Sex: A Black Feminist Critique of Antidiscrimination Doctrine, Feminist Theory and Antiracist Politics." *University of Chicago Legal Forum*, no. 1 (1989): 139-167.

Crenshaw, Kimberle. "Mapping the Margins: Intersectionality, Identity Politics, and Violence Against Women of Color." *Stanford Law Review* 43, no. 6 (1991): 1241-1299.

Dahlberg, Maija. "'The Lack of Such a Common Approach' - Comparative Argumentation by the European Court of Human Rights." *Finnish Yearbook of International Law* 23 (2012-2013): 73-111.

Danius, Sara, Stefan Jonsson, and Gayatri Chakravorty Spivak. "An Interview with Gayatri Chakravorty Spivak." *boundary 2* 20 (1993): 24-50.

Dann, Philipp, Maxim Bönnemann, and Tanja Herklotz. "Of Apples and Mangoes. Comparing the European Union and India." *Indian Yearbook of Comparative Law* (2016): 3-20.

Davis, Angela Y. *Women, Race & Class*. New York: Random House, 1983.

Dembour, Marie-Benedicte. *Who Believes in Human Rights? Reflections on the European Convention*. Cambridge: Cambridge University Press, 2006.

Devlin, Patrick. "Democracy and Morality." In *The Enforcement of Morals*, 86. Indianapolis: Liberty Fund, 2009.

Devlin, Patrick. "Morals and the Criminal Law." In *The Enforcement of Morals*, 1-25. Indianapolis: Liberty Fund, 2009.

Dietz, Chris. "Governing Legal Embodiment: On the Limits of Self-Declaration." *Feminist Legal Studies* 26, no. 2 (2018): 185-204.

Dijn, Annelien de. "Rousseau and Republicanism." *Political Theory* (2015): 1-22.

Djeffal, Christian. "Consensus, Stasis, Evolution: Reconstructing Argumentative Patterns in Evolutive ECHR Jurisprudence." In *Building Consensus on European Consensus. Judicial Interpretation of Human Rights in Europe and Beyond*, edited by Panos Kapotas and Vassilis Tzevelekos, 71-95. Cambridge: Cambridge University Press, 2019.

Donnelly, Jack. *Universal Human Rights*. 3rd ed. Ithaca and London: Cornell University Press, 2013.

Donoho, Douglas Lee. "Autonomy, Self-Governance, and the Margin of Appreciation: Developing a Jurisprudence of Diversity Within Universal Human Rights." *Emory International Law Review* 15 (2001): 391-466.

Dörr, Oliver. "Article 31." In *Vienna Convention on the Law of Treaties. A Commentary*, edited by Oliver Dörr and Kirsten Schmalenbach, 559-616. Berlin: Springer, 2018.

Dothan, Shai. "Comparative Views on the Right to Vote in International Law: The Case of Prisoners' Disenfranchisement." In *Comparative International Law*, edited by Anthea Roberts, Paul B. Stephan, Pierre-Hugues Verdier and Mila Versteeg, 379-395. Oxford: Oxford University Press, 2018.

Dothan, Shai. "How International Courts Enhance Their Legitimacy." *Theoretical Inquiries in Law* 14 (2013): 455-478.

Dothan, Shai. "In Defence of Expansive Interpretation in the European Court of Human Rights." *Cambridge Journal of International and Comparative Law* 3 (2014): 508-531.

Dothan, Shai. "Judicial Deference Allows European Consensus to Emerge." *Chicago Journal of International Law* (2017): 393-419.

Dothan, Shai. "Judicial Tactics in the European Court of Human Rights." *Chicago Journal of International Law* 12 (2011-2012): 115-142.

Dothan, Shai. "Margin of Appreciation and Democracy: Human Rights and Deference to Political Bodies." *Journal of International Dispute Settlement* 9 (2018): 145-153.

Dothan, Shai. "The Optimal Use of Comparative Law." *Denver Journal of International Law and Policy* 43 (2014): 21-44.

Dothan, Shai. "Three Interpretive Constraints on the European Court of Human Rights." In *The Rule of Law at the National and International Levels. Contestations and Deference*, edited by Machiko Kanetake and André Nollkaemper, 227-245. Oxford and Portland: Hart, 2016.

Douglas-Scott, Sionaidh. "Borges' *Pierre Menard, Author of the Quixote* and the Idea of a European Consensus." In *Building Consensus on European Consensus. Judicial Interpretation of Human Rights in Europe and Beyond*, edited by Panos Kapotas and Vassilis Tzevelekos, 167-186. Cambridge: Cambridge University Press, 2019.

Douglas-Scott, Sionaidh. "A Tale of Two Courts: Luxembourg, Strasbourg and the Growing European Human Rights Acquis." *Common Market Law Review* 43 (2006): 629-665.

Douzinas, Costas. "Adikia: On Communism and Rights." Critical Legal Thinking, 2010. Available at <http://criticallegalthinking.com/2010/11/30/adikia-on-communism-and-rights/>.

Douzinas, Costas. *The End of Human Rights*. Oxford: Hart, 2000.

Draghici, Carmen. “The Strasbourg Court between European and Local Consensus: Anti-democratic or Guardian of Democratic Process?”. *Public Law* (2017): 11-29.

Dworkin, Ronald. “Can Rights be Controversial?”. In *Taking Rights Seriously*, 335-348. London: Bloomsbury, 2013.

Dworkin, Ronald. “Constitutional Cases.” In *Taking Rights Seriously*, 163-184. London: Bloomsbury, 2013.

Dworkin, Ronald. “The Forum of Principle.” *New York University Law Review* 56 (1981): 469.

Dworkin, Ronald. “Hard Cases.” In *Taking Rights Seriously*, 105-162. London: Bloomsbury, 2013.

Dworkin, Ronald. “Justice and Rights.” In *Taking Rights Seriously*, 185-222. London: Bloomsbury, 2013.

Dworkin, Ronald. *Justice for Hedgehogs*. Cambridge, Mass.: Belknap Press of Harvard University Press, 2011.

Dworkin, Ronald. *Law's Empire*. Oxford: Hart, 1986.

Dworkin, Ronald. “Liberty and Moralism.” In *Taking Rights Seriously*, 289-310. London: Bloomsbury, 2013.

Dworkin, Ronald. “The Model of Rules II.” In *Taking Rights Seriously*, 65 103. London: Bloomsbury, 2013.

Dworkin, Ronald. “A New Philosophy for International Law.” *Philosophy & Public Affairs* 41 (2013): 2-30.

Dworkin, Ronald. “Objectivity and Truth: You'd Better Believe It.” *Philosophy & Public Affairs* 25 (1996): 87-139.

Dworkin, Ronald. “Reverse Discrimination.” In *Taking Rights Seriously*, 269-288. London: Bloomsbury, 2013.

Dworkin, Ronald. “Rights as Trumps.” In *Theories of Rights*, edited by Jeremy Waldron, 153-167. Oxford: Oxford University Press, 1984.

Dworkin, Ronald. “Taking Rights Seriously.” In *Taking Rights Seriously*, 223-247. London: Bloomsbury, 2013.

Dzehtsiarou, Kanstantsin. “Book Review of Shai Dothan, Reputation and Judicial Tactics. A Theory of National and International Courts.” *Human Rights Law Review* 15 (2015): 391-406.

Dzehtsiarou, Kanstantsin. “Does Consensus Matter? Legitimacy of European Consensus in the Case Law of the European Court of Human Rights.” *Public Law* (2011): 534-553.

Dzehtsiarou, Kanstantsin. “European Consensus and the Evolutive Interpretation of the European Convention on Human Rights.” *German Law Journal* 12 (2011): 1730-1745.

Dzehtsiarou, Kanstantsin. *European Consensus and the Legitimacy of the European Court of Human Rights*. Cambridge: Cambridge University Press, 2015.

Dzehtsiarou, Kanstantsin. "European Consensus: New Horizons." In *Building Consensus on European Consensus. Judicial Interpretation of Human Rights in Europe and Beyond*, edited by Panos Kapotas and Vassilis Tzevelekos, 29-41. Cambridge: Cambridge University Press, 2019.

Dzehtsiarou, Kanstantsin. "What Is Law for the European Court of Human Rights?". *Georgetown Journal of International Law* 49 (2017): 89-134.

Dzehtsiarou, Kanstantsin, and Alan Greene. "Legitimacy and the Future of the European Court of Human Rights: Critical Perspectives from Academia and Practitioners." *German Law Journal* 12 (2011): 1707-1715.

Dzehtsiarou, Kanstantsin, and Vasily Lukashevich. "Informed Decision-Making: The Comparative Endeavours of the Strasbourg Court." *Netherlands Quarterly of Human Rights* 30 (2012): 272-298.

Dzehtsiarou, Kanstantsin, and Pavel Repyeuski. "European Consensus and the EU Accession to the ECHR." In *The EU Accession to the ECHR*, edited by Vasiliki Kosta, Nikos Skoutaris and Vassilis P. Tzevelekos, 309-323. Oxford and Portland: Hart, 2014.

Easton, David. *A Systems Analysis of Political Life*. New York: Wiley, 1965.

Eisenberg, Avigail. *Reasons of Identity. A Normative Guide to the Political & Legal Assessment of Identity Claims*. Oxford: Oxford University Press, 2009.

Ely, John Hart. *Democracy and Distrust. A Theory of Judicial Review*. Cambridge, Mass.: Harvard University Press, 1980.

Ely, John Hart. "Professor Dworkin's External/Personal Preference Distinction." *Duke Law Journal* (1983): 959-986.

Engle, Karen. "Anti-Impunity and the Turn to Criminal Law in Human Rights." *Cornell Law Review* 100 (2015): 1069-1127.

Engle, Karen. "International Human Rights and Feminism: When Discourses Meet." *Michigan Journal of International Law* 13 (1992): 517-610.

Enright, Máiréad. "Symphysiotomies and an Overlooked Violation of Article 3 ECHR" *Irish Centre for Human Rights*, 2021. Available at <https://ichrgalway.wordpress.com/2020/12/21/symphysiotomies-and-an-overlooked-violation-of-article-3-echr/>

Epstein, Lee, and Jack Knight. "Toward a Strategic Revolution in Judicial Politics: A Look Back, A Look Ahead." *Political Research Quarterly* 53 (2000): 625-661.

Erdman, Joanna N. "The Deficiency of Consensus in Human Rights Protection: A Case Study of Goodwin v. United Kingdom and I. v. United Kingdom." *Journal of Law and Equality* 2 (2003): 318-347.

Estlund, David M. "Democratic Theory and the Public Interest: Condorcet and Rousseau Revisited." *The American Political Science Review* 83 (1989): 1317-1322.

Eynde, Laura Van den. "The Consensus Argument in NGOs' *Amicus Curiae* Briefs: Defending Minorities through a Creatively Used Majoritarian Argument." In *Building Consensus on European Consensus. Judicial Interpretation of Human Rights in Europe and Beyond*, edited by Panos Kapotas and Vassilis Tzevelekos, 96-119. Cambridge: Cambridge University Press, 2019.

Fallon, Richard H., Jr. "Legitimacy and the Constitution." *Harvard Law Review* 118 (2005): 1789-1853.

Fenwick, Helen. "Same-sex Unions at the Strasbourg Court in a Divided Europe: Driving Forward Reform or Protecting the Court's Authority via Consensus Analysis?". *European Human Rights Law Review* (2016): 248-272.

Fenwick, Helen, and Daniel Fenwick. "Finding 'East'/'West' Divisions in Council of Europe States on Treatment of Sexual Minorities: The Response of the Strasbourg Court and the Role of Consensus Analysis." *European Human Rights Law Review*, no. 3 (2019): 247-273.

Féron, Henri. "Human Rights and Faith: A 'World-wide Secular Religion'?". *Ethics & Global Politics* 7, no. 4 (2014): 181-200.

Finnemore, Martha, and Kathryn Sikkink. "International Norm Dynamics and Political Change." *International Organization* 52 (1998): 887-917.

Finnis, John. *Natural Law & Natural Rights*. 2nd ed. Oxford: Oxford University Press, 2011.

Fischl, Richard Michael. "The Question that Killed Critical Legal Studies." *Law and Social Inquiry* 17 (1992): 779-820.

Fleig Goldstein, Rachel M. "The Russian Constitutional Court versus the European Court of Human Rights: How the Strasbourg Court Should Respond to Russia's Refusal to Execute ECtHR Judgments." *Columbia Journal of Transnational Law* 56 (2017): 172-218.

Føllesdal, Andreas. "A Better Signpost, Not a Better Walking Stick: How to Evaluate the European Consensus Doctrine." In *Building Consensus on European Consensus. Judicial Interpretation of Human Rights in Europe and Beyond*, edited by Panos Kapotas and Vassilis Tzevelekos, 189-209. Cambridge: Cambridge University Press, 2019.

Føllesdal, Andreas. "The Legitimacy Deficits of the Human Rights Judiciary: Elements and Implications of a Normative Theory." *Theoretical Inquiries in Law* 14 (2013): 339-360.

Forowicz, Magdalena. *The Reception of International Law in the European Court of Human Rights*. Oxford: Oxford University Press, 2010.

Franck, Thomas M. "Legitimacy in the International System." *American Journal of International Law* 82 (1988): 705-759.

Frankenberg, Günter. "Critical Comparisons: Re-thinking Comparative Law." *Harvard International Law Journal* 26, no. 2 (1985): 411-455.

Frankenberg, Günter. "Tocqueville's Question. The Role of a Constitution in the Process of Integration." *Ratio Juris* 13, no. 1 (2000): 1-30.

Fredman, Sandra. "Foreign Fads or Fashions? The Role of Comparativism in Human Rights Law." *International and Comparative Law Quarterly* 64 (2015): 631-660.

Fredman, Sandra. "From Dialogue to Deliberation: Human Rights Adjudication and Prisoners' Rights to Vote." *Public Law* (2013): 292-311.

French, Duncan. "Treaty Interpretation and the Incorporation of Extraneous Legal Rules." *International and Comparative Law Quarterly* 55 (2006): 281-314.

Ganshof Van der Meersch, W.J. "La référence au droit interne des Etats contractants dans la jurisprudence de la Cour européenne des droits de l'homme." *Revue internationale de droit comparé* 32 (1980): 317-335.

Gearty, Conor. "Building Consensus on European Consensus." In *Building Consensus on European Consensus. Judicial Interpretation of Human Rights in Europe and Beyond*, edited by Panos Kapotas and Vassilis Tzevelekos, 448-467. Cambridge: Cambridge University Press, 2019.

Gerards, Janneke. "Diverging Fundamental Rights Standards and the Role of the European Court of Human Rights." In *Constructing European Constitutional Law*, edited by M. Claes and M. De Visser. Oxford: Hart. Available at <https://papers.ssrn.com/sol3/papers.cfm?abstract_id=2344626>.

Gerards, Janneke. "The European Court of Human Rights and the National Courts: Giving Shape to the Notion of 'Shared Responsibility'." In *Implementation of the European Convention on Human Rights and of the Judgments of the ECtHR in National Case-Law. A Comparative Analysis*, edited by Janneke Gerards and Joseph Fleuren, 13-93. Cambridge et al.: Intersentia, 2014.

Gerards, Janneke. *General Principles of the European Convention on Human Rights*. Cambridge: Cambridge University Press, 2019.

Gerards, Janneke. "Judicial Deliberations in the European Court of Human Rights." In *The Legitimacy of Highest Courts' Rulings*, edited by Nick Huls, Maurice Adams and Jacco Bomhoff, 407-436. The Hague: T.M.C. Asser Press, 2009.

Gerards, Janneke. "Margin of Appreciation and Incrementalism in the Case Law of the European Court of Human Rights." *Human Rights Law Review* (2018): 495-515.

Gerards, Janneke. "Pluralism, Deference and the Margin of Appreciation Doctrine." *European Law Journal* 17 (2011): 80-120.

Gerards, Janneke, and Sarah Lambrecht. "The Final Copenhagen Declaration: Fundamentally Improved With a Few Remaining Caveats". Strasbourg Observers, 2018. Available at <https://strasbourgobservers.com/2018/04/18/the-final-copenhagen-declaration-fundamentally-improved-with-a-few-remaining-caveats/>.

Gilabert, Pablo, and Holly Lawford-Smith. "Political Feasibility: A Conceptual Exploration." *Political Studies* 60 (2012): 809-825.

Glas, Lize R. "The European Court of Human Rights' Use of Non-Binding and Standard-Setting Council of Europe Documents." *Human Rights Law Review* 17 (2017): 97-125.

Glendon, Mary Ann. *Rights Talk. The Impoverishment of Political Discourse*. New York: The Free Press, 1991.

Gless, Sabine, and Jeannine Martin. "The Comparative Method in European Courts: A Comparison Between the CJEU and ECtHR?". *Bergen Journal of Criminal Law and Criminal Justice* 1 (2013): 36-52.

Golder, Ben. "Beyond Redemption? Problematising the Critique of Human Rights in Contemporary International Legal Thought." *London Review of International Law* 2, no. 1 (2014): 77-114.

Golder, Ben. "On the Varieties of Universalism in Human Rights Discourse." In *Human Rights Between Law and Politics: The Margin of Appreciation in Post-National Contexts*, edited by Petr Agha, 37-54. London: Hart, 2017.

Goldston, James A. "The Struggle for Roma Rights: Arguments that Have Worked." *Human Rights Quarterly* 32 (2010): 311-325.

Goldston, James A., and Shirley Pouget. "The Copenhagen Declaration: How Not to "Reform" the European Court of Human Rights." *European Human Rights Law Review*, no. 3 (2018): 208-210.

Gonzalez-Salzberg, Damian A. "The Accepted Transsexual and the Absent Transgender: A Queer Reading of the Regulation of Sex/Gender by the European Court of Human Rights." *American University International Law Review* 29 (2014): 797-829.

Gonzalez-Salzberg, Damian A. "Confirming (the Illusion of) Heterosexual Marriage: *Hämäläinen v Finland*." *Journal of International and Comparative Law* 2, no. 1 (2015): 173-186.

Gonzalez-Salzberg, Damian A. "An Improved Protection for the (Mentally Ill) Trans Parent: A Queer Reading of AP, Garçon and Nicot v France." *Modern Law Review* 81, no. 3 (2018): 526-538.

Grabenwarter, Christoph, and Katharina Pabel. *Europäische Menschenrechtskonvention*. 6th ed. München: Beck, 2016.

Gragl, Paul. *The Accession of the European Union to the European Convention on Human Rights*. Oxford: Hart, 2013.

Grear, Anna. "Challenging Corporate 'Humanity': Legal Disembodiment, Embodiment and Human Rights." *Human Rights Law Review* 7, no. 3 (2007): 511-543.

Green, Jeffrey Edward. "On the Co-originality of Liberalism and Democracy: Rationalist vs. Paradoxicalist Perspectives." *Law, Culture and the Humanities* 11 (2015): 198-217.

Greenhouse, Carol J. *A Moment's Notice. Time Politics across Cultures*. Ithaca: Cornell University Press, 1996.

Greer, Steven. *The Margin of Appreciation: Interpretation and Discretion under the European Convention on Human Rights*. Strasbourg: Council of Europe Publishing, 2000.

Griffin, James. *On Human Rights*. Oxford: Oxford University Press, 2008.

Grofman, Bernard, and Scott L. Feld. "Rousseau's General Will: A Condorcetian Perspective." *The American Political Science Review* 82 (1988): 567-576.

Grofman, Bernard, Guillermo Owen, and Scott L. Feld. "Thirteen Theorems in Search of the Truth." *Theory and Decision* 15 (1983): 261-278.

Gross, Aeyal. "Sex, Love, and Marriage: Questioning Gender and Sexuality Rights in International Law." *Leiden Journal of International Law* 21 (2008): 235-253.

Grossman, Nienke. "Legitimacy and International Adjudicative Bodies." *George Washington International Law Review* 41 (2009): 107-180.

Gutmann, Amy. "Introduction." In *Michael Ignatieff, Human Rights as Politics and Idolatry*, edited by Amy Gutmann, vii-xxviii. Princeton and Oxford: Princeton University Press, 2001.

Habermas, Jürgen. *Between Facts and Norms*. Translated by William Rehg. Cambridge: Polity Press, 1996.

Habermas, Jürgen. "Der europäische Nationalstaat - Zu Vergangenheit und Zukunft von Souveränität und Staatsbürgerschaft." In *Die Einbeziehung des Anderen. Studien zur politischen Theorie*, 128-153. Frankfurt a.M.: Suhrkamp, 1999.

Habermas, Jürgen. "Inklusion - Einbeziehen oder Einschließen? Zum Verhältnis von Nation, Rechtsstaat und Demokratie." In *Die Einbeziehung des Anderen. Studien zur politischen Theorie*, 154-184. Frankfurt a.M.: Suhrkamp, 1999.

Habermas, Jürgen. "On Law and Disagreement. Some Comments on 'Interpretative Pluralism'." *Ratio Juris* 16 (2003): 187-194.

Habermas, Jürgen. "Über den internen Zusammenhang von Rechtsstaat und Demokratie." In *Die Einbeziehung des Anderen. Studien zur politischen Theorie*, 293-308. Frankfurt a.M.: Suhrkamp, 1999.

Habermas, Jürgen. "Versöhnung durch öffentlichen Vernunftgebrauch." In *Die Einbeziehung des Anderen. Studien zur politischen Theorie*, 65-94. Frankfurt a.M.: Suhrkamp, 1999.

Habermas, Jürgen. "Volkssouveränität als Verfahren." In *Faktizität und Geltung. Beiträge zur Diskurstheorie des Rechts und des demokratischen Rechtsstaats*, 600-631. Frankfurt a.M.: Suhrkamp, 2014.

Hallström, Pär. "Balance or Clash of Legal Orders - Some Notes on Margin of Appreciation." In *Human Rights in Contemporary European Law*, edited by Joakim Nergelius and Eleonor Kristoffersson, 59-73. Oxford: Hart, 2015.

Hamilton, Frances. "Same-Sex Marriage, Consensus, Certainty and the European Court of Human Rights." *European Human Rights Law Review* (2018): 33-45.

Harasym, Sarah, ed. *Gayatri Chakravorty Spivak: The Post-Colonial Critic. Interviews, Strategies, Dialogues*. New York and London: Routledge, 1990.

Hare, R.M. "Rawls' Theory of Justice." In *Reading Rawls: Critical Studies on Rawls' 'A Theory of Justice'*, edited by Norman Daniels, 81-107. Stanford: Stanford University Press, 1989.

Hart, H.L.A. "Between Utility and Rights." *Columbia Law Review* 79 (1979): 828-846.

Hart, H.L.A. "Immorality and Treason." In *Morality and the Law*, edited by Richard A. Wasserstrom. Belmont: Wadsworth Publishing, 1971.

Hart, H.L.A. *Law, Liberty, and Morality*. Stanford: Stanford University Press, 1963.

Hartmann, Jacques. "A Danish Crusade for the Reform of the European Court of Human Rights". EJIL:Talk!, 2017. Available at <https://www.ejiltalk.org/a-danish-crusade-for-the-reform-of-the-european-court-of-human-rights/>.

Haslett, D.W. "What Is Wrong with Reflective Equilibria?". *The Philosophical Quarterly* 37 (1987): 305-311.

Hathaway, Oona A. "Treaties' End: The Past, Present, and Future of International Lawmaking in the United States." *Yale Law Journal* 117 (2008): 1236-1372.

Hauser, Gerard A. "The Moral Vernacular of Human Rights Discourse." *Philosophy & Rhetoric* 41 (2008): 440-466.

Helfer, Laurence R. "The Burdens and Benefits of Brighton". ESIL Reflections Vol. 1, issue 1 (2012). Available at <http://esil-sedi.eu/node/138>.

Helfer, Laurence R. "Consensus, Coherence and the European Convention on Human Rights." *Cornell International Law Journal* 26 (1993): 133-165.

Helfer, Laurence R. "Populism and International Human Rights Institutions: A Survival Guide." In *iCourts Working Paper Series, No. 133*, 2018. Available at <https://papers.ssrn.com/sol3/papers.cfm?abstract_id=3202633>.

Helfer, Laurence R. "Redesigning the European Court of Human Rights: Embeddedness as a Deep Structural Principle of the European Human Rights Regime." *European Journal of International Law* 19 (2008): 125-159.

Helfer, Laurence R., and Karen J. Alter. "Legitimacy and Lawmaking: A Tale of Three International Courts." *Theoretical Inquiries in Law* 14 (2013): 479-503.

Helfer, Laurence R., and Anne-Marie Slaughter. "Toward a Theory of Effective Supranational Adjudication." *Yale Law Journal* 107 (1997): 273-391.

Helfer, Laurence R., and Anne-Marie Slaughter. "Why States Create International Tribunals: A Response to Professors Posner and Yoo." *California Law Review* 93 (2005): 899-956.

Helfer, Laurence R., and Erik Voeten. "International Courts as Agents of Legal Change: Evidence from LGBT Rights in Europe." *International Organization* 68 (2014): 1-34.

Henrard, Kristin. "How the ECtHR's Use of European Consensus Considerations Allows Legitimacy Concerns to Delimit Its Mandate." In *Building Consensus on European Consensus. Judicial Interpretation of Human Rights in Europe and Beyond*, edited by Panos Kapotas and Vassilis Tzevelekos, 141-166. Cambridge: Cambridge University Press, 2019.

Henrard, Kristin. "How the European Court of Human Rights' Concern Regarding European Consensus Tempers the Effective Protection of Freedom of Religion." *Oxford Journal of Law and Religion* 4 (2015): 398-420.

Heringa, Aalt Willem. "The 'Consensus Principle': The Role of 'Common Law' in the ECHR Case Law." *Maastricht Journal of European and Comparative Law* 3 (1996): 108-145.

Hodson, Loveday. "A Marriage by Any Other Name? Schalk and Kopf v Austria." *Human Rights Law Review* 11 (2011): 170-179.

Hoffmann, Leonard. "The Universality of Human Rights." *Law Quarterly Review* 125 (2009): 416-432.

Hollinger, David A. "Debates with the PTA and Others." In *Michael Ignatieff: Human Rights as Politics and Idolatry*, edited by Amy Gutmann, 117-126. Princeton: Princeton University Press, 2001.

Hume, David. "A Treatise of Human Nature." In *Hume. The Essential Philosophical Works*. Ware: Wordsworth, 2011.

Hurd, Ian. "Torture and the Politics of Legitimation in International Law." In *The Legitimacy of International Human Rights Regimes. Legal, Political and Philosophical Perspectives*, edited by Andreas Føllesdal, Johan Karlsson Schaffer and Geir Ulfstein, 165-189. Cambridge: Cambridge University Press, 2013.

Hutchinson, Michael R. "The Margin of Appreciation Doctrine in the European Court of Human Rights." *International and Comparative Law Quarterly* 48 (1999): 638-650.

Hwang, Shu-Perng. "Grundrechtsschutz unter der Voraussetzung des europäischen Grundkonsenses?". *Europarecht* (2013): 307-322.

Iglesias Vila, Marisa. "Subsidiarity, Margin of Appreciation and International Adjudication within a Cooperative Conception of Human Rights." *International Journal of Constitutional Law* 15 (2017): 393-413.

Ignatieff, Michael. *Human Rights as Politics and Idolatry*. Princeton: Princeton University Press, 2001.

Janik, Ralph. "How Many Divisions Does the European Court of Human Rights Have? Compliance and Legitimacy in Times of Crisis." *Austrian Review of International and European Law* 20 (2015): 125-144.

Johns, Fleur. "Critical International Legal Theory." In *International Legal Theory: Foundations and Frontiers*, edited by Jeffrey L. Dunoff and Mark A. Pollack. Cambridge: Cambridge University Press, forthcoming. Available at <https://papers.ssrn.com/sol3/papers.cfm?abstract_id=3224013>.

Johnson, Paul. *Homosexuality and the European Court of Human Rights*. Abingdon: Routledge, 2013.

Kagiaros, Dimitrios. "When to Use European Consensus: Assessing the Differential Treatment of Minority Groups by the European Court of Human Rights." In *Building Consensus on European Consensus. Judicial Interpretation of Human Rights in Europe and Beyond*, edited by Panos Kapotas and Vassilis Tzevelekos, 283-310. Cambridge: Cambridge University Press, 2019.

Kakouris, C.N. "Use of the Comparative Method by the Court of Justice of the European Communities." *Pace International Law Review* 6 (1994): 267-283.

Kant, Immanuel. "Grundlegung zur Metaphysik der Sitten." In *Die Kritiken*, 641-705. Frankfurt a.M.: Zweitausendeins, 2008.

Kapotas, Panos, and Vassilis Tzevelekos. "How (Difficult Is It) to Build Consensus on (European) Consensus?". In *Building Consensus on European Consensus. Judicial Interpretation of Human Rights in Europe and Beyond*, edited by Panos Kapotas and Vassilis Tzevelekos, 1-26. Cambridge: Cambridge University Press, 2019.

Kapur, Ratna. *Gender, Alterity and Human Rights*. Cheltenham: Edward Elgar, 2018.

Kapur, Ratna. "Human Rights in the 21st Century: Take a Walk on the Dark Side." *Sydney Law Review* 28 (2006): 665-687.

Kelsen, Hans. *Allgemeine Staatslehre*. Berlin: Julius Springer, 1925.

Kelsen, Hans. *General Theory of Law and State*. Translated by Anders Wedberg. Cambridge, Mass.: Harvard University Press, 1945.

Kelsen, Hans. "Natural Law Doctrine and Legal Positivism." Translated by Wolfgang Herbert Kraus. In *General Theory of Law and State*, 389-446. Cambridge, Mass.: Harvard University Press, 1945.

Kelsen, Hans. *Reine Rechtslehre*. 2nd ed. Vienna: Deuticke, 1960.

Kennedy, David. *The Dark Sides of Virtue. Reassessing International Humanitarianism*. Princeton and Oxford: Princeton University Press, 2004.

Kennedy, David. "The International Human Rights Regime: Still Part of the Problem." In *Examining Critical Perspectives on Human Rights*, edited by Rob Dickinson, Elena Katselli, Colin Murray and Ole W. Pedersen, 19-34. Cambridge: Cambridge University Press, 2013.

Kennedy, David. "New Approaches to Comparative Law: Comparativism and International Governance." *Utah Law Review* (1997): 545-637.

Kennedy, David. "A New World Order: Yesterday, Today, and Tomorrow." *Transnational Law and Contemporary Problems* 4 (1994): 329-375.

Kennedy, David. "Turning to Market Democracy: A Tale of Two Architectures." *Harvard International Law Journal* 32, no. 2 (1991): 373-396.

Kennedy, David, and Chris Tennant. "New Approaches to International Law: A Bibliography." *Harvard International Law Journal* 35, no. 2 (1994): 417-460.

Kennedy, Duncan. *A Critique of Adjudication (fin de siècle)*. Cambridge, Mass.: Harvard University Press, 1997.

Kennedy, Duncan. "A Semiotics of Critique." *Cardozo Law Review* 22 (2001): 1147-1189.

Klabbers, Jan. *The Concept of Treaty in International Law*. The Hague et al.: Kluwer, 1996.

Klabbers, Jan. "Towards a Culture of Formalism? Martti Koskenniemi and the Virtues." *Temple International and Comparative Law Journal* 27, no. 2 (2013): 417-435.

Kleinlein, Thomas. "Consensus and Contestability: The ECtHR and the Combined Potential of European Consensus and Procedural Rationality Control." *European Journal of International Law* 28 (2017): 871-893.

Klocke, Daniel Matthias. "Die dynamische Auslegung der EMRK im Lichte der Dokumente des Europarats." *Europarecht* (2015): 148-169.

Knox, Robert. "Strategy and Tactics." *Finnish Yearbook of International Law* 21 (2010): 193-229.

Koch, Ida Elisabeth, and Jens Vedsted-Hansen. "International Human Rights and National Legislatures - Conflict or Balance?". *Nordic Journal of International Law* 75 (2006): 3-28.

Korhonen, Outi. "New International Law: Silence, Defence or Deliverance?". *European Journal of International Law* 7, no. 1 (1996): 1-28.

Koskenniemi, Martti. "Constitutionalism as Mindset: Reflections on Kantian Themes About International Law and Globalization." *Theoretical Inquiries in Law* 8 (2006): 9-36.

Koskenniemi, Martti. "The Effect of Rights on Political Culture." In *The Politics of International Law*, 133-152. Oxford: Hart, 2011.

Koskenniemi, Martti. "Epilogue. To Enable and Enchant - on the Power of Law." In *The Law of International Lawyers. Reading Martti Koskenniemi*, edited by Wouter Werner, Marieke de Hoon and Alexis Galán, 393-412. Cambridge: Cambridge University Press, 2017.

Koskenniemi, Martti. *From Apology to Utopia: The Structure of International Legal Argument*. Cambridge: Cambridge University Press, 2005.

Koskenniemi, Martti. "Human Rights Mainstreaming as a Strategy for Institutional Power." *Humanity* 1 (2010): 47-58.

Koskenniemi, Martti. "Human Rights, Politics and Love." In *The Politics of International Law*, 153-167. Oxford: Hart, 2011.

Koskenniemi, Martti. "International Law and Hegemony: A Reconfiguration." *Cambridge Review of International Affairs* 17 (2004): 197-218.

Koskenniemi, Martti. "International Law as Therapy: Reading The Health of Nations." *European Journal of International Law* 16 (2005): 329-341.

Koskenniemi, Martti. "'Intolerant Democracies': A Reaction." *Harvard International Law Journal* 37 (1996): 231-234.

Koskenniemi, Martti. "Law, Teleology and International Relations: An Essay in Counterdisciplinarity." *International Relations* 26 (2011): 3-34.

Koskenniemi, Martti. "Legitimacy, Rights and Ideology: Notes Towards a Critique of the New Moral Internationalism." *Associations* 7 (2003): 349-373.

Koskenniemi, Martti. "Letter to the Editors of the Symposium." *American Journal of International Law* 93 (1999): 351-361.

Koskenniemi, Martti. "The Pull of the Mainstream." *Michigan Law Review* 88 (1989-1990): 1946-1962.

Koskenniemi, Martti. "What is Critical Research in International Law? Celebrating Structuralism." *Leiden Journal of International Law* 29 (2016): 727-735.

Kotiaho, Paavo. "A Return to Koskenniemi, or the Disconcerting Co-optation of Rupture." *German Law Journal* 13, no. 5 (2012): 483-496.

Kovler, Anatoly, Vladimiro Zagrebelsky, Lech Garlicki, Dean Spielmann, Renate Jaeger, and Roderick Liddell. "The Role of Consensus in the System of the European Court of Human Rights." In *Dialogue between judges, European Court of Human Rights*, 11-19, 2008.

Kratochvíl, Jan. "The Inflation of the Margin of Appreciation by the European Court of Human Rights." *Netherlands Quarterly of Human Rights* 29 (2011): 324-357.

Krisch, Nico. *Beyond Constitutionalism: The Pluralist Structure of Postnational Law*. Oxford: Oxford University Press, 2010.

Kukavica, Jaka. "National Consensus and the Eigth Amendment: Is There Something to Be Learned from the United States Supreme Court?". In *Building Consensus on European Consensus. Judicial Interpretation of Human Rights in Europe and Beyond*, edited by Panos Kapotas and Vassilis Tzevelekos, 364-391. Cambridge: Cambridge University Press, 2019.

Künkler, Mirjam, and Tine Stein. "State, Law, and Constitution. Ernst-Wolfgang Böckenförde's Political and Legal Thought in Context." In *Ernst-Wolfgang Böckenförde: Constitutional and Political Theory. Selected Writings*, edited by Mirjam Künkler and Tine Stein, 1-35. Oxford: Oxford University Press, 2017.

Laborde, Cécile, and John Maynor. "The Republican Contribution to Contemporary Political Theory." In *Republicanism and Political Theory*, edited by Cécile Laborde and John Maynor, 1-28. Malden, Mass.: Blackwell, 2008.

Lafont, Cristina. "Is the Ideal of a Deliberative Democracy Coherent?". In *Deliberative Democracy and its Discontents*, edited by Samantha Besson and José Luis Martí, 3-25. Aldershot: Ashgate, 2006.

Lalor, Kay. "Making Different Differences: Representation and Rights in Sexuality Activism." *Feminist Legal Studies* 23 (2015): 7-25.

Lambert Abdelgawad, Elisabeth. "The Execution of the Judgments of the European Court of Human Rights: Towards a Non-coercive and Participatory Model of Accountability." *Zeitschrift für ausländisches öffentliches Recht und Völkerrecht* 69 (2009): 471-506.

Landemore, Hélène. *Democratic Reason. Politics, Collective Intelligence, and the Rule of the Many*. Princeton and Oxford: Princeton University Press, 2013.

Lau, Holning. "Rewriting Schalk and Kopf: Shifting the Locus of Deference." In *Diversity and European Human Rights. Rewriting Judgments of the ECHR*, edited by Eva Brems, 243-264. Cambridge: Cambridge University Press, 2012.

Legg, Andrew. *The Margin of Appreciation in International Human Rights Law: Deference and Proportionality*. Oxford: Oxford University Press, 2012.

Leijten, Ingrid. *Core Socio-Economic Rights and the European Court of Human Rights*. Cambridge: Cambridge University Press, 2018.

Lenaerts, Koen. "Interlocking Legal Orders in the European Union and Comparative Law." *International and Comparative Law Quarterly* 52 (2003): 873-906.

Lenaerts, Koen, and José A. Gutiérrez-Fons. "The Constitutional Allocation of Powers and General Principles of EU Law." *Common Market Law Review* 47 (2010): 1629-1669.

Letsas, George. "The ECHR as a Living Instrument: Its Meaning and Legitimacy." In *Constituting Europe. The European Court of Human Rights in a National, European and Global Context*, edited by Andreas Føllesdal, Birgit Peters and Geir Ulfstein, 106-141. Cambridge: Cambridge University Press, 2013.

Letsas, George. "No Human Right to Adopt?". *UCL Human Rights Review* 1 (2008): 135-154.

Letsas, George. “Strasbourg’s Interpretive Ethic: Lessons for the International Lawyer.” *European Journal of International Law* 21 (2010): 509-541.

Letsas, George. *A Theory of Interpretation of the European Convention on Human Rights*. Oxford: Oxford University Press, 2007.

Letsas, George. “The Truth in Autonomous Concepts: How To Interpret the ECHR.” *European Journal of International Law* 15 (2004): 279-305.

Letsas, George. “Two Concepts of the Margin of Appreciation.” *Oxford Journal of Legal Studies* 26 (2006): 705-732.

Lewis, Tom. “*Animal Defenders International* v *United Kingdom*: Sensible Dialogue or a Bad Case of Strasbourg Jitters?”. *Modern Law Review* 77 (2014): 460-492.

Lewis, Tom. “What not to Wear: Religious Rights, the European Court, and the Margin of Appreciation.” *International and Comparative Law Quarterly* 56 (2007): 395-414.

Linderfalk, Ulf. “Who Are ‘the Parties’? Article 31, Paragraph 3(C) of the 1969 Vienna Convention and the ‘Principle of Systemic Integration’ Revisited.” *Netherlands International Law Review* 55 (2008): 343-364.

List, Christian, and Robert E. Goodin. “Epistemic Democracy: Generalizing the Condorcet Jury Theorem.” *The Journal of Political Philosophy* 9 (2001): 277-306.

Little, Daniel. “Reflective Equilibrium and Justification.” *The Southern Journal of Philosophy* 22, no. 3 (1984): 373-387.

Lixinski, Lucas. “The Inter-American Court of Human Rights’ Tentative Search for Latin American Consensus.” In *Building Consensus on European Consensus. Judicial Interpretation of Human Rights in Europe and Beyond*, edited by Panos Kapotas and Vassilis Tzevelekos, 337-363. Cambridge: Cambridge University Press, 2019.

Lock, Tobias. “The Influence of EU Law on Strasbourg Doctrines.” *European Law Review* 41 (2016): 804-825.

De Londras, Fiona. “When the European Court of Human Rights Decides Not to Decide: The Cautionary Tale of *A, B & C* v. *Ireland* and Referendum-Emergent Constitutional Provisions.” In *Building Consensus on European Consensus. Judicial Interpretation of Human Rights in Europe and Beyond*, edited by Panos Kapotas and Vassilis Tzevelekos, 311-333. Cambridge: Cambridge University Press, 2019.

De Londras, Fiona, and Kanstantsin Dzehtsiarou. “Grand Chamber of the European Court of Human Rights: A, B & C v Ireland, Decision of 17 December 2010.” *International and Comparative Law Quarterly* 62 (2013): 250-262.

De Londras, Fiona, and Kanstantsin Dzehtsiarou. “Managing Judicial Innovation in the European Court of Human Rights.” *Human Rights Law Review* 15 (2015): 523-547.

Lovett, Frank. “Can Justice Be Based on Consent?”. *The Journal of Political Philosophy* 12 (2004): 79-101.

Luban, David. “Human Rights Pragmatism and Human Dignity.” In *Philosophical Foundations of Human Rights*, edited by Rowan Cruft, S. Matthew Liao and Massimo Renzo, 263-278. Oxford: Oxford University Press, 2015.

Lübbe-Wolff, Gertrude. "Homogenes Volk - Über Homogenitätspostulate und Integration." *Zeitschrift für Ausländerrecht und Ausländerpolitik* 27 (2007): 121-127.

Luca, Zoé. "Case of Lautsi v Italy. Religious Symbols in Public Schools and the (Lack of) Margin of Appreciation." *Maastricht Journal of European and Comparative Law* 17 (2010): 98-104.

Lugato, Monica. "The 'Margin of Appreciation' and Freedom of Religion: Between Treaty Interpretation and Subsidiarity." *Journal of Catholic Legal Studies* 52 (2013): 49-70.

Luhmann, Niklas. *Recht und Automation in der öffentlichen Verwaltung. Eine verwaltungswissenschaftliche Untersuchung*. Berlin: Duncker & Humblot, 1966.

Lupu, Yonatan. "International Judicial Legitimacy: Lessons from National Courts." *Theoretical Inquiries in Law* 14 (2013): 437-454.

Lyon, Arabella. *Deliberative Acts. Democracy, Rhetoric, and Rights*. University Park, PA: Pennsylvania State University Press, 2013.

Lyons, David. "Nature and Soundness of the Contract and Coherence Arguments." In *Reading Rawls: Critical Studies on Rawls' 'A Theory of Justice'*, edited by Norman Daniels, 141-167. Stanford: Stanford University Press, 1989.

MacCormick, Neil. *Legal Reasoning and Legal Theory*. Oxford: Clarendon Press, 1978.

MacCormick, Neil. *Rhetoric and the Rule of Law. A Theory of Legal Reasoning*. Oxford: Oxford University Press, 2005.

Macdonald, R. St. J. "The Margin of Appreciation." In *The European System for the Protection of Human Rights*, edited by R. St. J. Macdonald, Franz Matscher and Herbert Petzold, 83-124. Dordrecht: Nijhoff, 1993.

Maciejewski, Tim, and Jens T. Theilen. "Temporal Aspects of the Interaction between National Law and European Union Law: Reintroducing the Protection of Legitimate Expectations." *European Law Review* (2017): 706-721.

Madsen, Mikael Rask. "The Protracted Institutionalization of the Strasbourg Court: From Legal Diplomacy to Integrationist Jurisprudence." In *The European Court of Human Rights between Law and Politics*, edited by Jonas Christoffersen and Mikael Rask Madsen, 43-60. Oxford: Oxford University Press, 2011.

Madsen, Mikael Rask. "Rebalancing European Human Rights: Has the Brighton Declaration Engendered a New Deal on Human Rights in Europe?". *Journal of International Dispute Settlement* 9 (2018): 199-222.

Madsen, Mikael Rask, Pola Cebulak, and Micha Wiebusch. "Backlash Against International Courts: Explaining the Forms and Patterns of Resistance to International Courts." *International Journal of Law in Context* 14 (2018): 197-220.

Madsen, Mikael Rask, Pola Cebulak, and Micha Wiebusch. "Resistance to International Courts. Introduction and Conclusion." *International Journal of Law in Context* 14 (2018): 193-196.

Maduro, Miguel Poiares. *We The Court: The European Court of Justice and The European Economic Constitution. A Critical Reading of Article 30 of the EC Treaty*. Oxford: Hart, 1998.

Mahoney, Paul. "Judicial Activism and Judicial Self-Restraint in the European Court of Human Rights: Two Sides of the Same Coin." *Human Rights Law Journal* 11 (1990): 57-88.

Mahoney, Paul. "Marvellous Richness of Diversity or Invidious Cultural Relativism?". *Human Rights Law Journal* 19 (1998): 1-6.

Mahoney, Paul, and Rachael Kondak. "Common Ground. A Starting Point or Destination for Comparative-Law Analysis by the European Court of Human Rights?". In *Courts and Comparative Law*, edited by Mads Andenas and Duncan Fairgrieve, 119-140. Oxford: Oxford University Press, 2015.

Makaza, Dorothy. "Towards Afrotopia: The AU Withdrawal Strategy Document, the ICC, and the Possibility of Pluralistic Utopias." *German Yearbook of International Law* 60 (2017): 485-517.

Mälksoo, Lauri. "Concluding Observations. Russia and European Human-Rights Law: Margins of the Margin of Appreciation." In *Russia and European Human-Rights Law: The Rise of the Civlizational Argument*, edited by Lauri Mälksoo, 217-227. Leiden: Brill, 2014.

Mälksoo, Lauri. "Russia's Constitutional Court Defies the European Court of Human Rights." *European Constitutional Law Review* 12 (2016): 377-395.

Mann, Roni. "Non-ideal Theory of Constitutional Adjudication." *Global Constitutionalism* 7 (2018): 14-53.

Marks, Susan. "False Contingency." *Current Legal Problems* 62 (2009): 1-21.

Marks, Susan. "International Judicial Activism and the Commodity-Form Theory of International Law." *European Journal of International Law* 18, no. 1 (2007): 199-211.

Marks, Susan. *The Riddle of All Constitutions. International Law, Democracy, and the Critique of Ideology*. Oxford: Oxford University Press, 2000.

Marochkin, Sergei Yu. "A Russian Approach to International Law in the Domestic Legal Order: Basics, Development and Perspectives." *Italian Yearbook of International Law* XXVI (2016): 15-40.

Martens, Paul. "Perplexity of the National Judge Faced with the Vagaries of European Consensus." In *Dialogue between judges, European Court of Human Rights*, 53-65, 2008.

Martí, José Luis. "The Epistemic Conception of Deliberative Democracy Defended: Reasons, Rightness and Equal Political Autonomy." In *Deliberative Democracy and its Discontents*, edited by Samantha Besson and José Luis Martí, 27-56. Aldershot: Ashgate, 2006.

Martini, Stefan. *Vergleichende Verfassungsrechtsprechung. Praxis, Viabilität und Begründung rechtsvergleichender Argumentation durch Verfassungsgerichte*. Berlin: Duncker & Humblot, 2018.

Marx, Karl. "Thesen über Feuerbach." In *Karl Marx: Thesen über Feuerbach*, edited by Georges Labica. Hamburg and Berlin: Argument-Verlag, 1998.

Maus, Ingeborg. *Menschenrechte, Demokratie und Frieden. Perspektiven globaler Organisation*. Frankfurt a.M.: Suhrkamp, 2015.

Mavronicola, Natasa. "Taking Life and Liberty Seriously: Reconsidering Criminal Liability Under Article 2 of the ECHR." *Modern Law Review* 80, no. 6 (2017): 1026-1051.

Mayer, Franz C. "Constitutional Comparativism in Action. The Example of General Principles of EU Law and How They Are Made - A German Perspective." *International Journal of Constitutional Law* 11 (2013): 1003-1020.

McCrudden, Christopher. "Using Comparative Reasoning in Human Rights Adjudication: The Court of Justice of the European Union and the European Court of Human Rights Compared." *Cambridge Yearbook of European Legal Studies* 15 (2012-2013): 383-.

McGinnis, John O., and Michael Rappaport. "The Condorcet Case for Supermajority Rules." *Supreme Court Economic Review* 16, no. 1 (2008): 67-115.

McGoldrick, Dominic. "A Defence of the Margin of Appreciation and an Argument for its Application by the Human Rights Committee." *International and Comparative Law Quarterly* 65 (2016): 21-60.

McHarg, Aileen. "Reconciling Human Rights and the Public Interest: Conceptual Problems and Doctrinal Uncertainty in the Jurisprudence of the European Court of Human Rights." *Modern Law Review* 62 (1999): 671-696.

McLachlan, Campbell. "The Principle of Systemic Integration and Article 31(3)(C) of the Vienna Convention." *International and Comparative Law Quarterly* 54 (2005): 279-320.

McNeilly, Kathryn. "After the Critique of Rights: For a Radical Democratic Theory and Practice of Human Rights." *Law and Critique* 27 (2016): 269-288.

McNeilly, Kathryn. *Human Rights and Radical Social Transformation: Futurity, Alterity, Power*. London and New York: Routledge, 2018.

Meckled-García, Saladin. "Specifying Human Rights." In *Philosophical Foundations of Human Rights*, edited by Rowan Cruft, S. Matthew Liao and Massimo Renzo, 300-315. Oxford: Oxford University Press, 2015.

Meckled-García, Saladin, and Başak Çalı. "Lost in Translation. The Human Rights Ideal and International Human Rights Law." In *The Legalization of Human Rights. Multidisciplinary Perspectives on Human Rights and Human Rights Law*, edited by Saladin Meckled-García and Başak Çalı, 11-31. London and New York: Routledge, 2006.

Medda-Windischer, Roberta. "Dismantling Segregating Education and the European Court of Human Rights. *D.H. and Others vs. Czech Republic*: Towards an Inclusive Education?". *European Yearbook of Minority Issues* 7 (2007/8): 19-55.

Mégret, Frédéric. "The Apology of Utopia: Some Thoughts on Koskenniemian Themes, with Particular Emphasis on Massively Institutionalized International Human Rights Law." *Temple International and Comparative Law Journal* 27 (2013): 455-497.

Mégret, Frédéric. "Where Does the Critique of International Human Rights Stand? An Exploration in 18 Vignettes." In *New Approaches to International Law: The European and American Experiences*, edited by José María Beneyto and David Kennedy, 3-40. The Hague: T.M.C. Asser Press, 2012.

Meier, Severin. "The Influence of Utopian Projects on the Interpretation of International Law and the Healthy Myth of Objectivity." *German Yearbook of International Law* 60 (2017): 519-542.

Mena Parras, Francisco Javier. "Democracy, Diversity and the Margin of Appreciation: A Theoretical Analysis from the Perspective of the International and Constitutional Functions of the European Court of Human Rights." *Revista Electrónica de Estudios Internacionales* 29 (2015): 1-18.

Merkouris, Panos. *Article 31(3)(c) VCLT and the Principle of Systemic Integration*. Leiden and Boston: Brill, 2015.

Merrills, J.G. *The Development of International Law by the European Court of Human Rights*. Manchester: Manchester University Press, 1988.

Milanovic, Marko. "On Realistic Utopias and Other Oxymorons: An Essay on Antonio Cassese's Last Book." *European Journal of International Law* 23 (2012): 1033-1048.

Miles, Cameron A. "Indeterminacy." In *Concepts for International Law. Contributions to Disciplinary Thought*, edited by Jean d'Aspremont and Sahib Singh, 447-458. Cheltenham: Edward Elgar, 2019.

Mill, John Stuart. "De Tocqueville on Democracy in America [II]." In *The Collected Works of John Stuart Mill, Volume XVIII - Essays on Politics and Society*, edited by John M. Robson, 153-204. Toronto: University of Toronto Press, 1977.

Mill, John Stuart. "On Liberty." In *On Liberty and Other Essays*, 1-128. Oxford: Oxford University Press, 1991.

Miller, David. "Republicanism, National Identity, and Europe." In *Republicanism and Political Theory*, edited by Cécile Laborde and John Maynor, 133-158. Malden, Mass.: Blackwell, 2008.

Momirov, Aleksandar, and Andria Naudé Fourie. "Vertical Comparative Law Methods: Tools for Conceptualising the International Rule of Law." *Erasmus Law Review* 2, no. 3 (2009): 291-309.

Moravcsik, Andrew. "The Origins of Human Rights Regimes: Democratic Delegation in Postwar Europe." *International Organization* 54, no. 2 (2000): 217-252.

Morawa, Alexander. "The 'Common European Approach', 'International Trends', and the Evolution of Human Rights Law. A Comment on Goodwin and I v. the United Kingdom." *German Law Journal* 3 (2002).

Mouffe, Chantal. *The Democratic Paradox*. London and New York: Verso, 2005.

Mouffe, Chantal. "The Limits of John Rawls's Pluralism." *Politics, Philosophy & Economics* 4 (2005): 221-231.

Mowbray, Alastair. "The Creativity of the European Court of Human Rights." *Human Rights Law Review* 5, no. 1 (2005): 57-79.

Moyn, Samuel. *The Last Utopia. Human Rights in History*. Cambridge, Mass.: Belknap Press of Harvard University Press, 2012.

Moyn, Samuel. *Not Enough. Human rights in an Unequal World*. Cambridge, Mass.: Belknap Press of Harvard University Press, 2018.

Murray, John L. "Consensus: Concordance, or Hegemony of the Majority?" In *Dialogue between judges, European Court of Human Rights*, 25-48, 2008.

Mutua, Makau. “Savages, Victims, and Saviors: The Metaphor of Human Rights.” *Harvard International Law Journal* 42, no. 1 (2001): 201-245.

Myjer, Egbert. “The Succes[s] Story of the European Court: The Times They Are A-Changin’?”. *Netherlands Quarterly of Human Rights* 30, no. 3 (2012): 264-271.

Neuman, Gerald L. “Import, Export, and Regional Consent in the Inter-American Court of Human Rights.” *European Journal of International Law* 19 (2008): 101-123.

Nic Shuibhne, Niamh. “Consensus as Challenge and Retraction of Rights: Can Lessons Be Drawns from - and for - EU Citizenship Law?”. In *Building Consensus on European Consensus. Judicial Interpretation of Human Rights in Europe and Beyond*, edited by Panos Kapotas and Vassilis Tzevelekos, 421-447. Cambridge: Cambridge University Press, 2019.

Nickel, James W. *Making Sense of Human Rights*. Malden: Blackwell, 2007.

Nicola, Fernanda G. “National Legal Traditions at Work in the Jurisprudence of the Court of Justice of the European Union.” *American Journal of Comparative Law* 64 (2016): 865-889.

Nielsen, Kai. “Grounding Rights and a Method of Reflective Equilibrium.” *Inquiry* 25, no. 3 (1982): 277-306.

Nollkaemper, André. “International Adjudication of Global Public Goods: The Intersection of Substance and Procedure.” *European Journal of International Law* 23 (2012): 769-791.

Nolte, Georg. “Jurisprudence under Special Regimes Relating to Subsequent Agreements and Subsequent Practice.” In *Treaties and Subsequent Practice*, edited by Georg Nolte, 210-306. Oxford: Oxford University Press, 2013.

Nowlin, Christopher. “The Protection of Morals Under the European Convention for the Protection of Human Rights and Fundamental Freedoms.” *Human Rights Quarterly* 24 (2002): 264-286.

Nozawa, Junko. “Drawing the Line: Same-sex adoption and the jurisprudence of the ECtHR on the application of the “European consensus” standard under Article 14.” *Merkourios* 29 (2013): 66-75.

Nussbaum, Martha C. *From Disgust to Humanity. Sexual Orientation & Constitutional Law*. Oxford: Oxford University Press, 2010.

Nussbaum, Martha C. *Frontiers of Justice. Disability, Nationality, Species Membership*. Cambridge, Mass.: Belknap Press of Harvard University Press, 2006.

Nußberger, Angelika. “Auf der Suche nach einem europäischen Konsens – zur Rechtsprechung des Europäischen Gerichtshofs für Menschenrechte.” *Zeitschrift für rechtswissenschaftliche Forschung* 3 (2012): 197-211.

Nußberger, Angelika. “Hard Law or Soft Law - Does it Matter? Distinction Between Different Sources of International Law in the Jurisprudence of the ECtHR.” In *The European Convention on Human Rights and General International Law*, edited by Anne van Aaken and Iulia Motoc, 41-58. Oxford: Oxford University Press, 2018.

Nussberger, Angelika. *The European Court of Human Rights*. Oxford: Oxford University Press, 2020.

O'Boyle, Michael. "The Future of the European Court of Human Rights." *German Law Journal* 12 (2011): 1862-1877.

O'Cinneide, Colm. "Rights under Pressure." *European Human Rights Law Review* (2017): 43-48.

O'Connell, Paul. "Human Rights: Contesting the Displacement Thesis." *Northern Ireland Legal Quarterly* 69, no. 1 (2018): 19-35.

O'Connell, Paul. "On the Human Rights Question." *Human Rights Quarterly* 40, no. 4 (2018): 962-988.

Odermatt, Jed. "Patterns of Avoidance: Political Questions Before International Courts." *International Journal of Law in Context* 14 (2018): 221-236.

O'Hara, Claerwen. "Consensus, Difference and Sexuality: Que(e)rying the European Court of Human Rights' Concept of 'European Consensus'." *Law and Critique* (2020).

Oomen, B.M. "A Serious Case of Strasbourg-Bashing? An Evaluation of the Debates on the Legitimacy of the European Court of Human Rights in the Netherlands." *International Journal of Human Rights* 20 (2016): 407-425.

Orakhelashvili, Alexander. *The Interpretation of Acts and Rules in Public International Law*. Oxford: Oxford University Press, 2008.

Orford, Anne. "Embodying Internationalism: The Making of International Lawyers." *Australian Yearbook of International Law* 19 (1998): 1-34.

Örücü, Esin. "Whither Comparativism in Human Rights Cases?". In *Judicial Comparativism in Human Rights Cases*, edited by Esin Örücü, 229-242. London: UKNCCL, 2003.

Ost, François. "The Original Canons of Interpretation of the European Court of Human Rights." In *The European Convention for the Protection of Human Rights. International Protection versus National Restrictions*, edited by Mireille Delmas-Marty, 283-318. Dordrecht et al.: Kluwer, 1992.

Ostrovsky, Aaron A. "What's So Funny About Peace, Love, and Understanding? How the Margin of Appreciation Doctrine Preserves Core Human Rights within Cultural Diversity and Legitimises International Human Rights Tribunals." *Hanse Law Review* 1 (2005): 47-64.

Otto, Dianne. "Lost in Translation: Re-scripting the Sexed Subjects of International Human Rights Law." In *International Law and its Others*, edited by Anne Orford, 318-356. Cambridge: Cambridge University Press, 2006.

Otto, Dianne. "Queering Gender [Identity] in International Law." *Nordic Journal of Human Rights* 33 (2015): 299-318.

Paczolay, Péter. "Consensus and Discretion: Evolution or Erosion of Human Rights Protection?" In *Dialogue between judges, European Court of Human Rights*, 69-79, 2008.

Pascual-Vives, Francisco. *Consensus-Based Interpretation of Regional Human Rights Treaties*. Leiden and Boston: Brill, 2019.

Peat, Daniel. *Comparative Reasoning in International Courts and Tribunals*. Cambridge: Cambridge University Press, 2019.

Peroni, Lourdes. "Challenging Culturally Dominant Conceptions in Human Rights Law: The Cases of Property and Family." *Human Rights and International Legal Discourse* 4, no. 2 (2010): 241-264.

Peroni, Lourdes. "Religion and Culture in the Discourse of the European Court of Human Rights: The Risks of Stereotyping and Naturalising." *International Journal of Law in Context* 10, no. 2 (2014): 195-221.

Peroni, Lourdes, and Alexandra Timmer. "Vulnerable Groups: The Promise of an Emerging Concept in European Human Rights Convention Law." *International Journal of Constitutional Law* 11, no. 4 (2013): 1056-1085.

Perrone, Roberto. "Public Morals and the European Convention on Human Rights." *Israel Law Review* 47 (2014): 361-378.

Peters, Birgit. "The Rule of Law Dimensions of Dialogues Between National Courts and Strasbourg." In *The Rule of Law at the National and International Levels. Contestations and Deference*, edited by Machiko Kanetake and André Nollkaemper, 201-225. Oxford and Portland: Hart, 2016.

Petkova, Bilyana. "The Notion of Consensus as a Route to Democratic Adjudication." *Cambridge Yearbook of European Legal Studies* 14 (2011-2012): 663-695.

Pildes, Richard H. "Supranational Courts and The Law of Democracy: The European Court of Human Rights." *Journal of International Dispute Settlement* 9 (2018): 154-179.

Pinto de Albuquerque, Paulo. "Plaidoyer for the European Court of Human Rights." *European Human Rights Law Review*, no. 2 (2018): 119-133.

Pitea, Cesare. "Interpretation and Application of the European Convention on Human Right[s] in the Broader Context of International Law: Myth or Reality?". In *Human Rights and Civil Liberties in the 21st Century*, edited by Yves Haeck and Eva Brems, 1-14. Dordrecht: Springer, 2014.

Polakiewicz, Jörg. "Alternatives to Treaty-Making and Law-Making by Treaty and Expert Bodies in the Council of Europe." In *Developments of International Law in Treaty Making*, edited by Rüdiger Wolfrum and Volker Röben, 245-290. Heidelberg et al.: Springer, 2005.

Polakiewicz, Jörg, and Irene Suominen-Picht. "Aktuelle Herausforderungen für Europarat und EMRK: Die Erklärung von Kopenhagen (April 2018), das Spannungsverhältnis zwischen EMRK und nationalen Verfassungen und die Beteiligung der EU an dem europäischen Menschenrechtskontrollmechanismus." *Europäische Grundrechte-Zeitschrift* (2018): 383-390.

Popelier, Patricia. "Legitimate Expectations and the Law Maker in the Case Law of the European Court of Human Rights." *European Human Rights Law Review*, no. 1 (2006): 10-24.

Popelier, Patricia, and Catherine Van de Heyning. "Procedural Rationality: Giving Teeth to the Proportionality Analysis." *European Constitutional Law Review* 9 (2013): 230-262.

Posner, Eric A., and Cass R. Sunstein. "The Law of Other States." *Stanford Law Review* 59 (2006): 131-179.

Posner, Eric A., and John C. Yoo. "Judicial Independence in International Tribunals." *California Law Review* 93 (2005): 1-74.

Posner, Richard A. "The Supreme Court 2004 Term. Foreword: A Political Court." *Harvard Law Review* 119 (2005): 32-102.

Rachovitsa, Adamantia. "Fragmentation of International Law Revisited: Insights, Good Practices, and Lessons to be Learned from the Case Law of the European Court of Human Rights." *Leiden Journal of International Law* 28 (2015): 863-885.

Rachovitsa, Adamantia. "The Principle of Systemic Integration in Human Rights Law." *International and Comparative Law Quarterly* 66 (2017): 557-588.

Radačić, Ivana. "The Margin of Appreciation, Consensus, Morality and the Rights of the Vulnerable Groups." *Zb. Prav. fak. Rij.* 31 (2010): 599-616.

Rajagopal, Balakrishnan. "International Law and Social Movements: Challenges of Theorizing Resistance." *Columbia Journal of Transnational Law* 41 (2003): 397-433.

Rajagopal, Balakrishnan. *International Law from Below. Development, Social Movements and Third World Resistance*. Cambridge: Cambridge University Press, 2003.

De la Rasilla del Moral, Ignacio. "The Increasingly Marginal Appreciation of the Margin-of-Appreciation Doctrine." *German Law Journal* 7 (2006): 611-624.

Rawls, John. "The Independence of Moral Theory." In *John Rawls: Collected Papers*, edited by Samuel Freeman, 286-302. Cambridge, Mass.: Harvard University Press, 1999.

Rawls, John. *Justice as Fairness: A Restatement*. Cambridge, MA: Harvard University Press, 2001.

Rawls, John. *The Law of Peoples*. Cambridge, Mass.: Harvard University Press, 1999.

Rawls, John. "Outline of a Decision Procedure for Ethics." In *John Rawls: Collected Papers*, edited by Samuel Freeman, 1-19. Cambridge, Mass.: Harvard University Press, 1999.

Rawls, John. *Political Liberalism: Expanded Edition*. New York: Columbia University Press, 2005.

Rawls, John. *A Theory of Justice: Revised Edition*. Cambridge, Mass.: Belknap Press of Harvard University Press, 1999. 1971.

Raz, Joseph. "The Claims of Reflective Equilibrium." *Inquiry* 25 (1982): 307-330.

Raz, Joseph. "On the Authority and Interpretation of Cosntitutions: Some Preliminaries." In *Constitutionalism: Philosophical Foundations*, edited by Larry Alexander. Cambridge: Cambridge University Press, 1998.

Rees, Madeleine, and Christine Chinkin. "Exposing the Gendered Myth of Post Conflict Transition: The Transformative Power of Economic and Social Rights." *New York University Journal of International Law and Politics* 48 (2016): 1211-1226.

Regan, Daniel. "'European Consensus': A Worthy Endeavour for the European Court of Human Rights?". *Trinity College Law Review* 14 (2011): 51-76.

Rietiker, Daniel. "The Principle of 'Effectiveness' in the Recent Jurisprudence of the European Court of Human Rights: Its Different Dimensions and Its Consistency with Public International Law - No Need for the Concept of Treaty Sui Generis." *Nordic Journal of International Law* 79 (2010): 245-277.

Roberts, Anthea, Paul B. Stephan, Pierre-Hugues Verdier, and Mila Versteeg. "Comparative International Law: Framing the Field." *American Journal of International Law* 109 (2015): 467-474.

Robinson, William I. *Promoting Polyarchy: Globalization, US Intervention and Hegemony*. Cambridge: Cambridge University Press, 1996.

Rousseau, Jean-Jacques. *The Social Contract*. Translated by G.D.H. Cole. Milton Keynes: Jiahu Books, 2013.

Rozakis, Christos L. "The Accession of the EU to the ECHR and the Charter of Fundamental Rights: Enlarging the Field of Protection of Human Rights in Europe." In *The EU Accession to the ECHR*, edited by Vasiliki Kosta, Nikos Skoutaris and Vassilis P. Tzevelekos, 327-331. Oxford and Portland: Hart, 2014.

Rozakis, Christos L. "The European Judge as Comparatist." *Tulane Law Review* 80 (2005): 257-279.

Rozakis, Christos L. "Through the Looking Glass: An "Insider"'s View of the Margin of Appreciation." In *La conscience des droits: Mélanges en l'honneur de Jean-Paul Costa*, 527-537. Paris: Dalloz, 2011.

Rudolf, Beate. "European Court of Human Rights: Legal status of postoperative transsexuals." *International Journal of Constitutional Law* 1 (2003): 716-721.

Ryan, Clare. "Europe's Moral Margin: Parental Aspirations and the European Court of Human Rights." *Columbia Journal of Transnational Law* 56 (2018): 467-529.

Sadurski, Wojciech. *Constitutionalism and the Enlargement of Europe*. Oxford: Oxford University Press, 2012.

Said, Edward W. *Orientalism*. London: Penguin Books, 2003.

Sandholtz, Wayne. "Expanding Rights: Norm Innovation in the European and Inter-American Courts." In *Expanding Human Rights. 21st Century Norms and Governance*, edited by Alison Brysk and Michael Stohl, 156-176. Cheltenham: Edward Elgar, 2017.

Sandland, Ralph. "Crossing and Not Crossing: Gender, Sexuality and Melancholy in the European Court of Human Rights." *Feminist Legal Studies* 11 (2003): 191-209.

Saul, Matthew. "The European Court of Human Rights' Margin of Appreciation and the Processes of National Parliaments." *Human Rights Law Review* 15 (2015): 745-774.

Scalia, Antonin. "Keynote Address: Foreign Legal Authority in the Federal Courts." *Proceedings of the American Society of International Law* 98 (2004): 305-310.

Scanlon, T.M. "Rawls on Justification." In *The Cambridge Companion to Rawls*, edited by Samuel Freeman, 139-167. Cambridge: Cambridge University Press, 2003.

Scanlon, T.M. *What We Owe to Each Other*. Cambridge, Mass.: Belknap Press of Harvard University Press, 1998.

Schaffer, Johan Karlsson, Andreas Føllesdal, and Geir Ulfstein. "International Human Rights and the Challenge of Legitimacy." In *The Legitimacy of International Human Rights Regimes*, edited by Andreas Føllesdal, Johan Karlsson Schaffer and Geir Ulfstein, 1-31. Cambridge: Cambridge University Press, 2014.

Schlag, Pierre. "'Le hors de texte, c'est moi' - The Politics of Form and the Domestication of Deconstruction." *Cardozo Law Review* 11 (1990): 1631-1674.

Schliesky, Utz. *Souveränität und Legitimität von Herrschaftsgewalt. Die Weiterentwicklung von Begriffen der Staatslehre und des Staatsrechts im europäischen Mehrebenensystem*. Tübingen: Mohr Siebeck, 2004.

Schlüter, Alix. "Beweisrechtliche Implikationen der margin of appreciation-Doktrin." *Archiv des Völkerrechts* 54 (2016): 41-66.

Schmitt, Carl. *Der Begriff des Politischen*. Berlin: Duncker & Humblot, 2009.

Schwöbel-Patel, Christine. "Populism, International Law and the End of Keep Calm and Carry on Lawyering." *Netherlands Yearbook of International Law* (2018): 97-121.

Sedgwick, Eve Kosofsky. "Paranoid Reading and Reparative Reading, or, You're So Paranoid, You Probably Think This Essay Is About You." In *Touching Feeling: Affect, Pedagogy, Performativity*, 123-151. Durham: Duke University Press, 2002.

Seibert-Fohr, Anja. "The Effect of Subsequent Practice on the European Convention on Human Rights: Considerations from a General International Law Perspective." In *The European Convention on Human Rights and General International Law*, edited by Anne van Aaken and Iulia Motoc, 61-82. Oxford: Oxford University Press, 2018.

Sen, Amartya. "Elements of a Theory of Human Rights." *Philosophy & Public Affairs* 32 (2004): 315-356.

Sen, Amartya. *The Idea of Justice*. London: Penguin Books, 2010.

Senden, Hanneke. *Interpretation of Fundamental Rights in a Multilevel Legal System*. Cambridge: Intersentia, 2011.

Seyr, Sibylle. "Verfassungsgerichte und Verfassungsvergleichung. Der EuGH." *Journal für Rechtspolitik* 18 (2010): 230-239.

Shahid, Masuma. "The Right to Same-Sex Marriage: Assessing the European Court of Human Rights' Consensus-Based Analysis in Recent Judgments Concerning Equal Marriage Rights." *Erasmus Law Review*, no. 3 (2017): 184-198.

Shany, Yuval. "All Roads Lead to Strasbourg?: Application of the Margin of Appreciation Doctrine by the European Court of Human Rights and the UN Human Rights Committee." *Journal of International Dispute Settlement* 9 (2018): 180-198.

Shany, Yuval. "Assessing the Effectiveness of International Courts: A Goal-Based Approach." *American Journal of International Law* 106 (2012): 225-270.

Shany, Yuval. "Toward a General Margin of Appreciation Doctrine in International Law?". *European Journal of International Law* 16 (2006): 907-940.

Shelton, Dinah. "The Boundaries of Human Rights Jurisdiction in Europe." *Duke Journal of Comparative and International Law* 13 (2003): 95-153.

Siedentop, Larry. *Inventing the Individual. The Origins of Western Liberalism*. London: Penguin, 2015.

Simmons, A. John. "Ideal and Nonideal Theory." *Philosophy & Public Affairs* 38 (2010): 5-36.

Simmons, Beth A. *Mobilizing for Human Rights. International Law in Domestic Politics*. Cambridge: Cambridge University Press, 2009.

Simpson, Gerry. "Imagination." In *Concepts for International Law. Contributions to Disciplinary Thought*, edited by Jean d'Aspremont and Sahib Singh, 413-421. Cheltenham: Edward Elgar, 2019.

Singer, Peter. "Sidgwick and Reflective Equilibrium." *The Monist* 58 (1974): 490-517.

Singh, Sahib. "Koskenniemi's Images of the International Lawyer." *Leiden Journal of International Law* 29 (2016): 699-726.

Skouteris, Thomas. "Fin de NAIL: New Approaches to International Law and its Impact on Contemporary International Legal Scholarship." *Leiden Journal of International Law* 10, no. 3 (1997): 415-420.

Slaughter, Anne-Marie. "A Typology of Transnational Communication." *University of Richmond Law Review* 29 (1994): 99-137.

Soley, Ximena, and Silvia Steininger. "Parting Ways or Lashing Back? Withdrawals, Backlash and the Inter-American Court of Human Rights." *International Journal of Law in Context* 14 (2018): 237-257.

Spade, Dean. "Documenting Gender." *Hastings Law Journal* 59 (2008): 731-842.

Spano, Robert. "Universality or Diversity of Human Rights? Strasbourg in the Age of Subsidiarity." *Human Rights Law Review* 14 (2014): 487-502.

Spiekermann, Kai, and Robert E. Goodin. "Courts of Many Minds." *British Journal of Political Science* 42 (2011): 555-571.

Spielmann, Dean. "Allowing the Right Margin: The European Court of Human Rights and the National Margin of Appreciation Doctrine. Waiver or Subsidiarity of European Review?". *Cambridge Yearbook of European Legal Studies* 14 (2012): 381-418.

Spielmann, Dean. "The European Court of Human Rights: Master of the Law but not of the Facts?" In *Speech to the British Institute of International and Comparative Law*, 2014.

Spielmann, Dean. "Whither the Margin of Appreciation?". *Current Legal Problems* 67 (2014): 49-65.

Spivak, Gayatri Chakravorty. *In Other Worlds. Essays in Cultural Politics*. Abingdon: Routledge, 1998.

Steiner, Henry, and Philip Alston. *International Human Rights in Context: Law, Politics, and Morals*. 1st ed. Oxford: Oxford University Press, 1996.

Stone Sweet, Alec, and Thomas L. Brunell. "Trustee Courts and the Judicialization of International Regimes: The Politics of Majoritarian Activism in the European Convention on Human Rights, the European Union, and the World Trade Organization." *Journal of Law and Courts* 1 (2013): 61-88.

Sweeney, James A. "A 'Margin of Appreciation' in the Internal Market: Lessons from the European Court of Human Rights." *Legal Issues of Economic Integration* 34 (2007): 27-52.

Tedeschini, Michele. "The Politics of International Lawyers: Whose Legacy Is at Stake? Reflections on Martti Koskenniemi's Series on 'The Politics of International Law'." *Critical Legal Thinking*, 2019. Available at <http://criticallegalthinking.com/2019/07/15/politics-of-international-lawyers-whose-legacy-is-at-stake-martti-koskenniemi/>.

Theilen, Jens T. "Beyond the Gender Binary: Rethinking the Right to Legal Gender Recognition." *European Human Rights Law Review*, no. 3 (2018): 249-257.

Theilen, Jens T. "Depathologisation of Transgenderism and International Human Rights Law." *Human Rights Law Review* 14 (2014): 327-342.

Theilen, Jens T. "The Inflation of Human Rights: A Deconstruction." *Leiden Journal of International Law* 34 (2021): forthcoming.

Theilen, Jens T. "Levels of Generality in the Comparative Reasoning of the European Court of Human Rights and the European Court of Justice: Towards Judicial Reflective Equilibrium." In *Building Consensus on European Consensus: Judicial Interpretation of Human Rights in Europe and Beyond*, edited by Panos Kapotas and Vassilis Tzevelekos, 392-420. Cambridge: Cambridge University Press, 2019.

Theilen, Jens T. "The Long Road to Recognition: Transgender Rights and Transgender Reality in Europe." In *Transsexualität in Theologie und Neurowissenschaften. Ergebnisse, Kontroversen, Perspektiven*, edited by Gerhard Schreiber, 373-390. Berlin, Boston: de Gruyter, 2016.

Theilen, Jens T. "Of Wonder and Changing the World: Philip Allott's Legal Utopianism." *German Yearbook of International Law* 60 (2017): 337-367.

Theilen, Jens T. "Pre-existing Rights and Future Articulations: Temporal Rhetoric in the Struggle for Trans Rights." In *Cambridge Handbook of New Human Rights. Recognition, Novelty, Rhetoric*, edited by Andreas von Arnauld, Kerstin von der Decken and Mart Susi, 207-214. Cambridge: Cambridge University Press, 2020.

Theilen, Jens T. "Towards Acceptance of Religious Pluralism: The Federal Constitutional Court's Second Judgment on Muslim Teachers Wearing Headscarves." *German Yearbook of International Law* 58 (2015): 503-520.

Theilen, Jens T., Isabelle Hassfurther, and Wiebke Staff. "Towards Utopia - Rethinking International Law." *German Yearbook of International Law* 60 (2017): 315-335.

Thienel, Tobias. "The Burden and Standard of Proof in the European Court of Human Rights." *German Yearbook of International Law* 50 (2007): 543-588.

Timmer, Alexandra. "Toward an Anti-Stereotyping Approach for the European Court of Human Rights." *Human Rights Law Review* 11, no. 4 (2011): 707-738.

De Tocqueville, Alexis. *Democracy in America: Historical-Critical Edition of De la démocratie en Amérique*. Translated by James T. Schleifer. Indianapolis: Liberty Fund, 2010.

Tulkens, Françoise. "Execution and Effects of the Judgments of the European Court of Human Rights. The Role of the Judiciary." In *Dialogue between judges, European Court of Human Rights*, 8-14, 2006.

Tushnet, Mark. *Taking the Constitution Away from the Courts*. Princeton, N.J.: Princeton University Press, 1999.

Tzevelekos, Vassilis. "The Use of Article 31(3)(C) of the VCLT in the Case Law of the ECtHR: An Effective Anti-Fragmentation Tool or a Selective Loophole for the Reinforcement of Human Rights Teleology?". *Michigan Journal of International Law* 31 (2010): 621-690.

Tzevelekos, Vassilis, and Kanstantsin Dzehtsiarou. "International Custom Making and the ECtHR's European Consensus Method of Interpretation." *European Yearbook on Human Rights* (2016): 313-343.

Tzevelekos, Vassilis, and Panos Kapotas. "Book review of Dzehtsiarou, 'European Consensus'." *Common Market Law Review* 53 (2016): 1145-1148.

Tzouvala, Ntina. *Capitalism as Civilisation. A History of International Law*. Cambridge: Cambridge University Press, 2020.

Tzouvala, Ntina. "New Approaches to International Law: The History of a Project." *European Journal of International Law* 27, no. 1 (2016): 215-233.

Ulfstein, Geir. "Evolutive Interpretation in the Light of Other International Instruments: Law and Legitimacy." In *The European Convention on Human Rights and General International Law*, edited by Anne van Aaken and Iulia Motoc, 83-94. Oxford: Oxford University Press, 2018.

Von Ungern-Sternberg, Antje. "Anmerkung zu S.A.S. ./. Frankreich - Burkaverbot." *MenschenrechtsMagazin* (2015): 61-63.

Von Ungern-Sternberg, Antje. "Die Konsensmethode des EGMR. Eine kritische Bewertung mit Blick auf das völkerrechtliche Konsens- und das innerstaatliche Demokratieprinzip." *Archiv des Völkerrechts* 51 (2013): 312-338.

Valentine, David. *Imagining Transgender. An Ethnography of a Category*. Durham and London: Duke University Press, 2007.

Van Drooghenbroeck, Sébastien. *La Proportionnalité dans le Droit de la Convention Européenne des Droits de l'Homme*. Bruxelles: Bruylant, 2001.

Větrovský, Jaroslav. "Determining the Content of the European Consenus Concept: The Hidden Role of Language." In *Building Consensus on European Consensus. Judicial Interpretation of Human Rights in Europe and Beyond*, edited by Panos Kapotas and Vassilis Tzevelekos, 120-140. Cambridge: Cambridge University Press, 2019.

Vogiatzis, Nikos. "The Relationship Between European Consensus, the Margin of Appreciation and the Legitimacy of the Strasbourg Court." *European Public Law* 25, no. 3 (2019): 445-480.

Waldron, Jeremy. "The Core of the Case Against Judicial Review." *Yale Law Journal* 115 (2005-2006): 1346-1406.

Waldron, Jeremy. "Democratic Theory and the Public Interest: Condorcet and Rousseau Revisited." *The American Political Science Review* 83 (1989): 1322-1328.

Waldron, Jeremy. “Foreign Law and the Modern Ius Gentium.” *Harvard Law Review* 119 (2005): 129-147.

Waldron, Jeremy. *Law and Disagreement*. Oxford: Oxford University Press, 1999.

Waldron, Jeremy. “Rights and Majorities: Rousseau Revisited.” *Nomos* 32 (1990): 44-75.

Wasserstrom, Richard A. *The Judicial Decision. Toward a Theory of Legal Justification*. Stanford: Stanford University Press, 1961.

Weber, Cynthia. *Queer International Relations. Sovereignty, Sexuality and the Will to Knowledge*. Oxford: Oxford University Press, 2016.

Weber, Max. *Wirtschaft und Gesellschaft. Grundriss der verstehenden Soziologie*. 5th ed. Tübingen: Mohr Siebeck, 1972.

Weil, Prosper. “Towards Relative Normativity in International Law?”. *American Journal of International Law* 77 (1983): 413-442.

Weiler, J.H.H. “Does Europe Need a Constitution? Demos, Telos and the German Maastricht Decision.” *European Law Journal* 1 (1995): 219-258.

Wheatley, Steven. “Minorities under the ECHR and the Construction of a ‘Democratic Society’.” *Public Law* (2007): 770-792.

Wheatley, Steven. “On the Legitimate Authority of International Human Rights Bodies.” In *The Legitimacy of International Human Rights Regimes. Legal, Political and Philosophical Perspectives*, edited by Andreas Føllesdal, Johan Karlsson Schaffer and Geir Ulfstein, 84-116. Cambridge: Cambridge University Press, 2013.

Wildhaber, Luzius, Arnaldur Hjartarson, and Stephen Donnelly. “No Consensus on Consensus? The Practice of the European Court of Human Rights.” *Human Rights Law Journal* 33 (2013): 248-263.

Wintemute, Robert. "Consensus Is the Right Approach for the European Court of Human Rights." *The Guardian*, 12 August 2010.

Wittinger, Michaela. *Der Europarat: Die Entwicklung seines Rechts und der “europäischen Verfassungswerte”*. Baden-Baden: Nomos, 2005.

Yildiz, Ezgi. “A Court with Many Faces: Judicial Characters and Modes of Norm Development in the European Court of Human Rights.” *European Journal of International Law* 31 (2020): 73-99.

Yoshino, Kenji. “Of Stranger Spaces.” In *Law and the Stranger*, edited by Austin Sarat, Lawrence Douglas and Martha Merrill Umphrey, 211-234. Palo Alto: Stanford University Press, 2010.

Yourow, Howard Charles. *The Margin of Appreciation Doctrine in the Dynamics of the European Human Rights Jurisprudence*. The Hague: Martinus Nijhoff Publishers, 1996.

Zemanek, Karl. “Court Generated State Practice?”. *Austrian Review of International and European Law* 20 (2015): 3-14.

Ziemele, Ineta. “Customary International Law in the Case Law of the European Court of Human Rights - The Method.” *The Law and Practice of International Courts and Tribunals* 12 (2013): 243-252.

Ziemele, Ineta. "European Consensus and International Law." In *The European Convention on Human Rights and General International Law*, edited by Anne van Aaken and Iulia Motoc, 23-40. Oxford: Oxford University Press, 2018.

Ziyadov, Nazim. "From Justice to Injustice: Lowering the Threshold of European Consensus in Oliari and Others versus Italy." *Indiana Journal of Global Legal Studies* 26, no. 2 (2019): 631-672.

Zoethout, Carla M. "The Dilemma of Constitutional Comparativism." *Zeitschrift für ausländisches öffentliches Recht und Völkerrecht* 71 (2011): 787-806.

Zürn, Michael. "Perspektiven des demokratischen Regierens und die Rolle der Politikwissenschaft im 21. Jahrhundert." *Politische Vierteljahresschrift* 52 (2011): 603-635.

Zwart, Tom. "More Human Rights Than Court: Why the Legitimacy of the European Court of Human Rights is in Need of Repair and How It Can Be Done." In *The European Court of Human Rights and Its Discontents: Turning Criticism Into Strength*, edited by Spyridon Flogaitis, Tom Zwart and Julie Fraser, 71-95. Cheltenham: Edward Elgar, 2013.

Zysset, Alain. *The ECHR and Human Rights Theory: Reconciling the Moral and Political Conceptions*. Abington: Routledge, 2017.